ALL THE LADS

A Complete Who's Who of Sunderland A.F.C.

by Garth Dykes & Doug Lamming

DEDICATION

To our good friends
JIM CREASY and MIKE DAVAGE
who have assisted both of us many times in this and other publications. Unrivalled in their
dedication to the field of soccer research, they have enriched the works of numerous other
writers, in addition to our own. (G.D. & D.L.)

This edition published in Great Britain in 2000 by Sunderland AFC.

ISBN 1 899538 15 1

Edited by: Julian Baskcomb
Assistant Editor: Julia Byrne
Design & Layout: Trevor Hartley
Dust Jacket Designs: Two-Can Design

Printed and Produced for Sunderland AFC by
Polar Print Group Ltd
2, Uxbridge Road, Leicester LE4 7ST
Telephone: (0116) 2610800

Photographs and illustrations are courtesy of:
Sunderland AFC, Colorsport, Associated Sports Photography, Empics Ltd, Professional Sport
UK Ltd, Sportsphoto Ltd, Rufus Abajas, Brian Leng, Action Images, The D. Lamming Collection,
The G. Dykes Collection. Special research thanks to Andy Cowie, Ian Lilley, Ian Wright, David
Scranage and Tommy Hindley.
Many of the photographs reproduced are from original material in the archives at Sunderland
AFC who also retain the rights to official photocall pictures from the modern era taken by the
appointed Club Photographer. Most remaining photographs are from the private collections of
the authors or from albums owned by various Sunderland supporters or former players. We
have been unable to trace the sources of all these pictures, but any photographer involved is
cordially invited to contact the publishers in writing providing proof of copyright ownership.

By the same authors

Doug Lamming
❏ A Century of International Football, 1872-1972, with Morley
  Farror (Robert Hale, 1972)
❏ A Who's Who of Hull City AFC, 1904-1984 (Hutton Press, 1984)
❏ A Who's Who of Grimsby Town AFC, 1890-1985
  (Hutton Press, 1985)
❏ A Scottish Soccer Internationalists' Who's Who, 1872-1986
  (Hutton Press, 1987)
❏ Who's Who of Liverpool 1892-1989 (Breedon Books 1989)
❏ An English Internationalists' Who's Who (Hutton Press 1990)
❏ In Lincolnshire Long Ago, a memoir (Hutton Press, 1994)
❏ Forgotten Caps, England Football internationals of two
  World Wars, with Bryan Horsnell (Yore Publications, 1995)

Garth Dykes
❏ Oldham Athletic - A Complete Record, 1899-1988
  (Breedon Books, 1988)
❏ Exeter City - A Complete Record, 1904-1990, with the
  late Alex Wilson and Maurice Golesworthy
  (Breedon Books, 1990)
❏ New Brighton - A Complete Record, 1922-1951
  (Breedon Books, 1990)
❏ Accrington Stanley - A Complete Record, 1894-1962,
  with Mike Jackman (Breedon Books, 1991)
❏ The United Alphabet - A Complete Who's Who of
  Manchester United FC (Polar Publishing, 1994)

A FOREWORD BY BOB MURRAY
Chairman of Sunderland Association Football Club

It is with great pleasure that I have been asked to write the foreword to All The Lads. This excellent volume adds to the growing range of books exploring the Club's long history and makes a significant contribution to our knowledge by documenting the career of every player to have pulled on a Sunderland shirt.

With so many great players having turned out for Sunderland over the years, it is only fitting that a Sunderland AFC Who's Who should appear. Flicking through the pages of this book brings back some great memories of personal heroes. As a young lad, men such as Charlie Hurley and Brian Clough were the ones I wanted to see. Both were fantastic players and we have been lucky enough to see many others since.

But, this book is not just about memories. The heroes of yesteryear are recorded too. Most Sunderland fans will be too young to remember the great players who contributed to our early success, but the achievements of such men should not be lost in time. The names of Sunderland heroes should live forever, men such as Ted Doig, who kept goal for Sunderland during four championship seasons; Charlie Buchan, whose goals almost brought the double to Roker Park; and Raich Carter, the local lad whose intelligent play contributed greatly to our first F.A. Cup win.

Of course, we have also had players whose time at the Club was somewhat less successful than might have been the case, but this book details them all, from Monty with his record 623 appearances, through to those who made it onto the pitch for less than a handful of games. As such, this book is a real education for all Sunderland fans. I hope you enjoy it.

Best wishes

Bob Murray

ACKNOWLEDGEMENTS

Inevitably in works of this type, authors draw upon kindnesses from fellow statisticians. These take the form of details, embellishment and/or sometimes directing one on a completely new track.

Four gentlemen and one lady especially receive our thanks. They include Jim Creasy and Mike Davage, to whom our book is dedicated. Rob Mason, a man devoted to Sunderland AFC has proved an invaluable source of assistance supplying much colourful additional detail and wry observations, as well as giving up his time most generously to the book. Alex White's greatly appreciated contribution included the loan of his card index on Sunderland's players which gave us an invaluable check on our own records, beside supplying additional material. A personal thank you also, from Garth, to Ann for her unfailing help and support (and dexterous word-processing skills!)

The authors also wish to thank the Football League for access to their records and many friends, correspondents and former players who have supplied valuable details. Our sincere gratitude to:- David A. Allan, Mervin Baker, Stuart Basson, Nigel Bishop, Nigel D. Bond, Michael Braham, Michael Coady, Bill Cook, John D. Cross, Roy S. Davies, Jason S.K. Dickinson, John Fitzhugh, David Fleckney, Harry Greenmon, Malcolm Harley, Marcus Heap, Bryan Horsnell, Ian J. Hughes, Barry J. Hugman, Mike Jackman, Alan Jenkins, Paul Joannou, Trefor Jones, John Maddocks, Wade Martin, Gary Moore, Mrs Lorna Parnell, Dr. Stephen Phillips, the late Peter Pickup, Robert W. Reid, Dave Smith, David Sullivan, Paul Taylor, Mrs Ann Whitchelo, Peter Windle and Robert F. Wray.

Many books, records, newspapers and other public sources of reference, too numerous to mention, were used in our extensive research: particularly many studious publications produced by the Association of Football Statisticians. Our sincere thanks to all concerned.

Finally, our thanks to the directors and staff of the Polar Print Group, with a particular word of thanks to Julia Byrne for her help and support.

ALL THE LADS

INTRODUCTION

Sunderland must be counted among the great clubs of English football. They were champions of the Football League in their second season of membership and again the next term, 1892/93, when 100 goals were scored, 26 more than the next largest aggregate.

Three further titles were won before the Great War - 1894/95, 1901/02 and 1912/13. This last a season when the first twentieth century 'double' was almost accomplished: the Wearsiders lost the FA Cup final to Aston Villa by a goal to nil.

The winning of the Cup was to become a burning issue for the club with four semi-final defeats and this final defeat endured before Raich Carter's side at last landed the trophy in 1937.

The climb to early greatness was started by manager Tom Watson with the signing of Scots such as Campbell, Harvey, Auld, Porteous, John Smith, Stevenson and David Hannah. This Caledonian bedrock, eventually evolving into the famous 'Team of All the Talents', inaugurated the Sunderland style, well described in 1960 as "the classic Scottish method of controlled and unhurried ground-passing .... blended (with) the fast open English tactic." The Sunderland line-ups that won League championships in 1902 and 1913 vied with the 'nineties masters in many ways. Of the former, the great Ned Doig still held undisputed sway as goalkeeper. His full-backs, Scottish internationalists Andy McCombie and James Watson Snr, were the best defensive pairing in their time, with Billy Hogg and Jimmy Millar then the current attacking stars. Eleven years on and a completely changed team. A celebrated half-back line-up, Frank Cuggy, Charlie Thomson and Harry Low made up an ideal backbone, while a brilliant attack that included Jackie Mordue, an emerging Charlie Buchan and ace ball manipulator George Holley entranced spectators.

Between the wars, 1919-39, Sunderland continued to hold top class status. Besides winning the championship again in 1936 the club came runners-up twice and third on three occasions. And, most memorably in 1937, the FA Cup arrived at Roker Park for the first time. The personnel for those trophy-winning consecutive seasons recalled triumphs of the pre-Great War era. As in 1913 exceptionally gifted half-backs - Thomson, Johnston, McNab and Hastings - were available, while the great Raich Carter master-minded an attack that also included Patsy Gallacher, Bobby Gurney and the elusive, prodigiously popular Jimmy Connor. Gurney deserves a special mention for an extraordinary 22 years length of service to Sunderland. As does, of course, Bill Murray. And for prolific goalscoring Dave Halliday, a club record 43 in 42 League appearances in 1928/29 and a wonderful aggregate of 162 in 175 League and Cup appearances all told.

In the half-century and more since World War Two, the modern era, Sunderland's fortunes can best be described as varied. The club remained in the top flight until 1958, thereby creating a record for continuous First Division membership. There had been good seasons (3rd in 1949/50 and 4th in 1954/55) but the then lowest position, 20th, occurred in 1948 and again in 1957. The last as a foretaste of the vain struggle to avoid relegation in 1957/58. Three clubs - Newcastle United, Portsmouth and Sunderland - finished with 32 points but the latter's goals record (54 scored and 97 conceded) was easily the worst.

Life in Division Two took a while to assimilate. Lowly positions were endured in the first two seasons before a third place in consecutive years heralded the runners-up spot in 1963/64 and automatic promotion. Only 17 players were called on, the usual line-up reading Montgomery; Irwin and Ashurst; Harvey, Hurley and McNab; Usher, Herd, Sharkey, Crossan and Mulhall. There were four ever-presents while Hurley and Usher missed only one engagement. This was the age of goalkeeper 'Monty' and 'King' Charlie Hurley. Both were devoted contributors to the Roker cause with 17 and 12 years service respectively. In the period from the post-war resumption to the mid-sixties Sunderland's knock-out competition endeavours had three high points. They reached FA Cup semi-finals in successive seasons, 1954/55 and '55/56, losing 1-0 in turn to Manchester City and Birmingham City. And in the third year of a newly-founded League Cup lost at the same stage to old rivals Aston Villa.

The Wearsiders struggled in Division One's lower reaches after regaining top status, never in five seasons finishing higher than 15th and in the sixth, 1969/70, suffered relegation. There followed a similar curve to that of 1959-64: steady adaptation until promotion arrived again in 1975/76, this time being elevated as champions. The line-up was usually Montgomery; Malone and Bolton; Towers, Clarke and Moncur; Kerr, Holden, Halom, Robson and Porterfield with Ashurst, Greenwood and Hughes making significant numbers of appearances too.

But only a single season of the top grade ensued before a drop occurred again, the club placed a lowly 20th. This time, however, Sunderland proved 'street-wise' to Second Division conditions, finishing 6th, 4th and, in 1980, runners-up to return for a five-year stay. Next time Division Two proved a much tougher proposition. Sunderland struggled to 18th in 1985/86 and the following term worse in 20th and the ignominy of descent to Division Three. Such slides are not a unique happening in modern times to famous old clubs - Aston Villa, Blackburn Rovers, Wolves, Sheffield Wednesday and Manchester City are other examples - but this does not make the medicine any more palatable.

However, Sunderland buckled down, bouncing back right away as champions by a nine points margin over runners-up Brighton & Hove Albion. Players responsible for the happy outcome were Hesford; Kay and Agboola; Bennett, MacPhail and Owers; Lemon, Doyle, Gates, Gabbiadini and Armstrong, plus Atkinson's appearance on 21 occasions.

The Second Division spell, 1970-76, had been immensely brightened by an unexpected winning of the FA Cup in 1973. Early rounds against Notts County, Reading and Manchester City all required replays, then Luton were vanquished 2-0 at the quarter-final stage. Arsenal, for the Hillsborough semi-final, seemed odds-on favourites yet Sunderland won 2-1. And Leeds United, also a leading top flight side, were likewise strongly fancied to win the Wembley final but fell to an historic Ian Porterfield goal. The victorious line-up was Montgomery; Malone and Guthrie; Horswill, Watson and Pitt; Kerr, Hughes, Halom, Porterfield and Tueart, with David Young acting as substitute. A decade earlier the Rokerites reached the League Cup semi-final and were to go one better in 1985, losing the final to Norwich City, who triumphed thanks to an own goal registered by a mortified Sunderland player. Team: Turner, Venison, Pickering, Bennett, Chisholm, Corner, Daniel, Wallace, Hodgson, Berry, Walker; substitute Gayle.

Back to League matters and we find a real yo-yo pattern between the top divisions from 1988 onwards. Two seasons in Division Two were followed by immediate relegation and a further five with the championship won in 1996. The following qualified for medals: Agnew, Ball, Bracewell, Chamberlain, Given, Michael Gray, Philip Gray, Howey, Kubicki, Melville, Ord, Russell and Scott. Division One, taken over by the Football Association, became

the Premiership in 1992 and Sunderland now had a taste of this new elite section. But the club relinquished the coveted status immediately, finishing in a relegation position of 18th.

Season 1997/98 was exciting. Sunderland began moderately, eventually starting a dramatic surge, a main characteristic of which came from the goalscoring proclivities of Kevin Phillips: 29 goals in 42(1) League outings. So to the play-offs. Sheffield United were disposed of and then a Wembley final with Charlton Athletic to decide which club would compete in the 1998/99 Premiership.

The contest was described as perhaps the best ever seen at Wembley, and certainly the most exciting in the last thirty years. Continuous action, lots of goals, no definite result even after extra time and a shoot-out that went to fourteen shots. No wonder even neutral spectators found the tension almost unbearable. In brief, the score was 3-3 after 90 minutes, 4-4 after extra time and 7-6 to Charlton when the seventh Sunderland penalty-taker failed to score. So the prize of an immediate return to Premiership football eluded Sunderland at the last gasp.

But only for a year. Season 1998/99 proved one of the most momentous in the club's history. The First Division was won by an eight-point margin after heading the table for most of the campaign. Promotion came in mid-April with four fixtures still outstanding when a Kevin Phillips hat-trick clinched a handsome 5-2 win at Bury, and the championship was assured three days later. And it came about in spite of key players' absences for long spells through injury. Three were capped for the first time - Kevin Phillips (the club's most prolific scorer since Brian Clough), Allan Johnston and Michael Gray.

Since the unbroken 68-year top-flight membership ended in 1958, Sunderland had led a yo-yo existence, on 14 occasions experiencing promotion joys or relegation regrets in equal measure. Here, then, the fifteenth and happiest yet.

There is a well-known soccer cliché - a game of two halves - which may be adapted for Sunderland's 1999/2000 campaign: a season of two halves. After the runaway promotion success of 1998/99, and stark memories of 1997's immediate descent from the Premiership, supporters could not help but wonder what 1999/2000 held in store. Before the season even began it seemed prospects were not helped by the reluctance of two first-teamers, Michael Bridges and Allan Johnston, to agree new extended contracts. As a result

Bridges moved to Leeds United and Johnston, excluded from the Manager's plans, joined Bolton Wanderers on loan during October. Conversely, the Wearsiders paid a record fee for Stefan Schwarz of Valencia before the season opened.

Any forebodings may have been reinforced by Sunderland's first Premiership engagement when a visit to Chelsea brought a heavy 4-0 defeat. Happily such notions were soon allayed. Of the next 17 League matches, only two were lost and their position in the table from mid-September until December hovered between a lofty second and fourth. Indeed, Sunderland did not drop below fourth until Arsenal won 4-1 at Highbury on 15th January. And even amid a poor run, which began with a 5-0 Boxing Day defeat at Everton and lasted for three months without a victory, the team never fell below the halfway mark.

At the season's end The Lads finished a very creditable seventh. Creditable too for all concerned. Especially the ongoing excellence of Peter Reid's firm management. On the playing front mention must be made of Kevin Phillips' 30 League goals, proof that he is an ace natural scorer in any company. His signing of a five-year contract in March gave immense satisfaction. Paul Butler received his first Eire cap during February while a notable departure occurred in October when that fine servant, Kevin Ball, left for ambitious Fulham.

Finally we express the hope this volume will bring pleasure to Sunderland AFC's magnificent followers. We are both very conscious of the deep affection and passion the club holds for their supporters and vice-versa and have striven accordingly to produce a book worthy of them all.

Garth Dykes
Douglas Lamming

May 2000

NOTES ON THE TEXT

The order of information in each individual entry is that successfully adopted by the Editors in previous Polar publications. Additionally, in this instance, a player's peacetime representative and club honours (if any) have been listed at the end of his entry.

Abbreviations

apps.	appearances
gls.	goals
s'boy	schoolboy
am	amateur
app	apprentice
pro	professional
nc	Non-contract
Yth	Youth
sub	substitute
asst.	assistant
c.	circa
cs	close season
Sch	Schoolboys/schools
Div	Division
PL	The Premier League
FA	The Football Association
FL	The Football League
SL	Scottish League
SPL	Scottish Premier League
SC	Scottish Cup
WC	Welsh Cup
IC	Irish Cup
AIC	Anglo-Italian Cup
ASC	Anglo-Scottish Cup
AMC	Amateur Cup
AWT	Autoglass Windscreens Trophy
SVT	Sherpa Van Trophy
FAT	FA Trophy
FRT	Freight Rover Trophy
IL	Irish League
ECWC	European Cup Winners' Cup
ICFC	Inter Cities Fairs Cup
GMVC	GM Vauxhall Conference
Ire	Ireland
NIre	Northern Ireland
Eng	England
Scot	Scotland
q.v.	(quod vide) denotes a cross-reference

Nomenclature

Clubs have been given titles used at the time when the transfer or other event took place. For example, Small Heath/Birmingham City covers a single club. Also, Bradford refers to the defunct Bradford Park Avenue FC, Bradford City being accorded its full title throughout.

Position

Precise labelling using the classical 11-position goalkeeper to outside-left has been adopted where appropriate. Different modern concepts have necessitated broader terms (midfielder, defender, striker, etc) for recent and present-day players. Also for the early times before the 11 positions were precisely named (and a two-half-back system obtained) 'half-back' and 'forward' are used.

Transfer Fees

Many of the fees quoted here are known to be authentic. The remainder have been culled from newspapers and sporting journals and may be taken to be reasonably near the mark.

Players' statistics in the main body of the text are to the end of the 1998-99 season. However, the authors have added an appendix for 1999-2000 (see p472 onwards) plus incremental information regarding transfers etc to print deadline.

Every player who has appeared for Sunderland at senior competitive level is included, but this excludes the barely commenced season 1939-40. This was abandoned on the outbreak of war with Germany on 3rd September 1939, and subsequently deleted from FL records.

AGBOOLA, Reuben Omojola Folasanje

Role: Defender 1984-92
5'9" 11st.9lbs.
b. Camden, London, 30th May 1962

CAREER: Southampton app July 1978, pro Apr 1980/SUNDERLAND Jan 1985(Charlton Athletic loan Oct-Dec 1986)(Port Vale loan Nov 1990)/Swansea City Nov 1991/Woking Aug 1993/Gosport Borough Nov 1994.

Debut v Southampton (a) 29/1/1985
(Note: His initial appearance was on 12/1/1985 v Liverpool (h), but the game was abandoned).

The son of a Nigerian father and a Dorset mother, Agboola was born in North London and cost Sunderland £150,000 when Len Ashurst signed him in January 1985. A tough competitor whose speed and alertness had been successfully utilised by Southampton in a sweeper role, he nevertheless took some time to establish himself at Roker Park. He first appeared regularly in season 1987-88, under new manager Denis Smith, when the Third Division championship was secured. The Roker crowd certainly appreciated his wholehearted approach and Reuben became the first player capped by an African country whilst with the club when selected by Nigeria in 1990. Promotion was also won in his final season of first-team football (1989-90) when, despite defeat in the Play-off Final at Wembley, Sunderland were promoted. This came about when Swindon Town were relegated following Football League and Inland Revenue investigations into illegal payments.

Appearances:
FL: 131(11) apps.
0 gls.
FAC: 6(1) apps.
0 gls.
FLC: 12(2) apps. 0 gls.
Other: 6 apps. 0 gls.
Total: *155(14) apps. 0gls.*
Honours:
1 Nigerian cap/(Sunderland) Div 3 champs 1988.

AGNEW, David G.

Role: Goalkeeper 1950-51
b. Belfast, 31st March 1925

CAREER: Belfast Crusaders/
SUNDERLAND Jan 1950/
Blyth Spartans July 1953.

David Agnew

Debut v Aston Villa (h) 30/8/1950

His debut, in a 3-3 draw against Aston Villa, turned out to be David Agnew's solitary senior appearance in a three and a half year stay at Roker Park. And, indeed, he was third choice behind Johnny Mapson, Bob Robinson and, after his arrival in the 1952 close season, Harry Threadgold.

Appearances:
FL: 1 app. 0 gls.
Total: *1 app. 0 gls.*
Honours:
1 N.Ire am app. 1950.

AGNEW, Stephen Mark

Role: Midfield 1994-1998
5'10" 11st.9lbs.
b. Shipley, Yorkshire, 9th November 1965

CAREER: Barnsley & District Schoolboys (trials with Mancheser United, Leeds United, Sheffield Wednesday)/Barnsley assoc s'boy Apr 1982, app July 1982, pro Nov 1983/Blackburn Rovers June 1991(Portsmouth loan Nov/Dec 1992)/Leicester City Feb 1993/SUNDERLAND Jan 1995-June 1998/York City July 1998.

Debut v Oldham Athletic (a) 14/1/1995

Steve Agnew began with Barnsley, initially as a striker, making his first League appearance in April 1984. His debut must rank as one of the shortest

Reuben Agboola

ever, as he was on the pitch for only 15 seconds, when called on as a very late substitute against Charlton Athletic. He went on to record more than 200 League and Cup appearances for Barnsley before becoming Blackburn Rovers' record buy at £750,000 in June 1991. He was, however, injured almost immediately and had made only four senior appearances when Leicester City paid £250,000 in February 1993 and effectively resurrected his career. In his first full season at Filbert Street, Steve captained the Foxes to promotion into the Premiership, although injury prevented him from appearing in the Wembley play-off victory against Derby County. Joining Sunderland in January 1995 for £250,000 he helped his new side to avoid relegation and in the following term enjoyed a splendid season in the Division One championship winning side. Subsequently, however, the balding midfield link man spent two seasons of complete frustration. Mainly employed out of position, wide on the right, his unhappy Premiership term was curtailed by an ankle operation and later a fractured wrist. After only four starts in 1997-98 his season was ended in October by an Achilles injury. Out of contract at the end of June 1998, Steve was released and quickly snapped up, on a three year contract, by York City. By coincidence, Steve made his debut for the Minstermen against his former team mates at the Stadium of Light in a first round, second leg, Worthington Cup tie. In common with most affectionately regarded returning players he was given a warm reception by the crowd of over 22,000. In mid September Steve scored his first goals for York, striking twice at Fulham to earn his side a 3-3 draw against the eventual champions. Sadly, he was injured mid-season and unable to assist in an ultimately unsuccessful relegation battle, York losing their Division Two status following a 4-0 defeat at Manchester City in their final fixture of the season.

Appearances:
PL: 11(4) apps. 2 gls.
FL: 45(3) apps. 7 gls.
FAC: 3(1) apps. 1 gl.
FLC: 3 apps. 0 gls.
Total: *62(8) apps. 10 gls.*
Honours:
(Sunderland) Div 1 champs 1996.

Steve Agnew

AGNEW, William Barbour

Role: Right/Left-back 1908-10
5'8" 12st.8lbs.
b. New Cumnock, Ayrshire, 16th December 1880
d. Moffat, 20th August 1936

CAREER: Afton Lads (New Cumnock) and other minor sides prior to joining Kilmarnock Nov 1900/Newcastle United May 1902 £200/ Middlesbrough June 1904/Kilmarnock Sept 1906/SUNDERLAND May 1908/Falkirk Sept 1910-1912/Third Lanark Aug 1913 for a spell, coaching junior players/East Stirlingshire Sept 1913.

Debut v Manchester City 1/9/1908

A 1902 verdict on William Agnew was that "his tackling and clean kicking are of the highest class" to which qualities may be added the capacity for hard work. Against these was a deficiency of speed. Willie's best period was

undoubtedly the second Kilmarnock spell during which all his representative honours were won. He and his then partner, James Mitchell, were Scotland's full-backs against Ireland in 1908. Agnew is notable for being the first of only four players to assist the North-East's 'Big Three'.

Bill Agnew

Appearances:
FL: 28 apps. 0 gls.
Total: *28 apps. 0 gls.*
Honours:
3 Scot caps/2 SL apps.

AINSLEY, George Edward

Role: Inside-right 1932-34
6'1" 13st.4lbs.
b. South Shields, 15th April 1915
d. Seacroft, Leeds, April 1985

CAREER: Co. Durham Schools/South Shields St Andrews/SUNDERLAND Apr 1932/Bolton Wanderers Aug 1936 £2,500/Leeds United Dec 1936/guested for Birmingham, Blackpool,

George Ainsley

Bradford, Crewe Alexandra, Huddersfield Town, Liverpool, Manchester United, Southport & Sunderland during WW2/ Bradford Nov 1947 £5,000 incl G.H. Henry/ retired 1949. Subsequently held many coaching appointments at home (Cambridge University) and abroad - in India Jan 1950, USA, South Africa (Highland Park, Johannesburg) in the 1950's/Pakistan national coach to late 1962/Israel national coach 1963-Dec 1964/Workington manager June 1965-Nov 1966.

Debut v Chelsea (a) 6/5/1933

Big, powerfully built and able to occupy all three inside-forward positions, George Ainsley had great heading ability. His career really took off at Leeds, a fact demonstrated by selection for the FA's 1939 South African tour. He served in the RAF during the Second World War, reaching the high rank of Warrant Officer. Outside football, Ainsley had a reputation as an impersonator of near-professional standard, his repertoire embracing politicians and show business personalities.

Appearances:
FL: 4 apps. 0 gls.
Total: *4 apps. 0 gls.*

AISTON, Samuel James

Role: Winger 1996-date
6'2" 13st.4lbs.
b. Newcastle upon Tyne, 21st November 1976

CAREER: St.Cuthbert's School, Fenham/ Newcastle United Juniors/SUNDERLAND July 1995(Chester City loan Feb 1997)(Chester City loan Nov 1998)(Chester City loan Feb 1999).

Debut v Ipswich Town (a) 2/9/1995

A pacy, shock-haired wingman who enjoyed a splendid first season of senior football in 1995-96. Decent close control coupled with an ability to outstrip most defenders made him a dangerous raider in Sunderland's championship season. A loan spell to Chester City in Jan 1997 was designed to further his League experience and he assisted them to a place in the Division Three play-off semi finals. Sadly, in what was expected to be a season of further progress for the young wingman, he seriously damaged knee

Sam Aiston

AITKEN, George Gilbert Miller

Role: Half-back 1951-59
5'10" 13st.8lbs.
b. Lochgelly, Fife, 28th May 1925

CAREER: Lochore St Andrew's/Lochgelly
Albert(Wolverhampton Wanderers trial)/
East Fife 1943/Third Lanark Feb 1951/
SUNDERLAND Nov 1951 £19,500/
Gateshead Mar 1959 approx. £3,500/retired
1960.

Debut v Fulham (h) 24/11/1951

ligaments in a Central League match at the
Hawthorns in October 1997. His accidental
clash with the West Bromwich Albion
goalkeeper necessitated two operations and a
lengthy period of recuperation. Returning to
action in October 1998 after almost a year on
the sidelines, Sam was restricted to just two
substitute appearances for Sunderland in the
championship season. Two further separate
loan spells with Chester City, however, gave
him the opportunity to build his fitness levels.
Doubtless he will be hoping for a change of
fortune and some Premiership action in 1999-
2000.

Appearances:
PL: 0(2) apps. 0 gls.
FL: 5(13) apps. 0 gls.
FAC: 0(2) apps. 0 gls.
FLC: 0(2) app. 0 gls.
Total: *5(19) apps. 0 gls.*
Honours:
(Sunderland) Div 1 champs 1996/
6 Eng Sch caps.

Methil, a smallish town in Fifeshire linked
historically with coal exporting, is also
home to East Fife FC. And this football club
has a cup-tie past that few other lesser
Scottish League members can match. It
started in 1927 when the Scottish Cup final
was reached, an unheard-of feat for a
Second Division club. Eleven years later
they went one better, actually winning the
trophy and becoming the sole Second
Division side to do so. Then, after the War,
they contrived to carry off the Division 'B'
championship - by a considerable eleven
points margin - and the League Cup in the
same season, 1947-48. And followed this
again in 1950 and 1954, reaching the
Scottish Cup final as well in 1950. In two of
those memorable finals, those of 1948 and
1950, East Fife fielded a bed-rock half-back
line - Philp, William Finlay and George
Aitken - besides several forwards destined
to win Scotland caps. The latter included
Charlie Fleming, like Aitken eventually to
join Sunderland. The halves were tersely
and accurately summed up in print as
'daunting'. All three boasted good
physiques and performed with vigorous
command and style. George Aitken was the
heaviest of the trio and earned another
niche in the East Fife story as the club's
most capped player: five of his eight
Scotland appearances occured in his first
phase while on the Bayview register, the
remainder when at Roker Park. George,
however, did not come straight to
Sunderland from the Fifers. He went first
to the well-known, but sadly now defunct
outfit, Third Lanark. Thirds at the time
were in the top Division although in the
bottom half. George's stay at Cathkin was a

short one: a matter of only nine months covering a total of 20 League games. His costly move to Sunderland proved sound business. For a start, his spell at Roker Park lasted a lengthy seven and a half years with League appearances averaging 32 per season. And he had utility value in that he occupied all three half-back berths although predominantly at left-half, as in his East Fife days. A burly man and a hard competitor but nevertheless finely constructive, he possessed and exploited one of the longest throws of his time. Aitken had worked as a miner originally, continuing in the job after joining East Fife during wartime. He had attracted the attention of Wolves' manager, Major Buckley, when a junior with Lochgelly Albert. Brought to Wolverhampton on trial, he was unable to settle in the Black Country and so returned to his native Fife. Sunderland ended their record period in the top flight ten months before his transfer to nearby Gateshead. There he made 58 Division Four appearances, missing only two in his single full season at Redheugh Park. This season, 1959-60, turned out to be Gateshead's last in the Football League. After retiring from the game George worked in the motor trade in Sunderland.

Appearances:
FL: 245 apps. 3 gls.
FAC: 22 apps. 0 gls.
Total: *267 apps. 3 gls.*
Honours:
8 Scot caps/
(East Fife) SL Div 'B'
champs 1948/
SLC winner 1948,
1950/SC finalist 1950.

ALLAN, Adam McIlroy

Role: Centre-half 1927-30
6'0" 12st.6lbs.
b. Newarthill, Lanarks, 12th September 1904

CAREER: Regent Star (Glasgow) 1925/Falkirk 1926/SUNDERLAND Apr 1927 £5,000 incl Robert Thomson/Reading July 1930/Queen of the South Aug 1933-1937.

Debut v Portsmouth (h) 27/8/1927

Adam Allan had a handy physique for the pivotal role thus presenting an appreciable barrier to opposing attacks. He could head the ball a long, long way. Allan was seen to best effect in his native Scotland, quickly attracting attention on joining Falkirk and, finally, enjoying a run of 123 outings (3 goals) in the

George Aitken playing in the garden with son William.

four seasons immediately following Queen of the South's elevation to the Scottish League's top flight. Reports described him as having "... a ready wit and (to be) a great companion".

Appearances:
FL: 63 apps. 0 gls.
FAC: 2 apps. 0 gls.
Total: *65 apps. 0 gls.*

ALLAN, James

Role: Left-wing forward 1884-88
b. Scotland (possibly Ayrshire)
d. October 1912
Debut v Redcar (a) 8/11/1884 (FAC)

James Allan was the founder of Sunderland FC and therefore an imperishable name in the club's annals. He also later founded the short-lived, but distinguished, Sunderland Albion FC. The best and most renowned of the very earliest players, Allan acted at various times as club secretary and trainer. He was a schoolmaster by profession, a

James Allan

product of Glasgow University. After his arrival in Sunderland in 1877 he originally taught at the Hendon Board School and later at the Hylton Road School. A real personality player and team vice-captain, James scored many goals, often in unorthodox fashion and was selected for both County Durham and Northumberland County XIs. A bad injury during the season 1886/87 hastened the end of his playing career and he left the soccer scene in 1892 following the demise of Sunderland Albion.

Appearances:
FAC: 3 apps. 0 gls.
Total: *3 apps. 0 gls.*

Adam Allan

ALLAN, Robert

Role: Goalkeeper 1907-08
6'1" 12st.6lbs.

CAREER: Cronberry Eglington/ SUNDERLAND Aug 1907/ Heart of Midlothian cs 1908.

Debut v Aston Villa (a) 9/9/1907

A recruit from junior football, Robert Allan played in a number of practice games prior to the 1907/08 season under the name of Wilson but soon received a senior baptism. This occurred in the shape of a consecutive run of ten matches early in the 1907-08 campaign, starting with the third League fixture. The run comprised three wins, five defeats and two draws and Allan conceded 14 goals. His only remaining appearance came the following Boxing Day, in a 3-3 home draw against Bristol City. Interestingly, Robert left for Hearts, from which club Sunderland recruited another goalkeeping Allan, namely Tom (q.v.) in 1908.

NOTE: *In some records the player's surname is spelt Allen.*

Appearances:
FL: 11 apps. 0 gls.
Total: 11 apps. 0 gls.

Robert Allan

ALLAN, Thomas E.

Role: Goalkeeper 1908-11
5'8" 12st.0lbs.
b. Glasgow

Thomas Allan

CAREER: Wellwood Star/ Rutherglen Glencairn/ Heart of Midlothian 1905/SUNDERLAND Apr 1908 £350/Heart of Midlothian May 1911/Motherwell May 1914.

Debut v Bradford City (a) 20/2/1909

After commanding a then sizeable fee, Tom Allan's three years at Roker Park were largely spent in understudying the great L.R. Roose. He had joined Hearts at the tail end of their memorable 1890's/1900's epoch. Allan was an excellent goalkeeper, never more so than in his second Tynecastle spell when he regularly won high praise (and an inter-League medal) for bravery when under siege, this notwithstanding a moderate height and reach.

Appearances:
FL: 24 apps. 0 gls.
FAC: 2 apps. 0 gls.
Total: *26 apps. 0 gls.*
Honours:
4 Scot jnr apps./1 SL app. 1912.

ALLAN, W.M.

Role: Half-back 1884-85
Debut v Redcar (a) 8/11/1884 (FAC)

Allan played at centre-half in Sunderland's first ever FA Cup-tie. He also appeared at wing-half and made his debut, in the opening engagement of season 1881/82, at left-back. He was obviously a player of some versatility.

W.M. Allan

Appearances:
FAC: 1 app. 0 gls.
Total: *1 app. 0 gls.*

ALLARDYCE, Samuel

Role: Defender 1980-81
6'2" 14st.0lbs.
b. Dudley, 19th October 1954

CAREER: Bolton Wanderers app, pro Nov 1971/SUNDERLAND July 1980/Millwall Sept 1981/Tampa Bay Rowdies (USA) June 1983/ Coventry City Sept 1983/Tampa Bay (USA)/ Huddersfield Town July 1984/Bolton Wanderers July 1985/Preston North End Aug 1986/West Bromwich Albion coach June 1989/ Limerick (Ireland) manager cs 1990/Preston North End coach cs 1992, caretaker-manager Sept-Dec 1992/Blackpool manager July 1994-May 1996/SUNDERLAND youth manager Sept 1996/Notts County manager Jan 1997-Oct 1999/Bolton Wanderers manager Oct 1999.

Debut v Everton (h) 16/8/1980

As a Bolton player and team mate of Peter Reid in December 1975, Sam Allardyce scored one of the most memorable headed goals ever conceded by Sunderland. A £150,000 signing

Sam Allardyce

by Ken Knighton in the summer of 1980 following Sunderland's return to Division One, Allardyce was quickly appointed club captain. Before the end of the season, however, both Ken Knighton and his assistant Frank Clark were sacked and relegation was only avoided by virtue of a 1-0 victory against Liverpool at Anfield in the last match of the season. Four months later, Third Division Millwall paid £95,000 for his transfer. Fifteen years on Reid was instrumental in Sam's return to Roker as Director of Youth with responsibilities for restructuring the club's youth system. His stay proved brief however as he became Notts County's sixth manager within the space of 28 months in early 1997. He was unable to halt their slide into soccer's basement, however, their first win in 21 matches finally occurring against York City on 5th April 1997. In a truly remarkable transformation he led the Magpies to the championship of Division Three in 1997-98 by a massive 17 point margin but they were relegated again in 1998-99. Father of Craig Allardyce (P.N.E., Blackpool, Peterborough United and Mansfield Town).

Appearances:
FL: 24(1) apps. 2 gls.
FLC: 2 apps. 0 gls.
Total: *26(1) apps. 2 gls.*
Honours:
(Bolton Wanderers) Div 2 champs 1978.

ALLEN, Thomas

Role: Goalkeeper 1919-20
6'0" 10st.6lbs.
b. Moxley, Staffs, 1st May 1897
d. 10th May 1968

CAREER: Bilston United 1914/Old Park Works (Wednesbury)/Hickman's Institute FC (Birmingham League)/Wolverhampton Wanderers, on amateur forms during WW1/ SUNDERLAND May 1919/Southampton May 1920/Coventry City June 1928/Accrington Stanley July 1932/Northampton Town Sept 1933/Kidderminster Harriers Aug 1934-1936/ Cradley Heath Dec 1937.

Debut v Aston Villa (a) 6/9/1919

Tom Allen was a tall, slim custodian of no great physical presence, indeed, he acquired the nickname of 'Shadow' at Coventry because of his gangling frame. Yet his League career encompassed 15 years and well over 500 appearances. Allen had won recognition before turning professional, representing both North of England Juniors and, in 1916, the Birmingham League. Tom, brilliant as well as being extraordinarily consistent, was an ever-present in Southampton's 1921/22 championship side, conceding only 21 goals in 42 matches which must constitute some sort of record. During his year on Wearside Allen played in two winning derbies against Newcastle - both in front of record crowds.

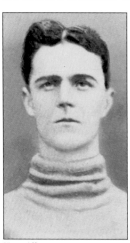

Tom Allen

Appearances:
FL: 19 apps. 0 gls.
FAC: 1 app. 0 gls.
Total: *20 apps. 0 gls.*
Honours:
(Southampton) FL Div 3 (Sth) champs 1922.

ANDERSON, George Albert

Role: Goalkeeper 1911-13
5'10" 12st.0lbs.
b. Haydon Bridge, Northumberland, 1887
d. Dundee, spring 1954

CAREER: Haydon Bridge FC for 3 seasons/ Mickley Colliery/SUNDERLAND May 1911/ Aberdeen May 1914-1922/Aberdeen director during the 1930's/Dundee manager during the 1950's.

Debut v Middlesbrough (a) 30/12/1911

George Anderson came to Roker from a successful Mickley side, proving a competent and daring deputy for Walter Scott and, in his first season, making eight appearances. However, thanks to the advent of Joe Butler, he made only a couple more in a three year stay, and moved on to Aberdeen shortly

George Anderson

before the outbreak of the First World War. The Scottish League maintained a full programme throughout the conflict, Anderson holding a regular place, and this continued after the Armistice. Altogether, Anderson grossed 213 Scottish League and Cup appearances for the Dons. After giving up playing, he went into business in Aberdeen and served as a town councillor. He was even caretaker-manager of Aberdeen F.C. for much of the World War Two period standing in for ex Sunderland scoring legend David Halliday who was away serving the war effort. George was also an excellent cricketer, good enough to act as wicket-keeper for Aberdeenshire County Cricket Club.

Appearances:
FL: 10 apps. 0 gls.
Total: *10 apps. 0 gls.*

ANDERSON, Stanley

Role: Right-half 1952-64
5'9" 11st.10lbs.
b. Horden, Co Durham, 27th February 1934

CAREER: East Durham Schools/Springwell United/Horden Colliery Welfare/ SUNDERLAND am June 1949, pro Feb 1951/ Newcastle United Nov 1963 £19,000/ Middlesbrough player-coach Nov 1965 £11,500, retired from playing and became manager Apr 1966/AEK(Athens) manager Jan 1973-Apr 1974/Queens Park Rangers coach June 1974, caretaker-manager Sept-Oct 1974/ Manchester City coach Dec 1974/Doncaster Rovers manager Feb 1975/Bolton Wanderers asst. manager Nov 1978, manager Feb 1980-May 1981, thereafter scouting for various clubs.

Debut v Portsmouth (h) 4/10/1952

Stan Anderson is a prominent personality from Sunderland's modern post-war history. Not only a member of a distinguished quartet that assisted all the North-East's 'Big Three' clubs, but, in addition, he skippered all three as well. The combined total of Stan's League appearances in these engagements came to a prodigious 504 of which four-fifths were in Sunderland's colours. Only Len Ashurst has played more League and Cup games for Sunderland as an outfield player. Anderson showed great potential from the start, graduating from his school team to represent East Durham Schools from where he progressed to schoolboy international status. Unsurprisingly, he captained the England Boys team. After school he worked as an apprentice plasterer and plumber but thoughts of a football career always loomed large in his mind. Turned down by Middlesbrough, he assisted a couple of minor teams before signing amateur forms for Sunderland two years prior to turning professional at 17. Stan's development into a class wing-half was both steady and assured, his senior debut coming after one-and-a-half years as a paid player. He was soon established as the regular right-half, a circumstance maintained during National Service as he was conveniently based at Catterick. Anderson's qualities were many -

resolution, vision, a notably relentless tackle and an all-pervading consistency. And, of course, eventually leadership on appointment as captain. His length of service stretched nearly 14 years. It also encompassed all his adult representative honours: an England 'B' appearance (1957), four Under-23 caps (1955-57) and, finally two full caps - the only Sunderland player capped by England in the 1960's. He was also captain at Under-23 level. Many thought the stigma of a sending-off in an Under-23 match, against Bulgaria in 1957, the reason for so meagre a haul of full caps. However, the truth about whether this misdemeanour was held against him is never likely to be revealed. What cannot be denied is that exceedingly tough competition existed at the time for the England wing-half spots, the age of Clayton, Moore, Flowers and Bobby Robson. Stan, almost the only local in a team of well-known players, felt the 1958 relegation more keenly than most. The way back proved far from easy. Don Revie relinquished the captaincy at the end of 1957/58, Charlie Hurley taking over with Stan as vice-captain. When Hurley was unfit Stan took charge, and did so well the generous Hurley, restored to fitness, argued he should keep the job. Stan scored twice in an unforgettable 2-1 FA Cup

Stan Anderson

third round win over Arsenal at Roker in 1961 and remained a regular until the actual promotion season of 1963-64 when, after ten League outings, he was replaced at right-half by Martin Harvey. Harvey, by then a full Northern Ireland international, had understudied Anderson for a long while, and aged 22 was a fine prospect. In such circumstances Sunderland reasoned they could afford to part with Anderson - which they did to rivals Newcastle United. The transfer created a sensation. Moves between North-East giants are not all that common but for one to involve such a long-serving icon, still under 30 and a powerful performer, caused a major furore. He did however, return for a well deserved testimonial shortly after. Newcastle though did an excellent piece of business. They were building for a promotion push which duly came in the shape of the 1964/65 Second Division championship. Stan's final playing move to Middlesbrough seemed a touch ironical in view of the Teessiders' rejection in his youth. Initially he found the differing demands of playing and coaching difficult. Appointed manager too late to avoid relegation, he nonetheless brought about a revival and gained promotion back to Division Two in 1967, not least by making training schedules far more enjoyable for the players. Several appointments followed, including a short-lived and rather unhappy one at Bolton, where Peter Reid was one of his young charges.

Appearances:
FL: 402 apps. 31 gls.
FAC: 34 apps. 4 gls.
FLC: 11 apps. 0 gls.
Total: *447 apps. 35 gls.*
Honours:
2 Eng caps/1 Eng B app./
4 Eng U-23 apps./3 Eng Sch apps./
(Newcastle United) FL Div 2
champs 1965.

Stan Anderson

ANGELL, Brett Ashley Mark

Role: Forward 1994-96
6'2" 13st.12lbs.
b. Marlborough, Wilts., 20th August 1968

CAREER: Portsmouth Aug 1986/Cheltenham Town/Derby County Feb 1988/Stockport County Oct 1988/Southend United Aug 1990 (Everton loan Sept 1993)/Everton Jan 1994/ SUNDERLAND Mar 1995(Sheffield United loan Jan 1996)(West Bromwich Albion loan Mar 1996)(Stockport County loan Aug 1996)/ Stockport County Nov 1996.

Debut v Barnsley (a) 24/3/1995

When Brett Angell joined Sunderland on transfer deadline day in 1995 he was just three goals short of a career century of goals in League and Cup competitions. Usually on the scoresheet when opposed to Sunderland, the powerfully built £750,000 striker spent an unhappy 20 months at Roker, completely losing his form and confidence. Within days of his signing, manager Mick Buxton was sacked, and Angell failed to impress new manager Peter Reid. Unrewarding loan spells to Sheffield United and West Bromwich Albion preceded a return to his former club Stockport County for a cut-price fee of £120,000. Happily, in familiar surroundings, he soon rediscovered his scoring ability. A memorable run to the semi-finals of the Coca Cola Cup was followed by promotion to Division One, clinched by his fifth minute

Brett
Angell

ANDREWS, Arthur

Role: Left-half 1922-31
5'9" 12st.2lbs.
b. Hylton, Sunderland, 12th January 1901
d. Sunderland, 3rd May 1971

CAREER: Lambton Star/Durham City am cs 1920, pro May 1921/ SUNDERLAND Nov 1922/Blyth Spartans Mar 1931/Spennymoor United later in the 1930's.

Debut v Everton (a) 9/12/1922

Arthur Andrews was a Roker regular for much of the 1920's and one-third of the redoubtable half-back line of Clunas, Parker and Andrews that held sway during seasons 1923/24-1926/27 inclusive. Arthur was an admirable clubman, a model of consistency and sound in all departments of half-back play. Indeed, in seven consecutive seasons from 1923/24 to 1929/30 he never made less than 27 League appearances. He first sampled Football League fare in Durham City's first two Northern Section campaigns. After leaving the game Arthur joined the police force.

Appearances:
FL: 227 apps. 2 gls.
FAC: 17 apps. 0 gls.
Total: *244 apps. 2 gls.*

goal against F.A.Cup semi finalists, Chesterfield, at the Recreation Ground. A goalscorer against Sunderland at the Stadium of Light in March 1998, Brett Angell's outstanding scoring record during the season was a key factor in helping unfashionable Stockport County to eighth place in Division One. Season 1998-99 proved less successful for the Edgeley Park club. Nevertheless, Brett again headed County's goalscoring lists, a feat he achieved in each of the last three seasons.

Appearances:
FL: 10 apps. 0 gls.
FLC: 1 app. 1 gls.
Total: *11 apps. 1 gl.*

ANNAN, Walter Archibald

Walter Annan

Role: Left -back 1902-03
5'9" 11st.10lbs.
b. Bathgate, West Lothian, circa 1880

CAREER: West Calder Aug 1899/Edinburgh St.Bernards May 1900/SUNDERLAND Apr 1902/Sheffield United Jan 1904/Bristol City May 1905/Burslem Port Vale July 1911-1912/ Mid-Rhondda FC manager 1912/Bristol City coach Mar 1921.

Debut v Notts County (h) 4/4/1903

Annan's solitary senior outing with Sunderland turned out to be the introduction to a decade of Football League activity. His best period was at Bristol City where he was first choice right-back for the bulk of a six-year stay, and where he earned his League and FA Cup medals. He was summed up in 1902 as "... a powerful back in any position and a most serviceable player all round". Annan later served in the Bristol police force.

Appearances:
FL: 1 app. 0 gls.
Total: *1 app. 0 gls.*
Honours: *(Bristol City) FL Div 2 champions 1906, FA Cup finalist 1909*

ARCHBOLD

Role: Right-back 1888-89
Debut v Elswick Rangers 27/10/1888 (FAC)

Archbold made two first team appearances for Sunderland in 1888/89, one being the above game in the FA Cup qualifying competition at home which was won 5-3. The other came a week later at home against Long Eaton Rangers when the lively Sunderland forwards again notched up a five in a 5-1 victory. Archbold played at right-back in the Cup-tie and on the left flank against Long Eaton.

Appearances:
FAC: 1 app. 0 gls.
Total: *1 app. 0 gls.*

ARMSTRONG, Gordon Ian

Role: Midfield 1984-96
6' 0" 12st.11lbs.
b. Newcastle-upon-Tyne, 15th July 1967

CAREER: Newcastle Schoolboys/ Northumberland Schoolboys/SUNDERLAND assoc s'boy June 1982 app, pro July 1985 (Bristol City loan August 1995)(Northampton Town loan Jan 1996)/Bury July 1996/Burnley Aug 1998.

Debut v West Bromwich Albion (a) 24/4/1985

An outstanding goalscoring midfielder and one of Sunderland's best ever local discoveries, Gordon Armstrong gave over a decade of service at Roker during which time he qualified as one of the club's top ten appearance makers. He was also the first

Sunderland midfielder since 1973 cup-winning skipper Bobby Kerr to score 50 League goals for the club. Twice voted Sunderland's Young Player of the Year, he made his debut as a 17-year-old in the final weeks of season 1984-85. A change of manager in the close season saw Gordon out of the picture until December of the following term when he was reintroduced by Lawrie McMenemy. He seized his opportunity by scoring in a 1-1 draw against Crystal Palace and thereafter became a regular first team squad member. As an attacking midfielder with outstanding aerial ability he scored 13 League and Cup goals in 1989-90 and within a total of 11 in 1991-92 was his memorable last-minute headed winner against Chelsea, which took Sunderland into the F.A. Cup semi-final. He appeared to be on his way out of Roker when listed by Terry Butcher but regained his first team place to extend his

ARDLEY, George Henry

Role: Right half 1919-20
5'8" 10st.9lbs.
b. Langley Park, Co Durham, 4th qtr 1897
d. Weardale, 3rd qtr 1927

CAREER: Langley Park FC/SUNDERLAND am 1919/20, pro Aug 1920/Shildon F.C. May 1921.

Debut v Liverpool (h) 1/5/1920

George Ardley was still an amateur when he made his sole League appearance, a 0-1 home defeat in the last fixture of the 1919/20 campaign. In the following close season, on signing him as a professional, manager Bob Kyle reported that the player was "quite good and was badly wanted by Oldham". That club's interest had apparently cooled before his release a year later.

>   **Appearances:**
>   *FL: 1 app. 0 gls.*
>   **Total:** *1 app. 0 gls.*

ARMSTRONG, Keith Thomas

Role: Wing Forward 1977-78
5'8" 11st.5lbs.
b. Corbridge, Northumberland, 11th October 1957

CAREER: Newcastle Schools/SUNDERLAND Jan 1975(Newport County loan Aug 1978)

(Scunthorpe United loan Oct 1978) Oulu Palloseura, Finland following release by Sunderland Mar 1979/Newcastle United June 1979/Hong Kong winter 1979/Oulu Palloseura (Newport County trial Oct 1980) (Workington trial Nov 1980) Oulu Palloseura.

Keith Armstrong

Debut v Cardiff City (h) 4/10/1977 (sub)

Basically a Reserve team player at Roker Park, Keith Armstrong's short run of consecutive League appearances spanned the final two months of season 1977-78 when Sunderland finished sixth in Division Two. Two separate loan spells did little to further his League experience in a career spanning a very modest 10(6) appearances and no goals. He found more success in Europe, winning a League championship with OPS Oulu (Finland). In 1980-81 he played for them

appearances to over 400, before joining Bury on a free transfer in July 1996. In his first season in Lancashire he assisted his new team to the championship of Division Two with an undefeated record in League matches at Gigg Lane, the only unblemished home record in the Nationwide and Premier Leagues in 1996-97. In August 1998 he followed his former Bury boss, Stan Ternent, to Burnley.

>   **Appearances:**
>   *FL: 336(18) apps. 50 gls.*
>   *FAC: 18 apps. 4 gls.*
>   *FLC: 25(4) apps. 3 gls.*
>   *Other: 13 apps. 4 gls.*
>   **Total:** *392(22) apps. 61 gls.*
>   **Honours:**
>   *1 FL app./(Sunderland) Div 3 champs 1988/*
>   *(Bury) Div 2 champs 1997*

Gordon Armstrong

against European Cup winners Liverpool in the first round of the competition. Surprisingly enough, in the same month, a trial with Newport County failed to win him a permanent engagement.

Appearances:
FL: 7(4) apps 0 gls.
Total *7(4) apps. 0 gls.*

ARNOTT, Kevin William

Role: Midfield 1976-82
5'10" 11st.12lbs.
b. Gateshead, 28th September 1958

CAREER: St. Aidan's, Sunderland/ Sunderland Schoolboys/SUNDERLAND assoc s'boy Oct 1973, app July 1975, pro Sept 1976 (Blackburn Rovers loan Nov 1981)/Sheffield United June 1982(Blackburn Rovers loan Nov 1982)(Rotherham United loan Mar 1983)/ Vasalund(Sweden) June-Oct 1987/Chesterfield n.c. Nov 1987-Mar 1988/Vasalund (Sweden) Mar-Aug 1988/Chesterfield Aug 1988-1991/ Playing in Sweden again in 1991/ Nykarbley(Finland) 1992-94/Hebburn F.C. 1994/Jarrow Roofing Boldon C.A. player-coach 1995 subsequently asst. manager/coach.

Debut v Wrexham (a) 12/1/1977 (sub) (FAC)

Kevin Arnott

Signed by Sunderland straight from school, Kevin Arnott's undoubted class and potential saw him elevated to the professional ranks at 18 years of age. His introduction into the League side, three days after his debut bow in a Cup replay at Wrexham, coincided with a six match unbeaten spell and a goal average of 17-1. Nevertheless, his best season came in 1979-80 when promotion to Division One was secured. The final game of the season against F.A.Cup winners West Ham clinched Sunderland's promotion, Arnott scoring one of the goals in a 2-0 victory before a capacity attendance of 47,129. Kevin proved an altogether stylish and highly skilful operator with a positive first touch that was stamped with genuine class. After a brief loan spell with Blackburn Rovers, he was transferred to Sheffield United, managed at that time by former team mate Ian Porterfield (q.v.). A knee injury ended his League career at Chesterfield, although he was able to resume playing during his spell in Finland, and subsequently in the North Eastern League.

Appearances:
FL: 132(1) apps. 16 gls.
FAC: 6(1) apps. 0 gls.
FLC: 7(1) apps. 1 gl.
Other: 1 app. 0 gls.
Total: *146(3) apps. 17 gls.*

ARTHUR, Joseph Ord

Role: Outside left 1910-12
5'8" 11st.4lbs.
b. South Shields, 11th July 1891
d. South Shields, 2nd qtr 1975

CAREER: South Shields Parkside/ SUNDERLAND May 1910/South Shields FC cs 1912(guested for Preston Colliery during WW1), later assisted Southport Central.

Debut v Bury (a) 14/4/1911

Joseph Arthur had two seasons at Roker Park with a League appearance in each. The second was also near the season's end - a 0-1 home defeat against Bolton Wanderers. He was a useful winger though much in the shadow of the great Arthur Bridgett and, from January 1912, that of another England cap, Harry Martin. Arthur was a rivetter by trade.

Appearances:
FL: 2 apps. 0 gls.
Total: *2 apps. 0 gls.*

ASHURST, John

Role: Central Defender 1971-80
6' 0" 12st.4lbs.
b. Coatbridge, 12th October 1954

CAREER: Renton Juniors/SUNDERLAND
app. 1969 pro Oct 1971/Blackpool Oct 1979/
Carlisle United Aug 1981/Leeds United July
1986/Doncaster Rovers Nov 1988/Bridlington
Town/Doncaster Rovers Nov 1990(Rochdale
month's trial Aug 1992).

Debut v Milwall (a) 9/9/1972

Long-serving central defender Jackie Ashurst
took some time to establish himself at Roker
Park. He had in fact sought a transfer before
becoming established during the last two
months of the promotion season 1975-76, in a
central defensive partnership with Bobby
Moncur as a place opened up following an
injury to Jeff Clarke. For the following two
seasons he was one of the first names on the
team sheet, but was out of the first team
picture when he became Blackpool's record
signing at £110,000 in October 1979. In a career
totalling 603(12) League appearances and 12
goals, he bowed out of senior football at 37
years of age, having appeared in 37 of
Doncaster Rovers 42 League engagements in
season 1991-92.

> **Appearances:**
> *FL: 129(11) apps. 4 gls.*
> *FAC: 8(3) apps. 0 gls.*
> *FLC: 8 apps. 0 gls.*
> *Others: 4 apps. 0 gls.*
> **Total:** *149(14) apps. 4 gls.*
> **Honours:** *(Sunderland) Div 2 champs 1976.*

*Jackie
Ashurst*

ASHURST, Leonard

Role: Left-back 1958-70
5'9" 11st.5lbs.
b. Aintree, Liverpool, 10th March 1939

CAREER: Liverpool Schools (Liverpool FC
am for four years and also on Wolves'
books as an am)/Prescot Cables/
SUNDERLAND Dec 1957/Hartlepool
United player-manager Mar 1971, retiring
from playing in 1973/Gillingham manager
May 1974/Sheffield Wednesday manager
Oct 1975-Oct 1977/Newport County
manager June 1978/Cardiff City manager
Mar 1982/SUNDERLAND manager Mar
1984-May 1985/Kuwait national coach
1985/Qatar coach/Blackpool assistant-
manager/Cardiff City manager Sept 1989-
May 1991/Weymouth manager to Apr
1993.

Debut v Ipswich Town (h) 20/9/1958

A long-time footballing man - 16 years a
Football League player and well over 20
years in coaching and administration, Len
grossed over 450 League and Cup
appearances in Sunderland's colours. He is
still one of only two outfield players to
record over 400 League games for the club.
As a player he was well described as

*Len
Ashurst*

"strong and difficult to beat" and, in 1964 when a member of the promotion team, "has established himself as one of the steadiest defenders in the League". Len attended the Fazackerley Secondary Modern School in Liverpool, shining at both cricket and football - he played for the Lancashire Schools Cricket X1 when 13. He was centre-half in the schools football team, eventually being called up for a trial for Liverpool Schools. There were three other boys, bigger and heavier than Len, also on trial for the pivotal spot, but he was able to take the place at right back of a lad who fortuitously for Len failed to turn up. At the time Ashurst was heavily reliant on his stronger left foot so was switched to left-back at half-time; thus left-back became his position from then on. He was a member of the Liverpool Schools side that won the English Schools trophy in 1953, which led to a place on the Anfield ground staff. Len remained on Liverpool's books for three years, during which time he served an apprenticeship as a printer. It was also in this period he made his seven England Youth appearances, so it came as a surprise and disappointment that the club decided not to offer a professional engagement.

However, George Curtis, the old Southampton forward who was then also on Sunderland's staff as well as running the England Youth team, came to the rescue. He was instrumental in arranging for Len to join Sunderland as a part-time professional whilst completing his apprenticeship as a compositor with a local printing firm. Len made his senior debut in September 1958 aged 19 in the very match that his future partner, Cecil Irwin, also made his first appearance. 'Cec' was a mere 16 years five months old on that date and still an amateur.

It is interesting to speculate if

Len
Ashurst

this was the first-class game's most youthful debutant full-back partnership. 'Lennie the Lion' always gave one hundred per cent commitment to the Sunderland cause and rarely missed a game. Indeed, he was ever-present in the 1964 promotion side. Len's years of sterling service were rewarded with a testimonial match against Newcastle before his 1971 free transfer to Hartlepool - his first managerial appointment which initially found him playing also. Before hanging up his boots a couple of years later he had made 42 League appearances and, besides managing and playing, had acted as trainer/coach as well. Such an all-round introduction into club administration was beneficial experience for future appointments. Len signed and developed several youngsters later to star with Sheffield Wednesday and steered Newport County to promotion. And, through winning the Welsh Cup, into European competition, County commendably reaching the Cup Winners' Cup quarter-final. He managed Cardiff City to promotion during his first spell at Ninian Park too. Ashurst's year as Sunderland's manager was not a happy one for, although the club reached the 1985 League Cup final, his Wembley team selection was controversial as Sunderland lost and the slump which followed saw the club relegated to Division Two, nine points adrift from the side in 20th place, Norwich City who also went down despite having beaten Sunderland in the League Cup Final. Perhaps not surprisingly, Ashurst was sacked. A major plus point, however, was the signing of Gary Bennett who he had managed at Cardiff. Since leaving the League scene Len, besides Weymouth, has managed a club further down the non-League ladder - Weston-super-Mare FC. He lives in the picturesque Wye Valley district.

Appearances:
FL: 403(6) apps. 4 gls.
FAC: 26 apps. 0 gls.
FLC: 23 apps. 0 gls.
Total: *452(6) apps. 4 gls.*
Honours:
1 Eng U-23 app./7 Eng Youth apps.

ATKINS, Ian Leslie

Role: Midfield 1982-84
6'0" 11st.3lbs.
b. Sheldon, Birmingham, 16th January 1957

CAREER: Sheldon Heath School/Leafield Athletic/Shrewsbury Town app June 1973,pro Jan 1975/SUNDERLAND Aug 1982/Everton Nov 1984/Ipswich Town Sept 1985 (Birmingham City loan Mar 1988)/ Birmingham City Apr 1988/Colchester United player-manager June 1990/Birmingham City player-asst. manager June 1991/Cambridge United manager Dec 1992-May 1993/ SUNDERLAND asst. manager June-Dec 1993/ Northampton Town manager Jan 1995-Oct 1999.

Debut v Aston Villa (a) 28/8/1982

An outstanding 1981-82 season with Shrewsbury Town (17 goals in 40 League appearances) had the scouts flocking to the Gay Meadow and it was Sunderland who were successful in securing Ian Atkins services. In a cash plus exchange deal, he cost

Ian Atkins

£30,000 with Alan Brown moving in the opposite direction. Hard-working, enthusiastic, and with highly developed competitive spirit, Atkins captained Sunderland to their highest post war position in Division One for sixteen years, but in the following term, which saw the departure of manager Alan Durban, relegation was only avoided by a win on the last day of the season at Leicester City. In a season of 'all change' in 1984-85, Atkins was just one of ten out-going players as new manager Len Ashurst financed his re-building programme. A second and short-lived spell at Roker came when Terry Butcher, who he'd worked with at Ipswich, appointed him as his assistant in the summer of 1993, a position terminated along with the sacking of Butcher in December of the same year. As Northampton Town's manager, he successfully guided them, via the Play-off Final at Wembley, to promotion from Division Three. Unfortunately, a second, successive, Wembley appearance in May 1998 saw the Cobblers beaten by Grimsby Town in the Second Division Play-off Final. In 1998-99 Northampton were relegated to Division Three, despite a nine-match unbeaten run at the end of the season - a dismal home record of just four wins, and a high percentage of drawn matches (18) significant contributory factors.

Appearances:
FL: 76(1) apps. 6 gls.
FAC: 4 apps. 0 gls.
FLC: 6 apps. 0 gls.
Total: 86(1) apps. 6 gls.
Honours:
(Shrewsbury Town) Div 3
champs 1979.

ATKINSON, Brian

Role: Midfield 1988-96
5'10" 12st.0lbs.
b. Darlington, 19th January 1971

CAREER: Avenue Comprehensive School, Newton Aycliffe/Bishop Auckland Schoolboys/Durham County Schoolboys/ Nunthorpe Athletic Juniors/SUNDERLAND

Brian Atkinson

assoc s'boy May 1985, app July 1987, pro July 1989(Carlisle United loan Jan 1996)/ Darlington Aug 1996 to date.

Debut v Plymouth Argyle (h) 4/4/1989

Signed as a schoolboy by George Herd, Brian Atkinson graduated so well that he was given his first League outing at 18 years of age before one of the club's lowest ever attendances. Only 8,003 fans witnessed Brian's disappointment when his third-minute 'goal' was ruled out for offside. In 1990 he made his international debut for England Under-21 and also appeared in the Division Two Play-off Final at Wembley. He returned two years later to play in the F.A. Cup Final defeat by Liverpool. An adaptable midfielder who covered a lot of ground, he passed well but lacked confidence when in goalscoring positions. A catalogue of injuries blighted his final two seasons at Roker, leading to his transfer to his home town club, Darlington, in the summer of 1996.

Appearances:
FL: 119(23) apps. 4 gls.
FAC: 13 apps. 2 gls.
FLC: 8(2) apps. 0 gls.
Other: 2(2) apps. 0 gls.
Total: *142 (27) apps. 6 gls.*
Honours:
6 Eng U-21 apps. 1990-91/
(Sunderland) FAC finalist 1992.

ATKINSON, Paul

Role: Wing Forward 1982-88
5'9" 10st.10lbs.
b. Chester-le-Street, 19th January 1966

CAREER: Pelton Rosebury School/Pelton Boys' Club/SUNDERLAND assoc s'boy May 1981, pro Nov 1983/Port Vale June 1988 (Stafford Rangers loan Jan 1989) (Hartlepool United loan Mar 1990) retired due to injury Jan 1991.

Debut v Norwich City (h) 27/8/1983

Paul Atkinson made his Sunderland debut in Division One but sampled both Second and Third Division fare before transferring to Port Vale shortly after collecting his Division Three championship medal. A stylish if lightweight winger or midfielder, Paul won England Youth honours but his full

potential was never realised. Something of a speed merchant, his game was all about pace and, when he cracked a fine goal against Wolves on only his fourth outing for The Lads, he looked destined for a bright future. He was extremely unfortunate to have his career terminated when only 25 years old due to a serious injury sustained shortly after his £20,000 transfer to Port Vale. Paul has remained a regular Sunderland supporter ever since.

Appearances:
FL: 46(14) apps. 5 gls.
FAC: 5 apps. 2 gls.
FLC: 2(1) apps. 0 gls.
Other: 7(1) apps. 0 gls.
Total *60(16) apps. 7 gls.*
Honours:
18 Eng Youth apps. (1982-85)/
(Sunderland) Div 3 champs 1988.

Paul Atkinson

AULD, John Robertson

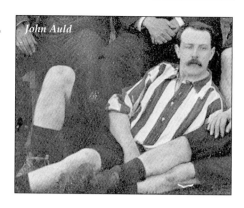

John Auld

Role: Centre-half 1889-95
b. Lugar, Ayrshire, 7th January 1862
d. Sunderland, 29th April 1932

CAREER: Kilmarnock 2nd XI/Lugar Boswell, early 1880's/Third Lanark c. 1883/Queen's Park Nov 1884/Third Lanark 1886/Queen's Park July 1887/SUNDERLAND pro May 1889/Newcastle United, reinstated am Oct 1896/retired cs 1897/Newcastle United director June 1897.

Debut v Burnley (h) 13/9/1890

A doughty Scot, John Auld was the first player to leave Sunderland for arch-rivals Newcastle United. But the parting came after seven excellent seasons when Auld was a veteran, and he retired after a season with the Tynesiders. A fine skipper and defender, determined and unyielding. His move to Sunderland was interesting; it involved £20 for turning professional, a £150 signing on fee, the establishing of a boot and shoe business (he was a shoemaker by trade) and a then substantial £300 wage over two years. An early representative honour was an appearance for Glasgow against Sheffield in 1887.

Appearances:
FL: 101 apps. 5 gls.
FAC: 15 apps. 0 gls.
Total: *116 apps. 5 gls.*
Honours:
3 Scot caps/(Queen's Park) SC winner 1889/(Sunderland) FL champs 1892, 1893.

BACH, Philip

Role: Right-back 1897-99
b. Ludlow, Salop, September 1872
d. Middlesbrough, 30th December 1937

CAREER: Middlesbrough Junior football/
Middlesbrough FC am/Reading pro Sept
1895/SUNDERLAND June 1897/
Middlesbrough Apr 1899/Bristol City 1900,
reinstated as am 1904 but did not play again/
Middlesbrough FC director Feb 1911-1925
(chairman July July 1911-1925 and again 1931-
35)/FA councillor 1925-37, serving on
international selection committee from Oct
1929/FL Management Committee from June
1929 and at various times President of the
North-Eastern League and Vice President of
the North Riding FA.

Debut v Sheffield Wednesday
(a) 4/9/1897

Philip Bach

Philip Bach was
distinguished both as a
player and an administrator.
In the former, his great
competence and consistency
won international recognition
in February 1899 when he was capped by
England against Ireland in an extraordinary
game which was actually staged at Roker Park
and resulted in a crushing 13-2 record rout by
England. In administration he took leading
roles over a quarter of a century span at club,
Football Association and Football League
levels. His own experience as a capped player
was especially valuable when serving as an
England selector. In business Mr Bach was a
hotel proprietor, first in Cheltenham and later
in Middlesbrough.

> **Appearances:**
> *FL: 43 apps. 1 gl.*
> *FAC: 3 apps. 0 gls.*
> **Total:** *46 apps. 1 gl.*
> **Honours:**
> *1 Eng cap.*

BAKER, Joseph Henry

Role: Centre-forward 1969-71
5'8" 11st.7lbs.
b. Woolton, Liverpool, 17th July 1940

CAREER: Motherwell and Wishaw Schools/
Edinburgh Thistle/Coltness United/

Armadale Thistle/
Chelsea one months trial
1955/Hibernian June
1956/AC Torino (Italy)
May 1961 £70,000/
Arsenal Aug 1962 £67,500/
Nottingham Forest Feb 1966 £60,000/
SUNDERLAND June 1969 £30,000/Hibernian
Jan 1971 £12,000/Raith Rovers June 1972-Oct
1974/Fauldhouse United manager-coach cs
1980/Albion Rovers manager July 1981-Feb
1982 and again Sept 1984-Dec 1985.

Debut v Coventry City (h) 9/8/1969

A precocious mid-fifties talent, Joe Baker was
much sought after, especially after netting 42
goals in 33 Scottish League outings for Hibs in
1959/60, and the subject of several then
substantial transfer fees. His honours read
somewhat oddly - a Scottish schoolboy cap
but an English international. However he was
Scottish in everything but birthplace and
reared in Motherwell from infancy. Not
surprisingly, Scottish in style - thrustful,
persistent and employing a degree of craft, he
also had a distinctive short-stepped gait. He is
perhaps best remembered at Sunderland for
the hat-trick scored against Charlton at Roker
in September 1970, following relegation to

Joe Baker

BALL, Kevin Anthony

Role: Defender/Midfield 1990-date
5'9" 12st.6lbs.
b. Hastings, 12th November 1964

CAREER: Hastings/Coventry City app
Sept 1981/Portsmouth Oct 1982/
SUNDERLAND July 1990 to date.
Debut v Tottenham Hotspur (h) 28/8/1990

Released by Coventry City when a
teenager, and without League experience,
Kevin Ball's career eventually took off with
Portsmouth, for whom he made his League
debut in January 1984. He helped them win
promotion from Division Two in 1987 and
cost Sunderland £350,000 in July 1990,
when manager Denis Smith signed him as
a replacement for John MacPhail. Despite
some initial struggles to find his feet, he
gradually settled, was voted club Player of
the Year in his first season and, aside from
enforced absences due to injuries and
suspensions, has rarely been out of the first
team picture since. In nine years of
exemplary service to date he has

successfully switched his playing role from
central defensive duty, where he was
strong in the air, despite what might be
conceived as a lack of height, to that of a
tough-tackling, ball-winning midfielder. In
either role his determination and never-
say-die attitude has justifiably made him
an all-time Wearside favourite, whose
natural leadership qualities and positive
attitude, both on and off the field, have
been key elements in Sunderland's return
to the top flight. Kevin's reward was a
richly deserved Testimonial Match against
Italian giants Sampdoria on 31st July 1999,
when a large crowd paid tribute to the
Lads' hugely popular skipper.

Appearances:
PL: 32 apps. 3 gls.
FL: 294(5) apps. 19 gls.
FAC: 16 apps. 0 gls.
FLC: 23(2) apps. 2 gls.
Other: 4 apps. 1 gl.
Total: *369(7) apps. 25 gls.*
Honours:
(Sunderland) FAC finalist 1992/
Div 1 champs 1996 & 1999.

Division Two. Joe was also tremendously
popular. At Forest, for instance, it is thought
that in modern times only Stuart Pearce has
exceeded him in the fans' affections. Since
leaving the game Joe has worked as a licensee
and in the building trade. He was the first to
play for England when with a 'foreign' club.

Appearances:
FL: 39(1) apps. 12 gls.
FAC: 2 apps. 0 gls.
FLC: 2 apps. 0 gls.
Total: *43(1) apps. 12 gls.*
Honours:
8 Eng caps/6 Eng U-23 apps./2 Scot Sch
apps./(Hibernian) SC finalist 1958.

BARNES, Peter Simon

Role: Winger 1988-89
5'10" 11st.10lbs.
b. Manchester, 10th June 1957

CAREER: Chorlton High G.S./Manchester &
District Schoolboys/Gatley Rangers/
Manchester City assoc. s'boy, app July 1972,

pro July 1974/West Bromwich Albion July
1979/Leeds United Aug 1981(Real Betis, Spain
loan Aug 1982)(Melbourne J.U.S.T. loan Apr
1984)(Manchester United loan May 1984)/
Coventry City Oct 1984/Manchester United
July 1985/Manchester City Jan 1987(Bolton
Wanderers loan Oct 1987)(Port Vale loan Dec
1987)/Hull City Mar 1988/Drogheda United
1988/Sporting Farense, Portugal Aug-Sept
1988/Bolton Wanderers Nov 1988/
SUNDERLAND Feb 1989/Tampa Bay
Rowdies, USA Apr-Aug 1990/Northwich
Victoria Aug-Oct 1990/Radcliffe Borough
1991/Mossley cs 1991-Oct 1991/Cliftonville
Nov 1992/Coached in Norway 1996.

Debut v Swindon Town (a) 18/2/1989

Peter Barnes made the last of 315 League
appearances in Sunderland's colours and was
substituted in a 4-1 defeat at Swindon Town.
He began as an immensely promising 17-year-
old with Manchester City, a flaxen-haired
flying wingman with a full repertoire of pace,
tricks and plenty of confidence. The son of
Ken Barnes, a stalwart wing half-back with

Kevin Ball, skipper of the record-breaking 1999 First Division champions.

31

Manchester City and Wrexham, Peter was voted Young Footballer of the Year by the PFA in 1975 and scored one of the goals - a crisp mid-air volley - in Manchester City's 2-1 League Cup Final victory against Newcastle United. He moved to West Bromwich Albion for £650,000 in July 1979 and two years later to Leeds United for £930,000. Thereafter he gathered no moss in a wandering path both at home and abroad without ever recapturing his earlier effervescent form.

Peter Barnes

Appearances:
FL: 1 app. 0 gls.
Total: *1 app. 0 gls.*
Honours:
22 Eng caps 1978-82/1 Eng 'B' app./9 Eng U-21 apps. 1977-78/Eng Youth/(Manchester City) FLC winner 1976.

BARRIE, Alexander W.

Role: Centre-half 1902-07
b. Parkhead, Glasgow, circa 1881
d. during 1914-18 War

CAREER: Parkhead Juniors/Edinburgh St Bernards Aug 1901/SUNDERLAND May 1902/Rangers June 1907/Kilmarnock May 1908/Abercorn Sept 1912.
Debut v Stoke (a) 8/11/1902

Alex Barrie

Alex Barrie came to Roker bringing a fine pedigree from a crack junior side of the time, Parkhead of Glasgow. He had won selection for Scotland at junior level and been a member (right-half) in Parkhead's Scottish Junior Cup-winning line-up of 1899. As a writer in a contemporary sporting journal,

BARTLEY, John

Role: Left-half 1926-30
5'9" 11st.3lbs.
b. Houghton-le-Spring, Co Durham, 15th January 1909
d. Houghton-le-Spring, Co Durham, 10th October 1929

CAREER: Houghton Catholic School/ Houghton St Michael's/Hetton Juniors/ SUNDERLAND Sept 1926 to his death.
Debut v Blackburn Rovers (h) 1/1/1927

John Bartley was a young wing-half who soon received his League baptism and thereafter proved a capable deputy for Arthur Andrews. His untimely demise at the age of only 20 years was much regretted.

Appearances:
FL: 19 apps. 1 gl.
Total: *19 apps. 1 gl.*

The Scottish Referee, remarked: "... a well-known junior figure in the Parkhead eleven when that organisation was top of the tree". He gave Sunderland an excellent five years' service, the *Athletic News* saying in 1907 on his transfer to Rangers he had played "... in many brilliant games". Alec could also take on both wing-half positions and was adept in headwork.

Appearances:
FL: 64 apps. 1 gl.
FAC: 5 apps. 1 gl.
Total: *69 apps. 2 gls.*

BAXTER, James Curran

Role: Left-half/Inside-left 1965-68
5'10" 10st.6lbs.
b. Hill of Beath, Fife, 29th September 1939

CAREER: Beath High School/Halbeath Boys' Club/Crossgates Primrose 1956/ Raith Rovers Apr 1957 £200/Rangers June 1960 £18,000/

Jim Baxter

SUNDERLAND May 1965 £72,500/ Nottingham Forest Dec 1967 approx £100,000/ Rangers May 1969 free/retired Nov 1970.
Debut v Leeds United (a) 21/8/1965

Jim Baxter was one of those cavalier characters touched by genius, much talked about and much relished, whose innate ball skills and other idiosyncrasies are recalled decades after they have left the scene. Indeed, his is one of the names paid tribute to in the banners which hang above the concourse at the Stadium of Light. Signed by new manager Ian McColl - a former Ibrox team mate - 'Slim Jim', as he was known, entranced the crowds, possessed a left foot described as a magic wand and a talent for improvisation best summed up as devastating. He was a master at reading a game, though ever cool, even at times appearing lethargic. To many, though, he was the perfect linkman between defence and attack, and few of the ecstatic crowd who saw it will ever forget his stunning second goal against Sheffield United on his first home appearance for the Lads in August 1965. A maverick entertainer, Baxter is also revered by Scots for his breathtaking Wembley display as World champions England were beaten 3-2 in April 1967. It was one of ten caps he won as a Sunderland player, making him the Lads' most capped Scottish international. Baxter had originally worked as a carpenter then as a miner and, for his National Service, joined the Black Watch. On leaving football he became a licensee and, through a drink problem, became seriously ill, undergoing two major operations. He is a cousin of George Kinnell (q.v.).

Appearances:
FL: 87 apps. 10 gls.
FAC: 6 apps. 2 gls.
FLC: 5 apps. 0 gls.
Total: *98 apps. 12 gls.*
Honours:
34 Scot caps/1 Scot U-23 app./(Rangers) 5 SL apps./EC finalist 1961/SL champs 1961, 1963, 1964/SC winner 1962, 1963, 1964/SLC winner 1961, 1962, 1964, 1965.

BEACH, Cyril Howard

Role: Inside-right 1932-33
5'9" 11st.0lbs.
b. Nuneaton, 28th March 1909

CAREER: Hounslow Town/Charlton Athletic
am Aug 1928, pro Mar 1929/SUNDERLAND
Sept 1932-cs 1933/Hayesco FC Jan 1936.

Debut v Blackburn Rovers (a) 1/10/1932

For Sunderland, Cyril Beach had League
outings on three consecutive Saturdays in
October 1932 that resulted in two defeats and
a draw. He left the professional scene the
following close season aged only 28 but re-
emerged as a permit player with a Middlesex
works side (Hayesco FC) in January 1936.
Prior to joining Sunderland, former clerk
Beach had been a handy reserve for Charlton
Athletic (31 League and FA Cup appearances,
five goals), performing in the half-back line in
addition to his usual inside-forward role.

Appearances:
FL: 3 apps. 0 gls.
Total: *3 apps. 0 gls.*

BEAGRIE, Peter Sydney

Role: Wing forward 1991-92
5'8" 9st.10lbs.
b. Middlesbrough, 28th November 1965

CAREER: Hartlepool United assoc. s'boy Jan
1980/Guisborough/Middlesbrough Sept
1983/Sheffield United Aug 1986/Stoke City
June 1988/Everton Nov 1989(SUNDERLAND
loan Sept 1991)/Manchester City Mar 1994/
Bradford City July 1997 to date(Everton loan
Mar 1998).

Debut v Middlesbrough (a) 28/9/1991

Peter Beagrie arrived at Roker on a temporary
transfer from Everton as Marco Gabbiadini
departed to Crystal Palace. After one month's
loan and five scintillating performances
Beagrie returned to Goodison Park, no
apparent moves being made to secure him on
a permanent basis. A traditional 'box of tricks'
wing-man with a hallmark, and totally unique,
backward somersault celebration after scoring.
Beagrie has made a good recovery from
persistent shin injury problems that blighted
much of his three year spell at Maine Road.
Signed by Bradford City for a bargain fee of

Peter Beagrie

£50,000 in July
1997, he made a
surprise return
to Everton, on
loan, on
transfer
deadline day
1998. Returning
to Valley
Parade after
just four starts
with Everton,
Peter was fully
involved in the
Bantams' First
Division
promotion
battle in 1998-
99, contributing 15 goals, and numerous
assists, in Bradford's memorable rise to the
Premiership, as runners up to Sunderland.

Appearances:
FL: 5 apps. 1 gl.
Total: *5 apps. 1 gl.*
Honours:
2 Eng 'B' apps./2 Eng U-21 apps. 1988.

BECTON, Thomas

Role: Inside-left 1899-1900
b. Preston, Lancs, 1878
d. Fulwood, nr Preston, 8th November 1957

CAREER: Junior football to Preston North End
cs 1897/New Brighton Tower Sept 1898/
SUNDERLAND May 1899/Kettering Aug
1900/Bristol Rovers June 1901/Kettering Oct
1902//Oswaldtwistle Rovers 1903/04/Colne
Dec 1905/Rossendale United May 1907.

Debut v Burnley (h) 16/9/1899 (scored)

Tommy Becton came from a noted footballing
family - a quartet of brothers that included the
Preston, Liverpool and England forward
Francis Becton. He was a thrustful inside-
forward in his own right, with an eye for the
scoring opportunity. After his year at
Sunderland there followed brief spells with
Southern League and non-League Lancashire
clubs.

Appearances:
FL: 15 apps. 6 gls.
Total: *15 apps. 6 gls.*

BEDFORD, Harry

Role: Inside-right 1931-32
5'9" 12st.4lbs.
b. Calow, nr Chesterfield, 15th October 1899
d. Derby, 24th June 1976

CAREER: Grassmoor Ivanhoe (Chesterfield
League)/Nottingham Forest am 1919, pro Aug
1919/ Blackpool Mar 1921 £1,500/ Derby
County Sept 1925 £3,500/ Newcastle United
Dec 1930 £4,000/ SUNDERLAND Jan 1932
£3,000/Bradford May 1932/Chesterfield June
1933/Heanor Town player/coach Aug 1934/
Newcastle United trainer/coach Oct 1937/
Derby County part-time masseur May 1938/
Belper Town manager Jan 1954/Heanor Town
manager Mar 1955-May 1956.

Debut v Everton (a) 16/1/1932

Harry Bedford had
made his name as a
prolifically scoring
centre-forward a
decade prior to
joining Sunderland. It
was at Derby where
he took the inside-
right berth to
accommodate the up
and coming Jack
Bowers. In all Harry
netted 308 goals in
486 League matches,
an outstanding
figure that included
four in three of
them and ten hat
tricks. And he twice
scored in inter-
league games. In
style he was dashing and difficult to contain.
Outside football Bedford was employed in
Derby as a licensee and, from 1941-64, the
Rolls-Royce company's fire service. Harry,
who was also a masseur to the Derbyshire
County Cricket Club for a time, had originally
started his working life as a miner. He served
on the committe of the Derby & District
Football League in 1948.

Appearances:
FL: 7 apps. 2 gls.
Total: *7 apps. 2 gls.*
Honours:
2 Eng caps/2 FL apps.

BEE, Francis Eric

Role: Inside-forward
1947-48
5'11" 10st.9lbs.
*b. Nottingham, 23rd January
1927*

CAREER: Nottingham
Boys' Brigade FC/
Nottingham Forest groundstaff
1940/ SUNDERLAND June 1947/Blackburn
Rovers Mar 1949/Peterborough United Aug
1950-cs 1952/Boston United 1953-55.

Frank Bee

Debut v Blackburn Rovers (a) 31/1/1948

Recruited by Forest at a very early age during
World War Two, Frank Bee subsequently
became a 'Bevin Boy' at Gedling Colliery and
played for their works team before returning
to the City Ground at the end of the war. An
inside-forward of willowy build, he made his
debut for Sunderland at Blackburn Rovers in
January 1948 but one week later was replaced
at inside-left by the great Len Shackleton,
newly arrived from Newcastle United.
Blackburn Rovers paid £6,000 for Frank in
March 1949 but he made only four League
appearances for them before joining non-
League Peterborough United (managed at that
time by former Sunderland favourite, Bobby
Gurney) in August 1950. Increasingly troubled
by shoulder injuries, he spent a year out of the
game after leaving Peterborough but was able
to resume his career with a final two year spell
with Boston United. For fifteen years a Vice-
President of his old club, Nottingham Forest,
Frank Bee is currently enjoying his retirement
in Nottingham, and keeps active with frequent
visits to the local golf course.

Appearances:
FL: 5 apps. 1 gl.
Total: *5 apps. 1 gl.*

BEESLEY, Colin

Role: Wing forward 1968-69
5'7" 9st.12lbs.
*b. Stockton on Tees, 6th
October 1951*

CAREER: SUNDERLAND
app, pro Jan 1969.

*Debut v Stoke City (h) 1969
(sub)*

Colin Beesley

Youngster Colin Beesley never started a senior match for Sunderland but was a substitute on three occasions during the 1968/69 tourney. He figured at outside-right in the club's Youth Cup-winning side of 1969.

Appearances:
FL: 0(3) apps. 0 gls.
Total: *0(3) apps. 0 gls.*

BELFITT, Roderick Michael

Role: Forward 1973-75
b. Doncaster, 30th October 1945

CAREER: Retford Town/Leeds United July 1963/Ipswich Town Nov 1971/Everton Nov 1972/SUNDERLAND Oct 1973(Fulham loan Nov 1974)/Huddersfield Town Feb 1975/ Worksop Town June 1976/Frickley Athletic/ Bentley Victoria/ Doncaster Rovers scout late 1970's.

Debut v Derby County (h) 29/11/1973 (sub)

Rod Belfitt served six League clubs as a wholehearted front-runner with pace, good constructive ideas and the ability to turn a defender. On the debit side, his League career return of 39 goals in 160(24) appearances was somewhat below average. His most productive spell was with Leeds United when, in 1967-68, his two goals against Derby County in the League Cup semi-final second leg took Leeds to Wembley and a 1-0 victory against Arsenal. In the same season he also appeared in the first leg of the Inter Cities Fairs Cup Final versus Ferencvaros which Leeds won 1-0 and on aggregate by the same scoreline. At Sunderland, Rod began up front but enjoyed an impressive spell partnering Dave Watson in central defence during the second half of season 1973/74. A qualified draughtsman, Belfitt returned to his profession when his football career ended.

Appearances:
FL: 36(3) apps. 4 gls.
FAC: 2 apps. 0 gls.
FLC: 0(2) apps. 0 gls.
Total: *38(5) apps. 4 gls.*
Honours:
(Leeds United) ICFC finalist 1967/ICFC winner 1968/FLC winner 1968.

Rod Belfitt

BELL, Edward

Role: Right-back 1905-08
5'10" 11st.10lbs.
b. Burnopfield, Co. Durham, 23rd December 1883

CAREER: West Stanley 1899/1900/Bishop Auckland 1902/03/Seaham White Star/ SUNDERLAND May 1905/Spennymoor United June 1908.

Debut v Everton (h) 18/11/1905

Almost all Ted Bell's Sunderland League and FA Cup appearances were made in his first (1905/06) season, with a good run from November to February. His association with the club actually dated from season 1904/05 when he skippered the 'A' team. He also held the captaincy in 1905/06 when the club won both the Durham Senior Cup and the Northern League Cup. Bell was a schoolmaster by profession.

Appearances:
FL: 19 apps. 0 gls.
FAC: 4 apps. 0 gls.
Total: *23 apps. 0 gls.*

BELL, John Cuthbert 'Paddy'

Role: Goalkeeper 1926-31
6'0" 12st.7lbs.
b. Seaham Harbour, Co. Durham, 24th October 1905

CAREER: Ryhope Colliery/Seaham Colliery/ SUNDERLAND am Sept 1924, pro Nov 1924/ Walsall Nov 1930/Accrington Stanley July 1931/Bradford Mar 1932-cs 1936 £250.

Debut v Leeds United (h) 26/3/1927

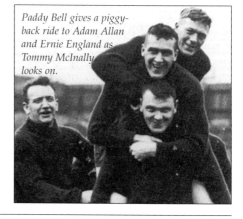

Paddy Bell gives a piggy-back ride to Adam Allan and Ernie England as Tommy McInally looks on.

A competent 'keeper, Paddy Bell was much in the shadow of Albert McInroy, of course, while at Roker, although his debut was particularly memorable as both Raich Carter and Stan Ramsay netted hat-tricks in a crushing 6-2 victory. He get much first team exposure at Walsall either, due to the presence of Welsh cap, Roy John. However, things perked up in his Accrington spell (28 League appearances) and 73 League and FA Cup appearances were spread over his four Park Avenue years. He played cricket for Seaham Harbour as a wicket-keeper. Jack's nickname, Paddy, is interesting but unexplained.

Appearances:
FL: 41 apps. 0 gls
Total: *41 apps. 0 gls.*

BELL, Richard

Role: Outside-left 1936-37
5'10" 10st.0lbs.
b. Greenock, Scotland

CAREER: Dawdon Juniors/Port Glasgow Athletic/SUNDERLAND June 1935/West Ham United May 1937/guest for Clapham and Southend United during WW2.

Debut v Leeds United (a) 24/4/1937

Actually an inside-forward, Richard Bell's only senior game for Sunderland was on the left wing. His League tally for West Ham was also one but this time at inside-left (against West Bromwich Albion at Upton Park in April 1939, when he scored one of the goals in a 2-1 win). Like many of the West Ham players Bell joined the Essex Regiment territorials in April 1939 and subsequently served in the Royal Artillery. During his Army career he rejoiced in the unfathomable nickname of 'Brindie'.

Richard Bell

Appearances:
FL: 1 app. 0 gls.
Total: *1 app. 0 gls.*

BENNETT, Gary Ernest

Role: Central Defender 1984-95
6'0" 13st.0lbs.
b. Manchester, 4th December 1961

CAREER: Ashton United/Manchester City Sept 1979/Cardiff City Sept 1981/SUNDERLAND July 1984/Carlisle United Nov 1995/Scarborough player-coach July 1996/Darlington July 1998.

Debut v Southampton (h) 25/8/1984 (scored)

Gary Bennett began at Maine Road but did not break through into League football until he joined Cardiff City, on a free transfer, when just short of his 20th birthday. Transferred to Sunderland in July 1984, his tribunal-set fee of £65,000 also covered a further £20,000 payable after 20 appearances; rather ironic in hindsight, considering 'Benno's' eventual total of 444 in Sunderland's colours! Only four Sunderland players have played more games. He immediately endeared himself

Gary Bennett

Gary Bennett

to the Roker faithful, scoring within two minutes of kick-off on his debut against Southampton's Peter Shilton. He appeared in the League Cup final in his first season, was voted Player of the Year in 1987 and 1994 and captained the Division Three championship side in 1988. A further Wembley appearance, in the FA Cup Final, followed in 1992. One year on, a crowd of almost 22,000 attended his testimonial game at Roker Park against Rangers. A consistently wholehearted performer throughout his eleven seasons, he will be fondly remembered not only for his sterling defensive qualities, but for his trademark forward runs, when he often stormed the opposition's rearguard single-handed. There were many memorable moments but few at Roker will forget his majestic last-minute header in the 1987 play-off with Gillingham that took the tie into extra time and seemed to have saved Sunderland from relegation to Division Three. Others may well recall Gary's brilliant last-minute winner against Manchester United in September 1990 when he lifted the ball over Gary Pallister and curled a shot around goalkeeper Gary Bailey. Bennett was only the second black player to appear for The Lads - after Roly Gregoire - and alongside other Len Ashurst signings, Reuben Agboola and Howard Gayle, 'Benno' was instrumental in ending racist chanting at Roker. Elder brother David Bennett, a first rate touchline dribbler, is best remembered for his scoring role in Coventry City's first FA Cup Final appearance against Spurs in 1987. Gary's summer 1998 move from Scarborough to Darlington saw him reunited with many Sunderland 'Old Boys' at Feethams, including Marco Gabbiadini and Brian Atkinson on the playing side, plus David Hodgson (manager) and Jim Montgomery (goalkeeping coach).

Appearances:
FL: 367(7) apps. 24 gls.
FAC: 17(2) apps. 0 gls.
FLC: 34(1) apps. 2 gls.
Other: 16 apps. 0 gls.
Total: *434(10) apps. 26 gls.*
Honours:
(Sunderland) FAC finalist 1992/FLC finalist 1985/Div 3 champs 1988.

BERRY, Stephen Andrew

Role: Midfield 1984-86
5'7" 11st.0lbs.
b. Gosport, Hampshire, 4th April 1963

CAREER: Gosport Borough/Portsmouth app 1979, pro Jan 1981(Aldershot loan Mar 1984)/ SUNDERLAND July 1984/Newport County Dec 1985/Swindon Town Mar 1987/Aldershot Oct 1987/Northampton Town Oct 1988/ Maidstone United 1991/Stevenage Borough 1995/Kettering Town player-manager Oct 1995/Stevenage Borough May 1998.

Debut v Southampton (h) 25/8/1984

A free transfer signing from Portsmouth in July 1984, Steve 'Chuck' Berry had little first team experience but acquitted himself well in Sunderland's midfield, always at the hub of things and with great enthusiasm for the game. The bulk of his appearances came in season 1984-85, when a Wembley appearance was followed by a run of defeats which ended in relegation from Division One. The arrival of new manager Lawrie McMenemy, and an

Steve Berry

influx of ex-international players of ripe experience, left Steve Berry surplus to requirements. In mid-season he departed to Third Division Newport County, and his League career concluded with Northampton Town. His career spanned 284 League appearances and 23 goals.

Appearances:
FL: 32(3) apps. 2 gls.
FAC: 1 app. 0 gls.
FLC: 10 apps. 0 gls.
Total: *43(3) apps. 2 gls.*
Honours:
(Sunderland) FLC finalist 1985.

BERTSCHIN, Keith Edwin

Role: Forward 1986-88
6'1" 11st.8lbs.
b. Enfield, Middlesex, 25th August 1956

CAREER: Mount Grace School/Barnet 1972/ Ipswich Town Oct 1973/Birmingham City July 1977/Norwich City Aug 1981/Stoke City Nov 1984/SUNDERLAND Mar 1987/Walsall Aug 1988/Chester City Nov 1990/Aldershot Town Aug 1991/Solihull Borough Mar 1992/ Evesham United 1993/Barry Town 1994/ Worcester City Aug 1994-Mar 1995/ Hednesford Town May 1995/Stafford Rangers Apr 1996, then retired.

Debut v Portsmouth (a) 28/3/1987

Keith Bertschin had a dream start to his League career when he scored with his first kick for Ipswich Town against Arsenal at Highbury in April 1976. He arrived at Roker Park much later in his career, and with over a century of League goals to his credit. A bustling, strong-running centre forward who cost Sunderland a reported fee of £32,000, his addition to the squad came too late to prevent relegation to Division Three for the first time in the club's long history. As the new season opened, Bertschin was Sunderland's first goalscorer in the Third Division. One month later, however, an injury at Fulham sidelined him and the subsequent success of the Gabbiadini/Gates partnership kept Bertschin out of the first team picture for the remainder of the season. A promotion winner with Birmingham and Norwich City, Keith was a player with an infuriating habit of scoring against Sunderland for other clubs and whilst with the Canaries was even involved in the

Keith Bertschin

accidental clash which fractured goalkeeper Chris Turner's skull. After leaving the top flight in 1992, he enjoyed a lengthy career in non-League football. Presently living in Solihull, Keith works as a financial advisor.

Appearances:
FL: 27(11) apps. 8 gls.
FAC: 0(1) app. 0 gls.
FLC: 2 apps. 0 gls.
Other: 1(1) apps. 2 gls.
Total: *30(13) apps. 10 gls.*
Honours:
Eng Youth/3 Eng U-21 apps./(Ipswich Town) FAYC winner 1975/(Sunderland) Div 3 champs 1988.

BERTRAM, A. Ernest

Role: Left-half 1903-04
b. 20th January 1885

CAREER: South Shields/SUNDERLAND Sept 1903/South Shields Aug 1906/Darlington Sept 1908.

Debut v Small Heath (a) 5/3/1904

In his initial season Bertram deputised for Dick Jackson in a match at Birmingham, which was lost 1-2. This was his sole first team outing in three years at Roker Park.

Appearances:
FL: 1 app. 0 gls.
Total: *1 app. 0 gls.*

BEST, Robert

Role: Outside-right/Centre-forward 1911-22
5'6" 10st.6lbs.
b. Mickley, Northumberland, 12th September 1891
d. Fulwell, Sunderland, 8th June 1947

CAREER: Mickley Colliery Welfare/
SUNDERLAND Aug 1911 £20/
Wolverhampton Wanderers Sept 1922/
Durham City Aug 1923/Hartlepools United
June 1924. retired cs 1927.
Debut v Aston Villa (a) 7/10/1911

Bobby Best was a perky little forward,
thrustful and an opportunist whose
Sunderland highlight was a hat-trick in a 5-2
Christmas win at Newcastle in 1914. Versatile
too, he was able to fill any position in the
attack. He spent the bulk of his first class
career at Roker Park and his appearance and
goals total would, of course, have been much
greater but for the intervention of the Great
War. In general, Bobby, who was a cousin to
Jerry Best of Leeds United, was first choice at
his other clubs. During the First World War he
guested for Sunderland Rovers. On leaving
football he worked for the Sunderland
Corporation.

Appearances:
FL: 90 apps. 23 gls.
FAC: 4 apps. 2 gls.
Total: *94 apps. 25 gls.*

Bobby Best

Fred Bett

BETT, Frederick

Role: Inside/outside-left 1937-39
5'7" 10st.2lbs.
b. Scunthorpe, 5th December 1920

CAREER: Scunthorpe Junior football/
Scunthorpe & Lindsey United/
SUNDERLAND Dec 1937/guest for Lincoln
City, Nottingham Forest and Chester during
WW2/Coventry City May 1946 £3,000/
Lincoln City Sept 1948 £2,000/Spalding
United Aug 1950/Holbeach United Aug 1953/
Bourne Town June 1954.
Debut v Liverpool (a) 12/3/1938

Fred Bett had two First Division games at
inside and one at outside-left for the Rokerites.
A diminutive but effective forward, and later a
deadly spot-kicker, Fred turned professional
two days after his 17th birthday. He made a
bright start at Coventry (four goals in his first
five matches) but his career was marred by
injury afterwards. Lincoln knew all about him
after a lengthy wartime association - 36 goals
in 77 appearances - but his contribution in this
second spell was limited to 14 outings (2
goals), all in season 1948/49. Fred rounded off
his career with a tour of south Lincolnshire
minor clubs.

Appearances:
FL: 3 apps. 0 gls.
Total: *3 apps. 0 gls.*

BINGHAM, William Laurie

Role: Outside-right 1950-58
5'7" 10st.2lbs.
b. Belfast, 5th August 1931

CAREER: Junior football to Glentoran Aug 1949/SUNDERLAND Oct 1950 £8,000/ Luton Town July 1958 £15,000+/Everton Oct 1960 £16,000 plus 2 players/Port Vale Aug 1963 £15,000, retired June 1965/ Southport trainer-coach/Southport manager Dec 1966/ Plymouth Argyle manager Feb 1968-Mar 1970/Linfield manager June 1970-71/Greece national coach 1971-May 1973/Everton manager May 1973-Jan 1977/Paok (Salonica) manager Apr-Oct 1977/Mansfield Town manager Feb 1978-July 1979.

Debut v Stoke City (h) 2/12/1950

Billy Bingham, a big name from the fifties, won the first 33 of his 56 Northern Ireland caps while with Sunderland and is one of the most capped players in the club's history. Billy was signed following an inter-leaguè appearance and gave Sunderland eight vintage years. He played in more

than 200 games for the club including the FA Cup semi-finals of 1955 and 1956. A small, elusive right winger, orthodox in style and a fine crosser, but with determination and dedication aplenty, his dribbling tricks included an intended (and practised) stumble that threw opponents off balance. Particularly notable was his international record; in a period of eight seasons he did not miss a single Northern Ireland game, a quite remarkable run which included five games in the 1958 World Cup Finals shortly before his summer transfer to Luton. Bingham is the only player to appear in the World Cup Finals whilst playing for The Lads. Eventually forced to retire from playing in 1965 after sustaining a broken leg he remained in the public eye for many years in important managerial and coaching posts. Between September 1967 and 1971, and again from February 1979, he enjoyed two separate spells as Northern Ireland's manager, leading them in the World Cup finals of 1982 and 1986. More recently Billy was for a spell Blackpool's director of football and their vice-chairman.

Appearances:
FL: 206 apps. 45 gls.
FAC: 21 apps. 2 gls.
Total: *227 apps. 47 gls.*
Honours:
56 NIre caps/2 IL apps/NIre Sch/NIre youth/(Luton Town) FAC finalist 1959/(Everton) FL champs 1963.

BIRCHAM, Walter Clive

Role: Outside-right 1958-60
5'6" 9st.2lbs.
b. Herrington, Co Durham, 7th September 1939

CAREER: Hetton-le-Hole schoolboy football/
Shiney Row Swifts/SUNDERLAND Sept
1956/Hartlepool United Feb 1960 small
fee/Boston United cs 1963.

Debut v Lincoln City (a) 23/8/1958

Little winger Walter Bircham made his League
debut in Sunderland's first-ever Second
Division match. He enjoyed much first team
exposure that term, indeed, all but two of his
eventual Roker total of appearances were
recorded then. On moving down the coast to
Hartlepool he had 105 League outings (scoring
15 goals) in a little over three seasons.

Appearances:
FL: 28 apps. 2 gls.
Total: *28 apps. 2 gls.*

BLACK, Alan Douglas

Role: Left-back 1964-66
5'10" 12st.6lbs.
b. Alexandria, Dunbartonshire, 4th June 1943

CAREER: Dunbartonshire schools/
Drumchapel Amateurs/Dumbarton am 1961/
Clydebank/Dumbarton 1962/SUNDERLAND
Aug 1964 free/Norwich City Sept 1966
£9,000/Dumbarton Jan 1974, retired through
injury 1975.

Debut v Manchester United (h) 24/2/1965

Alan Black

Alan Black was chiefly
notable for a long and
successful run at Norwich
City where he saw much
first team exposure at a
time when the club was
contending for League
and Cup honours. His
total appearance tally
there was 199 plus four
substitutions. Black was not the showy type of
defender, but quite reliable and consistent. His
eventual retirement was caused by a knee
injury.

Appearances:
FL: 4(2) apps. 0 gls.
Total: *4(2) apps. 0 gls.*

Walter Bircham

BLACK, John Ross

Role: Inside-right 1921-22
5'8" 11st.1lb.
b. Dunipace, Stirlingshire, 26th May 1900
d. Scunthorpe, December 1993

CAREER: Gordon Highlanders/Denny Hibs/
SUNDERLAND am Apr 1921, pro Aug 1921/
Nelson Aug 1922/Accrington Stanley Feb
1924/Chesterfield June 1924/Luton Town Aug
1926/Bristol Rovers Oct 1930-May 1932.

Debut v Birmingham (a) 1/10/1921

Red-haired John Black was a player of
considerable value if only for his versatility.

John Black

He competently occupied
most half-back and forward
positions for his several
League clubs and could
likely have done so in any
outfield berth. John broke a
leg while at Chesterfield
but recovered to make
nearly a century of

appearances for Luton. He was the younger brother of Adam Black, the well-known long-serving (1920-35) full-back of Leicester City.

Appearances:
FL: 2 apps. 0 gls.
Total: *2 apps. 0 gls.*
Honours:
Scot Jnr int/(Nelson)FL Div 3 Nth champs 1923.

BOE, James

Role: Goalkeeper 1914-15
6'0" 11st.7lbs.
b. Gateshead, 5th January 1891
d. Co Durham, late 1973

CAREER: Rodsley FC (Gateshead)/ SUNDERLAND May 1914-1915, later assisted Southport Central.

Debut v Everton (a) 21/11/1914

James Boe deputised once in that fateful 1914/15 season for an otherwise ever-present Leslie Scott. It was Boe's one and, perhaps not surprisingly, only senior appearance following a 7-1 hammering at Goodison Park. It is interesting to note that teenager Scott was Boe's junior by some four years.

Appearances:
FL: 1 app. 0 gls.
Total: *1 app. 0 gls.*

BOLDER, Robert John

Role: Goalkeeper 1985-86
6'3" 14st.7lbs.
b. Dover, Kent, 2nd October 1958

CAREER: Dover Town 1974/Sheffield Wednesday Mar 1977/Liverpool Aug 1983 (SUNDERLAND loan Sept 1985)/ SUNDERLAND Oct 1985(Luton Town loan Feb 1986)/Charlton Athletic Aug 1986-1991/ Dagenham & Redbridge/Charlton Community coach.

Debut v Shrewsbury Town (a) 21/9/1985

Bob Bolder's debut for Sunderland brought the season's first victory after a dismal opening of five defeats and two draws. Initially on loan from Liverpool, where Bruce Grobbelaar's form cast him into the role of permanent understudy, Bolder quickly

Bob Bolder

impressed at Roker and his move was made permanent when a fee of £30,000 was paid for his signature. Before the end of the season, however, he was deposed by on-loan Andy Dibble, from Luton Town, in a late season exchange which took Bolder to Kenilworth Road. He subsequently joined Charlton Athletic, where he rounded off his League career with 249 appearances in seven seasons of regular first team football. A promotion winner with Sheffield Wednesday in 1980, he was an unused substitute in the 1984 European Cup Final for Liverpool versus Roma.

Appearances:
FL: 22 apps. 0 gls.
FAC: 3 apps. 0 gls.
FLC: 2 apps. 0 gls.
Other: 2 apps. 0 gls.
Total: *29 apps. 0 gls.*

BOLLANDS, John Frederick

Role: Goalkeeper 1955-60
5'10" 11st.0lbs.
b. Middlesbrough, 11th July 1935

CAREER: South Bank/Oldham Athletic Mar 1953/SUNDERLAND Mar 1956 £2,500/Bolton Wanderers Feb 1960 £7,500/Oldham Athletic Sept 1961-June 1966 £2,500.

Debut v Birmingham City (h) 18/4/1956

A daring and agile custodian much admired by the schoolboy Jimmy Montgomery, John Bollands seemed set for full international honours when he sustained a broken leg while at Sunderland. He enjoyed just one full season as first choice, in 1956/57, when he missed only four League games. Despite his injury, John returned to render good service at Bolton (replacing another broken leg victim in England's Eddie Hopkinson) and his first love, Oldham. Bollands had genuine all-round ability and athleticism, dealing with high and low shots equally well.

Appearances:
FL: 61 apps. 0 gls.
FAC: 2 apps. 0 gls.
Total: *63 apps. 0 gls.*

BOLTON, Arthur Frederick

Role: Centre-forward 1938-39
5'10" 11st.10lbs.
b. Hexham, Northumberland, 1913

CAREER: Ashington/SUNDERLAND Nov 1938-1940.

Debut v Charlton Athletic (a) 26/11/1938

An ideally built centre-forward, Arthur Bolton was quickly given the opportunity of making the transition from the North-Eastern league to top flight soccer (within days, in fact). He had a run of half a dozen matches then another couple at the season's end, but he had little luck in the matter of goal scoring. Bolton was retained for the aborted 1939/40 campaign but he had disappeared from view when peacetime League football returned.

Appearances:
FL: 8 apps. 1 gl.
Total: *8 apps. 1 gl.*

John Bollands in action
for The Lads against
Arsenal at Roker Park.

BOLTON, Joseph

Role: Full-back 1971-81
b. Birtley, 2nd February 1955

CAREER: Chester-le-Street Schoolboys/
SUNDERLAND app, pro Feb 1972/
Middlesbrough July 1981/Sheffield United
Aug 1983-1985/Matlock Town manager late
1980's.

Debut v Watford (h) 17/4/1972

Joe Bolton

Locally born full-back Joe Bolton graduated
through junior ranks at Roker Park. He made
his League debut towards the close of season
1971-72 in a home fixture v Watford, which
resulted in the season's best victory, 5-0. In the
following term the tenacious, rugged-tackling
- opponents would often say 'dirty'! - defender
made his F.A. Cup debut in the third round tie
at Notts County, and held his place for the
replay. However, the vastly more experienced
Ron Guthrie was first choice during the
remainder of the season's Cup run, which
ended in memorable success at Wembley
against Leeds United. Joe was firmly
established as senior left full-back when
promotion to the First Division was achieved -
after a six year absence - in 1975-76, but
relegation immediately followed. A
fantastically popular player with the fans,
there is a legendary Lads' tale that Joe once
churned up the training pitch with his car in
the dead of night whilst chasing his errant
greyhounds! On the final day of the 1977-78
season Joe had scored twice in a win over
Charlton and when Sunderland won a penalty
the supporters chanted for him to complete a
hat-trick. In an unforgettable moment cult-
hero Joe blasted the ball over the bar and into
the fans at the Fulwell End!! It was not until
1979-80 that Ken Knighton's side regained
their First Division status. At the close of the
following term, in which he had appeared in
all but three of the seasons' League and Cup
engagements, Joe was transferred to
Middlesbrough for £200,000 after a decade of
sterling service during which fans never saw
him shirk a 50-50 challenge. He must have had
mixed feelings when he assisted his new club
to a 2-0 victory in the 100th Tees-Wear derby at
Roker Park in April 1982. After two years he
moved on to Sheffield United, where his
career was ended by a serious knee injury. He
settled with his family in Chesterfield where
his son Joe jnr. was reported to be showing
promise in Chesterfield Schoolboys rugby
team.

Appearances:
FL: 264(9) apps. 11 gls.
FAC: 20 apps. 1 gl.
FLC: 16(1) apps. 0 gls.
Other: 9 apps. 0 gls.
Total: *309(10) apps. 12 gls.*
Honours:
(Sunderland) Div 2 champs 1976.

Laurie Bolton

John Bone

BOLTON, Lyall 'Laurie'

Role: Wing-half 1955-57
b. Gateshead, 11th July 1932

CAREER: Windy Nook Juniors/
SUNDERLAND Aug 1950/Chelmsford City
July 1957.
Debut v Preston North End (h) 21/3/1956

Laurie Bolton had seven years on
Sunderland's books but had scant opportunity
with the likes of Stan Anderson, George
Aitken, Arthur Wright et all around. In the
event, the senior debut came nearly six years
after his joining. Laurie could usefully play on
either flank and did so in his three League
outings (two appearances at right-half and one
at left-half).

Appearances:
FL: 3 apps. 0 gls.
Total: *3 apps. 0 gls.*

BONE, John

Role: Centre-half 1954-57
6'1" 11st.10lbs.
b. Hartlepool, 19th December 1930

CAREER: Wingate/SUNDERLAND May
1951/Cambridge City July 1958.

Debut v Leicester City (a) 13/11/1954

An understudy to notable Sunderland pivots
Hall, Daniel and Aitken, John Bone's League
appearances were spread over three of his
seven Roker seasons. Admirably built for the
centre-half position, his best run was five
successive outings in the March and April of
1956.

Appearances:
FL: 11 apps. 0 gls.
Total: *11 apps. 0 gls.*

BONTHRON, Robert Pollock

Role: Right-back 1907-08
5'11" 13st.0lbs.
b. Burntisland, Fife, 1880

CAREER: Raith Athletic/
Raith Rovers July 1900/
Dundee May 1902/
Manchester United May
1903/SUNDERLAND May
1907/ Northampton Town
June 1908/Birmingham July
1910/Leith Athletic July 1912.

Robert Bonthron

Debut v Manchester City (h) 2/9/1907

Possessed of a hefty physique and naturally
robust and hard-tackling, Robert Bonthron

was apt to raise the ire of opposing supporters. This was particularly highlighted at Bradford in February 1906 when City fans, doubtless angered by a 5-1 home defeat, inflicted by Bonthron's then club, Manchester United, attacked him after the game. They were duly prosecuted. In his Sunderland season he played once on the left flank - against Woolwich Arsenal in December 1907. Besides his Northampton championship exploits, Bob was a key member of Manchester United's 1905-06 promotion-winning side.

Appearances:
FL: 23 apps. 1 gl.
FAC: 1 app. 0 gls.
Total: *24 apps. 1 gl.*
Honours:
(Northampton Town) Sthn Lge champs 1909.

BOWYER, Ian

Ian Bowyer

Role: Midfield 1980-82
5'10" 11st.11lbs.
b.Ellesmere Port, 6th June 1951

CAREER: Manchester City app, pro Aug 1968/Leyton Orient June 1971/Nottingham Forest Oct 1973/SUNDERLAND Jan 1981/ Nottingham Forest Jan 1982/Hereford United July 1987/Birmingham City coach.

Debut v Manchester United (h) 28/1/1981

Ian Bowyer first came into the limelight as a goalscoring teenager with Manchester City in 1969/70. He faded from the scene in the following term and moved to Orient where he finished as their leading goalscorer in 1971/72. In his first spell with Nottingham Forest he developed under manager Brian Clough into one of the game's outstanding midfielders with the priceless knack of scoring vital goals during Forest's greatest era. He joined Sunderland in January 1981, but suffered a knee injury two months later and failed to impress in a poor team battling against relegation. After just twelve months at Roker he returned to Forest and clocked up a second double-century of League appearances for them before ending his playing career in the colours of Hereford United in season 1989-90. His career aggregate of League appearances totalled 590 (38) and he scored 102 goals. As a coach, Ian was at the Stadium of Light with Birmingham City on the day Sunderland lifted

the 1999 Division One championship trophy. Son Gary, also a midfield player, has appeared in League football with Hereford United and Rotherham United.

Appearances:
FL: 15 apps. 1 gl.
FLC: 1 app. 0 gls.
Total: *16 apps. 1 gl.*
Honours:
(Manchester City) FLC winner 1970/ECWC winner 1970/(Nottingham Forest) Div 1 champs 1978/FLC winner 1978/EC winner 1979 & 1980/FLC finalist 1980.

BOYLE, Peter

Role: Left-back 1896-99
5'10" 12st.7lbs.
b. Carlingford, Co. Louth, 1877

CAREER: Coatbridge junior football/Gaelic Club (Ireland)/Albion Rovers Apr 1895/ SUNDERLAND Dec 1896/Sheffield United Dec 1898 £200/Motherwell May 1904/Clapton Orient Aug 1905/Wigan Town Aug 1907/ Chorley Nov 1907/Eccles Borough Dec 1907.

Debut v Blackburn Rovers (h) 19/12/1896

In 1902 Peter Boyle was described as "... a full-back of a very robust type: and "... paying a big price for his transfer Sheffield United secured his services and ever since he joined has done excellent service for them". His years at Bramall Lane were certainly the high point of his career, taking in, as it did, three FA Cup finals. Geographically, his career was interesting too with its several staging posts in Scotland, Ireland and England. Peter's haul of Irish caps could nearly have trebled - he was actually selected on 13 occasions. He is the father of Tommy Boyle, inside-right in Sheffield United's 1925 FA Cup-winning line-up.

Peter Boyle

Appearances:
FL: 32 apps. 0 gls.
FAC: 1 app. 0 gls.
Total: *33 apps. 0 gls.*
Honours:
5 Eire caps/(Sheffield United) FAC winner 1899, 1902/FAC finalist 1901.

BRACEWELL, Paul William

Role: Midfield 1983-97
5'8" 10st.9lbs.
b. Heswall, 19th July 1962

CAREER: Stoke City app Sept 1978, pro Feb 1980/SUNDERLAND July 1983/Everton May 1984(SUNDERLAND loan Aug 1989)/ SUNDERLAND Sept 1989/Newcastle United June 1992/SUNDERLAND player-asst manager May 1995/Fulham Oct 1997, appointed player-coach May 1998, manager May 1999.

Debut v Norwich City (h) 27/8/1983

Paul Bracewell made his debut for Sunderland as a 21-year-old having followed manager Alan Durban from Stoke City. A former team mate of Peter Reid during his Everton spell, Bracewell passed the 500 appearances milestone during the 1996-97 season. This despite a catalogue of career-threatening ankle injuries which saw him sidelined for the best part of two seasons during his Goodison Park spell. The injury stemmed from a challenge by battling ex Rokerite Billy Whitehurst during Billy's spell at Newcastle. In three separate

Paul Bracewell (right) was part of Sunderland's First Division championship-winning side in 1996.

periods with Sunderland, Paul was a stalwart performer in the midfield anchor role, his qualities as a ball-winner and director of operations seemingly undiminished despite his veteran status. In October 1997 he joined Kevin Keegan's Fulham in a £75,000 transfer, and in May 1998 was appointed their player-coach. Following Keegan's decision to take the England manager's position on a full-time basis, Paul was appointed Fulham's manager. He returned to his former club to make his first signing, Welsh international Andy Melville (q.v.). Paul's record of four appearances in FA Cup Finals is noteworthy, unfortunately on each occasion he finished on the losing side. In the last final he captained The Lads against Liverpool in 1992. Within a month of Wembley, Paul sensationally signed for the Magpies who offered him a lengthier contract than that proposed by Sunderland.

Paul Bracewell

Appearances:
FL: 191(1) apps. 6 gls.
FAC: 14 apps. 0 gls.
FLC: 17 apps. 0 gls.
Other: 3 apps. 0 gls.
Total: *225(1) apps. 6 gls.*
Honours:
3 Eng caps 1985-86/13 Eng U-23 apps. 1985-86/(Everton) FL champs 1985/FAC finalist 1985, 1986, 1989/ECWC winner 1985/ (Newcastle United) Div 1 champs 1993/ (Sunderland) FAC finalist 1992/Div 1 champs 1996/(Fulham) Div 2 champs 1999.

BRACKENRIDGE, John

Role: Forward 1888-89
b. Scotland, 1865
d. Sunderland, 22nd April 1925

CAREER: Joined SUNDERLAND in 1887 and played until the club was admitted to the Football League in 1890.

Debut v Elswick Rangers (FAC) 27/10/1888

John Brackenridge was an old-timer from the pre-League years, and very possibly a kinsman of Thomas Brackenridge, the Heart of Midlothian and Scotland forward. John collapsed and died when travelling on a Sunderland tram.

Appearances:
FAC: 2 apps. 3 gls.
Total: *2 apps. 3 gls.*

BRADSHAW, Thomas Dickinson

Role: Outside-right 1897-98
5'8" 11st.12lbs.
b. Hambleton, Lancs, 15th March 1879

CAREER: Lostock Hall/Preston North End Apr 1896/Blackpool Nov 1896/ SUNDERLAND May 1897/Nottingham Forest Jan 1898/Leicester Fosse Mar 1899/New Brighton Tower May 1900/Swindon Town Aug 1901/Reading Nov 1901/Preston North End Sept 1902/Wellingborough cs 1903/ Southport Central June 1904/Earlestown Dec 1904/Accrington Stanley/Leicester Fosse Oct 1905/Rossendale United Feb 1906/Glossop North End May 1907-1908.

Debut v Sheffield Wednesday 4/9/1897

legendary players and in his first season, 1949-50, Sunderland narrowly missed the championship. The following season Welsh international Trevor Ford arrived for £30,000 and the line-up with Len Shackleton and Broadis looked awesome, but amid rumours of personality problems the trio disappointed and failed to deliver. Manchester City revived their interest and took Ivor's skilful creative midfield play to Maine Road. He won England recognition and played in the 1954 World Cup finals following his return to the North-east with Newcastle. Ivor then retraced his steps to Carlisle and later continued in the Scottish League. After leaving active participation in football he became a successful sports journalist. He has since retired but continues to live in Carlisle. His nickname of 'Ivor' came about because the handwriting on a contract was mis-read. During the Second World War Ivor was a commissioned officer and a bomber pilot in the RAF.

Appearances:
FL: 79 apps. 25 gls.
FAC: 5 apps. 2 gls.
Total: *84 apps. 27 gls.*
Honours:
14 Eng caps/3 FL apps.

BRODIE, Stephen Eric

Role: Forward 1993-96
5'7" 10st.8lbs.
b. Sunderland, 14th January 1973

CAREER: SUNDERLAND assoc. s'boy May 1987, trainee July 1989, pro July 1991 (Doncaster Rovers loan Aug 1995) (Scarborough loan Dec 1996)/Scarborough Feb 1997 to date.

Debut v Notts County (a) 28/8/1993 (sub)

Stephen Brodie severed a long connection with Sunderland when he joined Scarborough on a free transfer almost ten years after his arrival at Roker as a 14-year-old schoolboy in 1987. The former Southmoor School pupil was an outstanding marksman at youth level, but his lack of height and lightweight build proved a disadvantage in senior football although he did impress on his only full start for the seniors against West Brom in May 1995. Impressive form in a short loan spell at Scarborough resulted in a permanent contract.

Stephen Brodie

In his first full season 10 goals in 43(1) League appearances helped The Boro' into sixth place and an appearance in the Division Three play-offs. Sadly, their twelve-year reign as a League club ended dramatically in May 1999, relegation to the Conference League following Carlisle United's widely publicised 'great escape' via their goalkeeper's injury-time winner. Despite having a year of his contract still to run, Stephen asked for a transfer but in fact did not leave the McCain Stadium as expected during the close season. A close friend of Michael Gray, Stephen still watches The Lads whenever possible.

Appearances:
FL: 1(11) apps. 0 gls.
Total: *1(11) apps. 0 gls.*

BROWN, Alan

Role: Forward 1976-82
6'0" 11st.11lbs.
b. Easington, Co Durham, 22nd May 1959

CAREER: SUNDERLAND app, pro Sept 1976 (Newcastle United loan Nov 1981-Jan 1982)/ Shrewsbury Town Aug 1982/Doncaster Rovers Mar 1984-1985.

Debut v Norwich City (h) 18/12/1976

Alan Brown was a tall, blond-haired centre forward who made his Sunderland debut as a 17-year-old in season 1976-77. He was to suffer the trauma of relegation in his first season, having made five initial appearances within a run of ten consecutive matches during which Sunderland failed to score, although Brown did rattle the crossbar at Anfield and Highbury. When he eventually did net his first goal,

Alan Brown

with a simple tap-in, Alan embarked on one of Roker's more memorable celebrations running almost the entire length of the Main Stand! A Durham County Cup winner with Easington School, Alan was dubbed the 'Easington Express' by the fans, and was one of many youngsters recruited by legendary talent-spotter Charles Ferguson. Brown became a first team regular during Ken Knighton's spell in charge. His best season was the 1979-80 promotion campaign in which he recorded 13 goals in League and Cup, with two - including a last minute equaliser - in a League Cup tie at Newcastle. His transfer to Shrewsbury Town in August 1982 was part of the exchange plus cash deal which brought Ian Atkins to Roker Park. Alan was Shrewsbury's leading goalscorer in his first season with 14 League and Cup goals. Transferred to Doncaster Rovers in March the following term he assisted them in their run-in to promotion from Division Three, as runners-up to York City.

Appearances:
FL: 87(26) apps. 21 gls.
FAC: 2(2) apps. 0 gls.
FLC: 7 apps. 4 gls.
Total: *96(28) apps. 25 gls.*

BROWN, Arthur Samuel

Role: Centre-forward 1908-10
5'9" 11st.12lbs.
b. Gainsborough, 6th April 1885
d. Gainsborough, 27th June 1944

CAREER: Gainsborough Church Lads Brigade/Gainsborough Trinity 1902 am/ Sheffield United May 1902 £350/ SUNDERLAND June 1908 £1,600, then a world record/Fulham Oct 1910/ Middlesbrough May 1912-1913.

Debut v Manchester City (a) 1/9/1908

Spotted playing in a boys' match when barely 13 years old by Gainsborough Trinity's trainer who was captivated by his nimbleness, Arthur 'Boy' Brown proved a precocious talent. So much so he was capped by England in February 1904 before his 19th birthday and remained our youngest international for half a century until Duncan Edwards came along. Arthur's main virtues were opportunism and accurate shooting power which included four goals against Sunderland in October 1907 at Bramall Lane. In later years, however, his career flagged and he had left the scene before reaching 30. Like his father, Arthur was a master builders' merchant and monumental mason.

Appearances:
FL: 50 apps. 21 gls.
FAC: 5 apps. 2 gls.
Total: *55 apps. 23 gls.*
Honours:
2 Eng caps.

BROWN, Cyril

Role: Centre-forward 1945-46
5'9" 11st.0lbs.
b. Ashington, 25th May 1918
d. Dover, 15th April 1990

Cyril Brown

CAREER: Felixstowe/Brentford Jan 1939/
SUNDERLAND Apr 1945/Notts County Aug
1946/Boston United 1947-48/Rochdale Aug
1948/Peterborough United cs 1951.

Debut v Grimsby Town (FAC) (a) 5/1/1946

Cyril Brown was a centre or inside-forward
who led Sunderland's attack in all the 1945/46
FA Cup ties. At that time, the last of the
wartime seasons, it was decided to run the
competition on a two-leg home and away
basis. Big crowds resulted; Sunderland, for
example, playing before gates of 45,000 in both
encounters with Birmingham. Cyril moved to
Notts County on the resumption of normal
peacetime soccer. His final League club was
Rochdale where, in an emergency, he
successfully switched to wing-half.

Appearances:
FAC: 6 apps. 5 gls.
Total: *6 apps. 5 gls.*

BROWN, Harold Archer

Role: Centre-forward 1921-22
5'11" 12st.0lbs.
b. Shildon, Co. Durham, 4th qtr 1897
d. Shildon, Co Durham, spring 1958

CAREER: Shildon FC/SUNDERLAND Jan
1922 £650/Leadgate Park Sept 1922/permit
player Chilton Colliery Oct 1922/Shildon FC
circa 1923/Queens Park Rangers May 1924-
1925.

Debut v Manchester United (h) 21/1/1922

Sunderland paid what was then a substantial
sum for non-League player Harold Archer and
included him in the first team right away.
Well-built and promising, Brown scored on his
debut but this was the only goal in half a
dozen consecutive Division One appearances.
After returning to the non-League scene, he
re-emerged with QPR in 1924/25, appearing in
all their first 13 Southern Section fixtures, in
which he netted three goals.

Appearances:
FL: 6 apps. 1 gl.
Total: *6 apps. 1 gl.*

BROWN, John

Role: Centre-forward 1897-99
5'9" 12st.0lbs.
b. Motherwell, 1877

John Brown

CAREER: Dalziel Rovers/
SUNDERLAND May 1897/Portsmouth cs
1899/ Middlesbrough June 1900/Wallsend
Park Villa Apr 1901/Kettering May 1902.

Debut v Sheffield Wednesday (a) 4/9/1897

Young Scot John Brown arrived with an
excellent reputation, having won junior
international honours and medals in the
Lanarkshire League and Cup competitions.
He performed quite well at Sunderland before
joining the newly-formed Portsmouth club.
At Middlesbrough John showed unusual
versatility: in his 21 League matches during
the 1990/01 campaign he appeared at right
and centre-half, both inside forward positions,
centre-forward and outside-left.

Appearances:
FL: 32 apps. 9 gls.
FAC: 1 app. 0 gls.
Total: *33 apps. 9 gls.*
Honours:
2 Scot Jnr int apps.

BROWN, Norman Liddle

Role: Outside-right 1904-07
5'7" 10st.8lbs.
b. Willington Quay, Co Durham, 1st qtr 1885

CAREER: Willington Athletic/
SUNDERLAND Nov 1904/Brentford May
1907/Luton Town May 1908/Southend United
cs 1909/Millwall Athletic 1910/North Shields
1911/Blackpool May 1913-1914.

Debut v Everton (a) 19/11/1904

Norman Brown was
a useful winger and
the great Billy
Hogg's understudy
for nearly three
years. Then he
undertook a mini-
tour of Southern
League clubs before
returning to the
North-East in the
shape of non-League

Norman Brown

North Shields. Norman for the most part enjoyed regular first team football with his four Southern League clubs. In his final (1913/14) Blackpool season he generally played at centre-forward, scoring twice in 13 Second Division engagements.

Appearances:
FL: 27 apps. 1 gl.
FAC: 2 apps. 1 gl.
Total: *29 apps. 2 gls.*

BROWN, Thomas

Role: Inside-right 1907-08
5'8" 12st.0lbs.
b. Sunderland

CAREER: Sunderland Royal Rovers/SUNDERLAND May 1907/St Mirren May 1908-1910.

Debut v Manchester City (h) 2/9/1907

Locally developed Tom Brown was able to also play centre-forward. His solitary League appearance was in the opening fixture of 1907/08 that resulted in a heavy home defeat (5-2) at the hands of Manchester City.

Tom Brown

Appearances:
FL: 1 app. 0 gls.
Total: *1 app. 0 gls.*

BUCHANAN, David

Role: Forward 1986-88
b. Newcastle upon Tyne, 23rd June 1962

CAREER: Leicester City app July 1978, pro July 1979(Northampton Town loan Oct 1982)/ Peterborough United Aug 1983/North Shields and Blyth Spartans during 1984/ SUNDERLAND n.c. 13 Aug, pro 21 Aug 1986 (York City loan Sept-Nov 1987) (Middlesbrough trial Apr 1988)(Norwegian football May 1988)/Blyth Spartans Aug 1988/

BUCHAN, Charles Murray

Role: Inside-right, occasionally centre-forward 1910-25
6'0" 12st.7lbs.
b. Plumstead, London, 22nd September 1891
d. Beaulieu-sur-Mer, France, 25th June 1960

CAREER: Bloomfield Road School, Woolwich/High Street School, Woolwich/ Elder Tree FC/St Nicholas FC/Woolwich Polytechnic/Plumstead FC(Woolwich Arsenal am dec 1908)/Northfleet Nov 1909/Leyton pro Mar 1910/ SUNDERLAND Mar 1911 £1,250/Arsenal July 1925 £4,100/retired May 1928.

Debut v Tottenham Hotspur (a) 1/4/1911

A legendary famous name that not only reverberates down the Sunderland years but those of our national game too. Buchan possessed immense skills in every aspect of inside-forward play - ball control, combination, speed of thought, natural scoring ability and (a speciality) the glancing header. Perhaps above all, however, were the quick-thinking subtleties, and here was a drawback not of Buchan's making. The subtleties could bamboozle colleagues as well as opponents! This was advanced as the reason his total of six England appearances was comparatively modest, even though he scored four times. (One could mention, too, the availability of Burnley's Bob Kelly (q.v.), a plausible factor, rarely highlighted). Buchan's 209 League goals for Sunderland has never been surpassed, and it is perhaps hard to believe he was barracked by the Roker crowd in his opening games for an apparent lack of commitment! Indeed, manager Bob Kyle was forced into a special trip to London but fortunately persuaded a disconsolate Charlie to return. It proved a

Newcastle Blue Star 1988/Bedlington/Whitley Bay.

Debut v Huddersfield Town (a) 23/8/1986

Initially signed on trial from Northern League club Blyth Spartans, David Buchanan, a fair-haired slightly-built forward, began impressively, netting five goals in an early masterstroke of negotiation as Buchan not only topped 400 appearances for the club, but finished top-scorer every year from the championship season of 1912-13 through to 1923-24. In 1922-23 Buchan was also the First Division's leading scorer. When the great manager Herbert Chapman moved to Highbury after a trio of titles at Huddersfield he made Buchan his first signing. Charlie's move to Arsenal, in his 34th year, was to prove a foundation stone of the London club's later inter-war successes. But it occasioned a much publicised and unusual transfer. Sunderland wanted a £4,000 fee for an outstanding player that manager Kyle was adamant would still score 20 goals a season. A deal was eventually struck at £2,000 plus £100 for every goal Buchan scored in his first season and he duly netted 21 times. Charlie went into journalism in 1928 as football and golf correspondent to the *Daily News*, a newspaper that amalgamated to become the *News Chronicle*. He was also an early commentator on BBC Radio. In 1951 he became editor of a new magazine, *Charles Buchan's Football Monthly*, which became a respected and unusually long-running publication. Buchan's biographical study, 'A Lifetime in Football' (Phoenix House 1955) is a most interesting book. Charlie was the brother of Tom Buchan (Bolton Wanderers, 1914-23) and a lifetime friend of his long-lived Sunderland team mate Joe Kasher. In the Great War, when he won the Military Medal, Buchan served in the Grenadier Guards before receiving a commission with the Sherwood Foresters.

Appearances:
FL: 380 apps. 209 gls.
FAC: 33 apps. 15 gls.
Total: *413 apps. 224 gls.*
Honours:
*6 Eng caps/1 Eng 'Victory' int app. 1919/10
FL apps./(Sunderland) FL champs 1913/FAC
finalist 1913/(Arsenal) FAC finalist 1927.*

season run of six matches. Thereafter both he and the team lost form and confidence, and the season ended in relegation to Division Three. Totally out of the picture under new manager Denis Smith, Buchanan was loaned to York City before being released in April 1988. An unsuccessful trial with Middlesbrough preceded a lengthy spell in

Norway and a subsequent circuit around the North-Eastern non-League scene. At the outset of his career, David played mainly on the wing and became Leicester City's youngest ever League player at the age of 16 years and 192 days, scoring against Oldham Athletic on his New Year's Day debut in 1979, the same afternoon that Gary Lineker made his League

David Buchanan

bow. Prior to his recruitment by Lawrie McMenemy, David had been capped by England at semi-professional level.

Appearances:
FL: 25(9) apps. 8 gls.
FAC: 2 apps. 3 gls.
Other: 2 apps. 0 gls.
Total: *29(9) apps.*
11 gls.

BUCKLE, Harold Redmond

Role: Outside-left 1902-06
5'10" 11st.12lbs.
b. Belfast, 1882

CAREER: Cliftonville Casuals/Cliftonville Olympic/Cliftonville FC May 1901/ SUNDERLAND Oct 1902/Portsmouth May 1906/Bristol Rovers May 1907/Coventry City June 1908, player-manager 1910-11/Belfast Celtic cs 1911/Glenavon cs 1914/Belfast United player-sec. manager Sept 1917/ Fordson's FC (Cork) Sept 1922.

Debut v Stoke (a) 8/11/1902

Harold Buckle was talked of in 1903 as "an exceedingly valuable player", and the statement held good for an abnormal while for he was still winning club honours more than 20 years on. Big as wingers go, he had speed, dexterity and a fair goals return, the

Harold Buckle

latter boosted by the exploitation of a rocket shot. On returning to Ireland in 1911 Harry, besides continuing his football career, worked in the Belfast shipyards for a time. As one of the very few Catholics so employed he endured an amount of persecution.

Appearances:
FL: 44 apps. 14 gls.
FAC: 2 apps. 1 gl.
Total: *46 apps. 15 gls.*
Honours:
2 Irish caps./4 IL apps./1 SL app./(Fordson's FC) Lge of Ire Cup winner 1926/Lge of Ire Cup finalist 1924.

BUCKLEY, Michael John

Role: Midfield 1978-83
5'5" 9st.6lbs.
b. Manchester, 4th November 1953

CAREER: Everton app, pro June 1971/ SUNDERLAND Aug 1978/Hartlepool United n.c. Aug 1983/Carlisle United Sept 1983/ Middlesbrough June 1984-1985.

Debut v Preston North End (h) 2/9/1978

A tenacious ball-winner, despite his lack of physical advantage, Mick Buckley made his Everton debut as an 18-year-old and was a member of the England Youth side that won

Mick Buckley

the European Youth Tournament in Spain in 1971-72. Team mates in the final against Germany in Barcelona included Trevor Francis, Kevin Beattie and John Gidman. In the Everton team the night The Lads were relegated at Goodison Park in 1977, Mick was a £60,000 signing by Sunderland in August 1978. A member of Sunderland's *Daily Express* Five-a-side winning team in 1979, Buckley was also a promotion winner in the 1979-80 season and, two years on, his timely winning goal, against Manchester City in the season's final fixture, ensured Division One survival.

Appearances:
FL: 117(4) apps. 7 gls.
FAC: 5 apps. 1 gl.
FLC: 8(1) apps. 0 gls.
Total: *130(5) apps. 8 gls.*
Honours:
2 Eng U-23 apps.1975-76/Eng Yth.

BURBANKS, William Edwin

Role: Outside-left 1934-48
5'8" 10st.7lbs.
b. Bentley, nr Doncaster, 1st April 1913
d. Hull, 26th July 1983

CAREER: Doncaster Grammar School/Thorne Town/ Doncaster YMCA/Denaby United June 1934/ SUNDERLAND Feb 1935 £750(guested for Doncaster Rovers, Blackpool, Manchester United, Leeds United and Chesterfield during WW2)/ Hull City June 1948/Leeds United July 1963/retired May 1954.

Debut v Portsmouth (h) 27/4/1935

Eddie Burbanks quickly graduated from Midland League soccer to the top flight with Sunderland and, in due course, became an automatic replacement for the great Jimmy Connor when The Lads' popular and worthy winger was badly injured in a 1937 FA Cup tie. Although he topped 150 League and Cup outings for

BURLEY, George Elder

Role: Full-back 1985-88
5'10" 11st.0lbs.
b. Cumnock, Ayrshire, 3rd June 1956

CAREER: Ayrshire Jnr football/Ipswich Town app 1971, pro June 1973/SUNDERLAND Sept 1985/Gillingham July 1988/Motherwell July 1989/Ayr United player-manager Jan 1991/ Falkirk Jan 1994/Motherwell Feb 1994/ Colchester United June 1994/Ipswich Town manager Dec 1994.

Debut v Huddersfield Town (a) 28/9/1985

As a crowd in excess of 36,000 packed into Old Trafford to witness the final home League appearance of superstar George Best, his immediate opponent on that December afternoon in 1973 was 17-year-old George

Sunderland Eddie's career was badly disrupted by the war. He did though score the club's last goal before the conflict and the first after it. More important was his first FA Cup goal which came three minutes from time to seal a 3-1 victory at Wembley in the 1937 final against Preston. Although naturally right-footed, Eddie played throughout a long career on the left flank: a polished performer he packed a hard shot in either foot. Signed later on by Raich Carter, the Hull City player/manager and an old Sunderland buddy, Eddie was a key man in the Tigers' 1949 championship side. He settled in Hull and ran a sweet shop until retiring in November 1979.

Appearances:
FL: 131 apps. 25 gls.
FAC: 21 apps. 3 gls.
Total: *152 apps. 28 gls.*
Honours:
(Sunderland) FAC winner 1937/(Hull City) FL Div 3 Nth champs 1949.

Burley, making his first League appearance for Ipswich Town. The calm and assured display of the former Scottish Schoolboy international was a precursive view of a career which spanned over 500 appearances for Bobby Robson's fine Ipswich Town sides of the seventies and eighties. He arrived at Roker a vastly experienced 29-year-old but in Lawrie McMenemy's mix of former international and bargain signings he was, despite some personally stylish performances, unable to prevent a downward momentum which ended in relegation to Division Three in May 1987. Burley made his final League appearance, at the age of 38, with Third Division Colchester United in December 1994. During the same month he returned to familiar territory as manager of Ipswich Town. In 1998-99, for the third season in succession, Burley's attractive Ipswich side cruelly lost out on promotion to the Premiership at the play-off stage. This latest misery followed a 4-3 victory against Bolton Wanderers, which levelled the aggregate score in the semi-final to 4-4, but saw Ipswich miss out, yet again, on the away goals ruling.

Appearances:
FL: 54 apps. 0 gls.
FAC: 5 apps. 1 gl.
FLC: 2 apps. 0 gls.
Other: 5 apps. 1 gl.
Total: *66 apps. 2 gls.*
Honours:
11 Scot caps 1979-82/Scot Sch & Yth/5 Scot U-21 apps./2 Scot U-23 apps./(Ipswich Town) FAC winner 1978.

George Burley

BURLINSON

Role: Left-half 1884-85
Debut v Redcar (a) (FAC) 8/11/1884

Burlinson appeared in Sunderland's first FA Cup tie, a 3-1 defeat at Redcar. He also played at left-half the following week and, all told, had five outings that season. The others were one at inside-left (in September) and two at centre-forward (in December). Something of a utility man it would seem

> **Appearances:**
> *FAC: 1 app. 0 gls.*
> **Total:** *1 app. 0 gls.*

BUTCHER, Terence Ian

Role: Central defender 1992-93
6'4" 14st.5lbs.
b. Singapore, 28th December 1958

CAREER: Lowestoft Schools/Ipswich Town Aug 1976/Rangers Aug 1986/Coventry City player-manager Nov 1990/Halesowen Town player-coach Jan 1992/Sheffield Wednesday reserves and Scout Apr 1992/SUNDERLAND Aug 1992, appointed player-manager Feb 1993, manager later in the same month. Contract terminated Nov 1993.

Debut v Swindon Town (a) 15/8/1992

Born in Singapore when his father was serving in the Royal Navy, Terry Butcher was raised in Lowestoft and spotted in schools football by Ipswich Town. He made his League debut in April 1978, in the memorable season that Ipswich won the FA Cup by beating Arsenal 1-0. A tall, commanding, physically-equipped central defender, he made his international debut, at Under-21 level, against Sweden in June 1979, and won the first of his 77 full England caps against Australia in Sydney in May 1980. A UEFA Cup-winner's medal in 1981 seemed scant reward for ten seasons with Ipswich, whose near misses included the runners-up spot in Division One in consecutive seasons 1981 and 1982. An Ipswich record fee of £725,000 took him to Rangers and he skippered them to success on all domestic fronts during his four year stay despite some occasionally unsavoury on field antics. A £450,000 fee then took him to Coventry City as player-manager in November 1990. Injury problems restricted his

Terry Butcher

playing to just six League appearances, and he resigned in January 1992 after being asked to accept a cut in wages. Signed for Sunderland by Malcolm Crosby on a free transfer, Butcher quickly replaced the outgoing manager in the hot seat but although clearly vastly experienced as a player, he was past his best. He did, however, have an appealing regular end of match routine where he conducted cheers from the Sunderland fans. Relegation to Division Three was only narrowly avoided and, despite a £2 million investment in new players in the 1993 close season, the new campaign began with an opening day club record 5-0 drubbing at Derby. A subsequent run of five consecutive defeats inevitably led to Butcher's dismissal in November 1993.

Appearances:
FL: 37(1) apps. 0 gls.
FAC: 2 apps. 0 gls.
FLC: 2 apps. 1 gl.
Total: *41(1) apps. 1 gl.*
Honours:
77 Eng caps 1980-1990/7 Eng U-21 apps.
1979-80/(Ipswich Town) UEFAC winner
1981/(Rangers) SPL champs 1987, 1989,
1990/SC finalist 1989/SLC winner 1987,
1988, 1989.

BUTLER, Geoffrey

Role: Left-back 1967-69
5'8" 11st.0lbs.
b. Middlesbrough, 29th September 1946

CAREER: Middlesbrough schools football/ Middlesbrough FC am, pro May 1964/ Chelsea Sept 1967 £57,000/SUNDERLAND Jan 1968 £65,000/Norwich City Oct 1968 £25,000(Baltimore Comets lona May 1974-Aug 1975)/AFC Bournemouth Mar 1976/ Peterborough United non-contract Aug 1981/ Trowbridge Town July 1982/Salisbury City player-manager Feb 1983, later becoming commercial manager.

Debut v Burnley (h) 20/1/1968

Geoff Butler

A promising schoolboy, Geoff Butler represented the North Riding at that level and was said to have been "developed by Middlesbrough as a stolid, clean-kicking full-back". After a thorough introduction to the senior game at Ayresome Park, Geoff moved on in quick succession to Chelsea and then Sunderland. Although both transfers were occasioned with very high fees by 1960s standard, he grossed only nine League appearances plus three substitutions at the two venues. There followed periods at Norwich - a sterling long stay - Bournemouth and Peterborough where he was generally first choice.

Appearances:
FL: 1(2) apps. 0 gls.
FAC: 2 apps. 0 gls.
Total: *3(2) apps. 0 gls.*
Honours:
(Norwich City) FL Div 2 champs 1972/ FLC finalist 1973.

BUTLER, Joseph

Role: Goalkeeper 1912-14
5'9" 12st.0lbs.
b. Horsehay, Salop,

CAREER: Junior football/Stockport County 1898/Clapton Orient May 1905/Stockport County Feb 1906/Glossop North end Mar 1908 £150/ SUNDERLAND Oct 1912/ Lincoln City May 1914 (guested for Rochdale and Stockport County during WW1).

Debut v Chelsea (a) 5/10/1912

A great favourite at Stockport where he received his League baptism, Joe Butler had three separate spells there and actually played for them 21 years after originally signing. Agile and brave, Joe made 152 consecutive League appearances for Glossop, also helping that club reach the FA Cup quarter-finals. His high point, though, was the part he played in Sunderland's wonderful 1912/13 championship season. An ever-present following his October arrival, he also played in all ten FA Cup ties including the narrow defeat in the

Joe Butler

fiercely contested final with Aston Villa at The Crystal Palace which cost Sunderland the chance of the 'Double'. To date, no goalkeeper in the club's history with more than 50 appearances can better Butler's record of conceding just 84 goals in 79 games. Indeed, he only once conceded more than three in a game. In a long career Joe eventually grossed over 450 League appearances. Prior to professional football he had worked as a miner.

Appearances:
FL: 65 apps. 0 gls.
FAC: 14 apps. 0 gls.
Total: *79 apps. 0 gls.*
Honours:
(Sunderland) FL Champs 1913/FAC finalist 1913.

BUTLER, Paul

Role: Central Defender 1998-date
6' 2" 13st. 0lbs.
b. Manchester, 2nd November 1972

CAREER: Moston Brook H.S./ Manchester Schoolboys/Bradford City trainee 1989/ Rochdale trainee Aug 1990, pro July 1991/ Bury July 1996/ SUNDERLAND July 1998-date.

Debut v Queens Park Rangers (h) 8/8/1998

Promotion to the Premiership and international recognition combined to make season 1998-99 a truly memorable one for Sunderland's strapping central defender. Paul began with Rochdale making his first League appearance as a 17-year-old in September 1990. He cost Bury £100,000 in July 1996 and marshalled the Shakers' defence so successfully in his first season they won the Division Two championship with the best defensive record in their section. Outstanding in Bury's initial First Division campaign, he was a target for both Ipswich Town and Charlton Athletic, but it was Sunderland's £1 million bid that ultimately proved successful. Paul was a key member of Sunderland's miserly defence all season, and the fact that promotion to the Premiership was stylishly clinched on the ground of his former club, Bury, was obviously a matter of supreme satisfaction for the commanding, no-nonsense defender who has so successfully negotiated his first season on Wearside.

Appearances:
FL: 44 apps. 2 gls.
FAC: 2 apps. 0 gls.
FLC: 6(1) apps. 0 gls.
Total: *52(1) apps. 2 gls.*
Honours:
Eire B 1999/(Bury) Div 2 champs 1997/(Sunderland) Div 1 champs 1999.

Paul Butler

BYRNE, Christopher

Role: Forward 1997-98
5'9" 10st.8lbs.
b. Manchester, 9th February 1975

CAREER: Manchester Schoolboys/Crewe Alexandra assoc. s'boy Dec 1989, trainee Aug 1991, pro June 1993-June 1994/Flixton FC (South Manchester League)/Droylsden FC Nov 1995/Macclesfield Town Feb 1996/ SUNDERLAND June 1997/Stockport County Nov 1997.

Debut v Sheffield United (a) 10/8/1997 (sub)

A lightly-built, pacy midfielder whose shoot-on-sight policy did much to assist Macclesfield Town to the championship of the Vauxhall Conference in 1996-97. Ten goals in 18 League appearances included a hat-trick in the final promotion-clinching game. His first senior club was Crewe Alexandra where he graduated from schoolboy to professional but left, aged 19 years, without

Chris Byrne

having made a League appearance. In the week of his Sunderland debut, Byrne also netted a hat-trick for the Reserves in their opening Pontin's League fixture at Manchester City, but his stay on Wearside proved brief. Despite his undoubted potential he was unable to settle in the North-East. Having reluctantly decided to release him, Sunderland made a handsome profit of £200,000 when Byrne moved homeward to join Stockport County. In September 1997 Chris Byrne missed a Coca-Cola Cup tie against Bury when he assisted the police in their enquiries into a murder case. More recently he was sentenced to 240 hours community service for his part in a burglary at a pharmacy. Caught on the premises, he assaulted a policeman in an effort to escape. A serious knee ligament injury sustained in a match against Huddersfield Town in September 1998 resulted in Chris being sidelined for much of season 1998-99.

Appearances:
FL: 4(4) apps. 0 gls.
FLC: 1(1) apps. 0 gls.
Total: *5(5) apps. 0 gls.*
Honours:
(Macclesfield Town) VC champs 1997.

BYRNE, John Frederick

Role: Forward 1991-93
6'0" 12st.3lbs.
b. Wythenshawe, Cheshire, 1st February 1961

CAREER: York City app July 1977, pro Jan 1979/Queens Park Rangers Oct 1984/Le Havre, France May 1988/Brighton & Hove Albion Sept 1990/SUNDERLAND Oct 1991/Millwall Oct 1992(Brighton & Hove Albion loan Mar 1993)/Oxford United Nov 1993/Brighton & Hove Albion Feb 1995/Crawley Town Aug 1996/Shoreham FC (Sussex County League) Mar 1997, appointed joint manager (with Russell Bromage) Aug 1997.

Debut v Bristol Rovers (h) 26/10/1991

Eighteen-year-old John Byrne was recruited from Manchester junior football by fellow Mancunian and York City manager, Wilf McGuinness. In a seven year spell at Bootham Crescent, the tousle-haired striker netted 64 goals in 199 appearances, the highlight coming in 1983-84 when his significant contribution of 27 League goals earned him a Division Four championship medal. Early in the following season, Queens Park Rangers paid £100,000 for his signature, and it was during his spell at Loftus Road that he was first capped by the Republic of Ireland - the country of his father's birth. The French club, Le Havre, paid £175,000 for him in May 1988 and he joined Sunderland for £225,000, after spending a year with Brighton which included a Wembley appearance in the season's Division Two play-off final, won by Notts County. His season at Roker was certainly eventful: manager Denis Smith, who had tried several times to sign Byrne before he succeeded, was replaced by Malcolm Crosby, while relegation from Division Two was only narrowly avoided as Sunderland also reached the final of the FA

Cup. John Byrne's record of seven FA Cup goals in eight matches included strikes in every round up to and including the semi-final, but the fairy-tale ended at Wembley where Byrne fluffed a fine chance with the game scoreless and Liverpool ran out comfortable winners by 2-0. Sold by manager Crosby to Millwall for £275,000 after almost exactly one year at Roker, his best subsequent spell was with Oxford United. Increasingly troubled by injuries during his third spell at Brighton, Byrne was released during the 1996 close season. His League career totalled 503 appearances and he scored 134 goals.

Appearances:
FL: 33 apps. 8 gls.
FAC: 8 apps. 7 gls.
FLC: 2 apps. 0 gls.
Total: *43 apps. 15 gls.*
Honours:
23 Eire caps 1985-93/(York City) Div 4 champs 1984/(QPR) FLC finalist 1986/(Sunderland) FAC finalist 1992.

John Byrne

CAMPBELL, *John Middleton*

Role: Centre-forward 1889-97
5'9"
b. Renton, Dunbartonshire, 19th February 1870
d. Sunderland, 8th June 1906

CAREER: Renton Union/Renton FC/
SUNDERLAND cs 1889/Newcastle United
May 1897 £40/retired Oct 1898.

Debut v Blackburn Rovers (h) 20/9/1889 (FAC)
FL Debut v Burnley (h) 13/9/1890

John Campbell was a prominent member of 'The Team of All the Talents' and was regarded, as one authority says, "as the most dangerous centre-forward of his day". Campbell had a bustling, no-nonsense style and a great penchant for goalscoring, in his heyday topping the League's scoring list in three seasons out of four. It is a measure of his potency as a forward that he remains the fifth highest goalscorer in Sunderland's history. Clearly a confident fellow he is easily spotted in team photographs of the era, usually lounging unconventionally on the ground at the front in relaxed pose. In the evening of his career Johnny helped Newcastle win promotion, leaving the Magpies because he had become a licensee, thus breaking club rules. In the 1890's many good judges were mystified as to why he had never received international recognition. His brother, Robert Campbell, was Sunderland's manager from 1896 to 1899.

Appearances:
FL: 190 apps. 133 gls.
FAC: 25 apps. 17 gls.
Total: *215 apps.*
150 gls.
Honours:
(Renton) SC winner
1889/(Sunderland)
FL champs 1892, 1893,
1895.

John Campbell

CAMPBELL, William Gibson

Role: Outside-left 1965-66
5'6" 9st.10lbs.
b. Belfast, 2nd July 1944

CAREER: Junior football/Distillery am, pro cs1964/SUNDERLAND Sept 1964 £8,000/ Dundee May 1966 £3,000/Motherwell July 1970/Linfield player-manager 1974.

Debut v Sheffield United (a) 21/11/1964

Bill Campbell, a nippy little Irish winger, was mostly employed as stand-in for Mike Hellawell and Brian Usher in his two terms at Roker Park. He had arrived, aged 20, shortly after taking the professional ticket. Billy enjoyed a lot more first team

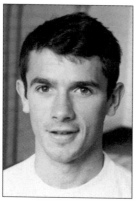

Bill Campbell

exposure with his two Scottish clubs and was at Dundee during a period of domestic success. Recognition of his talents at international level was justified.

Appearances:
FL: 5 apps. 0 gls.
Total: *5 apps. 0 gls.*
Honours:
6 NIre caps/3 NIre U-23 apps./(Dundee) SLC finalist 1968/(Linfield) IC finalist 1975.

CARMICHAEL, Robert

Role: Inside-right 1906-07
5'7" 12st.0lbs.
b. Scotland, 1885

CAREER: Shettleston FC (Glasgow)/ SUNDERLAND Jan 1907/St Mirren cs 1908/ Oldham Athletic May 1909 £90/Third Lanark cs 1910-1911/Shelbourne(Ireland) 1915

Debut v Bury (h) 20/4/1907

Robert Carmichael was a reserve inside-forward of short though heavy build. The 5-2 home defeat inflicted by Bury in April 1907

was his sole Sunderland first team outing, while at Oldham he appeared five times, scoring one goal. Carmichael's time at Shelbourne included an appearance in a Belfast City Cup final in May 1915. In July 1943 it was reported that

Robert Carmichael

Carmichael had been appointed assistant trainer to Glasgow Rangers.

Appearances:
FL: 1 app. 0 gls.
Total: *1 app. 0 gls.*

CARR, Henry

Role: Centre-forward 1910-11
5'8" 12st.0lbs.
b. South Bank, Middlesbrough, 1st qtr 1887

CAREER: South Bank FC/SUNDERLAND Oct 1910/Middlesbrough Nov 1910-1912/ South Bank. As an amateur the player, of course, had never really left the latter club.

Debut v Blackburn Rovers (a) 8/10/1910

Henry Carr deputised for George Holley (unavailable because of an inter-league fixture) for his solitary Sunderland League appearance. The local press thought he was the first amateur centre-forward to represent the club in their then 21-year Football League history. Harry belonged to the famous quartet of Carr brothers, all of whom played for Middlesbrough. (The other three turned professional and included Jackie, a full England cap).

Appearances:
FL: 1 app. 0 gls.
Total: *1 app. 0 gls.*
Honours:
1 Eng am int app./(South Bank FC) AMC winner 1913/AMC finalist 1910.

CARTER, Horatio Stratton 'Raich'

Role: Inside-forward 1932-39
5'7" 10st.6lbs.
b. Hendon, Sunderland, 21st December 1913
d. Hull, 9th October 1994

CAREER: Hendon School/Sunderland
Schools/Whitburn St Mary's/Leicester City
trial/Sunderland Forge/Esh Winning/
SUNDERLAND am Nov 1930, pro Nov 1931/
Derby County Dec 1945 £8,000/Hull City
player-asst. manager Mar 1948 £6,000, player-
manager May 1948-Sept 1951, player only to
Apr 1952/Cork Athletic Jan-May 1953/Leeds
United manager May 1953-June 1958/
Mansfield Town manager Feb 1960/
Middlesbrough manager Jan 1963-Feb 1966.

Debut v Sheffield Wednesday (a) 15/10/1932

A superb inside-forward, amongst the greatest
and most complete this country has produced:
ice cool, possessor of magnificent ball control,
scoring power in either foot (although
naturally left-footed) and innate vision that
intelligently created for others. A true
Sunderland and indeed, national legend, Raich
Carter was pure class. An outstanding, if
diminutive, schoolboy player, as the four-cap
haul demonstrates, an unsuccessful trial at
Leicester City was a blow. Things were
difficult at home. His widowed mother had
been left with three young children, an uncle
was looking after the family and secured
Raich an apprenticeship as an electrician. In
his autobiography, 'Footballer's Progress'
(Sporting Handbooks, 1950), Raich relates how
he overcame the disappointment. He took
advantage of being on Sunderland's books as
an amateur and worked his way with steely
resolve to a professional contract. The
resultant wage enabled him to leave his
electrician's apprenticeship, with its miniscule
wages, for good, becoming the main financial
prop of his family. Raich's subsequent career
at Roker Park from then on became the stuff of

*Raich Carter skippered The Lads to
FA Cup success in 1937, scoring the
decisive second goal against Preston.*

Raich Carter

legend. He made his League bow two months short of his 19th birthday. By the age of 24 he had won all the top honours then open to a player: international caps, a League championship medal, an FA Cup winners' medal and appearances for the Football League in inter-league representative games. In Sunderland's 1936 championship season he was joint top-scorer with Bobby Gurney and continued to head the scoring charts in the seasons that followed before the war. In 1937 against Preston at Wembley Raich not only scored the decisive second goal as Sunderland became the first team to come from behind to win the trophy, but he also skippered Sunderland to their first FA Cup final victory with an eleven containing only two members (Mapson and Duns) younger than himself. First picked by England in 1934 he won 13 caps and scored seven times but he also netted 19 goals in 18 unofficial, mainly wartime internationals. On one occasion he scored four goals at Roker Park playing in a trial match for 'The Rest' against England. Although he assisted Sunderland during wartime seasons the appearances were spasmodic. He had joined the RAF at the outbreak, playing as a guest for Derby County when serving at Loughborough and helping to rehabilitate injured airmen. Another Derby guest was the celebrated Irish cap, Peter Doherty, and their inside-forward partnership - although their styles differed markedly - immediately gelled and became famous. Indeed it was the main feature in the Derby side that lifted the first post-war FA Cup in 1946. Raich actually signed for the Rams soon after hostilities ended and so was a 'permanent' Derby County player when acquiring his second Cup winners' medal. At Hull he had an equally dramatic effect. Signed by the renowned Major Buckley as player-assistant manager, aged 34, he succeeded Buckley in the manager's chair two months later. Raich continued to play, captaining the Tigers to the Third Division (North) title in 1949. The club's home crowds rocketed to the 40,000 mark, the team a mixture of experienced men and up-and-coming youngsters, the former well exampled by a left wing of Carter and his old

Sunderland partner, Eddie Burbanks. Raich, his hair rapidly greying, was dubbed 'the silver-haired maestro' by the local press. He left the managership in 1951 but continued playing until 1952, having a final playing fling early the following year, picking up a medal at Cork in the process. His subsequent forays into the managerial field were quite successful, including as they did promotions with Leeds United (1956) and Mansfield Town (1963). But the career can be summed up as efficient rather than spectacular. Carter, a perfectionist,

WILLS'S CIGARETTES

H. CARTER (SUNDERLAND)

did not willingly accept the foibles of lesser men, in particular those of moderately talented footballers. On leaving the game he managed the sports department of a Hull store and later ran a credit business in that City. Raich was no mean cricketer (he had won honours when at school at swimming and athletics also) attaining Minor Counties standard and being awarded his cap by Durham CCC in 1933. In 1946 he played for Derbyshire on three occasions. In June 1998, just one day before they were due to be auctioned at Christie's, Glasgow, Sunderland City Council purchased Raich Carter's medal collection which has since been displayed with his shirts in the City Library. It was a fitting gesture as it is doubtful a better player than Carter has ever graced Sunderland's red and white stripes.

Appearances:
FL: 245 apps. 118 gls.
FAC: 31 apps. 9 gls.
Total: *276 apps. 127 gls.*
Honours:
13 Eng caps/17 Eng wartime int apps./4 Eng Sch apps./4 FL apps./(Sunderland) FL champs 1936/FAC winner 1937/(Derby County FAC winner 1946/(Hull City) FL Div 3 Nth champs 1949/(Cork Athletic) FA of Ire Cup winner 1953.

CARTER, Timothy Douglas

Role: Goalkeeper 1987-93
6'2" 13st.11lbs.
b. Bristol, 5th October 1967

CAREER: Bristol Rovers app, pro Oct 1985
(Newport County loan Dec 1987)/
SUNDERLAND Dec 1987(Carlisle United loan
Mar-Apr 1988)(Bristol City loan Sept 1988)
(Birmingham City loan Nov 1991)/Hartlepool
United Aug 1992(Millwall loan Jan 1994)/
Millwall Mar 1994/Blackpool Aug 1995/
Oxford United Aug 1995/Millwall Dec 1995/
Halifax Town July 1998-May 1999.
Debut v Bristol City (h) 23/4/1988

An ideally-built goalkeeper with quick
reflexes, Tim Carter won England Youth caps
against the USSR, Italy and Holland in April
1985, and in December of the same year made
his Football League debut for Bristol Rovers as
an 18-year-old. He established himself in the
following season with 44 senior appearances,
and on Christmas Eve 1987 joined Sunderland
for an initial fee of £35,000 with a further
£15,000 payable, linked to first team
appearances. Signed as cover for Iain Hesford,
Carter found few opportunities. He enjoyed a
run of senior outings in the first half of season
1989-90 before Tony Norman regained his
position as Number One goalkeeper. In season
1996-97, Carter's 46 Division Two appearances
for Millwall were his highest seasonal return
for ten years. Signed by Halifax Town for their
initial season back in the League, Tim was not
retained at the end of the season in which the
Shaymen had at one stage looked capable of
mounting a serious
promotion challenge and
both senior goalkeepers
were amongst the close
season departures.

Appearances:
FL: 37 apps. 0 gls.
FLC: 9 apps. 0 gls.
Other: 4 apps. 0 gls.
Total: *50 apps. 0 gls.*
Honours:
3 Eng Youth apps.
1985.

Norman Case

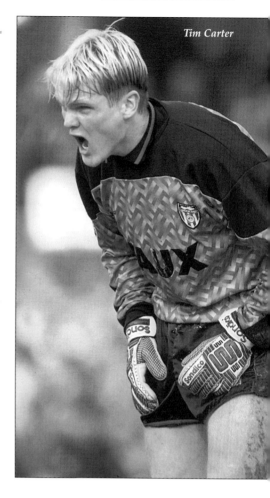

Tim Carter

CASE, Norman

Role: Centre-forward 1949-51
b. Prescot, Lancs, 1st September 1925
d. Watford, 1973

CAREER: Junior football/Sheffield United
Aug 1948/Leyton Orient Oct 1948/Rochdale
Nov 1948-Feb 1949/Ards 1949/
SUNDERLAND Sept 1949/Watford Dec 1950
(Yeovil Town loan Aug 1951)/Rochdale Feb
1952/Cheltenham Town cs 1952/Canterbury
City Aug 1953.
Debut v Stoke City (h) 26/10/1949 (scored)

Although he had been on the books of three
Football League clubs previously, it was
Sunderland who provided Norman Case's
League debut. (And he scored in a 3-0 win

over Stoke). Case arrived at Roker Park after a bright, if brief, spell in Ireland with Ards. A five-goal spree against Coleraine attracted attention, notably selection for the Irish League against the Scottish League at Ibrox. The Scots were rampant, winning 8-1: Norman netted the Irish consolation goal. He did not achieve regular first team football subsequently at either Watford or Rochdale and his aggregate Football League records reads 16 appearances, six goals. Yet he had the 'goal touch', in his short Yeovil loan period, for example, scoring 23 times.

Appearances:
FL: 4 apps. 2 gls.
Total: *4 apps. 2 gls.*
Honours:
1 IL app.

CHALMERS, James

Role: Outside-left 1897-99
5'9" 12st.0lbs.
b. Old Luce, Wigtownshire, 3rd December 1877

CAREER: Beith/Morton July 1896/ SUNDERLAND May 1897/Preston North End Oct 1898/Notts County June 1899/Beith Sept 1900/Partick Thistle Oct 1900/Watford July 1901/Tottenham Hotspur May 1902/Swindon Town May 1904/Norwich City May 1906/ Beith cs 1907/Bristol Rovers May 1908/Clyde Nov 1908.

Debut v Sheffield Wednesday (a) 4/9/1897

James Chalmers

A much-travelled forward, James Chalmers was formidably built for a wingman, making his forays difficult to contain and, despite the brevity of his stays, he nonetheless recorded at least double figures of first team appearances for six of his eight English clubs. Another physical circumstance was that he had become grey-haired by his mid-twenties (it must have been all that travelling!). And from the above roll-call of clubs it would seem Beith FC would always welcome him home.

Appearances:
FL: 27 apps. 4 gls.
FAC: 1 app. 0 gls.
Total: *28 apps. 4 gls.*

CHAMBERLAIN, Alec Francis Roy

Role: Goalkeeper 1993-96
6'2" 13st.9lbs.
b. March, Cambs, 20th June 1964

CAREER: Ramsey Town/Ipswich Town July 1981/Colchester United Aug 1982/Everton July 1987(Tranmere Rovers loan Nov 1987)/ Luton Town July 1988(Chelsea loan Sept 1992)/SUNDERLAND July 1993(Liverpool loan Mar 1995)/Watford July 1996-date.

Debut v Derby County (a) 14/8/1993

The son of a Cambridgeshire farmer, Alec Chamberlain began with Ipswich Town as a teenager. Without League experience when he joined Colchester United in 1982, he was virtually ever-present for four seasons before Everton paid £80,000 to take him to Goodison in 1987. He had actually turned down Sunderland in favour of the First Division Toffeemen, and despite the fact he had not featured in a senior match during his year on

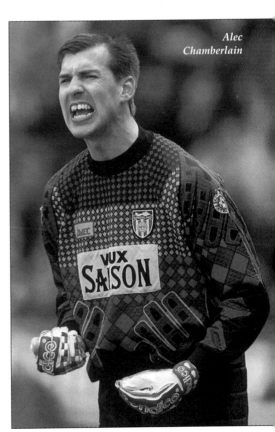
Alec Chamberlain

Merseyside, Luton Town paid £150,000 for him in 1988. After five seasons at Kenilworth Road he was brought to Sunderland by Terry Butcher, a former colleague at Ipswich Town. His three year contract proved eventful. Statistically, Alec Chamberlain's percentage of clean sheets ranked him as Sunderland's best goalkeeper since the 1960's. Recovering from a mauling at Derby County on his debut he proved a commanding presence in a season which saw the exit of Butcher. Under managers Buxton and Reid in 1994-95 he vied with Tony Norman for first team duties, and in his final season collected a First Division championship medal for 29 appearances which included five clean sheets in his season's final six fixtures. Sold to Watford for £40,000 in the close season, he found few opportunities due to the impressive form of Kevin Miller. Alec claimed the first team spot in 1997-98, however, appearing in all League matches during the Second Division championship campaign. Additionally, he was selected for the PFA Second Division team and was voted Watford's Player of the Year. Very much the hero in Watford's 1999 penalty shoot-out victory against Birmingham City, his string of fine saves throughout the match ending crucially with his diving stop to keep out Chris Holland's spot kick , thereby booking the Hornet's trip to Wembley. Having sat on the bench on his two previous visits to Wembley (with Everton when they won the Charity Shield in 1987 and with Liverpool when they won the League Cup in 1995) Alec was fully involved in the 1999 Division One play-off final against Bolton. His stunning 31st minute save from a point-blank rocket from Eidur Gudjohnsen proved a pivotal moment in the match which Watford went on to win 2-0, and book a place in the Premiership. The fact they were immediately dubbed the bookies' relegation favourites is unlikely to dampen the enthusiasm of Watford's veteran 'keeper, who will be keen to add to his 500 plus career appearances total in the Premier League.

Appearances:
FL: 89(1) apps. 0 gls.
FAC: 8 apps. 0 gls.
FLC: 9 apps. 0 gls.
Other: 1 app. 0 gls.
Total: *107(1) apps. 0 gls.*
Honours:
(Sunderland) Div 1 champs 1996/(Watford) Div 2 champs 1998.

CHAMBERS, Brian Mark

Role: Midfield 1970-73
5'10" 10st.12lbs.
b. Newcastle upon Tyne, 31st October 1949

CAREER: Newcastle Schoolboys/ SUNDERLAND pro Aug 1967/Arsenal June 1973/Luton Town July 1974/Millwall July 1977/AFC Bournemouth July 1979/Halifax Town Mar-May 1981/Poole Town July 1981/ Salisbury City Nov 1985/Dorchester Town 1986/Swanage player-manager/Poole Town July 1989, player-manager June 1991.

Debut v Luton Town (a) 31/10/1970 (sub)

England Schoolboy international Brian Chambers celebrated his 21st birthday and Football League debut on the same date. To make the day even more memorable, Sunderland recorded their first away win of the season, 2-1 at Luton Town. One of the many young players introduced into senior football by manager Alan Brown, Brian enjoyed quite lengthy spells of first team football before departing Roker in a £30,000 transfer to Arsenal, in the week following Sunderland's famous FA Cup Final victory over Leeds United. Rather curiously, having

Brian Chambers

been an unused Sunderland substitute against Arsenal in the epic Cup semi-final, he then played for the Gunners in the held over third place play-off match between the two losing semi-finalists. A similar fee took him to Luton Town after just one season at Highbury. In a career spanning ten campaigns and six League clubs, Chambers recorded 251 appearances and scored 31 goals. His final move in League circles took him to Halifax Town for a small fee on transfer deadline day in 1981. In what proved his final League appearance (versus Aldershot on 2.5.1981) he scored the only goal of the game.

Appearances:
FL: 53(10) apps. 5 gls.
FAC: 4(1) apps. 2 gls.
FLC: 0(1) apps. 0 gls.
Other: 0(1) apps. 0 gls.
Total: *57(13) apps. 7 gls.*
Honours:
7 Eng Sch apps. 1965.

CHAPMAN, Lee Roy

Role: Forward 1983-84
6'2" 13st.0lbs.
b. Lincoln, 5th December 1959

CAREER: Stoke Schoolboys/Stafford Rangers/Stoke City June 1978(Plymouth Argyle loan Dec 1978)/Arsenal Aug 1982/SUNDERLAND Dec 1983/Sheffield Wednesday Aug 1984/Niort, France June 1988/Nottingham Forest Oct 1988/Leeds United Jan 1990/Portsmouth Aug 1993/West Ham United Sept 1993(Southend United loan Jan 1995)/Ipswich Town Jan 1995(Leeds United loan Jan 1996)/Swansea City Mar-May 1996.

Debut v Luton Town (h) 31/12/1983

Lee Chapman's career aggregate of 196 League goals in 552 appearances successfully carried on a family tradition started by father Roy in the 1950s and 1960s. An inside-forward who assisted six League clubs, Chapman Snr. registered 202 League goals in 415 appearances, including 78 in 136 appearances with Mansfield Town. Lee began with Stoke City, moved briefly to Arsenal for £500,000 and joined Sunderland for a cut-price £200,000 some sixteen months later. He joined a struggling side who needed to win the season's final fixture, at Leicester City, to

Lee Chapman

avoid relegation. Goals from Chapman and Bryan Robson ensured safety, but a close season clear-out saw Chapman among those discarded, Sheffield Wednesday paying just £100,000 for his transfer. At this point his career took a much-needed upturn, his reputation as a powerful attack leader being reflected in his escalating transfer fees (£350,000 to Nottingham Forest and £400,000 to Leeds United). He retired in the close season of 1996 to run a wine bar in Chelsea and to concentrate on TV commitments. He is married to Lesley Ash, the well-known film and TV actress who appears as 'Debs' in the popular series 'Men Behaving Badly'.

Appearances:
14(1) apps. 3 gls.
FAC: 2 apps. 1 gl.
Total: *16(1) apps. 4 gls.*
Honours:
1 Eng U-21 app. 1981/(Nottingham Forest)
FLC winner 1989/Simod Cup winner 1989/
(Leeds United) Div 2 champs 1990/
FL champs 1992.

CHILTON, Frederick

Role: Left-back 1956-58
5'9" 12st.2lbs.
b. Washington, Co Durham, 10th July 1935

CAREER: Usworth Colliery/SUNDERLAND May 1953/North Shields May 1959.

Debut v Wolverhampton Wanderers 12/9/1956

Fred Chilton

A reserve left-back of good physique on Sunderland's books for six years but Fred Chilton had only three League outings to show for it. A not surprising circumstance as, after developing, Chilton had to compete firstly with internationalists Joe McDonald and Billy Elliott and, lastly, with the emerging Len Ashurst.

Appearances:
FL: 3 apps. 0 gls.
Total: *3 apps. 0 gls.*

CHISHOLM, Kenneth McTaggart

Role: Inside-left 1953-56
5'11" 12st.7lbs.
b. Glasgow, 12th April 1925
d. Chester-le-Street, 30th April 1990

CAREER: Junior football/Queen's Park Feb 1942(guested for Leicester City, Chelsea, Portsmouth and Bradford during WW2)/ Partick Thistle pro May 1946/Leeds United Dec 1947 £8,000/Leicester City Dec 1948 £10,000/Coventry City Mar 1950 £16,500+/ Cardiff City Mar 1952 nearly £10,000/ SUNDERLAND Dec 1953 approx. £15,000/ Workington Aug 1956 £6,000/Glentoran player-manager Jan 1958/Spennymoor United June 1958/Los Angeles Kickers, USA 1959.

Debut v Aston Villa (h) 1/1/1954

CHISHOLM, Gordon William

Role: Central Defender 1978-86
6'1" 12st.7lbs.
b. Glasgow, 8th April 1960

CAREER: Glasgow schoolboys/Possil Y.M./SUNDERLAND Apr 1978/Hibernian Sept 1985/Dundee Sept 1987/Partick Thistle July 1992, appointed asst. manager Aug 1995, re-appointed asst. coach June 1997/Clydebank asst. coach Aug 1997/ Ross County May 1999 asst. manager.

Debut v Charlton Athletic (h) 19/8/1978

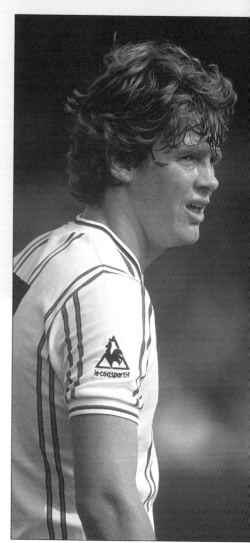

Sunderland won promotion to Division One in Gordon Chisholm's second season of League football, and he was a regular in the heart of The Lads' defence in the next five seasons in the top flight. Recruited from Glasgow Juvenile ranks as a 16-year-old, he was a first team regular at 18, versatile enough to operate in either midfield or defence. He tackled well, distributed intelligently and was always a fine, steadying and authoritative influence. In Sunderland's run to the League Cup final in 1985, his vital goal at White Hart Lane in the fourth round disposed of Tottenham. Unfortunately his cruelly-deflected own goal in the final, and Clive Walker's missed penalty, were the key elements in a Wembley game which Norwich City won 1-0. In May 1999 it was announced that Gordon had resigned his position on Clydebank's coaching staff due to the serious financial problems being encountered by the Bankies. Later in the same month he was reported to have joined Ross County, with assistant manager responsibilities at Victoria Park.

Appearances:
FL: 192(5) apps. 10 gls.
FAC: 9 apps. 2 gls.
FLC: 20(4) apps. 4 gls.
Other: 3 apps. 0 gls.
Total: *224(9) apps. 16 gls.*
Honours:
(Sunderland) FLC finalist 1985.

Ken Chisholm

Early in 1949 a critic wrote: "Ken Chisholm is a very forceful player on his day, possessing a fast, direct dribble and a pile-driving left foot", which was a fair and accurate description of a player whose wandering career always maintained a good ratio of goals scored to games played. Originally an outside-left for Queen's Park, he developed in the inside position with Partick Thistle. In Scotland he qualified for a Physical Training diploma and, when a Leeds player, acted as a coach under the West Riding FA. During the war Ken flew with the RAF, a commissioned officer in bomber command. After leaving football, he worked in the insurance industry, based in the North-East.

Appearances:
FL: 78 apps. 33 gls.
FAC: 8 apps. 4 gls.
Total: *86 apps. 37 gls.*
Honours:
1 Scot Victory int app./(Leicester City) FAC finalist 1949.

CLACK, Charles Edward

Role: Outside-right 1921-23
5'9" 10st.7lbs.
b. Highworth, Wiltshire, 4th June 1896
d. Cirencester, April 1984

CAREER: Pontypridd Jan 1921/ SUNDERLAND May 1921/Bristol City May 1923-24. subsequently assisting Nuneaton Town and Hinckley Town cs 1926. Afterwards a permit player with Holywell Amateurs Aug 1933.

Debut v Cardiff City (a) 3/12/1921

All but one of Ted Clack's League appearances came in the first year: after the above debut consecutive runs of four (January-February 1922) and three (March 1922). Sunderland fielded four outside-rights that season - James Stephenson, Bobby Best and Alec Donaldson being the others. For Bristol City Clack played in a couple of Second Division matches.

Ted Clack

Appearances:
FL: 9 apps. 0 gls.
Total: *9 apps. 0 gls.*

CLARK, Henry

Role: Inside-left 1956-57
5'7" 10st.4lbs.
b. Sunderland, 11th September 1934

CAREER: St Benet's FC (Sunderland)/RAF
football/SUNDERLAND May 1956/Blyth
Spartans June 1958.

Debut v Chelsea (h) 23/3/1957

A local lad, Harry Clark's half-dozen Division
One outings all occurred towards the end of
the 1956/7 campaign. Competition for the
inside-left spot was pretty hot in Harry's time
with the likes of Shack, 'Cannonball' Fleming,
Alan O'Neill et al around. And the Eire star,
Ambrose Fogarty, arrived the following
autumn to provide an even richer mix.

> **Appearances:**
> *FL: 6 apps. 0 gls.*
> **Total:** *6 apps. 0 gls.*

Harry Clark

CLARK, James McNichol Cameron

Role: Centre-half 1934-37
5'10" 11st.9lbs.
b. Cathcart, Glasgow, 1913

CAREER: Clydebank Juniors/SUNDERLAND
June 1933/Plymouth Argyle Oct 1937
£3,250/retired during WW2.

Debut v Derby County (a) 2/2/1935

In the mid-thirties Jimmy Clark was described
as " ... a young player of splendid physique
(who) made rapid progress after going to
Wearside ... soon found a senior place but
dogged by injury ... His grandfather used to
play for Sunderland 44 years ago". (This must
have been his maternal grandfather). He
shared the first team pivotal role with Bob
Johnston, the pair even sharing the high
honours then acquired. Jimmy got a
championship medal while Bob appeared in
the 1937 Cup final. After serving with the RAF
during the war, Jimmy emigrated to South
Africa. It was reported in the 1960s he was
managing a soccer side there.

> **Appearances:**
> *FL: 49 apps. 0 gls.*
> *FAC: 1 app. 0 gls.*
> **Total:** *50 apps. 0 gls.*
> **Honours:**
> *(Sunderland) FL champs 1936.*

Jimmy Clark

CLARK, Lee Robert

Role: Midfield 1997-99
5'7" 11st.7lbs.
b. Wallsend, 27th October 1972

CAREER: Wallsend Boys' Club/Newcastle United assoc. s'boy Dec 1986, trainee July 1989, pro Nov 1989/SUNDERLAND June 1997/Fulham July 1999.

Debut v Sheffield United (a) 10/8/1997

Lee Clark

Lee Clark was first spotted by Newcastle United as a nine-year-old with Wallsend Boys' Club. Taken into their Centre of Excellence two years later, he went on to captain England Schoolboys. In the black and white jersey he was playing for Newcastle United Reserves whilst still at school, and made his League debut at 17. Voted North-East Footballer of the Year at 19, he completed over 200 senior appearances for the Magpies despite spending ten months on the sidelines following a serious foot injury sustained at Blackburn Rovers in February 1994. Sunderland's record signing at £2.75 million in June 1997, Clark fully justified his huge fee. A midfielder with all the necessary attributes of ball control, vision and passing skills, an additional bonus of 13 League goals in his first season, plus a mid-season spell as skipper soon earned him the crowd's respect at the Stadium of Light. A view shared by Lee's fellow professionals who voted him into the 1997-98 First Division Select Team, perhaps curiously the only Sunderland player so honoured. Despite suffering a broken fibia in the first League match of 1998-99 versus Queens Park Rangers, Lee was able to return within three months but took several more weeks to rediscover his best form. Again selected in the PFA Division One team he was joined on this latest occasion by four other Sunderland players, a fair reflection of the strength of the squad at the Stadium of Light. In summer 1999 however, it was revealed Clark had been photographed at Newcastle's FA Cup final defeat in May wearing a tee-shirt displaying a message derogatory towards Sunderland's supporters. It was clearly an intolerable situation for the club. Clark was summarily transfer listed and for a £3 million fee quickly moved on to join Fulham, newly promoted to Division One and managed by ex-Sunderland stalwart Paul Bracewell.

Appearances:
FL: 73(1)apps. 16 gls.
FAC: 4 apps. 0 gls.
FLC: 4(1) apps. 0 gls.
Total: *81(2) apps. 16 gls.*
Honours:
Eng Sch/Eng Yth/11 Eng U-21 apps. 1992-94/ (Newcastle United) Div 1 champs 1993/(Sunderland) Div 1 champs 1999.

CLARK, William

Role: Outside-right 1908-10
5'7" 10st.0lbs.
b. Airdrie, 1881
d. Bristol, 17th March 1937

CAREER: Port Glasgow Athletic Aug 1900/ Bristol Rovers May 1904/ SUNDERLAND May 1908/Bristol City Oct 1910 (in exchange for John Cowell)/Leicester Fosse Aug 1911-1912.

Willie Clark

Debut v Manchester City 1/9/1908

"Knows the whereabouts of the goal posts," was a pithy soccer annual comment on the little Scot, Willie Clark. Bristol Rovers signed him after he had aggregated 35 goals on Port Glasgow Athletic's behalf, and he won a Southern League championship medal in his very first season at Eastville. In four seasons there he scored 35 times in 133 Southern League outings. Two terms with Sunderland and another with Bristol City followed. Willie settled in Bristol on retiring, working as a licensee holding a couple of posts in the Clifton area of the city.

Appearances:
FL: 41 apps. 4 gls.
FAC: 3 apps. 0 gls.
Total: *44 apps. 4 gls.*
Honours:
(Bristol Rovers) SL champs 1905.

CLARKE, Norman Samson

Role: Outside-left 1962-63
5'10" 11st.0lbs.
b. Ballyloughan, Co Antrim, 1st April 1942

CAREER: Boys Brigade football/Ballymena United/SUNDERLAND Feb 1962 £6,000/ retired through injury 1965.

Debut v Middlesbrough (h) 18/8/1962

Norman Clarke

Norman Clarke was capped at three levels by Northern Ireland (and very young for his amateur selections) in addition to a couple of inter-league games before arriving at Roker Park. All his League appearances for Sunderland occurred in the opening weeks of season 1962/63, the one in the League Cup coming the following November. Otherwise he understudied the popular George Mulhall, very much the regular man for the outside-left spot. Nevertheless, it was extremely unfortunate that Norman Clarke had to retire aged only 23.

Appearances:
FL: 4 apps. 0 gls.
FLC: 1 app. 0 gls.
Total: *5 apps. 0 gls.*
Honours:
2 NIre U-23 apps./2 NIre am apps./NIre Yth/2 IL apps.

CLARKE, Jeffrey Derrick

Role: Central Defender 1975-82
6'1" 13st.8lbs.
b. Hemsworth, nr Pontefract, 18th January 1954

CAREER: Manchester City app Aug 1971, pro Jan 1972/SUNDERLAND June 1975/ Newcastle United Aug 1982(Brighton & Hove Albion loan Aug 1984)/MKE Ankaragucu, Turkey cs 1987/Whitley Bay Feb 1988/ Newcastle United Community Officer Nov 1988, appointed asst. coach cs 1993/Nissan FC physio Sept 1997/ Sunderland Academy physio Aug 1998.

Debut v Chelsea (h) 16/8/1976

A formidably-built fair-haired pivot, Jeff Clarke lacked League experience when he joined Sunderland from Manchester City. His arrival was part of the deal that took Sunderland's international centre-half Dave Watson to Maine Road, with Sunderland receiving a cash adjustment of £200,000. Clarke settled swiftly into the heart of Sunderland's defence, aided and abetted by the ripe experience of Scottish international defender, Bobby Moncur. Despite recurring knee injuries, the most serious of which sidelined him for the full season of 1980-81, Clarke's dominance in the air and calm distribution out of defence were key factors in the promotion seasons of 1975-76 and particularly 1979-80 when he and Shaun Elliott formed a brilliant defensive pairing. Released on a free transfer to Newcastle United after seven years at Roker Park, Jeff ably assisted the Magpies to promotion in 1984 and subsequently joined their coaching staff. In September 1997 he joined Nissan of the Vauxhall Wearside League as physiotherapist and part-time coach to their youth team. Currently back with Sunderland as Academy physio, Jeff has wide ranging responsibilities for over 150 young players. These include his son, Jamie, who made his debut for the Under 17s v Everton in February 1999.

Appearances:
FL: 178(3) apps. 6 gls.
FAC: 15 apps. 0 gls.
FLC: 14 apps. 0 gls.
Other: 3 apps. 0 gls.
Total: *210(3) apps. 6 gls.*
Honours:
(Sunderland) Div 2 champs 1976.

Jeff Clarke

CLOUGH, Brian Howard

Role: Centre-forward 1961-65
5'10" 11st.12lbs.
b. Middlesbrough, 21st March 1935

CAREER: Great Broughton Juniors (North
Yorks)/Billingham Synthonia/Middlesbrough
am Nov 1951, pro May 1952/SUNDERLAND
July 1961 £45,000/retired through injury Nov
1964 and joined club's training staff/
Hartlepool United manager Oct 1965/Derby
County manager June 1967/Brighton & Hove
Albion manager Nov 1973/Leeds United
manager July-Sept 1974/Nottingham Forest
manager Jan 1975-May 1993.

Debut v Walsall (a) 19/8/1961 (scored)

Brian Clough is an unusual case, having been
outstanding as a player but infinitely more so
as a manager, in a long period extending over
half a lifetime. The managerial fame stemmed
deservedly from his many successes (Clough
surely ranks with the likes of Chapman,
Busby, Paisley and Ferguson) but also the
legend was much gilded by relentless media
attention. Publicity-conscious Clough and his
club's were never long out of the limelight. In
his prime he was funny, abrasive, provocative,
exasperating and always good for an often
controversial off-the cuff quote, be it on TV,
radio or to a newspaper columnist. As to
managerial achievements (and here it should
be mentioned an astute colleague from his
Middlesbrough days, Peter Taylor, was his
assistant for 14 of his management years) this
tabulation provides a summary. His greatest
triumphs came with firstly Derby County and
then Nottingham Forest - both clubs that were
meandering aimlessly in Division Two when
he took control and galvanised them to glory.
Surely no club of such relatively modest
means will ever repeat Forest's dream pair of
back to back European Cups. Under
Cloughie's guidance his clubs have won or
reached:

European Cup: won two (1979, 1980)
European Super Cup: won one (1980),
runners-up 1981
World Club Championship: runners-up 1981
Simod/Zenith Cup: winners 1989, 1992
FL champions: twice (1972, 1978)
FL Div 2: champions 1969, promotion 1977
FA Cup: runners-up 1991
FL Cup: won four (1978, 1979, 1989, 1990),
runners-up 1980, 1992

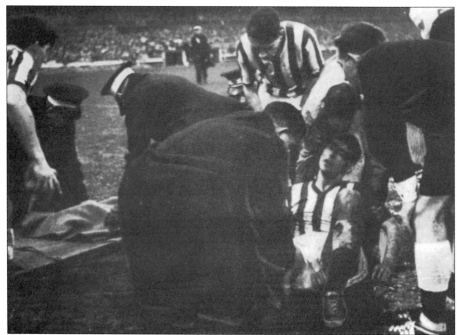

*Brian Clough lies injured after a collison with Bury goalkeeper Chris Harker on Boxing Day 1962. He
suffered cruciate ligament damage which effectively ended his playing career.*

As a courageous, determined player his outstanding attribute was quite simply a rare natural talent for goal-scoring. Like the legendary Jimmy Greaves he would often do comparatively little in a match, yet finish with a couple of goals. This is well demonstrated by his career figures in League and Cup competition. For Middlesbrough he scored a staggering 204 goals in 222 matches which added to the equally extraordinary Sunderland figures below give a career tally of 267 goals in 269 games. Such a record is quite exceptional, even more so in a playing career cruelly curtailed early by a serious knee injury. Brian Clough came from a family of nine children and worked as a clerk with the well-known local firm, ICI, before taking up football professionally. In his first season with Sunderland in 1961-62 he became a firm crowd favourite following his summer transfer from his hometown Middlesbrough and netted five hat-tricks. He had already rattled in 28 League and Cup goals the following season to set Sunderland on a likely promotion course before fate took a hand and, chasing a loose ball into the box, he suffered a shattering knee injury in a collision with the Bury goalkeeper Chris Harker in a top of the table promotion clash at Roker on Boxing Day 1962. The cruciate ligament injury effectively ended Clough's playing career although after a 20 month absence he bravely attempted a comeback with his only outings in Division One - three games and one further goal in September 1964. It was a brave but vain hope, and like so many other sportsmen then, was unsuccessful in an era prior to today's more advanced surgery. His testimonial match reward in September 1966 at Roker saw Sunderland draw 6-6 with The Charlton's XI. World Cup hero Bobby scored three while Jimmy Montgomery got two for The Lads! It is therefore pleasant to record how Clough's achievements have ultimately been recognised locally and nationally. He was granted a honorary degree by Nottingham University in 1990 ("for services to Nottingham"), awarded

Brian Clough

the OBE in the Birthday Honours list of 1991 and, in March 1993, made a Freeman of the City of Nottingham. Later dogged by ill-health, not helped by lengthy but unproven FA allegations about his transfer dealings at Forest, Clough now lives quietly in retirement in Derbyshire. His Sunderland-born son Nigel, also a forward, won 14 England caps and played for Forest, Liverpool and Manchester City.

Appearances:
FL: 61 apps. 54 gls.
FAC: 4 apps. 0 gls.
FLC: 9 apps. 9 gls.
Total: *74 apps. 63 gls.*
Honours:
*2 Eng caps/1 Eng B app./3 Eng U-23 apps./
2 FL apps.*

CLUNAS, William McLean

Role: Right-half 1923-31
5'9" 11st.10lbs.
b. Johnstone, Renfrewshire, 29th April 1899
d. Johnstone, Renfrewshire, 1st September 1967

CAREER: Kilbarchan Athletic/Johnstone
FC/St Mirren Mar 1921/SUNDERLAND Oct
1923 £2,500/Morton Aug 1931/Inverness
Thistle player/coach Sept 1934, subsequently
having a spell as the Johnstone FC secretary
June 1938.

Debut v Nottingham Forest (h) 1/11/1923

Billy Clunas was a
prominent figure in
the Twenties, the
undisputed occupant
of the senior right-
half spot from his
arrival in the
autumn of 1923
through to 1930. He
had all-round
ability and was
excellent at
distribution and in
defence. But the
attribute most
commented upon
was his capacity as
a deadly penalty-
taker, missing only
two while at
Roker. Ten of his

WILLIAM CLUNAS
SUNDERLAND

12 goals in 1928/29 were from the spot and
Raich Carter rated Billy the best penalty-taker
he had ever seen. Billy also held the club's
seasonal record of goals (12) from a non-
forward for some sixty years until equalled by
John McPhail in the late 1980s. Besides
winning a couple of caps, he also scored for
his country, making him one of only four
players to have netted for Scotland whilst on
Sunderland's books. Billy acted as a Scotland
travelling reserve on several occasions when
with St Mirren. Early in his career he had a
trial with Luton Town.

Appearances:
FL: 256 apps. 42 gls.
FAC: 16 apps. 2 gls.
Total: *272 apps. 44 gls.*
Honours:
2 Scot caps.

COADY, Michael Liam

Role: Defender 1976-80
5'11" 11st.0lbs.
b. Dipton, Co Durham, 1st October 1958

CAREER: Lanchester St Bedes/Durham
Schools/SUNDERLAND assoc. s'boy Feb
1975, app July 1975, pro July 1976/Carlisle
United July 1980/Sydney Olympics, Australia
Apr 1982/Wolverhampton Wanderers Jan
1985/Sydney Olympics Mar 1986(Lincoln City
2-week trial Aug 1986)/Retired from playing
and returned to the UK in 1990.

Debut v Leeds United (a) 9/4/1977

Sunderland faced considerable
opposition for the signature of Michael
Coady on schoolboy forms, as the
sixteen-year-old defender had
previously had trials with Everton,
Ipswich Town and West Bromwich
Albion. He was first introduced at
League level as an 18-year-old, but
despite a most impressive debut, was
unable to maintain that level of form
and found few subsequent
opportunities. It was not until his
£20,000 move to Carlisle United that he
finally sampled regular first team
football. In the company of many ex
Rokerites at Brunton Park (manager
Stokoe and players 'Pop' Robson, Trevor
Swinburne and Graham Winstanley),
Coady made 45 League appearances in
1980-81 but had departed to Australia
prior to the close of the following promotion
campaign. Returning to League football to join
struggling Wolverhampton Wanderers in
January 1985, he was unable to halt their slide
into Division Three. He was released in
February of the following term (which ended
with once-proud Wolves relegated to Division
Four) and returned to Australia. A brief trial
with Lincoln City
ended when he failed a
medical but his career
in Australia continued
for a further four years
prior to retirement.

Appearances:
FL: 4(2) apps. 0 gls.
Total: *4(2) apps.*
0 gls.

Michael Coady

COGLIN, Stephen

Role: Inside-left 1924-27
5'7" 10st.1lb.
b. Willenhall, Staffs,
14th October 1903

Steve Coglin

CAREER: Moxley White Star/Darlaston/
Lichfield City/Wednesbury Old Athletic/
Willenhall FC cs 1923/SUNDERLAND May
1924/Grimsby Town Feb 1927/Notts County
May 1931/Worcester City Aug 1932/Hereford
United May 1935/Cannock Town Dec 1935/
Bromsgrove Rovers, subsequently (Sept 1936)
a permit player for Archdales FC (Worcs).

Debut v Liverpool (a) 25/10/1924

As a glance at his career details reveals, Steve
Coglin played for a remarkable number of
West Midlands non-League clubs both before
and after the eight-year senior spell. "Small,
fast and a good ball player", as he was
consistently summed up, his peak was
reached at Grimsby. There he was a regular
member of the side that won promotion to the
top flight in 1929, his promptings a major
contribution to Joe Robson's prolific goal
scoring. Immediately following his Notts
County season Steve popped in 42 goals in 123
appearances for Worcester City.

Appearances:
FL: 21 apps. 10 gls.
Total: *21 apps. 10 gls.*

COLEMAN, John George 'Tim'

Role: Inside-right 1910-11
5'6" 11st.4lbs.
b. Kettering, Northamptonshire, 26th October 1881
d. Kensington, London, 20th November 1940

CAREER: Kettering St Mary's/Kettering FC/
Northampton Town May 1901/Woolwich
Arsenal May 1902/Everton Feb 1908 £700/
SUNDERLAND May 1910/Fulham June
1911/Nottingham Forest July 1914/retired
during WW1 but was assisting Tunbridge
Wells Rangers c.1920/Maidstone United
manager 1921-22, later in the 1920s was
coaching in Holland.

Debut v Newcastle United (h) 1/9/1910

A short though sturdily built inside-forward,
Tim Coleman was a consistent scorer
throughout a somewhat nomadic career. He

Tim Coleman

was also deft in footwork and a good team
man. fitting in admirably with fellow
attackers. Tim served in the Footballers
Battalion during the First World War, at one
stage being posted as missing. He lost his life
early in the second war through an industrial
accident. At the outset of Tim's career he was
nicknamed 'Tiddy'.

Appearances:
FL: 32 apps. 20 gls.
FAC: 1 app. 0 gls.
Total: *33 apps. 20 gls.*
Honours
1 Eng cap/3 FL apps.

COLEMAN, Keith

Role: Full-back 1971-73
5'9" 11st.5lbs.
b. Washington, Co Durham, 24th May 1951

CAREER: Washington Youths/
SUNDERLAND app, pro June 1968/
West Ham United Sept 1973/K.V. Mechelen,
Belgium cs 1977/Darlington July 1979-Aug
1980.

Debut v Swindon Town (h) 11/9/1971

Introduced to senior football by manager Alan
Brown, Keith Coleman succeeded long-serving

full-back Cec Irwin and made 32 League appearances in his first season. When Alan Brown was replaced as manager by Bob Stokoe in December 1972, one of his earliest signings was Ron Guthrie who took over from Coleman as first team left full-back. A £20,000 transfer to West Ham United provided more opportunities, although Keith was unfortunate to miss out when West Ham won the FA Cup in 1975. Despite having made 27(2) First Division appearances during the same season, he made only one FA Cup appearance, McDowall and Lampard being the preferred pairing. Some compensation came twelve months later when he appeared in the European Cup-Winners' Cup Final, played at the Heysel Stadium in Brussels. Although the Hammers took the lead, they eventually succumbed to a star-studded Anderlecht side by 4-2. After four seasons at Upton Park and 111(6) League and Cup appearances, Keith moved into the Belgian Second Division. He returned homewards in 1979 and spent his final season of senior football with Darlington in Division Four. In the 1980's Keith was reported to be working in a sports centre in Brentwood, Essex.

Appearances:
FL: 49 apps. 2 gls.
FAC: 4 apps. 0 gls.
FLC: 1 app. 0 gls.
Other: 0(1) app. 0 gls.
Total: *54(1) apps. 2 gls.*
Honours:
(West Ham United) ECWC finalist 1976.

COLLIN, George

Role: Left-back 1936-37
5'9" 11st.0lbs.
b. Oxhill, Co Durham, 13th September 1905
d. Derby, 1st February 1989

CAREER: Junior football (West Ham United am)/West Stanley/Arsenal pro Feb 1923/West Stanley 1924-25/Bournemouth & Boscombe Athletic Aug 1925 £100/West Stanley Aug 1927/Derby County Nov 1927 £500/ SUNDERLAND June1936 £1,500/Port Vale June 1938/Burton Town player/manager Aug 1939.

Debut v Sheffield Wednesday (a) 29/8/1936

Early on, while at Bournemouth, George Collin sustained a badly broken leg, which was thought to have ended his career. However, he came back to render Derby County a near nine-season spell of First Division service, making 334 League and Cup appearances in total. At the Baseball Ground George was a first-rate partner to England's Tom Cooper - unruffled, dependable, consistent and quick to the tackle. He was mostly first choice in his initial season with Sunderland (but did not make the Cup final side) when all his senior outings occurred. George was a former blacksmith and a good amateur cricketer.

Appearances:
FL: 31 apps. 0 gls.
FAC: 1 app. 0 gls.
Total: *32 apps. 0 gls.*

Keith Coleman

George Collin

COLLINS, John Douglas

Role: Midfield 1976-78
5'9" 10st.6lbs.
b. Newton, nr Doncaster, 28th August 1945

CAREER: Pinxton Colliery Welfare/
Rotherham United app/Grimsby Town am
Mar 1963, pro June 1963/Burnley Sept 1968/
Plymouth Argyle May 1976/SUNDERLAND
Mar 1977/Tulsa Roughnecks, USA Feb 1978/
Derby County coach 1978/Rochdale player-
manager Jan-Nov 1979, Sydney Olympics,
Australia coach 1981.

Debut v Aston Villa (a) 23/3/1977

One of several ex Burnley personnel who
assisted Sunderland during Jimmy Adamson's
spell in charge at Roker Park. A lightweight
but combative midfielder, the fair-haired
Collins had over 300 League appearances to
his credit, but his influence proved insufficient
to keep Sunderland in the top flight. Unable to
hold a first team place he was released after
eleven months to sign for Tulsa Roughnecks,
prior to taking his first steps into coaching and
management. At the outset of his career, he
was developed by Grimsby Town, where he
made exactly 100 League appearances.
Burnley paid a fee in the region of £30,000 for
him in 1968 and he assisted them to the
Second Division Championship during his
stay which took in over 200 senior outings.

Appearances:
FL: 4(2) apps. 0 gls.
FLC: 1 app. 0 gls.
Total: *5(2) apps. 0 gls.*
Honours:
(Burnley) Div 2 champs 1973.

*Doug
Collins*

COLQUHOUN, John Mark

Role: Wing-forward 1992-93
5'8" 11st.2lbs.
b. Stirling, 14th July 1963

CAREER: St Moden's High School/
Grangemouth Inter Boys' Club/Stirling Albion
July 1980/Celtic Nov 1983/Heart of
Midlothian May 1985/Millwall Aug 1991/
SUNDERLAND July 1992/Heart of
Midlothian July 1993/St Johnstone Apr-May
1997.

Debut v Swindon Town (a) 15/8/1992

John Colquhoun followed in his father's

footsteps when he signed for Stirling Albion as a teenager. John Snr was a versatile inside or wing forward whose Football League career with Oldham Athletic and Scunthorpe United covered 382 appearances and 64 goals. Aside from two seasons in English football, John Jnr spent the majority of his career in Scottish football, most notably in two separate spells with Heart of Midlothian (345 Scottish League appearances and 64 goals). Signed from Millwall for £220,000 as part of manager Crosby's re-building programme, Colquhoun had made only two appearances in Sunderland's starting line-up by mid-season. When Terry Butcher took over the managerial reins, Colquhoun was given an extended run

in the number nine jersey, but was not alone in his failure to impress in a very poor side that narrowly avoided relegation from Division One. In a close season of many comings and goings, John returned to Hearts when he was part of the £460,000 deal that brought Derek Ferguson to Roker Park. John now works as a journalist with the *Scotland on Sunday* newspaper.

Appearances:
FL: 12(8) apps. 0 gls.
FLC: 2 apps. 0 gls.
Other: 1 app. 0 gls.
Total: *15(8) apps. 0 gls.*
Honours:
1 Scot cap 1988.

COMMON, Alfred

Role: Inside-right/Centre-forward 1900-05
5'8" 13st.0lbs.
b. Millfield, Sunderland, 25th May 1880
d. Darlington, 3rd April 1946

CAREER: Jarrow 1897/South Hylton Juniors/SUNDERLAND Aug 1900/ Sheffield United Oct 1901 £325/ SUNDERLAND June 1904 £520 (a record)/ Middlesbrough Feb 1905 £1,000 (the first 4-figure fee)/Woolwich Arsenal Aug 1910 £250/Preston North End Dec 1912-14 £250.

Debut v Wolverhampton Wanderers 15/9/1900

Alf Common is a significant historical footballing figure in that he was famously the controversial first subject of a four-figure transfer fee and also a few months earlier, the first £500 plus fee. The then enormous £1,000 paid by Middlesbrough in February 1905 certainly caused a major national sensation at the time, but proved a good investment as he was a vital factor in the club's avoidance of a looming relegation. In fact Sunderland had sold Common prior to this, collecting £325 from Sheffield United, for whom he scored in the initially drawn 1902 FA Cup final with Southampton, before buying him back amid much publicity for a new national record fee of £520. Although a heavy man Common was exceptionally quick in movement and possessed great stamina. An England international (but not capped at Roker) Common, other than his

transfers, did not in truth command a major part in Sunderland's playing history. Although aggressive on the field he was said to be jovial and humorous off it, no doubt useful qualities later in his capacity as a Darlington licensee for many years until his retirement in 1943.

Appearances:
FL: 41 apps. 11 gls.
FAC: 2 apps. 1 gl.
Total: *43 apps. 12 gls.*
Honours:
3 Eng caps/1 FL app./(Sheffield United)
FAC winner 1902/(Preston North End)
FL Div 2 champs 1913.

CONNER, John

Role: Centre-forward 1912-14
5'8" 10st.4lbs.
b. Rutherglen, Lanarks, 27th December 1891

CAREER: Central Half Holiday FC/Perth
Violet/SUNDERLAND May 1912/Distillery
May 1914 and later, during WW1 assisting
Glentoran and Belfast Celtic/Crystal Palace
July 1919/Newport County Nov 1922/
Bristol City Dec 1924/Millwall June 1925-Jan
1926/ Chatham Mar 1926/Yeovil & Petters
United cs 1926/Southend United cs 1927/
Yeovil & Petters United Jan 1929.

Debut v Blackburn Rovers (h) 18/9/1912

John Conner, a former grocer and lookalike
of boxer Jimmy Wilde, enjoyed a long career
embracing clubs from all four home
countries. He was a skilled performer
possessing speed and thoughtful
distribution, and he could also fill the other
inside berths. An ever-present in Palace's
fine 1921 championship side, scoring 29
goals, Conner was a leading figure of
Newport County's early seasons of Football
League membership.

Appearances:
FL: 5 apps. 2 gls.
FAC: 4 apps. 3 gls.
Total: *9 apps. 5 gls.*
Honours:
*Scot Jnr int/(Crystal Palace) FL Div 3
champs 1921.*

John Connor

CONNOR, James

Role: Outside-left 1930-39
5'7" 10st.4lbs.
b. Renfrew, 1st June 1909
d. Sunderland, 8th May 1980

CAREER: Paisley Schools/Paisley Carlisle
(Juvenile side)/Glasgow Perthshire/
St Mirren pro 1926/SUNDERLAND May
1930/retired through injury cs 1939.

Debut v Manchester City (h) 30/8/1930

It is probable there has never been a more
popular player at Roker Park than this
dazzling little Scot. Jimmy Connor was
succinctly described in 1933 as "fast, elusive
and has the art of cutting-in and having a shot
at goal". And a couple of years later a critic
observed: "a thoughtful player with few frills
but a set purpose: he quickly gets into his
stride, makes ground quickly and does not
miss chances to cut inside and shoot. He has a
powerful shot with the left foot." This left foot,
indeed, was legendary, the prime factor in
Jimmy's immaculate control. So predominant
was it that on occasion he was dubbed 'one-
footed'. Jimmy, who worked originally as a
joiner, made an early impact at St Mirren (99
Scottish League outings, 17 goals) and it was
said "Sunderland had to pay heavily for his
signature". The actual fee was not revealed
but can reasonably be estimated at £5,000
upwards. A Scottish international, injuries
sustained from 1933/34 onwards gradually
took their toll and, although Jimmy was an
ever-present in the 1935/36 championship
side, his League appearances thereafter
totalled only 31. Even so he created many
marvellous memories, none more so than his
part in one of the greatest games in
Sunderland's history. Champions Arsenal had
won the title three seasons running but in late
December 1935 were beaten 5-4 in a thriller at
Roker Park with Jimmy delighting the 59,000
crowd by crashing in the dramatic deciding
goal. Sunderland, of course, went on to take
the Gunners' title crown. His career and hopes
of another medal were ended by an appalling
tackle in the fourth round of the successful
1937 Cup run after he had already scored - his
13th FA Cup goal - in the 3-1 home win over
Luton. Later a season ticket holder at Roker
and also a local newsagent for many years, it
was reported Jimmy had said that when he
died he hoped his late wife - a Sunderland girl

- would be waiting for him between two golden goalposts. It is fair to say his glittering skills certainly provided Sunderland fans with a slice of Heaven on Earth.

Appearances:
FL: 254 apps. 48 gls.
FAC: 30 apps. 13 gls.
Total: *284 apps. 61 gls.*
Honours: *Scot Jnr int/4 Scot caps/(Sunderland) FL champs 1936.*

COOKE, Frederick Robert

Role: Centre-forward/Inside-left 1919-21
5'8" 11st.10lbs.
b. Kirkby-in-Ashfield, Notts, 5th July 1896
d. Kirkby-in-Ashfield, Notts, 1976

CAREER: East Kirkby FC (Notts)/ SUNDERLAND July 1919/Swindon Town May 1921/Accrington Stanley 1923-May 1924 £40/Bangor City Oct 1924.

Debut v Bradford (h) 24/4/1920 (scored)

Fred Cooke scored on his debut and five times in 11 League outings the following term before sampling Third Division fare at Swindon. In two seasons there he made 33 Southern Section appearances, scoring 15 goals. Cooke was a regular at Accrington (25 appearances in League matches, five goals) until the arrival of another Sunderland 'old boy' in the shape of John Ross Black. Cooke's goal touch had apparently faltered.

Fred Cooke

Appearances:
FL: 12 apps. 5 gls.
Total: *12 apps. 5 gls.*

COOKE, John

Role: Forward 1979-85
5'8" 11st.0lbs.
b. Salford, Manchester, 25th April 1962

CAREER: Barhill Boys' Club, Manchester/ SUNDERLAND app Dec 1978, pro Nov 1979(Carlisle United loan Nov 1984)/Sheffield Wednesday June 1985/Carlisle United Oct 1985/Stockport County July 1988/Chesterfield July 1990-1992/Gateshead/Spennymoor/ SUNDERLAND kit manager 1993-date.

Debut v Bristol Rovers (h) 24/11/1979

A prominent scorer for Sunderland at youth level, Salford-born John Cooke won England Youth recognition whilst at Roker and made his League debut in the promotion season of 1979-80. In his second senior outing he scored the winner in a vital match against second placed Luton Town. This proved to be the start of a 14-match unbeaten run to the end of the season, which culminated in promotion to Division One. Never able to establish himself firmly in the top flight, he found more opportunities with Carlisle United but could not halt their slide from Division Two to the Fourth Division in the space of three seasons. John's career wound up in Division Four, although with Stockport County in 1989-90, fourth place and subsequent defeat in the play-off semi-final was a disappointing end to a good season.

Appearances:
FL: 42(13) apps. 4 gls.
FAC: 3(1) apps. 0 gls.
FLC: 3 apps. 1 gl.
Total: *48(14) apps. 5 gls.*
Honours:
3 Eng Youth apps. 1981.

Terry Cooke

John Cooke

COOKE, Terence John

Role: Forward 1995-96
5'7" 9st.9lbs.
b. Marston Green, Birmingham, 5th August 1976

CAREER: Manchester United from school, trainee July 1992, pro July 1994 (SUNDERLAND loan Jan-Feb 1996) (Birmingham City loan Nov 1996-Jan 1997) (Wrexham loan Oct 1998)(Manchester City loan Jan 1999)/Manchester City Apr 1999.

Debut v Tranmere Rovers (h) 30/1/1996

A goalscorer in both legs of the FA Youth Cup Final won by Manchester United against Tottenham on penalties in 1994-95, lively winger Terry Cooke spent a month's loan at Roker in Sunderland's Division One championship season. His loan linked him again with one of his earliest mentors in the game, 'Pop' Robson, who was on the Old Trafford coaching staff when Cooke arrived as a raw but talented 14-year-old. An England Under-21 international, Terry made his Manchester United debut at 19 and impressed with his pace, skill on the ball and distribution. Season 1998-99 proved eventful for Terry Cooke. An outstanding three month loan spell with Manchester City was followed by a permanent move to Maine Road after seven years at Old Trafford. His £1 million transfer involved a down payment of £600,000 with the balance linked to the player's future success with City. Just four days after Manchester United had administered a 90th minute knock-out blow in Europe, City followed their example, stunning Gillingham with two late, late goals to take the Second Division play-off final into extra time. One of City's successful marksmen in the subsequent penalty shoot-out, Terry will now take the field in Division One, a more fitting stage for his burgeoning talents.

Appearances:
FL: 6 apps. 0 gls.
Total: *6 apps. 0 gls.*
Honours:
4 Eng U-21 apps. 1996/Eng Yth.

CORNER, David Edward

Role: Central Defender 1984-88
6'1" 12st.3lbs.
b. Sunderland, 15th May 1966

CAREER: St Thomas Aquinas School/Sunderland Schoolboys/Oldham Athletic assoc. s'boy/SUNDERLAND app, pro Apr 1984(Cardiff City loan Sept 1985)(Peterborough United loan Mar 1988)/Leyton Orient July 1988/Darlington July 1989-1991.

Debut v Nottingham Forest (a) 1/9/1984

David Corner had made only four first team appearances - including being substituted on his debut after Forest's Peter Davenport scored a hat-trick - when he was selected to play in the 1985 League Cup Final. The 18-year-old local defender came into the Wembley side against Norwich as a replacement for suspended skipper Shaun Elliott. Unfortunately, his inexperienced efforts to shepherd the ball to defensive safety saw him robbed and, as this led directly to the only goal of the game, David shouldered much of the blame. It is fair to say his Sunderland career never really recovered from it. Shortly after representing England in the World Youth International championships in Russia in

August 1985 he was loaned to Cardiff City to gain further League experience. After 17 first team appearances for Sunderland in 1986-87 he faded from the scene under new manager Denis Smith and appeared only four times in the Division Three promotion campaign of 1987-88. His final season in League football with Darlington earned him a Fourth Division Championship medal, along with other ex Sunderland team mates, Mark Prudhoe and Frank Gray. In the late 1990's David was reported to be working in the north east as an insurance salesman.

Appearances:
FL: 34(1) apps. 1 gl.
FAC: 3(1) apps. 1 gl.
FLC: 3 apps. 0 gls.
Other: 2(1) apps. 1 gl.
Total: *42(3) apps. 3 gls.*
Honours:
Eng Yth/(Sunderland) FLC finalist 1985/(Darlington) GMVC champs 1990/Div 4 champs 1991.

David Corner

CORNFORTH, John Michael

Role: Midfield 1984-91
6'1" 12st.8lbs.
b.Whitley Bay, 7th October 1967

CAREER: Monkseaton High School/Whitley
Bay/SUNDERLAND app, pro Oct 1985
(Doncaster Rovers loan Nov 1986)(Shrewsbury
Town loan Nov 1989)(Lincoln City loan Jan
1990)/Swansea City Aug 1991/Wycombe
Wanderers Dec 1996(Peterborough United
loan Feb 1998), released May 1999.

Debut v Ipswich Town (h) 11/5/1985

John Cornforth made his debut in an
unfamiliar right-back role as a 17-year-old in
the final Division One fixture of 1984-85. A
gate of 9,398 constituted the worst attendance
at Roker Park for eleven seasons, as the final
rites of a relegation term were played out.
Despite his ability to create chances from
central midfield thanks to his excellent passing

*John
Cornforth*

skills, it was not until Denis Smith arrived at
Roker that Cornforth finally enjoyed a more
prolonged involvement at senior level. With
eight starts and four substitute appearances in
1987-88 he qualified for a Third Division
championship medal and in the same season
opened his account as a goalscorer with two
against York City in a 4-2 win. After spending
almost six years as a Sunderland professional
Swansea City paid £50,000 for his transfer and
it was during his spell at Vetch Field that he
caught the eye of the Welsh selectors.
Birmingham City paid £350,000 for him in
March 1996 but in December of the same year,
and after just eight senior appearances, they
transferred him to Wycombe Wanderers for a
bargain £50,000. In the same month he made a
court appearance when Stockport County
midfielder Brian McCord was awarded
damages estimated at £250,000 for an horrific
leg injury. Tackled by Cornforth in a Second
Division game at Swansea in March 1993,
McCord's multiple fracture ended his playing
career. Season 1998-99 began shakily at
Adams Park, and Wycombe looked unlikely to
preserve their Second Division status, but
fortunes revived under new manager Lawrie
Sanchez. During the season Cornforth spent
some time out with a niggling knee injury,
faded from the first team picture, and was
released in summer 1999.

Appearances:
FL: 21(11) apps. 2 gls.
FAC: 1 app. 0 gls.
Other: 1(3) apps. 0 gls.
Total: *23(14) apps. 2 gls.*
Honours:
*2 Welsh caps 1995/(Sunderland) Div 3
champs 1988/(Swansea City) AMC winner
1994.*

COTON, Anthony Philip

Role: Goalkeeper 1996-98
6'2" 13st.7lbs.
b. Tamworth, Staffs, 19th May 1961

CAREER: Tamworth/Mile Oak Rovers/
Birmingham City Oct 1978(Hereford United
loan Oct 1979)/Watford Sept 1984/Manchester
City July 1990/Manchester United Jan 1996/
SUNDERLAND July 1996, appointed Reserve
Team coach Feb 1998, contract cancelled
Oct 1998/Manchester United coaching staff
Oct 1998.

Tony Coton

Debut v Leicester City (h) 17/8/1996

Tony Coton passed the significant milestone of 500 League appearances whilst wearing Sunderland's colours, but one game later in October 1996, suffered an horrific injury after an accidental collision with Southampton striker Egil Ostenstad. Stretchered off with his leg broken in five places, his recovery necessitated further interim surgery and a lengthy rehabilitation period. Signed after a spell at Manchester United, where he had the relatively thankless task of understudy to Peter Schmeichel, Coton had made an excellent start as he sought to re-establish himself in the top flight despite his goal-kicking being hampered by a troublesome Achilles tendon injury. Considered unfortunate not to have gained full international honours, Tony Coton cost Manchester City £1 million in 1990, after six excellent seasons with Watford. His career had kicked-off with Birmingham for whom he saved a first minute penalty - against Sunderland - on his debut. At Maine Road he was first associated with Peter Reid, City's then player-manager, and as the Blues' fortunes faded it was Reid who influenced Coton's decision to move to Sunderland, when Wolves were also interested in signing him. In

charge of Sunderland's Reserve team when they won promotion in 1998, Coton departed the Stadium of Light in October of the same year, following reports in the national press that he had initiated High Court proceedings against the club, alleging failure to provide suitable disability cover at the time of his injury in 1996.

Appearances:
PL: 10 apps. 0 gls.
FLC: 2 apps. 0 gls.
Total: *12 apps. 0 gls.*

COVERDALE, Robert

Role: Wing-half 1914-21
5'8" 11st.6lbs.
b. West Hartlepool, 16th January 1892
d. Hull, 7th January 1969

CAREER: Rutherglen Glencairn/ SUNDERLAND Aug 1912(guest player for Hull City during WW1)/Hull City May 1921/ Grimsby Town Sept 1924/Bridlington Town 1925.

Debut v Blackburn Rovers (a) 17/10/1914

Bobby Coverdale

Bobby Coverdale was something of a utility man: he made his debut at outside-left and in the League played on both wing-half flanks and at inside-left for Sunderland. A gritty, two-footed performer, he could take both sides with equal facility. Coverdale served in the Army during the First World War, in the Durham Light Infantry, representing his regiment at soccer. He played for Scotland in a junior international before the selectors discovered that, being English born he was ineligible. Bobby went to Hull on a free transfer in lieu of benefit. The aggregate figure for his four years with the Humberside clubs were 96 first team outings, eight goals.

Appearances:
FL: 20 apps. 0 gls.
FAC: 1 app. 0 gls.
Total: *21 apps. 0 gls.*
Honours
Scot Jnr int.

COWAN, James Clews

Role: Goalkeeper 1953-54
5'11" 11st.7lbs.
b. Paisley, 16th June 1926
d. 20th June 1968

CAREER: Paisley schools football/Mossvale
Juniors (Paisley)/St Mirren while still at
school/Morton May 1944/SUNDERLAND
June 1953 £8,000/Third Lanark Nov 1955-1956.

Debut v Charlton Athletic (a) 19/8/1953

Jimmy Cowan built an enormous reputation
as a class 'keeper in the immediate post-war
period. He had originally been a centre-
forward and, on joining St Mirren as a
goalkeeper, still led his school team's attack.
When home on leave in 1947 while serving
with the BAOR he was a last-minute
replacement for Morton, saved two penalties
and became first choice from then on. Jimmy's
long run of international duty had ended by
the time of the transfer to Sunderland and his
first team activity at Roker Park was confined
to season 1953/54. An early appraisal had
related how Cowan gained stature playing in
Forces' representative matches, making
miracle saves through lightning reactions, and
being acrobatic, agile and daring.

Appearances:
FL: 28 apps. 0 gls.
FAC: 1 app. 0 gls.
Total: *29 apps. 0 gls.*
Honours:
*25 Scot caps/3 SL apps./(Morton) SC finalist
1948.*

COWAN, Walter Gowans

Role: Inside-right 1895-97
b. Dalziel, Lanarks, 1874

CAREER: Motherwell/SUNDERLAND May
1895/Motherwell May 1897.

*Debut v
Blackburn
Rovers (h)
7/9/1895*

Walter
Cowan
appeared in
roughly a
third of
Sunderland's
League
programme
during his
two-year
service. He
shared the
inside-right
spot with a
mixed bag of
attacking
talent that
included John
Harvey and Scotland's Jimmy Miller. Cowan
combined well and produced a fair goals
return.

Walter Cowan

Appearances:
FL: 19 apps. 7 gls.
Total: *19 apps. 7 gls.*

Jimmy Cowan

COWELL, John

Role: Centre-forward 1910-11
5'8" 11st.0lbs.
b. Blyth, Northumberland, 9th June 1887

CAREER: Springwell FC/Rowland's Gill/
Spen Black & White/Castleford Town/Selby
Mizpah/Rotherham Town 1907-08/Bristol
City Apr 1909/SUNDERLAND Oct 1910
(exchange for Wm Clark)/Distillery May
1911/Belfast Celtic Nov 1914.

Debut v Manchester City (a) 22/10/1910

John Cowell certainly
had a tour of sundry
North-East and
Yorkshire junior clubs
before attaining League
status. From around
1903, for the most part
spending a season with
each, the centre-
forward picked up a
few trophies in the
process, at Selby
memorably netting 23

John Cowell

goals in a mere 11 appearances - he scored
prolifically during these 'prentice years. John
did well at Bristol too, his haul of 20 in 37
League matches, including a four (against
Nottingham Forest in April 1910) and a hat-
trick (against Middlesbrough in September
1909).

> **Appearances:**
> *FL: 14 apps. 5 gls.*
> **Total:** *14 apps. 5 gls.*

COXFORD, John

Role: Centre-half 1924-27
5'9" 12st.6lbs.
b. Seaton Hirst, Northumberland, 25th July 1904
d. Bury St Edmunds, Suffolk, 1978

CAREER: North Seaton Colliery/Stakeford
United/SUNDERLAND May 1924/
Birmingham Apr 1927/Bournemouth &
Boscombe Athletic May 1930/Poole Town May
1934/Northfleet Aug 1934.

Debut v Blackburn Rovers (a) 18/4/1925

For John Coxford a period of three years as a
reserve at Roker was followed by another
three in like mode with Birmingham (16

John Coxford

League appearances there). Things looked up
for John on the south coast as he was
Bournemouth's regular centre-half in his four
years at Dean Court, grossing over 130
Southern Section appearances. "The mainstay
of the side, a strong player, defence his chief
line," said one commentator in 1933. He
played but a couple of games for Poole prior
to serving his last club, Northfleet.

> **Appearances:**
> *FL: 11 apps. 0 gls.*
> **Total:** *11 apps. 0 gls.*

CRADDOCK, Jody Darryl

Role: Central Defender 1997-date.
6'2" 12st.4lbs.
b. Redditch, Worcs, 25th July 1975

CAREER: Christchurch/Cambridge United
Aug 1993/SUNDERLAND July 1997.

Debut v Bury (h) 16/9/1997 (FLC)

Jody Craddock joined Sunderland from

Jody Craddock

Cambridge United on the day the Stadium of Light was opened for an initial payment of £300,000 with a further £200,000 payable linked to appearances. The 22-year-old central defender was considered 'one for the future' when signed, and faced stiff competition from Ord and Melville in the centre of Sunderland's defence. In the event, circumstances contrived to give him an early opportunity at senior level, which he seized to great effect. A talented all-round defender, his game owed much to early coaching by former England centre-half Roy McFarland, Cambridge United's manager during Craddock's spell at the Abbey Stadium. Good in the air and a constructive passer out of defence, his partnership with Darren Williams did much to kick-start Sunderland's 1997-98 campaign after an indifferent opening, which ultimately cost the side an automatic promotion spot. At 6ft. 2ins. and built to match, it seems inconceivable that Jody was once turned down by Yeovil because he was considered too small. At 18 he left non-League football to join Cambridge United on a free transfer. Consistent performances saw him rewarded by a place in the PFA Third Division team in 1997 after three seasons in which he recorded over 150 league and Cup appearances. Season 1998-99 proved frustrating for Jody, despite his starring role in the Reserves championship-winning side. Sidelined with a calf strain after appearing in the season's opening two fixtures, he was unable to regain his first team

spot due to the outstanding form of Butler and Melville in the heart of the Lads' backline but still earned praise from manager Peter Reid for his ultra-professional response to the situation.

Appearances:
FL: 36(4) apps. 0 gls.
FAC: 2 apps. 0 gls.
FLC: 6(2) apps. 0 gls.
Total: *44(6) apps. 0 gls.*

CRAGGS, John

Role: Outside-right 1900-04
5'9" 11st.10lbs.
b. Trimdon Grange, Co Durham, circa 1880

CAREER: Trimdon Grange FC/ SUNDERLAND Mar 1900/Reading May 1902/SUNDERLAND Aug 1903/Nottingham Forest Nov 1904/Sutton Town Dec 1906/ Houghton Rovers June 1907/West Stanley Sept 1907.

Debut v Everton (h) 16/11/1901

John Craggs

John Craggs was mostly in Sunderland's 'A' team and, with half a dozen League appearances to his name, moved to Reading and regular first team football. He did well - a critic remarking that he was "... a smart player on the wing, (he) centres quickly and combines well" - so the Roker management persuaded him to return. He moved on again after little more than a season, although generally first choice and a frequent scorer. But John was appreciated in Nottingham, the local authoritative *Post Guide* reckoning him to be the best outside-right the club had had for four years. He seems to have just 'missed out' with the honours, i.e. Sunderland's 1901/02 championship and Forest's 1906/07 Division Two winning sides.

Appearances:
FL: 42 apps. 16 gls.
FAC: 1 app. 1 gl.
Total: *43 apps. 17 gls.*

CRAIG, J. Robert

Role: Left-back 1949-50
5'9" 10st.8lbs.
b. Consett, Co Durham, 16th June 1928

CAREER: Leadgate Juniors/SUNDERLAND
Aug 1948/Headington United cs 1951.

Debut v West Bromwich Albion (h) 24/9/1949

Robert Craig was at
Sunderland in the
immediate post-war era
when the full-back duo
of Stelling and Hudgell
reigned supreme at
Roker Park. Reserve
defenders' outings
therefore, were
infrequent. Such is the
case here: Craig's debut
(a 2-1 win over West
Bromwich) was his 'one
and only' appearance in League football. He
had originally been on Sunderland's books in
November 1945.

Robert Craig

    Appearances:
    FL: 1 app. 0 gls.
    Total: *1 app. 0 gls.*

CRAWFORD, James

Role: Outside-right 1898-1900
5'6" 11st.0lbs.
b. Leith, circa 1877

CAREER: Abercorn/Reading 1897/
SUNDERLAND May 1898/Derby County
May 1900/Middlesbrough Nov 1901-1903.

Debut v Preston North End (a) 13/9/1898

In 1902 a commentator wrote James Crawford
was " ... a tricky and speedy outside-right but
somewhat uncertain". The commentator did
not say precisely where uncertainty lay. Was it
when to middle the ball? Or in picking out a
colleague to pass to? Or to his exact role in a
team's scheme of things? No matter, Crawford
had a decent appearance record. Besides the
Sunderland figures below he made 43 at
Derby and 26 at Middlesbrough.

    Appearances:
    FL: 55 apps. 5 gls.
    FAC: 2 apps. 1 gl.
    Total: *57 apps. 6 gls.*

CRESSWELL, Frank

Role: Inside-left 1926-29
5'7" 10st.6lbs.
*b. South Shields,
5th September 1908
d. Jesmond, Newcastle upon Tyne,
2nd December 1979*

Frank Cresswell

CAREER: South Shields Schools/Durham
Schoolboys/Tyne Dock/SUNDERLAND Nov
1925/West Bromwich Albion June 1929 £975/
Chester July 1930('fee' affected in June 1931,
when Chester entered the Football League, it
took the form of an exchange with another
player Arthur Gale)/Notts County Jan 1934/
Chester June 1934-1938 when he retired
through injury/Northampton Town asst.
manager.

Debut v Huddersfield Town (a) 14/9/1926

Frank Cresswell was awarded four schoolboy
caps in 1921 an 1922 - two against Scotland
and two against Wales - and captained the
side in all four. An obvious recruit for senior
status, therefore, and where better to go than
to the local big shots, Sunderland? Frank,
however, never gained a regular spot but did
so in his West Brom season before moving to
the then non-League Chester. This club was
elected to the Football League a year later,
Cresswell becoming one of their key players
before retiring through injury in the close
season of 1937. An attempted come-back in
1937/38 was unsuccessful, finishing with
aggregate Chester figures of 168 Northern
Section appearances, 57 goals. In the brief
Notts County interlude he had 16 Second
Division outings, scoring four goals. He won
praise for his clever footwork, constructive
ideas and goal awareness. On leaving football
Frank worked in the insurance industry until
1973. Younger brother of the celebrated
Warney Cresswell (q.v.).

    Appearances:
    FL: 13 apps. 1 gl.
    Total: *13 apps. 1 gl.*
    Honours:
    *4 Eng Sch apps. 1922-23/(Chester) WC
    winner 1933/WC finalist 1935.*

*Right: Warney Cresswell
in action (nearest the
camera)*

CRESSWELL, Warneford

Role: Right-back 1921-27
5'9" 10st.6lbs.
b. South Shields, 5th November 1897
d. South Shields, 20th October 1973

CAREER: Stanhope Road School/South Shields Schools/South Shields Junior football/North Shields Athletic 1914(guest player for Morton, Heart of Midlothian, Hibernian and Tottenham Hotspur during WW1)/South Shields May 1919/SUNDERLAND Mar 1922 £5,500 (a record at the time)/Everton Feb 1927/retired May 1936/Port Vale coach, manager to Apr 1937/Northampton Town manager Apr 1937-Sept 1939/Dartford manager cs 1946-Jan 1947.

Debut v Sheffield United (h) 4/3/1922

Warney Cresswell was a renowned figure from inter-war years over whom critics regularly waxed lyrical. Some stock phrases: "the prince of full-backs" ... "one of the most talented backs" ... "a master of positional play" ... and so on. What is certain is that his cool, unruffled demeanour, coupled with finely judged tackles and intelligent measured clearances were unsurpassed. Warney's outstanding talents brought bids from Spurs and Aston Villa but South Shields would not part, eventually capitulating to a record offer from neighbouring Sunderland. Cresswell made the Roker right-back position his own and he was capped by England every year between 1923 and 1927. On one occasion he played for his country when goalkeeper and club mate Albert McInroy was also selected. An even larger sum - although the player was in his 30th year - took him to Everton and a string of club honours until aged 38. (A prime example of brains saving legs). At Goodison he eventually made the transition to left-back, thus accommodating, in turn, the Welsh cap, Ben Williams, and the Irish cap, Willie Cook. These were enduring partnerships reminiscent of the Cresswell/Ernie England duo at Roker. His managerships were competent rather than spectacular. In the 1914/18 war Warney served in the Royal Artillery; in World War Two as an Army PT instructor. Outside football he worked as manager of a Liverpool cinema and in the licensed trade at Dartford. Brother of Frank Cresswell (q.v.).

Appearances:
FL: 182 apps. 0 gls.
FAC: 8 apps. 0 gls.
Total: *190 apps. 0 gls.*
Honours:
7 Eng caps/5 FL apps./1 Eng Sch app./(Everton) FL champs 1928, 1932/FL Div 2 champs 1931/FAC winner 1933.

CRINGAN, William

Role: Wing-half 1910-15
5'9" 11st.7lbs.
b. Muirkirk, Ayrshire, 15th May 1890
d. 12th May 1958

CAREER: Douglas Water Thistle/
SUNDERLAND June 1910(Wishaw Thistle
loan Aug 1915)(Ayr United temp transfer Jan
1916)(Celtic loan)/Celtic Sept 1917 £600/Third
Lanark Oct 1923/Motherwell May 1924-Feb
1925/Inverness Thistle Mar 1925/Bathgate
Nov 1925.

Debut v Tottenham Hotspur (h) 26/11/1910

Billy Cringan achieved
fame as a Celtic
centre-half but this
came after a long
apprenticeship at
Roker Park where he
had developed into a
capable wing-half,
mostly on the left
flank. He enjoyed an
amount of first team
exposure which
included a run of three
games at centre-
forward, an experiment not repeated. As a
pivot Billy's play was outstanding, especially
so in its defensive aspects. His departure from
Parkhead apparently came from an off-the-
field matter. Perhaps because of being team

Bill Cringan

captain, he acted as spokesman for the Celtic
players when meeting directors over bonus
payment. Within a month he was transferred
to Third Lanark. Willie served in the Army
during the First World War and, after leaving
football, was a Bathgate licensee. Brother of
Jimmy Cringan, the long-serving (1922-34)
Birmingham half-back.

Appearances:
FL: 77 apps. 2 gls.
FAC: 5 apps. 0 gls.
Total: *82 apps. 2 gls.*
Honours:
5 Scot caps/1 Scot Victory int app./
4 SL apps./(Celtic) SL champs 1919, 1922/
SC winner 1923.

CROSSAN, John Andrew

Role: Inside-left 1962-65
5'8" 11st.5lbs.
b. Londonderry, 29th November 1938

CAREER: Junior football to Derry City/
Coleraine/Sparta Rotterdam 1959/Standard
Liege 1960/SUNDERLAND Oct 1962 approx
£27,000/Manchester City Jan 1965 £40,000/
Middlesbrough Aug 1967 £32,500/Tongren FC
(Belgium) cs 1970.

Debut v Grimsby Town (h) 3/11/1962

Johnny Crossan experienced a most eventful
early career in that, when with Coleraine, he
signed for Bristol City but the registration was

Johnny Crossan in action at Roker Park.

not accepted by the Football League. Aged only 19, and accused of taking payment while officially an amateur, he was banned for life by the Irish League. Crossan thereupon moved to the continent which brought no little benefit and breadth to his game as he assisted top Dutch and Belgian clubs. With Standard Liege, for instance, he sampled European Cup soccer in 1961-62 up to and including the semi-final stage where he marked Real Madrid legend Alfredo di Stefano. Sunderland swiftly engaged him a few days after the life ban was lifted and as an ever present and top scorer with 22 League goals he proved a major force in the 1964 promotion team. His final tally of 48 goals in 99 games is mighty impressive for an influential player who created as many as he scored. Johnny won a dozen of his 24 Northern Ireland caps and netted half his ten international goals whilst at Roker, including one against England at Wembley in 1963. Equally successful at Manchester, he skippered City's 1966 Division Two championship side under Joe Mercer and Malcolm Allison. Crossan cost Middlesbrough their then record fee but had subsequent health problems, first from insomnia and then undergoing major surgery in 1969 for the removal of duodenal ulcers. Johnny was a highly skilled performer able to take the inside-right berth also. And it seems a long lasting one: in August 1980 he was reportedly turning out for Foyle Harps (Londonderry), well into his 42nd year.

Appearances:
FL: 82 apps. 39 gls.
FAC: 10 apps. 8 gls.
FLC: 7 apps. 1 gl.
Total: *99 apps. 48 gls.*
Honours:
24 NIre caps/1 NIre B app./4 NIre am apps./(Manchester City) FL Div 2 champs 1966.

CROSSLEY, Charles Arthur

Role: Inside-forward 1913-20
5'7" 12st.2lbs.
b. Wolverhampton, 1892
d. Wolverhampton, 29th April 1965

CAREER: Hednesford Town/Walsall 1913/SUNDERLAND Feb 1914(guest player for Tottenham Hotspur, Clapton Orient and Huddersfield Town during WW1)/Everton Apr 1920/West Ham United June 1922/

Swindon Town July 1923/Ebbw Vale player-manager Sept 1925.

Debut v Tottenham Hotspur (h) 14/3/1914

Charlie Crossley was a short, thickset man whose broad shoulders and substantial weight could make his presence felt. He belonged to the foraging type with an eye for the scoring chance - he headed Everton's scoring list in his first Goodison season. And a player of recognised quality - he appeared in an England trial match shortly before leaving Sunderland. Crossley played in exactly one-third of West Ham's 1922/23 promotion-winning programme but did not make their Wembley Cup final side that season. During the First World War he was a stoker on a submarine destroyer and in February 1920 represented the North versus England.

Charlie Crossley

Appearances:
FL: 43 apps. 17 gls.
FAC: 3 apps. 0 gls.
Total: *46 apps. 17 gls.*

CUGGY, Francis

Role: Right-half 1909-21
5'9" 11st.4lbs.
b. Walker-on-Tyne, Northumberland, 16th June 1889
d. Walker-on-Tyne, Northumberland, 27th March 1965

CAREER: Willington Athletic Dec 1907/SUNDERLAND Mar 1909/Wallsend player-manager May 1921-cs 1922/Celta Vigo (Spain) coach, appointed Nov 1923.

Debut v Aston Villa (a) 12/2/1910

The apex of the famous Cuggy, Jackie Mordue and Charlie Buchan triangle whose extraordinarily skilful combination so entranced contemporary critics, especially during the vintage 1912-13 season when

Sunderland vied with Aston Villa in an effort to clinch the much-prized League and Cup 'Double'. As an individual Frank Cuggy was aptly described as "an attacking wing-half with superb ball control who delighted in the Scottish style of triangular play between wing-half, winger and inside-forward." Not mentioned in this quote is tenacity and persistence - as Sunderland's regular choice right-half he simply never gave up on the cause. But for the interruption of the Great War Frank would almost certainly not only have topped 300 outings for the club but also gained more than his initial pair of England caps. After leaving football, Frank worked in the local shipyards.

CUGGY, SUNDERLAND

Appearances:
FL: 166 apps. 4 gls.
FAC: 24 apps. 0 gls.
Total: *190 apps. 4 gls.*
Honours:
2 Eng caps/3 FL apps./(Sunderland) FL champs 1913/FAC finalist 1913.

CULLEN, Anthony

Role: Winger 1988-92
5'6" 11st.7lbs.
b. Gateshead, 30th September 1969

CAREER: Newcastle United trainee/ SUNDERLAND Sept 1988 (Carlisle United loan Dec 1989)(Rotherham United loan Jan 1991)(Bury loan Oct 1991)/Swansea City Aug 1992/Doncaster Rovers n.c. Aug-Sept 1993.

Tony Cullen

Debut v Swindon Town (a) 18/12/1989 (sub)

Tony Cullen made his first senior appearance towards the close of the 1988-89 season, and when the new campaign opened he was in the starting line-up for matches against Swindon Town and Ipswich Town. He then lost his

number seven jersey to Paul Bracewell, newly arrived from Everton for his second spell at Roker Park. In the first of his subsequent loan moves, Tony scored his first senior goal for Carlisle United on his debut at Brunton Park. Swansea City manager (and former Sunderland coach) Frank Burrows recruited him in August 1992, and his season at the Vetch was spent in the company of a number of ex-Sunderland players including Reuben Agboola, John Cornforth and Colin West. A month's trial with Doncaster Rovers wound up Tony's League career which, including substitute appearances, totalled 65 matches and five goals.

Appearances:
FL: 11(18) apps. 0 gls.
FLC: 0(5) apps. 1 gl.
Total: *11(23) apps. 1 gl.*

CUMMINS, Stanley

Role: Forward/Midfield 1979-85
5'6" 9st.1lb.
b. Sedgefield, Co Durham, 6th December 1958

CAREER: Middlesbrough app, pro Dec 1976 (Minnesota Kicks, USA loan May 1977)/ SUNDERLAND Nov 1979 (Seattle Sounders, USA loan May 1981)/ Crystal Palace Aug 1983/SUNDERLAND Oct 1984/Minnesota Strikers, USA Aug 1985.

Debut v Notts County (h) 17/11/1979 (scored)

Stan Cummins, a mighty atom in terms of size, was an extremely skilful performer who made an immediate impact at Roker Park, following his £300,000 move from First Division Middlesbrough where it had been predicted he might become the game's first £1 million player. A goalscorer on his debut, he totalled 12 League goals in 26 appearances (including four against Burnley) in his first season, Sunderland winning promotion from Division Two, as runners-up to Leicester City. During the following three seasons in Division One, relegation fears were never far away despite - or because of - a large turnover of playing personnel. Several times linked with a possible move to Manchester City, Stan did in fact leave to join Crystal Palace, after failing to agree a new contract. It was a most

Stan and Anne Cummins and the ball Stan scored four with against Burnley in February 1980.

controversial departure as Sunderland had offered terms no better than those that already existed and therefore Stan was entitled to a free transfer. It proved a fairly brief stay, as ten matches into his second season at Selhurst he returned to Roker, in the campaign that Sunderland reached the League Cup Final. His appearances during the season were limited by injury and the fact he was cup-tied.

Appearances:
FL: 145(5) apps. 29 gls.
FAC: 8(1) apps. 0 gls.
FLC: 6 apps. 3 gls.
Total: *159(6) apps. 32 gls.*

CUNNING, Robert Robertson I.

Role: Outside-left 1950-51
b. Dunfermline, 12th February 1930

CAREER: Port Glasgow/SUNDERLAND June 1950/Hamilton Academical Oct 1951/Rangers Sept 1954-1956.

Debut v Middlesbrough (a) 14/10/1950

Blond Scot Bob Cunning was concisely labelled "a progressive winger". He was a stand-in for Tommy Reynolds in his sixteen months at Roker Park, and his League duty was confined to five consecutive appearances in October and November 1950. The move to

Hamilton proved advantageous, the Accies winning promotion as runners-up in Division 'B', to which Cunning contributed a valuable 16 goals. Continuing good form brought a glamour transfer to Rangers but he had only seven first team outings, all in season 1954/55: three in the League and four in cup competitions.

Bob Cunning

Appearances:
FL: 5 apps. 0 gls.
Total: *5 apps. 0 gls.*

CUNNINGTON, Shaun Gary

Role: Midfield/Full-back 1992-95
5'9" 11st.2lbs.
b. Bourne, Lincs, 4th January 1966

CAREER: Bourne Town/Wrexham app 1982, pro Jan 1984/Grimsby Town Feb 1988/ SUNDERLAND July 1992/West Bromwich Albion Aug 1995/Notts County Mar 1997/ Kidderminster Harriers Aug 1998.

*Shaun
Cunnington*

appearances were a valued contribution in a campaign which ended with Sunderland one point above the Division One relegation places. A catalogue of injuries and illness followed after he was initially hurt in a meaningless Anglo-Italian Cup tie. His senior outings in the following two seasons were severely restricted. He was similarly plagued by knee and ankle injuries during his spell with West Bromwich Albion who recouped only £25,000 of their original £220,000 outlay when they transferred him to Notts County in March 1997. Sadly, a succession of injuries blighted Shaun's time at Meadow Lane, and he did not qualify for a championship medal from Notts runaway success in 1997-98, having appeared in only 3(6) of the season's Division Three matches. Released at the end of his contract, he joined Kidderminster Harriers of the Conference League in the summer of 1998.

Appearances:
FL: 52(6) apps. 8 gls.
FAC: 2 apps. 1 gl.
FLC: 3 apps. 0 gls.
Other: 2 apps. 0 gls.
Total: *59(6) apps. 9 gls.*
Honours:
(Wrexham) WC winner 1986/WC finalist 1982, 1983.

CURRAN, Edward 'Terry'

Role: Winger 1986-87
5'10" 12st.4lbs.
b. Kinsley, 20th March 1955

CAREER: Doncaster Rovers pro July 1973/ Nottingham Forest Aug 1975(Bury loan Oct 1977)/Derby County Nov 1977/Southampton Aug 1978/Sheffield Wednesday Mar 1979/ Sheffield United Aug 1982(Everton loan Dec 1982)/Everton Sept 1983/Huddersfield Town July 1985/SUNDERLAND Nov 1986/ Grantham Town June 1987/Grimsby Town Nov 1987/Chesterfield n.c. Mar 1988/Goole Town manager Nov 1989/Mossley manager Nov-Dec 1992.

Debut v Grimsby Town (a) 15/11/1986

Very much a rolling stone who gathered no moss, Terry Curran flitted briefly across the Roker scene in season 1986-87, the term in which Sunderland were relegated to Division Three. A talented but controversial wingman,

Debut v Swindon Town 15/8/1992

Very much an early developer, Shaun Cunnington was in Bourne Town Reserves team at 15 years old. He made his League debut for Wrexham when he was 16, and when he left the Racecourse at 22, had appeared in over 250 matches, including eight ECWC ties and two Welsh Cup finals. He cost Grimsby Town just £50,000 in February 1988 and in four seasons captained the Mariners to successive promotions from Division Four to Division Two. Signed by Malcolm Crosby for £650,000, he showed very patchy form in his first season, although seven League goals in 39

Terry Curran

CURRAN, Patrick Joseph

Role: Inside-right 1937-38
5'8" 10st.3lbs.
b. Sunderland, 13th November 1917

CAREER: Sunderland St Patrick's/
SUNDERLAND am Jan 1936, pro Sept 1936/
Ipswich Town Oct 1938 £750/Watford June
1939 £300 (guested for South Shields during
WW2)/Bradford City June 1947-cs 1948.
Debut v Birmingham (a) 26/2/1938

Local product Pat Curran was transferred to
Ipswich Town after only one senior
appearance with Sunderland and made nine
first team appearances for the Suffolk club,
scoring one goal. He joined Watford just
before the outbreak of war and played in a
number of wartime games for them. In his
Bradford City season he had five Northern
Section outings, scoring a single goal.

Appearances:
FL: 1 app. 0 gls.
Total: *1 app. 0 gls.*

curly-haired Curran was a match winner on
his day, but was far too often at odds with
managers and coaches. Indeed, barracked by
Roker fans at a reserve match he flicked up
two fingers in a V-sign and was subsequently
sacked by the club. Difficult to fit into any
specific team formation or role, he remained a
maverick throughout his career which
spanned thirteen League clubs and an
aggregate 394(18) appearances and 72 goals.
The undoubted highlight was his sparkling 22
League goals in 44 appearances for Sheffield
Wednesday in a brilliant 1979-80 season when
the Owls won promotion from Division Three.
Earlier in his career Curran helped Brian
Clough's Nottingham Forest win promotion
from Division Two in 1976-77 and was a squad
member (eight appearances, four as substitute)
of Everton's League championship side in
1984-85. A cruciate ligament injury ended his
career and outside the game he has been
variously involved in a pallet hire business,
worked as an hotelier near to Wetherby and as
a salesman.

Appearances:
FL: 9 apps. 1 gl.
Total: *9 apps. 1 gl.*

Pat Curran

CURTIS, John Joseph

Role: Outside-right 1906-07
5'6" 11st.0lbs.
b. Settle, Yorkshire, 13th December 1888
d. Wimbledon, London 1st qtr 1955

CAREER: South Bank St Peter's/South Bank
FC/SUNDERLAND Dec 1906/Shildon Dec
1907/Gainsborough Trinity May 1908/
Tottenham Hotspur Apr 1909/Fulham cs
1913/Brentford June 1914/Stockport County
Sept 1914(guest player for Brentford during
WW1)/Middlesbrough July 1919/Shildon Oct
1920.

Debut v Sheffield Wednesday (h) 8/12/1906

Not very tall, but solidly built, John Curtis
made the rounds of Football and Southern
League clubs after leaving Sunderland. The
best spell was at Tottenham, his thrustful no-
nonsense approach a distinct adjunct to a side
on the point of promotion to the top flight. It
was around this time that Curtis's talents were
recognised by selectors and, in January 1910,
he played in an England trial. However, the
unlucky Curtis developed injury problems
that took the gloss off his performances. He
served in the Royal Field Artillery during the
First World War.

Appearances:
FL: 1 app. 0 gls.
Total: *1 app. 0 gls.*

John Curtis

DALE, Fred

Role: Half-back 1885-88
Debut v Redcar (a) 24/10/1885 (FAC)

Fred Dale

Fred Dale was an old-time stalwart who occupied all three half-back positions for Sunderland in FA Cup ties. He had, like goalkeeper Bill Kirtley, joined them from a disintegrating nearby club, Workmen's Hall of Monkwearmouth, and later captained Sunderland. Twenty years on he vied with Bob Kyle for the club managership, but Kyle was the successful applicant and held the post for almost 23 years.

> **Appearances:**
> *FAC: 9 apps. 0 gls.*
> **Total:** *9 apps. 0 gls.*

DALTON, James J.

Role: Right-back/centre-half 1893-94
b. Canada, circa 1891

CAREER: Canadian touring side of 1891/ SUNDERLAND Sept 1891 (at the time of his League debut was assisting Pawtucket FC, USA)/Nelson cs 1894.

James Dalton

Debut v Sheffield Wednesday (a) 2/9/1893

James Dalton's League debut - the opening match of 1893/94 - was at centre-half, and the other two games, in October 1893, at right-back. Dalton was a very early example of soccer cosmopolitanism that now, a century later, has reached world-wide proportions. And he must surely have a claim to be the first Canadian to play first-class football in England.

> **Appearances:**
> *FL: 3 apps. 0 gls.*
> **Total:** *3 apps. 0 gls.*

DANIEL, Peter William

Role: Midfield/Full-back 1984-86
5'9" 11st.6lbs.
b. Hull, 12th December 1955

CAREER: Hull City assoc. s'boy Oct 1969, app 1971, pro Sept 1973/Wolverhampton Wanderers May 1978/Minnesota Kicks May 1984/SUNDERLAND Aug 1984/Lincoln City Nov 1985, appointed caretaker-manager Mar-May 1987/Burnley July 1987, retired May 1989/North Ferriby player-coach and manager June 1981/Winterton Rangers manager.

Debut v Tottenham Hotspur (h) 4/9/1984

Peter Daniel

Bearded Peter Daniel, a bargain £18,000 signing by manager Len Ashurst, spent an eventful 15 months at Roker Park. Always a hard-working, neat passer of the ball during his time with The Lads, the former Wembley winner - with Wolves in 1980 - helped take Sunderland to the same venue in 1985, where they were beaten by Norwich City. To compound the disappointment relegation worries became reality, and Sunderland (along with Norwich) lost their top flight status. Drastic measures were called for as 1985-86 opened with five consecutive defeats, and Peter Daniel was one of the players off-loaded. At the outset of his career, with hometown club Hull City, the former painter and decorator won England Under-21 honours, and cost Wolves £182,000 in May 1978. At Molineux he experienced relegation and promotion in successive seasons, 1982 and 1983, before joining Sunderland after a brief spell in America with Minnesota Kicks. In May 1987 Peter was in temporary charge at Lincoln City when they became the first League club to be relegated to the Vauxhall Conference. In his final spell of League football with Burnley he made a third visit to Wembley where his former club, Wolves, beat the Clarets 2-0 in the Sherpa Van Trophy in May 1988 before a crowd in excess of 80,000.

Appearances:
FL: 33(1) apps. 0 gls.
FAC: 1 app. 0 gls.
FLC: 10 apps. 0 gls.
Other: 1 app. 0 gls.
Total: *45(1) apps. 0 gls.*
Honours:
7 Eng U-21 apps. 1977-78/(Wolverhampton Wanderers) FLC winner 1980/(Sunderland) FLC finalist 1985/(Burnley) SVT finalist 1988.

DANIEL, William Raymond

Role: Centre-half 1953-57
6'0" 12st.9lbs.
b. Swansea, 2nd November 1928
d. 6th November 1997

CAREER: Swansea Schools/Plasmarl Youth Club (Swansea)/Swansea Town am during WW2/Arsenal am Aug 1946, pro Oct 1946/SUNDERLAND June 1953 £27,500/Cardiff City Oct 1957 approx. £7,500/Swansea City Mar 1958 approx

£3,000/Hereford United player-manager July 1960-1963, continuing as a Hereford player to cs 1967.
Debut v Charlton Athletic (a) 19/8/1953

A strong, assured pivot, in his heyday Ray Daniel was deemed the best in the United Kingdom. He preferred the attacking style and, indeed, it was said he left Arsenal because he "wished to play a more venturesome game". Originally a wing-half, Ray understudied Leslie Compton at Highbury. At Roker he became Sunderland's captain and made a few appearances at centre-forward. (Towards the end of his career he played at full-back). His brother Bobby, also a promising footballer, lost his life in a 1943 RAF bombing raid. After leaving football Ray worked as a representative of a Swansea brandy importing firm and, later, as a sub-postmaster until 1989.

Appearances:
FL: 136 apps. 6 gls.
FAC: 17 apps. 1 gl.
Total: *153 apps. 7 gls.*
Honours:
21 Welsh caps/Welsh Sch/(Arsenal) FL champs 1953/FAC finalist 1952.

Ray Daniel

Peter Davenport

DAVENPORT, Peter

Role: Forward 1990-93
5'10" 11st.6lbs.
b. Birkenhead, 24th March 1961

CAREER: Cammell Laird F.C./Everton am/
Nottingham Forest Jan 1982/Manchester
United Mar 1986/Middlesbrough Nov 1988/
SUNDERLAND July 1990/Airdrieonians Aug
1993/St Johnstone July 1994/Stockport
County Mar 1995/Southport Aug 1995,
appointed player-asst. manager June 1996,
caretaker-manager Dec 1996/Macclesfield
Town Jan 1997, appointed player-coach cs
1997, re-signed as n.c. player Sept 1998
(St Helens Town n.c. loan Feb 1999) .

Debut v Norwich City (a) 25/8/1990 (scored)

Peter Davenport signed professional forms
with Nottingham Forest in January 1982,
having failed to graduate beyond amateur
status with Everton. He made a promising
start with Forest, scoring four goals in his first
five matches. His ability to hold up the ball
plus a commendable total of 54 League goals
in 118 appearances - which included a City

Ground hat-trick against Sunderland in 1984 -
prompted Manchester United to pay £570,000
for him to replace Barcelona-bound Mark
Hughes. Davenport eventually reached
Sunderland via Middlesbrough for a £300,000
fee in July 1990 as a replacement for the
ageing Eric Gates. Viewed as an ideal man to
continue the supply line to Marco Gabbiadini,
Peter's time at Roker Park saw the club's
fortunes at a generally low ebb, aside from the
FA Cup run to Wembley in 1992. A popular,
fully committed performer, Davenport has
registered a total in excess of 100 goals in
English and Scottish League football. Joining
Macclesfield Town after failing to secure the
post of manager with Southport, he scored his
100th goal in the Football League in the
Silkmen's final game of 1997-98, which saw
them promoted in their first season as a
League club. In the 1998-99 season Peter made
only one substitute appearance for
Macclesfield, and in February 1999 was
permitted to play for St. Helens Town on a
temporary basis, to assist them out of a short-
term fixture backlog.

Appearances:
FL: 72(27) apps. 15 gls.
FAC: 9(1) apps. 2 gls.
FLC: 5(2) apps. 1 gl.
Other: 3(1) apps. 0 gls.
Total: *89(31) apps. 18 gls.*
Honours:
1 Eng cap 1985/1 Eng 'B' app./(Sunderland)
FAC finalists 1992/(Macclesfield Town)
GMVC champs 1997.

DAVIS, Herbert 'Bert'

Role: Outside-right 1932-37
5'5" 10st.8lbs.
b. Bradford, 11th August 1906
d. Yeadon, Leeds, 17th July 1981

CAREER: Bradford Schools/Guiseley/
Bradford Nov 1927/SUNDERLAND Apr 1932
£4,000/Leicester City Dec 1936 £2,000/Crystal
Palace June 1937/Bradford Apr 1939 (guested
for Huddersfield Town and York City during
WW2).

Debut v Manchester City (h) 27/8/1932

Bert Davis enjoyed a superb start to his
professional career, being drafted straight into
the Park Avenue side that romped away with

the Northern Section championship. He then held a regular first team place until a move to top flight Sunderland and a League title medal. However, he lost his place to an emerging Len Duns before the historic 1937 Wembley win. David, diminutive in stature and with no weight advantage, was still a handful for opposing defences all the same, and his goalscoring record was good for a winger. He once worked in a woollen mill, and in the 1930s ran a sports outfitting business not far from Roker Park. A rather unexpected Bert Davis statistic: he was twice sent off in the '35/6 championship run - at Wolverhampton in October and at Middlesbrough in March.

Appearances:
FL: 151 apps. 38 gls.
FAC: 12 apps. 2 gls.
Total: *163 apps. 40 gls.*
Honours:
(Bradford) FL Div 3 Nth champs 1928/(Sunderland) FL champs 1936.

Bert Davis

DAVIS, Richard Daniel

Role: Inside-right/centre-forward 1946-54
5'8" 11st.2lbs.
b. Aston, Birmingham, 22nd January 1922
d. Bishop's Stortford, 11th August 1999

CAREER: Saltley Schools/Morris Jacobs FC (Birmingham Works League)/ SUNDERLAND Feb 1939/Darlington May 1954-1957.

Debut v Leeds United (a) 7/12/1946

Dickie Davis was a valuable inside-forward with a natural opportunist's nose for goals. Thanks to the war his League debut was delayed nearly eight years, afterwards sharing the inside-right and centre appearances with a wide variety of Roker developments and seasoned signings (e.g. Jackie Robinson, Harry Kirtley and Cliff Whitelum). Dickie had made a name guesting for Aston Villa in wartime, this experience making for an easy settling-in when peacetime soccer returned. His best Sunderland season was 1949-50 when 25 League goals saw him finish as the First

Division's leading scorer. It is the last time to date that a Sunderland player has finished as leading scorer in the top flight Division. After fifteen years on Sunderland's books he made a short move to

Dickie Davis

Darlington (for a fee described as 'three figure'). In a three-year stint at The Feethams his Football League figures were 93 appearances and 32 goals.

Appearances:
FL: 144 apps. 72 gls.
FAC: 10 apps. 7 gls.
Total: *154 apps. 79 gls.*
Honours:
1 Eng Sch app.

DAVISON, Arnold

Role: Wing-forward 1886-89
d. Sunderland 1910, aged 46
Debut v Morpeth Harriers 16/10/1886
(FAC)

Arnold Davison was among the most prominent of the early pre-League performers; a dashing winger, highly popular with Sunderland supporters. When displaced, albeit temporarily, by the club's Scots recruitment policy, Arthur Appleton tells us, in his informed *Hotbed of Soccer* (Rupert Hart-Davis, 1960), a local poet was inspired to write:

> *'Who played right well in former days
> For love of play and honour's praise
> Before the dawn of the Scottish craze?
> 'Twas Arnie.'*

Years later the unfortunate Arnie fell on hard times and died in the workhouse.

Appearances:
FAC: 10 apps. 3 gls.
Total: *10 apps. 3 gls.*

DAVISON, James Hawkins

Role: Outside-right 1959-63
5'11" 12st.0lbs.
b. Sunderland, 1st November 1942

CAREER: Sunderland Schools/ SUNDERLAND Nov 1959/Bolton Wanderers Nov 1963 approx. £15,000/Queen of the South Feb 1965.
Debut v Scunthorpe United (a) 21/11/1959

Jimmy Davison did not have long to wait for his initial Division Two game. However, he never had any extended runs of appearances as the first choice outside-right during his Roker sojourn. Perhaps this is not surprising for well-known players with representative honours, such as Fogarty and Harry Hooper, were available at this time. At Bolton Jimmy made 21 League appearances, scoring a single goal before travelling north "for a nominal fee" to Dumfries. He was blessed with an unusually hefty physique for a winger.

Appearances:
FL: 62 apps. 10 gls.
FAC: 3 apps. 1 gl.
FLC: 7 apps. 0 gls.
Total: *72 apps. 11 gls.*

DAYKIN, Thomas

Role: Left-back 1904-09
5'8" 12st.0lbs.
b. Shildon, Co Durham, August 1882

CAREER: Bishop Auckland/Newcastle United trial/Hobson Wanderers/ SUNDERLAND am Mar 1905, pro soon afterwards/ Birmingham Dec 1908/South Shields 1912/retired 1915.
Debut v Manchester City (h) 1/4/1905

Tom Daykin was a useful man to have around as he could also fill both wing-half positions most adequately. This versatility maybe militated against automatic selection and it must be said there was stiff competition for the left-back spot with Jim Watson snr. and Dusty

Jimmy Davison

Tom Daykin

Rhodes on hand. At Birmingham Tom played mainly at left-half with a few spells at right-back. His record there reads 88 League appearances (1 goal) plus six in the FA Cup.

Appearances:
FL: 47 apps. 0 gls.
FAC: 2 apps. 0 gls.
Total: *49 apps. 0 gls.*

DEATH, William George

Role: Outside-left 1924-28
5'8" 11st.5lbs.
b. Rotherham, 13th November 1899
d. Nottingham, 3rd July 1984

CAREER: Broome Athletic(Rotherham Town guest 1918)/Rotherham Town Sept 1920/Notts County Mar 1921 £400/Mansfield Town cs 1923/SUNDERLAND Mar 1924 £500/Exeter City Sept 1928/Gillingham July 1930/Mansfield Town June 1931/Grantham cs 1932/Sutton Town Feb 1933/Afterwards a permit player for City Transport FC (Nottingham) Aug 1934 and played in minor football until the war.

Debut v Burnley (a) 29/9/1924

Billy Death spent much of his professional career in the Midlands, a local soccer annual mentioning in successive years (1921 and '22)

Billy Death

that he "centres well on the run and shoots hard" and was "a speedy outside-left and a capital marksman", which sums up his style very well. Sunderland forked out what was then a considerable amount for a non-League player, having assessed his worth in the course of Mansfield's successful 1923/4 bid for the Midland League title. It could be argued that Billy kept his most important Sunderland contribution until the end. In his very last game - an absolutely crucial Wear-Tees derby at Ayresome Park in May 1928 - Billy scored in a 3-0 relegation showdown that not only kept Sunderland up, and protected their proud record of only having played in the top flight, but also sent Middlesbrough down. In one of the tightest tables ever, only three points separated relegated Spurs from tenth placed Arsenal. Billy learned the game during the 1914/18 war and played until he was 40. The player was wont to present his surname as De'ath, which is understandable.

Appearances:
FL: 53 apps. 14 gls.
FAC: 3 apps. 2 gls.
Total: *56 apps. 16 gls.*

DEMPSTER, James Barclay

Role: Goalkeeper 1919-22
5'9" 11st.7lbs.
b. Newarthill, Lanarks, 30th January 1896

CAREER: Newarthill Thistle/SUNDERLAND Mar 1920/Airdrieonians June 1922/St Johnstone Jan 1924/Dundee United Feb 1927/Bo'ness cs 1927/Bathgate Dec 1928/Bo'ness Dec 1929.

Debut v Blackburn Rovers (h) 5/4/1920

Sunderland FC has never been averse to blooding recently signed junior talent early. Jimmy Dempster is a case in point, making the League side a month after joining. And it was a successful debut: he played in the final five fixtures of 1919/20, letting in only three goals

Jimmy Dempster

and keeping three clean sheets. Another fact worth recording - besides, of course, that of being an adept and sound custodian - was an association with clubs newly risen from Scotland's Division Two. He joined St Johnstone during their promotion campaign, Dundee United the season following their title win and Bo'ness immediately after theirs. And all within a period of three and a half years.

Appearances:
FL: 40 apps. 0 gls.
FAC: 3 apps. 0 gls.
Total: *43 apps. 0 gls.*
Honours:
(St Johnstone) SL Div 2 champs 1924.

DEVINE, Joseph Cassidy

Role: Left-half/inside-left
5'8" 10st.7lbs.
b. Dalziel, Lanarks, 9th August 1905
d. Chesterfield, 9th May 1980

CAREER: Motherwell Watsonians/Cleland Juniors/Bathgate/Burnley May 1925 £250/ Newcastle United Jan 1930 £5,500/

Joe Devine

SUNDERLAND Jan 1931 £3,000/Queens Park Rangers May 1933 £2,500/Birmingham Jan 1935 £2,000/Chesterfield May 1937-1938, becoming coach to cs 1950. Also coached in Iceland, scouted for Bristol City and was a referee in Highland League football.

Debut v Southampton (FAC) (h) 3/1/1931

Originally an inside-right, from his Bathgate days Joe Devine was a noted tactician employing excellent ball control and a fair shot. He attracted a very large transfer fee by 1930 standards from Newcastle, adopting a wing-half role also during his two years at Roker Park. Joe captained both Birmingham and QPR but, despite a lengthy career spent mainly in the top flight, he won neither representative nor club honours. A broken leg sustained in a 1938 cup tie brought his playing days to an end. Apart from football, at different times he ran a London sports outfitting business and worked as a licensee in the Chesterfield area. Nephew of Joe Cassidy, the Celtic and Scotland forward.

Appearances:
FL: 67 apps. 7 gls.
FAC: 9 apps. 0 gls.
Total: *76 apps. 7 gls.*

DIBBLE, Andrew Gerald

Role: Goalkeeper 1985-86
6'2" 13st.7lbs.
b. Cwmbran, Monmouthshire, 8th May 1965

CAREER: Llantarman Schoolboys/Torfan Schoolboys/Cardiff City app July 1981, pro Aug 1982/Luton Town July 1984 (SUNDERLAND loan Feb-May 1986) (Huddersfield Town loan Mar 1987)/ Manchester City July 1988(Aberdeen loan Oct 1990)(Middlesbrough loan Feb 1991)(Bolton Wanderers loan Sept 1991)(West Bromwich Albion loan Feb 1992)(Oldham Athletic loan Apr 1993)(Sheffield United loan Feb 1997) (Glasgow Rangers loan Mar 1997)/Sheffield United Aug 1997/Luton Town Sept 1997/ Middlesbrough Jan 1998-May 1998/ Altrincham FC(Barry Town loan)/Hartlepool United Mar-May 1999.

Debut v Huddersfield Town (a) 1/3/1986

Andy Dibble represented Wales Schoolboys at Rugby Union but switched successfully to soccer and first came to prominence as a 17-

Andy Dibble

on a playing surface believed to have been contaminated with chemicals. Happily, he made a full recovery, and in March 1999 was offered a short-term contract with Hartlepool United, managed by ex-Sunderland goalkeeper, Chris Turner.

Appearances:
FL: 12 apps. 0 gls.
Total: *12 apps. 0 gls.*
Honours:
Wales Sch & Yth/3 Welsh U-21 caps 1983-84/3 Welsh caps 1986-89/(Luton Town)FLC winner 1988*.

*In this final, Andy Dibble was a late replacement for Les Sealey. At a crucial stage of the game he saved a Nigel Winterburn penalty, and Luton went on to beat Arsenal 3-2 thanks to a last-minute winner from Brian Stein.

DICHIO, Daniele Salvatore Ernest

Role: Forward 1997-date
6'3" 12st.3lbs.
b. Hammersmith, London, 19th October 1974

CAREER: Queens Park Rangers assoc. s'boy Mar 1989, trainee July 1991(Welling United loan) pro May 1993(Barnet loan Mar 1994)/Sampdoria, Italy cs 1997(Lecce, Italy loan later in 1997)/SUNDERLAND Jan 1998.

Debut v Norwich City (a) 28/1/1998 (sub)

Danny Dichio was first noted by Sunderland's manager Peter Reid when he was a player at Queens Park Rangers in the late 1980s and Danny was showing promise in their youth set-up. Efforts to bring him to Sunderland failed in the summer of 1997 when his contract ended at QPR and he opted for a move into Italy's Serie A with Sampdoria. Despite a debut at Barcelona's Nou Camp in a pre-season friendly and an early UEFA Cup appearance as substitute for Jürgen Klinsmann, Dichio failed to establish himself with Sampdoria and was loaned to newly-promoted Lecce. Despite a scoring debut for his new club he again found himself out of the first team picture. When made available by Sampdoria, clubs from England, Scotland and France sought his services. Following his £750,000 transfer to Sunderland in January 1998, Danny battled manfully despite limited opportunities, the bulk of his first season's appearances coming from the substitutes'

year-old in Cardiff City's 1982-83 promotion team managed by former Roker stalwart Len Ashurst. He joined Luton Town for £125,000 in July 1984, but had lost his first team place to Les Sealey at the time of his loan move to Sunderland. As part of the loan agreement, Bob Bolder moved to Kenilworth Road. Dibble appeared in a dozen Division Two matches for Sunderland in the closing stages of season 1985-86, when victory in each of the last three home matches ensured Second Division survival. A series of outstanding performances during those tense relegation haunted days made 'Officer' Dibble enormously popular at Roker and he was always afforded a generous reception whenever he returned with other clubs. At Manchester City in the late 1980's Dibble had two seasons as first-choice 'keeper, but his subsequent career has been most notable for a succession of temporary moves. Seven appearances for Rangers at the close of 1996-97 began with a clean sheet in the old firm derby at Celtic Park, and three other shut-outs saw Rangers safely to their ninth successive championship. A bizarre accident in January 1999, which occurred when Andy was playing on loan with Barry Town, necessitated a fortnight's stay in hospital and skin grafts to cover burns on his chest and arms. These were sustained after he had dived team and reserves, however, proved doubly rewarding and resulted in two championship medals for his season's efforts, a Division One award and a Pontin's League Premier Division medal.

Appearances:
FL: 18(32) apps. 10 gls.
FAC: 1(1) apps. 0 gls.
FLC: 4(1) apps. 2 gls.
Total: *23(34) apps. 12 gls.*
Honours:
Eng Sch/1 Eng U-21 app. 1996/(Sunderland) Div 1 champs 1999.

DILLON, John

Role: Outside-left 1960-62
5'8" 11st.4lbs.
b. Coatbridge, 9th November 1942

CAREER: Bellshill Athletic/SUNDERLAND am, pro Nov 1959/Brighton & Hove Albion July 1962/Crewe Alexandra July 1963/Albion Rovers July 1964.

Debut v Middlesbrough (a) 24/9/1960

A teenage debutant and useful stand-in for Jack Overfield, most of John Dillon's senior appearances were recorded in season 1960/61. In his Brighton year he had 21 League outings

Danny Dichio

bench. Whilst continuing to face stiff competition from the established and highly successful striking duo of Quinn and Phillips, he showed a marked improvement during 1998-99. A bright start in pre-season was followed by an early first team opportunity - made possible by an injury to Niall Quinn - which was seized to such good effect that Danny won a Nationwide Player of the Month award. One of four Sunderland strikers who notched double figures in the Championship season, he would surely have been a first-choice player at most other First Division clubs. Regular involvement with both first

John Dillon

(3 goals) and, in a similar period with Crewe five appearances (1 goal). As often happens, the wanderer then returned to his native heath. Dillon was quite adaptable, being listed as an inside-right at Crewe and a centre-forward with Albion Rovers. Later on he scouted for Sunderland and recommended Kieron Brady and others to the club.

Appearances:
FL: 18 apps. 1 gl.
FAC: 4 apps. 0 gls.
FLC: 1 app. 0 gls.
Total: *23 apps. 1 gl.*

DITCHBURN, John Hurst

Role: Right-half/centre-half 1923-26
5'10" 11st.6lbs.
b. Hunslet, Leeds, 13th March 1897
d. Exeter, January 1992

CAREER: Blantyre Thistle/Cambuslang/ Blantyre Victoria/ SUNDERLAND Aug 1923/ Exeter City May 1926/Exeter Loco Sept-Nov 1928/retired cs 1934.

Debut v Sheffield United (a) 26/1/1924

Jock Ditchburn

Always known as Jock because although Leeds born, John Ditchburn was of Scottish parentage and lived in Scotland from the age of three. He had a fair sampling of the Scottish junior scene before reaching Roker Park and a spot as understudy for Clunas and Charlie Parker. He came into greater prominence as the Exeter City centre-half until knee injuries took their toll. Ditchburn was not retained for season 1928/29 but fine displays for Exeter Loco, where he was a permit player, induced the Grecians to re-engage him the following November. In his comeback he was included in the Grecians' Reserve team who won 12-3! All told he made 91 Football League and FA Cup appearances before his retirement in 1934, when he joined the club's ground staff. He was awarded a benefit match in May 1934, Second Division Notts County providing the opposition at St James' Park

Appearances:
FL: 6 apps. 0 gls.
Total: *6 apps. 0 gls.*

DOCHERTY, Michael

Role: Full-back 1976-79
5'7" 10st.5lbs.
b. Preston, Lancs, 29th October 1950

CAREER: Chelsea app/Burnley app Apr 1967, pro Nov 1967/Manchester City Apr 1976/ SUNDERLAND Dec 1976, retired from playing Sept 1979 subsequently appointed coach-caretaker-manager from Apr until June 1981/Hartlepool United manager June-Dec 1983/Wolverhampton Wanderers coach/ Blackpool asst. manager 1988/Burnley asst. manager Jan 1989/Hull City asst. manager July 1990/Rochdale coach 1991, appointed caretaker-manager Nov 1994, manager Jan 1995-May 1996.

Debut v Coventry City (h) 3/1/1977

Mick Docherty, the son of larger-than-life Tommy Docherty, began with his father's club, Chelsea, as a 16-year-old in 1966. Transferred to Burnley he developed so rapidly that he made his League debut at 18 and was firmly established as senior right full-back a year later. He injured knee ligaments at Huddersfield in April 1973 and, in the opening game of the following season, more seriously, damaged both cruciate and medial ligaments in his left knee and was effectively

Mick Docherty

on borrowed time thereafter. A brief spell at
Manchester City preceded his transfer to
Sunderland, where he teamed up with his
former manager Jimmy Adamson. His arrival
in mid-season 1976-77 came amid a grim club
record run of ten games without a goal. On his
debut the defence appeared bolstered by
Mick's presence but Sunderland still lost to a
last minute blunder. Improved form followed,
but the campaign ended sadly, one point short
of a miraculous escape. Enforced retirement at
28 years of age ended on a winning note at
Wrexham in Sunderland's final game of 1978-
79, but with the side one point adrift of a
promotion place. During his subsequent spell
on the coaching staff Mick was briefly
appointed caretaker-manager, following the
dismissal of Ken Knighton and Frank Clark.
Two wins in his four games in charge,
including a crucial final game 1-0 victory at
Anfield in May 1981, guaranteed top flight
survival.

Appearances:
FL: 72(1) apps. 6 gls.
FAC: 2 apps. 0 gls.
FLC: 3 apps. 0 gls.
Other: 2 apps. 1 gl.
Total: *79(1) apps. 7 gls.*
Honours:
*4 Eng Yth apps./(Burnley) Div 2 champs
1973.*

DODDS, Leslie

Role: Goalkeeper 1954-56
5'9" 13st.0lbs.
*b. Lemington, Newcastle upon Tyne, 12th October
1936*

CAREER: Newburn Schools/SUNDERLAND
am Aug 1952, pro Oct 1953-1960/
Stamfordham FC Nov 1960.
Debut v West Bromwich Albion (h) 21/8/1954

Leslie Dodds was a weighty young 'keeper
whose League outings were confined to two
seasons (1954/5 and '55/6). During his seven
years as a Sunderland professional the first
team goalkeeping spot was principally the
domain of Willie Fraser, Johnny Bollands and,
latterly, Peter Wakeham. Yet Les Dodds had a
pedigree, as his several England schoolboy
appearances testify.

Appearances:
FL: 6 apps. 0 gls.
Total: *6 apps. 0 gls.*
Honours:
4 Eng Sch apps.

Leslie Dodds

DOIG, John Edward 'Ned'

Role: Goalkeeper 1890-1904
5'9" 12st.9lbs.
b. Letham, Forfarshire, 29th October 1866
d. Prescot, Lancs, 7th November 1919

CAREER: St Helens FC (Arbroath)/Arbroath
FC 1883 (1 app. for Blackburn Rovers Nov
1889)/SUNDERLAND Sept 1890/Liverpool
Aug 1904/retired 1908 but had a final spell,
from cs 1909, with St Helens Recreation, Lancs,
when past his 42nd birthday.
Debut v West Bromwich Albion (a) 20/9/1890

Ned Doig is, by general consent, counted
among the game's greatest goalkeepers of all
time, a master of all the goalkeeping arts. He
was first in the long line of Sunderland's
Scottish internationalists and established a
record for the number of seasons with a single
club (a record eventually broken by another
Scotland cap, Andrew Wilson of Sheffield
Wednesday). Doig arrived from Arbroath with
a massive reputation, cited when there as "one
of the finest, coolest and most resourceful
'keepers in Scotland." This arrival was not,
however, an unalloyed joy because of an
improper registration. Ned had signed for
Blackburn Rovers and, indeed, had played for
the Lancashire club in a League match during
the previous season, 1889/90. The Wearsiders
were fined £25 and two points were deducted
from their record, the first time a points
deduction penalty had been imposed. The
number of 'firsts' associated with Ned seems
unusually high. What was so remarkable
about Doig, though, apart from the brilliant
qualities previously mentioned, was his
astounding consistency (and incidentally,
freedom from injury). From his debut against
West Bromwich Albion on September 20th,
1890 (Sunderland's first-ever League victory)
to January 1894 he did not miss a League or
FA Cup appearance. After a one-match
absence he completed another run of
consecutive matches to the third League game
of 1895/96. This was one of just two missed
appearances that term and there were precious
few more absences right up to the stage where
former Sunderland boss Tom Watson took him
to Liverpool in August 1904. This outstanding
service in 14 seasons with the Wearsiders
included seven as an ever-present and only
one where more than two games were missed
- the final season, 1903/04, when he appeared

in 29 out of a possible 34. A quite astonishing
record. He was an ever-present in his first
Liverpool campaign too, when the Anfielders
finished as Division Two champions, Ned
adding a final medal to a noteworthy
collection. Thereafter, his 40th birthday
looming and a reserve, he made 15 top-flight
appearances spread over three seasons. He
joined his last club, non-League St.Helens
Recreation, in his 42nd year. There is an
apocryphal tale concerning Ned's coolness. It
is that this admirable quality was diminished
only when he lost his cap in a goalmouth
melée. Being mighty sensitive about a balding
pate his keeness to recover his cap seemed
almost as important as the defence of his net!
It is thought that, taking into account all the
friendlies Sunderland played in Doig's time,
his tally of first class appearances would
constitute the club's record.

Appearances:
FL: 421 apps. 0 gls.
FAC: 35 apps. 0 gls.
Total: *456 apps. 0 gls.*
Honours:
5 Scot caps/(Sunderland) FL champs 1892,
1893, 1895, 1902/(Liverpool) FL Div 2
champs 1905.

DONALDSON, Alexander Pollock

Role: Outside-right 1921-23
5'7" 10st.0lbs.
b. Gateside, Renfrews, 4th December 1890

CAREER: Belgrave Primitive Methodists
(Leicester)/Belgrave FC/Balmoral
United/Ripley Town Athletic 1910-
11/Sheffield United Apr 1911/Bolton
Wanderers Dec 1911 £50 (guested for Leicester
Fosse, Arthurlie and Port Vale during
WW1)/SUNDERLAND Mar 1922 over
£2,000/Manchester City May 1923-May 1924
when he left the first class game due to injury
following a trial with Crystal Palace in the
same month/Chorley Feb 1925/Ashton
National 1928-29 season/Chorley 1929-1931.
Debut v Preston North End (a) 1/4/1922

The slightly built Alex Donaldson was a canny
winger, specialising in accurate centres and
disconcerting swerves. In April 1914 he was
selected for an England trial, the mistake
arising from his having been a Leicester
resident from the age of 10. Donaldson was

Ned Doig

plagued by injuries after the war, culminating in a broken right knee-cap sustained in February 1921 and leading to retirement from top-class football. All the same it will be noted he played in good class non-League soccer,

Alex Donaldson

namely the Lancashire Combination, into his 41st year. In fact, as late as 1930, *The Lancashire Daily Post Handbook* said he was still more than a match for many young defenders. Alec worked as a Bolton publican during the 1950s. In the 1914/18 war he worked in a munitions factory.

Appearances:
FL: 43 apps. 1 gl.
FAC: 2 apps. 0 gls.
Total: *45 apps. 1 gl.*
Honours:
6 Scot caps/3 Scot Victory apps.

DOUGALL, Thomas

Role: Outside-right 1948-49
b. Wishaw, Lanarks, 17th May 1921
d. January 1997

CAREER: Morris Motors FC/ Coventry City Sept 1945/ Brentford Aug 1947/ SUNDERLAND Nov 1948/ Yeovil Town May 1950.

Debut v Chelsea (h) 4/12/1948

Tom Dougall made his League bow with Second Division Brentford and had another

Tom Dougall

outing before he arrived at Roker Park. He sampled top flight soccer with Sunderland a month later with appearances in three consecutive fixtures during December 1948. For the record they resulted in a win (3-0 against Chelsea), a draw (0-0 at Birmingham) and a defeat (1-4 at Bolton). Manager of Kingstonian FC in the late 1960s.

Appearances:
FL: 3 apps. 0 gls.
Total: *3 apps. 0 gls.*

DOWSEY, John

Role: Inside-right 1927-29
5'9" 11st.8lbs.
b. Willington, Co Durham, 1st May 1905
d. Costock, Notts, 27th October 1942

Jack Dowsey

CAREER: Hunswick Villa/Newcastle United June 1924/West Ham United May 1926 £250/ Carlisle United July 1927/SUNDERLAND Nov 1927/Notts County Feb 1929 £500 incl Ike McGorin/Northampton Town Nov 1931/ Nuneaton Town Aug 1934.

Debut v Bury (h) 11/2/1928

Jack Dowsey did not enjoy regular first team football until reaching Notts County nearly five years after he had turned professional. Yet the player had obvious potential and was a frequent goalscorer (54 in two seasons) in Newcastle' successful North Eastern League line-up. At Nottingham he grossed 103 League and FA Cup appearances and was converted into a competent, effective right-half. Jack occupied this berth in County's 1930/31 Southern Section championship side, missing only three matches during the campaign.

Appearances:
FL: 11 apps. 1 gl.
Total: *11 apps. 1 gl.*
Honours:
(Notts County) FL Div 3 Sth champs 1931.

DOYLE, Stephen Charles

Role: Midfield 1986-89
5'9" 11st.11lbs.
b. Port Talbot, Glamorgan, 2nd June 1958

CAREER: Preston North End app, pro June 1975/Huddersfield Town Sept 1982/ SUNDERLAND Sept 1986 £60,000/Hull City Aug 1989 £75,000/Rochdale Nov 1990-Mar 1995/ Chorley 1995, appointed caretaker-manager Nov 1996.

Debut v Ipswich Town (a) 20/9/1986

In a League career that totalled 626 appearances, Steve Doyle won promotion from the Third Division on three occasions and with three different clubs. A ball-winning midfield anchorman who made his debut for

Preston as a 16-year-old in November 1974, he was promoted with Preston in 1978, with Huddersfield in 1983 where perhaps he played his best football, and finally with Sunderland in 1988. Sold to The Lads by Terriers boss Mick Buxton for £60,000, Steve was a consistent enough performer as a regular during his three seasons at Roker Park, and came close to winning a full cap in 1986-87 when called up into the full Welsh squad for the match against Russia, but he did not gain a place in the team.

Appearances:
FL: 101(1) apps. 2 gls.
FAC: 5 apps. 0 gls.
FLC: 4 apps. 0 gls.
Other: 4 apps. 0 gls.
Total: *114(1) apps. 2 gls.*
Honours:
2 Welsh U-21 caps 1979, 1984 (the latter as an over-age player)/Wales Yth/(Sunderland) Div 3 champs 1988.

Steve Doyle

DUNCAN, Cameron

Role: Goalkeeper 1985-87
6'1" 11st.12lbs.
b. Shotts, 4th August 1965

CAREER: Shotts F.C. (Motherwell trial 1984)/ SUNDERLAND pro July 1984/Motherwell June 1987/Partick Thistle Oct 1989/Ayr United Mar 1991/Albion Rovers Nov 1996-98.

Debut v Grimsby Town (a) 22/3/1986

Briefly on trial with Motherwell before signing professional forms with Sunderland, Cammy Duncan won Scottish Youth honours whilst at Roker. Despite saving a penalty on his first team debut in a display showing great all-round confidence, he failed to establish himself at senior level and was given a free transfer in June 1987. A move back to Motherwell and his native Lanarkshire proved successful and two years on Partick Thistle paid a club record fee of £60,000 for his transfer.

Appearances:
FL: 1 app. 0 gls.
FLC: 2 apps. 0 gls.
Total: *3 apps. 0 gls.*
Honours:
Scot Yth 1984.

Cameron Duncan

DUNLOP, William

Role: Wing-half 1892-99
b. Annbank, Ayrshire

CAREER: Annbank FC/ SUNDERLAND Jan 1893/Rangers cs 1899/ Partick Thistle June 1900/Annbank FC Nov 1900.

Debut v Sheffield Wednesday (h) 28/1/1893

A most adaptable player mostly seen as a right-half at Sunderland, William Dunlop had a fair number of games on the opposite flank, and he could fill in as pivot or forward also. A similar story evolved in his Rangers season, appearing in all three half-back positions. Dunlop then moved to the newly-promoted Partick Thistle but stayed only a few months before returning to his native Annbank.

William Dunlop

Appearances:
FL: 134 apps. 6 gls.
FAC: 10 apps. 1 gl.
Total: *144 apps. 7 gls.*
Honours:
(Sunderland) FL champs 1895.

Note: *Sunderland FC had two William Dunlops: the player dealt with above and a trainer appointed in January 1922. The latter had been a player too, and a noted one - a Scottish cap who won four championship medals in Liverpool's cause.*

DUNN, Barry

Role: Winger 1979-82
5'8" 10st.5lbs.
b. Sunderland, 5th February 1952

CAREER: Tow Law Town/Bishop Auckland/ Blue Star/SUNDERLAND Sept 1979/Preston North End Oct 1981-Mar 1982/Darlington Aug 1982-May 1983.

Debut v Preston North End (h) 29/9/1979 (sub)

A former Gas Board servicing engineer who played weekend football for Wearside League club Blue Star, Barry Dunn was a latecomer to senior football at 27 years of age. A proposed move to Peterborough United, when he was 21, had fallen through when manager Noel Cantwell left the club before negotiations were completed. In Barry's first season at Roker Sunderland were just a point adrift of champions Leicester City, and won promotion to Division One. In 15(5) League appearances Dunn's busy style was often impressive in many of the campaign's emphatic victories. Subsequent management upheavals as top-flight football proved an uphill struggle saw Dunn out of the first team picture and he stepped down into Division Three in a £15,000 transfer to Preston in October 1981. Two months on, the manager who had signed him - Tommy Docherty - had been dismissed and new manager Gordon Lee released Barry before the season's close. A scoring debut for Darlington in Division Four marked his final season of League football in which he scored four goals in 16 appearances. These days Barry is still regularly watching Sunderland.

Appearances:
FL: 16(7) apps. 2 gls.
FLC: 2 apps. 0 gls.
Total: *18(7) apps. 2 gls.*

Barry Dunn

Len Duns

DUNS, Leonard

Role: Outside-right 1935-52
5'8" 11st.9lbs.
b. Newcastle upon Tyne, 26th September 1916
d. Ponteland, Northumberland, 20th April 1989

CAREER: Newcastle West End /
SUNDERLAND am Sept 1933, pro Oct 1933
(guested for Aldershot, Brentford, Newcastle
United, Notts County, Reading, West
Bromwich and Wrexham during WW2) /
retired June 1952.

Debut v Portsmouth (a) 2/11/1935

It is a somewhat odd fact that in the 20-year
inter-war period, after the departure of Jackie
Mordue and Bobby Best, the outside-right
berth was never properly filled by a really
consistent operator. Frankly, no other position
had so may aspirants. This was certainly not
due to unwillingness on the Wearsiders' part
to fork out the transfer fees. Donaldson,
Grimshaw, Wilks, Eden and Bert Davis all cost
appreciable fees at the time. Two further
developments from non-League sources, Jack
Prior and George Robinson, both left after four
years' Roker service to help Grimsby Town
and Charlton Athletic respectively in
successful promotion campaigns. Matters on
the right-wing at the outset of season 1935/36
were much the same as they had been since
the Great War ended. The man in possession,
Bert Davis, had arrived three years before, and
performed well enough without earning
eulogies like those reserved for Jimmy Connor
on the opposite flank. Then, three months into
the season, Len Duns, a young right-winger
from nearby Newcastle, got his League
blooding. He came in at a propitious moment.
The great Sunderland side of the mid-Thirties
had taken shape. The previous season
(1934/35) had seen them finish runners-up to
Arsenal. It was a combination containing
players who had established themselves fairly
recently such as young 'keeper Jimmy Thorpe,
the all-Scottish half-back line of Thomson,
Johnston and Hastings, plus youthful skipper,
Raich Carter. Duns had 17 League outings in
his inaugural 1935/36 season. Len could not
have timed it better for the Wearsiders walked
off with the League title, a hefty eight points
clear of runners-up Derby County, and he won
a championship medal at the age of 19. The
following campaign, 1936/37, with Duns an
acknowledged first-teamer and Davis

departed to Leicester, another trophy materialised. Sunderland won the FA Cup for the very first time, with Len occupying the outside-right position at Wembley. So, in his first two senior seasons and before reaching the age of 21 he had won the two most coveted domestic club honours. Len would have been the first to acknowledge the benefits he received from partnering a genius like Carter, and the promptings from his wing-half, the diminutive but sagacious Scot, Charlie Thomson. This is not to say Duns did not bring his own valuable contributions to the team's success. He possessed good attacking instincts aided by a handy physique. He knew where the opposing goal lay too. In the Cup-winning season he cracked in 21 goals in 44 League and FA Cup games, including five en route to Wembley, a splendid return for a winger. Len was almost 30 when peacetime soccer resumed after the Second World War. He had clocked up well over a hundred senior appearances for Sunderland before the outbreak, and was to double the figure by the time he retired six years later. It is pure speculation but he would surely have topped the 400 mark but for the war. A fine, durable servant, Sunderland was his only senior club although he guested for many others during the conflict.

Appearances:
FL: 215 apps. 45 gls.
FAC: 29 apps. 9 gls.
Total: *244 apps. 54 gls.*
Honours:
(Sunderland) FL champs 1936/FAC winner 1937.

EDEN, William

Role: Outside-right 1929-32
5'7" 10st.3lbs.
b. Stockton-on-Tees, 1st July 1905
d. Darlington, November 1993

CAREER: Loftus Albion/Darlington Mar 1928/SUNDERLAND Oct 1929 £1,250/ Darlington Nov 1932 £500/Tranmere Rovers Mar 1935 (guested for New Brighton and Crewe Alexandra during WW2, and retired before peace returned).

Debut v Newcastle United (h) 19/10/1929

Billy Eden was well-known to North-East soccer fans between the wars. A nippy little right-winger with a scoring touch, in his first full League season, 1928/29, he topped Darlington's list netting 11 goals in 30 appearances. He spent three years at Sunderland - the best of which was season 1930-31 - without fully establishing himself in what was something of a on-going problem role at the club. It turned out, however, he was not confined to one position, in the 'Thirties taking the inside berth and, in Tranmere's title-winning 1937/38 line-up, often played outside-left. Apart from football Billy performed in a dance band.

Appearances:
FL: 60 apps. 18 gls.
FAC: 11 apps. 3 gls.
Total: *71 apps. 21 gls.*
Honours:
(Tranmere Rovers) FL Div 3 Nth champs 1938.

Billy Eden

EDGAR, Daniel

Role: Left-half 1931-35
5'9" 11st.5lbs.
b. Jarrow, Co Durham, 3rd April 1910
d. Jarrow, Co Durham, 23rd March 1991

CAREER: Jarrow St Bede's/SUNDERLAND am May 1930, pro Aug 1930 (Walsall loan Nov 1930-May 1931)/Nottingham Forest June 1935/retired through injury 1938.

Debut v Bolton Wanderers (h) 19/3/1932

Dan Edgar would likely have been kept by Sunderland but for the proliferation of budding wing-half talent (Alex Hastings, Chas. Thomson et al.). As it was Forest acquired a player of marked versatility, deservedly a prime favourite at Trent Bridge. The crowd doted on his crisp tackling, stamina and kicking power (he spent much time there at right-

Dan Edgar

back as well as right-half). Cartilage trouble caused Dan's untimely retiral, this type of injury a common ender of careers then. He had originally been a shipyard worker.

Appearances:
FL: 43 apps. 0 gls.
FAC: 3 apps. 0 gls.
Total: *46 apps. 0 gls.*

EDGAR, James Henry

Role: Outside-right 1905-06
b. Birtley, Co Durham, 1882

CAREER: Birtley FC/SUNDERLAND Dec 1905/Birtley Aug 1906/Hebburn Argyle Oct 1906/Birtley Jan 1907.

Debut v Bolton Wanderers (a) 17/2/1906

Winger James Edgar was briefly in the League limelight before returning to the comparative obscurity of Northern Alliance etc football. Both his outings with Sunderland resulted in heavy away defeats (not necessarily Edgar's fault, of course!). In the Bolton Wanderers debut above the Wearsiders lost 6-2 and at Manchester on 21st April 1906 City won 5-1.

Appearances:
FL: 2 apps. 0 gls.
Total: *2 apps. 0 gls.*

ELLIOTT

Role: Right/left-back
1884-87
Debut v Redcar (a) 8/11/1884 (FAC)

An early Sunderland defender who participated in the club's first-ever FA Cup-tie, playing at left-back.

Elliott

In the three Cup ties of 1886/87 he appeared at right-back, revealing two-footed adaptability. His appearances during his time with the club were mostly on the right flank.

Appearances:
FAC: 4 apps. 0 gls.
Total: *4 apps. 0 gls.*

ELLIOTT, David

Role: Left-half 1963-67
5'9" 11st.3lbs.
b. Tantobie, Co Durham, 10th February 1945

CAREER: Co Durham Schools/Wallsend Corinthians (Gateshead am circa 1960)/ SUNDERLAND app 1961, pro Feb 1962/ Newcastle United Dec 1966 £10,000/Southend United Jan 1971/Newport County player-manager Apr 1975-Feb 1976/Bangor City player-manager 1977/Newport County Oct

David Elliott

1978/Bangor City player-manager late 1978-
Oct 1984/subsequently had spells as coach
with Cardiff City and manager of Caernarfon
Town.

Debut v Derby County (h) 22/2/1964

David Elliott made his debut in the 1963/64
promotion season, aged 19, moving on to
neighbouring Newcastle nearly three years
later. Regular first team football came with a
further transfer, this time to Southend, where
he played 190 League and Cup games plus
four substitutions. There followed a round of
Welsh clubs in playing, managerial and
coaching capacities. Dave was an incisive
wing-half, strong in defence and a full 90-
minute man. After leaving school he had
worked as a motor mechanic prior to taking
up football full time.

Appearances:
FL: 30(1) apps. 1 gl.
FAC: 4 apps. 0 gls.
FLC: 1 app. 0 gls.
Total: *35(1) apps. 1 gl.*

ELLIOTT, Shaun

Role: Central Defender 1976-86
6'0" 11st.6lbs.
b. Haltwhistle, 26th January 1957

CAREER: Haydon Bridge/SUNDERLAND
app Jan 1974, pro Jan 1975(Seattle Sounders,
USA loan May-Aug 1981)/Norwich City Aug
1986/Blackpool Aug 1988/Colchester United
Mar 1991/Gateshead Aug 1992/Bishop
Auckland Aug 1993/Whitley Bay Mar 1995/
Durham City.

Debut v Wrexham (a) 12/1/1977 (FAC 3r)

Fair-haired Shaun Elliott was one of several
younger players thrown into the deep end by
manager Jimmy Adamson in mid-season 1976-
77. Alert and mobile, he combined pace and
skill with an acute positional sense and an
assured touch on the ball. From the time of his
debut - made when he was a fortnight away
from his 20th birthday - Shaun
remained an almost automatic
selection and in a decade of
loyal service recorded in
excess of 300 League
appearances. Combining
brilliantly in central defence
with Jeff Clarke in one of the

Shaun Elliott

club's best-ever backline pairings, he missed only one match in the 1979-80 promotion season during which Sunderland remained unbeaten at home. One of his trio of England 'B' caps came against Spain in a match staged at Roker Park in 1980. Shaun's lowest ebb with The Lads was his acute disappointment in 1984-85 when suspension robbed him of his hard-earned Wembley place in the League Cup Final against Norwich City. Then at the outset of what would have been his testimonial season, Lawrie McMenemy sold him to Norwich, for a fee in the region of £150,000. A catalogue of injuries restricted his League appearances to a modest 29(2) in two

seasons at Carrow Road, and he spent his final two seasons of senior football with Blackpool. He assisted Colchester United to win the GM Vauxhall Conference title in season 1991-92, but left them in the close season for a homeward move to Gateshead.

Appearances:
FL: 316(5) apps. 11 gls.
FAC: 14 apps. 0 gls.
FLC: 28 apps. 0 gls.
Total: *358(5) apps. 11 gls.*
Honours:
3 Eng 'B' apps. 1979-81/(Colchester United)
GMVC champs 1992.

ELLIOTT, William Henry

Role: Outside-left/left-back/left-half
1953-59
5'7" 11st.2lbs.
b. Bradford, 20th March 1925

CAREER: Bradford Schools/Yorkshire Schools/Bradford am 1939-40, pro Mar 1942/Burnley Aug 1951 £23,000/ SUNDERLAND June 1953 £26,000/ Wisbech Town July 1959-1961/Libyan national coach Oct 1961-1963/Sheffield Wednesday scout 1963-1964/US Forces (Germany) coach 1964-1966/Daring FC (Brussels) trainer July 1966/Sunderland coach Jan 1968-June 1973/Brann FC (Norway) coach 1974-1978/Sunderland caretaker manager Dec 1978-May 1979/ Darlington manager June 1979-June 1983.

Debut v Charlton Athletic (a) 19/8/1953

Billy Elliott was a top class left-winger with left flank versatility - he appeared at left-half when still at Park Avenue and with Sunderland, from November 1956 onwards, was often at left-back. He made his senior debut for Bradford when only 15 at half-back, eventually moving to outside-left with enormous success. Billy scored the historic goal for Bradford at Highbury that saw mighty Arsenal crash out of the FA Cup third round in January 1948. He first asked for a transfer in November 1950. It was refused and the request repeated several times before Burnley, then a well-established Division One outfit, paid a big

fee for him. It was while at Turf Moor that all his representative honours but one accrued (the exception a 1954/55 appearance against the Irish League, when a Sunderland player.) Indeed, he scored three times in his five England outings. A fast, determined, tough performer. After giving up playing Billy had a most varied footballing managerial and coaching career both at home and abroad. Besides being varied it was also lengthy and all but continuous over a span of 22 years. He was Sunderland's trainer when the Cup was won in 1973, having briefly been caretaker-manager earlier in the season, and in 1979 was in charge as caretaker for 23 games, winning 13 and narrowly missing out on promotion. In retirement he settled in Sunderland but more recently suffered a suspected heart attack when a guest of manager Peter Reid at the Stadium of Light in 1999. Happily he was back watching The Lads before the season ended.

Appearances:
FL: 193 apps. 23 gls.
FAC: 19 apps. 3 gls.
Total: *212 apps. 26 gls.*
Honours: *5 Eng caps/4 FL apps.*

ELLIS, William Thomas

Role: Outside-left 1919-28
5'9" 11st.4lbs.
b. Wolverhampton, 5th November 1895
d. Sunderland, 18th November 1939

CAREER: Highfield Villa/Willenhall Swifts/
Bilston Juniors/Hickman's Works FC
(Birmingham Works League)/SUNDERLAND
Mar 1919/Birmingham Nov 1927/Lincoln City
Aug 1929/York City Nov 1930-Jan 1931/Blyth
Spartans May 1931, retired 1932.

Debut v Middlesbrough (a) 6/3/1920

In 1922, when the player was getting
established, a critic wrote that Bill Ellis
"...with proper
training has soon
developed into an
exceedingly clever
winger, and today
is a most valuable
asset". And he
went on to say he
was a tricky and
crafty dribbler,
with a rare turn
of speed, and
many of his
dandy crosses
have meant goals
for Buchan. Over
some four
seasons he had a
noted left-wing
partnership
with 'Tricky'
Hawes, and
Hawes too
could thank
him for

W. ELLIS

supplying chances. In his
Birmingham spell his League and FA Cup
appearances totalled 35 (8 goals), at Lincoln 33
(12 goals) and at York two (1 goal). His son,
Billy jnr., a Dorking schoolmaster, played for
Dorking FC and assisted Sunderland reserves
on occasion.

Appearances:
FL: 192 apps. 31 gls.
FAC: 10 apps. 0 gls.
Total: *202 apps. 31 gls.*
Honours:
1 FL app.

ELLISON, Raymond

Role: Full-back 1972-74
5'7" 11st.6lbs.
b. Newcastle upon Tyne, 31st December 1950

CAREER: Newcastle United app, pro Oct
1968/SUNDERLAND Mar 1973/Torquay
United July 1974/Workington July
1975/Gateshead United Feb 1977/Tow Law
Town/Whitley Bay player-coach June
1980/Alnwick Town manager Nov 1983-84.

Debut v Oxford United (h) 3/10/1973

Signed for £10,000
from Newcastle
United as full-back
cover in 1972-73,
the year of
Sunderland's
FA Cup
triumph,
Ellison made
two
consecutive
senior
appearances
shortly after
his arrival at
Roker. He was

Ray Ellison

exclusively in reserve during
1973-74 and when released on a free
transfer in the close season he travelled
south to join Fourth Division Torquay
United. Released after one season at
Plainmoor he returned north to sign for
Workington. Ray's first two goals in senior
football, in 37 appearances, in 1975-76 could
not prevent the Reds from the ignominy of
bottom place in Division Four and a re-
election application. His penalty goal in the
opening fixture of 1976-77 was sufficient to
ensure a winning start against Crewe
Alexandra, but Workington then failed to win
another match until New Year's Day. Prior to
their almost inevitable demise as a League
outfit, Ellison himself stepped into non-League
circles with Gateshead United. After leaving
football he became a meat wholesaler.

Appearances:
FL: 2 apps. 0 gls.
Total: *2 apps. 0 gls.*

ELLISON, Samuel Walter

Role: Outside-right 1946-47
5'9" 11st.3lbs.
b. Leadgate, Co Durham, 27th April 1923
d. Isle of Wight, December 1994

CAREER: Middlesbrough Crusaders/
SUNDERLAND Oct 1945/Consett circa 1947/
Reading June 1949-1950.

Debut v Blackpool (a) 18/1/1947

Sam Ellison's complement of League outings
for Sunderland occurred in the January and
February of 1947. The run started with a
thumping 5-0 victory at Blackpool. The others
were another away win (2-1 at Blackburn) and
a goalless draw at home against Portsmouth.
In his Reading season Ellison made four
Southern Section appearances.

Appearances:
FL: 3 apps. 0 gls.
Total: *3 apps. 0 gls.*

ENTWISTLE, Wayne Peter

Role: Forward 1977-80
5'11" 11st.8lbs.
b. Bury, Lancs, 6th August 1958

CAREER: Bury app, pro Aug 1976/
SUNDERLAND Nov 1977/Leeds United Oct
1979/Blackpool Nov 1980/Crewe Alexandra
Mar 1982/Wimbledon July 1982/Grays
Athletic Feb 1983/Bury Aug 1983/Carlisle
United June 1985/Bolton Wanderers Oct 1985
(Burnley loan Aug 1986)/Stockport County
Oct 1986/Bury n.c. Aug 1988/Wigan Athletic
Oct 1988/Altrincham/Hartlepool United n.c.
Sept 1989.

ENGLAND, Ernest

Role: Left-back 1919-30
5'8" 11st.6lbs.
b. Shirebrook, Derbyshire, 3rd February 1901
*d. Radcliffe-on-Trent, Notts, 22nd February
1982*

CAREER: Forester's FC (works side)/
Shirebrook FC cs 1919/SUNDERLAND
Dec 1919 £100/West Ham United Oct 1930
£500/Mansfield Town June 1931 £350/
Frickley Colliery Aug 1935/Mansfield
Town asst. trainer Aug 1936/Notts County
asst. trainer May 1937, trainer June 1938-
Aug 1944.

Debut v Manchester City (a) 27/12/1919

Ernie England was a major figure in the
1920s: resolute, busy and unusually grim-
visaged, an ideal foil to the cool, more
stylish positional ploys of Warney
Cresswell and Bill Murray. A no-nonsense
full-back straight from the 'take no
prisoners' mould of that era, he gave
Sunderland a decade of devoted, consistent
service. Actually right-footed, he had asked
to take the left-back position at school
(when promising enough to earn England
trials). Ernie once explained: "It suited me
to go on the side of the weaker foot. I could
collect corners better, and I'd clear upfield
towards centre - and I could tackle the

centre-forward better too". He also
developed a formidable - and noted - right-
legged sliding tackle, perfectly timed. Ernie
made his League debut at 18, after only a
couple of games with the reserves, and
once he became the
regular left-back the
following season,
1920/21, it was the
start of an impressive
run that lasted
throughout the 1920's.
He later had a
miserable six months
at West Ham,
separated from his
family, and
contemplated
retirement. However,
Mansfield Town,
newly elected to the
Football League,
offered an
engagement and
Ernie played 137
League and FA Cup
game for the Stags from 1931/32 to '34/35
inclusive. All in all a quite admirable club
man.

LAMUERT & BUTLER'S CIGARETTES

E. ENGLAND (SUNDERLAND)

Appearances:
FL: 335 apps. 0 gls.
FAC: 16 apps. 0 gls.
Total: *351 apps. 0 gls.*

Wayne Entwistle

Debut v Charlton Athletic (a) 3/12/1977 (scored)

Former England Youth international Wayne Entwistle joined Sunderland from Bury for £30,000. The fair-haired striker scored on his debut, but failed to hold down a first team place in his initial season. He did much better in the following term 1978/79 with 34(2) appearances, scoring 11 League goals including the one which complemented Gary Rowell's hat-trick in a memorable 4-1 win at Newcastle. He linked again with his former boss, Jimmy Adamson, when he left Roker to join Leeds United, but found little success at Elland Road, leaving on a free transfer after 13 months to join Third Division Blackpool. There then followed a succession of moves around the lower divisions, a second spell with hometown club Bury his most productive - 21 goals in 45 appearances in 1984-85 being a significant contribution to the Shakers' promotion from Division Four. Wayne's final League career encompassed twelve clubs, 280(49) appearances and 81 goals.

Appearances:
FL: 43(2) apps. 13 gls.
FAC: 4(1) apps. 1 gl.
FLC: 2 apps. 0 gls.
Total: *49(3) apps. 14 gls.*
Honours:
Eng Yth.

ERIKSSON, Jan

Role: Defender 1997-98
6'0" 13st.0lbs.
b. Sundsvall, Sweden, 24th August 1967

CAREER: GIF Sundsvall/IFK Sundsvall/AIK Stockholm 1986/IFK Norrkoping 1990-91 (trials with Newcastle United and Tottenham Hotspur in 1991)/IFC Kaiserslautern, Germany cs 1992 (loaned to a Japanese J League side, also to AIK Stockholm and Servette FC, Geneva, Switzerland) /Helsingborgs IF, Sweden 1996/ SUNDERLAND Jan 1997/Tampa Bay Mutiny, USA Jan 1998.

Debut v Aston Villa (a) 1/2/1997

Jan Eriksson spent a frustrating year with Sunderland, in which he made one senior appearance at Aston Villa, shortly after his £250,000 transfer from Helsingborgs IF. In addition to being booked on his debut, Aston Villa's winner was a Savo Milosevic strike helped by a slight deflection from the hapless Eriksson. Having joined Sunderland in the Swedish close season, he was lacking match fitness, but his spell in the Reserves became permanent, as Melville and Ord, with Howey

Jan Eriksson

as deputy, dominated the central defensive duties. Originally signed on a two-and-a-half year contract, Eriksson was linked with a possible return to Helsingborgs in April 1997. The holder of 35 international caps for his country, the right-sided defender made his full international debut in February 1990 at the age of 22. He helped Sweden to the semi-finals of Euro '92, scoring twice in the tournament, against England and France. In his second season in the Bundesliga, Eriksson assisted Kaiserslautern to the runners-up position in the League championship.

Appearances:
FL: 1 app. 0 gls.
Total: *1 app. 0 gls.*
Honours:
18 Swedish U-18 apps./15 Swedish U-21 apps./35 Swedish caps 1990-94.

ERSKINE, W.

Role: Outside-right 1885-87
Debut v Redcar (a)
24/10/1885 (FAC)

Sunderland's first choice outside-right from the tail end of season 1884/85 until the end of November

W Erskine

1887. Erskine had a fair scoring record for a winger, enjoying a particularly fruitful period at the commencement of the 1886/87 term, scoring in each of the first four engagements.

Appearances:
FAC: 4 apps. 1 gl.
Total: *4 apps. 1 gl.*

EVANS, John

Role: Inside-left 1954-55
b. Hetton-le-Hole,
Co Durham, 21st October
1932

CAREER: Junior football to Norwich City Oct 1949/SUNDERLAND Aug 1954/Chesterfield May 1956-1957.

John Evans

Debut v Portsmouth (a) 11/9/1954

A free transfer signing whose sole senior game for the Wearsiders was also the sum total of his League appearances. For he did not get an opportunity at either Norwich or Chesterfield (which was a free transfer move too). Evans could also take the centre-forward position.

Appearances:
FL: 1 app. 0 gls.
Total: *1 app. 0 gls.*

FAIRLEY, Thomas

Role: Goalkeeper 1952-53
5'10" 12st.0lbs.
b. Houghton-le-Spring, Co Durham, 12th October 1932

CAREER: Bankhead Juniors/SUNDERLAND Oct 1951/Carlisle United May 1956/ Hartlepool United June 1959/Cambridge City Aug 1960.

Debut v Stoke City (a) 28/3/1953

Tom Fairley experienced an unfortunate League baptism with Sunderland: successive heavy away defeats at Stoke and Bolton, the scores being 3-0 and 5-0 respectively. Tom did not get another League outing until his move to Carlisle, where he saw a fair amount of Northern Section action (56 FL appearances), largely in the 1956/57 season. His year at Hartlepool was confined to their reserve team.

Appearances:
FL: 2 apps. 0 gls.
Total: *2 apps. 0 gls.*

Tom Fairley

FALL, William

Role: Left-half 1924-25
5'9" 11st.7lbs.
b. Tyne Dock, Northumberland, 3rd qtr 1900

CAREER: Tyne Dock FC/SUNDERLAND am Aug 1923, pro Aug 1924/West Stanley Oct 1925.

Debut v Preston North End (h) 3/9/1924

William Fall deputised for the ubiquitous Arthur Andrews in three consecutive Football League fixtures early in season 1924/25, his other appearances being right at the end, the last match but one. It was at West Ham and Fall played inside-left. He actually received his League baptism only eight days after joining the paid ranks.

Appearances:
FL: 4 apps. 0 gls.
Total: *4 apps. 0 gls.*

FARQUHAR, James William

Role: Half-back/forward 1898-1907
5'7" 11st.5lbs.
b. Elgin, Morayshire, 1879

CAREER: Elgin City/ SUNDERLAND Jan 1899/retired May 1907.

William Farquhar

Debut v Sheffield Wednesday (a) 18/2/1899

Described in 1902 as a "Sunderland reserve, one of the handymen. Can play a good game anywhere except goal." High praise this last sentence but the handiness was not proven over Farquhar's eight and a half years in a Sunderland jersey. However, he did take both wing-half and all three inside-forward berths in the League side, with a predominance of appearances at right-half. And he did become something more than a reserve as a regular selection from 1903-1906 inclusive. Unluckily for Farquhar, a first team place came just too late for a 1902 championship medal.

Appearances:
FL: 187 apps. 18 gls.
FAC: 8 apps. 0 gls.
Total: *195 apps. 18 gls.*

FEENAN, John Joseph

Role: Right/left-back 1936-39
5'10" 11st.4lbs.
b. Newry, Co. Down, 1st July 1914
d. Gloucester, October 1994

CAREER: Junior football/Belfast Celtic/
SUNDERLAND Aug 1936 £2,000/returned to
Ireland during WW2 and retired before peace
was established.

Debut v Brentford (h) 19/9/1936

A nicely built Irishman, John Feenan was an
excellent stand-in for either John Gorman or
Alex Hall. He did not, however, really break
into the senior side - it was the peak 1930's
period when League and Cup honours
accrued. Both of Freeman's Republic of Ireland
caps, though, were gained in his Roker Park
days. He appeared against France and
Switzerland.

> **Appearances:**
> *FL: 28 apps. 0 gls.*
> *FAC: 1 app. 0 gls.*
> **Total:** *29 apps. 0 gls.*
> **Honours:**
> *2 Eire caps 1937.*

John Feenan

FERGUSON, Derek

Role: Midfield 1993-95
5'8" 11st.12lbs.
b. Glasgow, 31st July 1967

CAREER: Blue Star/Burbank Boys' Club/
Gartcosh United/Rangers Aug 1983(Dundee
loan Jan 1990)/Heart of Midlothian Aug 1990/
SUNDERLAND July 1993/Falkirk Sept 1995/
Dunfermline Athletic July 1998-May 1999.

Debut v Derby County (a) 14/8/1993

Scottish international midfielder Derek
Ferguson was brought to Roker from Heart of
Midlothian by former Rangers team mate
Terry Butcher. A fee of £460,000 changed
hands plus John Colquhoun, who returned to
Tynecastle. Three years earlier, Hearts paid a
record £750,000 for the stylish midfield
provider who began with Rangers as a 17-
year-old and enjoyed six successful campaigns
at Ibrox until restricted by a shoulder injury
and competition from midfielders of the
calibre of Ray Wilkins and Graeme Souness.

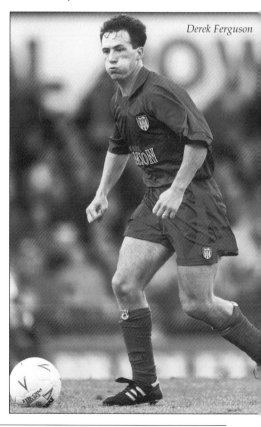

Derek Ferguson

Fortunate to escape serious injury in a car crash with three other Sunderland players in August 1993, when returning home from a pre-season testimonial game at Middlesbrough, Ferguson was able to line up with his new team mates for the season's opener at Derby County. Surviving a 5-0 hammering at the Baseball Ground - Sunderland's worst ever opening day performance - he completed 41 League appearances in his first season, but injuries curtailed his total to 23 in 1994-95. Transferred for £150,000 to Falkirk in September 1995 Ferguson suffered relegation from the Premier Division in his first season at Brockville, and in mid-term 1996-97 a serious knee injury saw him sidelined for the remainder of the season. After three seasons with Falkirk, in the last of which he made only four substitute appearances, Derek departed Brockville Park to join Dunfermline Athletic of the Scottish Premier League. It proved an unhappy season for the Pars, who won only four of their 32 League games and were relegated. Inevitably, the list of players released was lengthy, and Ferguson was amongst those forced to seek pastures new.

Appearances:
FL: 64 apps. 0 gls.
FAC: 6 apps. 1 gl.
FLC: 3 apps. 0 gls.
Other: 2 apps. 0 gls.
Total: *75 apps. 1 gl.*
Honours:
Scot Sch/Scot Yth/5 Scot U-21 apps. 1986-89/2 Scot caps 1988/(Rangers) SPL champs 1987 & 1989/SLC winner 1987, 1988, 1989.

FERGUSON, Matthew

Role: Right-half 1896-1902
5'7" 11st.4lbs.
b. Bellshill, Glasgow, circa 1873
d. Sunderland, 12th June 1902

CAREER: Bellshill Hawthorn/Mossend Brigade/SUNDERLAND May 1896 to his death.

Debut v Bury (h) 1/9/1896

Not long before his sudden and untimely death at the age of 29, Matthew Ferguson was described as one of the neatest half-backs around and a strong candidate for an international cap. Such an honour would have

been appropriate. He had been given a League opportunity at the earliest possible moment, was an ever-present in this initial season, and held first team status with considerable distinction from then on, winning a championship medal in 1902. Matthew made his debut at inside-right, moving to right-half for his second match and keeping the position until the end of season 1901/02.

Appearances:
FL: 171 apps. 5 gls.
FAC: 11 apps. 0 gls.
Total: *182 apps. 5 gls.*
Honours:
Scot Jnr int/(Sunderland) FL champs 1902.

Matthew Ferguson

FERGUSON, Robert Gibson

Role: Wing-half 1922-25
5'9" 11st.2lbs.
b. Blythswood, Glasgow, 5th January 1902

CAREER: Battlefield Juniors, Queen's Park Junior side (guest player for Third Lanark during WW1)/Cambuslang Rangers July 1920 (Falkirk trial Aug 1921)/SUNDERLAND Aug 1921, originally trial/Middlesbrough Jan 1925

Bob Ferguson

(Crystal Palace trial Sept 1932, Barrow trial Oct-Dec 1932)/Northwich Victoria player/ manager July 1933/Peterborough United.

Debut v Newcastle United (h) 11/11/1922

Although Ferguson had a nodding acquaintance with the pivotal role, almost all his League outings with Sunderland were at wing-half, and most of them on the right. At Middlesbrough, however, he played centre-half, earning a couple of championship medals in the process. All told he made 159 League and FA Cup appearances for the 'Boro. A steady player and a good team man, Bob Ferguson was the son of a Glasgow policeman. A brother played for Third Lanark, and another, Harry, was Glasgow Junior Registration Secretary.

Appearances:
FL: 30 apps. 1 gl.
FAC: 4 apps. 0 gls.
Total: *34 apps. 1 gl.*
Honours:
(Middlesbrough) FL Div 2 champs 1927, 1929.

FINLAY, John

Role: Inside-right 1946-47
b. Birtley, Co. Durham, 16th February 1919
d. Co. Cleveland, 5th March 1985

CAREER: Ouston Juniors/SUNDERLAND May 1938-1947 (guest player for Carlisle United 1939/40).

Debut v Charlton Athletic (a) 11/9/1946

Like Dickie Davis, John Finlay joined Sunderland shortly before the war and, as a consequence, had to wait until 1946 for his League bow. However, unlike Davis (a 150-plus appearance man) the debut was his sole senior game. A dispiriting one also - Charlton won 5-0.

Appearances:
FL: 1 app. 0 gls.
Total: *1 app. 0 gls.*

FINNEY, Thomas

Role: Midfield 1974-76
5'11" 11st.8lbs.
b. Belfast, 6th November 1952

CAREER: Crusaders/Luton Town Aug 1973/ SUNDERLAND July 1974/Cambridge United Aug 1976/Brentford Feb 1984/Cambridge United Dec 1984/Cambridge City July 1986/ Ely City/March Town/Histon Town.

Debut v Bolton Wanderers (h) 21/9/1974 (sub)

Tom Finney made an explosive start to his League career, scoring twice in his first full appearance for Luton, and once in each of his next three matches. The Hatters won promotion to Division One (as runners-up to Middlesbrough) but Finney was allowed to join Sunderland in the close season. He made only one appearance in the starting line-up during his first season at Roker. Nevertheless, he made his full international debut in the close season and scored Northern Ireland's winner against Wales in only his second appearance for his country. In Sunderland's promotion campaign of 1975-76 he made seven League and five Cup appearances, scoring the goal which disposed of Hull City in the fourth round of the FA Cup. Transferred to Cambridge United for £50,000 in August 1976 Finney appeared in 332 League matches, and scored 61 goals for them in two spells, broken only by a brief stay with Brentford. He remains Cambridge United's most capped player, winning seven of his 15 Northern Ireland caps whilst at the Abbey Stadium. Tom, who married a Sunderland girl, now works for a security firm.

Appearances:
FL: 8(7) apps. 1 gl.
FAC: 6 apps. 1 gl.
Total: *14(7) apps. 2 gls.*
Honours:
15 NIre caps 1975-80/
(Cambridge United) Div 4
champs 1977.

Tom Finney

FLEMING, Charles 'Legs' or 'Cannonball'

Role: Centre/inside-forward 1954-58
5'11" 11st.10lbs.
b. Blairhall, Fife, 12th July 1927
d. 15th August 1997

CAREER: Blairhall Colliery/East Fife 1947/
SUNDERLAND June 1955 £7,000 plus Tommy
Wright/Bath City July 1958/Trowbridge Town
manager to Sept 1965/Hakoah (Sydney,
Australia) coach 1971-Oct 1972.

Debut v Blackpool (a) 5/2/1955

Charlie Fleming

An unusual, maybe
unique, case of a
player with two well-
known nicknames,
both stemming from
noticeable traits.
'Legs' from a
distinctive galloping
action and
'Cannonball' for the
ferocity and power of
his famed shooting.
Charlie was a major
contributor to East
Fife's post-war Cup
success, continuing a
rich scoring vein after
arriving at Roker Park, not least in the
reaching of the 1955 and 1956 FA Cup semi-
finals. Indeed, his first goals for the club were
a brace in a 2-1 win at Newcastle in February
1955 and he struck 32 goals in 1955/56 and
followed up with 27 the next season. In his
non-League foray with Bath City, Fleming
notched 44 goals in their 1959/60 Southern
League championship winning campaign.
Prior to his retirement, when he settled in the
village of Oakley near Dunfermline in his
native Fifeshire, Charlie held coaching
appointments in America and Canada. He
died on the day the Stadium of Light hosted
its first League game.

Appearances:
FL: 107 apps. 62 gls.
FAC: 15 apps. 9 gls.
Total: *122 apps. 71 gls.*
Honours:
1 Scot cap/Rest of Gt Britain v Wales
1951/(East Fife) SL Div 'B' champs 1948/SC
finalist 1950/SLC winner 1950, 1954.

Ambrose Fogarty

FOGARTY, Ambrose Gerald

Role: Inside-forward 1957-64
5'7" 11st.0lbs.
b. Dublin, 11th September 1933

CAREER: Home Farm/Bohemians (Dublin)/
Glentoran pro 1955/SUNDERLAND Oct 1957
£3,000/Hartlepools United Nov 1963 £10,000/
Cork Hibernian player-manager to mid-season
1968-69/Cork Celtic player-manager
1969/Drumcondra manager early 1971/
Athlone Town manager 1974-75 mid-season-
March 1996.

Debut v Birmingham City (a) 9/11/1957

A talented Republic of Ireland international,
Ambrose Fogarty possessed excellent utility
value. Mainly an inside-forward, he could also
take either wing and lead the attack. At
Sunderland he played in both inside-forward
berths and outside-right. Ambrose, slimly built
and a forager, had a nose for goalscoring

opportunities as his statistics show. He was a development of that famous nursery, Home Farm, in his native Eire, graduating in familiar sequence to the Dublin club, Bohemians. With the Bohs he experienced League of Ireland football, scoring eight goals in that competition before crossing the border to turn professional for Glentoran. He played inside-right for the Glens in the Irish Cup final of 1956, a long drawn out affair that required two replays before Distillery emerged as winners. Fogarty's time with Sunderland started early in the 1957/58 season that brought relegation gloom to Roker Park for the first time. In the six years before top-flight football returned, he won ten of his 11 Eire caps, the first against West Germany in May 1960. He was, of course, an international team mate of club colleague and skipper, the great Charlie Hurley. Ambrose made 24 League appearances in that initial season but in the next - the club's first-ever in Division Two - only three. Thereafter he played much first team football, missing only one game in 1960/61, the season that began the climb back to the First Division.

Alan Foggon

It was also the season in which the League Cup was launched and Fogarty scored in Sunderland's first ever tie - a 4-3 defeat at Brentford. In his last full term 1962/63, he shared the inside-forward berths with George Herd and Johnny Crossan, who filled those places in the 1964 promotion line-up. His penultimate move involving an English club mildly surprised the football world. No great distance in miles - just down the coast to Hartlepool - yet in soccer terms from marble halls to labourer's cottage. Hartlepools United had always been a cinderella outfit, invariably anchored in the lowest reaches of the League and often forced to seek re-election (once five times in a row). Yet here they were expending their top fee of £10,000 - a record which stood for 22 years - on an international aged 30 but with enough steam left to stir the populace. Ambrose did a good job for Hartlepools. He played in 127 League matches, scoring 22 goals and won his final Republic of Ireland cap and, in so doing, became the club's one and only international. Ambrose later returned to Eire for 25 years of managerial work that included a lengthy spell in charge of Athlone Town.

Appearances:
FL: 152 apps. 37 gls.
FAC: 12 apps. 3 gls.
FLC: 10 apps. 4 gls.
Total: *174 apps. 44 gls.*
Honours:
11 Eire caps/(Glentoran) IC finalist 1956.

FOGGON, Alan

Role: Forward 1976-77
b. West Pelton, Co Durham, 23rd February 1950

CAREER: Newcastle United app Aug 1965, pro Nov 1967/Cardiff City Aug 1971/ Middlesbrough Oct 1972/Rochester Lancers, NASL, Apr 1976/Hartford Bi-Centennials, NASL, June 1976/Manchester United July 1976/SUNDERLAND Sept 1976/Southend United June 1977(Hartlepool United loan Feb 1978)/Consett Aug 1978/Whitley Bay.
Debut v West Ham United (a) 25/9/1976

Probably the most remarkable feature of Alan Foggon's brief stay at Roker Park was the fact he served under three different managers in ten months. Bob Stokoe, Ian MacFarlane (as caretaker) and Jimmy Adamson were the trio who were unable to prevent Sunderland from dropping out of Division One. After a handful of first team appearances, two of which were made against his previous club Manchester United, Foggon who looked overweight and woefully out of touch, departed to Southend in a general close season clear-out. At the outset of his career he won England Youth honours when he burst onto the scene at Newcastle in the late Sixties. Characterised by his flowing locks, shirt worn outside his shorts and socks around his ankles, Foggon was an exciting forward, pacy and direct with an eye for goal. One of a fairly select band of players to have represented the North-East's 'Big Three' undoubtedly his best days were at Middlesbrough. He was their leading goalscorer with 19 in 41 League appearances in the 1973-74 Division Two championship side and was similarly successful in Division One the following term with 16 League and two FA Cup goals. His career aggregate figures were a commendable 220(24) League appearances and 62 goals, but the fact he was a non-League player at 28 years of age suggests his potential was not fully realised. Alan is presently employed as a security manager in Jarrow.

Appearances:
FL: 7(1) apps. 0 gls.
FAC: 2 apps. 0 gls.
Total: *9(1) apps. 0 gls.*
Honours:
Eng Yth 1968/(Newcastle United) ICFC winner 1969/(Middlesbrough) FL Div 2 champs 1974.

FORD, Anthony

Role: Winger/Midfield 1984-85
5'9" 12st.7lbs.
b. Grimsby, 14th May 1959

CAREER: Grimsby Town app July 1975, pro May 1977(SUNDERLAND loan Mar 1986)/ Stoke City July 1986/West Bromwich Albion Mar 1989/Grimsby Town Nov 1991(Bradford City loan Sept 1993)/Scunthorpe United player-coach Aug 1994/Barrow Aug 1996/ Mansfield Town player-coach Oct 1996, appointed asst. manager cs 1998/ Rochdale asst. manager June 1999.

Debut v Bradford City (h) 29/3/1985 (sub) (scored)

Tony Ford joined his local team, Grimsby

Tony Ford

Town, as an apprentice in July 1975. In October of the same year he became the youngest-ever Grimsby player to make a full League appearance at 16 years and 164 days. He began as a winger but was equally at home in midfield or as an out-and-out striker, in which role he scored 16 League goals in 1978-79, when promotion from Division Four was secured. Placed on the Mariners' transfer list after 408 appearances and 62 goals in eleven seasons, he joined Sunderland on two months' loan, just prior to the transfer deadline in March 1986. Despite a goalscoring debut, from the substitutes' bench, he was not signed permanently after his loan spell, and Stoke City paid £35,000 for his transfer in the close season. After three successful terms in the Potteries his value had increased to £145,000, when West Bromwich Albion signed him in March 1989. Released into non-League football by Scunthorpe United at the age of 37 in the close season of 1996, Tony proved anything but a spent force when he quickly returned to League circles with Mansfield Town. In this latest instalment of a remarkable career, he occupied the wing-back position with no lack of sound judgement, dash and enthusiasm. His appearance against Rochdale in early January 1998 was his 900th League and Cup appearance, making him the fifth player in the history of the game to reach this milestone. In terms of English League outings alone, Tony surpassed Terry Paine's earlier record (for an outfield player) of 814 appearances on 16th January 1999. In Scottish football, incidentally, Graeme Armstrong the player-coach of Stenhousemuir played his 864th Scottish League game on Boxing Day 1998 to pass the record for English & Scottish appearances, previously held by the former Scottish international Tommy Hutchison.

Appearances:
FL: 8(1) apps. 1 gl.
Total: *8(1) apps. 1 gl.*
Honours:
2 Eng 'B' apps. 1989/(Grimsby Town) Div 3 champs 1980.

FORD, Trevor

Role: Centre-forward 1950-54
6'0" 12st.10lbs.
b. Swansea, 1st October 1923

CAREER: Swansea Schools/Tower United
(Swansea)/Swansea Town am May 1942, pro
Dec 1944 (guested for Clapton Orient during
WW2)/Aston Villa Jan 1947 £9,500 plus
Tommy Dodds/SUNDERLAND Oct 1950
£29,500/Cardiff City Dec 1953 £29,500/retired
Nov 1956 but joined PSV Eindhoven Mar 1957
£5,000/Newport County July 1960
£1,000/Romford Mar-cs 1961.

Debut v Chelsea (a) 28/10/1950

A celebrity from the immediate post-war
years, Trevor Ford was the subject of large
transfer fees as befits a proven goalscorer; the

£29,500 paid out and then received for him
from Cardiff remained a record until 1970.
Ford began making a name 'guesting' for
Orient at inside-right, blossoming into a hot
property when peace returned. Critical
comment into the 'fifties was flattering and
typical examples were: "the most fiery
forward of his decade", "one of football's most
dangerous centre-forwards, tremendously
thrustful", "probably Britain's best centre-
forward" and "a ninety-minute player who
never spares himself". Ford's time at Roker
was not considered his peak because of a clash
of styles with Len Shackleton. All the same, his
ratio of goals to appearances was eminently
satisfactory during his three full seasons in the
early 'fifties and is bettered by few forwards in
Sunderland's history. He endeared himself to
the Wearside public with a hat-trick on his
home debut in a 5-1 win over Sheffield

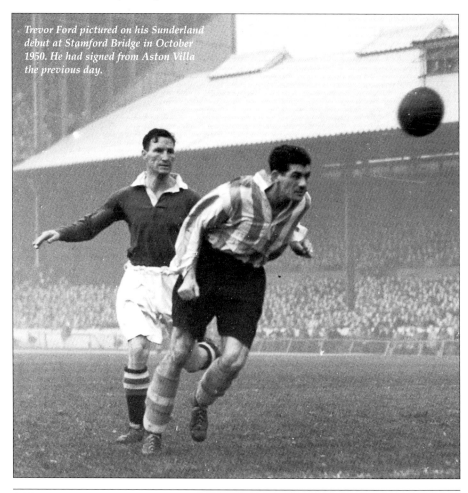

*Trevor Ford pictured on his Sunderland
debut at Stamford Bridge in October
1950. He had signed from Aston Villa
the previous day.*

Wednesday when one of his shots managed to dislodge a post! He also won 13 of his Welsh international caps whilst at Sunderland and in November 1950 scored twice at Roker Park as England beat Wales 4-2. Trevor commenced working in the motor trade when at Sunderland and continued so on his return to Wales. He also wrote for a national Sunday newspaper. Trevor shares with Ivor Allchurch Wales' aggregate goals record (23).

Appearances:
FL: 108 apps. 67 gls.
FAC: 9 apps. 3 gls.
Total: *117 apps. 70 gls.*
Honours
38 Welsh caps.

FORD

Role: Right-back 1887-88

Debut v Morpeth Harriers (h) 15/10/1887 (FAC)

Ford played in all five ties of Sunderland's controversial 1887/88 FA Cup run, all but one of them in the right-back position. An exception was the tie against Newcastle West End on November 5, 1887, when he appeared at centre-half. Sunderland were actually expelled from the competition for breaking the English Cup rules over paid players. Like so many of Sunderland's pre-League men Ford was no slave to a single role. In this season - apparently his only one with the club - he played at left-back a number of times and at inside-right.

Appearances:
FAC: 5 apps. 0 gls.
Total: *5 apps. 0 gls.*

FOREMAN, John James

Role: Outside-right/outside-left
5'9" 11st.4lbs.
b. Tanfield, Co. Durham, last qtr 1913

CAREER: Co. Durham Schools/Tanfield Lea/Crook Town Apr 1933/SUNDERLAND May 1933/West Ham United Sept 1934/Bury March 1937/Swansea Town Dec 1937 (Workington loan cs 1938)/Hartlepools United June 1939 (guested for Crewe Alexandra during WW2).

Debut v Manchester City (h) 11/4/1934

John Foreman

Fast moving John Foreman made his maiden League appearance at outside-left and his second three days later, on the opposite wing (a home match against Middlesbrough). This was the sum total of Foreman's first team activity for Sunderland. Reserve wingers were rather restricted in this heyday of Bert Davis and Jimmy Connor. He did, however, enjoy a fair amount of Second Division action at West Ham, Bury and Swansea, grossing 67 appearances (10 goals).

Appearances:
FL: 2 apps. 0 gls.
Total: *2 apps. 0 gls.*

FORSTER, Derek

Role: Goalkeeper 1964-72
5'9" 11st.2lbs.
b. Newcastle upon Tyne, 19th February 1949

CAREER: Newcastle Schools/SUNDERLAND app June 1964, pro Feb 1966/Charlton Athletic July 1973/Brighton & Hove Albion July 1974-1976/Later a permit player in Wearside League football.

Debut v Leicester City (h) 22/8/1964

It would be hard to visualise a more romantic start to a football career. An England schoolboy goalkeeper (after being an outfield player), Derek Forster joined Sunderland as an apprentice professional and, because of an injury to Jim Montgomery, was pitchforked into the League side at the age of 15 years and 185 days, thus

Derek Forster

becoming the First Division's youngest-ever player. The remainder of Forster's career was an anti-climax; he understudied Montgomery and Sandy McLaughlan for the next nine years, then came spells at Charlton and Brighton and he was first choice at neither. His League appearances total after a dozen years was only 30. In later life Derek worked as assistant manager of the Washington Leisure Centre in County Durham.

Appearances:
FL: 18 apps. 0 gls.
FAC: 1 app. 0 gls.
Total: *19 apps. 0 gls.*
Honours:
5 Eng Sch apps.

FORSTER, Henry

Role: Right/left-back 1906-12
5'8" 12st.0lbs.
b. Annfield Plain, Co Durham, 1883

CAREER: West Stanley/Annfield Plain FC/ SUNDERLAND July 1905/West Ham United May 1912-1914.

Debut v Sheffield United (a) 9/2/1907

Henry Forster

An able, two-footed player possessing versatility, in the four League appearances of his debut season (1906/07) Henry Forster appeared in four different positions, both full-back and each wing-half. Thereafter his frequent outings were fairly evenly divided between the full-back berths. It was never plain sailing with Rhodes still in post to 1908, and Bonthron, Milton and Ness arriving with proven senior records during Forster's time at Roker. His figures at West Ham were 40 Southern League appearances plus four in the FA Cup.

Appearances:
FL: 102 apps. 2 gls.
FAC: 9 apps. 0 gls.
Total: *111 apps. 2 gls.*

FOSTER, John Samuel

Role: Centre-forward 1907-08
5'9" 12st.0lbs.
b. Rawmarsh, Yorks, 19th November 1877
d. Grimsby, 5th February 1946

CAREER: Rotherham Church Institute/ Thornhill United May 1900/Blackpool May 1901/Rotherham Town May 1902/Watford May 1905/SUNDERLAND Dec 1907 £800/ West Ham United May 1908/Southampton Mar 1909, in exchange for F Costello/ Huddersfield Town May 1909/Castleford Town 1910/Morley FC 1911/Huddersfield Town asst. trainer cs 1912, then manager/ Bradford City asst. manager Aug 1926/ Portsmouth scout 1938.

Debut v Birmingham 7/12/1907

John Foster

John Foster was signed by Sunderland from Watford for a fee so high that a Watford FC historian described it as "an astounding increase on previous figures fetched for outgoing players." He went on " ... it was to be 14 years before Watford were to spend anything like that figure on a player." However, Foster was a hot property, an effective opportunist, with a record up to that point of the 1907/08 season of 12 goals in 13 Southern League appearances. Sadly his Roker Park tenure was a brief one. Jack's health deteriorated, so did his form and the medical advice suggested a return to the south. Hence the move after a mere six months to West Ham. He subsequently held appointments as assistant trainer at Huddersfield Town, later becoming their assistant manager under Herbert Chapman and, in August 1926, became Bradford City's assistant manager. During the 1930's Foster scouted for Portsmouth.

Appearances:
FL: 8 apps. 3 gls.
Total: *8 apps. 3 gls.*

FOSTER, John Thomas F.

Role: Outside-right 1920-21
5'6" 9st.13lbs.
*b. Southwick, Sunderland, 21st
March 1903*

John Foster

CAREER: Sunderland Schools/
Murton Colliery Welfare/
SUNDERLAND Aug 1920/
Ashington June 1921/Halifax Town Sept
1923/Grimsby Town May 1925/Bristol City
June 1926/Brentford May 1929/Barrow July
1933-1936(Ashford trial Oct 1937)/Joined
Brentford's ground staff cs 1938 and soon after
WW2, in 1946, went to Belgium to join the
staff of the Royal Racing Club.

Debut v Huddersfield Town (a) 25/9/1920

John Foster was associated with three Third
Division championship sides (Grimsby Town
1926, Bristol City 1927 and Brentford 1933) but
qualified for a medal only with the latter. At
Bristol he understudied Cyril Gilhespy (q.v.).
Small and canny, Foster enjoyed 16 years of
League fare, his best run coming late with
Brentford (141 League appearances). At that
period the Bees were a high-flying Southern
Section outfit who, after nudging promotion
for three years, finally made it, going on to the
top flight two seasons later.

Appearances:
FL: 5 apps. 0 gls.
FAC: 1 app. 0 gls.
Total: *6 apps. 0 gls.*
Honours:
(Brentford) FL Div 3 Sth champs 1933.

FOTHERINGHAM, Alexander

Role: Left-back 1898-99
b. Inverness

CAREER: Inverness Caledonians/
SUNDERLAND Mar 1899/ Inverness
Caledonians Apr 1899.

Debut v Bury (a) 31/3/1899

Alex Fotheringham was with Sunderland on
trial and called upon to deputise for Bob
McNeill less than two weeks after his
registration with the Football League. The
event was a happy one - Sunderland won 2-1.

Appearances:
FL: 1 app. 0 gls.
Total: *1 app. 0 gls.*

FRASER, John Watson

Role: Outside-left 1958-60
5'8" 11st.0lbs.
b. Belfast, 15th September 1938

CAREER: Junior football to Glentoran/
SUNDERLAND Mar 1959 £3,500/Portsmouth
June 1960 c. £1,500/Margate cs 1961/Watford
July 1962, originally on trial/Durban City
(South Africa) 1964/South African national
trainer-coach.

Debut v Huddersfield Town (h) 28/2/1959

John Fraser was one of several possible
successors to the long-serving Billy Bingham
but he was transferred after little more than a
season to Pompey. At Fratton Park he had
only one League outing, drifting to non-
League Margate. Given another senior chance
by Watford, matters improved when he
moved to the inside-right position. He had a
deal of coaching and administrative
experience following his emigration to South
Africa, assisting many clubs there and
eventually becoming a manager.

Appearances:
FL: 22 apps. 1 gl.
Total: *22 apps. 1 gl.*
Honours:
NIre 'B'/NIre Sch.

John Fraser

FRASER, William Alexander

Role: Goalkeeper 1953-59
6'0" 11st.13lbs.
b. Melbourne, Australia, 24th February 1929
d. Kirkcaldy, 7th March 1996

CAREER: Cowie FC/Stirling Juniors/Third Lanark circa 1946/Airdrieonians 1950 £350/ SUNDERLAND Mar 1954 £5,000/Nottingham Forest Dec 1958-1959 £5,000.

Debut v Tottenham Hotspur (a) 20/3/1954

Willie Fraser qualified for Scotland by reason of Scottish parentage: his mother was born in Stirling, his father in Inverness. Willie had arrived in Scotland from Australia at the age of six and lived in Stirling from then on. He was an excellent 'keeper, a clean and safe

Willie Fraser

handler, fully capable of the occasional 'impossible' save. Perhaps the highlights of Fraser's time with Sunderland were his appearances in the FA Cup semi-finals of both 1955 and 1956 - two seasons when in an expensive and talented line-up he remained firmly first choice between the posts racking up 45 outings each term in both League and Cup. Both his caps were also earned while at Roker, in season 1954/55 against Wales and Northern Ireland.

Appearances:
FL: 127 apps. 0 gls.
FAC: 16 apps. 0 gls.
Total: *143 apps. 0 gls.*
Honours:
2 Scot caps.

FULLARTON, William M.

Role: Centre-half 1903-06
5'9" 12st.4lbs
b. Fifeshire, circa 1882

CAREER: Vale of Leven Aug 1901/Queen's Park 1901-02/SUNDERLAND Dec 1903/ Nottingham Forest Nov 1905 £500/Plymouth Argyle player-manager July 1906/New Brompton July 1907-1910.

Debut v Notts County (A) 12/12/1903

William Fullarton came to Roker Park with a good pedigree having played for both of Scotland's early top clubs. He vied with the two Alecs, McAllister and Barrie, for the senior centre-half spot before transferring to Forest, a then noteworthy fee changing hands. Following a score of First Division appearances at Nottingham, an appointment as Plymouth Argyle's manager unluckily coincided with financial straits, and a decision to replace a salaried manager by an unpaid management committee. Fullarton could also perform usefully as a back or wing-half. His brother, David, assisted New Brompton before the First World War.

Appearances:
FL: 31 apps. 0 gls.
FAC: 2 apps. 0 gls.
Total: *33 apps. 0 gls.*

William Fullarton

FULTON, William

Role: Centre/inside-forward 1898-1900
5'8" 11st.6lbs.
b. Alva, Clackmannanshire, circa 1877

CAREER: Alva Albion Rangers (Preston North End trial)/SUNDERLAND May 1898/Bristol City June 1900/Derby County May 1901/ Alloa Athletic July 1902, reinstated as amateur 1904.

Debut v Stoke (h) 26/11/1898

William Fulton's handy capacity for filling each inside position was nicely illustrated at Sunderland, having runs in all three. He was at Bristol in 1900/01, when City enjoyed a highly successful season finishing runners-up to Southampton in the Southern League's First Division. Fulton scored eight goals in 24 appearances, mostly playing inside-left (which was apparently his favourite berth). His Derby County campaign was marred by injury. After returning to his native Clackmannanshire he became a licensee.

Appearances:
FL: 26 apps. 4 gls.
FAC: 5 apps. 3 gls.
Total: *31 apps. 7 gls.*

GABBIADINI, Marco

Role: Forward 1987-92
5'10" 13st.4lbs.
b. Nottingham, 20th January 1968

CAREER: Nunthorpe G.S./York City app Nov 1984, pro Sept 1985/SUNDERLAND Sept 1987/Crystal Palace Oct 1991/Derby County Jan 1992(Birmingham City loan Oct-Nov 1996) (Oxford United loan Jan 1997)/Stoke City Dec 1997/York City Feb-May 1998/Darlington July 1998.

Debut v Chester City (h) 26/9/1987

Marco Gabbiadini cost Sunderland £80,000 in September 1987, and in his first season at Roker, he scored 21 of Sunderland's 92 League goals as they swept to the Third Division championship under new manager Denis Smith. Excellent acceleration and foraging skills, coupled with a fine positional sense, made Gabbiadini a difficult opponent in all areas of the field. A hot property throughout his stay in Wearside, he was eventually sold to Crystal Palace for £1.8 million after six years as a firm crowd favourite and only a week after hitting a six minute hat-trick against Charlton. By contrast, his four months at Selhurst Park proved an extremely unhappy sojourn. Derby County paid £1 million to resurrect his career and he spent five years with the Rams, during which time he scored against Sunderland in a miserable 5-0 opening day defeat in August 1993. Gradually his role switched from that of an out and out striker to one of a provider. Troubled by knee injuries and out of the first team picture during 1996-97, he had loan spells at Birmingham City and Oxford United before being given a free transfer by Derby in the close season. At the end of 1997-98 Marco was released by York City following a brief second spell at Bootham Crescent. Signed by Darlington in July 1998 Marco enjoyed a highly successful first season with the Quakers, as his return of 25 League and Cup goals made him joint leading scorer in Division Three. To cap it off, he turned out for a 'Sunderland XI' and netted a splendid hat-trick at the Stadium of Light in May 1999 against Sunderland in Jimmy McNab's Testimonial match.

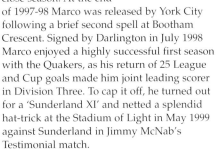

> **Appearances:**
> *FL: 158(2) apps. 75 gls.*
> *FAC: 5 apps. 0 gls.*
> *FLC: 14 apps. 9 gls.*
> *Other: 6 apps. 3 gls.*
> **Total:** *183(2) apps. 87 gls.*

GABBIADINI, Ricardo

Role: Forward 1989-90
5'11" 13st.6lbs.
b. Newport, Monmouthshire, 11th March 1970

CAREER: York City trainee, pro July 1986/SUNDERLAND June 1988(Blackpool loan Sept 1989)(Grimsby Town loan Oct 1989)(Brighton & Hove Albion loan Mar 1990)(Crewe Alexandra loan Oct 1990)/Hartlepool United Mar 1991/Scarborough Mar 1992/Carlisle United Aug 1992/Chesterfield n.c. Dec 1993.

Debut v Leeds United (a) 14/10/1989 (sub)

Younger brother of Marco, Ricardo Gabbiadini followed him from York City to Sunderland as an 18-year-old. He had loan spells with four other League clubs during his stay of almost three seasons at Roker Park, but made only one substitute appearance for Sunderland when he replaced his brother Marco in a 2-0 defeat at Leeds United in October 1989. Although not on the pitch together, the Gabbiadini boys did play in the same game and so became the first brothers to play for The Lads at

Marco Gabbiadini

first team level since Billy and John Hughes. Earlier the same month Ricardo had completed a brief but successful loan with Third Division Blackpool for whom he netted three goals in five League appearances. Rather surprisingly, his best season in League football was his last -

Ricardo Gabbiadini

five goals in 27 League and Cup appearances for Third Division Carlisle United in season 1992-93 constituting a high proportion of his modest career total of 58 League appearances and 10 goals. Last traced as a non-contract player with Chesterfield in 1993-94, he did not appear at League level with the Spireites.

Appearances:
FL: 0(1) app. 0 gls.
Total: *0(1) app. 0 gls.*

GALBRAITH, Thomas D.

Role: Outside-right 1897-98
b. Fifeshire, circa mid-1870's

CAREER: Renton May 1896/Vale of Leven Nov 1896/SUNDERLAND Jan 1898/Leicester Fosse Aug 1898-cs 1900/Vale of Leven Nov 1902.

Debut v Bury (h) 15/1/1898

Thomas Galbraith

Resident at Roker for little more than half a year, Thomas Galbraith was a first team member at Leicester, making 62 Football League appearances in two campaigns there. A main asset was a propensity for scoring goals. In his first Fosse season he netted 16 in 32 League games, heading the scoring sheet - and from the outside-right position. However, in 1899/1900 the flow all but ceased with a return of a single goal in 30 outings. And this despite a move to the inside berth.

Appearances:
FL: 3 apps. 0 gls.
Total: *3 apps. 0 gls.*

GALLACHER, Patrick

Role: Inside-forward 1929-39
5'6" 9st.4lbs.
b. Bridge of Weir, Renfrewshire, 21st August 1909
d. Greenock, 4th January 1992

CAREER: Linwood schoolboy football/ Linwood St Conval's Church/Bridge of Weir FC/SUNDERLAND ground staff 1927, pro Sept 1928/Stoke City Nov 1938 £5,000/retired during WW2 after guesting for Aldershot, Bournemouth, Brentford, Bristol City, Charlton, Crystal Palace, Crewe Alexandra, Fulham, Luton, Leyton Orient, Leicester City, Millwall, Notts County, Newcastle United & Stoke/ Weymouth player-manager.

Debut v Arsenal (h) 21/9/1929

Once established, Patsy Gallacher attracted very favourable comment: "Sunderland's best inside-left since Holley" and (in 1922) "shows touches of real brilliance" being typical. In style 'The Mighty Atom' was of traditional Scottish mould, ball control aiding fine dribbling skills and he possessed a natural body swerve. It speaks volumes for his talent that Patsy, who was a Scottish Cup-winner at only 17, was the boyhood hero of Arsenal and Scotland legend

Patsy was known to entertain his team-mates with a song on away trips.

Alex James. Patsy saw no point in dashing around needlessly expending energy and made his League debut at outside-left, moving to inside-right when Raich Carter emerged. But the two switched positions later: Patsy's best place was on the left flank. His peak, of course, coincided with the Wearsiders' great League and Cup triumphs of the 'Thirties and he scored the 1937 Cup semi-final winner in a 2-1 victory over Millwall at Leeds Road, Huddersfield. His goal tally, which included half a dozen hat-tricks, reached double figures in six successive seasons from 1931-32 to 1936-37 with a best return of 20 League goals as

Sunderland were championship runners-up in 1935 and a healthy 19 the following title year as the League crown was finally wrested from Arsenal's grasp. Patsy scored on his only international outing for Scotland against Ireland in 1935 when he was partnered by Roker team mate Jimmy Connor on the left flank. After leaving the game he went into business in London but returned to Scotland for his final years. Patsy served in the RAF during the Second World War, and his daughter was still living in Sunderland in the late 1990's.

Appearances:
FL: 274 apps. 101 gls.
FAC: 33 apps. 7 gls.
Total: *307 apps. 108 gls.*
Honours:
1 Scot cap/(Sunderland) FL champs 1936/FAC winner 1937.

GATES, Eric Lazenby

Role: Forward/Midfield 1985-90
5'6" 10st.4lbs.
b. Ferryhill 28th June 1955

CAREER: Bishop Auckland schoolboys/
Ipswich Town app, pro Oct 1972/
SUNDERLAND Aug 1985/Carlisle United
June 1990, retired May 1991/Hartlepool
United asst. manager to 1993.

Debut v Blackburn Rovers (h) 17/8/1985

Eric Gates was Lawrie McMenemy's star
signing in the summer of 1985, and the
£150,000 outlay proved a very sound
investment. In almost 13 seasons as a
professional with Ipswich Town the slightly-
built, long-haired midfielder-cum-striker won
two England caps in the World Cup qualifying
games against Norway and Rumania in 1981
after progressing through from the 1973 FA
Youth Cup winning squad at Portman Road.
Eric is probably best remembered by
Sunderland fans for his sparkling strike
partnership with Marco Gabbiadini, the pair
sharing 40 of Sunderland's 92 League goals in
the championship campaign of 1987-88. Gates'
19 goals included four against Southend
United in a 7-0 win in November 1987, which
made him the first Sunderland player to score
four in a game since Stan Cummins' quartet
against Burnley in February 1980. Eric's final
goal came in the memorable 1990 play-off
semi-final win at Newcastle when he also
cleverly created the winner for Gabbiadini.
Released after five seasons at Roker Park, Eric
Gates' career wound up with a final campaign
in the colours of Carlisle United. His League
aggregate (including substitute appearances)
totalled 515 and he scored 124 goals. Now
involved in media work, Eric is part of the
Metro FM and Magic 1152 team who comment
on live Sunderland matches; he also writes for
a local newspaper and appears on Tyne Tees
Television.

Appearances:
FL: 167(19) apps. 45 gls.
FAC: 7 apps. 2 gls.
FLC: 18 apps. 6 gls.
Other: 7 apps. 1 gl.
Total: *199(19)apps. 54 gls.*
Honours:
*2 Eng caps 1981/(Ipswich Town) UEFAC
winner 1981/(Sunderland) FL Div 3 champs
1988.*

Eric Gates

GAUDEN, Allan

Role: Outside-left 1965-68
5'7" 10st.10lbs.
b. Langley Park, Co Durham, 20th November 1944

CAREER: Esh Winning Juniors/Langley Park
Juniors/SUNDERLAND ground staff cs 1961,
pro Mar 1962/Darlington Oct 1968 £5,000/
Grimsby Town Feb 1972 about £2,000/
Hartlepool Aug 1973/Gillingham Dec 1974/
retired 1975.

Debut v Tottenham Hotspur (a) 6/10/1965

As a youth Allan Gauden earned a reputation
by one season's work alone. In the Durham &
District Junior League he scored an amazing
105 goals for Esh Winning Juniors - and from
the wing! In due course he became a member
of the blossoming Sunderland youth team
which also included Jim Montgomery and
Nick Sharkey. Allan stayed at Roker Park
seven years before sampling life in the lower
divisions. He has one particular record of note
to his name, becoming Sunderland's first ever
substitute when he replaced Mike Hellawell
against Aston Villa on 6th September 1965.

Allan Gauden

Debut v Leeds United (a) 4/12/1937

Bernard Gaughran went to Southampton at the second time of asking - Celtic had nipped in and thwarted the first attempt. The Saints then got him on a free transfer, however, and so received a tidy profit from Sunderland's coffers a few months later. Sunderland signed him on the strength of a promising start at The Dell: he had netted four goals in only seven Second Division fixtures. Besides the Leeds debut game recorded above, Gaughran played at Portsmouth a week later (both were lost) and that was the extent of his involvement in the League for Sunderland. For Notts County he made two Southern Section appearances (1 goal). The subsequent tour in wartime of Irish clubs did not lack variety.

Appearances:
FL: 2 apps. 0 gls.
Total: *2 apps. 0 gls.*

GAYLE, Howard Anthony

Role: Forward 1984-86
5'10" 10st.9lbs.
b. Liverpool, 18th May 1958

CAREER: Liverpool app June 1974, pro Nov 1977(Fulham loan Jan 1980)(Newcastle United loan Nov 1982)(Birmingham City loan Jan 1983)/Birmingham City June 1983/ SUNDERLAND July 1984/Dallas Sidekicks, USA cs 1986/Stoke City Mar 1987/Blackburn Rovers July 1987/Halifax Town Sept 1992 (Carlisle United trial Oct 1992)/Accrington Stanley Sept 1993.

Debut v Southampton (h) 25/8/1984

Howard Gayle spent nine years with Liverpool after joining them from junior Sunday League circles, but in six seasons as an Anfield professional he made only four League appearances. He did, however, receive a European Cup winners' medal in 1981 as an unused substitute in the 1-0 win against Real Madrid. He had a number of loan moves before joining Birmingham City where he won England Under-21 recognition as well as something of a tabloid 'bad boy' reputation. He joined Sunderland for £65,000 and won a League Cup finalist's medal in 1985 when he replaced David Corner in the 1-0 defeat by Norwich City. Despite the Cup final appearance, Sunderland were relegated and

Darlington paid what was for them a significant sum for his services, but Grimsby proved a more profitable venue personally in that he qualified there for a championship medal. Allan completed his playing career down in Kent with Gillingham prior to a return to his native North-East and employment in the fire service.

Appearances:
FL: 40(4) apps. 6 gls.
FAC: 2(1) apps. 1 gl.
FLC: 3(1) apps. 0 gls.
Total: *45(6) apps. 7 gls.*
Honours:
(Grimsby Town) FL Div 4 champs 1972.

GAUGHRAN, Bernard Michael

Role: Centre-forward 1937-38
5'8" 11st.10lbs
b. Dublin, 29th September 1915
d. Dundalk, 20th September 1977

CAREER: Bohemians (Dublin) 1935/Celtic Nov 1936/Southampton June 1937/SUNDERLAND Nov 1937 £1,000/Notts County May 1938/Dundalk Aug 1939/Portadown Feb 1940/St James Gate (Dublin) Aug 1941/Distillery June 1942/Brideville Mar 1943.

came perilously close to a repeat performance the following term. In a poor side, Gayle's form was inconsistent; on good days he was a handful for the best defenders with his searing pace and explosive shooting - few will forget his brilliant winner against Forest in the 1985 League Cup run - but the fact he made only 39 League starts in two seasons accurately reflects his in-and-out form. With Blackburn he enjoyed a vintage season in 1988-89, scoring 19 League goals in 45 appearances. Sadly, however, in the play-off finals against Crystal Palace he missed an important penalty in the Ewood Park leg and Rovers' 3-1 advantage proved insufficient as Palace, in extra time, won the second leg 3-0. Howard now works guiding under-privileged youngsters in difficult social areas of his home town Liverpool.

Appearances:
FL: 39(9) apps. 4 gls.
FAC: 1(2) apps. 0 gls.
FLC: 6(2) apps. 1 gl.
Other: 2 apps. 0 gls.
Total: *48(13) apps. 5 gls.*
Honours:
3 Eng U-21 apps. 1984.

Howard Gayle

GEMMELL, James

Role: Centre/inside-forward 1900-07 & 1910-12
5'9" 11st.12lbs.
b. Glasgow, 17th November (year unknown, may be circa 1880)

CAREER: Duntocher Hibernian (Glasgow)/ Clyde Aug 1900/SUNDERLAND Nov 1900/ Stoke May 1907/Leeds City Nov 1907/ SUNDERLAND May 1910/Third Lanark Apr 1912/West Stanley player-manager July 1913.
Debut v Sheffield Wednesday (h) 8/12/1900

Around the time of his championship season which he finished as joint top scorer with ten goals, Jimmy Gemmell was described as "a very smart forward who can play in any inside-forward position; combines well and shoots with great accuracy." To this may be added a consistency quality that continued throughout the bulk of a career still to be experienced. For Leeds City, the other senior club for whom he had a more than brief

Jimmy Gemmell

connection, he made 73 League and FA Cup appearances, scoring 14 goals. It would seem Gemmell preferred an inside berth rather than leading the attack judging from the positional data from his Leeds and (two) Sunderland spells. Father of James Gemmell jnr, a stout defender (left-back) for Bury throughout the 1930s (over 250 Second Division outings).

Appearances:
FL: 212 apps. 46 gls.
FAC: 15 apps. 0 gls,
Total: *227 apps. 46 gls.*
Honours:
(Sunderland) FL champs 1902.

GEORGE, William Samuel

Role: Right-half 1920-21
5'8" 11st.0lbs.
b. Aston, Birmingham, 3rd qtr 1895
d. Selly Oak, Birmingham, 29th September 1962

CAREER: Austin Motor Works (Birmingham) (guested for Leicester Fosse during WW1)/ Merthyr Town cs 1919/ SUNDERLAND Aug 1920/Shildon July 1921/ Burton All Saints. Later a permit player with Birmingham Corporation Trams (May 1923).

Debut v Huddersfield Town (h) 2/10/1920

William George was signed by Sunderland after making eight appearances out of a possible 42 for a Merthyr Town side that finished one rung from the Southern League basement in 1919/20. In the ensuing season George was one of half a dozen players to perform as Sunderland's right-half in the League programme - a somewhat unsettled picture. George's other League outing was another home fixture a fortnight later: a 2-0 defeat inflicted by Newcastle United.

Appearances:
FL: 2 apps. 0 gls.
Total: *2 apps. 0 gls.*

GIBB, Thomas

Role: Midfield 1975-77
5'10" 11st.2lbs.
b. Bathgate, Lothian, 13th December 1944

CAREER: Wallhouse Rose/Armadale Thistle/ Partick Thistle June 1963/Newcastle United Aug 1968/SUNDERLAND July 1975/ Hartlepool United July 1977-July 1979.

Debut v Chelsea (h) 16/8/1975

A product of Armadale Thistle, Tommy Gibb joined Partick Thistle as an 18-year-old half-back. A forceful, spirited linkman in midfield, he ripened during five seasons at Firhill into one of

Tommy Gibb

the best middle men in the country, and commanded a fee of £45,000 when he moved to Newcastle United in August 1968. His 250 plus appearances in all competitions for the Magpies included a record-breaking 171 in succession and 24 in European competitions. Tommy made the short move to Roker Park, on a free transfer, in June 1975 but lost his place after appearing in the opening six matches in the Division Two championship-winning season. Released after two seasons, he joined Hartlepool United on a free transfer. They reached round four of the FA Cup but were re-election applicants in his first term, and Gibb departed at the end of the following campaign, not having added to his 40 appearances and four goals, registered in 1977-78.

Appearances:
FL: 7(3) apps. 1 gl.
Total: *7(3) apps. 1 gl.*
Honours:
1 Scot U-23 app. 1968/(Newcastle United) ICFC winner 1969/FAC finalist 1974.

GIBSON, Frederick Thomas Bertrand

Role: Outside-left 1909-10
5'6" 10st.7lbs.
b. Pilgrims Rest, Johannesburg, South Africa, 8th December 1888
d. Nuneaton, 15th March 1952

CAREER: Bablake School/Lichfield Grammar School/Bedworth Town/Sunderland Royal Rovers 1907/SUNDERLAND May 1909/Raith Rovers July 1910/Dunfermline Athletic cs 1911/Raith Rovers cs 1912/Heart of Midlothian 1917/Coventry City May 1919/ Nuneaton Town cs 1922/Atherstone Town.

Fred Gibson

Debut v Tottenham Hotspur (a) 25/3/1910

Frederick Gibson came to England, aged 11, with his family who settled in Bedworth, Warwickshire. Both his schools (Bablake School, Coventry and Lichfield Grammar School) were rugger-playing but he played soccer for Bedworth Town during vacations. He moved to Wearside to take up am engineering apprenticeship, Sunderland spotting his potential in local junior circles. Chances, though, were in short supply with great wingers like Bridgett and Mordue around. So Scotland beckoned and Fred's high point - a Cup final appearance - reached. Obviously a man of parts: he won a bronze medal shooting at Bisley in 1906. And he became president of Bedworth Town FC in January 1934.

Appearances:
FL: *1 app. 0 gls.*
Total: *1 app. 0 gls.*
Honours:
(Raith Rovers) SC finalist 1913.

GIBSON, George Eardley

Role: Centre-forward 1932-33
5'9" 10st.3lbs.
b. Biddulph, Staffs, 29th August 1912
d. Blackburn, 30th December 1990

CAREER: Kidderminster Harriers (Stoke City trial)/Frickley Colliery/SUNDERLAND Apr 1931/Leicester City Nov 1934/US Valenciennes, France, July 1935/Distillery Jan 1936/RC Roubaix cs 1936/Shelbourne Dec 1936/Workington June 1937/Bradford City May 1938-1939.

Debut v Bolton Wanderers (a) 11/3/1933

George Gibson was a centre-forward whose light 10 stone 3 pounds weight of 1933 had, according to the records, reached a quite formidable 12 stone two and a half pounds two years later. This did not, however, bring any better return in the way of League appearances - as at Sunderland, he made a couple for Leicester, and only three for Bradford City. (Workington had yet to achieve

League status.) George's best time came in France, the Valenciennes fans reckoning him a hit and where there was a distinguished colleague in the form of England's Peter O'Dowd.

Appearances:
FL: *2 apps. 1 gl.*
Total: *2 apps. 1 gl.*

George Gibson

GIBSON, John Rutherford

Role: Right-back 1920-22
5'9" 11st.5lbs.
b. Philadelphia, USA, 23rd November 1898
d. Luton, July 1974

CAREER: Netherburn/Blantyre Celtic/SUNDERLAND Nov 1920/Hull City May 1922/Sheffield United Mar 1929 £5,000/Luton Town Aug 1933/Vauxhall motors, Luton Oct 1934.

Debut v Everton (a) 20/11/1920

Born in the States of Scottish parentage, Jock Gibson's family moved to Sheffield when he was two, and up to Scotland (Hamilton) when 13. He learned his football in Lanarkshire and made his League bow for Sunderland a fortnight after signing. But Bert Hobson

Jock Gibson

remained first choice for right-back and then the matchless Warney Cresswell arrived in March 1922. So Jock made an advantageous move to Hull City, linking up to form a celebrated full-back partnership with Matt Bell which lasted seven seasons and eventually attracted a large fee from Sheffield United (at 31 years of age). On leaving football he worked as an inspector for Vauxhall Motors in Luton, retiring in 1964.

Appearances:
FL: 4 apps. 0 gls.
FAC: 1 app. 0 gls.
Total: *5 apps. 0 gls.*

GIBSON, William

Role: Left-half 1888-94 & 1895-96
5'9" 14st.4lbs.
b. Scotland circa 1868
d. Lincoln, 15th September 1911, aged 43

CAREER: Flemington Thistle/Cambuslang 1887/SUNDERLAND Aug 1888/Rangers May 1894/SUNDERLAND May 1895/Notts County May 1896/Lincoln City May 1898/ retired 1903.

Debut v Burnley (h) 13/9/1890 (FL)

Turning the scales at over 14 stone when in his mid-20s, William Gibson's formidable weight had risen to around 17 stones in 1898. Obviously not an opponent to be trifled with, but Gibson also possessed great skill. Even when only a year off retirement his kicking

William Gibson

was praised for its certainty and accuracy. Willie moved to left-back after joining Notts County, remaining in that position for the remainder of his career. He settled in Lincoln, and was employed as a licensee there until his death in early middle age. His moves to and from Rangers involved an exchange with Andrew McCreadie on both occasions.

Appearances:
FL: 93 apps. 7 gls.
FAC: 9 apps. 0 gls.
Total: *102 apps. 7 gls.*
Honours
1 SL app. 1895/(Sunderland) FL champs 1892, 1893/(Notts County) FL Div 2 champs 1897.

GIBSON, William Kennedy

Role: Right-back 1901-02
b. Ireland, 1876

CAREER: Cliftonville 1893/SUNDERLAND Mar 1902/Bishop Auckland May 1902/ Sunderland Royal Rovers Apr 1908. NOTE: It should be appreciated that, Gibson being an amateur, the foregoing dates are those when he joined a named club but that his liaison with previous clubs did not necessarily lapse. For example, his name appears on Sunderland's seasonal retained lists up to and including 1904/05. And in lists of Irish internationalists his club is consistently given as Cliftonville. In other words he was a Cliftonville player throughout, from his first cap in 1893/94 to his last in 1901/02.

Debut v Bury 16/4/1902

W.K. Gibson holds a special place in the game's annals as he was for long considered to be the youngest player in the home countries to be capped - he was 17 when first honoured (Ireland v Wales on February 24, 1894). However, in the absence of a precise birth-date, some authorities consider the palm passed to Norman Kernaghan of Belfast Celtic, aged 17 years, 80 days when he played for Northern Ireland against Wales on March 11, 1936. What is beyond dispute is that Gibson was a fine, all-round defender, especially for Cliftonville when that club was a major power in Irish football from the earliest times to the Great War.

Appearances:
FL: 2 apps. 0 gls.
Total: *2 apps. 0 gls.*
Honours:
13 Irish caps/5 IL apps/ (Cliftonville) IC winner 1897/1901.

GILBERT, Timothy Hew

Role: Full-back 1976-80
5'9" 11st.3lbs.
b. South Shields, 28th August 1958
d. Cleadon, 29th May 1995

CAREER: Tynemouth Schoolboys/ SUNDERLAND app Sept 1973, pro Aug 1976/ Cardiff City Feb 1981/ Darlington Aug 1982-84.

Debut v Newcastle United (a) 27/12/1976 (sub)

Tim Gilbert made his debut at St James Park in the 101st Tyne-Wear derby, won 2-0 by Newcastle United, replacing Bob Lee in the second half. He had exactly a year to wait for his next chance and he made the most of it, scoring Sunderland's goal in a 1-1 draw at Blackburn Rovers. Largely in reserve due to the consistency of Joe Bolton, Tim eventually moved to Cardiff for a small fee. Injuries restricted his appearances at Ninian Park, and he was released at the close of 1981-82 when Cardiff lost their Second Division status. He moved homewards to join Darlington and in two seasons at the Feethams recorded 62(3) appearances and three goals. Tim Gilbert's sudden death, at the early age of 36 years, came when he was coaching a schoolboys team in Cleadon. An exhibition match for the benefit of his dependents was held at Roker Park in August 1995.

Tim Gilbert

Appearances:
FL: 34(2) apps. 3 gls.
FAC: 5 apps. 0 gls.
Other: 2 apps. 0 gls.
Total: *41(2) apps. 3 gls.*

GILHESPY, Thomas William Cyril

Role: Outside-right 1920-21
5'9" 11st.0lbs.
b. Fencehouses, Co Durham, 18th February 1898
d. Lancaster, March 1985

CAREER: Fencehouses FC/Chester-le-Street/ SUNDERLAND Aug 1920/ Liverpool Aug 1921 £250/Bristol City May 1925/Blackburn Rovers June 1929/Reading June 1930/Mansfield Town July 1931 £150/ Crewe Alexandra Aug 1932-1933.

Cyril Gilhespy

Debut v Bradford City (h) 30/10/1920

After his Sunderland season and a four-year stint as a Liverpool reserve, Cyril Gilhespy had a like stretch with Bristol City, his best years. At Ashton Gate he had a regular first team place, picked up a medal and a reputation as a fast, capable wingman, his performances aided by physical development. Cyril was transferred to Mansfield for their inaugural Football League season in July 1931 along with two other former Sunderland notables, Ernie England and Billy Death.

Appearances:
FL: 16 apps. 1 gl.
Total: *16 apps. 1 gl.*
Honours:
(Bristol City) FL Div 3 Sth champs 1927.

GILHOOLEY, Michael

Role: Centre-half 1921-24
6'1" 12st.0lbs.
b. Glencraig, Fife, 26th November 1896

CAREER: Glencraig Thistle/Celtic 1913/Vale of Leven/Clydebank during WW1/Hull City July 1920 £2,500/SUNDERLAND Mar 1922 £5,250/Bradford City May 1925/Queens Park Rangers May 1927 -1928/Troon Athletic Feb 1929.

Debut v Sheffield United (h) 4/3/1922

Michael Gilhooley cost Hull City their highest outlay to date at the time and on leaving attracted what was the highest national transfer fee (a record soon to be broken). Gilhooley was a lithe, effective pivot whose supreme heading ability earned him the nickname 'Rubberneck' at Hull. And his form there was such as to win attention from Scotland selectors. Unluckily for the player (and Sunderland) he sustained a bad knee injury not long after arriving at Roker Park and was never the same again, having lost his confidence. He served with the Highland Light Infantry in France during the First World War.

Appearances:
FL: 20 apps. 0 gls.
Total *20 apps. 0 gls.*
Honours:
1 Scot cap 1922.

Michael Gilhooley

GILLESPIE, John

Role: Left-back 1892-93
b. probably Scotland

CAREER: Morton/SUNDERLAND Sept 1892/
Sunderland Albion 1893. Possibly had a spell
with Stenhousemuir in the mid-1890s.
Debut v Blackburn Rovers (a) 18/2/1893 (FAC)

John Gillespie made his debut in an important
game - an FA Cup quarter-final which
unfortunately ended in an emphatic 3-0 defeat.
Shortly afterwards Gillespie played in a string
of five consecutive League games that resulted
in three wins, a draw and only one defeat.
That first victory is worth a mention - 5-0 at
Newton Heath. Also reference must be made
to the more famous James Gillespie (below)
who also joined from Morton and assisted
Sunderland Albion. As far as is known the
pair were not related. John's final appearance
was in the penultimate League fixture.

Appearances:
FL: 6 apps. 0 gls.
FAC: 1 app. 0 gls.
Total: *7 apps. 0 gls.*

GILLESPIE, James

Role: Outside-right 1890-91 & 1892-97
b. Scotland
d. Bearsden, nr Clydebank, August 1932

CAREER: Morton/SUNDERLAND
1890/Sunderland Albion 1891/
SUNDERLAND Aug 1892/Third Lanark
May 1897-1900/Ayr FC Sept 1902.

Debut v Wolverhampton Wanderers (h)
15/9/1890

Although usually at outside-right James
Gillespie turned out for Sunderland's
League side in all the other four attack
positions, so exhibiting versatility in
addition to high skill. Also he was a proven
goalscorer as the statistics below
demonstrate. For some strange,
unexplained reason known as 'Taffy'
(perhaps because his sole Scottish cap was
against Wales). Gillespie was a cabinet
maker by trade.
See also the entry for John Gillespie. (q.v.)

Appearances:
FL: 135 apps. 50 gls.
FAC: 14 apps. 1 gl.
Total: *149 apps. 51 gls.*
Honours:
1 Scot cap/SL app./
(Sunderland) FL champs
1893/1895

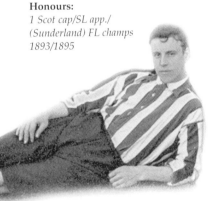

GIVEN, Seamus
John James 'Shay'

Role: Goalkeeper 1995-96
6'2" 13st.4lbs.
b. Lifford, Co Donegal, 20th April 1976

CAREER: Murlog Primary School/St
Columbus College/St Patricks Schoolboys/
Lifford/Lifford Celtic(trials with Manchester
United and Bradford City)/Celtic app Sept
1992/Blackburn Rovers Aug 1994(Swindon
Town loan Aug 1995)(SUNDERLAND loan
Jan-Apr 1996)/Newcastle United June 1997.

Debut v Leicester City (a) 14/1/1996

Shay Given joined Celtic as a 16-year-old and
spent two years at Parkhead when Pat Bonner
was first choice goalkeeper. He refused terms
for a professional contract and had returned to
Ireland when Blackburn persuaded him to try
again at Ewood Park. With Tim Flowers and

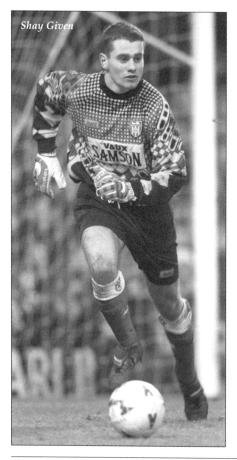

Shay Given

Bobby Mimms heading the queue, Shay
gained League experience in a successful loan
spell at Swindon Town. Arriving at Roker Park
on a similar basis his form was a revelation, as
twelve clean sheets in 17 appearances not only
earned instant cult hero status with the fans
but prompted a scramble for his signature and
elevated him from virtual obscurity to first
choice goalkeeper for his country. Indeed,
Shay's full international debut came during
his Roker loan spell. Sunderland's reported
bid of £1.5million was rejected, but it seemed
only a matter of time before Given would
move on, with regular first team football
necessary to keep him in the eye of Ireland
manager, Mick McCarthy. Ex-Blackburn boss
Kenny Dalglish succeeded in luring Given to
Newcastle in June 1997, the £1.5 million fee
decided by tribunal. A Wembley appearance
rewarded Shay's successful first season at St
James Park, although an injury sustained
whilst on international duty cost him his place
for a lengthy mid-term spell, when Shaka
Hislop seized his opportunity. In late season
1998-99 an unexpected loss of confidence by
Given resulted in promotion for local
understudy Steve Harper eight matches prior
to the FA Cup final against Manchester
United. Harper deservedly held his place and
Given's second successive FA Cup final
appearance was restricted to a role on the
bench that suddenly cast his long-term
Magpies' future into some doubt.

Appearances:
FL: 17 apps. 0 gls.
Total: *17 apps. 0 gls.*
Honours:
*21 Eire caps 1996-99/Eire U-21/Eire
Yth/(Sunderland) FL Div 1 champs
1996/(Newcastle United) FAC finalist 1998.*

GLADWIN, Charles Edward

Role: Right-back 1912-15
5'10" 12st.6lbs.
b. Worksop, Notts, 9th December 1887
d. Rotherham, February 1952

CAREER: Dinnington Main Colliery Oct
1907/Blackpool Dec 1908/SUNDERLAND
Oct 1912/Watford cs 1919, club trainer Jan
1920-cs 1920.

Debut v Middlesbrough (h) 12/10/1912

It is appropriate to quote a critic of the

Charlie Gladwin

immediate pre-First World War days on the subject of big Charlie Gladwin: "his fearless tackling and vitality were a major influence on the (Sunderland) side. He used his awesome physique to full advantage, dominating the whole penalty area and giving the wing halves freedom to attack." Rather unappealingly it was claimed Gladwin "used to push his finger down his throat and make himself sick before a game as a way to conquer his nerves." But once on the field Gladwin didn't care about reputations - even on his own side - and made an enormous difference to the team. Sunderland reportedly paid close on £3,000 in an autumn deal that brought Gladwin and goalkeeper Joe Butler from Blackpool. The pair, particularly Gladwin, were crucial and regular back-line pieces in the jigsaw of the great Sunderland side which blossomed that

season to take the League title, and Gladwin played in all ten ties as Sunderland reached the FA Cup final only to see the 'Double' slip away with defeat by Aston Villa at the Crystal Palace. The former's temporary position as Watford trainer resulted from the appointed trainer's illness.

Appearances:
FL: 54 apps. 0 gls.
FAC: 10 apps. 1 gl.
Total: *64 apps. 1 gl.*
Honours:
(Sunderland) FL champs 1913/FAC finalist 1913.

GLOAG

Role: Centre/inside-forward 1887-88
Debut v Middlesbrough 26/11/1887 (FAC) (scored)

Gloag's other Cup appearance was also against Middlesbrough a week later, when he played inside-left. In the first game he was the centre-forward scoring twice. Gloag was a regular Sunderland player that 1887/88 season, his appearances evenly distributed between the three inside-forward berths.

Appearances:
FAC: 2 apps. 2 gls.
Total: *2 apps. 2 gls.*

GODBOLD, Harry

Role: Outside-left 1957-60
5'8" 10st.5lbs.
b. Springwell, Co. Durham, 31st January 1939

CAREER: Usworth Colliery/SUNDERLAND May 1956/Hartlepool United Jan 1961/Boston United Aug 1963/Boston FC cs 1964/Lincoln City Mar 1966/Spalding United cs 1966/Boston FC Dec 1967/Gateshead 1968.
Debut v Leicester City (h) 4/9/1957

Three years a Sunderland reserve and understudy to Colin Grainger for the bulk of that time, Harry Godbold made his senior debut in the dire 1957/58 season when top flight status was lost. On moving to neighbours Hartlepool he enjoyed regular first team action with a total of 66 League outings (8 goals) before transferring to non-League circles. Unusually he returned to League fare after almost three years, signing for Lincoln

City. In 22 League appearances for the Imps he scored three goals.

Appearances:
FL: 12 apps. 1 gl.
FAC: 1 app. 0 gls.
Total: 13 apps. 1 gl.

GODDARD, George Charles

Role: Inside-right/centre-forward 1934-36
5'11" 12st.4lbs.
b. Gomshall, Surrey 20th December 1903
d. Kingston-upon-Thames, 23rd April 1987

CAREER: Surrey junior football/Redhill/Queens Park Rangers am 1925, pro June 1926/Wolverhampton Wanderers Dec 1933/SUNDERLAND Oct 1934/Southend United July 1935.

Debut v Birmingham (h) 8/12/1934

George Goddard had built and deserved a big reputation as a fast goal-scoring centre-forward with Queens Park Rangers. Indeed his figures over a lengthy period of seven and a half seasons were eye-catching (189 goals in 259 League and FA Cup

George Goddard

appearances). And they included, in 1929/30, a seasonal total of 37 in 41 League outings that made him the Southern Section's top scorer. One wonders whether his move to top flight football came too late - he was 30 when transferred to Wolves - for his stays there and at Sunderland were comparatively brief. This thought is not to denigrate a fine player in any way. George had been a crack amateur when at Redhill, representing the Athenian League and winning a county cap with Surrey. Outside football he had been a butcher's boy and had also worked in a local bus garage.

Appearances:
FL: 14 apps. 5 gls.
Total: 14 apps. 5 gls.

GOODCHILD, George

Role: Outside-right 1894-95
b. Ryhope, Co. Durham, 1st qtr 1875

CAREER: Ryhope Colliery/SUNDERLAND June 1894/Derby County June 1896/Nottingham Forest Mar 1897/Burton Swifts Oct 1897/Jarrow July 1899/Whitburn Sept 1900/South Shields Athletic July 1901/Later with Ashington July 1904.

Debut v Sheffield United (a) 9/3/1895

George Goodchild's only League appearance with Sunderland was followed by four for Forest (in Division One) and nine for Burton Swifts (in Division Two). At Derby Goodchild was not selected for the League side. He eventually returned to his native North-East for a round of the local non-League clubs.

Appearances:
FL: 1 app. 0 gls.
Total: 1 app. 0 gls.

GOODCHILD, John

Role: Inside-right 1957-61
5'9" 10st.12lbs.
b. Gateshead, 2nd January 1939

CAREER: Ludworth Juniors/SUNDERLAND Sept 1956/Brighton & Hove Albion May 1961/York City June 1966/Darlington July 1967-1968.

Debut v Leicester City (h) 4/9/1957 (scored)

A teenage debutant, on which occasion John Goodchild, appearing at outside-left, scored. During his five years at Roker Park, although the bulk of appearances were at inside-right, he played on both wings and at inside-left also. And it was at outside-left that Brighton used his attacking talents, where he had 162 League outings (plus one substitution), scored 45 goals and won a medal. The York season produced 29 League outings (6 goals). John's career took in all four Football League divisions including two with Sunderland.

Appearances:
FL: 44 apps. 21 gls.
FAC: 1 app. 0 gls.
Total: 45 apps. 21 gls.
Honours:
(Brighton & Hove Albion) FL Div 4 champs 1965.

GOODMAN, Donald Ralph

Role: Forward 1991-95
5'10" 13st.2lbs.
b. Leeds, 9th May 1966

CAREER: Leeds Schoolboys/Collingham/
Bradford City app Oct 1983, pro July 1984/
West Bromwich Albion Mar 1987/
SUNDERLAND Dec 1991/Wolverhampton
Wanderers Dec 1994/Hiroshima, Japan June
1998(Barnsley loan Dec 1998-Mar 1999)/
Motherwell May 1999.

Debut v Wolverhampton Wanderers (a) 7/12/1991

Don Goodman won a Division Four
championship medal with Bradford City in his
first season as a professional. Always a
determined competitor and a natural athlete,
his all-round game developed considerably
following his £50,000 deadline transfer to West
Bromwich Albion in March 1987. Signed by

Sunderland to replace Marco Gabbiadini for a
club record £900,000 he settled quickly at
Roker, scoring a hat-trick against Millwall on
his seventh appearance, and leading the
goalscoring list with 11 in 22(2) appearances.
He was cup-tied and disappointed to miss out
on a Wembley FA Cup final place in 1992, but
his 16 goals in 41 appearances in 1992-93 were
a major contribution in a season when
relegation was narrowly avoided. At the time
of his £1.1 million transfer to Wolves, Don's
goalscoring touch seemed to have deserted
him, nevertheless he passed the landmark of a
century of League goals during his spell at
Roker. Don led the Wolves goalscoring lists in
1995-96 with 20 and thankfully made a full
recovery from a depressed fracture of the
skull, sustained in an accidental clash of heads

*Don
Goodman*

*n Goodchild (centre) jumps
a high ball against Swansea.*

at Huddersfield in April 1996. Out of contract with Wolves in May 1998, Don accepted a lucrative offer from Japanese J League club, Hiroshima, but was back in England for a three month loan with Barnsley in mid season, linking up with player-manager John Hendrie, an old friend from his Bradford days. In March 1999 Don's travels continued when he joined Motherwell, and despite failing to impress immediately at Fir Park, was on the scoresheet in Well's final match of the season, a 2-1 victory at Dunfermline.

Appearances:
FL: 112(4) apps. 40 gls.
FAC: 3 apps. 1 gl.
FLC: 9 apps. 4 gls.
Other: 4 apps. 2 gls.
Total: *128(4) apps. 47 gls.*
Honours:
(Bradford City) Div 3 champs 1985.

GORMAN, James Joseph

Role: Right-half 1936-39
5'9" 11st.9lbs.
b. Liverpool, 3rd March 1910
d. Sunderland, 1st February 1991

CAREER: Liverpool schoolboy football/Skelmersdale United/Burscough Rangers/Blackburn Rovers am Mar 1929, pro Aug 1930 £100/SUNDERLAND Jan 1937 £6,250 (guest player for Hartlepools United, Middlesbrough and Carlisle United during WW2/Hartlepools United Oct 1945-1946.

Debut v Brentford (a) 23/1/1937

Jimmy Gorman

Originally a centre-forward, Jimmy Gorman became a full-back when assisting Skelmersdale, soon attracting the scouts. He had half a dozen years of top flight football before arriving at Roker Park in exchange for a hefty fee. While with Blackburn he was described as a "strong and hard tackler, reckoned to be one of the fastest backs in the country". This speed enabled Jimmy to adapt to the then newly fashionable role of attacking, or overlapping full-back. He took a short time to settle in with Sunderland but proved a tower of strength in the successful FA Cup run the following Spring, not least with thoughtful positional play. Good at cricket and baseball, the latter a favourite Liverpudlian pastime, Jimmy was a cabinet maker by trade.

Appearances:
FL: 82 apps. 0 gls.
FAC: 17 apps. 1 gl.
Total: *99 apps. 1 gl.*
Honours:
(Sunderland) FAC winner 1937.

GOW, Donald Robertson

Role: Right/left-back 1891-92 & 1893-97
5'10" 12st.8lbs.
b. Blair-Atholl, Perthshire, 8th February 1868
d. Middlesbrough, 1945

CAREER: Cessnock Bank (Glasgow)/Rangers Oct 1885/SUNDERLAND pro Sept 1891/Rangers May 1892/SUNDERLAND Oct 1893/New Brighton Tower June 1897/Millwall Athletic Aug 1898-1899/Girvan Oct 1899.

Debut v Bolton Wanderers (a) 9/9/1891

A leading amateur sprinter in Scotland, it naturally followed that Don Gow's footballing action was extremely fast. He also employed a strong, clean kick and infinite resource. Gow was considered able to take any position and not be restricted to any particular style of play. He captained Scotland in his sole international appearance and when, remarkably, but five weeks past his 20th birthday. And he was possibly the first - and certainly among the very first - non-Englishmen to represent the Football League. Donald was older brother to John Robertson Gow of Rangers and Scotland.

Appearances:
FL: 99 apps. 1 gl.
FAC: 12 apps. 0 gls.
Total: *111 apps. 1 gl.*
Honours:
1 Scot cap/FL app./(Rangers) Joint SL champs 1891/(Sunderland) FL champs 1892.

Right: Don Gow

GRAHAM, Allan

Role: Right-back 1957-58
b. Ryhope, Co Durham, 23rd October 1937

CAREER: Silksworth Juniors/SUNDERLAND
May 1955/Horden Colliery Welfare June 1958.

Debut v Wolverhampton Wanderers 31/8/1957

Allan Graham spent three years at Roker Park,
his three senior appearances concentrated into
season 1957/58, that dismal season when top
flight status was lost for the first time in 68
years. Graham's debut saw a crushing 5-0
defeat by Wolves but his second appearance a
few days later was in a 3-2 home win over
Leicester City. His final outing, on the 12th
October, at Burnley was worse than the
Wolves' debacle - Sunderland lost 6-0.

Appearances:
FL: 3 apps. 0 gls.
Total: *3 apps. 0 gls.*

GRAINGER, Colin

Role: Outside-left 1956-60
5'10" 10st.2lbs.
b. Havercroft, West Yorkshire, 10th June 1933

CAREER: South Elmsall/Wrexham ground
staff 1949, pro Oct 1950/Sheffield United July
1953 £2,500/SUNDERLAND Feb 1957 £17,000
plus Sam Kemp/Leeds United July 1960
£13,500/Port Vale Oct 1961 £6,000/Doncaster
Rovers Aug 1964/Macclesfield Town cs - Oct
1966.

Debut v Tottenham Hotspur (a) 9/2/1957

Colin Grainger came from a famous soccer
family: brother of Jack (England 'B'), uncle of
Edwin Holiday (England), brother-in-law of
Jim Iley (England Under-23) and cousin of two
other League players, one of whom introduced
him to Wrexham. Colin played only five times
in Wrexham's League side before being
snapped up by Sheffield United. All but one of
his representative honours were obtained
whilst at Bramall Lane. The Blades pocketed a
handsome profit on his transfer to Sunderland
where he was held in high regard and has
been bracketed with Dennis Tueart as one of
The Lads' finest post-war operators on the left
flank. His abilities neatly summed up as "fast
moving and keen to score", Grainger slotted in
55 goals in an aggregate of 325 League

matches. He possessed an excellent singing
voice and sang professionally. After leaving
football Colin worked as regional manager for
a cash register company and later as a
representative for a firm of wine merchants.

Appearances:
FL: 120 apps. 14 gls.
FAC: 4 apps. 0 gls.
Total: *124 apps. 14 gls.*
Honours:
7 Eng caps/3 FL apps.

Colin Grainger

Frank Gray

medal and appeared in the starting line-up in the final seven matches, six of which were convincingly won. Released towards the close of the following season, he joined Darlington as player-coach. Frank Gray made his final Football League appearance in February 1992 at 37 years of age. Including substitute appearances, his commendable career aggregate was 647 League appearances and 48 goals. Brother of Eddie Gray who, rather unusually, was Frank's manager during his second spell with Leeds United.

Appearances:
FL: 120(28) apps. 8 gls.
FAC: 4(1) apps. 0 gls.
FLC: 6(1) apps. 0 gls.
Other: 7 apps. 0 gls.
Total: *137(30) apps. 8 gls.*
Honours:
Scot Sch/5 Scot U-23 apps. 1974-76/32 Scot caps 1976-1983/(Leeds United) ECWC finalist 1973/EC finalist 1975/(Nottingham Forest) EC winner 1980/FLC finalist 1980/(Sunderland) FL Div 3 champs 1988.

GRAY, Francis Tierney

Role: Full-back 1985-89
5'10" 11st.10lbs.
b. Castlemilk, Glasgow, 27th October 1954

CAREER: Glasgow Schools/Leeds United app 1970, pro Nov 1971/Nottingham Forest July 1979/Leeds United May 1981/SUNDERLAND July 1985/Darlington player-coach July 1989, manager June 1991-Feb 1992/Wetherby Athletic/Harrogate Town player-manager Dec 1993.

Debut v Blackburn Rovers (a) 17/8/1985

A £100,000 signing by new Sunderland manager, Lawrie McMenemy, in July 1985, Frank Gray survived a dreadful start to his Sunderland career, as the season opened with five straight defeats, and a goal average of 0-10. It must have been something of a culture shock for the vastly experienced Scottish international whose glittering career began in the early seventies with Leeds United. He was a member of the Leeds party for the 1973 FA Cup Final, famously won against all the odds by Sunderland. Rarely absent in his first two seasons at Roker, Frank Gray lost out to Reuben Agboola in 1987-88 and was largely employed as a substitute. He nevertheless qualified for a Division Three championship

GRAY, Martin David

Role: Midfield 1990-96
5'9" 11st.4lbs.
b. Stockton on Tees, 17th August 1971

CAREER: Durham County Schools and Youth(Middlesbrough trial 1988)/Ferryhill Athletic/SUNDERLAND Feb 1990(Aldershot loan Jan-Feb 1991)(Fulham loan Oct 1996)/Oxford United Mar 1996.

Debut v Blackburn Rovers (a) 29/4/1992 (sub)

Captain of Durham County Under-18's at 16 years of age, Martin Gray's progress was under review by a number of League clubs before he joined Sunderland in February 1990. A hardworking utility midfielder Martin also appeared in central defence and midfield and could always be relied upon to give 100% wherever selected. He actually made his League debut as a substitute in Aldershot's colours during a loan spell in season 1990-91, fourteen months prior to his first senior outing for Sunderland, again as a substitute, in a 2-2 draw at Blackburn Rovers. In five years as a Sunderland professional, Martin enjoyed extended spells of first team action during seasons 1993-94 and 1994-95, but he had made only four starting appearances and three as a substitute in the championship season 1995-96

Martin Gray

GRAY, Michael

Role: Midfield/Full-back 1992-date
5'7" 10st.10lbs.
b. Sunderland, 3rd August 1974

CAREER: Castle View School/Sunderland Schoolboys/Durham County U-18/ Manchester United assoc. s'boy Oct 1988/ SUNDERLAND trainee July 1990, pro July 1992.

Debut v Derby County (a) 21/11/1992 (sub)

Nine different League clubs sought Michael Gray's signature when he was released from Manchester United's School of Excellence at 15 years of age. There was, however, little consideration given to other interested parties when Sunderland offered him a traineeship. A Sunderland supporter from the age of six, Michael fulfilled his youthful ambition by joining his hometown club. His first team debut at Derby County was made doubly memorable when he faced his boyhood hero, Marco Gabbiadini. In his first full appearance, against Barnsley in December 1992, Michael scored a stunning goal, fired in from outside the penalty area, in the first minute of the match. His subsequent progress under five different managers has been quite outstanding. In the attacking facets of play, his skill, pace and repertoire of tricks make him a handful for any defence. Able to play in midfield or at left back, his workrate and stamina were fully rewarded during a memorable 1998-99 season, as he showed great character to overcome the dreadful disappointment of his crucial sudden-death penalty miss in the Wembley play-off final defeat of 1998 against Charlton. His excellent overlapping left wing play in partnership with Allan Johnston was a feature of Sunderland's success throughout the season, and his call-up into the England squad and subsequent international debut in Budapest followed by further caps against Bulgaria and Sweden, proved to be the icing on the cake.

and was transferred to Oxford United for £100,000 in March of that term. Appearing in seven of the season's closing matches, Martin assisted his new team - managed by ex-Sunderland duo, Denis Smith and Malcolm Crosby, to promotion into Division One. Sadly, their tenure ended on the last Sunday of the League programme in May 1999 when, despite recording their best victory of the season - 5-0 against Stockport County - Oxford were relegated to the Second Division.

Appearances:
FL: 46(18) apps. 1 gl.
FAC: 0(3) apps. 0 gls.
FLC: 6(2) apps. 0 gls.
Other: 3(1) apps. 0 gls.
Total: *55(24) apps. 1 gl.*

Appearances:
PL: 31(3) apps. 3 gls.
FL: 177(19) apps. 11 gls.
FAC: 9(1) apps. 1 gl.
FLC: 17(3) apps. 0 gls.
Total: *234(26) apps. 15 gls.*
Honours:
1 FL U-21 XI app./3 Eng caps 1999/ (Sunderland) FL Div 1 champs 1996 & 1999.

GRAY, Philip

Role: Forward 1993-96
5'9" 12st.5lbs.
b. Belfast, 2nd October 1968

CAREER: Belfast Schools/Northern Ireland Schools/Ballyclare Comrades/Tottenham Hotspur app Apr 1985, pro Aug 1986(Barnsley loan Jan 1990)(Fulham loan Dec 1990)/Luton Town Aug 1991/SUNDERLAND July 1993/Nancy-Lorraine F.C., France July 1996/Fortuna Sittard, Holland Dec 1996/Luton Town Sept 1997.

Debut v Notts County (a) 28/8/1993 (sub)

'Tippy' Gray (from the PG initials!) began with Tottenham and made his League debut at 18

Philip
Gray

years of age in the final game of 1986-87, five days prior to Spurs appearance in the 1987 FA Cup Final. A combination of injuries and the very stiff competition at White Hart Lane eventually led to his £275,000 transfer to Luton Town, managed by ex-Spurs boss David Pleat. His full international debut followed and in the season prior to his move to Sunderland he scored 19 of Luton's 48 League goals, the next highest being Scott Oakes with five. Linked with Chelsea before the transfer deadline and later with West Ham, Phil did in fact sign for Sunderland boss Terry Butcher for a fee of £775,000. Despite being involved in a car crash that delayed his debut, Gray led the goalscoring lists in each of his first two seasons at Roker and passed the milestone of 50 League goals during 1995-96 despite missing the run-in to the championship after being injured in February. At the end of his contract in the close season and a free agent, he moved to French club Nancy-Lorraine. After scoring the winner against Paris Saint-Germain in December he was surprisingly on the move again in a £400,000 transfer to Fortuna Sittard in Holland who bought out his contract. In September 1997 he rejoined Luton Town.

Appearances:
FL: 108(7) apps. 34 gls.
FAC: 8 apps. 3 gls.
FLC: 9 apps. 4 gls.
Total: *127(7) apps. 41 gls.*
Honours:
NIre Sch & Yth/1 NIre U-21 app.1990/21 NIre caps 1994-1999/(Sunderland) FL Div 1 champs 1996.

GRAYSTON, John

Role: Centre-forward 1884-85
Debut v Redcar (a) 8/11/1884 (FAC)

John Grayston participated in Sunderland's first-ever FA Cup tie and has a place in the club's history on two other counts. He was a club founder and, eight years later, secretary at the time when it

John Grayston

momentously turned professional. As he wrote some years afterwards it was a 'veiled professional' club, some players being paid and found jobs, an arrangement looked after by an informal sub-committee. Particularly important too was his part in bringing Tom Watson, the man who had made Newcastle West End a leading club, to Sunderland. John Grayston, like other founders a school teacher by profession, became headmaster of the Stansfield Road School, Roker.

Appearances:
FAC: 1 app. 0 gls.
Total: *1 app. 0 gls.*

GREENWOOD, Roy Thornton

Role: Winger 1975-79
5'10" 11st.0lbs.
b. Leeds, 26th September 1952

CAREER: Pudsey Juniors/Hull City app Aug 1968, pro Oct 1970/SUNDERLAND Jan 1976/Derby County Jan 1979/Swindon Town Feb 1980/Huddersfield Town Aug 1982(Tranmere Rovers loan Nov 1983)/Scarborough June 1984.

Debut v West Bromwich Albion (a) 10/1/1976

Roy Greenwood

Considering the fact that Roy Greenwood cost Sunderland £140,000 - marginally less than their record fee at that time, his spell with The Lads was disappointing. This, despite the fact he qualified for a Second Division championship medal within four months of joining the Roker Park brigade. A long term leg injury restricted him to only 50 appearances in the starting line-up in his three years with the club, and in January 1979 he departed to Derby County for a cut-price fee of £50,000. Once left out of an official club team photograph when he refused to shave off his beard, Roy was an independent type, but his refusal to join Arsenal (managed by his old Hull City boss Terry Neill) in 1977 seemed a most baffling decision. In terms of his total

career, Roy Greenwood's initial spell with Hull City (24 goals in 118(8) appearances) was undoubtedly his best.

Appearances:
FL: 45(11) apps. 9 gls.
FLC: 3 apps. 0 gls.
Other: 2 apps. 0 gls.
Total: *50(11) apps. 9 gls.*
Honours:
(Sunderland) Div 2 champs 1976.

GREGOIRE, Roland B.

Role: Forward 1977-79
5'9" 10st.6lbs.
b. Liverpool, 23rd November 1958

CAREER: Bradford Junior football/Halifax Town Aug 1976/SUNDERLAND Nov 1977-July 1980.

Debut v Hull City (h) 2/1/1978

Taken onto Halifax Town's ground staff at 17 years of age, Roly Gregoire had made only five League appearances when Sunderland paid £5,000 for him in November 1977. A spectacular hat-trick against Sunderland Reserves had prompted manager Jimmy

Roly Gregoire

Adamson to sign the youngster and he became the first black player to represent the Wearsiders when he made his League debut two months later. Injuries to Wilf Rostron and Roy Greenwood gave Roly his big chance, and a late run in the seniors in April 1978 saw him net his first League goal in a 3-1 win at Luton Town. A clever ball player with a deceptive body swerve, he unfortunately lacked physical advantage and subsequently faded from the scene, his contract being cancelled in July 1980.

Appearances:
FL: 6(3) apps. 1 gl.
FAC: 0(1) app. 0 gls.
Total: *6(4) apps. 1 gl.*

GREGORY, Clarence

Role: Inside-left 1920-21
5'8" 12st.0lbs.
b. Aston Manor, Birmingham, 1900

CAREER: Aston Schools/Wellington Town/ SUNDERLAND Mar 1920 £300/Queens Park Rangers June 1922/Yeovil & Petters United 1923/Wellington Town cs 1924/Hereford United subsequently before joining Leamington Town cs 1927/Rugby Town 1930.

Clarence Gregory

Debut v Tottenham Hotspur (a) 2/4/1921

Clarence Gregory was one of a trio of brothers, all of whom became professional footballers. The others were Howard (Football League championship medal with West Bromwich Albion, 1920) and John (Queens Park Rangers 1912-23). Clarence, a colleague of John's with QPR for a season, assisted the club in his main position, outside-left, bringing an unusual 12 stone weight to its execution. He scored a single goal in 24 Southern Section appearances, which included sole outings at inside-left and centre-forward. Whilst with Hereford United John netted 50 goals in the 1926-27 season.

Appearances:
FL: 1 app. 0 gls.
Total: *1 app. 0 gls.*
Honours:
1 Eng Sch app. 1914.

GREY, Thomas

Role: Centre-half 1907-08
5'9" 12st.0lbs.
b. Whitley Bay, Northumberland, 1st qtr 1885

CAREER: Whitley Bay Athletic/ SUNDERLAND am July 1907/Bedlington United/Newcastle United am Jan 1908/Blyth Spartans June 1909/Newcastle United am cs 1911-1915/Newcastle Bohemians 1919.

Debut v Preston North End (a) 18/1/1908

A leading North-East amateur from the immediate pre-First World War days, Thomas Grey spent his soccer career assisting local clubs. Besides the Sunderland debut he made one other First Division appearance - in his second Newcastle spell, against Aston Villa (a) in

Thomas Grey

April 1914 when United won 3-1, standing in for Scottish cap Wilf Low. As is usual with amateurs, his periods with various clubs would overlap if they were contesting in different competitions. Grey was sound in attack and defence.

Appearances:
FL: 1 app. 0 gls.
Total: *1 app. 0 gls.*
Honours:
3 Eng am apps.

GRIMSHAW, William

Role: Outside-right 1923-27
5'9" 11st.0lbs.
b. Burnley, 30th April 1890
d. Burnley, 6th May 1968

CAREER: St John's RC School Burnley/
Livingstone United/Barnoldswick United/
Burnley June 1910/Colne circa 1911(guested
for Hull City during WW1)/Bradford City
June 1912/Cardiff City cs 1919/
SUNDERLAND Dec 1923 £3,500/retired from
first class football May 1927, later playing as a
permit player in Bradford/J.S. Driver's FC
(Bradford) Oct 1933.

Debut v Huddersfield Town (a) 8/12/1923

"A clever, industrious player with a good turn
of pace " and " ... a fleet-footed and dangerous
raider" were typical critical comments when
Billy Grimshaw was at his zenith. Son of an
old Blackburn Olympic man, he had some

Billy Grimshaw

experience with
Burnley's reserves
and minor
Lancashire sides
prior to the
Bradford City
engagement. He
found chances
there limited with
the inimitable
Dickie Bond
available, but
made a name in
Wales with a rising
Cardiff City that
won top flight
status and Cup

glories during the 'Twenties. Billy's transfer to
Sunderland occasioned some surprise but the
management felt the right-wing spot had
never been really satisfactorily filled since the
halcyon days of Jackie Mordue. However, Billy
did not really reproduce his Cardiff form at
Roker Park. He became a Bradford licensee
following the 1927 retiral. In the Great War he
served in the Royal Garrison Artillery.

Appearances:
FL: 71 apps. 6 gls.
FAC: 4 apps. 0 gls.
Total: *75 apps. 6 gls.*
Honours:
1 FL app.

GUNSON, Joseph Gordon

Role: Outside-left 1929-30
5'10" 11st.4lbs.
b. Chester, 1st July 1904
d. Broughton, Clwyd, 13th September 1981

CAREER: Chester Schools/Brickfields FC
(Chester)/Nelson am cs 1923/Wrexham pro
Aug 1926/SUNDERLAND May 1929 £1,500/
Liverpool Mar 1930/Swindon Town June
1934/Wrexham May 1935/Bangor City player-
manager cs 1936.

Debut v Portsmouth (a) 14/9/1929

Gordon Gunson had a highly satisfactory
initial professional engagement with
Wrexham, scoring 90 goals in 190 League and
FA Cup matches - an excellent return for a
wingman. This did not go unnoticed
elsewhere, a selection for Wales transpiring
but having to be foregone because of a Chester
birth-place. He shared a first team spot with
Adam McLean during his Roker Park years,
then had a much longer top flight spell at
Liverpool where he supplanted the long-
serving Fred Hopkin. It was there also that a
cartilage injury developed which shortened
his playing career. Gunson was a talented
winger who, besides delivering what were
described as inch-perfect centres for the inside
men, was a marksman himself. After his stint
as player-manager at Bangor City, Gunson
held a number of football appointments in
post Second World War days, including trainer
of Crewe Alexandra in the 1940s, managerial
posts with Flint Town, Welshpool and
Dolgellau and as a scout for Coventry City

Gordon Gunson

and other
clubs.

Appearances:
FL: 19 apps.
11 gls.
FAC: 4 apps.
1 gl.
Total: *23 apps.*
12 gls.

GURNEY, Robert

Role: Centre/inside-forward 1925-39
5'8" 11st.0lbs.
b. Silksworth, Co Durham, 13th October 1907
d. Sunderland, 14th April 1994

CAREER: Silksworth Council School/
Co Durham Schools/Hetton Juniors/
Seaham Harbour/Bishop Auckland June
1924/SUNDERLAND pro May 1925/
retired and joined club training staff May
1946/Horden Colliery FC manager 1947/
Peterborough United manager Feb 1950/
Darlington manager Mar 1952-Oct 1957/
Leeds United scout/Horden Colliery
Welfare FC manager 1960-63/Hartlepools
United manager Apr 1963-Jan 1964.

Debut v West Ham United (a) 3/4/1926

Must always come into the reckoning when
any list of outstanding club servants is
under consideration, Bobby Gurney's
devotion to Sunderland FC extended over a
remarkable 22 years including the war
period, the bulk of them as part of the first
team. Spotted originally and recommended
by Charlie Buchan while assisting Bishop
Auckland, 'Boy' Gurney, as he was initially
dubbed by 'keeper Albert McInroy, proved
able to take all three inside berths, doing so
from the beginning as stand-in for Dave
Halliday, Bob Marshall et al with equal
facility. It was the advent of Carter and
Gallacher as regular inside men that
Gurney became 'full-time' centre-forward.
To all positions he brought enthusiasm,
wholeheartedness, consistency and the
resource to escape from his markers and
send goal-potential passes from the wings.
He broke both legs in the course of his
career, early on at Workington when still 19
and again much later on, returning on both
occasions without any apparent diminution
of powers. So full marks for bravery also.
Top scorer for seven successive seasons
during the 1930's, he is Sunderland's
record goalscorer - 228 goals in 388 League
and FA Cup appearances, which includes
10 hat-tricks and two fours. He was joint
top-scorer with Raich Carter in the 1936
championship season. Then in 1937 Bobby
scored a vital last minute FA Cup equaliser
against Wolves and went on to net

Sunderland's first ever goal at Wembley, deftly glancing in Carter's header from a corner, as the Cup was won. Scoring goals came naturally it seems - he had slotted in an amazing 131 in his Hetton Junior season and notched nine for the reserves in his first game at Roker! Capped just once by England he did score twice for The Rest v England at Roker in 1934 and for England against Scotland at Hampden in an unofficial international in 1935. Gurney was latterly employed as a brewery representative. A most modest, likeable man Bobby was a magnificent ambassador for Sunderland both on and off the pitch and kept close ties with the club until his death.

Appearances:
FL: 348 apps. 205 gls.
FAC: 40 apps. 23 gls.
Total: *388 apps. 228 gls.*
Honours:
1 Eng cap/(Sunderland) FL champs 1936/FAC winner 1937.

The team pictured (below) circa 1914 is the Silksworth Independant Order of Grand Templars, named after a chapel in New Silksworth, a colliery village on the outskirts of Sunderland. The goalkeeper in the centre of the back row is Ralph Gurney and the small boy on the right of the middle row is Ralph's younger brother Bobby 'Boy' Gurney.

GUTHRIE, Ronald George

Role: Full-back 1972-75
5'10" 12st.12lbs.
b. Burradon, Newcastle upon Tyne, 19th April 1944

CAREER: Newcastle United July 1963/ SUNDERLAND Jan 1973/Ashington June 1975/Gateshead United 1975/Lusitano, South Africa 1976/Blyth Spartans cs 1977/North Shields Sept 1981.

Debut v Swindon Town (a) 20/1/1973

A fringe player with Newcastle United, the solidly-built left full-back was a Bob Stokoe signing in January 1973. Four months later he was a proud FA Cup winner, one of his very rare goals helping to account for Luton Town in

Ron Guthrie

the sixth round of the competition. After a further two seasons during which Sunderland were most pundits' tip for promotion, but in fact finished disappointingly sixth and fourth, a very busy close season in 1975 saw many departures (including Ron Guthrie), and an influx of new players. In season 1977-78 Ron helped Blyth Spartans to reach round five of the FA Cup. They drew 1-1 at Wrexham and in the replay at St James Park, Newcastle, were narrowly defeated by 2-1 before a crowd of 42,157. Once his football days were over Ron was employed as a milkman.

Appearances:
FL: 66 apps. 1 gl.
FAC: 7 apps. 1 gl.
FLC: 2 apps. 0 gls.
Other: 2(1) apps. 0 gls.
Total: *77(1) apps. 2 gls.*
Honours:
(Sunderland) FAC winners 1973.

Alex Hall

172

HAGGAN, John

Role: Wing-half 1919-20
5'8" 11st.6lbs.
b. Chester-le-Street, Co Durham, 16th December 1896
d. Gateshead, 2nd qtr 1982

CAREER: Pelaw FC, Tyneside/
SUNDERLAND Dec 1919/Brentford May
1922/Preston Colliery cs 1923/Hamilton
United (Canada)/Usworth Colliery Sept 1931.
Later a permit player with Washington Co-op
Wednesday July 1933.
Debut v West Bromwich Albion (a) 26/12/1919

Both John Haggan's senior appearances were
made very soon after joining, the Boxing Day
fixture above and the other eight days later.
This was at Derby and both games were lost
convincingly (4-0 at West Brom and 3-1 at
Derby). Haggan was left-half in the former
and right-half on the other occasion. For
Brentford Haggan played 21 Southern Section
and FA Cup matches (all at left-half), scoring
one League goal.

Appearances:
FL: 2 apps. 0 gls.
Total: *2 apps. 0 gls.*

*Alex Hall (extreme left) listens along with Patsy Gallacher,
Eddie Burbanks and Bert Johnston as Manager Johnny
Cochrane talks tactics on a Cup Final Eve visit to Wembley in
1937.*

HALL

Role: Right-back 1884-85
Debut v Redcar (a)
8/11/1884 (FAC)

Another member of the side that fought
Sunderland's first-ever FA Cup-tie. It was one
of Hall's nine reported
appearances for the club in
that 1884/85 non-League
season. Eight of his
outings were at right-back,
the other (against Erimus
FC of South Bank) being at
left-back.

Hall (George)

Appearances:
FAC: 1 app. 0 gls.
Total: *1 app. 0 gls.*

** It is more than likely his first name was George,
as news of a pre-1900 Sunderland player was noted
in 1937 as living in the USA at Ashley Fallas
where he was working as a monumental sculptor.*

HALL, Alexander Webster

Role: Right/left-back 1928-39
5'10" 11st.8lbs.
*b. Kirknewton, Midlothian, 6th
November 1908*
*d. Kirknewton, Midlothian, 5th
September 1991*

CAREER: East Calder Swifts/
Oakbank Amateurs/Wallyford
Bluebell/Dunfermline Athletic Dec
1928/SUNDERLAND Apr 1929
£750/Hibernian Oct 1945 coach
(after being a wartime guest from
Oct 1939)/ Sliema Wanderers
coach.
Debut v Sheffield United (a) 4/5/1929

Pithily summed up as "a robust,
straightforward back", Alex Hall
had been snapped up by
Sunderland after a bare four
months in senior soccer. "Spotted
comparatively raw", as one account
has it. He made his Sunderland
League bow very soon afterwards:
in the final fixture of 1928/29. The
club then cannily allowed him to
mature with the reserves a whole

season and a half before his next Football League appearance, on 27 December 1930 against Manchester City. And it was not until the 1934/35 campaign that his first team place was assured. Hall's virtues were several - he was strong in both feet, playing mostly right-back until Gorman's arrival, powerful in the tackle and decisive as when to make it. When he had finished playing Alex became Hibernian's third team coach before taking up a coaching position with Sliema Wanderers in Malta for a time from 1950. He originally worked as an engineer.

Appearances:
FL: 206 apps. 1 gl.
FAC: 27 apps. 0 gls.
Total: *233 apps. 1 gl.*
Honours:
(Sunderland) FL champs 1936/FAC winner 1937.

HALL, Frederick Wilkinson

Role: Centre-half 1946-55
5'11" 13st.12lbs.
b. Chester-le-Street, Co Durham, 18th November 1917
d. Stanley, Co Durham, 8th January 1989

CAREER: Ouston Juniors/Blackburn Rovers Nov 1935/SUNDERLAND Aug 1946/Barrow Sept 1955/Ransome & Marles (Newark) Aug 1956.

Debut v Derby County (h) 31/8/1946

Fred Hall was a pivot of weighty proportions, having risen to a near 14 stones from a recorded 12 stone 4 pounds in 1938. In those pre-war years Hall had made 29 Second Division appearances (debut 1936/37) of which eight were at right-back, five right-half, 14 centre-half and two left-half, revealing a very handy versatility. During the War, besides serving in the RAF, he had assisted a number of clubs as a guest. One of these, Spurs, impressed with Fred's ability, tried to obtain his transfer but their offer did not match Rovers' valuation. He requested a transfer in 1946 following a dispute over terms. Blackburn refused at first, then agreed reluctantly. Sunderland stepped in, soon appointing Fred skipper and he

HALL, Gareth David

Role: Defender 1995-98
5'8" 10st.7lbs.
b. Croydon, Surrey, 20th March 1969

CAREER: Woking S.F.A./Chelsea app July 1985, pro Apr 1986(SUNDERLAND loan Dec 1995)/SUNDERLAND Jan 1996(Brentford loan Oct 1997)/Swindon Town May 1998.

Debut v Derby County (a) 23/12/1995 (sub)

Gareth Hall spent nine-and-a-half years with Chelsea, making his League debut at 18 years of age and winning his first cap for Wales at 19. In all, he played in 138 games and scored four goals for the Pensioners. He joined Sunderland in a £300,000 transfer in mid-season 1995-96 and appeared in 8(6) Division One matches during the promotion campaign. After replacing Kubicki at right full-back in

Fred Hall

proved a most influential and commanding figure at centre-half during the early post-war years, finally completing more than 200 outings for the club. In 1945 Hall was a reserve for the Victory International match in France.

Appearances:
FL: 215 apps. 1 gl.
FAC: 9 apps. 0 gls.
Total: *224 apps. 1 gl.*

Gareth Hall

the following September, he held his position throughout the season, and his regular involvement in Premiership football earned him a recall to the Wales squad after a gap of four years. Sunderland began the new season with Chris Makin at right full-back, and at the time of Hall's loan to Brentford, he had not featured in the first team. It was not until the February 1998 visit to Molineux that he was given his first start of the season in an unfamiliar line-up, hit by four suspensions, that battled hard to secure a vital 1-0 victory against promotion rivals Wolves. Released in May 1998, following a season of severely restricted opportunities, Gareth was quickly snapped up, signing a three-year contract with Swindon Town.

Appearances:
PL: 32 apps. 0 gls.
FL: 9(7) apps. 0 gls.
FAC: 2 apps. 0 gls.
FLC: 3(1) apps. 0 gls.
Total: *46(8) apps. 0 gls.*
Honours:
8 Eng Sch apps. 1984/1 Wales U-21 app. 1990/9 Welsh caps 1988-92/(Chelsea) Div 2 champs 1989/FMC winner 1990/ (Sunderland) Div 1 champs 1996.

HALL, Matthew

Role: Inside-left 1906-07
5'8" 10st.0lbs.
b. circa 1886

CAREER: St Mirren 1904/SUNDERLAND May 1906/Clyde May 1907.

Debut v Newcastle United (a) 1/9/1906

Matthew Hall played in the first seven League fixtures of 1906/07, Jim Gemmell took over for the next three, then Hall came back for the eleventh and was not selected for the first team again. An analysis of results that coincided with his appearances gives two wins, two draws and four defeats. The inside-left berth gives a little unsettled picture that term, five players sharing the 38 appearances. On signing for Clyde, the club said of him: 'He's a forward possessed of great speed and very clever on the ball.'

Matthew Hall

Appearances:
FL: 8 apps. 1 gl.
Total: *8 apps. 1 gl.*

HALL, Thomas

Role: Centre-forward/inside-left 1910-13
5'8" 10st.2lbs.
b. Newburn, Northumberland, 4th September 1891

CAREER: Newburn Manor School/Newburn Grange 1908/Newburn Alliance late 1908/ SUNDERLAND Jan 1909/Newcastle United May 1913 £425 (Leeds City guest during WW1)/Gillingham May 1920/Gillingham trainer July 1926.

Debut v Notts County (a) 17/12/1910

A prolific scorer for his school team, Newburn Manor, Thomas Hall averaged 30 goals per season over a three year span. He continued in this scoring vein in his brief acquaintance with the junior scene so was quickly snapped up by Sunderland. At Newcastle (58 League and FA Cup outings, 16 goals) he made a dream debut at Roker Park, finding the net

Tom Hall

in a 2-1 victory over his old buddies. Moving south after the Great War, Tom proved an excellent signing for Gillingham, appearing in 190 Third Division matches in which he slotted in 47 goals - he was credited with Gillingham's first-ever hat-trick versus Norwich City on 11th February 1922. An industrious forward who could adequately fill all five attacking positions, Tom was the brother of Bertie Hall (Hartlepools United/Norwich City/Bristol City).

Appearances:
FL: 30 apps. 8 gls.
Total: *30 apps. 8 gls.*
Honours:
(Sunderland) FL champs 1913.

HALLIDAY

Role: Right-back/Centre-half 1887-88

Debut v Newcastle United (h) 5/11/1887 (FAC) (scored)

Halliday appeared at right-back in his first FA Cup tie and at centre-half in the other two, positions he occupied in the friendly and local cup-ties that composed the rest of match programmes in pre-League seasons. It seems not unlikely his couple of goals were from penalties. What is established is that they were scored on his debut, chronicled above, and in the last tie of that campaign, against Middlesbrough away. This was won 4-2 but Sunderland were subsequently disqualified.

Appearances:
FAC: 3 apps. 2 gls.
Total: *3 apps. 2 gls.*

HALLIDAY, David

Role: Centre-forward 1925-30
6'0" 12st.4lbs.
b. Dumfries, 11th December 1897
d. Banchory, nr Aberdeen, 5th January 1970

CAREER: Dumfries schools football/ Tayleurians FC (Dumfries) during WW1/ Queen of the South Wanderers 1919-20/ St Mirren June 1920/Dundee June 1921/ SUNDERLAND Apr 1925 £3,500/Arsenal Nov 1929 £6,500/Manchester City Nov 1930 £5,700/Folkestone July 1933/Clapton Orient Dec 1933/Yeovil & Petters United player-manager July 1935/Aberdeen manager Dec 1937/Leicester City manager June 1955, retired Nov 1958, thence scout.

Debut v Birmingham (h) 29/8/1925

Down the years there have always been players well worthy of international honours who, in the event, did not get them. Such a one was surely David Halliday, a centre-forward whose seasonal and aggregate scoring figures speak volumes. Doubtless the fact that he was a contemporary of Hughie Gallacher and James McGrory was a prime cause but nevertheless. For Sunderland he still remains the highest seasonal scorer (43 in 42 Division One games in 1928/29) and his grand total of 153 includes three fours and a dozen hat-tricks. Not only

that, he was top scorer in each of his four seasons with the Lads - and no Sunderland player since has even equalled his *worst* seasonal tally of goals! Overall he is one of the six greatest strikers Britain has known: 347 in 464 Football and Scottish League appearances. Big and powerful and dashing, Halliday thrilled the crowds and was, it almost goes without saying, a deadly marksman. At Arsenal he was part of a very expensive front line but stayed only a year before joining Manchester City. Prolific even in his last match for the Gunners, he netted four times in a remarkable 6-6 draw with Leicester - a record result which still stands as the League's joint-highest scoring draw. He had not always been a centre-forward but an inside-left at school, outside-right for Queen of the South and St Mirren and outside-left for Dundee, the latter instituting the change to centre. Unlike many great players, Halliday was also a highly successful manager, presiding over both Aberdeen (Cup and Championship) and Leicester City (Second Division champions) when honours were won. He worked as a motor mechanic after leaving school, and latterly was the proprietor of a hotel at Bieldside, Aberdeen. A younger brother, John, assisted Queen of the South, Lincoln City and other clubs between the wars.

Appearances:
FL: 166 apps. 153 gls.
FAC: 9 apps. 9 gls.
Total: *175 apps. 162 gls.*
Honours:
1 SL app./(Dundee) SC finalist 1924.

HALOM, Victor Lewis

Role: Forward 1972-76
5'10" 12st.10lbs.
b. Coton Park, Burton upon Trent, 3rd October 1948

CAREER: Burton & South Derbyshire Boys/ Charlton Athletic app Apr 1964, pro Jan 1966 (Orient loan Aug 1967)/ Orient Oct 1967/ Fulham Nov 1968/Luton Town Sept 1971/ SUNDERLAND Feb 1973/ Oldham Athletic July 1976/Rotherham United Feb 1980. Career ended by injury during 1980-81 season/ Northwich Victoria briefly during 1981-82/ Frederikstad, Norway coach 1982/ Barrow manager 1983/Rochdale manager May 1984-Dec 1986/Burton Albion manager Sept-Oct 1987/North Shields. (In July 1991 reported to be playing in the Vaux Bluebell Over-40's League).

Debut v Sheffield Wednesday (a) 10/2/1973

Within three months of his arrival at Roker Park Vic Halom became the proud possessor of an FA Cup winners' medal. In the run-in to the 1973 Wembley final against Leeds United, Halom scored two vital goals. The first against Cup favourites Manchester City at Roker Park in the fifth round replay remains part of Sunderland folklore - a blistering angled drive

Vic Halom's goal in the FA Cup against Manchester City was one of Roker Park's finest.

Vic Halom

appearances and 131 goals. Outside the game Vic Halom stood for the Liberal Democrats in Sunderland North in the 1992 General Election, but finished third behind the Labour and Conservative candidates.

Appearances:
FL: 110(3) apps. 35 gls.
FAC: 10(1) apps. 2 gls.
FLC: 6 apps. 3 gls.
Other: 4 apps. 0 gls.
Total: *130(4) apps. 40 gls.*

HAMILTON, Andrew

Role: Outside-left 1896-97
5'10" 11st.4lbs.
b. Glasgow, circa 1874
d. Glasgow, October 1929

CAREER: Cambuslang/Falkirk May 1894/ SUNDERLAND May 1896/New Brighton Tower Aug 1897/Warmley May 1898/Ryde IOW Sept 1900/Watford Nov 1900-May 1901.
Debut v Bury (h) 1/9/1896

Andrew Hamilton played in the second and last League fixtures of 1896/97 with five other appearances at intervals throughout the season. All were in Hamilton's customary left-wing position except the last which was at inside-right. Ostensibly his handy physique would have lent itself to an inside-forward role rather than a winger's. Hamilton's best feat for Sunderland was in scoring a couple of goals in the 4-3 home victory over Liverpool on October 17, 1896.

Appearances:
FL: 7 apps. 2 gls.
Total: *7 apps. 2 gls.*

HAMILTON, James

Role: Midfield 1971-74
5'11" 11st.4lbs.
b. Uddingston, 14th June 1955

CAREER: Coatbridge Juniors (with a spell on West Bromwich Albion's ground staff)/ SUNDERLAND app June 1971, pro June 1972 (Plymouth Argyle loan Nov 1975)/Plymouth Argyle Jan 1976/Bristol Rovers Dec 1976/ Carlisle United Sept 1977(Morton loan)/ Australian Football Sept 1981/Gretna Aug 1982/Hartlepool United Nov 1982/Gretna Aug 1986.

to crown a quality move that sent the 51,000 crowd delirious. His second was the first goal against Arsenal in a memorable semi-final at Hillsborough. A strong, aggressive striker, he was one of Bob Stokoe's earliest signings, and proved terrific value for his £35,000 transfer fee. His chirpy character also endeared Vic to the Roker faithful who bestowed on him unconditional cult status. Vic repaid them with further classic moments such as his marvellous home hat-trick to beat a quality Derby side 3-0 in the second replay of a League Cup tie in October 1973. Increasingly troubled by injuries in his final season, he nevertheless qualified for a Division Two championship medal in 1975-76 before departing in the close season to Oldham Athletic for £25,000. At Boundary Park he scored 23 League and Cup goals in his first season and passed the 100 League goals milestone in the Latics' colours. He later linked up again with Cup final team mate Ian Porterfield who was boss at Rotherham with Halom as his player-coach. His career aggregate figures were 435 Football League

Debut v Preston North End (h) 25/9/1971 (sub) (scored)

Jimmy Hamilton, Sunderland's youngest outfield League player at 16 years, 103 days, made a dream start when, in his first substitute appearance, he headed a last minute winning goal against

Jimmy Hamilton

Preston North End in a 4-3 victory. Unfortunately 'Chico' - a nickname pinched from the Aston Villa player of that era - did not progress and was subsequently transferred to Plymouth Argyle, and quickly on to Bristol Rovers. His career finally took off with Carlisle United where he recorded 150(4) appearances and 12 goals. In recent years Jimmy Hamilton has been employed as a Dumfries hotelier and in the antiques trade in Beverley.

Appearances:
FL: 8(8) apps. 2 gls.
Total: *8(8) apps. 2 gls.*

HANNAH, David

Role: Inside-forward/outside-left 1889-94
5'6" 11st.3lbs.
b. Raffrey, Co Down, 28th April 1867
d. January 1936

CAREER: Renton/SUNDERLAND cs 1889/ Liverpool Nov 1894/Dundee cs 1897/ Woolwich Arsenal Oct 1897/Renton Aug 1899.

Debut v Blackburn Rovers (a) 18/1/1890

Signed a year before Sunderland obtained admission to the Football League, David Hannah coped easily with the demands that

David Hannah

higher status made. He had moved with his family to Renton when a child, worked in a local dye works from the age of 13 and eventually joined the then famous Renton FC, for the most part assisting their reserves. David, short, thickset and usefully versatile, was an early Sunderland notability. He went on to Liverpool, enjoying another championship season there.

Appearances:
FL: 75 apps. 21 gls.
FAC: 14 apps. 4 gls.
Total: *89 apps. 25 gls.*
Honours:
(Sunderland) FL champs 1892, 1893/(Liverpool) FL Div 2 champs 1896.

HANNAH, James 'Blood'

Role: Outside-right/outside-left 1891-97
b. Glasgow, circa 1868

CAREER: Glasgow junior football/Third Lanark 1888/Sunderland Albion Sept 1890/ SUNDERLAND Aug 1891/Third Lanark May 1897/Queens Park Rangers Nov 1899/ Dykehead Aug 1900/Sunderland Royal Rovers Jan 1901.

Debut v Everton (h) 3/10/1891

James Hannah was soon among the honours after joining Thirds and arrived at Sunderland after first linking up with neighbours Albion, after winning both a cap and a Scottish Cup medal. Like so many of his Sunderland team mates Hannah was not

James Hannah

limited to any one position, e.g. He performed in the '92 side at outside-right, and at outside-left, to accommodate the newly acquired Jim Gillespie, the following campaign. And he could take an inside berth. Hannah's stay with Sunderland, though not of course of Doig-like length, was still a significant six years - a fair span for that time. It would be illuminating to learn the derivation, and meaning, of that odd nickname 'Blood'.

Appearances:
FL: 156 apps. 67 gls.
FAC: 16 apps. 10 gls.
Total: *172 apps. 77 gls.*
Honours:
1 Scot cap/(Third Lanark) SC winner 1889/(Sunderland) FL champs 1893, 1895.

HANNIGAN, John Leckie

Role: Outside-right/outside-left 1955-58
5'10" 11st.0lbs.
b. Glasgow, 17th February 1933

CAREER: Junior football to Morton circa 1952-53/SUNDERLAND June 1955, around £8,000/Derby County May 1958 £3,250/Bradford June 1961 £2,400/Weymouth July 1964/Bath July 1968, retired 1969.

Debut v Birmingham City (a) 8/10/1955

Handy cover for both Billy Bingham and Billy Elliott, John Hannigan was concisely analysed in the 'Fifties as "a young player with a powerful direct style". He found a third string

John Hannigan

to his bow at Derby when switched in season 1958/59 to centre-forward with some success. In all his while at the Baseball Ground he played in 75 League and FA Cup matches, scoring 19 goals. With Bradford Park Avenue Hannigan also saw much first team duty, his figures there being 122 League and Cup outings, and ten goals. And whilst with Weymouth the club won the championship and John also collected a League Cup finalist's medal in 1964/65. The club retained the title the following year and went close again in 1966/67. At Bath, he won promotion with them in 1968/69 before retiring.

Appearances:
FL: 33 apps. 8 gls.
FAC: 2 apps. 2 gls.
Total: *35 apps. 10 gls.*

HANNING, James

Role: Inside-right 1897-98

CAREER: Dalziel Rovers/SUNDERLAND Jan 1898/Hamilton Academical Sept 1898/Carfin Emmett Sept 1899.

Debut v Notts County (a) 5/2/1898

It is a high probability James Hanning was another of Sunderland's myriad Scots - he certainly hailed from a Scottish junior club that supplied recruits in those early times. Hanning's sole run-out in the League, at Nottingham against the County, resulted in a 1-0 victory. Incidentally, his appearance interrupted a splendid run in the inside-right position by Jim Leslie from November 27, 1897 to the end of the season that took in 20 League and one FA Cup match.

Appearances:
FL: 1 app. 0 gls.
Total: *1 app. 0 gls.*

HARDWICK, Steven

Role: Goalkeeper 1987-88
5'11" 13st.0lbs.
b. Mansfield, 6th September 1956

CAREER: Chesterfield July 1974/Newcastle United Dec 1976(Detroit Express loan May-Aug 1978)/Oxford United Feb 1983(Crystal Palace loan Mar 1986)(SUNDERLAND loan Aug 1987)/Huddersfield Town July 1988/

Steve Hardwick

Paul Hardyman

Kettering Town cs 1991/Scarborough trial Aug 1991/Emley F.C./Kettering Town Mar 1992/ Boston United Sept 1992.

Debut v Brentford (a) 15/8/1987

Steve Hardwick, a loan signing from Oxford United, was Sunderland's first goalkeeper in Division Three. He starred in the opening six League fixtures which yielded three wins and three draws. He also played in both legs of the League Cup against Middlesbrough (lost 2-1 on aggregate). The fact that Oxford had allowed him to become cup-tied indicated he was available for a permanent move, and it was somewhat surprising he rejected Sunderland's offer of a contract at the end of his loan agreement. A product of the famous Chesterfield Academy of Goalkeeping, Hardwick became Newcastle United's record goalkeeper signing at £80,000 in December 1976. After a lengthy spell in reserve he finally established himself but although often cruelly criticised and never a crowd favourite, had made 101 senior appearances when Oxford United paid a bargain £30,000 to take him to the Manor. He proved an inspiration, winning successive championship medals in Oxford's meteoric rise from Division Three to Division One, recording 158 consecutive appearances along the way. Three seasons with Huddersfield Town wound-up Steve Hardwick's League career which totalled 404 appearances.

Appearances:
FL: 6 apps. 0 gls.
FLC: 2 apps. 0 gls.
Total: *8 apps. 0 gls.*
Honours:
Eng Yth/(Oxford United) Div 3 champs 1984/Div 2 champs 1985.

HARDYMAN, Paul George

Role: Defender 1989-92
5'8" 11st.2lbs.
b. Portsmouth, 11th March 1964

CAREER: Fareham/Waterlooville 1982/ Portsmouth app July 1983, pro May 1984/ SUNDERLAND July 1989/Bristol Rovers July 1992/Wycombe Wanderers Aug 1995/Barnet Aug 1996-July 1997(Slough Town loan Feb 1997).

Debut v Swindon Town (a) 19/8/1989

Paul Hardyman joined Sunderland from his hometown club, Portsmouth, for a tribunal-set fee of £130,000 in July 1989. Included in his 72 League appearances for Portsmouth, for whom he signed as a pro on the same day as Kevin Ball, were 33 in 1986-87 when they won promotion to Division One as runners-up to Derby County. He had an excellent beginning with Sunderland with 42 League starts and seven goals in his initial season. He also scored twice in League Cup ties, five of his total of nine goals coming from the penalty spot. The one most recalled however, is the last minute penalty he missed in the goalless home leg of the tense 1990 play-off semi-final with Newcastle when John Burridge saved and Paul was sent-off for a reckless follow-up challenge. Primarily a left full-back, Hardyman was equally at home in midfield and was a regular first team player during his three years at Roker Park, but was devastated only to be named on the bench for the 1992 FA Cup final against Liverpool after playing in every round prior to Wembley. Bristol Rovers paid £160,000 for him in August 1992, but his subsequent moves were without a fee and he was released by Barnet in the close season of 1997, after ending the campaign on loan to Slough Town. More recently he was spotted supporting The Lads at Wembley in the 1998 Division One Play-Off final.

Appearances:
FL: 102(5) apps. 9 gls.
FAC: 8(1) apps. 1 gl.
FLC: 11 apps. 2 gls.
Other: 2 apps. 0 gls.
Total: *123(6) apps. 12 gls.*
Honours:
2 Eng U-21 apps. 1985-86/
(Sunderland) FAC finalist 1992.

HARFORD, Michael Gordon 'Mick'

Role: Forward 1992-93
6'2" 14st.5lbs.
b. Sunderland, 12th February 1959

CAREER: Sunderland Schoolboys/Lincoln City July 1977/Newcastle United Dec 1980/Bristol City Aug 1981/Newcastle United Mar 1982/Birmingham City Mar 1982/Luton Town Dec 1984/Derby County Jan 1990/Luton Town Sept 1991/Chelsea Aug 1992/SUNDERLAND Mar 1993/Coventry City July 1993/Wimbledon Aug 1994, retired from playing Aug 1998, and appointed first team coach, appointed caretaker-manager Apr 1999.

Debut v Barnsley (a) 21/3/1993

Mick Harford began with Lincoln City, initially as a midfield player. He was quickly and successfully converted into a striker and had scored 40 goals in 115 appearances for the Imps when Newcastle paid a fee in the region of £200,000 for his signature. It was a record at the time, but his spell at St James Park was not distinguished and he moved quickly on to cash-strapped Bristol City. This eventually led to an unusual transfer move. To facilitate his move to Birmingham City and to recoup monies owed to Newcastle, Harford was transferred (on paper only) back to Newcastle before signing for Birmingham. Always a willing and enthusiastic worker and an excellent muscular target man, his all-round game improved dramatically during his first spell at Luton Town, a fact recognised by the England selectors who awarded him two full caps in 1988-89. A supporter of The Lads from the age of seven, by comparison Mick's spell as a Sunderland player lasted only a matter of months. A transfer deadline buy from Chelsea (fee £250,000), he was pitched headlong into a relegation scrap successfully, if unconvincingly, negotiated as Sunderland won only one of the season's final ten fixtures. In the close season a fee of £200,000 was recouped when he signed for Coventry City. At the age of 35 he joined Wimbledon and, in a new role operating between midfield and defence, continued to exhibit his battling qualities while his strength in the air further made him a great danger at set pieces. In April 1999 Mick was appointed caretaker-manager of Wimbledon, with a brief to continue until Joe Kinnear was fit to resume work, following his heart attack in March.

Appearances:
FL: 10(1) apps. 2 gls.
Total: *10(1) apps. 2 gls.*
Honours:
2 Eng caps 1988-89/1 Eng 'B' app./(Luton Town) FLC winner 1988/FLC finalist 1989.

HARGREAVES, Leonard

Role: Outside-left 1927-29
5'10" 11st.2lbs.
*b. Kimberworth, nr Rotherham,
7th March 1906
d. Sheffield, 3rd qtr 1980*

CAREER: Blackburn Wesleyans (Doncaster), Sheffield Sunday Schools League/Doncaster Rovers Mar 1925/ SUNDERLAND Apr 1927 £2,000/ Sheffield Wednesday Mar 1929/ Workington Oct 1931/Doncaster Rovers July 1932/Luton Town Aug 1933/Peterborough & Fletton United July 1934.

Debut v West Ham United (a) 1/9/1927

In the spring of 1925 Doncaster Rovers recruited two young wingmen, one an outside-right, the other an outside-left. The pair joined Sunderland two years later at a then significant fee and were respectively Alwyne Wilks and this present subject, Len

Hargreaves. It was hoped he would take the mantle of Bill Ellis (transferred to Birmingham the following November) and in fact Len was first choice in 1927/28 (28 First Division appearances). But Adam McLean took over in 1928/29, Hargreaves moving on to Sheffield Wednesday where chances proved rare due to the rise of future England winger, Ellis Rimmer. A few months with non-League Workington and a return to Doncaster brought no great change to his fortunes and the drift out of the big time was completed at Luton (no senior appearances). Hargreaves was once a locomotive fitter.

Appearances:
FL: 36 apps. 12 gls.
FAC: 4 apps. 1 gl.
Total: *40 apps. 13 gls.*

HARKER, J.

Role: Inside-right 1898-99

CAREER: Thornaby FC/SUNDERLAND Mar 1899/Thornaby Apr 1899.

Debut v Blackburn Rovers (h) 3/4/1899

Harker has proved to be a real mystery man who, according to one source, was with Sunderland a matter of six days only. His name does not appear on the club's lists of the period and very possibly Harker was an amateur recruited for just one match. What is known is that Blackburn won 1-0.

Appearances:
FL: 1 app. 0 gls.
Total: *1 app. 0 gls.*

Len Hargreaves

HARPER, George Spencer

Role: Inside-left 1902-03
5'6" 12st.7lbs.
*b. Birmingham
d. Birmingham, 14th July 1949*

CAREER: Saltley Gas Co (Birmingham)/ Burton United/Aston Villa/Hereford Thistle Apr 1896/Wolverhampton Wanderers cs 1897/

Grimsby Town May 1902/SUNDERLAND Nov 1902/retired through injury May 1904.

Debut v West Bromwich Albion (h) 29/11/1902

George Harper

George Harper was introduced into the first class game by Wolves - he saw only reserve team football with Villa - and had quite a good run at Molineux with 66 League and Cup games (21 goals) under his belt. He headed their score sheet for the 1899/1900 campaign. He moved to Grimsby to participate in their first-ever top flight season, doing moderately well (25 League and Cup games, three goals). Transferred to Sunderland with Bobby Hogg moving in the opposite direction, all his first team appearances were concentrated into the 1902/03 season. George was on the short side but possessed of twelve and a half stones weight wise; he had to be treated with respect by any opposition.

Appearances:
FL: 10 apps. 1 gl.
FAC: 1 app. 0 gls.
Total: *11 apps. 1 gl.*

HARPER, William

Role: Goalkeeper 1921-23
5'10" 11st.5lbs.
b. Wishaw, Lanarkshire, 15th November 1900

CAREER: Wishaw/ SUNDERLAND Sept 1921/ Manchester City May 1923/ Crystal Palace May 1924/ Luton Town Oct 1926/ Weymouth 1927/Callender Athletic Feb 1930.

Debut v Manchester City (h) 14/1/1922

Scot Willie Harper was a highly competent goalkeeper who, once he had got into the League side, missed but one League game to the end of 1921/22, an 18-match sequence. The next season Ned Robson had the edge. Harper's career was a varied one after leaving Roker Park. J.F. Mitchell, an amateur but soon to be a full England cap, held sway at Maine Road and the next move, to Crystal Palace, proved a good one. Willie missed only a single League game in 1924/25 and, after holding the first team spot for almost half of 1925/26, gave way to the rich promise of Billy Callender. The latter went on to become a Palace celebrity. Again at Luton, fortune smiled, Harper gaining the senior spot and clocking up 31 League appearances in a truncated season there.

Appearances:
FL: 28 apps. 0 gls.
Total: *28 apps. 0 gls.*

Willie Harper

HARRIS, Gordon

Role: Inside-forward
1967-72
5'9" 11st.2lbs.
b. Worksop, Notts, 2nd June 1940

CAREER: Worksop Schools/Firbeck Colliery/Burnley Jan 1958/SUNDERLAND Jan 1968 £65,000/South Shields July 1972.

Debut v Everton (h) 11/1/1969

Of Gordon Harris a scribe wrote "ten years at Turf Moor where he has progressed from a speedy outside-left into a thoughtful midfield general." And again, in the programme for an inter-league match "an inside-forward of great determination and ability." Gordon had been coveted by other clubs in the early part of his Burnley decade when understudy to the

Gordon Harris

Gerry Harrison

England cap, Brian Pilkington, but offers were refused. When Pilkington moved to Bolton in February 1961 Harris took over. It was in the season of 1963/64 that a switch to inside-left occurred, followed by runs in other positions. His lone England cap came in 1966 against Poland. Gordon's aggregate figures with Burnley were 313 senior appearances, 81 goals. His first games in a Sunderland shirt, for instance, were at left-half, but he was criticised with a degree of justification by some during his Roker spell for being too slow when operating in a more foward role. 'The General' Gordon was nonetheless one of Sunderland's most skilful players during the disappointing 1969/70 relegation season. He later worked in the coal industry as a driver.

Appearances:
FL: 124(1) apps. 16 gls.
FAC: 3 apps. 0 gls.
FLC: 3 apps. 0 gls.
Other: 4 apps. 0 gls.
Total: *134(1) apps. 16 gls.*
Honours:
1 Eng cap/2 Eng U-23 apps./2 FL apps./
(Burnley) FAC finalist 1962.

HARRISON, Gerald Randall 'Gerry'

Role: Defender/Midfield 1998-date
5'10" 12st.2lbs.
b. Lambeth, London, 15th April 1972

CAREER: South London Schools/West Norwood/Watford ass. sch. Feb 1987, trainee July 1989, pro Dec 1989/Bristol City July 1991 (Cardiff City loan Jan 1992)(Hereford United loan Nov 1993)(Bath City loan Feb 1994)/ Huddersfield Town Mar 1994/Burnley Aug 1994/SUNDERLAND July 1998(Luton Town loan Dec 1998)(Hull City loan Mar 1999).

Debut v York City (h) 18/8/1999 (FLC)

A versatile all-round sportsman, Gerry Harrison won schoolboy international honours in both football and athletics. He won the English Schools javelin championship at 15 and later the Great Britain title, and was county standard at both cricket and hockey. Despite the many career options, football claimed him and he made his League debut for Watford as a 17-year-old. Able to occupy almost any outfield position, he began as a striker but has operated with equal faculty in defence or midfield. Gerry has been associated with nine different League clubs in his career to date. Four seasons with Burnley have made up the bulk of his 200 plus League appearances, and it was from Turf Moor that Sunderland signed him, on a free transfer, in July 1998. He failed to impress on his Sunderland debut, but was subsequently found to be suffering from the Hepatitis A virus. Happily he made a full recovery but was then unable to break into the very strong first team squad. Just prior to Christmas 1998 he joined Luton Town on a three-month loan, and this was immediately followed by a further loan to Hull City. Pitched headlong into a relegation struggle, Gerry was able to assist the Tigers in their ultimately successful efforts to avoid relegation from Division Three.

Appearances :
FLC: 1 app. 0 gls.
Total: *1 app. 0 gls.*
Honours:
2 Eng Sch apps. 1987.

HARTLEY, James Milburn

Role: Centre/inside-forward 1895-97
5'6" 11st.4lbs.
b. Dumbarton, 29th October 1876

CAREER: Junior football to Dumbarton FC 1894/SUNDERLAND Oct 1895/Burnley Nov 1896 in company with Wm. Longair (Lincoln City loan Mar 1897)/Tottenham Hotspur May 1897/Lincoln City May 1899/Rangers cs 1903/Port Glasgow Athletic cs 1904/Brentford cs 1905/New Brompton May 1906-1908.

Debut v Sheffield Wednesday (a) 19/10/1895

James Hartley enjoyed a somewhat roving career, taking in clubs from Scotland to Kent with stays varying in length from a matter of months to four years. He made the most impact at Lincoln, the City club stepping in for his services two years after a short loan period (the City management apparently had noted his abilities). Hartley became their first player to register 50 League goals and they valued his capacity to play in four forward positions (the 'blind spot' was outside-left). He had actually started out as a defender. His brother, Abraham Hartley, was Everton's centre-forward in the 1897 FA Cup final.

Appearances:
FL: 11 apps. 1 gl.
Total: *11 apps. 1 gl.*

HARTNESS, George

Role: Inside-right 1896-1897

CAREER: Monkseaton FC/SUNDERLAND Nov 1895-1897.

Debut v Sheffield Wednesday (h) 5/12/1896

A debut made a year after joining, Hartness's other appearance occurred a week later: another home fixture, this time against Everton. Both games were drawn, 0-0 and 1-1 respectively. Another player named Hartness (no first team appearances) was signed by Sunderland in October 1909, first name Henry, but whether he was related to George is not known.

Appearances:
FL: 2 apps. 0 gls.
Total: *2 apps. 0 gls.*

HARVEY, John

Role: Outside/inside-right 1889-81 & 1892-97
5'4"
b. Scotland

CAREER: Renton/SUNDERLAND cs 1889/Clyde Jan 1891/SUNDERLAND Sept 1892/Newcastle United May 1897 £40 including J M Campbell, retired cs 1899 becoming United's asst trainer until a year later.

Debut v Blackburn Rovers (a) 18/1/1890 (FAC)
Debut v Aston Villa (a) 17/9/1892

John Harvey was a little terrier of a Scot prominent in Sunderland's rise of the 1890s. During those years a feature was the understanding and combination developed between the diminutive Harvey and the burly John Campbell. The pair moved to Newcastle together, there to participate in United's promotion line-up of '97/8. This was the third club to field a Harvey/Campbell pairing that had commenced at Renton. Strangely neither achieved a Scotland cap. Harvey's surname

John Harvey

has often appeared in print as Harvie, but the -ey ending is the one used both in Football League and club records. John was a fitter by occupation.

Appearances:
FL: 96 apps. 14 gls.
FAC: 12 apps. 3 gls.
Total: *108 apps. 17 gls.*
Honours:
(Sunderland) FL champions 1893.

HARVEY, Martin

Role: Wing-half 1959-72
5'9" 11st.3lbs.
b. Belfast, 19th September 1941

CAREER: Belfast schools football/ SUNDERLAND Sept 1958, retired through injury 1971, becoming a club coach/Carlisle United asst manager-coach 1978, caretaker-manager Feb 1980, manager Apr 1980-Sept 1980/Plymouth Argyle coach July 1981-1989/ Raith Rovers asst. manager/Millwall asst. manager Feb 1996.

Debut v Plymouth Argyle (a) 24/10/1959

Martin Harvey was a top class wing-half who usually operated on the right flank. A telling

Martin Harvey

tackle, constructive approach and thoughtful distribution were prominent among his qualities. Honoured with half a dozen caps at schoolboy level, he went to Burnley for a trial at 15 but was not made an offer as, at 5'3", he was considered too small. (Sunderland had a profitable penchant for snapping up ex-Burnley trialists - Martin's team mates, Jim Montgomery and Cec Irwin, had likewise sampled Turf Moor). Sunderland manager, Alan Brown, quickly stepped in, signing Martin as a professional without preliminaries such as amateur or ground staff status. As Stan Anderson's understudy, he served a long apprenticeship. Anderson was club captain at the height of his considerable powers. Martin played in Sunderland sides at every grade before making his senior debut in October 1959. It was to be precisely four years and a mere 20-odd League games before he replaced Anderson. He was 22, ambitious and had been a full international since 1960/61. October 1963 proved a memorable month for Martin as he also replaced the renowned Danny Blanchflower in the Northern Ireland line-up. He had then represented his country at four different levels. Anderson departed to Newcastle United and season 1963/64 turned out to be a wonderful term for Harvey to finally make his mark. Sunderland finished as Division Two runners-up, five points clear of third-placed Preston North End, and so returned to the top flight. It was a fine side - from ubiquitous Jim Montgomery in goal to perky George Mulhall on the extreme left. The half-back line, comprised of Martin, the great Charlie Hurley and Jimmy McNab, filled an essential role and was the fulcrum around which attack and defence functioned. Martin, often a left-back in later years, grossed a total of 353 senior appearances (plus 4 subs) before injury, collected making a last-ditch clearance at Norwich in 1972, forced his retirement. He was only 30 and his total would surely have easily exceeded the 400 mark and perhaps have included a 1973 FA Cup medal had a full playing span been possible. There seems little doubt it would also have been spent in Sunderland's red and white stripes and he was honoured with a testimonial against Newcastle three years later. After his enforced retirement from the playing arena, Martin undertook a variety of behind-the-scenes appointments, especially as assistant manager. His sole managerial appointment was with Carlisle United. He had been assistant to

Bobby Moncur at Brunton Park and on taking over saw the club reach a comfortable sixth in the Third Division. Harvey resigned early the following season (1980/81), however, after a poor start, making him the club's shortest serving manager. In the event Carlisle, however, were not relegated.

Appearances:
FL: 310(4) apps. 5 gls.
FAC: 25 apps. 0 gls.
FLC: 15 apps. 0 gls.
Other: 3 apps. 0 gls.
Total: *353(4) apps. 5 gls.*
Honours:
34 NIre caps/2 NIre 'B' apps./2 NIre U-23 apps./6 NIre Sch apps.

HASTINGS

Role: Utility player 1887-88
Debut v Morpeth Harriers (h) 15/10/1887 (FAC)

Hastings played in four of the five FA Cup ties Sunderland contested in 1887/88 and remarkably occupied a different position in all of them. His appearance in the third round tie with Middlesbrough was, however, not without great controversy. After a 2-2 draw, Sunderland won the replay 4-2 but Boro' later protested, apparently following a conversation overheard in a pub, that Hastings, Monaghan (q.v.) and Richardson (q.v.) - all Scotsmen who had been drafted in - had breached the English Cup rules (which stated professionals should be born locally or have lived nearby for at least two years) and been paid to play. Sunderland somehow successfully argued the trio were amateurs but were found guilty of paying their train-fares from Dumfries. The club were ejected from the Cup competition and the players suspended for three months. The incident proved a major factor in Sunderland operating on a full professional basis from then on.

Appearances:
FAC: 4 apps. 0 gls.
Total: *4 apps. 0 gls.*

Alex Hastings

HASTINGS, Alexander Cockburn

Role: Left-half 1930-46
5'11" 12st.8lbs.
b. Falkirk, 17th March 1912
d. South Australia, 26th December 1988

CAREER: Falkirk schools football/Carron Welfare/Rosewell Rosedale/Stenhousemuir/ SUNDERLAND Aug 1930 (guested for Hartlepools United during WW2)/retired 1946/Kilmarnock manager Mar 1948-Apr 1950/Stoke City scout during 1960s.

OGDEN'S CIGARETTES

A. HASTINGS (SUNDERLAND)

Debut v Portsmouth (a) 6/9/1930

The 1930's were vintage years at Roker Park for the production of young half-backs. A prime example was Alex Hastings, establishing himself in his very first season and soon to be a very youthful and successful captain. He had started as a boy at right-back, moved to centre-half and finally centre-forward from which berth he scored 54 goals in his last nine months at school. As a senior, Alex was clever, deft and high spirited in performance, and indeed, mature for his years as perhaps the early captaincy shows. A stalwart and loyal Sunderland servant throughout the 1930's he had competition for a regular Roker place from Sandy McNab but won two Scottish caps, both against Ireland, in 1935 and 1937. However, like so many players of the era Alex lost key years of his career to World War Two and he played only very briefly once hostilities had ceased. The Kilmarnock appointment was his sole managerial post after which he ran a Monkton hotel. He later was employed as a Falkirk licensee and managed an Edinburgh bookshop. Hastings emigrated to Australia in 1965 and football claimed him again; he became President of the South Australian Soccer Federation.

Appearances:
FL: 263 apps. 2 gls.
FAC: 37 apps. 4 gls.
Total: *300 apps. 6 gls.*
Honours:
2 Scot caps/(Sunderland) FL champs 1936.

Alex Hastings receives the League championship trophy in 1936.

HASTINGS, John George

Role: Right-back 1908-09
5'8" 11st.7lbs.
b. Thornaby-on-Tees, N.Yorkshire, 1887

CAREER: Darlington St Augustine's/
SUNDERLAND Feb 1909/retired 1913.

Debut v Preston North End (h) 24/4/1909

On Sunderland's books
for some four years, John
Hastings played only
one senior game for the
club: the last League
fixture of season 1908/09
which was won 2-1. It
must be said, however,
that stiff competition
was on hand with the
arrival of Trougher and,
later, Charlie Gladwin.

John Hastings

Appearances:
FL: 1 app. 0 gls.
Total: *1 app. 0 gls.*

HAUSER, Thomas

Role: Forward 1988-92
6'3" 12st.6lbs.
b. Schopfhain, Germany, 10th April 1965

CAREER: Schopfhain/F.C. Basle, Switzerland
1982/Old Boys Basle, Switzerland 1988/
SUNDERLAND Feb 1989/Cambuur Oct 1992.

Debut v Hull City (h) 25/2/1989 (sub)

The son of a former professional footballer,
Thomas Hauser was born in Germany some 30
miles from the Swiss border. He began with
his father's old club, F.C. Basle, at 17 years of
age and scored twice on his debut. He cost
Sunderland a reported £200,000 in February
1989 and was seen as a strike partner for
Marco Gabbiadini. In the event, he failed to
dislodge veteran Eric Gates and became
almost a fixture on the substitutes' bench, so
much so that bemused Roker fans dubbed him
with the nickname 'U-Boat'.

Appearances:
FL: 22(32) apps. 9 gls.
FAC: 0(1) apps. 0 gls.
FLC: 3(6) apps. 2 gls.
Other: 1 app. 0 gls.
Total: *26(39) apps. 11 gls.*

HAWES, Arthur Robert 'Tricky'

Role: Inside-left 1921-27
5'8" 10st.7lbs.
b. Swanton Morley, Norfolk, 2nd October 1895
d. Norwich, 11th October 1963

CAREER: Thorpe Hamlet School/Junior
Institute/Norwich CEYMS/Boulton & Paul's
(works side)/Norwich City Sept 1915/Norfolk
County/South Shields May 1920/
SUNDERLAND Dec 1921 £1,750/Bradford
Aug 1927 £650/Accrington Stanley July 1929
£100/Nelson July 1920 £50/Hyde United Sept
1931/Wombwell Dec 1931/Rochdale Feb
1932/Goole Town Aug 1932/Frost's Athletic
July 1935/Gothic trainer to 1958, Vice-
chairman 1961.

Debut v West Bromwich Albion (h) 24/12/1921

Son of a long-time Norwich City assistant
trainer, Arthur had a thorough grounding in
that area's junior football prior to joining the
club. A reputation for goal-scoring was
enhanced with City - he notched 79 in
wartime friendlies, a total that included seven

Thomas Hauser

hat-tricks. An accomplished one and a half seasons with South Shields attracted a big money move to Sunderland and the start of a noted left-wing partnership with Billy Ellis. He had heralded his arrival at Roker Park by scoring a couple of goals in a 5-0 thumping of West Brom. Hawes' progress was such that he appeared in an England trial match (for the Rest v England in February 1925). At the end of his playing career he returned to League football with a few months at Rochdale when in his 37th year (13 Northern Section appearances). An idiosyncrasy was the carrying of a handkerchief in his left hand throughout a match. A word on that nickname: one source tells us it was given to Arthur at Thorpe Hamlet School. However, another recalls that the surname Hawes attracts the nickname 'Tricky' in the same fashion a Murphy is automatically 'Spud' and a Clark 'Nobby'.

Appearances:
FL: 139 apps. 39 gls.
FAC: *8 apps. 0 gls.*
Total: *147 apps. 39 gls.*
Honours:
(Bradford) FL Div 3 Nth champs 1928.

HAWKE, Warren Robert

Role: Forward 1988-93
5'10" 10st.11lbs.
b. Durham, 20th September 1970

CAREER: Monkseaton High School/ SUNDERLAND assoc. s'boy Oct 1987, trainee Dec 1987, pro Nov 1988(Chesterfield loan Sept 1991)(Carlisle United loan Oct 1992) (Northampton Town loan Mar 1993)/Raith Rovers Aug 1993/Scarborough nc trial Dec 1993/Berwick Rangers Dec 1993/Greenock Morton July 1995.

Debut v Portsmouth (a) 8/4/1989 (sub)

Warren Hawke progressed quickly from schoolboy to professional ranks and had his first experience of League football at 19. He came off the bench to score Sunderland's second goal in a 2-0 victory at Swindon Town on the opening day of 1989-90, but with Eric Gates and Marco Gabbiadini as competition, found few opportunities. A substitute in the 1992 FA Cup final against Liverpool, Warren was a stylish player with a decent touch who was perhaps not quite good enough to

Warren Hawke

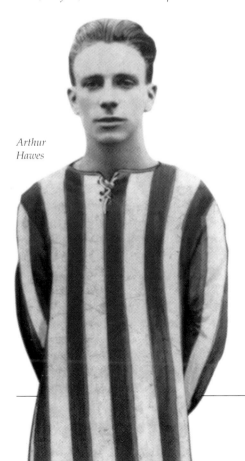

Arthur Hawes

succeed at top level. A series of loan moves and very brief spells with Raith Rovers and Scarborough did nothing to further his ambitions, but a mid-term transfer to Berwick Rangers in 1993-94 effectively resurrected his flagging career. Twelve goals in 20 appearances for the Borderers took them to the runners-up spot in Division Two of the Scottish League, and he followed up with 16 in 35 appearances in 1994-95. His tally included a late season hat-trick against the eventual Division Two champions, Greenock Morton. Three months later, Warren moved to Cappielow and scored 13 goals in 35 Division One appearances in his first season.

Appearances:
FL: 8(18) apps. 1 gl.
FAC: 1(1) apps. 0 gls.
FLC: 1 app. 0 gls.
Total: *10(19) apps. 1 gl.*
Honours:
(Sunderland) FAC finalist 1992.

HAWLEY, John East

Role: Forward 1979-81
6'1" 13st.5lbs.
b. Withernsea, 8th May 1954

CAREER: Hull, West Riding & Yorkshire Schoolboys/Hull City am Apr 1972, pro Aug 1976/Leeds United May 1978/SUNDERLAND Oct 1979/Arsenal Sept 1981(Orient loan Oct 1982)(Hull City loan Dec 1982)/Happy Valley F.C., Hong Kong 1983/Bradford City Sept 1983/Scunthorpe United July 1985, retired 1986.

Debut v Manchester City (h) 3/10/1979 (FLC 3r)

A relatively late arrival to the professional game, John Hawley remained over four years as an amateur with Hull City as football vied with the family antiques business, joining the paid ranks at 22. Signed for Leeds by Jimmy Armfield, who quickly resigned, John played under Jock Stein and then former Sunderland boss Jimmy Adamson and scored 16 goals during his single season at Elland Road. Newly-appointed Sunderland manager Ken Knighton, who John knew from his Hull days, splashed a club record £200,000. A dangerous strike forward with an admirably consistent goalscoring record, John made a spectacular start and netted a hat-trick on his League debut for Sunderland in a 4-0 win over Charlton. Sadly, injury restricted him to only a further eight League appearances in his first season as Sunderland won promotion. When 1980-81 opened, he scored his second hat-trick, this time at Manchester City, but six games into the season suffered a hamstring injury which sidelined him for three months. Few fans will forget John's return to the team before Christmas with a fabulous forty-yard strike past Arsenal's Pat Jennings. But Sunderland struggled on only to narrowly avoid the drop. Indeed, John joined the Gunners in a £100,000 deal when judged surplus by new boss Alan Durban but the move was never a success. In a late flourish with Bradford City John netted 13 goals in ten consecutive League wins, including four against Wimbledon, and in 1984-85 won a Third Division championship medal - albeit against the horrific background of the Bradford Fire Disaster. His League career covered seven clubs and his aggregate figures were 256(31) appearances, 89 goals. John now lives on Humberside and runs a thriving antiques business in York.

Appearances:
FL: 25 apps. 11 gls.
FAC: 3 apps. 0 gls.
FLC: 3 apps. 0 gls.
Total: *31 apps. 11 gls.*
Honours:
(Bradford City) Div 3 champs 1985.

John Hawley (centre) poses for the cameras with Alan Brown and Stan Cummins after the trio registered a hat-trick of Roker Park hat-tricks in 1979-80. Hawley's treble came on his League debut against Charlton (4-0), Brown followed with three against Oldham (4-2) and Cummins scored four against Burnley (5-0).

HAY, Alan Browning

Role: Full-back 1988-89
5'11" 11st.3lbs.
b. Dunfermline, 28th November 1958

CAREER: Riverside Boys' Club/Dundee/
Bolton Wanderers Mar 1977/Bristol City July
1978(St Mirren loan 1981-82)/York City Aug
1982/Tranmere Rovers Aug 1986/Hill of
Beath/York City nc Dec 1988/SUNDERLAND
trial Feb 1989/Torquay United Sept 1989-
1991/South Tyneside United/Hartlepool asst.
manager Mar 1994.

Debut v Ipswich Town (h) 25/3/1989

Alan Hay was signed by Sunderland on a
monthly contract during a spell when injuries
and suspensions depleted the senior ranks. He

appeared just
once in the first
eleven and shone
in a 4-0 victory
against Ipswich
Town.
Unfortunately he
was unable to
complete the 90
minutes and did
not feature again
in the League
side. In early days
a Scottish Under-
16 Cup winner
with Riverside

Alan Hay

Boys' Club, Alan was briefly on Dundee's
books before signing for Bolton
Wanderers whilst still a teenager.
He made his League debut with
Bristol City, but enjoyed the best
spell of his career with York City.
At Bootham Crescent he totalled
178(4) appearances in a four-year
period and missed only one match
during 1983-84 when history was
made. In securing the
championship of Division Four,
York City won the first major
honour in the club's history.

Appearances:
FL: 1 app. 0 gls.
Total: *1 app. 0 gls.*
Honours:
(York City) Div 4 champs 1984.

HEALEY, Richard

Role: Inside-right 1909-12
5'11" 12st.5lbs.
b. Darlington, 20th September 1889
d. Darlington, 3rd qtr 1974

CAREER: Darlington Grammar School/
Bishop Auckland Aug 1908/SUNDERLAND
am Feb 1910/Stockton Aug 1910/Bishop
Auckland 1912/Middlesbrough am Mar
1914/Darlington 1920-1923. (As is customary
with amateurs, there would be overlaps in
times spent with various clubs.)

Debut v Manchester United (a) 16/4/1910

In September 1910 the local sports edition ran
a feature on Richard Healey describing him as
"a bright and dashing player who can use his
head as well as his feet." A product of
Darlington Grammar School, an institution
that proved itself a soccer nursery, he was for
four seasons a member of the school XI,
eventually becoming captain. He left in 1908 to
take a science course at the Armstrong
College, Newcastle. The Stockton transfer of
1910 was occasioned by his family's move to
take up residence in that town. He made three
First Division appearances for Middlesbrough
in 1914/15, scoring one goal, and completed
his League career with Darlington assisting
that club post-war. It was in their first couple
of seasons as a League club, 1921/2 and '22/3
(22 appearances, 5 goals). He was also a useful
cricketer, assisting Darlington CC and Durham
in the Minor Counties championship.

Appearances:
FL: 3 apps. 1 gl.
Total: *3 apps. 1 gl.*
Honours:
4 Eng am
apps./(Bishop
Auckland) AMC
finalist 1911.

Richard Healey

HEATHCOTE, Michael

Role: Central Defender 1987-90
6'2" 12st.5lbs.
b. Kelloe, Co Durham, 10th September 1965

CAREER: Spennymoor United/
SUNDERLAND Aug 1987(Halifax Town loan
Dec 1987)(York City loan Jan 1990)/
Shrewsbury Town July 1990/Cambridge
United Sept 1991/Plymouth Argyle Aug 1995
to date.

Debut v Southend United (h) 3/11/1987 (sub)

A £15,000 signing from Spennymoor United,
Michael Heathcote made his League debut as
a substitute in Sunderland's best win of the
1987-88 Third Division championship season,
a 7-0 annihilation of Southend United. Despite
the bright start, he found it was tough going at
Roker Park as he had two years to wait for a
second League outing. Transferred to
Shrewsbury Town for £55,000 in the summer
of 1990, his value had almost trebled fourteen
months later when he moved up to Division
One with Cambridge United. In 1995-96
Heathcote's outstanding form in the centre of
Plymouth Argyle's defence earned him

Mike Heathcote

election for the PFA's Third Division team. He
also appeared on the winning side in the
Division Three play-off final at Wembley,
Plymouth beating Darlington 1-0 to clinch
promotion.

Appearances:
FL: 6(3) apps. 2 gls.
Total: *6(3) apps. 2 gls.*

HEDLEY, John Robert

Role: Right-back 1950-59
5'8" 11st.7lbs.
*b. Willington Quay, Co Durham, 13th December
1923*
d. Northumberland, 2nd June 1985

CAREER: Willington Quay FC/North
Shields/Everton Apr 1945/SUNDERLAND
Aug 1950 £10,000/Gateshead July 1959-1960.

Debut v Liverpool (a) 26/8/1950

Jack Hedley was a
solid defender,
equally at home on
the left flank - in fact
most of his 61
League and FA Cup
appearances for
Everton were at left-
back. The
Merseysiders would
have been unlikely
to sanction the
transfer, but for
Hedley being among
the players lured to

Jack Hedley

South America in the summer of 1950 in a
notorious episode that came to be known as
the Bogota affair. The professional clubs of
Colombia broke away from their national
association and so from FIFA also. Neil
Franklin and George Mountford of Stoke City
signed for the Santa Fe club of Bogota for
wages far exceeding those permitted by our
Football League. Others followed, including
Hedley, but in the event he refused the terms
offered by the Millionaires Club of Bogota and
returned home. A loyal servant to Sunderland
Jack went on to register close to 300 games for
the club.

Appearances:
FL: 269 apps. 0 gls.
FAC: 26 apps. 0 gls.
Total: *295 apps. 0 gls.*

HEGAN, Daniel

Role: Inside-forward 1961-63 & 1973-74
5'6" 11st.3lbs.
b. Coatbridge, 14th June 1943

CAREER: Coatbridge Schools/Glasgow
Schools/Albion Rovers 1960/SUNDERLAND
Sept 1961 £6,000/Ipswich Town June 1963
£4,000/West Bromwich Albion May 1969
£30,000 plus Ian Collard/Wolverhampton
Wanderers May 1970 £27,000/SUNDERLAND
Nov 1973 £5,000/Highlands Park
(Johannesburg) cs 1974(Partick Thistle trial late
1974)/Coleshill Town Aug 1975/retired 1978
and became soccer coach at Butlin's Holiday
Camp, Clacton on Sea.

Debut v Millwall (a) 15/12/1973

Danny Hegan

A naturally
talented
player - a
potential
general in
modern soccer
parlance -
who could
well have had
a greater
career. What
has been
described as 'a
hectic social
life' interfered.
Hegan had
actually been
dismissed by
Wolves just
prior to the
second signing by Sunderland. He did not get
a first team game during the his initial Roker
spell, Ipswich providing a senior debut, and it
was at Portman Road that Danny made most
League appearances and won a championship
medal.

Appearances:
FL: 3(3) apps. 0 gls.
FAC: 0(2) apps. 0 gls.
Total: *3(5) apps. 0 gls.*
Honours:
*7 NIre caps/(Ipswich Town) Div 2 champs
1968/(Wolves) UEFAC finalist 1972.*

HELLAWELL, Michael Stephen

Role: Outside-right 1964-67
5'11" 11st.0lbs.
b. Keighley, Yorkshire, 30th June 1938

CAREER: Yorkshire Schools/Salts FC
(Saltaire)/Huddersfield Town am/Queens
Park Rangers Aug 1955/Birmingham City
May 1957 fee under £10,000 plus C W Finney/
SUNDERLAND Jan 1965 £27,500/
Huddersfield Town Sept 1966 £15,000/
Peterborough United Dec 1968 £4,000/
Bromsgrove Rovers Aug 1969, later assisting
Nuneaton Borough before retiring.

Debut v Blackpool (h) 6/2/1965

An incisive right-
winger noted for
his great pace -
he had been a
champion
sprinter when at
school - Mike
Hellawell
represented
Yorkshire Schools
at cricket also,
and originally
counted cricket
his main interest.
But once at QPR
professional
football prevailed
and he soon won
a representative

Mike Hellawell

honour by playing for the Division Three
South XI against the Division Three North.
And Mike progressed to earn a couple of
England caps. Cricket, though, still loomed
large in his sporting life. A fast bowler, he
became professional to the Walsall CC and in
1962 played for Warwickshire in a first class
match. After leaving football Mike returned to
his native Keighley and established a
greengrocery business. A younger brother,
John, played for Bradford City and other
clubs.

Appearances:
FL: 43(1) apps. 2 gls.
FAC: 2 apps. 0 gls.
Total: *45(1) apps. 2 gls.*
Honours
*2 Eng caps/(Birmingham City) FLC winner
1963.*

HENDERSON, George Brown

Role: Centre-half 1925-29
6'0" 12st.4lbs.
b. Keilty, Fife, 9th January 1902

CAREER: Edinburgh St Bernards/
SUNDERLAND Aug 1924 £750/Barnsley Mar
1929 £1,300/Glenavon trial Aug 1937/
Cowdenbeath Feb 1938.

Debut v Liverpool (a) 31/10/1925

George Henderson proved a first-rate deputy
for Charlie Parker and then Adam Allan
before departing to Barnsley. Powerfully built
and effective, the embodiment of what a 'sheet
anchor' pivot should be, George made 262
League and FA Cup appearances (12 goals) in
his eight years at Oakwell. These figures
illustrate both consistency in performance and
freedom from injury. The fee Barnsley paid for
George was moderate and extremely well
spent.

Appearances:
FL: 45 apps. 1 gl.
FAC: 3 apps. 0 gls.
Total: *48 apps. 1 gl.*
Honours:
(Barnsley) Div 3 Nth champs 1934.

George Henderson

HENDERSON, Michael Robert

Role: Defender 1975-79
5'10" 11st.4lbs.
b. Gosforth, Northumberland, 31st March 1956

CAREER: SUNDERLAND assoc. s'boy May
1972, app July 1972, pro Apr 1974/Watford
Nov 1979/Cardiff City Mar 1982/Sheffield
United Aug 1982/Chesterfield Jan 1985,
appointed player-coach cs 1987, caretaker-
manager Oct 1988/Matlock Town Sept 1989.

Debut v York City (a) 1/11/1975

Signed on schoolboy forms in 1972, Mick
Henderson progressed through junior and
reserve ranks and made his first team debut at
19 in the promotion season 1975-76. Strong in
the tackle, two-footed and with plenty of

Mick Henderson

stamina, his one weakness was a lack of pace, made particularly evident when opposed to a speedy wingman. He cost Watford £120,000 in November 1979 but thereafter moved without a transfer fee. His League career ended at Chesterfield, for whom he made 136 League appearances (10 goals). He subsequently joined the Sheffield police force. A brother, Kenny Henderson, who once won a televised penalty competition at Wembley, was on Sunderland's books as a centre-forward but did not graduate to senior level.

Appearances:
FL: 81(3) apps. 2 gls.
FAC: 6(1) apps. 0 gls.
FLC: 2(1) apps. 0 gls.
Other: 1 app. 0 gls.
Total: *90(5) apps. 2 gls.*
Honours:
(Chesterfield) Div 4 champs 1985.

HEPWORTH, Maurice

Role: Full-back 1970-71
5'9" 11st.5lbs.
b. Hexham, 6th September 1953

CAREER: SUNDERLAND app, pro Sept 1970 (Darlington loan Jan-Feb 1975)/Arcadia, Pretoria, S. Africa Feb 1975.

Debut v Bolton Wanderers (a) 12/4/1971

Maurice Hepworth made two Second Division appearances in April of 1971 as deputy for long-serving full-back Cec Irwin. His debut at Bolton Wanderers resulted in a 3-1 victory, and The Lads were also successful in his second match, 2-1 at Sheffield Wednesday. Almost four years later, and whilst on a month's loan with Fourth Division Darlington, Hepworth had his final experience of League football in four appearances for the Quakers. In the same month his Sunderland contract was cancelled, and he left with his family bound for soccer in the sun in South Africa.

Maurice Hepworth

Appearances:
FL: 2 apps. 0 gls.
Total: *2 apps. 0 gls.*

HERD, George

Role: Outside/Inside-right 1960-69
5'8" 11st.2lbs.
b. Gartcosh, Glasgow, 6th May 1936

CAREER: Gartcosh Thistle/Inverness Thistle/ Queen's Park Aug 1956/Clyde pro May 1957/ SUNDERLAND Apr 1961 £42,500/Sunderland trainer/coach May 1969 but joined Hartlepool as a player June 1970-1971. Subsequently held a number of appointments including part-time coach to Newcastle United juniors July 1974-Oct 1976/Sunderland youth team in the late 1970s/Queen of the South manager cs 1980/ Darlington coach cs 1981. After this he coached in Kuwait (two spells) and for Sunderland and Middlesbrough.

Debut v Liverpool (h) 29/4/1961

Unlike most of his schoolboy contemporaries George Herd did not harbour ambitions to become a professional footballer. Indeed he then had little time for the game, working as a shop messenger boy every weekday evening and on Saturday mornings. However, he joined Gartosh Thistle at 15 and was played at outside-right where it was thought his slight physique might attract less buffeting. George's dedication to the sport continued to flower during National Service in the army, along with a belated ambition to join the paid ranks. The aim was ultimately realised by way of junior Inverness Thistle and the once famous amateur Queen's Park of the Scottish League. With Queen's George won his first representative honour - an amateur cap. He worked as a railway ganger at this juncture. Clyde signed him as a professional in May 1957, an engagement that lasted four years to the mutual satisfaction of club and player. They were good times at Shawfield in 1957/58, the club finished fourth in Division One and won the Scottish Cup, their second win in three years and third final in nine. Herd won a winners' medal in that 1958 final playing outside-right. He won all his representative honours with Clyde apart from the amateur cap. Such a now well-established forward attracted a big fee as Sunderland's outlay illustrates. It was a thoughtful investment. George was in his mid-twenties and at his peak, slight of build with the intelligence and vision to see several options ahead. He was equally able in both right flank attack berths and had been capped in both. The team had recovered from the trauma of 1958's descent to the Second Division and were to finish sixth the month after Herd's arrival. In the next two seasons they went tantalisingly close to promotion. Sunderland were third both years, a single point behind promoted Leyton Orient in 1962 and merely an inferior goals record to promoted Chelsea in 1963. But persistence paid off at last in 1963/64 with the Wearsiders runners-up to Leeds United. George, a prominent member of that team, scored 13 goals in 39 outings, forged a telling partnership with winger Brian Usher and fed the free-scoring centre-forward, Nick Sharkey. At one stage, rather surprisingly, George was criticised for not scoring more goals, this despite all his nippy bright service to colleagues. George ended his playing days - as did several other Sunderland favourites - at West Hartlepool. Amid other later appointments, he had spells at Roker Park coaching the youngsters. He returned to Scotland in 1980 for his one brief spell in club management with Queen of the South. The Dumfries club had a good season in 1980/81, as runners-up to Queen's Park in Division Two of the Scottish League. More recently during the 1990's George coached Sunderland Youths alongside his lifelong friend Jim Montgomery.

George Herd

Appearances:
FL: 275(3) apps. 47 gls.
FAC: 21 apps. 4 gls.
FLC: 19 apps. 4 gls.
Total: *315(3) apps. 55 gls.*
Honours:
5 Scot caps/1 Scot am app./3 SL apps./(Clyde) SC winner 1958.

HESFORD, Iain

Role: Goalkeeper 1986-89
6'2" 14st.10lbs.
b. Noola, Kenya, 4th March 1960

CAREER: Blackpool app, pro Aug 1977/ Sheffield Wednesday Aug 1983(Fulham loan Jan 1985)(Notts County loan Nov 1985(SUNDERLAND loan Aug 1986)/ SUNDERLAND Sept 1986/Hull City Dec 1988/Maidstone United Aug 1991/ Eastern, Hong Kong late 1992.
Debut v Huddersfield Town (a) 23/8/1986

Largely first choice goalkeeper during his two-and-a half seasons with Sunderland, Iain Hesford made his debut whilst on loan from Sheffield Wednesday against his father's old club, Huddersfield Town. Hesford Snr, also a goalkeeper, was a one-club man whose 220 appearances included the 1938 FA Cup Final, won in the last minute of extra time by Preston North End, thanks to a penalty converted by Scottish international George Mutch. Iain Hesford began at Blackpool where he won England Youth and Under-21 honours before Sheffield Wednesday signed him. Three years on, and without a League appearance for the Owls, as Martin Hodge clocked up 126

Iain Hesford

consecutive matches, Sunderland revived Iain's career when Lawrie McMenemy paid £80,000 for his transfer. Hesford sampled both relegation from Division Two via a play-off in his first season and then immediate promotion as his roller-coaster spell at Roker saw mixed press reviews as he dropped the odd 'clanger', was left out for the opening six games of 1987-88, yet then finished runner-up to Player of the Year Eric Gates. He nevertheless commanded a six-figure sum when he joined Hull City in December 1988, departing in a deal which also included Billy Whitehurst and brought Tony Norman to Roker Park. Hesford's final season was spent with Maidstone United who resigned from the League in August 1992. During 1991-92 Maidstone won only eight matches; Iain scored the winning goal in one of them, his punt stealing a 3-2 home victory against Hereford United. Unfortunately his big moment was witnessed by only 846 spectators.

Appearances:
FL: 101 apps. 0 gls.
FAC: 3 apps. 0 gls.
FLC: 4 apps. 0 gls.
Other: 6 apps. 0 gls.
Total: 114 apps. 0 gls.
Honours:
7 Eng U-21 apps. 1982-83/1 Eng Yth app. 1978/(Sunderland) Div 3 champs 1988.

HESLOP, Brian

Brian Heslop

Role: Half-back 1967-71
5'9" 11st.5lbs.
b. Carlisle, 4th August 1947

CAREER: Junior football to Carlisle United app, pro Aug 1965/SUNDERLAND May 1967 £5,000/ Northampton Town Mar 1971 £5,000/ Workington Sept 1972-1976.

Debut v Leeds United (a) 19/8/1967

Brian Heslop made his Sunderland first team debut on the opening day of season 1967/68 at centre-forward. He was a fortnight past his twentieth birthday and with a mere five Second Division outings for Carlisle under his belt. Thereafter he proved an effective reserve for all three half-back positions. After four years he moved to Northampton at the same

transfer fee (49 League appearances plus one substitution) and finally did a good stint for Workington (139 League appearances plus one substitution).

Appearances:
FL: 57(1) apps. 0 gls.
FAC: 1 app. 0 gls.
FLC: 4 apps. 0 gls.
Other: 4 apps. 0 gls.
Total: 66(1) apps. 0 gls.

HETHERINGTON, Harold

Role: Outside-right 1947-48
b. Chester-le-Street, Co Durham, 7th November 1928

CAREER: Shiney Row FC/SUNDERLAND May 1946/Gateshead Jan-May 1949.

Debut v Chelsea (a) 10/9/1947

In his two and a half seasons at Roker Park, Hetherington deputised for Len Duns in a couple of successive matches. His debut game resulted in a 1-1 draw and Harold's other outing - a midweek home game against Blackburn Rovers three days later - ended in a 1-0 defeat. For Gateshead he made two Northern Section appearances, scoring one goal.

Appearances:
FL: 2 apps. 0 gls.
Total: 2 apps. 0 gls.

HETZKE, Stephen Edward Richard

Role: Central Defender 1985-87
6'2" 13st.4lbs.
b. Marlborough, Wilts, 3rd June 1955

CAREER: Hungerford Town/Reading app, pro June 1973(Vancouver Whitecaps loan cs 1976)/Blackpool July 1982/SUNDERLAND Mar 1986/Chester City June 1987/Colchester United Mar 1988-Dec 1989/Chesterfield coach.

Debut v Charlton Athletic (h) 8/3/1986

Steve Hetzke, an uncompromising pivot of the 'They shalt not pass' breed, moved up a level when he joined Sunderland's relegation dogfight in March 1986. A vastly experienced defender - all of Hetzke's 400 plus appearances were made in Division Three and Four and, if lacking in the finer points, he was

Steve Hetzke

quick to clear his lines and certainly proved a formidable barrier to opposing forwards. He began with Reading, where he made his debut whilst still an apprentice at 16 years of age in December 1971. He spent eleven seasons at Elm Park and won a Fourth Division championship medal with them in 1978-79, scoring nine League goals in 42 appearances during that term. He joined Blackpool for £12,500 in July 1982 and assisted them to promotion to Division Three in 1985 as runners-up to Chesterfield. Steve's spell at Roker ended after the club faced the prospect of Third Division football for the first time. After a brief period with Chester City his playing career wound up with Fourth Division Colchester United, a goal in his final League appearance at Torquay United taking his career total to 43 in 466(9) appearances.

Appearances:
FL: 32 apps. 0 gls.
Other: 1 app. 0 gls.
Total: *33 apps. 0 gls.*
Honours:
(Reading) Div 4 champs 1979.

Joe Hewitt (front right) pictured in 1903 next to the enormous Sheriff of London Shield and with the Durham County Cup at his feet.

HEWITT, Joseph

Role: Inside/outside-left 1901-04
5'8" 11st.6lbs.
b. Chester, 3rd May 1881
d. Liverpool, November 1971

CAREER: Chester works team/ SUNDERLAND Sept 1901/Liverpool Jan 1904/Bolton Wanderers Aug 1910-1911/ Liverpool FC coaching staff 1911/12, continued to serve the club in various capacities until 1964.

Debut v Blackburn Rovers (a) 1/3/1902

Joe Hewitt's chief claim to fame was his marvellous service to Liverpool FC that added up to an astonishing 60 years. It commenced with four and a half years on the playing strength and ended in 1964 as press box attendant aged 83, when the club gave him a pension. He had come to be an Anfield institution, an enormously popular figure. Latterly he had been living in an old people's home in Croxteth. With Sunderland Joe, who could play in any forward position, did so. A critic wrote in 1903 that Joe was " ... very clever indeed, both in combination and trickiness. Shoots well and scored the highest number of goals for his side last season."

Appearances:
FL: 36 apps. 11 gls.
Total: *36 apps. 11 gls.*
Honours:
(Liverpool) FL champs 1906.

HEYES, James T.

Role: Inside-right 1925-26
5'8" 11st.0lbs.
b. Northwich, Cheshire, circa 1902

James Heyes

CAREER: Northwich Victoria
(Bolton Wanderers trial Jan 1922)/
SUNDERLAND Apr 1925 £100/West Ham
United June 1927/ Connah's Quay Aug
1928(Bangor City trial Jan 1929)/Ashton
National Feb 1929/Mossley Sept 1929.

Debut v Tottenham Hotspur (h) 26/9/1925

Heyes spent a quite long apprenticeship with
his local Northwich Victoria, as witness the
three-year interval between his Bolton trial
and the signing for Sunderland in the spring
of 1925. Chances at Roker for inside-rights
were naturally limited with contenders like
Bobby Marshall and Bob Kelly on the books.
Opportunities at West Ham were also rare and
he made no first team appearances there.

> **Appearances:**
> *FL: 4 apps. 0 gls.*
> **Total:** *4 apps. 0 gls.*

HEYWOOD, Albert Edward

Role: Goalkeeper
1938-39
6'0" 11st.3lbs.
*b. West Hartlepool,
12th May 1913
d. West Hartlepool,
May 1989*

CAREER: Hartlepool
Expansion (Hartlepools
United am Dec 1931)/

Albert Heywood

Trimdon Grange (Manchester City trial Feb
1934)/Luton Town May 1934 (Wolverhampton
Wanderers trial Dec 1935)/Spennymoor
United circa 1936/SUNDERLAND Mar 1937
(guest player for Hartlepools United and
Middlesbrough during WW2)/Hartlepools
United May 1946-1947.

Debut v Charlton Athletic (h) 1/4/1939

Albert Heywood had a rather odd 'thirties
career; non-League engagements interspersed
with leading clubs' trials, a brief Luton stay
before becoming a 'permanent', Sunderland
signing ... and all this over some eight years. It

was Sunderland who provided the League
debut and three more outings in the last pre-
war season. They all occurred in April 1939,
successive games that resulted in a draw and
three defeats. Something of a regular for
Sunderland in war-time games, Heywood was
first choice for his post-war Hartlepools
campaign, appearing in 39 Northern Section
matches.

> **Appearances:**
> *FL: 4 apps. 0 gls.*
> **Total:** *4 apps. 0 gls.*

HINDMARCH, Robert

Role: Central Defender 1977-84
6'1" 13st.4lbs.
b. Stannington, Morpeth, 27th April 1961

CAREER: Wallsend Boys' Club/
SUNDERLAND app June 1977, pro May 1978
(Portsmouth loan Dec 1983)/Derby County
July 1984/Wolverhampton Wanderers June
1990-cs 1993.

Debut v Orient (a) 14/1/1978

Rob Hindmarch

One of the club's brightest prospects, Rob Hindmarch made an excellent impression when he made his League debut as a 16-year-old in Division Two in season 1977-78. England Youth honours followed when he took part in the Las Palmas tournament. He was a member of the 1979-80 promotion-winning team and had four seasons in Division One before, rather surprisingly, being allowed to join Derby County on a free transfer in July 1984. Quickly established as club captain, Rob led the Rams to successive promotions in 1986 and 1987. After six years at the Baseball Ground he joined Wolverhampton Wanderers for £300,000, but appeared in their League side in only one of his three seasons at Molineux.

Appearances:
FL: 114(1) apps. 2 gls.
FAC: 5 apps. 0 gls.
FLC: 6(2) apps. 1 gl.
Total: *125(3) apps. 3 gls.*
Honours:
7 Eng Yth apps. 1978/(Derby County)Div 2 champs 1987.

HINDMARSH, James Lyons

Role: Inside-left 1905-06
5'11" 12st.9lbs.
b. South Shields, 2nd qtr 1885
d. Luton, 16th March 1959

CAREER: Whitburn Colliery/SUNDERLAND Mar 1905/Fulham May 1906 £20/Watford Dec 1907/Plymouth Argyle May 1908/Stockport County June 1910 £100/Manchester City Dec 1912/Newport County reserves player-coach, Sept 1919, first team coach 1920, secretary-manager May 1922-May 1935.

Debut v Notts County (h) 30/9/1905

James Hindmarsh had an indifferent start to his professional playing career, not getting regular first team football until reaching Plymouth. He headed Argyle's scoring list in 1909/10 with 16 goals in 40 Southern League appearances. Altogether with Argyle

James Hindmarsh

he played 60 Southern League and FA Cup matches, scoring 25 goals. He moved to wing-half at Stockport and continued there for Manchester City of the First Division (35 League and FA Cup outings). Hindmarsh is mainly remembered as a long-serving and resilient Newport County manager, seeing the Welsh club through many crises. A pillar of the playing staff in his early managerial days was Jack Conner (q.v.).

Appearances:
FL: 1 app. 0 gls.
Total: *1 app. 0 gls.*

HINNIGAN, Joseph Peter

Role: Full-back 1979-83
6'0" 12st.7lbs.
b. Liverpool, 3rd December 1955

CAREER: South Liverpool/Wigan Athletic July 1979/SUNDERLAND Feb 1980/Preston North End Dec 1982/Gillingham Aug 1984/Wrexham July 1987/Chester City Aug 1988, retired 1990 and appointed club physiotherapist.

Debut v Luton Town (h) 23/2/1980

Joe Hinnigan

Joe Hinnigan's form in the last line of Wigan Athletic's defence earned the Springfield Park club a record fee for a Fourth Division player when Sunderland splashed out £135,000 for his transfer in February 1980. At Roker he took the not inconsiderable step from Division Four to Division Two in his stride, and three months and 14 appearances later celebrated promotion to Division One with his new team mates having not tasted defeat. With Joe Bolton restored to fitness and the experienced Steve Whitworth still first choice at right-back, Joe Hinnigan was cast as an understudy during the 1980/81 season back in the top flight, but returned with a bang in March 1981 when he netted four goals in three League matches, a significant contribution to the team's successful fight to avoid relegation. After leaving Sunderland for Preston in a £15,000 transfer in December 1982, Hinnigan made three further moves, giving each club his customary full value and professional approach. His League career in total spanned 359(8) appearances and he scored 32 goals.

Appearances:
FL: 63 apps. 6 gls.
FAC: 1 app. 0 gls.
FLC: 1 app. 0 gls.
Total: *65 apps. 6 gls.*

HIRD, Robert Keith Bryan

Role: Goalkeeper 1960-61
5'11" 11st.12lbs.
b. Annfield Plain, Co Durham,
25th November 1939
d. Newcastle upon Tyne, 3rd qtr 1967

CAREER: Annfield Plain FC/
SUNDERLAND Sept 1957/
Darlington July 1963-64.

Debut v Liverpool (h) 29/4/1961

Hird stood in for Peter Wakeham in the final League match of 1960/61 (the only senior game Wakeham missed that term), the result a 1-1 draw. For Darlington Hird made 17 Fourth Division appearances. He died in tragic circumstances aged only 27.

Appearances:
FL: 1 app. 0 gls.
Total: *1 app. 0 gls.*

Robert Hird

HOBSON, Herbert Bertie 'Bert'

Role: Right-back 1912-22
5'8" 11st.7lbs.
b. Tow Law, Co Durham, 1890
d. Tow Law, Co Durham, November 1963

CAREER: Tow Law Juniors/Tow Law FC/
Stanley United/Crook Town/SUNDERLAND
Aug 1912 (guest player for Stoke and
Wolverhampton Wanderers during WW1)/
West Stanley Jan 1923/Rochdale Mar 1923/
Jarrow player-coach circa 1924/Darlington Feb
1925-1926/Jarrow Aug 1926/Spennymoor
United Sept 1928.

Debut v Sheffield United (a) 24/3/1913

A solid, reliable defender, Bert Hobson secured
a regular place at Roker from October 1913,
and retained it in the post-war era until his
departure. He was offered maximum terms in
May 1922 (the move to Rochdale the previous
March was obviously 'on loan'), but these
were refused unless granted a benefit. He was
later transfer-listed in the first instance at
£1,500. Five months later this was reduced to
£750. Bert came back to League soccer late in
his career, making half a dozen Northern
Section appearances for Darlington - three in
1924/5 and three in '25/6. During the First
World War, Bert was awarded the Military
Medal.

> **Appearances:**
> *FL: 160 apps. 0 gls.*
> *FAC: 12 apps. 0 gls.*
> **Total:** *172 apps. 0 gls.*

*Bert
Hobson*

HODGSON, David James

Role: Forward 1984-86
5'10" 12st.2lbs.
b. Gateshead, 1st November 1960

CAREER: Redheugh Boys' Club, Gateshead
(Ipswich Town trial)(Bolton Wanderers
trial)(Sheffield Wednesday trial)/
Middlesbrough app Aug 1976, pro Aug 1978/
Liverpool Aug 1982/SUNDERLAND Aug
1984/Norwich City July 1986(Middlesbrough
loan Feb 1987)/Jerez Club de Portivo, Spain
July 1987/Sheffield Wednesday Aug 1988/
Mazda, Japan July 1989/Metz, France/
Swansea City nc Mar 1992(Mainz, Germany
trial Aug 1992)/Rochdale n.c. Sept 1992/
Darlington coach June-Dec 1995, manager Nov
1996.

Debut v Chelsea (a) 27/8/1985 (sub)

David Hodgson won six England Under-21
caps during his early days with
Middlesbrough where he made his first
appearance in Division One as a richly-
promising striker. He cost Liverpool £450,000
in August 1982, and made his debut for the
Reds as a substitute in the Charity Shield final
at Wembley. He had followed the trail of

*David
Hodgson*

Graeme Souness and Craig Johnston from Middlesbrough to Anfield, but failed to emulate their success and departed for a cut price sum of £125,000 after two seasons, in the last of which he appeared only once in the starting line-up in League matches. A return to the North-East failed to recapture his lost form and Sunderland were relegated at the end of his first season at Roker. Under new manager Lawrie McMenemy, Hodgson was on the transfer list and playing for the Reserves shortly after the disastrous opening to the new campaign - five straight defeats and no goals scored. Released on a free transfer he joined Norwich City but this and subsequent moves proved to be downhill all the way. In a tabloid newspaper in 1992, David ruefully admitted he had "thrown it all away". More recently he has had a spell operating as a players agent.

Appearances:
FL: 32(8) apps. 5 gls.
FAC: 1 app. 0 gls.
FLC: 8(1) apps. 1 gl.
Other: 1(1) apps. 1 gl.
Total: *42(10) apps. 7 gls.*
Honours:
6 Eng U-21 apps. 1980-82/(Liverpool) FL champs 1983/(Sunderland) FLC finalist 1985.

HODKIN, Ernest

Role: Right-half 1910-11
5'6" 10st.11lbs.
b. Grassmoor, Chesterfield, 1889

CAREER: Clay Cross/
Mansfield Mechanics 1909/
SUNDERLAND Aug 1910/Stoke Apr 1912/
Billingham 1913.

Ernest Hodkin

Debut v Oldham Athletic (a) 21/1/1911

The short but sturdily-built half-back Ernest Hodkin signed after a successful term with Mansfield Mechanics when they topped the Notts & Derby League. Lack of height did not prevent Hodkin appearing at centre-half on occasion. He played in a couple of First Division games for Sunderland during January 1911: the debut above and against Woolwich Arsenal at home a week later. For Stoke he made 29 Southern League and FA Cup appearances, scoring one goal.

Appearances:
FL: 2 apps. 0 gls.
Total: *2 apps. 0 gls.*

HOGG, James William

Role: Centre-forward 1923-25
5'9" 11st.0lbs.
b. Sunderland, 9th August 1900
d. Sunderland, 3rd qtr 1974

CAREER: Whitburn, where he was an amateur/SUNDERLAND Nov 1923 pro to 1925. It was reported in May 1925 that he had joined Sheffield United, but in fact the move was not confirmed and the player disappeared from the League scene.

Debut v Sheffield United (h) 19/1/1924 (scored)

James Hogg had an unusually fine scoring record in a debut top flight season: eight goals in eight League appearances. Interestingly, three of his total nine outings were against Sheffield United and he scored in two of them - his initial appearances, which may explain in part the intended, though aborted, 1925 transfer. And why did not Sunderland hang on to such a talent? Brian Hastings' *Whitburn 1882-1989* tells us Hogg's "... last game for Sunderland was against Sheffield United in 1925. He swore after this game he would never kick a ball for Sunderland again, due to a personal clash with his fellow forward Marshall". Outside football James Hogg worked as a clerk in the offices of the Sunderland Corporation Tramways.

Appearances:
FL: 9 apps. 8 gls.
Total: *9 apps. 8 gls.*

HOGG, Robert

Role: Inside-right/
centre-forward 1899-1903
5'8" 12st.7lbs.
*b. Whitburn, Co Durham,
2nd qtr 1877*
d. Malton, Yorkshire, 14th March 1963

Bobby Hogg

CAREER: Selbourne Rovers/Whitburn FC/
SUNDERLAND June 1899/Grimsby Town Nov 1902/Blackpool cs 1904/Luton Town cs 1905.

Debut v Sheffield United (a) 2/10/1899

"A fast and clever forward," said a commentator of the early 1900s. Bobby Hogg gained an inter-league medal early in his professional career while enjoying a fair slice of first team action at Roker Park. Without doubt his best season with Sunderland was the 1901-02 championship triumph when he made 29 appearances and scored six goals. At Grimsby, though, who he joined early the following season, he saw very little (three appearances, one goal) due to a recurring knee injury. He recovered sufficiently to play 26 times in Blackpool's Second Division line-up but after 1905 faded from the senior scene. He is not related to the great Billy Hogg (q.v.).

Appearances:
FL: 67 apps. 17 gls.
FAC: 6 apps. 2 gls.
Total: *73 apps. 19 gls.*
Honours:
1 FL app. v Irish League 1901/(Sunderland) FL champs 1902.

HOGG, William

Role: Outside right/centre-forward
1899-1909
5'9" 11st.10lbs.
b. Newcastle upon Tyne, 29th May 1879
d. Sunderland, 30th January 1937

CAREER: Willington Athletic 1897/ SUNDERLAND Oct 1899/Rangers May 1909 £100/Dundee May 1913/Raith Rovers player-manager cs 1914, but on the outbreak of war returned to Sunderland and was employed in an engineering works/Montrose post-war/ SUNDERLAND coach Oct 1927-1934.

Debut v Notts County (h) 2/12/1899

"A large, well-built player, Hogg was nevertheless noted for his speed and ball skills," wrote a contemporary critic. John Allan in the first volume of his captivating *Story of the Rangers* (1923) relates that Billy, despite his physical advantages, did not in fact like charging, either as receiver or giver. Also that outside-right was the position in which he excelled most although his capabilities at inside right and leading the attack were considerable. A regular goalscorer from his introduction at the turn of the century Hogg, an England international with Sunderland, scored ten goals as the club won the 1902 championship title. Another highspot came further towards the end of his Roker career

HOLDEN, Melville George

Role: Forward 1975-78
b. Dundee, 25th August 1954
d. Penwortham, Lancs, 31st January 1981

CAREER: Preston North End app, pro Sept 1972/SUNDERLAND May 1975/Blackpool July 1978/Pec Zwolle, Holland Sept 1978.
Debut v Chelsea (h) 16/8/1975 (sub)

Mel Holden scored on his second appearance for Preston North End, and his prowess as a marksman prompted Sunderland manager Bob Stokoe to pay £120,000 for the 20-year-old Scot. His return of 15 League and Cup goals in his first season was a significant contribution with a hat-trick in The Lads' famous 9-1 win over Newcastle at St James Park in December 1908, just a fortnight after he had bagged another treble in a 4-0 win at Woolwich Arsenal. As a person it is said he bubbled over with high spirits. Hogg was no mean cricketer either, once winning a newspaper prize for taking seven wickets for

Billy Hogg

no runs. Apart from football he worked for some years as a licensee in the Sunderland district and elsewhere.

Appearances:
FL: 281 apps. 83 gls.
FAC: 21 apps. 2 gls.
Total: *302 apps. 85 gls.*
Honours:
3 Eng caps/3 FL apps./(Sunderland) FL champs 1902/(Rangers) SL champs 1911, 1912, 1913.

to Sunderland's championship of Division Two, and their good FA Cup run (to round six) in the same term. Sadly, life in the First Division proved less rewarding and when Mel scored against Bristol City on 11th February 1977 it was Sunderland's first

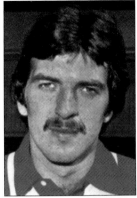

Mel Holden

goal in eleven League matches. Amazingly, the next three games were won, 4-0, 6-1 and 6-0, Holden scoring four of the 16 goals. Not without his detractors during his spell at Roker, Mel was an inconsistent performer but always likely to conjure up a goal, however out of touch he might appear. He left Roker to team up again with Bob Stokoe at Blackpool, but stayed for only three months and was sold to Dutch club Pec Zwolle for £40,000. He was only with them for a short time before returning to England. Sadly, he was struck down by a fatal illness some three years later.

Appearances:
FL: 66(7) apps. 23gls.
FAC: 7 apps. 3 gls.
FLC: 3 apps, 2 gls.
Total: *76(7) apps. 28 gls.*
Honours:
(Sunderland) Div 2 champs 1976.

HOLDEN, William

Role: Centre-forward 1955-56
5'11" 11st.6lbs.
b. Bolton, 1st April 1928

CAREER: Radcliffe Works (Bolton)/Bolton Wanderers trial/Everton am/Burnley part-time pro Nov 1949/SUNDERLAND Dec 1955 £12,000/Stockport County Oct 1956 £6,000/Bury Mar 1959, part exchange for 2 players/Halifax Town June 1962/Rugby Town July 1963/Hereford United 1964.

Debut v Newcastle United (a) 27/12/1955

Bill Holden attended the same school as the great Tommy Lawton and was spotted by

former Burnley player, Jack Marshall, becoming a trialist at Turf Moor. There he graduated from the 'A' team to the Central League side and, in 1950, the League side. Holden impressed as a budding star, exhibiting intelligence, good ball control, a powerful shot and an aerial threat. It has to be recorded, however, that this rich promise did not lead to the heights predicted. Bill was an above average talent that could have gone further. Later he also played at inside-right.

Appearances:
FL: 19 apps. 5 gls.
FAC: 5 apps. 2 gls.
Total: *24 apps. 7 gls.*
Honours:
1 Eng 'B' app. v Scotland 1953/(Bury) Div 3 champs 1961.

Bill Holden

HOLLEY, George

Role: Inside-forward/outside-left 1904-15
5'9" 12st.4lbs.
b. Seaham Harbour, Co Durham,
20th November 1885
d. Heath Town, Wolverhampton,
27th August 1942

CAREER: Seaham Athletic/Seaham Villa/
Seaham White Star 1903-04/
SUNDERLAND Nov 1904 (guest for
Fulham during WW1)/ Brighton & Hove
Albion July 1919/ SUNDERLAND coach

Jan 1921/ Wolverhampton Wanderers
trainer July 1922/ Barnsley trainer 1932.
Debut v Sheffield Wednesday (a) 27/12/1904

The story has been told many times about
George Holley entertaining spectators with
his consummate skills, a ball artist of the
first rank. And not only spectators - the
great Charlie Buchan (a super practitioner
himself) was said to have been sometimes
open-mouthed in sheer admiration.
Moreover, Holley's performances were by
no means mere occasional flashes in the
pan - in other words, he had genuine
consistency - and most importantly, was
simply deadly in front of goal. George hit
nine hat-tricks for Sunderland including
one in a legendary 9-1 win in front of
60,000 at St James Park in December 1908.
It is a measure of his worth that only Bobby
Gurney, Charlie Buchan and Dave Halliday
have scored more goals for the club than
George's tally of 154. Top scorer in five
separate seasons he also finished as leading
marksman in Division One in 1911-12. A
year later he was vice-captain of the team
who came so close to the coveted League
and Cup 'Double' but perhaps unwisely
was played in the FA Cup final against
Aston Villa when clearly not fully fit - a
gamble that backfired badly in the days
before any substitutes were permitted. As a
Sunderland player he scored eight goals in
ten international appearances for England
and played three games as a member of the
FA touring party to South Africa in 1910.
Later on after the Great War he spent a
decade as trainer at Wolverhampton and
several years with Barnsley. George was the
father of Tom Holley, a well-known half-
back with Barnsley (1932-36) and Leeds
United (1936-49). George had originally
worked as a ship's plater.

Appearances:
FL: 279 apps. 145 gls.
FAC: 36 apps. 9 gls.
Total: *315 apps. 154 gls.*
Honours:
10 Eng caps/5 FL apps./(Sunderland) FL
champs 1913/FAC finalist 1913.

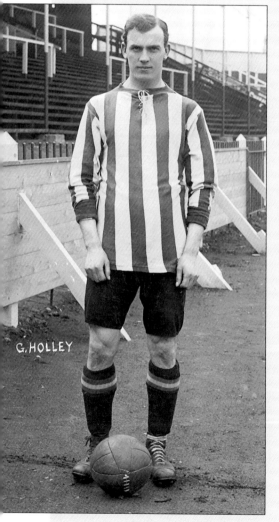

George Holley

Darren Holloway

HOLLOWAY, Darren

Role: Defender 1997-date
6'0" 12st.5lbs.
b. Bishop Auckland, 3rd October 1977

CAREER: Parkside School/Hilda Park Boys/ Crook & Bishop Auckland Schoolboys/ Manchester United Centre of Excellence 1988- 91/York City Juniors/SUNDERLAND trainee July 1994, pro Oct 1995(Carlisle United loan Aug 1997).

Debut v Stoke City (a) 25/10/1997

Introduced at senior level during an injury crisis in October 1997, Darren Holloway performed so well on his debut at Stoke City that he became a fixture in the side for the remainder of the season. His Sunderland

debut followed a highly successful loan spell with Carlisle United. The Cumbrians gave Darren his first taste of League football, and were sufficiently impressed to offer Sunderland a reported fee of £400,000 for his permanent transfer. This was not entertained and shortly after his return, Darren made his long overdue debut for The Lads. A mark of the progress he made in his first season came when, along with team mate Darren Williams, he appeared for the England Under-21 side in Switzerland in March 1998. Sadly, Darren was absent from first-team duty for much of 1998- 99. A pre-season back injury caused him to pull out of the West Country tour, and after a lengthy spell on the sidelines he found himself unable to break back into the first team. His first start in the League was not, in fact, until February, when he deputised for Michael Gray at Oxford United. He showed up well in this match and in five subsequent appearances from the bench, and is certain to be pressing for a first team place in the Premiership.

Appearances:
FL: 36(5) apps. 0 gls.
FAC: 2 apps. 0 gls.
Total: *38(5) apps. 0 gls.*
Honours:
1 Eng U-21 app. 1998.

HOLTON, James Alan

Role: Half-back 1976-77
6'1" 13st.5lbs.
b. Lesmahagow, 11th April 1951
d. Bagington, Coventry, 5th October 1993

CAREER: Celtic ground staff/West Bromwich Albion Apr 1968/Shrewsbury Town June 1971/Manchester United Jan 1973(Miami Toros loan June-Aug 1976)(SUNDERLAND loan Sept 1976)/SUNDERLAND Oct 1976/ Coventry City Mar 1977(Detroit Express loan May-Aug 1980)/Sheffield Wednesday May 1981, retired cs 1982.

Debut v West Ham United (a) 25/9/1976

Although a member of West Bromwich Albion's Youth Cup Final side in 1969, Jim Holton was released by the Baggies and his League career began modestly in Shrewsbury Town's colours. Manchester United's manager Tommy Docherty paid £80,000 for him in January 1973, and the rugged, no-nonsense centre-half enjoyed his best days at Old

Trafford. The battle cry from the Stretford End ran "Six foot two, eyes of blue, big Jim Holton's after you!" Although in fact his eyes were brown the rest of the song was not far off the mark! A broken leg in December 1974 was followed by a similar injury nine months later in a comeback with the Reserves, and after a spell in America Jim joined Sunderland for £40,000, following a month's loan. Manager Bob Stokoe resigned in the month of Holton's signing and new manager Jimmy Adamson began with a poor run of results and few goals scored. In 15 League starts for Sunderland, Holton had only twice appeared on the winning side, and was probably relieved to join Coventry City after only seven months on Wearside. Shortly before his departure, Jim enjoyed his finest game for The Lads as he and Jeff Clarke somehow restricted Newcastle to merely a 2-0 win at St James Park in December 1976 when it could have been ten. He appeared in exactly 100 League and Cup matches for the Sky Blues and retired in 1982 during his spell with Sheffield Wednesday where he did not appear in the League side. He was later a publican in Coventry, prior to his sadly premature death at the wheel of a car, apparently from a heart attack, when aged 42.

Jim Holton

Appearances:
FL: 15 apps. 0 gls.
FAC: 2 apps. 1 gl.
FLC: 2 apps. 0 gls.
Total: *19 apps. 1 gl.*
Honours:
1 Scot U-23 app. 1973/15 Scot caps 1973-75/(Manchester United) Div 2 champs 1975.

HOOD, Henry Anthony

Role: Centre-forward 1964-67
5'9" 11st.4lbs.
b. Glasgow, 3rd October 1944

CAREER: St Aloysius College/Holyrood Senior Secondary/Campsie Black Watch/St Roch's (Glasgow) July 1961/Brunswick Boys' Club (Edinburgh) later in 1961/Clyde June 1962/SUNDERLAND Nov 1964 £26,000/Clyde Oct 1966 £12,000/Celtic Mar 1969/St Antonio Thunder May 1976/Motherwell Aug 1976/Queen of the South Sept 1977, retired Sept 1978/Albion Rovers manager Feb 1981-Apr 1981/Queen of the South manager Feb 1982-Apr 1982.

Harry Hood

Debut v Burnley (h) 14/11/1964

Jock Stein, the celebrated Celtic manager, reckoned Harry had all the required technical and physical qualities " ... but he must force himself into the action." Maybe this cost him a full cap. It is interesting to note too that this gifted player, who could take any forward role, had been in the big time some seven years without gaining a club honour and that, on joining the Celts, acquired a remarkable cache of medals. His brother, Jack Hood, was the first Scottish junior to command a £1,000+ fee (Shettleston to Everton for £1,200 in 1956). Astonishingly, Harry is said to have never played soccer at school. And he must have established some sort of record for the brevity of his two managerships.

> **Appearances:**
> *FL: 31 apps. 9 gls.*
> *FAC: 1 app. 1 gl.*
> *FLC: 1(1) apps. 0 gls.*
> **Total:** *33(1) apps. 10 gls.*
> **Honours:**
> *1 Scot U-23 app./(Celtic) SL champs 1970, 1971, 1972, 1973/SLC winner 1970, 1975/SLC finalist 1971, 1972, 1973, 1974.*

HOOPER, Harry

Role: Outside-right 1960-63
5'8" 10st.7lbs.
b. Pittington, Co Durham, 14th June 1933

CAREER: Co Durham Schools/Hylton Colliery/West Ham United am 1949, pro Nov 1950/Wolverhampton Wanderers Mar 1956 £25,000/Birmingham City Dec 1957 £19,000/SUNDERLAND Sept 1960 £17,000/Kettering Town May 1963/Dunstable Town cs 1965/Heanor Town.

Debut v Plymouth Argyle (a) 1/10/1960

Harry Hooper was a real crowd-pleaser with his exceptional speed and strong shooting - "a dazzling wing raider," as someone once wrote. He received an early senior baptism with the Hammers, against Barnsley at Upton Park on February 3rd 1951, aged 17, and later played on the opposite flank with like facility. Son of Harry Hooper Snr of Sheffield United's 1936 Cup Final side and subsequent Halifax Town manager. Harry was later employed by an electronics company in Bedford.

Appearances:
FL: 65 apps. 16 gls.
FAC: 8 apps. 2 gls.
FLC: 7 apps. 1 gl.
Total: *80 apps. 19 gls.*
Honours:
6 Eng 'B' apps./2 Eng U-23 apps./3 FL apps./ (Birmingham City) ICFC finalist 1960.

Harry Hooper

HOPE, James William

Role: Inside-right 1908-09
b. Kelloe, Co Durham

CAREER: Kelloe FC/South Moors Violet (West Stanley)/ Birtley/West Stanley/ Horden Colliery/ Horden Athletic/SUNDERLAND Jan 1908-cs 1909.

James Hope

Debut v Leicester Fosse (a) 20/3/1909

James Hope was a Sunderland player for a season and a half following a successful time in the minor circles of County Durham - most notably in helping Birtley win the Gateshead League championship. Hope's only senior outing for Sunderland, at Leicester against the Fosse, resulted in a 4-3 defeat.

Appearances:
FL: 1 app. 0 gls.
Total: *1 app. 0 gls.*

HOPKINS, William

Role: Centre-half 1913-15
5'10" 11st.7lbs.
b. Esh Winning, Co Durham, 11th November 1888
d. Blackpool, 26th January 1938

CAREER: Esh Winning Rangers/ Crook Town 1907/Derby County trial/Esh Winning Rangers/Stanley United/SUNDERLAND May 1912/Leeds City July 1919 £50/South Shields Oct 1919 £600/Hartlepools United May 1921/ Durham City Aug 1923-1925, player-coach from Aug 1924/Sheffield United asst. trainer/ Charlton Athletic trainer/Grimsby Town trainer June 1931/Port Vale trainer 1935/ Barnsley trainer July 1936 to his death.

Debut v Liverpool (a) 13/9/1913

Bill Hopkins also appeared at right-half for Sunderland and he could take a forward position. An efficient performer, at

Bill Hopkins

the outset of his senior career he was praised for being strong and fearless. Hopkins was one of the players sold at the famous auction when the Leeds City club collapsed and it is interesting to reflect on the fee paid by Leeds and that obtained three months later at auction - a twelve-fold increase! At the time of his sudden demise, Hopkins was with a Barnsley FC party preparing for a cup-tie against Blackpool.

Appearances:
FL: 10 apps. 0 gls.
Total: *10 apps. 0 gls.*

HORNBY, Cecil Frederick

Role: Half-back/inside-right 1935-37
5'10" 11st.7lbs.
b. West Bromwich, 29th April 1907
d. West Bromwich, 3rd qtr 1964

CAREER: Oakengates Town/Leeds United May 1929/SUNDERLAND Feb 1936 £1,000/ Oakengates Town player-manager July 1937/ Brierley Hill Alliance Dec 1937/Cradley Heath Aug 1938.

Cecil Hornby

Debut v Grimsby Town (h) 19/2/1936

An acknowledged utility man before joining Sunderland, Hornby's dozen League appearances for the club were divided between right-half (once), centre-half (five times) and inside-right (six). He did however score one of the goals in Sunderland's 7-2 romp at Birmingham City on the day the 1936 championship was clinched. His single cup-tie was at inside-right and he scored in the 3-2 win at Southampton which began the successful 1937 Cup run. At Leeds, besides the foregoing, he appeared at inside-left (his Oakengates berth) and left-half, which was said to be his primary position. In all Hornby played 89 League and Cup matches for Leeds United, scoring five goals. He was described at various times as "a robust and willing worker" and a player with "smart ball control and plenty of pluck and speed."

Appearances:
FL: 12 apps. 2 gls.
FAC: 1 app. 1 gl.
Total: *13 apps. 3 gls.*

HORSWILL, Michael Frederick

Role: Midfield 1971-74
5'10" 11st.0lbs.
b. Annfield Plain, 6th March 1953

CAREER: Stanley Boys/Annfield Plain/ SUNDERLAND app July 1968, pro Mar 1970/ Manchester City Mar 1974/Plymouth Argyle June 1975/Hull City July 1978/Happy Valley, Hong Kong Mar 1982/Barrow 1982-83/ Carlisle United n.c. Aug 1983.

Debut v Preston North End (a) 4/4/1972

Micky Horswill began with Sunderland from twelve years of age when he commenced on a twice-weekly training programme. Three years later he signed apprentice forms and graduated through the ranks, making his League debut in Division Two, in a 3-1 victory at Preston in April 1972. In the following season under new manager Bob Stokoe, he appeared in every round of the season's unforgettable FA Cup run to Wembley and the historic victory over Leeds United. A versatile ball-winner in midfield, the lean, red-haired link-man combined strong tackling with the ability to cut down opponents' space, and pass constructively out of defence. A major

contributor to the Cup run, Horswill blunted opponents of the calibre of Manchester City's Colin Bell, Alan Ball of Arsenal and in the final, Leeds United's Johnny Giles. His long association with Sunderland ended in March 1974 when, along with Dennis Tueart, he joined Manchester City in a major deal which valued Horswill at £100,000 but also included Tony Towers' move to Sunderland. After a relatively short stay at Maine Road he had good spells with Plymouth Argyle (90 appearances, 3 goals) and Hull City (82 appearances, 6 goals). His final appearance, before a troublesome knee injury forced his retirement, was for Carlisle United, managed by his former Sunderland boss, Bob Stokoe. Micky later ran a pub in Sunderland.

Appearances:
FL: 68(1) apps. 3 gls.
FAC: 10 apps. 1 g.
FLC: 5 apps. 0 gls.
Other: 8 apps. 1 gl.
Total: *91(1) apps. 5 gls.*
Honours:
(Sunderland) FAC winner 1973.

Micky Horswill

HOUSAM, Arthur

Arthur Housam

Role: Wing-half 1937-48
5'8" 10st.0lbs.
b. Sunderland, 10th October 1917
d. Sunderland, 31st December 1975

CAREER: Hylton Colliery/SUNDERLAND
May 1937(guested for Chesterfield and
Sheffield Wednesday during WW2)/Horden
Colliery Welfare June 1948.

Debut v Preston North End (h) 4/5/1938

Arthur Housam played mainly at right-back
but in 1946/47 he had a number of games on
the left flank to accommodate Ken
Willingham. Housam first made Sunderland's
League side in the final two matches of
1937/38 and the following term was
recognised as a half-back of great promise.
That pillar of inter-war football journalism,
Topical Times, selected him as one of their
twelve 'Best Discoveries of 1938/39' finishing
its eulogy as follows: "He was born within
shouting distance of the Roker Park ground,
and he had a hero in half-back Billy Clunas,
one of the best of recent times. Housam
modelled his play on that of Clunas, and thus
has all the finer touches which a top grade
half-back can always use and, in addition,
there is a natural hard-working, grafting spirit.
These combined virtues have helped Housam
to get to the front. He should stay there now."
The war, with its interruption of budding
promise, had much to answer for.

> **Appearances:**
> *FL: 55 apps. 2 gls.*
> *FAC: 12 apps. 1 gl.*
> **Total:** *67 apps. 3 gls.*

HOWEY, Lee Matthew

Role: Utility 1992-96
6'2" 13st.9lbs.
b. Sunderland, 1st April 1969

CAREER: St Cuthbert's Primary School/
Sunderland Schoolboys/Ipswich Town Oct
1986/AC Hemptinne, Belgium/Seaham Red
Star/Blyth Spartans Mar 1988/Gateshead/
Bishop Auckland 1992(Doncaster Rovers
trial)/SUNDERLAND Mar 1993/Burnley Aug
1997(Northampton Town loan Nov 1998)/
Northampton Town Feb 1999.

Debut v Portsmouth (h) 1/5/1993 (sub)

Lee Howey

Elder brother of Newcastle United's Steve Howey, Lee was a member of the Sunderland Schoolboys side that shared the English Schools FA Trophy in 1983. He arrived at Roker ten years later, and after a variety of experience which included three years in Belgium. Following his return to England, contractual problems led to a lengthy suspension and when he resumed his playing career it was in non-League circles. Nineteen goals for Bishop Auckland in 1992-93 alerted senior interest, and it was Terry Butcher - a former playing colleague at Ipswich Town - who arranged trials at Roker which resulted in Lee becoming a Sunderland player just prior to the transfer deadline in March 1993. As either striker or defender his strength, physical presence and wholehearted approach made him a crowd favourite, particularly so after moments such as his bullet header from a corner which beat Middlesbrough at Roker in January 1994. But Lee was never able to establish a regular starting place in the side. In the close season of 1997, following Sunderland's relegation from the Premiership, an influx of new signings led to Howey's £200,000 transfer to Burnley, where he re-joined forces with Chris Waddle, newly appointed player-manager of the Clarets after his brief stay at Roker Park. Lee scored on his debut for Burnley, but injury in mid season restricted his League outings. Following a loan

spell with Northampton Town in November 1998, he rejoined the Cobblers on a permanent basis later in the season, but was unable to prevent their subsequent relegation to Division Three.

Appearances:
FL: 39(31) apps. 8 gls.
FAC: 2(4) apps. 1 gl.
FLC: 1(4) apps. 2 gls.
Other: 0(1) apps. 0 gls.
Total: *42(40) apps. 11 gls.*
Honours:
(Sunderland) Div 1 champs 1996.

HUDGELL, Arthur John

Role: Left-back 1946-57
5'9" 11st.13lbs.
b. Hackney, London, 28th December 1920

CAREER: Hackney Schools/Eton Manor/ Crystal Palace Dec 1937/SUNDERLAND Jan 1947 £10,000 (Silkworth Juniors coach [loan] 1957)/retired 1958.

Debut v Blackburn Rovers (a) 1/2/1947

Arthur Hudgell

A stylish, fair-haired full-back, Arthur Hudgell was Jack Stelling's partner for seven years. Hudgell made no pre-war senior appearances for Crystal Palace, being still only 18 when war broke out, but did so in wartime. His peacetime (i.e. 1946/47) figures for the Glaziers were 25 Southern Section outings (one goal) plus one in the FA Cup. He cost Sunderland what was then a record transfer fee for a defender but it was certainly money well spent on a solid player who became an often unsung stalwart of a Sunderland side containing some outstanding individuals. Arthur had played in the same boys' club team as Ivor Broadis (q.v.) and could fill the right-back position most capably.

Appearances:
FL: 260 apps. 0 gls.
FAC: 15 apps. 0 gls.
Total: *275 apps. 0 gls.*

HUGGINS, Jack W.

Role: Outside-left 1906-08
5'8" 12st.0lbs.

CAREER: Bede College/Leadgate/
SUNDERLAND am June 1906, pro June 1907/
Reading May 1908/SUNDERLAND Sept 1909-
1910.

*Debut v Manchester
United (h)
20/10/1906 (scored)*

Unusually weighty
for a left-winger,
Jack Huggins
heralded his senior
blooding by
contributing a goal
in an emphatic 4-1
home win over
Manchester
United. All of his

Jack Huggins

League appearances took place in the first
Roker Park spell: seven in each season. He
played when Arthur Bridgett was either
unavailable or occupying another forward
berth. Huggins, a school teacher, was an
excellent cricketer good enough to assist
Durham CCC.

Appearances:
FL: 14 apps. 2 gls.
Total: *14 apps. 2 gls.*

HUGHES, Ian James

Role: Defender 1979-80
5'9" 11st.1lb.
b. Sunderland, 24th August 1961

CAREER: Sunderland Schoolboys/Durham
County Schoolboys/SUNDERLAND app Aug
1977, pro Aug 1979/Barnsley July 1981/
SUNDERLAND nc cs 1982. Injured in pre-
season and taken onto coaching staff. Youth
and reserve team coach until June 1985/
Newcastle United asst. coach to 1986/
West Ham United senior scout.

Debut v Swansea City (a) 10/11/1979

In early days Ian Hughes represented
Sunderland Schoolboys at Primary and
Secondary levels, and was a Durham County
Under-15 representative. (A youthful team
mate was goalkeeper Stephen Pears who

subsequently
progressed to
Manchester
United and
Middlesbrough.)
Ian's League
debut, at 18 years
of age, came
during the
promotion season
of 1979-80. He
was one of four
team changes in
an unfamiliar
line-up that went
down 3-1 at
Swansea City.
After a season
with Barnsley he
returned to

Ian Hughes

Sunderland but an injury in a pre-season
friendly ended his playing career. In both part
and full-time roles he coached at Roker until
the arrival of Lawrie McMenemy in 1985. West
Ham United's senior scout in the North-East
since 1986, Ian Hughes currently lives in
Sunderland and is a business manager with a
pharmaceutical company.

Appearances:
FL: 1 app. 0 gls.
Total: *1 app. 0 gls.*

HUGHES, John

Role: Winger 1972-73
6'2" 13st.7lbs.
b. Coatbridge, 3rd April 1943

CAREER: Kirshaw Amateurs/Shotts Bon
Accord Aug 1959/Celtic Oct 1959/Crystal
Palace Oct 1971/SUNDERLAND Jan-May
1973/Baillieston Juniors coach Jan 1974/
Stranraer manager Jan 1975-Apr 1976/
Baillieston Juniors coach May 1976/Scottish
FA Juniors coach Sept 1978-Jan 1982.

Debut v Millwall (h) 27/1/1973

An elder brother of Sunderland's Billy Hughes
(q.v.). John 'Yogi Bear' Hughes ended his
distinguished career at Roker Park. Sadly, he
appeared only once in Sunderland's colours
before an injury, suffered a mere three minutes
into his debut, forced his retirement. He began
with Celtic at 16 years of age and scored on
his first team debut at 17. Surprisingly nimble

John Hughes

HUGHES, William

Role: Forward 1966-77
5'9" 10st.12lbs.
b. Coatbridge, 30th December 1948

CAREER: Coatbridge schools football/
SUNDERLAND ground staff Dec 1965, pro
Feb 1966(Derby County loan)/Derby
County Sept 1977 £30,000/Leicester City
Dec 1977 £45,000(Carlisle United loan Sept-
Oct 1979)/San Jose Earthquakes, California
Apr 1980/Corby Town.

Debut v Liverpool (h) 4/2/1967

Leeds United manager Don Revie once
summed up Billy Hughes' style very well
when seeking the striker's services.
"Hughes," said Revie, "is one of the most
exciting players I've seen. He loves to go
forward. He runs straight at opponents
forcing them to commit themselves and can
shoot with either foot." Billy had other
virtues as well. He possessed subtlety and,
importantly, versatility that enabled him to
combine well with other players. During
his long stay at Roker Park he appeared in
all five forward positions. Don Revie was
keen to take the player to Leeds but, with
Hughes then at the height of his
considerable powers, Sunderland refused
the overture for one of their top men. Billy
arrived at Roker Park aged 16 after being
spotted in Coatbridge schools soccer by
Sunderland
scout, Tom
Rutherford.
His earliest
days at Roker
were
interrupted
briefly by a
flirtation with
Celtic. Billy's
elder brother
John was then
a star at
Parkhead and
their parents
wanted the
pair to be
together.

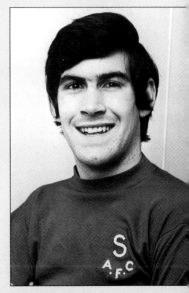

Billy Hughes

for his size, his game was characterised by his
unstoppable charging runs and ferocious
shooting. On the debit side, he was an
inconsistent performer but 189 goals in 416
appearances for Celtic and six consecutive
championships suggest there were many more
good days than bad. John's unhappy single
appearance for Sunderland came in the 1972-
73 season, and the man signed to replace him
in the number nine jersey, Vic Halom, was an
FA Cup winner within three months of
joining. It is interesting to speculate that, in
different circumstances, Sunderland might
have fielded brothers at Wembley. After
retiring John coached and was manager of
Scotland's Junior international squads, and
more recently has been a publican in Glasgow
and Coatbridge.

Appearances:
FL: 1 app. 0 gls.
Total: *1 app. 0 gls.*
Honours:
*6 Scot FL apps./4 Scot U-23 apps. 1961-64/8
Scot caps 1965-70/(Celtic) EC finalist 1970/
SL champs 1966-71 incl/SC winner 1965/
SC finalist 1961, 1963, 1966, 1970/SLC
winner 1966, 1967, 1968, 1970/SLC finalist
1965.*

However, Billy soon decided a career with Sunderland was the better option and returned to Roker. He made his senior debut against Liverpool shortly after his 18th birthday, deputising for the injured George Mulhall in a line-up that included seven Scots. By 1968/69 he was an established first team regular, but Sunderland were then in decline and were relegated to Division Two the following season. It turned out to be a lengthy six-year spell in the lower division but this was lightened by the unexpected FA Cup triumph of 1973. Billy was very much a star of the Cup run. The Wearsiders accounted for three first-class teams en route to their Wembley triumph and Billy notched four fine goals - firstly against Manchester City at Maine Road in round five with a brace in the replay at Roker, and another against Arsenal in the classic Hillsborough semi-final - that are now part of Sunderland folklore. Billy also took the corner from which Sunderland scored in the final against Leeds. Billy Hughes at his best was an absolutely magnificent player and when linked with Dennis Tueart, the duo formed a truly quicksilver forward pairing. Both scored in Sunderland's opening European Cup Winners' Cup tie in Hungary in September 1973. Billy's two goals that silenced 60,000 Manchester United fans at Old Trafford in November 1974 also stick in the memory before he qualified for a Divison Two championship medal in the following season 1975/76. Billy's brother, the famous 'Yogi', had transferred to Sunderland in January 1973 following a 15-month sojourn at Crystal Palace. He had won a cartload of honours at Celtic Park that included eight full Scotland caps and an appearance in a European Cup final. Disappointingly, the brothers were destined to play in the same side only once. It was at Millwall on January 27, 1973, when John, on his debut, sustained the knee injury that ended his career. Billy left Sunderland after nearly 12 years on the club's books, Derby County paying £30,000 for his services.

His stay at the Baseball Ground was brief. He had made only eight appearances before new Derby manager, Tommy Docherty, inexplicably released his leading scorer to East Midlands neighbours Leicester City. Billy played no first team football for his final League club, Carlisle United. After leaving the game Billy returned to Derby where he worked some years as a licensee. He subsequently returned to the North-East as clubhouse manager and steward at the Stressholme Golf Club, Darlington.

Appearances:
FL: 264(23) apps. 74 gls.
FAC: 21(1) apps. 4 gls.
FLC: 12(3) apps. 3 gls.
Other: 7(1) apps. 1 gl.
Total: *304(28) apps. 82 gls.*
Honours:
1 Scot cap/(Sunderland) Div 2 champs 1976/FAC winner 1973.

Billy Hughes tests Arsenal goalkeeper Bob Wilson in the 1973 FA Cup semi-final at Hillsborough.

HUNTER, George

Role: Right-half 1921-23
6'0" 12st.4lbs.
b. Hylton Colliery, Sunderland, circa 1902

CAREER: Hylton Colliery Welfare/ SUNDERLAND Apr 1921/Exeter City May 1923/Workington cs 1924/Southend United Feb 1925/Doncaster Rovers Oct 1925/ Scunthorpe & Lindsay United cs 1926.

Debut v Liverpool (h) 7/1/1922 (FAC)

George Hunter

Tall and well-built, wing-half George Hunter's second League appearance, a home game against Sheffield United on March 4, 1922, was at outside-right. He played in both of the FA Cup ties that season. In season 1922/23 he had a run of five consecutive League outings, October 7 - November 4 inclusive, which included three wins and a draw. George's first team record with Exeter was 24 appearances, made up of 18 in the League and six in the FA Cup. In 1922 it was said that when "tried at right-half became an immediate success." His career petered out with brief spells at Southend and Doncaster Rovers, but he did not appear in League matches with either club.

Appearances:
FL: 9 apps. 0 gls.
FAC: 2 apps. 0 gls.
Total: *11 apps. 0 gls.*

HUNTER, James

Role: Left-back 1885-86
Debut v Redcar (a)
24/10/1885 (FAC)

James Hunter played at left-back for his cup-tie - the only one in 1885/86 when Sunderland were

James Hunter

eliminated in the first round by Redcar, just as they had been in the previous season. But

continued on p222>

HURLEY, Charles Joseph

Role: Centre-half 1957-69
6'1" 13st. 5lbs.
b. *Cork, 4th October 1936*

CAREER: Essex Schools/
Rainham Youth Club
(Essex)/Millwall am May
1953, pro Oct 1953/
SUNDERLAND Sept 1957
£20,000/Bolton Wanderers
June 1969/retired Jan
1972/Reading manager Jan
1972-Feb 1977.

Debut v Blackpool (a)
5/10/1957

An all time Sunderland
celebrity, idolised by young
and old alike, who came to
be dubbed 'The King' because of his loyalty
and leadership. Readers of the magazine
Northern Football, elected Charlie the 'North
East's Player of the Year' for 1963 in a poll
remarkable for the fact he was the choice of
many Newcastle United and Middlesbrough
fans too. He headed a similar Tyne Tees TV
poll in the mid-'Sixties, and was runner-up to
Bobby Moore as The Football Writers'
Association 'Player of the Year' for 1964. In
1979, seven years after retiring, he was elected
by Sunderland supporters as their 'Player of
the Century'. The fans never had any inkling
of doubt about Charlie's worth and he is
arguably Sunderland's most famous and
valuable player. At the time of those 1960s
polls they lauded him in print as "the best
centre-half in Europe" and even went further,
citing him as "the best centre-half in the
world". Yet the player could hardly have had
a more depressing introduction to life at Roker
Park. In his first appearance, an away League
fixture against Blackpool, the Wearsiders were
annihilated 7-0 and, a week later at Turf Moor,
Burnley triumphed by 6-0. Such dire form led
inevitably at the season's end to Sunderland's
first relegation and extinguished the longest
top-flight run any club had enjoyed. But in
Charlie Sunderland now had the rock around
which a side could be re-built to regain its
rightful status. Big, tall and commanding,
constructive to a degree, and a regal
inspiration to his team, he was described as
"brilliant in defence, a good surprise attacker
and, above all, a gentleman on the field of

play in the true sense of the word". Although
born in Eire, he left aged seven months and
was brought up in Rainham, Essex. After
joining Millwall on amateur forms in May
1953 he turned professional five months later,
spurning overtures from West Ham United.
Charlie was first selected for Eire when aged
19 but was unable to play because of a
cartilage injury. It stemmed from a mishap in
Army football during national service in 1955.
Happily, successful surgery meant a great
career was not unduly interrupted. An
international debut soon materialised a year
later. The prospect of a move to Sunderland
did not arouse much enthusiasm on Charlie's
part. He has since related, in typically
humorous fashion, how he was completely
unaware of Sunderland's precise location on
the map. But the club's redoubtable manager,
Alan Brown, fortunately possessed
considerable persuasive powers and spent
hours convincing him. He never did a better
piece of business. In spite of suffering
relegation so soon Charlie stayed loyal to the
Wearsiders, never requesting a transfer
although other clubs were always angling for
his talents. His ambition was to bring back
top-flight football to Roker Park, and he took
over the captaincy when Stan Anderson
moved to Newcastle, a natural progession as
Anderson had instructed him well in the art of
leadership. It was a six-season slog before First
Division status returned, and Charlie's
personal high spot was skippering the 1964
promotion team (of which he was the only
member to have appeared in the 1958
relegation season). "That day meant so much
to the people of Sunderland. I remember the
team doing a lap of honour at the end of the
game, and seeing grown men, miners,
shipbuilders and the like in tears. No money
in the world could replace the memories I
have of Sunderland, Roker Park and all those
marvellous supporters - I wouldn't change a
thing." Charlie's magnificent twelve-year stint
at Sunderland ended with a transfer to Bolton
Wanderers. He had 41 League outings for the
Burnden Park club before hanging up his
boots to taste managerial life at Reading. His
five years there included an FA Cup tie at
Roker in 1973 when his tumultuous reception
from the home fans almost defied belief, and a
promotion campaign (1975-76). Charlie later
became sales manager of a packaging
company in Hertfordshire, but still returns on
occasions to watch his beloved Sunderland.

His younger brother, Chris, was on Millwall's books in the 1960s. It is a measure of the mutual regard and respect between club and player that Sunderland's training ground is named The Charlie Hurley Centre, which he opened. Also on the emotional occasion of Roker Park's final game, it was 'King Charlie' who dug up the centre-spot which was duly replanted at the Stadium of Light.

Appearances:
FL: 357(1) apps. 23 gls.
FAC: 26 apps. 3 gls.
FLC: 17 apps. 0 gls.
Total: *400(1) apps. 26 gls.*
Honours:
40 Eire caps.

Hunter had great versatility. This quality was quite widespread in those early days and he could more than match most. In 1885/6 he made four appearances at left-back, five at centre-half, one at inside-right, one at centre-forward, six at inside-left and one at outside-left. For a guess one would say he favoured the left flank.

Appearances:
FAC: 1 app. 0 gls.
Total: *1 app. 0 gls.*

HUNTLEY, Richard Bernard

Role: Right-half 1968-69
5'9" 10st.0lbs.
b. Sunderland, 5th January 1949

CAREER: Junior football to SUNDERLAND, pro Aug 1967/Cambridge City May 1969.

Debut v Everton (a) 2/11/1968

Richard Huntley was centre-half in Sunderland's 1967 Youth Cup-winning side and continued the natural progression to the club's professional staff. It transpired the debut League match was to be his only one, the result a 2-0 defeat in front of a handsome crowd of 40,492. Six months later Huntley disappeared into non-League obscurity.

Appearances:
FL: 1 app. 0 gls.
Total: *1 app. 0 gls.*

HURDMAN, Arthur Stanley

Role: Outside-right 1906-08
b. Sunderland, 3rd qtr 1882
d. Sunderland, 20th May 1953

CAREER: Sunderland schools football/ Sunderland Old Boys' League/Sunderland Black Watch/SUNDERLAND am May 1906, pro Dec 1906/Darlington June 1908.

Debut v Woolwich Arsenal (a) 1/12/1906

Arthur Hurdman was one of the Wearside League's star turns before joining the Roker Park brigade and he captained the Sunderland Black Watch side in 1905/06. (Which club, incidentally, was to go out of existence soon afterwards.) Hurdman's regular position then was centre-forward, but he switched to outside-right for Sunderland 'A' and it was

there that he made his League appearances. In 1907 the local press wrote that Hurdman " ... is on the small side but lack of inches is made up for by plenty of go and energy. A capital shot and tricky with the ball, he has so far proved a dangerous opponent and his promotion to first class company is fully merited."

Appearances:
FL: 8 apps. 3 gls.
Total: *8 apps. 3 gls.*

HYSLOP, Thomas

Role: Inside-left 1893-95
6'0"
b. Mauchline Ayrshire,
22nd September 1874
d. Elderslie, nr Paisley,
April 1936

Tom Hyslop

CAREER: Elderslie FC/Army football (Scots Guards) (5 matches for Millwall Athletic 1892-93)/SUNDERLAND Jan 1894/Stoke Feb 1895/ Rangers May 1896/Stoke Apr 1898/Rangers May 1899/Partick Thistle May 1900/ Wanderers (Scotland) Sept 1902/Johnston Nov 1902. Later played in America and in December 1908 it was reported he was assisting Phildelphia Thistle FC.

Debut v Everton (h) 6/2/1894

Tall, as befitted a former Guardsman, Tom Hyslop was an exceptionally fine marksman, and fast. On his occasional appearances at outside-left opposing wing-halves found Hyslop a rare handful with his speed and physique. It is noteworthy that in the first Rangers spell, Tom was a member of an all-Scottish international vanguard, the other four being Tom Low, 'Kitey' McPherson, Jimmy Millar and Alec Smith. But Tom had made his reputation with Sunderland and Stoke before going to Ibrox, winning his first cap when at Stoke. The Wanderers FC mentioned in Hyslop's career details is almost certainly the future Dundee Wanderers FC.

Appearances:
FL: 18 apps. 10 gls.
Total: *18 apps. 10 gls.*
Honours:
2 Scot caps/(Sunderland) FL champs 1895/(Rangers) SC winners 1897, 1898.

INGLIS, J.

Role: Right-back 1885-86
Debut v Redcar (a) 24/10/1885 (FAC)

Historians have been able to unearth line-ups for all matches but one the club played in that far-off pre-League season when friendlies formed most items in a fixture list. It would appear Inglis's FA Cup tie was his sole appearance that term: it resulted in a 3-0 defeat.

Appearances:
FAC: 1 app. 0 gls
Total: *1 app. 0 gls.*

IRWIN, Cecil

Role: Right-back 1958-72
6'1" 13st.6lbs.
b. Ellington, Northumberland, 8th April 1942

CAREER: East Northumberland Schools (Burnley trial)/SUNDERLAND am, pro Apr 1959/Yeovil Town player-manager June 1972-1975.

Debut v Ipswich Town (h) 20/9/1958

A fine prospect from the beginning. Cec Irwin's first taste of representative football was with the East Northumberland Under-11's. On moving to his senior (11-15) school, Hirst East C S, he played for the East Northumberland Schools at that level, making five appearances for the county team during his last term there. He was courted by several top flight clubs, having a month's trial with one of them (Burnley). Afterwards, in 1958, Cec signed amateur forms for Sunderland, an understandable move in view of his boyhood support for the Wearsiders from the Roker End terraces. Subsequently Cec played for the England Youth team on eight occasions. He made his first team debut aged 16 years, 165 days, standing in for Jack Hedley, which made him Sunderland's youngest ever senior debutant. His partner that day and in a myriad of later games, Len Ashurst, aged 19, was also making his senior bow. Such a youthful debutant full-back pairing surely has to be some sort of a record! The couple came through with credit despite the 2-0 reverse. After this, manager Alan Brown allowed Irwin to mature with the reserves, wisely preventing a possible drain on the young player's

confidence. He had only seven outings in 1959/60 and two in 1960/61. The following season he became a regular, replacing Colin Nelson. Progress was halted by a broken wrist in September 1962 but he had returned by 1963/64 as a valued member of the promotion line-up, missing only three games. Once again Cec lost his place when John Parke, the Northern Ireland international, arrived from Hibs, but he reclaimed the right-back spot the next season. Despite such fluctuations in his long 14-year spell at Sunderland he was a splendidly reliable right-back who employed a hard, determined tackle and possessed good positional sense. He aggregated 349 senior appearances (plus 3 subs), scoring a solitary goal in October 1968 during a 3-1 win over Nottingham Forest. Once recalling this memorable goal in the *Echo,* he related how, after Charlie Hurley had passed him the ball, he moved into the opponents' half, discovered no options available and so blasted the ball goalwards. A breeze was blowing from the Fulwell End and

Cecil Irwin

the sun may have affected the goalkeeper, Gordon Marshall, but Cec's speculative long shot sailed over Marshall and into the net. Blessed with a fine muscular physique during his playing days, Cec used the tactic of marauding down the right flank and lofting in accurate centres for the likes of Neil Martin in what was, in hindsight, an early example of the more modern 'wing-back' ploy. After leaving football he became a newsagent in Ashington. An unexpected return as part-time manager of Ashington FC, the local non-Leaguers, occurred in the autumn of 1996 following the departure of their manager.

Appearances:
FL: 312(3) apps. 1 gl.
FAC: 20 apps. 0 gls.
FLC: 13 apps. 0 gls.
Other: 4 apps. 0 gls.
Total: *349(3) apps. 1 gl.*
Honours:
8 Eng Yth apps.

IVES, Albert Edward

Role: Left-back 1932-34
5'11" 11st.6lbs.
b. Newcastle upon Tyne, 1st qtr 1909

CAREER: Spen Black & White/ SUNDERLAND Mar 1930/Barnsley Feb 1936-1938/Blyth Spartans 1938.
Debut v Aston Villa (h) 7/9/1932

Understudy to the consistent Harold Shaw for the whole of his six years at Roker Park, Bert Ives was described in 1933 as " a serviceable player who likes to get into it." Which presumably meant he went readily into a challenge. A report the following year said he had been sought by other clubs: an understandable development in view of his reliability at top level. For Barnsley Ives made nine Second Division appearances, deputising for their long-serving Bob Shotton.

Appearances:
FL: 12 apps. 0 gls.
Total: *12 apps. 0 gls.*

Bert Ives

JACKSON, Archibald

Role: Centre-half 1922-24
5'9" 11st.0lbs.
b. Plumstead, London, 25th January 1901
d. Chester, 11th November 1985

CAREER: Rutherglen Glencairn/
SUNDERLAND July 1922/Southend United
May 1924/Third Lanark Nov 1924/Chester
1925/Tranmere Rovers May 1928/Accrington
Stanley July 1930/Walsall Nov 1930/
Southport Feb-Mar 1931/Northwich Victoria
Nov 1931/Manchester North End/Rossendale
United July 1935.

Debut v Middlesbrough (a) 18/4/1923

Archie Jackson was on the books of a number
of League clubs for varying periods ranging
from two years to a few weeks but did not, in
some instances, make the first teams. In his
best spell, at Tranmere, he was first choice in
1928/29 and made 37 Northern Section
appearances all told for the Birkenhead club.
He was a prominent figure in a three-year stint
with a then non-League Chester and made one
Scottish League top flight appearance for
Third Lanark. Archie came from a sporting
family - his father played for Newcastle
United and other top clubs in pre-World War
One years, and he was a brother of the well-
known James ('Parson') Jackson (Liverpool
1925-33); a cousin, also named Archie Jackson,
was a famous Australian Test cricketer.

> **Appearances:**
> *FL: 6 apps. 0 gls.*
> **Total:** *6 apps. 0 gls.*

JACKSON, Richard William

Role: Left-half 1898-1905
5'8" 11st.9lbs.
b. Middlesbrough, 1877

CAREER: Middlesbrough/SUNDERLAND
May 1898/Portsmouth May 1905-1907/
Darlington manager May 1912-1919/
Middlesbrough asst. manager/Durham City
manager July 1926-1927.

Debut v Sheffield United (a) 17/12/1898

A centre-half earlier and, indeed, that was the
position occupied when Dicky Jackson won
his Amateur Cup medal. At Sunderland,
however, he made his many senior

Dicky Jackson

appearances on the left
flank, a lively and
capable performer
during one of the club's
finest periods. His

splendid Sunderland service was duly
honoured by a joint benefit with Billy Hogg in
December 1904. As manager of two clubs with
limited resources, Dicky had his successes.
With Darlington the North-Eastern League
championship was won in 1912/13 by five
clear points, 116 goals were scored and only
23 conceded in a 38 match tourney (a strong
competition containing, inter alia, the reserve
sides of Sunderland, Newcastle United and
Middlesbrough). And in his brief tenure at
Durham City - a club soon to lose its Football
League status - he produced jewels in Sammy
Crooks (Derby County and England) and
Fulham's Syd Elliott.

> **Appearances:**
> *FL: 163 apps. 10 gls.*
> *FAC: 6 apps. 0 gls.*
> **Total:** *169 apps. 10 gls.*
> **Honours:**
> *(Middlesbrough) AmC winner 1898/*
> *(Sunderland) FL champs 1902.*

JAMES, Leighton

Role: Winger 1982-84
5'9" 12st.6lbs.
b. Llechwyr, Swansea, 16th February 1953

CAREER: Swansea Schoolboys/Neath Boys'
Club/Burnley app Oct 1968/pro Feb 1970/
Derby County Nov 1975/Queens Park
Rangers Oct 1977/Burnley Sept 1978/Swansea
City May 1980/SUNDERLAND Jan 1983/
Bury Aug 1984/Newport County player-coach
Aug 1985/Burnley Aug 1986, appointed youth
coach June 1987, released May 1989/Bradford
City coach Feb 1990/Gainsborough Trinity
manager/Haslingden F.C. coach cs 1991/
Morecambe manager Jan-June 1994/Darwen/
Netherfield manager/Ilkeston Town manager
1995-Feb 1996/Accrington Stanley manager to
Feb 1998.

Debut v Aston Villa (h) 15/1/1983

Leighton James

against Sunderland Youth in the Roker Park final of the eight team Sunderland International Youth Tournament in 1972. He won his first full Wales cap at 18 in October 1971, and his final one of 54 during his spell at Roker. His playing career ended where it began, at Burnley, in May 1989. He appeared in 630(2) Football League games and scored 123 goals.

Appearances:
FL: 50(2) apps. 4 gls.
FAC: 1 app. 0 gls.
FLC: 4 apps. 0 gls.
Total: *55(2) apps. 4 gls.*
Honours:
Wales Sch & Yth/17 Wales U-23 apps. 1972-75/54 Welsh caps 1972-83/(Burnley) Div 2 champs 1973/ASC winner 1978/ (Swansea City) WC winner 1981, 1982.

JARVIE, Gavin

Role: Left-half 1907-12
5'8" 12st.0lbs.
b. Newton, Lanarkshire, 1879

CAREER:
Airdrieonians Oct 1901/Bristol Rovers Apr 1904/SUNDERLAND June 1907/Hamilton Academical Mar 1912.

Debut v Manchester City (h) 2/9/1907

Gavin Jarvie

One of several shrewd signings by manager Alan Durban during season 1982-83, Leighton James arrived at Roker Park on a free transfer and immediately became an influential figure in Sunderland's successful struggle against relegation. A vastly experienced international wing-man who registered his 100th League goal in Sunderland's colours, James proved an excellent short-term signing. Less individualistic than in his heyday, and with a more even temperament, the bulky wing-man proved a fine team player. Still capable of bewildering footwork he was also a masterly striker of the dead ball, particularly dangerous from free-kicks and corners. His magnificent career began with Burnley where he was a League debutant at 17 years of age. Indeed, he netted the winning goal for Burnley Youth

Gavin Jarvie also played centre-half on occasion - he occupied that position on the above Sunderland debut. He came to Roker Park following a capital three years at Eastville, which took in membership of Rovers' 1904/05 Southern League title-winning side. Gavin's aggregate SL figures for Bristol Rovers were 89 appearances, one goal and he had 28 Scottish League First Division outings with Hamilton Accies in the 1912/13 campaign. An efficient half-back, strong all round and, as has been indicated, adaptable.

Appearances:
FL: 96 apps. 2 gls.
FAC: 7 apps. 0 gls.
Total: *103 apps. 2 gls.*
Honours:
(Bristol Rovers) Sthn Lge champs 1905.

JOHNSON, Joseph

Role: Left-back 1919-21
5'8" 13st 0lbs.
b. Felling, Co Durham

CAREER: Felling Colliery/SUNDERLAND
July 1919/Ebbw Vale May 1921.

Debut v Preston North End (h) 10/4/1920

Joe Johnson

Joe Johnson was one of five left-backs fielded by Sunderland in League fixtures in the initial inter-war season. But only one of three in 1920/21 when Ernie England had got into his stride for a long occupancy. Joe, a local recruit of weighty proportions, played in three of the final four 1919/20 games and two during the next season.

Appearances:
FL: 5 apps. 0 gls.
Total: *5 apps. 0 gls.*

JOHNSTON, Allan

Role: Midfield/Winger 1996-date
5'10" 11st.0lbs.
b. Glasgow, 14th December 1973

CAREER: Lenzie Boys' Club/Eastercraigs Boys' Club/Glasgow Rangers Juniors/ Tynecastle Boys' Club/Heart of Midlothian June 1990/Rennes, France cs 1996/ SUNDERLAND Mar 1997.

Debut v Newcastle United (a) 5/4/1997

Allan Johnston made a goalscoring debut for Hearts against Airdrieonians in May 1993 and became a senior squad member in the following season. In his first full campaign he made five starts and 23 substitute appearances, but in 1995-96, his last at Tynecastle, where he was known as 'Sticky', he missed only three League matches and the undoubted highlight was his hat-trick against champions Rangers at Ibrox. A season in France with Rennes broadened Allan's experience as he was used in a variety of positions, including centre-forward and behind the front two strikers. Sunderland paid £550,000 for his signature and 'Magic' quickly

endeared himself to the fans. His skilful wingplay, versatility and eye for a scoring chance made him a key member of Sunderland's free-scoring side, and he won deserved recognition when called up by Scotland 'B' in March 1998. Consistently outstanding form at club level, where he formed a dangerous left-sided attacking partnership with the overlapping Michael Gray, was rewarded in October 1998 when Allan was capped by Scotland against Estonia and the Faroe Islands. He was the first Sunderland player capped by Scotland since Billy Hughes in 1975, and has since also appeared against the Czech Republic. Allan also scored against the Faroe's and Czech's, making him not only the first Sunderland player to score twice for Scotland, but also the first to do so since 1934. He would most probably have played against Bosnia, but the match was called off due to hostilities and the

Allan Johnston

political situation. His appearances at international level have drawn high praise from Scotland's manager, Craig Brown, who recently said: "Allan Johnston can play either right, left or in a free role and rarely wastes a ball. He has a shot in both feet and crosses the ball quite brilliantly." The summer of 1999 brought unexpected problems however, with Johnston transfer listed after refusing to consider any extension to his current contract with Sunderland.

Appearances:
PL: 4(2) apps. 1 gl.
FL: 81(2) apps. 18 gls.
FAC: 2 apps. 0 gls.
FLC: 6(1) apps. 1 gl.
Total: *93(5) apps. 20 gls.*
Honours:
4 Scot caps 1998-99/3 Scot U-21 apps.
1994-96/2 Scot 'B' apps. 1998/
(Heart of Midlothian) SC finalist 1996/
(Sunderland) Div 1 champs 1999.

JOHNSTON, Harry W.

Role: Left-half 1894-98
5'9" 12st.0lbs.
b. Glasgow, 1871
d. Glasgow, 10th December 1936

CAREER: Airdrieonians 1888-89/Clyde 1892/SUNDERLAND May 1894/Aston Villa Aug 1897/Grimsby Town Oct 1897/ Gravesend Feb 1898/Third Lanark later in 1898.

Debut v Derby County (h) 1/9/1894

Sunderland had the best of Harry Johnston, his engagements thereafter being of a short term nature. And his earlier ones were by way

Harry Johnston

of being an apprenticeship. Yet Harry was on Wearside in the 'Team of All the Talents' era, a regular (29 appearances) in the 1895 championship line-up. He was first choice in 1895/96 too. A powerful, incisive wing-half in those years.

Appearances:
FL: 60 apps. 4 gls.
FAC: 6 apps. 0 gls.
Total: *66 apps. 4 gls.*
Honours:
(Sunderland) FL champs 1895.

JOHNSTON, John

Role: Right-back 1908-09
b. probably in Scotland

CAREER: Cambuslang Rangers/ SUNDERLAND Aug 1907/Motherwell cs 1909.

Debut v Blackburn Rovers (a) 22/3/1909

John Johnston

No fewer than eight different players occupied the first team right-back berth in season 1908/09, which superficially would indicate either desperation or a depressingly long injury list. However, it was not desperation for Sunderland finished a creditable third in the League and reached the FA Cup quarter-finals. John Johnston played his sole Football League game for the Wearsiders that term. It turned out to be an historic occasion: Blackburn won 8-1, a result that remained Sunderland's record defeat for decades.

Appearances:
FL: 1 app. 0 gls.
Total: *1 app. 0 gls.*

JOHNSTONE, Robert

Role: Outside-left 1896-97
5'7" 10st.3lbs.
b. Renton, Dunbartonshire, circa 1897

CAREER: Renton FC/SUNDERLAND May 1896/Third Lanark May 1897/Dunfermline Athletic Oct 1899.

Debut v Sheffield Wednesday (a) 10/10/1896

A typical little Scottish forward possessing gifts of ball control and combination, a couple

JOHNSTON, Robert

Role: Centre-half 1930-39
5'11" 11st.8lbs.
b. Falkirk, 2nd June 1909
d. Sunderland, 27th September 1968

CAREER: Alva Albion Rangers/
SUNDERLAND Aug 1929 (guested for
Hartlepools United and Lincoln City
during WW2, retired from playing
before peace returned)/Sunderland
trainer June 1951-July 1957.

Debut v West Ham United (a)
25/4/1931

Bert Johnston cost merely a small
donation to his junior club's
funds when signed, but proved a
wonderful investment in
retrospect considering his length
of service on the field and
behind the scenes. Originally
Johnston understudied the
redoubtable Jock McDougall
and, even when the latter moved
on to Leeds United in 1934, had to
compete with Jimmy Clark for the
senior pivotal role until Clark
transferred to Plymouth Argyle.
Johnston was a fine defensive player
though he preferred to introduce an
attacking element into his
performance. An engineer by
calling and father of David
Johnston who played
professionally for
Exeter City and
Stockport County
during the 1960s.

Appearances:
FL: 145 apps. 0 gls.
FAC: 18 apps. 0 gls.
Total: *163 apps. 0 gls.*
Honours:
1 Scot cap v Czechoslovakia
1938/(Sunderland) FAC winner 1937.

of Bob Johnstone's Sunderland Football
League appearances were in his other position,
inside-left. Rather confusingly his Sunderland
season coincided with one of Harry Johnston's
and they met up again in Third Lanark's
colours (which may have caused a little
confusion at Cathkin also).

Appearances:
FL: 12 apps. 0 gls.
FAC: 2 apps. 0 gls.
Total: *14 apps. 0 gls.*

JONES, John Edward

Role: Left-back 1945-47
5'9" 11st.10lbs.
b. Bromborough, Cheshire, 3rd July 1913
d. Sunderland, 26th January 1995

CAREER: Bebington/Bromborough Pool/
Ellesmere Port/Everton Mar 1932(guested for
Chester, Southport, Tranmere, Wigan and
Wrexham in WW2)/SUNDERLAND Dec 1945,

Jack Jones

Ken Jones

retired 1947 and became club asst-trainer to May 1969.

Debut v Grimsby Town (a) 5/1/1946 (FAC)

Although he did not pick up any medals with Everton's 1930's trophy-winning sides, Jack Jones still clocked up 108 League and FA Cup appearances for the Toffees when rivals included internationalists. This was achieved by dint of application, his intuition and reliability not to be gainsaid. Jones guested for several clubs during the 1939-45 war, including Sunderland who thus had a good opportunity to assess his worth, and who secured his transfer shortly after the war ended. Following one peacetime season at Roker Park, Jack started a long stint on the training staff.

Appearances:
FL: 24 apps. 0 gls.
FAC: 7 apps. 0 gls.
Total: *31 apps. 0 gls.*

JONES, Kenneth

Role: Left-back 1959-60
5'8" 11st.0lbs.
b. Easington, North Yorkshire, 1st October 1936

CAREER: Sunderland Schools/ SUNDERLAND Oct 1953/Hartlepools United Jan 1961-1962.

Debut v Bristol Rovers (a) 23/1/1960

Over seven years on Sunderland's books, all of Ken Jones' League outings occurred during the second half of season 1959/60 standing-in for the ubiquitous Len Ashurst. He had an outstanding career as a schoolboy that peaked in the winning of three England caps in 1951-52, playing against Eire and Scotland twice. Ken made 33 Fourth Division appearances for Hartlepools before disappearing from the League scene.

Appearances:
FL: 10 apps. 0 gls.
Total: *10 apps. 0 gls.*
Honours:
3 Eng Sch int apps.

JOPLING

Role: Outside-left 1888-89
Debut v Newcastle East End 17/11/1888 (FAC) (scored)

Jopling made four appearances for Sunderland in that long ago pre-League campaign, which included the above FA Cup-tie and all took place in November 1888. In two of them he played at inside-right (against Durham University on the 14th and Lincoln City on the 24th). The other, against Long Eaton Rangers on the 3rd November was at outside-left as in the Cup-tie.

Appearances:
FAC: 1 app. 1 gl.
Total: *1 app. 1 gl.*

KASHER, Joseph

Role: Centre-half 1919-23
5'10" 11st.6lbs.
b. Willington, Co Durham, 14th January 1894
d. Middlesbrough, 8th January 1992

CAREER: Hunwick Juniors/Willington/
Crook Town (Sunderland trial pre-WW1)/
SUNDERLAND May 1919/Stoke Oct 1922/
Carlisle United July 1924/Accrington Stanley
June 1925/retired May 1927/Bishop Auckland
FC committee 1940.

Debut v Arsenal (a) 20/9/1919

The oldest in a
family of ten
children, Joe went
to work in the
mines when 14. He
played in local
junior soccer until
graduating to the
well-known
amateur outfit
Crook Town, but a
professional
engagement was
delayed by the war.

Joe Kasher

Kasher served in the Naval Division,
becoming a prisoner of war in 1917. Thrilled to
sign for Sunderland, the club he'd supported
since boyhood, Joe always told the tale how at
Crook he deliberately avoided meeting a keen
Middlesbrough scout because he knew of
Sunderland's interest. He reached the
professional ranks at the relatively late age of
25 but soon received his League baptism with
the Wearsiders. Joe once recalled how he
received the then almost regulation tot of
whisky from trainer Billy Williams to calm his
debut nerves. Lean and wiry, Joe was perhaps
a little lightweight when compared to
defenders of his era, but remained a regular
for the three seasons after the Great War until
displaced by Charlie Parker. He then moved
on to Stoke but a year and a half later, unable
to agree terms for season 1924/25, he joined
Carlisle United, then a North-Eastern League
club, on a part-time basis. Joe returned to
Football League action with Accrington
Stanley (47 appearances), retiring after a
couple of terms at Peel Park. Joe earned a
reputation as an upstanding centre-half and in
his Accrington days was described in a local
handbook as "a true pivotal man, breaking up

neatly and plying his
wings with consummate
judgement." After
leaving football, he
spent a dozen years as
licensee of the Peel Park
Hotel in Accrington, but returned to the
North-East as mine host at The Three Tuns in
Coundon and also served on the Bishop
Auckland FC committee. A lifelong friend of
Charlie Buchan, it is virtually certain Joe
Kasher, who died only days short of his 98th
birthday, is the longest-lived Sunderland
player. He was certainly the oldest ex-
professional from any club at the time of his
death.

> **Appearances:**
> *FL:* 85 apps. 0 gls.
> *FAC:* 4 apps. 0 gls.
> **Total:** 89 apps. 0 gls.

KAY, John

Role: Full-back 1987-94
5'10" 11st.6lbs.
b. Great Lumley, Co Durham, 29th January 1964

CAREER: Chester-le-Street Schoolboys/
Durham Schoolboys/Arsenal assoc. s'boy
1979, app 1980, pro Aug 1981/Wimbledon July
1984(Middlesbrough loan Jan 1985)/
SUNDERLAND July 1987(Shrewsbury Town
loan Mar 1996)/Preston North End Aug 1996/
Scarborough Sept 1996, released May 1999.

Debut v Brentford (a) 15/8/1987

As a schoolboy John Kay was North of
England 200 metres champion but his football
career began in the South with Arsenal, where
he won a Football Combination championship
medal in 1984. He had made his Gunners
League debut in the previous season at West
Bromwich Albion in a game that marked the
1000th appearance of goalkeeper Pat Jennings.
Transferred to Wimbledon for £25,000 in July
1984, John made 26 League appearances for
the Dons in 1985-86 when they won
promotion to Division One. A loan spell with
Middlesbrough preceded his £22,500 transfer
to Sunderland in 1987. He was an immediate
success at Roker, ever-present in his first
season when the championship of Division
Three was won in style. Ever a joker and
eccentric, he was popular with both fans and
team mates alike. John was though unlucky to

John Kay

KEETON, William Walter

Role: Inside-right 1930-32
b. Shirebrook, Derbyshire, 30th April 1905
d. Forest Town, Mansfield, 10th October 1980

CAREER: Grantham Town/SUNDERLAND
Oct 1930-Dec 1931 £450/Nottingham Forest
Sept 1932-1933/Loughborough Corinthians
Jan 1933.

Debut v Arsenal (a) 17/1/1931

A useful inside-right whose time at Roker Park
was ended by the player's request for a
transfer. He wished to return south because of
his wife's ill-health. Walter Keeton was much
better known as the Notts and England
cricketer (two Tests, v Australia 1934 and the
West Indies 1939). He first played for
Nottinghamshire in 1926, becoming a regular
team member in 1931, an attractive right-
handed opening batsman and a brilliant deep
field. Despite illness and injuries - the most
serious being knocked down by a lorry in 1935
- his cricket career lasted until 1952. Keeton
made 54 centuries, scored 1,000 runs in a
season 12 times (on six occasions exceeding
2,000) and scored a century against every

miss the 1992 FA Cup final through injury, but
remained a mainstay of Sunderland's defence
until a badly broken leg, sustained at
Birmingham in October 1993, effectively
ended his involvement at senior level, just one
short of 200 league appearances. While on
loan at Shewsbury he did appear at Wembley,
against Rotherham in the Auto Windscreens
Shield final. Released on a free transfer in the
summer of 1996, he was briefly with Preston
North End before joining a number of former
Sunderland colleagues at Third Division
Scarborough. After two excellent seasons at
The McCain Stadium, in the last of which the
play-off semi-finals were reached, season 1998-
99 ended in heartbreak with relegation to the
Football Conference on the last day of the
season. John Kay was one of several players
released as a consequence.

Appearances:
FL: 196(3) apps. 0 gls.
FAC: 12 apps. 0 gls.
FLC: 19 apps. 0 gls.
Other: 6 apps. 1 gl.
Total: *233(3) apps. 1 gl.*
Honours:
(Sunderland) Div 3 champs 1988.

*Walter Keeton (right) walks out to bat for England
with legend Len Hutton at The Oval in 1939.*

county. And he is also the only Notts player to score 300 in an innings (312 not out v Middlesex 1939) and he hit six other double centuries. After retiring he ran a sports shop for a time, later working for the National Coal Board.

Appearances:
FL: 11 apps. 1 gl.
Total: *11 apps. 1 gl.*

KELLY, David Thomas

Role: Forward 1995-96
5'11" 11st.3lbs.
b. Birmingham, 25th November 1965

CAREER: Alvechurch/Walsall Dec 1983/West Ham United July 1988 £600,000/Leicester City Mar 1990 £300,000/Newcastle United Dec 1991 £250,000/Wolverhampton Wanderers June 1993 £750,000/SUNDERLAND Sept 1995/Tranmere Rovers Aug 1997-date.

Debut v Millwall (a) 23/9/1995

Republic of Ireland international David Kelly made his name with Walsall where 26 goals in 1986-87 brought a big-money move to Upton

Park but he disappointed at both West Ham and, later, Leicester before flourishing under Kevin Keegan at Newcastle. His eleven vital goals helped save the Magpies from relegation in 1991-92 and he was top scorer with 24 strikes as Newcastle stormed to the championship, and promotion a year later. Dumped from the Magpies' Premiership plans, Kelly cost Sunderland £900,000 from Wolves, where he had spent two years, and this sum was topped up to £1 million when Sunderland won promotion to the Premiership at the end of his first season. Unfortunately, Kelly had spent a frustrating first term at Roker, a troublesome ankle injury restricting his League appearances to just 9(1) and two goals. Although signed on a three-year contract, he was made available for transfer in the close season of 1996. In the event, and the absence of any significant offers, he spent a further season at Roker Park, won back his place in the starting line-up, but for the first time in his career failed to find the net during the season which ended in Sunderland's relegation from the Premier League. No doubt this lack of success was in part attributable to his wide berth in right midfield, and he quickly rediscovered his goalscoring touch following his £350,000 transfer to Tranmere Rovers in August 1997. Goals in each of his first three appearances got him off to a flying start, and despite some injury problems David finished his first season at Prenton Park as leading goalscorer with 11 League and three FLC goals. Appointed club captain in mid season 1997-98, he continued to work hard in an attack which at times appeared lightweight, lacking a goalscorer of the calibre of their present manager, and former player-manager, John Aldridge.

Appearances:
PL: 23(1) apps. 0 gls.
FL: 9(1) apps. 2 gls.
FAC: 3 apps. 0 gls.
FLC: 2(1) apps. 0 gls.
Total: *37(3) apps. 2 gls.*
Honours:
1 Eire 'B' app./1 Eire U-21 app./3 Eire U-23 apps./26 Eire caps 1988-date/(Newcastle United) Div 1 champs 1993.

David Kelly

KELLY, Peter W.

Role: Left-back 1908-09
5'11" 11st.7lbs.

CAREER: North Shields Athletic/
SUNDERLAND May 1908-1909
Debut v Liverpool (h) 1/1/1909

Peter Kelly was a locally recruited defender -
and very possible locally born also - making
his League bow on a New Year's Day,
occupying the position usually taken by Harry
Forster or Albert Milton. The result was a
heavy 4-1 home defeat and also Kelly's
solitary first team outing.

> **Appearances:**
> *FL: 1 app. 0 gls.*
> **Total:** *1 app. 0 gls.*

KELLY, Robert

Role: Outside/inside-right 1925-27
5'7' 10st. 0lbs.
*b. Ashton-in-Makerfield, Lancs, 16th November
1893*
d. Fylde area of Lancashire, 22nd September 1969

CAREER: Ashton White Star/Ashton Central/
Earlestown Rovers (Liverpool County
Combination) Aug 1912/St Helens Town Aug
1913/Burnley Oct 1913 £275/SUNDERLAND
Dec 1925 £6,550, a record/Huddersfield Town
Feb 1927 £3,500/Preston North End July 1932/
Carlisle United player-manager Mar 1935/
retired from playing during 1935-36/Stockport
County manager Nov 1936-Jan 1939/Bury
Town (Suffolk) manager from Dec 1960/
coaching appointments in Switzerland and the
Channel islands.

Debut v Manchester United (h) 5/12/1925

When the great Charlie Buchan joined Arsenal
in 1925, Sunderland's management must have
pondered how to replace what must have
seemed an irreplaceable player. After six
months one obvious solution presented itself:
go for England's first-choice inside-right of the
early 1920's even if a record transfer fee had to
be paid. And so Bob Kelly came to Roker Park,
32 years of age but still at the height of his
powers and still with a decade of playing
years to run. He could take the outside-right
role too and had done so for England when it
was rare for anyone to represent their country

Bob Kelly

in different positions. It is an undoubted fact
Bob was a complete inside-forward. As late as
1934 a critic described him as "still an astute,
quick-thinking forward with twinkling feet
even in the twilight of his great career ... and
now needs thrustful colleagues to be an
effective schemer but at 41 remains a
remarkable footballer, as he proved last
season." Kelly, like his father, had been a
miner. At football he played at full-back and
centre-half before switching to inside-forward
with Earlestown. In his brief time at St Helens
both Spurs and Preston North End coveted
him but Burnley stepped in, fielding him in
their League side after only a single run-out
with the reserves. His career really took off
after the war, during which he served in the
Royal Artillery.

> **Appearances:**
> *FL: 50 apps. 10 gls.*
> *FAC: 5 apps. 4 gls.*
> **Total:** *55 apps. 14 gls.*
> **Honours:**
> *14 Eng caps/7 FL apps./(Burnley) FL champs
> 1921/(Huddersfield Town) FAC finalist 1928,
> 1930.*

KELLY, Thomas

Role: Left-half 1905-06

CAREER: Seaham White Star/SUNDERLAND Aug 1905/Murton Red Star May 1906/Seaham Albion May 1907, later assisted Seaham Harbour.

Debut v Liverpool (h) 16/9/1905

Kelly soon made his League debut - in the third League fixture of 1905/06, which resulted in a 2-1 defeat against the eventual champions. He was one of seven players to occupy the left-half position before October was out. But then Dave Willis took over for the rest of the season, grossing 29 appearances out of a possible 38.

Appearances:
FL: 1 app. 0 gls.
Total: *1 app. 0 gls.*

KELSALL, Josiah

Role: Centre-forward 1913-14
5'6" 11st.0lbs.
b. Maryport, Cumberland, 20th May 1892
d. Beeston, Notts, 24th April 1974

CAREER: Maryport/SUNDERLAND am Nov 1913-1914 when he joined the Army.

Debut v Sheffield Wednesday (h) 4/4/1914

A Cumberland amateur, Josiah Kelsall was not very tall though possessed of a sturdy build. His solitary League appearance for Sunderland resulted in a 1-0 win for the Wednesday. The centre-forward berth saw many changes of occupant that season; ten players in all were called upon including Willie Cringan, invariably a half-back, for the final three league games.

Appearances:
FL: 1 app. 0 gls.
Total: *1 app. 0 gls.*

KEMP, Samuel Patrick

Role: Outside-right 1952-57
5'9" 10st.8lbs.
b. Stockton-on-Tees, 29th August 1932

CAREER: Whitby Town/SUNDERLAND Mar 1952/Sheffield United Feb 1957 (in part exchange for Colin Grainger)/Mansfield Town May 1958 £2,000/Gateshead Oct 1958-1959

Debut v Tottenham Hotspur (h) 18/4/1953

Samuel Kemp was among Billy Bingham's many understudies during that star's long reign as Sunderland's outside-right. Kemp did not get an extended run at Bramall Lane either. There he deputised for another renowned Irish winger in Alf Ringstead (who, incidentally, also left the Blades for Mansfield Town eventually). Kemp's League appearances for Sheffield United totalled 16 (1 goal), in the brief spell at Mansfield three (1 goal) and for Gateshead seven (1 goal). His aggregate, therefore, including the Sunderland contribution, is 43 with five goals scored.

Appearances:
FL: 17 apps. 2 gls.
FAC: 2 apps. 0 gls.
Total: *19 apps. 2 gls.*

Samuel Kemp

KENNEDY, Alan Phillip

Debut v Swindon Town (h) 24/9/1985 (FLC 2)

Role: Full-back 1985-87
5'10" 10st.7lbs.
b. Sunderland 31st August 1954

CAREER: Newcastle United app July 1971, pro Sept 1972/Liverpool Aug 1978/ SUNDERLAND Sept 1985/Husquvana, Sweden cs 1987/Hartlepool United Oct 1987/ K Beerschot VAV Belgium Nov 1987/ Grantham Town/Wigan Athletic Dec 1987/ Colne Dynamoes Aug 1988/Wrexham Mar 1990/Morecambe Mar 1991/Netherfield player-manager 1991-Aug 1992/Northwich Victoria/Radcliffe Borough 1992/Netherfield Nov 1993/Barrow 1994-96.

One of a number of richly-experienced players signed by new manager Lawrie McMenemy, Alan Kennedy - a £100,000 recruit from Liverpool - had spent seven years at Anfield and won numerous awards which included five League championships and two European Cup winners' medals. The strong-running full-back was recruited one month into the 1985-86 season which had opened disastrously with five straight defeats and no goals scored. In February Alan netted twice against Carlisle at Roker - one an absolute humdinger of a shot - and an eventual eighteenth position in Division Two ensured survival. But in the following term the unthinkable happened

Alan Kennedy

when Sunderland were relegated to Division Three for the first time in their 108-year existence. Alan Kennedy was just one of several discarded players in the close season. At the age of 33 he embarked on a wandering path which took in European and non-League football; his final League appearance, at 36, was for Wrexham at Gillingham in October 1991. It brought his League career aggregate, including substitute appearances, to 506 and he scored 26 goals. Elder brother Keith, also a full-back, was a similarly durable performer. He also began with Newcastle United but most notably completed 405 League appearances for Bury.

Appearances:
FL: 56 apps. 2 gls.
FAC: 4 apps. 0 gls.
FLC: 2(1) apps. 0 gls.
Other: 4 apps. 1 gl.
Total: *66(1) apps. 3 gls.*
Honours:
8 Eng 'B' apps./6 Eng U-23 apps./2 Eng caps 1984/(Newcastle United) FAC finalist 1974, FLC finalist 1976/(Liverpool) EC winners 1981, 1984/EC finalist 1985/FL champs 1979, 1980, 1982, 1983, 1984/FLC winners 1981, 1982, 1983, 1984.

KERR, Andrew

Role: Centre-forward 1962-64
5'10" 11st.6lbs.
b. Lugar, Ayrshire, 29th June 1931
d. Aberdeen, 31st December 1997

CAREER: Wishaw High School/Lugar Boswell Thistle/Partick Thistle May 1952/ Manchester City June 1959 £11,000/ Kilmarnock Dec 1959 £6,000/SUNDERLAND Apr 1963 £22,250/Aberdeen Apr 1964 £8,000/ Glentoran trial July 1965/ Inverness Caledonians Aug 1965-1967.

Debut v Preston North End (a) 6/4/1963

Particularly noted for his outstanding versatility although, with Sunderland, 18 of Andrew Kerr's 19 senior appearances were at centre-forward, with just one elsewhere - at centre-half. However, he was a proven performer in both full-back, all half-back and centre-forward roles, and there is little doubt he could have made a show in all positions. Andy did not regularly lead attacks until 1958/59, his best years - those spent at

Kilmarnock - following. He scored 113 goals in 137 matches for Killie (including five versus Airdrie in September 1962), a magnificent return, many conjured out of apparent 'impossible' situations. Andy was an elegant footballer and a highly individual character. He was unfortunate in being on the losing side in all five of his major finals (in which by the way, he played in three different positions: right-back, left-half and centre-forward). Outside football Andrew worked for a firm manufacturing aeroplane parts and as a club steward.

Appearances:
FL: 18 apps. 5 gls.
FLC: 1 app. 0 gls.
Total: *19 apps. 5 gls.*
Honours:
2 Scot caps/2 SL apps./(Partick Thistle) SLC finalist 1954, 1957/(Kilmarnock) SC finalist 1960/SLC finalist 1961, 1963.

Andy Kerr

KERR, Robert

Role: Midfield 1966-79
5'5" 9st.3lbs.
b. Alexandria, Dunbartonshire, 16th November 1947

CAREER: Dumbarton Schools/Dumbarton Castle Rovers/Balloch Juniors/ SUNDERLAND app cs 1963, pro Nov 1964/ Blackpool Mar 1979/Hartlepool United July 1980-1982.

Debut v Manchester City (h) 31/12/1966 (scored)

A small man, but one who looms large in Sunderland's post-World War Two history mainly for the fact he captained the team in the 1970s when the FA Cup and Division Two championship were won. Bobby Kerr was dubbed 'the little general' by Bob Stokoe for his leadership, tactical know-how and competence as an all-round footballer. And he was also renowned and rightly so, for his big heart and sheer guts in bouncing back after twice breaking the same leg during his early career. A member of Sunderland's 1966 FA Youth Cup final team, Bobby's leg was first broken in a reserve match and again a year later, on 11th March 1967, in a fifth round FA Cup-tie collision with Leeds' Norman Hunter. Accordingly he lost a whole season - the last appearance of his senior debut campaign divided from the next by over eighteen months (17 September 1968). Bobby had been in sprightly form in 1966/67, scoring the only goal on his debut to beat Manchester City at Roker, and totalled seven in his first eleven games, including a brace in a 3-0 home win over Newcastle. It is interesting to note his consistent League appearance record from 1970/71, when he headed the scoring list, to his last season (1978/79). Including that first regular 1970/71 campaign, up to and including his last full season (1977/78) he appeared in 307(6) out of a possible 336. In five consecutive seasons, 1971/72 to 1975/76, he never made less than 40 appearances. He certainly more than made up for that period lost to injury. In his sixteen years at Roker the highs were obviously the unforgettable FA Cup victory of 1973 and the 1976 Division Two championship. Bobby had a leading role in this historic cup run, appearing in all nine ties - there were three replays plus the six rounds. His non-stop running typified the team's spirit and his link with right-back Dick Malone helped blunt the threat of Leeds' predicted match-winner Eddie Gray in the final. The 1976 championship had been building up for four years and was widely anticipated after the Wembley success. The promotion line-up contained five survivors from Wembley (plus Billy Hughes, who appeared in a third of the programme) and Bobby Kerr, still giving his best in the No.7 shirt. The low points, of course, were the relegations of 1970 and 1977, while the very early seasons were none too bright with the club consistently wallowing in the wrong end of the table. Nearly three years later, aged 32, Bobby left Sunderland for Third

Bobby Kerr - the 1973 FA Cup winning captain.

Division Blackpool, immensely popular and acknowledged as one of the club's greatest ever servants. He had 18(4) League outings, and scored two goals before returning to Co Durham and Hartlepool United, where he stayed for two years, played in 48(1) Fourth Division games and scored another two goals. He thus sampled all sections of the Football League in his long career. Outside football Bobby has worked in the licensed trade and currently runs The Copt Hill in Houghton. His brother George Kerr played for and managed several lower division League clubs. In the 1970s, manager Bob Stokoe recommended

Bobby be considered for a Scottish cap, but that honour did not materialise. A pity, it was richly deserved.

Appearances:
FL: 355(13) apps. 56 gls.
FAC: 29(1) apps. 5 gls.
FLC: 14 apps. 1 gl.
Other: 15 apps. 5 gls.
Total: *413(14) apps. 67 gls.*
Honours:
(Sunderland) FAC winner 1973/Div 2 champs 1976.

KICHENBRAND, Donald Basil 'Rhino'

Role: Centre-forward 1957-60
5'11" 12st.9lbs.
*b. Germiston, Transvaal, South Africa,
13th August 1933*

CAREER: Delfos FC, Transvaal/Rangers Sept 1955/SUNDERLAND Mar 1958 £8,000/returned to S.A. cs 1960 and assisted Johannesburg Wanderers, returned to Scotland and assisted Forfar Athletic Dec 1962-May 1963.

Debut v Sheffield Wednesday (h) 8/3/1958 (scored)

'Rhino' Kichenbrand

In the mid-1950s it was reported that "Rangers' burly centre-forward from Boksburg, South Africa, has in one season become the most talked-about player in Scotland. Dashing and eager, he makes up for his lack of artistry by his speed and powerful shooting". In the season referred to, 1955/56, Kichenbrand netted 24 goals in 25 League outings, an exceptional tally that included five in an 8-0 thrashing of Queen of the South. A game, incidentally, notable also for being the first Scottish League match played under floodlights. But the next season the South African was replaced by Max Murray, a recruit from amateur Queen's Park, and quickly transferred to Sunderland, his time in the Caledonian limelight limited in duration. Unable to save Sunderland from the drop in 1958 despite six goals in 10 games, Don's best Roker season was 1958-59 when as a regular he scored 21 goals in Division Two. The nickname, Rhino, given by the Ibrox faithful, is self-explanatory.

Appearances:
FL: 53 apps. 28 gls.
FAC: 1 app. 0 gls.
Total: *54 apps. 28 gls.*
Honours:
(Rangers) SL champs 1956.

KIERNAN, Joseph

Role: Left-half 1962-63
5'9" 11st.7lbs.
b. Coatbridge, 22nd October 1942

CAREER: Junior football to SUNDERLAND Nov 1959/Northampton Town July 1963 £2,000/Kettering Town July 1972/Atherstone Dec 1973, player-manager Apr 1977/Wellingborough Town/Irthlingborough Diamonds/Northampton Town asst manager to Apr 1992, later youth coach.

Debut v Southampton (a) 22/9/1962

Joe Kiernan's sole League outing for Sunderland (the above Southampton game, a 4-2 away win) was a prelude to a long and most eventful stay at Northampton. The Cobblers had just won the Third Division championship and Joe saw them rise to the top flight and descend back to the basement. His figures for Northampton are impressive, totalling 352 appearances, 14 goals, made up of FL 308(13), FAC 19, FLC 25(1). A good, reliable wing-half and a splendid club man. Whilst at Kettering, Joe skippered the Southern League championship side under manager Ron Atkinson.

Appearances:
FL: 1 app. 0 gls.
FLC: 1 app. 0 gls.
Total: *2 apps. 0 gls.*

Joe Kiernan

KINNELL, George

Role: Centre-half 1966-69
5'11" 11st.11lbs.
b. Cowdenbeath, 22nd December 1937

CAREER: Crossgates Primrose/Aberdeen Feb 1959/Stoke City Nov 1963 £27,000/Oldham Athletic Aug 1966 £26,000 incl Keith Bebbington/SUNDERLAND Oct 1966 £20,000/Middlesbrough Oct 1968 £20,000/Juventus FC, Melbourne, Australia June 1969.

Debut v Stoke City (h) 25/10/1966

A sound pivot of rangy build especially good in the air, George Kinnell had considerable utility value too, occupying both full-back, all half-back and inside-right berths for his first senior club, Aberdeen. He also captained the Dons, aggregating 164 League and Cup games and scoring 25 goals while at Pittodrie. Following a successful three years at Stoke, George spent a bare two months with Oldham before joining Sunderland. This move

George Kinnell

proved unpopular with Latics supporters - he was fast becoming a favourite having scored eight goals in 12 Third Division outings. And occupying four different positions, three of them in the forward line. (It is perhaps not too much to class Kinnell's versatility with that of Andy Kerr?) George is a cousin of the celebrated Jim Baxter (q.v.).

Appearances:
FL: 67(2) apps. 3 gls.
FAC: 7 apps. 0 gls.
FLC: 3 apps. 3 gls.
Total: *77(2) apps. 6 gls.*
Honours:
(Stoke City) FLC finalist 1964.

KIRBY, Frederick

Role: Centre-forward 1911-12
5'9" 12st.0lbs.
b. County Durham

CAREER: Bishop Auckland/SUNDERLAND am July 1911/Bishop Auckland Dec 1911/Durham City circa 1912/Middlesbrough Oct 1913/Halifax Town 1914/Bradford Nov 1914-circa 1920.

Debut v Woolwich Arsenal (a) 18/11/1911

Unusually for an amateur, Frederick Kirby played League football with three different clubs. After his one-match initiation for Sunderland he appeared twice for Middlesbrough in 1913/14 and an appreciable ten times (3 goals) in 1914/15 with Bradford Park Avenue, and all in the First Division. But then Fred was a first-class amateur from that ever-productive organisation, Bishop Auckland FC. As was customary with these unpaid folk, Kirby never actually left the Bishops (as witness his 1913/14 Amateur Cup medal), his connection with professional brethren brief diversions that likely extended his soccer horizons - and performances - a great deal. A surveyor by trade, Kirby served in the RAMC during World War One, joining up in 1915.

Appearances:
FL: 1 app. 0 gls.
Total: *1 app. 0 gls.*
Honours:
1 Eng am app. v Denmark 1914/(Bishop Auckland) AmC winner 1914.

KIRTLEY, John Henry M.

Role: Inside-forward 1948-55
5'9" 10st.10lbs.
b. Washington, Co Durham, 23rd May 1930

CAREER: Fatfield Juniors/SUNDERLAND am, pro May 1949/Cardiff City May 1955/Gateshead Mar 1957 £3,000, contract terminated Dec 1959 and later that season joining Rhyl/Sankey's FC (Wellington, Salop) July 1962.

Debut v Manchester City (a) 16/4/1949

A critic said in 1951 that "despite Sunderland's expensive forward purchases a place at inside-forward must be found for 'Harry'. It was

Harry Kirtley

initial Football League season, the first couple of matches in fact. In the second of these, Sunderland lost 4-3 to Wolves after leading 3-0 and Kirtley was blamed. Hence the move to neighbouring Sunderland Albion with a successor for many years to come, Ted Doig, installed. Bill Kirtley's contribution to the pre-

Bill Kirtley

League season should not be minimised, however. He first played for Sunderland in 1882/83. Fifty years on, up to the mid-1930s, he looked after the billiards room in the old corner offices at Roker Park.

Appearances:
FL: 2 apps. 0 gls.
FAC: 13 apps. 0 gls.
Total: *15 apps. 0 gls.*

certainly true his alertness, speed in thought and action, and general effectiveness in both inside berths warranted a regular first team showcase. With Cardiff Harry played 38 League games (4 goals) and for Gateshead 96 (14 goals). Originally he had worked as an apprentice colliery electrician.

Appearances:
FL: 95 apps. 18 gls.
FAC: 6 apps. 0 gls.
Total: *101 apps. 18 gls.*

KIRTLEY, William

Role: Goalkeeper 1884-91

CAREER: Workmen's Hall FC (Monkwearmouth)/SUNDERLAND circa 1882/Sunderland Albion Sept 1890

FAC debut v Redcar (a) 8/11/1884
FL debut v Burnley (h) 13/9/1890

Bill Kirtley holds a unique place in Sunderland's history, being the sole amateur from the earliest years to play through to the League era. He made two appearances in that

KNOWLES, Joseph

Role: Left-back 1896-97
5'6" 11st.6lbs.
b. Monkwearmouth, Sunderland, 1872

CAREER: Monkwearmouth FC 1892/ SUNDERLAND Nov 1895/Tottenham Hotspur May 1897/South Shields cs 1898/ Queens Park Rangers Aug 1899-1900.

Debut v Bury (a) 16/4/1897

A thickset defender, Joe Knowles played his solitary senior game for Sunderland in the final League fixture of the normal programme (there were four Test matches to follow). Things looked up for Knowles with Spurs, though, and he made 19 out of a possible 22 Southern League games, mostly at right-back. He was not retained nonetheless, coming back to the North-East for a year with South Shields. Then a return to the first-class game for Queens Park Rangers' first Southern League outings, all of them at right-back.

Appearances:
FL: 1 app. 0 gls.
Total: *1 app. 0 gls.*

KUBICKI, Dariusz

Role: Full-back 1993-96
5'10" 11st.7lbs.
b. Kozuchow, Poland, 6th June 1963

CAREER: Zastal/Mielec/Legia Warsaw 1983/
Aston Villa Aug 1991(SUNDERLAND loan
Mar 1994)/SUNDERLAND July 1994/
Wolverhampton Wanderers Aug 1997
(Tranmere Rovers loan Mar 1998)/Carlisle
United July-Sept 1998/ Darlington n.c. Oct
1998.

Debut v Notts County (h) 5/3/1994

A £100,000 bargain signing from Aston Villa in
July 1994, Dariusz Kubicki was secured on a
permanent contract following his successful
loan spell, at the end of the 1993-94 season. He
first moved into English football with Aston
Villa, whose new manager Ron
Atkinson paid £200,000 for him
shortly after his appointment at
Villa Park. Kubicki made 23
consecutive League appearances in
1991-92 but lost his place when Villa
paid £1.7 million for Earl Barrett in
February of the same season.
Considering Kubicki had played
virtually no senior football for two
seasons when he joined Sunderland,
his class was immediately apparent,
and he embarked on a remarkable
run of 124 consecutive appearances.
He controversially lost his place to
Gareth Hall in September 1996
when one game short of equalling
George Mulhall's post-war record of
125 consecutive appearances. He
quickly returned to the side and
ended Sunderland's first
Premiership term with 28(1)
appearances to his credit. Released
at the age of 34 in the close season
he joined Wolves on a free transfer.
In early season he returned with his
new club to play against
Sunderland at the Stadium of Light
and received a warm reception from
his former supporters despite
supplying the cross from which
Andy Melville scored an own goal!
Shortly afterwards, however, he lost
his first team place and ended the
season on loan with Tranmere
Rovers. Released by Wolves in
summer 1998, his League career appears to
have wound down, following two months
with Carlisle United and a non-contract
arrangement with Darlington. Kubicki won 47
caps for his country, making his first
international appearance as a 19-year-old. He
was twice a Polish Cup winner with Legia
Warsaw and in his last season in Poland
played in the semi-final of the ECW Cup when
Legia lost to the eventual winners Manchester
United.

Appearances:
PL: 28(1) apps. 0 gls.
FL: 107 apps. 0 gls.
FAC: 7 apps. 0 gls.
FLC: 7 apps. 0 gls.
Total: *149(1) apps. 0 gls.*
Honours:
47 Polish caps.

Dariusz Kubicki

CAREER: Talbot Steelworks/ Bloxwich Strollers cs 1923/ Walsall May 1925/Burton Town 1926/ Merthyr Town Aug 1927/ Dundee Jan 1928/ SUNDERLAND May 1929 £350/ Swindon Town May 1931/ Worcester City July 1932/ Shrewsbury Town Aug 1933/ Brierley Hill Alliance Aug 1934, later assisted Dudley Town.

Debut v Derby County (a) 31/8/1929

George Lawley was a short though well-built winger usually found on the right flank. He was secured by Sunderland following a good run at Dundee (34 Scottish League appearances, three goals). There were several rivals during his two years at Roker Park, notably Billy Eden, and his activities were restricted largely to the reserves. George, as a general rule, changed clubs annually, his travels taking him to Scotland and Wales besides widely spaced English venues. His appearances in Football League and Scottish League matches totalled 115, in which he scored 12 goals. And he had a noticeably high count of spells with Midlands non-League clubs.

> **Appearances:**
> *FL: 10 apps. 1 gl.*
> **Total:** *10 apps. 1 gl.*

LAWRENCE, James Hubert

Role: Winger 1993-94
6'0" 12st.6lbs.
b. Balham, London, 8th March 1970

CAREER: Cowes, I.O.W./SUNDERLAND Oct 1993/Doncaster Rovers Mar 1994/Leicester City Jan 1995/Bradford City June 1997-date.

Debut v Middlesbrough (a) 17/10/1993 (sub)

A flying wing-man with a very distinctive hairstyle, ex convict Jamie Lawrence was recruited by Terry Butcher after serving two years in Parkhurst prison on a charge of armed robbery. Lawrence began brightly at Roker Park until an ankle injury and a change of management (Mick Buxton replaced Terry Butcher) saw him on the sidelines. His career took off following his £25,000 transfer to Doncaster Rovers and his value had increased to £125,000 when Leicester City signed him, less than a year later.

Intermittently used at Filbert Street, he nevertheless had the supreme satisfaction of laying on Leicester's first goal of their 1995-96 promotion season, in his team's 2-1 victory at Roker Park. In the summer of 1997, Bradford City paid £50,000 for his transfer and, two years on, he helped the Bantams clinch promotion to the Premiership as runners up to Sunderland.

Appearances:
FL: 2(2) apps. 0 gls.
FLC: 0(1) app. 0 gls.
Total: *2(3) apps. 0 gls.*
Honours:
(Leicester City) FLC winners 1997.

Jamie Lawrence

LAWTHER, William Ian

Role: Centre-forward 1959-61
5'9" 11st.3lbs.
b. Belfast, 20th October 1939

CAREER: Belfast Crusaders/
SUNDERLAND Mar 1958/
Blackburn Rovers July 1961
£18,000/Scunthorpe United July
1963 £12,000/ Brentford Nov
1964 £15,000/Halifax Town Aug
1968 £3,000/Stockport County
July 1971-cs 1976/Bangor City
late 1976.

Debut v Aston Villa (a) 31/8/1959

At age 15 Ian was taken under
Manchester United's wing but,
becoming homesick, he returned
to Belfast after a couple of
months. United held on to his
registration for six months
hoping he might return. The fact
he did not do so was a cause of
regret later. However, once in
Sunderland's first team for
1959/60 Lawther's career took
off and he scored 17 League
goals with a further 24 the
following season. It eventually
lasted 16 seasons, encompassed

Ian Lawther

all four divisions of the Football League and,
in total, 577 appearances plus 21 substitutions
in which he scored 178 goals. A high point was
the helping of Halifax Town to their only
League promotion in 1968/69. Another was a
unique happening when he signed for
Brentford in the committee room of the House
of Commons. The Bees' chairman at the time,
Jack Dunnett, being an MP, made this possible.
Curiously, he had also scored against
Brentford at Griffin Park in Sunderland's first
ever League Cup tie in October 1960. Nephew
of Fred Roberts, an Irish international who
netted a record 96 goals in 1930/31 wearing
Glentoran's colours. Ian at one period had a
tailor's shop in Halifax.

Appearances:
FL: 75 apps. 41 goals.
FAC: 7 apps. 2 gls.
FLC: 1 app. 1 gl.
Total: *83 apps. 44 gls.*
Honours:
4 NIre caps/2 NIre 'B' apps./2 NIre Yth apps.

LEE, Robert Gordon

Role: Forward 1976-80
6'1" 12st.5lbs.
b. Melton Mowbray, Leics, 2nd February 1953

CAREER: Blaby Boys' Club/Leicester City
app July 1971, pro Feb 1972(Doncaster Rovers
loan Aug 1974)/SUNDERLAND Sept 1976/
Bristol Rovers 1980/Carlisle United July
1981/Southampton May 1983/Hong Kong/
Darlington Aug 1983/Boston United Oct
1983/Hong Kong cs 1984/Boston United 1984.

Debut v Everton (h) 2/10/1976

A record £200,000 signing from Leicester City
in September 1976, Bob Lee joined a side
struggling to come to terms with First Division
football, following their promotion winning
season, 1975-76. A well-built striker who
possessed all the necessary physical attributes,
he was perhaps not aggressive enough in the

penalty area but was still leading scorer in his first season with 13 League goals in 32(1) appearances. During four years at Roker he averaged a goal every three games and netted a treble as WBA were beaten 6-1 in February 1977 - a rare highspot in a relegation season. Too often however he was ineffective, especially for such a major signing, and consequently sometimes became a target for the disappointed home crowd. In his final appearance early in the 1979-80 promotion campaign, Bob scored against his old club Leicester City. He assisted Carlisle United to promotion from Division Three in 1981-82 and at the end of his career appeared at Wembley in the FA Trophy Final of 1985. Bob later became a publican in Loughborough.

Appearances:
FL: 101(8) apps. 32 gls.
FAC: 5 apps. 1 gl.
FLC: 4 apps. 0 gls.
Other: 2 apps. 0 gls.
Total: *112(8) apps. 33 gls.*
Honours:
(Boston United) FAT finalist 1985.

Bob Lee

LEE, Thomas

Role: Left-half 1897-98
5'8" 11st.7lbs.
b. Alnwick, Northumberland, 1876

CAREER: Alnwick Town, SUNDERLAND Mar 1897/Bristol Rovers cs 1899/Hebburn Argyle May 1901/Millwall Athletic Aug 1902/ Ashington Mar 1903.

Debut v Everton (a) 11/4/1898

Thomas Lee played in the final two games of 1897/98: the above debut and a home fixture against Nottingham Forest, but this was his first team quota as a Sunderland player. The debut was a 2-0 defeat and the Forest game a resounding 4-0 win. Lee fared better with Bristol Rovers, making 22 Southern League appearances, in so doing revealing a marked utility value, playing in both full-back and all three half-back roles. At Millwall, Lee had five Southern League outings, four at left-back and one at left-half.

Appearances:
FL: 2 apps. 0 gls.
Total: *2 apps. 0 gls.*

LEMON, Paul Andrew

Role: Forward/Midfield 1984-90
5'11" 11st.6lbs.
b. Middlesbrough, 3rd June 1966

CAREER: Burton Ramsey School, Middlesbrough/Middlesbrough Schoolboys/ SUNDERLAND assoc. s'boy, app 1982, pro May 1984(Carlisle United loan Dec 1984) (Walsall loan Nov 1989)(Reading loan Dec 1989(Chesterfield loan Sept 1990)Chesterfield Nov 1990/Tromso (Norway) 1993/Derry City, Rep of Ire, Sept 1993/Telford United Dec 1993.

Debut v Aston Villa (a) 1/12/1984 (sub)

An excellent goalscoring record in both the Northern Intermediate and Central Leagues saw Paul Lemon initially drafted into the first team as an 18-year-old. It took him some time, however, to establish himself as a regular in the League side, the bulk of his senior appearances spanning two seasons, the 1986-87 relegation campaign and the following season's Division Three championship in which he scored nine of Sunderland's 92 League goals. He was also on target in Cup

Paul Lemon

competitions that year and netted two beauties in a Freight Rover Trophy tie at Scarborough. Indeed, Paul was one of four Sunderland players that campaign to record a double figures goal tally. With his final League club, Chesterfield, 'Jack' Lemon, as he was popularly known, recorded 85 League appearances and scored ten goals. His career total of League matches amounted to 199 (25 goals). Paul was latterly employed in the insurance industry in Chesterfield.

Appearances:
FL: 92(16) apps. 15 gls.
FAC: 2(1) apps. 0 gls.
FLC: 6(1) apps. 0 gls.
Other: 6 apps. 2 gls.
Total: *106(18) apps. 17 gls.*
Honours:
(Sunderland) Div 3 champs 1988.

LEONARD, James 'Hookey'

Role: Inside-left 1930-32
5'6" 11st.0lbs.
b. Paisley, Renfrewshire
d. 1958

CAREER: Saltcoats Victoria/Cowdenbeath 1923 (spells in USA football with Indiana Flooring Dec 1926-1927 and the same club, now re-named New York Nationals Sept 1928-Dec 1929)/SUNDERLAND Oct 1930 £2,750 (Rhyl Athletic May 1931)(Cowdenbeath July 1931)Colwyn Bay Oct 1931, returning to Sunderland that month, registration cancelled Apr 1932/Greenock Morton Oct 1932-Jan 1933.

Debut v Leeds United (a) 4/10/1930 (scored)

'Hookey' Leonard arrived at Sunderland as an established player after years of experience in Scotland and the States. He had joined Cowdenbeath in time for their 1923/24 runners-up promotion run, finishing as second top scorer with 15 goals. Despite two spells in America he had made 105 Scottish League First Division appearances (60 goals) for the Fifeshire club. In 1981 a Sunderland FC publication said Leonard was "a little man

'Hookey' Leonard

with slightly turned-in feet ... he could pass beautifully" and that "he touched the tops and one day the depths, was hero and villain". The latter remark may have referred to off-the-field matters, for Hookey left Roker Park "owing to various breaches of discipline" the official phrase. About that nickname: a popular inter-war weekly published by the Amalgamated Press, *The Football & Sports Favourite*, ran a series by Stanton Hope on a fictitious Pompey naval rating named Hookey Walker, naturally a super footballer and, equally naturally, an inside-forward (THE glamour position). Could Mr Leonard's appellation stem from him?

Appearances:
FL: 35 apps. 18 gls.
FAC: 7 apps. 2 gls.
Total: *42 apps. 20 gls.*

LESLIE, James

Role: Inside-right 1897-1901
5'7" 11st.7lbs.
b. Barrhead, Renfrewshire
d. Sunderland, September 1920,
aged 47

Jim Leslie

CAREER: Clyde/Bolton Wanderers May 1895/Clyde Sept 1895/SUNDERLAND May 1897 £40/Middlesbrough May 1901/Clyde Oct 1902.

Debut v Sheffield Wednesday (a) 4/9/1897

Extremely popular on Wearside with his Scottish craft and incisive action, Sunderland certainly had the cream of Jimmy Leslie's English career. His place in the club's history was secured as the scorer of Sunderland's first goal at the newly opened Roker Park on 10th September 1898 in a 1-0 win over Liverpool. Curiously, he had also notched the final goal at the old Newcastle Road ground in a 1-0 win over Sheffield United in April 1897. He played no first team football during his brief Bolton Wanderers acquaintance, which seems to have been merely a trial period. And in the Middlesbrough season he only played seven League games, scoring three goals. Jim does appear to have had an attachment for Clyde FC, emanating from the Glasgow club and twice returning.

Appearances:
FL: 93 apps. 24 gls.
FAC: 6 apps. 2 gls.
Total: *99 apps. 26 gls.*

LEWIS, Albert Edward Talbot 'Tal'

Role: Goalkeeper 1904-05
6'1" 13st.10lbs.
b. Bedminster, Bristol, 20th January 1877
d. Redland, Bristol, 22nd February 1956

CAREER: Bedminster FC Jan 1896/Bristol City cs 1897/Everton cs 1898/Bristol City 1899/Walsall Aug 1901/Sheffield United May 1902/SUNDERLAND June 1904/Luton Town May 1905/Leicester Fosse July 1906/Bristol City Oct 1907-1908.

Debut v Preston North End (a) 3/9/1904

A fine, upstanding figure of a man and a reserve with most of his clubs, 'Tal 'Lewis' best spell came late - at Leicester (38 League appearances plus a Cup-tie). Signed in a joint deal with Alf Common, at Sunderland his quartet of League outings were the opening fixtures of 1904/05, T.S. Rowlandson and Isaac Webb mostly filling the breach thereafter. Unusually, 'Tal' played at full-back for Bristol City and Everton and did not turn goalkeeper until his spell at Walsall. Perhaps more

'Tal' Lewis

renowned as a cricketer with Somerset 1899-1914 (208 matches), 'Tal' scored a double century against Kent in 1909. After the Great War he coached in India and was reputed to be a highly skilled billiards player.

Appearances:
FL: 4 apps. 0 gls.
Total: *4 apps. 0 gls.*

LILLEY, Thomas

Role: Left-back 1927-28
5'11" 12st.4lbs.
b. New Herrington, Co Durham, 1st qtr 1900
d. New Herrington, Co Durham, 3rd qtr 1964

CAREER: Methley Perseverance/ Huddersfield Town Nov 1922/Nelson Nov 1923/Hartlepools United Aug 1924/ SUNDERLAND May 1926/St Mirren Aug 1928/Fulham July 1930 £250/Annfield Plain Aug 1931/New Herrington Welfare Feb 1932/ Shiney Row Swifts/Sunderland District Omnibus Company Nov 1933.

Debut v Portsmouth (h) 27/8/1927

Tom Lilley also played at right-back. He was a man of many clubs who had senior outings with all of them but was a reserve with Huddersfield and Sunderland. His best spells were at Hartlepools

Tom Lilley

(60 Northern Section appearances and an ever-present in 1925/26) and St Mirren. With the latter he appeared in 62 Scottish League top flight matches, scoring seven goals, in two seasons when the Paisley club finished in top half positions and reached the semi-final and quarter-final of the Scottish Cup.

Appearances:
FL: 1 app. 0 gls.
Total: *1 app. 0 gls.*

LINDSAY, Albert Fowler

Role: Goalkeeper 1902-04
b. West Hartlepool, 26th September 1881
d. West Hartlepool, 1961

CAREER: West Hartlepool FC/ SUNDERLAND June 1902/Luton Town June 1904/Glossop North End Mar 1906/ Sunderland Royal Rovers Nov 1906.

Debut v Notts County (h) 4/4/1903

It must have been a thankless task understudying a masterly and invariably fit Ned Doig, an obstacle which several custodians faced over the years, including this present subject, Albert Lindsay, who started out as a centre-half in his Hartlepool days. He left Sunderland the day 'Tal' Lewis was signed, but a change of fortune came with the move to Luton. He was the regular 'keeper in 1904/05, making 33 Southern League appearances, but second string to Platt in 1905/06. For Glossop he appeared twice in League Division Two matches.

Albert Lindsay

Appearances:
FL: 3 apps. 0 gls.
Total: *3 apps. 0 gls.*

LINDSAY, David

Role: Right-back 1946-47
5'10" 11st.9lbs.
b. Cambuslang, Lanarks, 29th June 1926

CAREER: Blantyre Victoria/SUNDERLAND Aug 1946/Southend United May 1948/Yeovil Town July 1951.

Debut v Preston North End (a) 5/4/1947

Ideally built and signed for the first post-war season, David Lindsay had also played centre-half for the Blantyre Vics. His sole League game in a Sunderland jersey resulted in a 2-2 draw. He made 52 Southern Section appearances and one in the FA Cup for Southend United, scoring one League goal.

Appearances:
FL: 1 app. 0 gls.
Total: *1 app. 0 gls.*

LIVINGSTON, George Turner

Role: Inside-left 1900-01
5'9" 11st.10lbs.
b. *Dumbarton, 5th May 1876*
d. *Helensburgh, Dunbartonshire, 15th January 1950*

CAREER: Sinclair Swifts for 3 seasons/ Artizan Thistle (Dumbarton)/Parkhead FC (Glasgow)/Dumbarton circa 1895/Heart of Midlothian June 1896/SUNDERLAND May 1900 £175/Celtic May 1901/Liverpool May 1902/Manchester City May 1903/Rangers Nov 1906/Manchester United Jan 1909/retired during WW1/Dumbarton manager Jan 1919/ Clydebank manager Aug 1919/Rangers trainer July 1920-July 1927/Bradford City trainer July 1928-May 1935, when he retired.

Debut v Notts County (a) 1/9/1900

Not only a fine robust player but also the possessor of a sunny disposition that made for dressing-room harmony and a role as team joker. On the field Livingston's main qualities lay in team work and astute, accurate distribution. A contemporary writer described his play thus "close and powerful on the ball and using his weight if necessary when near

George Livingston

goal". He enjoyed a long career both as a player and later in managerial and training capacities. It will be noticed that, apart from the war period, his career was interrupted by only one year, 1927-28. Away from football George ran a plumbing and gas-fitting business. During WW1 he served with the RAMC in East Africa.

Appearances:
FL: 30 apps. 12 gls.
FAC: 1 app. 0 gls.
Total: *31 apps. 12 gls.*
Honours:
2 Scot caps/1 SL app./(Celtic) SC finalist 1902/(Manchester City) FAC winner 1904.

LLOYD, Thomas

Role: Left-back 1925-27
5'9" 12st.0lbs.
b. *Wednesbury, Staffs, 17th November 1903*
d. *Bradford, 20th January 1984*

CAREER: Junior football to Walsall Aug 1922/ Willenhall 1924/ SUNDERLAND Feb 1925/Bradford May 1927/Burton Town player-manager May 1937-Feb 1938.

Debut v Leicester City (h) 27/3/1926

Tommy Lloyd was best known, of course, as Bradford's stalwart left-back for a decade. In that time he played in 328 League matches, in which he scored 22 goals, and 17 FA Cup-ties. Not bad for a free transfer signing! Tommy could perform just as well at right-back - all his five League outings for Walsall in his earliest senior days were on the right flank. And so was one of his Sunderland appearances. A critic recorded in 1933 that Tommy was a "very plucky type of player. Is never beaten physically or morally. Times his tackles and is quick on recovery." He qualified as a masseur.

Tommy Lloyd

Appearances:
FL: 4 apps. 0 gls.
Total: *4 apps. 0 gls.*

LLOYD, William Stanley

Role: Inside-forward 1946-48
5'6" 10st.4lbs.
b. West Auckland, Co Durham, 1st October 1924

CAREER: East Durham Schools/
SUNDERLAND Dec 1941/Grimsby Town Aug
1948 £6,000/Worksop Town cs 1953/
Scunthorpe United July 1954-1955.

Debut v Derby County (h) 31/8/1946

Thrice capped as a schoolboy in 1939, Stan
Lloyd joined the Sunderland staff two years
into World War Two. Consequently his real
debut was delayed nearly five years. He
started in the first team on the resumption of
peacetime
football in
1946/47 at
inside-right,
gave way to
the newly
acquired Jackie
Robinson,
afterwards
acting as
stand-in
inside-left for
Willie Watson.
Transferred to
Grimsby
following only
a few League
outings in
1947/48, Stan

Stan Lloyd

was a regular for five seasons, playing on both
wings besides the inside berths. Possessing no
physical advantages he did have vision, was a
canny dribbler and his distribution excellent.
Returning to the League scene after a year
with Midland League Worksop he made just
one appearance for Scunthorpe.

Appearances:
FL: 24 apps. 5 gls.
Total: *24 apps. 5 gls.*
Honours:
3 Eng Sch apps.

LOCKIE, Alexander James

Role: Centre-half 1936-46
5'10" 11st.13lbs.
b. South Shields, 11th April 1915

CAREER: South Shields St Andrews/
SUNDERLAND Aug 1935/Notts County Sept
1946-1947.

Debut v Manchester City (h) 14/4/1937

The War caused
sorry
interruptions to
a myriad of
burgeoning
football careers
and Alec Lockie
provides a
prime example.
After ranking as
No.3 centre-half
behind Jim
Clark and Bert
Johnston, he
had seen the
former depart
to Plymouth
and just

Alec Lockie

established himself in Sunderland's first team,
having made 29 League appearances in
1938/39 to Johnston's 12. Lockie was still a
Sunderland player for the initial post-war
season, 1946/47, but Fred Hall had arrived
from Blackburn Rovers. So he moved to Notts
County, making 23 Southern Section
appearances in what turned out to be his final
senior term. An excellent pivot ideally built for
the role.

Appearances:
FL: 40 apps, 1 gl.
FAC: 10 apps. 0 gls.
Total: *50 apps. 1 gl.*

LOGAN, D.

Role: Inside-left 1885-86
Debut v Redcar (a) 24/10/1885 (FAC)

The Cup-tie could have been Logan's sole
appearance for Sunderland in 1885/86 (not all
line-ups are known for that long ago pre-
League season - so he was possibly 'imported'
specially for the match). It was the club's
second venture into the competition and
resulted in a 3-0 defeat.

Appearances:
FAC: 1 app. 0 gls.
Total: *1 app. 0 gls.*

LOGAN, Henry Morrison

Role: Inside-right 1909-10
5'7" 10st.0lbs.
b. Glasgow, May 1888

CAREER: Cathcart Windsor, Myrtle XI (one of Queen's Park's junior sides)/Glasgow Benburb/Shettleston 1908/SUNDERLAND June 1909/Woolwich Arsenal July 1910-1911.

Debut v Chelsea (h) 30/10/1909

Henry Logan

A good representative record in minor soccer - besides his junior international caps, Henry Logan appeared in inter-league matches and, more notably, for the Glasgow Association against Perthshire. He started as a centre-forward, switching to inside-right when with Glasgow Benburb. He played in 11 First Division matches for Woolwich Arsenal, taking the inside-left position also. Unfortunately it was a depressing record: only one of the eleven resulted in victory. His brother, a right-back, assisted Vale of Leven and Queens Park Rangers during the 1900s.

Appearances:
FL: 1 app. 0 gls.
FAC: 1 app. 0 gls.
Total: *2 apps. 0 gls.*
Honours:
2 Scot Jnr caps.

LOGAN, James

Role: Outside-right/outside-left 1891-92
5'8" 11st.12lbs.
b. Troon, Ayrshire, 24th June 1870
d. Loughborough, 25th May 1896

CAREER: Ayr FC/SUNDERLAND Aug 1891/Ayr FC Nov 1891/Aston Villa July 1892/Notts County Oct 1893 £15/Dundee Mar 1895/Newcastle United June 1895/Loughborough Jan 1896.

Debut v Preston North End (a) 12/9/1891

Actually a centre-forward, but in Jimmy Logan's two League outings he was at outside-right in the above debut and outside-left against West Bromwich Albion five weeks later. A centre-forward of repute, he was a dangerous opportunist with a nose for goals, one of only three

Jimmy Logan

players to notch a hat-trick in an FA Cup final. Logan's untimely demise, only two years after his moment of national glory, was caused by a chill caught when playing for Loughborough against Newton Heath which developed into pneumonia. Without kit, which failed to turn up, he had to play in torrential rain in his own clothes and then wear the sodden garments after the match. Brother of Peter Logan, outside-right in Bradford City's 1911 FA Cup winning team, Jimmy scored on his international debut, and lone appearance, for Scotland.

Appearances:
FL: 2 apps. 0 gls.
Total: *2 apps. 0 gls.*
Honours:
1 Scot cap/(Notts County) FAC winner 1894.

LONGAIR, William 'Plum'

Role: Centre-half 1896-97
b. Dundee, 19th July 1870
d. Dundee, 28th November 1926

CAREER: Rockwell FC (Dundee) 1887/Dundee East End 1888/Dundee 1893/Newton Heath Feb 1895/Dundee Apr 1895/SUNDERLAND Feb 1896/Burnley Nov 1896 £50/Dundee May 1897/Brighton United Apr 1898/Dundee Apr 1899, trainer Aug 1900-1922, groundsman Sept 1924-1926.

Debut v Bury (h) 1/9/1896

Like James Logan, 'Plum' Longair made a mere couple of League appearances for Sunderland although a Scottish internationalist to boot. Longair's career, though, is more notable for its association with Dundee FC: four separate playing spells and, on retirement from the playing arena, 22 years as a trainer and two as a groundsman. A remarkable sequence. He had originally been a centre-forward, moving to centre-half late in

1890. 'Plum' developed into a first-rate pivot particularly strong defensively. Late in his playing career a Scottish journal called him "the well-beloved of all the centre-halves in Scotland" showing he was held in affection too.

Appearances:
FL: 2 apps. 0 gls.
Total: *2 apps. 0 gls.*
Honours:
1 Scot cap v Ireland 1894.

LONGHORN, Dennis

Role: Midfield 1973-77
6'0" 11st.1lb.
b. Southampton, 12th September 1950

CAREER: Bournemouth app 1966, pro Aug 1968/Mansfield Town Dec 1971/ SUNDERLAND Feb 1974(Sheffield United loan Oct 1976)/Sheffield United Nov 1976/ Aldershot Feb 1978/Colchester United May 1980/Chelmsford City/Halstead Town manager 1989.

Debut v Middlesbrough (h) 2/3/1974 (sub)

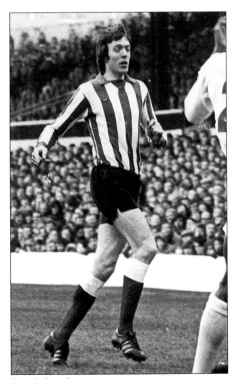

Dennis Longhorn

Dennis Longhorn joined Sunderland from Fourth Division Mansfield Town, in a deal which took John Lathan (q.v.) to Field Mill. A tall midfielder built on willowy lines, who possessed a strong shot from outside the area, he took over the number four jersey of the departed Micky Horswill in the final months of season 1973-74. Increased competition for places in the following season saw him out of the first team picture for quite lengthy spells, and in the championship winning season of 1975-76 he made only 6(2) League appearances. A keen all-round sportsman who also enjoyed cricket and golf, Dennis gave good value to each of his six League clubs in a career which spanned 293(33) League appearances and 13 goals.

Appearances:
FL: 35(5) apps. 3 gls.
FAC: 2 apps. 0 gls.
FLC: 1 app. 0 gls.
Total: *38(5) apps. 3 gls.*

LORD

Role: Inside-left 1886-87
Debut v Morpeth Harriers 16/10/1886 (FAC) (scored)

Lord scored a couple of goals in each of his first two Cup-ties: the 7-2 drubbing of Morpeth Harriers and a 2-1 victory over Newcastle West End. The latter result brought a protest from West End which was upheld. The resulting replay produced a 1-0 defeat for Sunderland.

Appearances:
FAC: 3 apps. 4 gls.
Total: *3 apps. 4 gls.*

LOW, Henry Forbes

Role: Centre/wing-half 1907-15
5'9" 12st.0lbs.
b. Old Machar, Aberdeen, 1882
d. Sunderland, 26th September 1920

CAREER: Orion FC (Aberdeen) Aug 1901/ Aberdeen 1903/SUNDERLAND May 1907/ retired May 1919.

Debut v Manchester City (h) 2/9/1907

One of those gifted individuals who can literally make a show in any position, Harry Low disported himself mainly in Sunderland's

Harry Low

LOWREY, Patrick

Role: Centre/inside-forward 1968-72
5'8" 12st.3lbs.
b. Newcastle upon Tyne, 11th October 1950

CAREER: Newcastle upon Tyne Schools/
Newcastle United app/SUNDERLAND pro
Nov 1967-1972/RU Bruges (Belgium)/
Darlington Aug 1975/Workington July 1976-
1977.

Debut v Arsenal (h) 5/4/1969

Paddy Lowrey is noteworthy for a goodly
haul of schoolboy caps - five - all acquired
during season 1965/66, preceding a brief spell
as a Newcastle United apprentice. It was with
Sunderland, however, that Paddy took the
professional ticket. He made his League bow
aged 18 but never broke into the first team on
a regular basis. He was however, one of the
scorers in a 3-2 friendly win over the Great
Britain Olympic squad at Roker in April 1971.
For Darlington he appeared in 14 Fourth
Division games (plus six substitutions),
scoring twice, and for Workington, in the same
competition, 15 games, scoring three goals. In
the latter season, 1976/77, the Cumberland
club were wooden spoonists for the second
successive season and lost their League status
to Wimbledon.

Appearances:
FL: 13(2) apps. 3 gls.
Total: *13(2) apps. 3 gls.*
Honours:
5 Eng Sch apps.

half-back line and there mostly as left-half. He
had started with junior Orion, one of three
minor organisations (the others were
Aberdeen and Victoria United) which
amalgamated in 1903 to form Aberdeen FC
and, in so doing, enter the Scottish League.
Making 103 League and Scottish Cup
appearances for the Dons, he was a seasoned
campaigner when Sunderland secured his
signature. A regular fixture in Sunderland's
1913 championship-winning side, Harry also
turned out in all ten FA Cup ties that same
year, including the final against Aston Villa at
Crystal Palace which was lost 0-1 and cost the
club the coveted 'Double' of League and Cup.
A further blow was that Sunderland's second
Cup replay saga with rivals Newcastle clashed
with Harry's selection by Scotland in March
for a match in Ireland and he pulled out of the
international party. Unfortunately, he was
never picked again. Brother of Wilf Low, the
Newcastle United and Scotland star, and
cousin of Willie Low (Aberdeen 1909-1917).
Sad to say, Harry died distressingly young.

Appearances:
FL: 202 apps. 34 gls.
FAC: 26 apps. 4 gls.
Total: *228 apps. 38 gls.*
Honours:
*(Sunderland) FL champs 1913/FAC finalist
1913.*

Paddy Lowrey

Chris Lumsdon

LUMSDON, Christopher

Role: Midfield 1997-date
5'11" 10st.6lbs.
b. Killingworth, Newcastle upon Tyne, 15th December 1979

CAREER: George Stephenson High School, Killingworth/North Tyneside Schoolboys/Northumberland Schoolboys/SUNDERLAND assoc s'boy Nov 1995, trainee July 1996, pro July 1997.

Debut v Wolverhampton Wanderers (a) 7/2/1998

Red-haired teenage wing-back Chris Lumsdon is an exciting prospect who has shone at every level. With a competitive attitude to complement his maturing skills, Chris made his senior debut and quickly found his feet in one of the 1997-98 season's outstanding results, a 1-0 victory at Molineux. Decimated by injuries and suspensions, the unfamiliar Sunderland line-up nevertheless fought magnificently to take the points. As a highly-rated schoolboy, Chris received offers from many clubs in both England and Scotland, including Rangers, Coventry City and Nottingham Forest. His decision to remain in the North-East has to date proved beneficial. He made only one Worthington Cup appearance in 1998-99, but Chris helped the

Reserves clinch the Pontin's Premier League championship, despite a troublesome groin injury which required surgery in late season. Contracted to the club until 2003 and highly rated by manager Peter Reid, Chris will be hoping for more opportunities at senior level in 1999-2000. His father Arthur was on Newcastle's books in the 1960's.

> **Appearances:**
> *FL: 1 app. 0 gls.*
> *FLC: 0(1) apps. 0 gls.*
> **Total:** *1(1) apps. 0 gls.*
> **Honours:**
> *Eng U-18 1998.*

LYNAS, John

Role: Outside-right 1928-29
5'4" 10st.0lbs.
b. Blantyre, Lanarks, 18th January 1907

CAREER: Shettleston/Rutherglen Glencairn/Bo'ness/SUNDERLAND May 1928 £310/Third Lanark Oct 1929/retired 1936 and appointed Blackpool trainer, an appointment that lasted well into the post-war period.

Debut v Burnley (a) 25/8/1928

Small, compactly built Scottish right-winger, Johnny Lynas stayed not quite a season at Roker Park. He played for Sunderland in the first nine League fixtures of 1928/29 and a final one against West Ham in the penultimate game on April 27 1929. Lynas stayed some six years with Third

John Lynas

Lanark after this at a time when Thirds were yo-yoing between the Scottish First and Second Divisions (his top-flight figures were 61 appearances, 18 goals). On retirement Johnny became a highly regarded Blackpool trainer, especially during the post-war years when the club reached the FA Cup final on three occasions. A quiet, unassuming man but none the worse for that, he had spent much of the war as a POW after the Japanese captured Singapore.

Appearances:
FL: 10 apps. 1 gl.
Total: *10 apps. 1 gl.*
Honours:
Scot Jnr int/(Third Lanark) SL Div 2 champs 1931, 1935.

NOTE: *It is very possible the player won a Scottish League Division Two medal with Bo'ness in 1926/27, but it cannot be proved at the time of writing. If Lynas did win three medals it would likely have created a Division Two record.*

LYNCH, Thomas Michael

Role: Defender 1988-90
6'0" 12st.6lbs.
b. Limerick, 10th October 1964

CAREER: Limerick/SUNDERLAND Aug 1988 (Shrewsbury Town loan Jan 1990)/Shrewsbury Town Feb 1990-cs 1997.

Debut v Chelsea (a) 12/11/1988

A Republic of Ireland Olympic international, Tommy Lynch spent a season and a half in reserve at Roker, following his £20,000 transfer from Limerick in the summer of 1988. In his first season he appeared in four League matches as deputy for Reuben Agboola. In the following term his first senior outing was on 6th January in the 2-1 defeat at Reading in the FA Cup third round. Later in the same month he was loaned to Shrewsbury Town and, by coincidence, Reading again provided the opposition when he made his first appearance for his new club. Signed on a permanent basis by Shrewsbury following his loan spell, Tommy enjoyed a long and successful career

Tommy Lynch

at Gay Meadow. At either left full-back or in central defence he proved a popular figure, strong in the tackle, completely dominant in the air, and a set-piece specialist. He appeared in 234 League matches for the Shrews and scored 14 goals.

Appearances:
FL: 4 apps. 0 gls.
FAC: 1 app. 0 gls.
Total: *5 apps. 0 gls.*
Honours:
(Shrewsbury Town) Div 3 champs 1994.

MAIN, David

Role: Centre-forward 1910-11
b. Falkirk, 1888

CAREER: Falkirk/SUNDERLAND Oct 1910/ Aberdeen May 1911-1917.

Debut v Notts County (a) 17/12/1910 (scored)

Scot David Main stayed only briefly at Roker Park. His only first team outing apart from the debut occurred a week later on Christmas Eve 1910 against Manchester United, a 2-1 home reverse. Against Notts County Main scored Sunderland's goal in a 1-1 draw. He did well for Aberdeen subsequently as first choice centre-forward or inside-left, grossing 158 League and Cup appearances in which he scored 58 goals. Although not exactly a speed merchant, David had the valuable trait of positional know-how, netting many opportunist goals as a result. He left Aberdeen when the club shut down temporarily.

> **Appearances:**
> *FL: 2 apps. 1 gl.*
> **Total:** *2 apps. 1 gl.*

MAKIN, Christopher Gregory

Role: Full back 1997-date
5'11" 11st.0lbs.
b. Manchester, 8th May 1973

CAREER: Manchester Schoolboys/Boundary Park Juniors/FA National School, Lilleshall whilst Oldham Athletic assoc s'boy June 1987, trainee Aug 1989, pro Nov 1991(Wigan Athletic loan Aug-Nov 1992) (Preston North End loan 1993)/ Marseille, France cs 1996/ SUNDERLAND Aug 1997.

Debut v Sheffield United (a) 10/8/1997

Chris Makin joined Oldham Athletic from school, but made his League debut with the Division Three 'Latics', Wigan Athletic, during a loan spell at the beginning of season 1992-93. He made an impressive start, scoring twice, and Wigan were anxious to sign him permanently, but Oldham refused to entertain the approach. He made his Oldham debut in the Premiership versus Arsenal at Boundary Park in October 1993 and was a losing FA Cup semi-finalist in the same season. During the summer of 1996 Chris moved to one of Europe's top clubs, Marseille, on a free transfer under the Bosman ruling. A superb move for the player, but a financial disaster for the hard-up Latics. He cost Sunderland £500,000 a year later, his transfer coinciding with Kubicki's move to Wolves. Excellent pace and distribution, plus the ability to occupy both full-back positions and midfield, have made Chris Makin a top class defender. His crisp tackling ability helped further cement Wearside popularity,

Chris Makin

but he was unfortunate to suffer ligament damage in October 1997 which sidelined him for some weeks. Not alone in his misfortune, Makin was just one of a complete back four who began the season and were replaced, albeit with great success, by the more youthful quartet of Holloway, Williams, Craddock and Gray. Although missing the start of the 1998-99 season due to a kidney infection, Chris then enjoyed an uninterrupted run of first team duty from the end of September. He displayed consistently outstanding form throughout the championship campaign in Sunderland's water tight defence, and richly deserved his Division One winners' medal.

Appearances:
FL: 61(4) apps. 1 gl.
FAC: 3 apps. 0 gls.
FLC: 10 apps. 0 gls.
Total: *74(4) apps. 1 gl.*
Honours:
Eng Sch/Eng Yth/5 Eng U-21 apps.
1994/(Sunderland) Div 1 champs 1999.

MALEY, Mark

Role: Defender 1998-date
b. Newcastle upon Tyne, 26th January 1976

CAREER: St. Cuthberts, Benwell/Wallsend Boys' Club/Centres of Excellence at Manchester United, Middlesbrough and Newcastle United/SUNDERLAND assoc s'boy Nov 1995, trainee Aug 1997, pro Jan 1998-date.

Debut v York City (h) 18/8/1998 (FLC)

Former Northumbrian Schools 400 metres champion Mark Maley made considerable progress during season 1998-99. The ex-England Schoolboys captain - he appeared in 30 internationals - made his senior debut at 17 years of age and successfully graduated through the youth sides to appear in over half the season's Reserve team fixtures.

Mark Maley

Able to play at full-back, centre-back or in midfield, he is comfortable in possession, tackles well and is quick to react to dangerous situations. Certainly Mark is one of the brightest young prospects at the Stadium of Light, and one for the future.

Appearances:
FLC: 1 app. 0 gls.
Total: *1 app. 0 gls.*
Honours:
30 Eng Sch apps.

MALONE, Richard Philip

Role: Full-back 1970-77
6'0" 12st.2lbs.
b. Motherwell, 22nd August 1947

CAREER: Ayr United/SUNDERLAND Oct 1970/Hartlepool United July 1977/Blackpool Nov 1978, retired May 1980.

Debut v Bristol City (h) 17/10/1970

Scotland Under-23 international Dick Malone cost £30,000 when he joined Sunderland from Ayr United in October 1970. He had an unlucky start, as he was injured on his debut and took some time to regain full fitness. He recounted that during all his time in Scotland he had never been injured, but 50 minutes into his first game in England he was crocked! His Sunderland career blossomed under Bob Stokoe's management and he appeared in every round of the 1973 FA Cup adventure which saw Sunderland winners of the famous old trophy for the first time in 36 years. The Wembley final was surely Malone's finest match. It was widely predicted the class of Leeds' flying winger, Eddie Gray, would prove decisive, but Malone, neatly assisted by Bobby Kerr, marked Gray out of the game so effectively he was substituted. A fine attacking full-back Malone, who was affectionately dubbed 'Superdick' by the fans in a Roker retort to Tyneside's 'Supermac', was an early exponent of the overlapping run and his final ball into opponents' penalty areas was more often than not accurate. He scored only twice but both goals were collectors' items at the Roker End. One was a forty-yard rocket, the other ended a neat passing movement which included a burst of Dick's delightfully unorthodox dribbling! A fixture in Sunderland's defence for six seasons, he eventually lost his place in 1976-77, the season which ended in relegation from Division One. After a term with Hartlepool, Malone joined Blackpool and was reunited with former Sunderland manager, Bob Stokoe. It was reported that Malone's outstanding display in a testimonial match for Ian Porterfield had prompted his former manager to offer him a contract. Later on Malone worked for haulage firm TNT and has remained a regular visitor on home matchdays.

Appearances:
FL: 235(1) apps. 2 gls.
FAC: 22 apps. 0 gls.
FLC: 10 apps. 0 gls.
Other: 8 apps. 0 gls.
Total: *275(1) apps. 2 gls.*
Honours:
1 Scot U-23 app. 1970/(Sunderland) FAC winners 1973/Div 2 champs 1976.

MALTBY, John

Role: Inside-forward 1956-61
5'9" 11st.4lbs.
b. Leadgate, Co Durham,
31st July 1939

CAREER: Crookhall Juniors/ SUNDERLAND am June 1955/ pro Aug 1957/Darlington June 1961/Bury July 1965 £5,000/ Southern Suburbs, South Africa early 1967.

Debut v Chelsea (h) 10/11/1956

John Maltby also played outside-left and was a local development, mostly in the reserves as stand-in for Shack, 'Legs' Fleming and the rest. He went to Darlington for a small fee, making 115 Fourth Division appearances (32 goals). The Quakers had a moderate side at this juncture but Jack did well enough as an individual for Bury to lay out a significant fee. At Gigg Lane he played in 56 Second Division matches plus a substitution (eight goals). The club was heading for relegation when Maltby left for South Africa.

Appearances:
FL: 22 apps. 1 gl.
FAC: 1 app. 0 gls.
Total: *23 apps. 1 gl.*

Dick Malone

John Maltby

MAPSON, John

Role: Goalkeeper 1935-53
5'11" 12st.10lbs.
b. Birkenhead, 2nd May 1917
d. Washington, Tyne & Wear, 19th August 1999

CAREER: Swindon Schools/Highworth Town/Westrop Rovers/Swindon Town am/Reading Apr 1935 (Guildford City loan)/SUNDERLAND Mar 1936 £2,000/retired May 1954.

Debut v Portsmouth (h) 4/4/1936

It read like fiction. The young Sunderland goalkeeper, Jimmy Thorpe, had died suddenly and unexpectedly. An emergency replacement was called for, manager Johnny Cochrane's choice a youngster of 18 with a mere couple of Third Division appearances to his name. The youngster made his First Division debut shortly afterwards in a star-studded side of awesome quality pressing for the championship. The championship is won although he didn't quite make enough appearances to warrant a medal, but for good measure the young 'keeper goes on to win a Cup-winners' medal the following term the day before his 20th birthday. Really the stuff of the inter-war *Sports Budget* authors! Johnny moved to Swindon from his native Birkenhead as a lad, eventually working in succession as a grocer's boy, in a bakehouse and as a milk boy. The strongest aspect of his goalkeeping style was his positional sense which was so astute he only rarely had to make a last-ditch dive. He also had a distinctive method of catching the ball - one arm over the other to one side of his body - and possessed a most robust clearance kick. In 1939 he went with the FA touring party to South Africa, playing against the national side. During World War Two he moved back south to employment in an engineering works. When work allowed Johnny assisted Reading in wartime football and helped them win the London War Cup in 1941 and that year played for England against Wales in a wartime international. Johnny returned between the posts at Roker Park once peacetime football resumed and remained The Lads' first-choice goalkeeper for a further six seasons before hanging up his boots in summer 1953. In retirement Johnny lived with his daughter in Washington, Tyne & Wear, and his death in August 1999 saw the passing of the last remaining member of the 1937 FA Cup-winning side.

Appearances:
FL: 346 apps. 0 gls.
FAC: 36 apps. 0 gls.
Total: 382 apps. 0 gls.
Honours:
(Sunderland) FAC winners 1937.

Johnny Mapson pictured at the age of 78.

Johnny Mapson

263

MARANGONI Claudio O.

Role: Forward 1979-81
6'1" 13st.0lbs.
b. Argentina, 17th November 1974

CAREER: San Lorenzo,
Argentina/SUNDERLAND Dec 1979-Dec
1980/Hurracan, South America Jan 1981.

Debut v Cardiff City (h) 8/12/1979

Signed for a record £320,000 by manager Ken
Knighton, the tall elegant Argentinian Claudio
Marangoni struggled desperately to come to
terms with the vastly different style of English
football. He made 16 appearances and scored
three goals in his first season but had made
only 3(1) First Division appearances in 1980-
81, when agreement was reached to rescind
his contract after just twelve largely miserable
months at Roker. The terms of his contract
saved Sunderland a great deal of money, as
the substantial balance outstanding on his fee
became null and void when he returned to his
home country. The Argentinian international,
who took out Italian citizenship just prior to
coming to England was quickly fixed up with
a new club when he returned to the South
American sunshine. The fact that Marangoni
was later voted Footballer of the Year in
Argentina may remain a source of complete
disbelief to Sunderland fans, but is perhaps in
some way, a measure of how unfortunate it
was things simply did not work out for him at
Roker.

Appearances:
FL: 19(1) apps. 3 gls.
FAC: 1 app. 0 gls.
FLC: 1 app. 0 gls.
Total: *21(1) apps.*
3 gls.
Honours:
Argentina full cap.

MARPLES, Emmerson Arthur

Role: Right-back 1907-08
5'8" 13st.0lbs.
b. Chesterfield, 1879
d. Chesterfield, 1964

CAREER: Dronfield Town Aug 1899/
Chesterfield Town Oct 1901/SUNDERLAND
Feb 1908 £350/Chesterfield Town Oct 1910.

Debut v Chelsea (a) 29/2/1908

Emmerson Marples

A weighty defender who
arrived rather late in the
big time at aged 29.
However, Marples had
experienced an amount
of Second Division fare
in the ranks of
Chesterfield Town (146
appearances plus 11 in
FA Cup-ties). His League
outings with Sunderland
consisted of the final ten
fixtures of 1907/08, six of these being wins
and the rest defeats. Marples certainly enjoyed
longevity in football as well as in actual years:
he was turning out for Eckington Works when
in his early 40s.

Appearances:
FL: 10 apps. 0 gls.
Total: *10 apps. 0 gls.*

*Claudio Marangoni
(centre) with his wife,
Monica, and the
Sunderland manager
who signed him,
Ken Knighton.*

MARRIOTT, Andrew

Role: Goalkeeper 1998-date
6'1" 13st.0lbs.
b. Sutton-in-Ashfield, 11th October 1970

CAREER: Arsenal assoc sch Oct 1985, trainee
July 1987, pro Oct 1988/Nottingham Forest
June 1989(West Bromwich Albion loan Sept
1989)(Blackburn Rovers loan Dec 1989-Jan
1990)(Colchester United loan Mar 1990)
(Burnley loan Aug 1991)(Wrexham loan Oct
1993)/Wrexham December 1993
(SUNDERLAND loan Aug 1998)/
SUNDERLAND Oct 1998.

Debut v Grimsby Town (a) 13/3/1999

Andy Marriott was the second Wrexham
player to join Sunderland for season 1998-99,
when he followed Neil Wainwright to the
Stadium of Light. A goalkeeper of ripe
experience, Andy, who tasted early success
with Brian Clough's Nottingham Forest, had
the benefit of ten years as a professional,
almost half of which had been spent at the
Racecourse Ground with in excess of 200
League appearances for Wrexham. A number
of loan stints have featured in his League
career to date, and one such noteworthy spell
was spent at Turf Moor. In the maximum
period allowed (three months) he played 17
times for Burnley and won a Division Four
championship medal. In his first season on
Wearside, the outstanding form of Thomas
Sorensen restricted Andy to a single senior
appearance, but he responded with an
impressive clean sheet. Nevertheless, his
outstanding form in Sunderland's Reserve
team earned him a call-up into the Wales Euro
2000 training camp, after six months in the
international wilderness. Despite having
played for England U-21 in a friendly
international, Andy qualified for Wales
through his grandparents.

> **Appearances:**
> *FL: 1 app. 0 gls.*
> **Total:** *1 app. 0 gls.*
> **Honours:**
> *Eng Sch & Yth/1 U-21 app. 1992/*
> *5 Welsh caps 1996-98/*
> *(Nottingham Forest) FLC finalist 1992/*
> *ZDS winner 1992/(Burnley) Div 4 champs*
> *1992/(Wrexham) WC winner 1995.*

Andy Marriott

MARSDEN, William

Role: Inside-left 1920-24
5'8" 10st.6lbs.
b. Silksworth, Co Durham, 10th November 1901
d. Sheffield, 1983

CAREER: Ryhope FC/Silksworth Colliery/
SUNDERLAND Oct 1920/Sheffield
Wednesday May 1924, retired through injury
1930/Gateshead trainer cs 1934/Hartlepools
United coach Aug 1934 and then a club coach
in Holland (Be Quick FC and DWS 1938, and an
assistant coach to the Netherlands FA before
WW2)/Doncaster Rovers manager Apr 1944-Jan
1946/Worksop Town manager May 1953.

Debut v Derby County (a) 28/3/1921

A classic case of a young player leaving his
first big club for another, switching positions
and going on to gain international caps and
the rest. Billy Marsden, naturally right-footed,
by assiduous practice became adept with his
left. A move to left-half in a side destined for
the highest honours was the result. Billy,
together with Alf Strange and Tony Leach,

Bill Marsden

MARSHALL, Robert Samuel

Role: Inside-forward 1920-28
5'9" 11st.0lbs.
b. Hucknall, Notts, 3rd April 1903
d. Glapwell, Derbyshire, 27th October 1966

CAREER: Hucknall Olympic/SUNDERLAND
May 1920/Manchester City Mar 1928/retired
Mar 1939 on appointment as Stockport County
manager/Chesterfield manager Feb 1949-July
1952.

Debut v Bradford City (a) 23/10/1920 (scored)

Played mostly at inside-right but from 1925-27
Bobby Marshall made some League
appearances at centre-half, a position he was
to occupy regularly for Manchester City from
1936. Bobby's first-class career covers
practically the whole of the twenty inter-war
seasons and it was spent almost entirely in
the top flight. His aggregate figures are
impressive: League 521 appearances, 138
goals; FA Cup 39 appearances, 15 goals,
making a grand total of 560 appearances, 153
goals. It can be taken for granted a high
consistency was maintained over these
nineteen years. In addition
Marshall had superb ball
control and, as an inside
man, an eagle eye for the
scoring chance. Bobby
latterly worked as a
licensee. He
collapsed and died
when serving at his
bar. Elder brother
of W H Marshall
who played for
Port Vale, Wolves
and other clubs
between the wars.
Bob's League career
covers 32 unbroken
years.

Appearances:
FL: 196 apps. 68 gls.
FAC: 9 apps. 5 gls.
Total: *205 apps. 73 gls.*
Honours:
(Manchester City)
FL champs 1937/
FL Div 2 champs 1928/
FAC winner 1934/
FAC finalist 1933.

formed an all-England half-back line.
A dreadful injury when playing for
England against Germany in May
1930 - it involved spinal damage
and a broken neck - brought an
abrupt and untimely end to an
outstanding career. A German
surgeon saved his life.
Afterwards, besides coaching
and managerial appointments,
he was employed as a licensee
in Sheffield. Marsden actually
left Sunderland FC by refusing
the terms offered. It is worth
mentioning the date of his debut
and that of his second League
appearance for the Wearsiders is
separated by two and a half years.

Appearances:
FL: 3 apps. 2 gls.
Total: *3 apps. 2 gls.*
Honours:
3 Eng caps/1 FL app./(Sheffield Wednesday)
FL Div 2 champs 1926/FL champs 1929,
1930.

Bobby Marshall

MARSHALL, W.

Role: Centre-half 1885-86
Debut v Redcar (a)
24/10/1885 (FAC)

Marshall was the pivot
in the line-up for
Sunderland's second
FA Cup-tie, which was
almost a repeat of the
first - a 3-0 (instead of a

W. Marshall

3-1) defeat at Redcar. He played centre-half in
the first three fixtures of 1885/86, thereafter
appearing at right and left-back, left-half and
inside-right, left-back being the most favoured.

Appearances:
FAC: 1 app. 0 gls.
Total: *1 app. 0 gls.*

MARSTON, Maurice

Role: Right-back 1951-53
b. Trimdon, Co Durham, 24th March 1929

CAREER: Silksworth Juniors/SUNDERLAND
June 1949/Northampton Town July 1953
£6,000 incl. Wm. Walsh/Kettering Town 1957.

Debut v Tottenham Hotspur (a) 15/3/1952

Maurice Marston

The bulk of Maurice Marston's League outings
in a Sunderland jersey came towards the end
of season 1951/52: a clutch of seven
consecutive matches from mid-March to mid-
April. It was not a bad run either, with three
wins, three draws and only a single defeat (his
debut at White Hart Lane). In his last
appearance, against Charlton Athletic in
December 1952, he played at left-back.
Maurice put in four good years with
Northampton (149 Southern Section
appearances, two goals). A good, reliable back.

Appearances:
FL: 9 apps. 0 gls.
Total: *9 apps. 0 gls.*

MARTIN, Henry

Role: Outside-left 1911-22
5'10" 12st.0lbs.
b. Selston, Notts, 5th December 1891
d. Sandiacre, Notts, 31st December 1974

CAREER: Sutton Junction
1909/SUNDERLAND Jan 1912 (guested for
Nottingham Forest during WW1)/Nottingham
Forest May 1922/Rochdale June 1925-cs 1929
when appointed club trainer/York City
trainer-coach Aug 1931/Mansfield Town coach
Nov 1933, manager Dec 1933-Mar
1935/Newport County trainer Nov
1935/Swindon Town trainer cs 1936,
remaining on their training staff into the 1950s.

Debut v Liverpool (a) 5/4/1912 (scored)

As late as 1924 Harry Martin was still
receiving favourable reviews such as this: "His
great raking stride carries him past most
opposing backs, and he centres brilliantly as in
the days when he was at the height of his
fame with Sunderland." And a year before
"one of the finest outside-lefts who ever laced
a boot." An excellent left-wing replacement for
the great Arthur Bridgett, Harry scored on his
Good Friday debut when Bridgett stood down
for religious reasons, and soon flourished with
the Wearsiders, gaining club honours and an
England cap within little more than two years
of joining. He was to stay at Roker for a
decade but his best years were interrupted by
the Great War. He did, however, collect a
championship medal in 1913 and played in
Sunderland's first FA Cup final the same year.
Forest knew all about his capabilities from a
series of wartime guest appearances and at the

Harry Martin

George 'Pompey' Martin

£120/Boulton & Paul works team Sept 1928/Norwich CEYMS Oct 1928.

Debut v Leicester Fosse (a) 20/3/1909

A couple of Martin's Sunderland Football League appearances were at right-half while at Norwich City, where he stayed a noteworthy 14 years and became skipper, he played centre-half. A strong, unyielding performer justly popular with the Canaries' following. As Martin himself said "being a man of few words, it is on the field I like to make my presence felt. I think I may say that I never don the yellow and green jersey of Norwich City without a full determination that the Canaries are going to win." Some puzzlement has been expressed elsewhere concerning the nickname 'Pompey'. The explanation is given by Martin himself in a symposium by club captains published circa 1920. The nickname was applied on his arrival at Norwich from Portsmouth (where he had spent a year mostly on the injured list). The inference is it was coined to differentiate him from George Harlow Martin, a locally famous amateur of the time who had assisted the Canaries during the late 1900s. Our subject, George (Pompey) Martin served in the Royal Engineers and worked in a munitions factory during World War One. He had two benefits whilst on the Norwich books.

Appearances:
FL: 14 apps. 1 gl.
Total: *14 apps. 1 gl.*

City Ground he struck up a brilliant partnership with ex Roker team mate Walter Tinsley (q.v.). During the war Harry had served in the Army. His long football career concluded in a remarkably lengthy stint as part of Swindon Town's support staff.

Appearances:
FL: 211 apps. 23 gls.
FAC: 20 apps. 1 gl.
Total: *231 apps. 24 gls.*
Honours:
1 Eng cap v Ireland 1914/2 Eng 'Victory' apps. 1919/2 FL apps./(Sunderland) FL champs 1913/FAC finalist 1913.

MARTIN, Isaac George 'Pompey'

Role: Left-half 1908-12
5'8" 11st.7lbs.
b. Gateshead, 25th May 1889
d. Norwich, 6th May 1962

CAREER: Rodsley Gateshead FC /Windy Nook/SUNDERLAND Feb 1908/Portsmouth Aug 1912 £100/Norwich City July 1913-1927

MARTIN, Neil

Role: Centre/inside-forward 1965-68
6'0" 11st.8lbs.
b. Tranent, East Lothian, 20th October 1940

CAREER: Tranent Juniors/Alloa Athletic 1959/Queen of the South late 1961 £2,000/Hibernian July 1963 £6,000/SUNDERLAND Oct 1965 £45,000/Coventry City Feb 1968 £90,000/Nottingham Forest Feb 1971

Neil Martin

£65,000/Brighton & Hove Albion July 1975/
Crystal Palace Mar 1976/St Patrick's Athletic
later in 1976/Al-Arabi Sporting Club, Kuwait
asst manager 1978/Walsall youth coach
afterwards until appointed their joint manager
July 1981, manager 1982.

Debut v Sheffield Wednesday (a)
23/10/1965 (scored)

Neil Martin's spell at Sunderland did not
coincide with a flourishing time for the club.
In the three seasons that encapsulated his two-
and-a-half year Roker spell they finished 19th,
17th and 15th in the First Division. Despite
some famous names, Jim Baxter and Ralph
Brand, for example, and others of genuine
potential, results were moderate to say the
least. Not much blame, however, could be laid
at Neil's door. His 46 goals in 99 League and
Cup encounters were a healthy return and
local verdicts were nothing other than
favourable. He was described as "every inch a
thoroughbred footballer, very good at taking
his chances" and "with the right kind of
support could become the side's top

personality." Before crossing the border, Neil
had built a solid reputation. Whilst attached to
his first senior club, Alloa Athletic, he served
an apprenticeship as a mining engineer, but
his promise induced Queen of the South - a
club of small means - to pay a significant sum
for his services. Neil's 33 goals in 61 League
outings persuaded Hibernian to treble that fee.
The Easter Road club, a useful side in the mid-
Sixties, reached the semi-finals of both Scottish
and League Cups during Neil's stay, and he
earned two Scotland caps, a just reward for
netting 53 goals in only 65 League
appearances. An ideally proportioned striker,
Neil's height and imposing physique made
him a dangerous customer in the air and he
held his line well. At Sunderland he enhanced
his reputation, despite playing for a moderate
side, and just a month after his arrival won his
last cap alongside team mate Jim Baxter in a
1-0 World Cup qualifier win over Italy in front
of 100,000 at Hampden Park. In 1966-67 he hit
20 top-division League goals for Sunderland,
the last player to do so, and his hat-trick in a
7-1 FA Cup fourth round rout of Peterborough
at Roker was the club's only post-war FA Cup
treble until Kevin Phillips' four against
Rotherham in early 1998. He moved to
Coventry City, another struggling outfit, for
double the fee Sunderland had paid. There is
no doubt Neil's 18 League goals in 15 games
kept Coventry in the top flight during the final
months of 1967/68. However, things improved
a couple of seasons later when the Sky Blues
reached the dizzy heights of sixth in 1970/71.
Neil, however, seemed fated to be mostly
associated with English strugglers. At
Nottingham Forest, he experienced relegation
to Division Two and was then discarded by
Brian Clough. His aggregate Football League
figures were 329(8) appearances with 115
goals. He is one of a select band who have
scored a century and more goals in both
Leagues. Neil's subsequent experience on the
football administration side extended
geographically from Kuwait to Walsall where
he assumed complete control for a few
months.

Appearances:
FL: 86 apps. 38 gls.
FAC: 8 apps. 6 gls.
FLC: 5 apps. 2 gls.
Total: *99 apps. 46 gls.*
Honours:
3 Scot caps/2 SL apps./1 Scot U-23 app.

MATTEO, Dominic

Dominic Matteo

Role: Defender 1994-95
6'1" 11st.8lbs.
b. Dumfries, 28th April 1974

CAREER: Liverpool assoc. s'boy Sept 1989, trainee June 1990, pro May 1992 (SUNDERLAND loan Mar 1995).

Debut v Barnsley (a) 24/3/1995

Dominic Matteo's only appearance for Sunderland cost the club a £2,500 fine due to a registration error (he actually played when ineligible) and he returned to Anfield after just one First Division appearance. At the time, the 20-year-old Matteo was facing stiff competition at Liverpool and it was not until season 1996-97 that he finally established himself. He has since developed into a polished defender in either central or left-sided defence, comfortable on the ball and composed when under pressure. Outstanding form in the early stages of season 1996-97 led to a call-up by Glenn Hoddle into England's senior squad, but he has yet to figure at full international level. Matteo's single appearance for Sunderland marked the debut of Brett Angell, and the 2-0 defeat at Oakwell proved Mick Buxton's last as manager, his replacement, Peter Reid, being the twenty-first boss in Sunderland's history.

Appearances:
FL: 1 app. 0 gls.
Total: *1 app. 0 gls.*
Honours:
Eng Yth/4 Eng U-21 apps. 1994-98/
1 Eng 'B' app 1998.

MAXWELL, William Sturrock

Role: Inside-forward 1902-03
5'10" 11st.7lbs.
b. Arbroath, 21st September 1875
d. Bristol, 14th July 1940

CAREER: Hearts Strollers/Arbroath FC am 1893-94/Dundee am 1894-95 (1 game for Heart of Midlothian during that season)/Stoke pro Aug 1895/Third Lanark July 1901 £250/SUNDERLAND May 1902/Millwall Athletic May 1903/Bristol City May 1905/retired cs

Bill Maxwell

1909/Leopold FC (Belgium) coach Sept 1909, afterwards coach to the Belgian national side into the 1920s.

Debut v Nottingham Forest (h) 1/9/1902

Bill Maxwell had acquired a terrific reputation by the time he reached Sunderland as one of the finest forwards ever to leave Scotland. Extremely versatile - he could take any attack berth - Bill was a splendid dribbler and able to gather a pass when going full tilt. Yet Maxwell's service to the Wearsiders was confined to a single season in which he appeared in a mere seven League matches. He later, however, became a firm favourite at Bristol, described in a programme obituary as "a brilliant exponent of inside-forward play, a master craftsman, clever shot, sportsman and gentleman. His skill gave pleasure to thousands". Maxwell showed exceptional talent early, twice representing Angus in county matches when only 17.

Appearances:
FL: 7 apps. 3 gls.
Total: *7 apps. 3 gls.*
Honours:
1 Scot cap v England 1898/
(Bristol City) FL Div 2 champs 1906.

MEARNS, Frederick Charles

Role: Goalkeeper 1901-02
5'10" 12st.8lbs.
b. Sunderland, 31st March 1879
d. Sunderland, 22nd January 1931

CAREER: Whitburn/SUNDERLAND Jan 1901/Kettering May 1902/Tottenham Hotspur Mar 1903/Bradford City May 1904/Southern United Apr 1905/Grays United cs 1905/Southern United Dec 1905/Barrow Mar 1906/Bury Apr 1908/Stockton cs 1908/Hartlepools United 1908/Barnsley May 1909/Leicester Fosse Jan 1911 (in exchange for George Travers)/Newcastle City cs 1913/Sunderland West End Oct 1919/Durham City trainer.

Debut v Aston Villa (h) 5/10/1901

Fred Mearns was a working joiner before and

after a roving football career that alternated between Football League, Southern League and sundry other clubs of varying status over many years. At Sunderland he deputised for the perennial Ted Doig a couple of times in 1901/02, conceding one goal (the debut above was a 1-0 victory, the other appearance, against Derby County in April 1902, a defeat by the same score). Mearns, a capable goalie, enjoyed his best spell, and made a Cup final appearance, with Barnsley. Earlier, at Kettering, he reputedly saved 17 penalties during season 1902/03 and became known (and rightly!) as 'The Penalty King.'

Fred Mearns

Appearances:
FL: 2 apps. 0 gls.
Total: *2 apps. 0 gls.*
Honours:
(Barnsley)FAC finalist 1910.

MEECHAN, Peter

Role: Right-back 1893-95
5'9" 13st.13lbs.
*b. Broxburn, West Lothian,
28th February 1872
d. Nova Scotia, Canada,
July 1915*

Peter Meechan

CAREER: Broxburn Shamrock Sept 1891/ Hibernian Feb 1892/SUNDERLAND Aug 1893/Celtic May 1895/Everton Jan 1897 £450 - £250 paid to Celtic, £200 to Sunderland, thought to be a then record/Southampton May 1898 £200/Manchester City Dec 1900/ Barrow cs 1901/Broxburn Athletic Mar 1902/ Clyde Aug 1903/Broxburn Shamrocks May 1904.

Debut v Aston Villa (h) 9/9/1893

A former miner, Peter Meechan (referred to as Meehan in some record books) was a formidable back if not exactly the soul of consistency. Variable too it appears as his weight was also given in the period as 13st 13lbs. (perhaps close season indulgences

caused the fluctuation?) All the same Meechan's record of honours speaks for itself. In total they are well above average and evenly spread over service with four of his first-class clubs. He was said to have been in indifferent health after he left Sunderland, where he enjoyed arguably the best on-field form of his career, and he did indeed die in middle age.

Appearances:
FL: 42 apps. 1 gl.
FAC: 6 apps. 0 gls.
Total: *48 apps. 1 gl.*
Honours:
1 Scot cap v Ireland 1896/1 SL app. v Irish Lge 1896/(Celtic) SL champs 1896/ (Sunderland) FL champs 1895/(Everton) FAC finalist 1897/(Southampton) Sth Lge champs 1899, FAC finalist 1900.

MELVILLE, Andrew Roger

Role: Central defender 1993-99
6'0" 13st.3lbs.
b. Swansea, 29th November 1968

CAREER: Lonlas Boys' Youth Club/Swansea Schoolboys/Swansea City pro July 1986/ Oxford United July 1990/SUNDERLAND Aug 1993(Bradford City loan Feb 1998)/Fulham May 1999.

Debut v Derby County (a) 14/8/1993

Sunderland's most capped Welsh international, central defender Andy Melville made his first senior appearance for Swansea City in the FA Cup and his League debut followed shortly afterwards, both milestones being passed before his 17th birthday. International recognition at 'B' and Under-21 level followed, and his first full cap versus West Germany at Cologne came just a fortnight before his 21st birthday. After 185 League appearances for the Swans, Andy joined Oxford United for a fee of £275,000. Three seasons on, he arrived at Roker, signed by Terry Butcher in a cash-plus-exchange deal (Anton Rogan moving to Oxford along with an initial fee of £500,000). Under three different managers in his first two seasons, Melville's power in the air and sound distribution made him an automatic choice in central defence. This remained the position until early season 1997-98, when the side's

Andy Melville

Bracewell, newly appointed manager of Fulham. At Craven Cottage Andy was expected to line up in a three-man central defensive formation featuring two other Welsh internationals, Kit Symons and Chris Coleman.

Appearances:
PL: 30 apps. 2 gls.
FL: 174 apps. 12 gls.
FAC: 11 apps. 0 gls.
FLC: 18(1) apps. 0 gls.
Other: 2 apps. 0 gls.
Total: *235(1) apps. 14 gls.*
Honours:
1 Wales 'B' app./2 Wales U-21 apps. 1990-91/32 Welsh caps 1990-date/(Swansea City) WC winner 1989/(Sunderland) FL Div 1 champs 1996 & 1999.

METCALF, George William

Role: Centre-half 1906-07
5'8" 11st.0lbs.
b. Easington, Co Durham, 1885

CAREER: Sunderland Black Watch/ SUNDERLAND Dec 1905/North Shields Athletic 1909/Huddersfield Town Feb 1910-May 1913.

Debut v Bolton Wanderers 16/2/1907

Reserve half-back for over three years at Roker Park, George Metcalf's first team experience was confined to season 1906/07. With Huddersfield Town he made six Second Division appearances, plus two in the FA Cup. All but one were at right-half - in the other (against Blackpool in March 1911) he played centre-half.

Appearances:
FL: 2 apps. 0 gls.
Total: *2 apps. 0 gls.*

MIDDLETON, Matthew Young

Role: Goalkeeper 1933-39
5'9" 12st.4lbs.
b. Boldon Colliery, Co Durham, 24th October 1907
d. Sunderland, 19th April 1979

CAREER: Newcastle Swifts/Boldon Colliery Welfare/Southport am Jan 1931, pro Mar 1931/SUNDERLAND Aug 1933/Plymouth Argyle May 1939/Horden Colliery Welfare/ Bradford City Aug 1946/York City Feb 1949/

indifferent start saw him dropped after ten appearances. It is unlikely Andy would have refused the offer of first team football when Bradford City moved to sign him after a six game loan spell at the end of 1997-98 but the Bantams blanched at the £1 million asking price. In the event, he returned to the North-East and worked hard on his fitness during the close season. An injury to Jody Craddock presented him with an early opportunity, which was firmly seized. Once back in the side Andy quickly developed a strong partnership with Paul Butler at the heart of Sunderland's defence, and his form was so good he was recalled to the Welsh squad for the March fixture in Switzerland. Available on a Bosman free transfer at the end of the season, Andy declined a one-year offer to remain at the Stadium of Light in order to team up with former Sunderland assistant boss Paul

Blyth Spartans 1950-52/
Murton Colliery/
Hartlepools United asst
trainer.

*Debut v Wolverhampton
Wanderers (h) 20/1/1934*

Accurately described by
the Southport FC
historians as "an agile
fearless 'keeper with a
spectacular style", Matt

Matt Middleton

Middleton was an outside-right as a junior,
played goalkeeper in an emergency and
remained in that position for the rest of a long
career. At Southport Matt quickly became first
choice, registering 71 League and FA Cup
appearances whilst at Haig Avenue. With
Sunderland he vied with Jimmy Thorpe for
the first team spot, then understudied the
newly signed John Mapson prior to joining
Plymouth Argyle shortly before the outbreak
of war. Returning to his original occupation as
a Boldon Colliery miner, Matt still turned out
for the Devon club in wartime football (as a
result likely becoming wartime's champion
traveller!). Older brother of Ray Middleton,
the Chesterfield, Derby County and England
'B' goalkeeper. Matt's grandson Grant Brown
played for Lincoln City against Sunderland in
an FA Cup tie in January 1999.

Appearances:
FL: 56 apps. 0 gls.
FAC: 2 apps. 0 gls.
Total: *58 apps. 0 gls.*

MIDDLETON, Robert Connan

Role: Goalkeeper 1930-33
5'11" 12st.6lbs.
b. Brechin, Angus, 15th January 1904
d. Kirkcaldy, early 1996

CAREER: Brechin City/Cowdenbeath am Dec
1928, pro cs 1929/SUNDERLAND Nov 1930
£2,400/Burton Town Sept 1933/Chester Feb
1934/retired 1937-38.

Debut v Bolton Wanderers (a) 15/11/1930

"A class 'keeper who is the possessor of a very
safe pair of hands," wrote a critic in 1933. Bob
Middleton came to Sunderland with 72
Scottish League First Division appearances to
his name. He had reached the first-class game
comparatively late, signing professional when

in his 27th year. He played for non-League
Burton Town for almost a season before
linking up with Chester of the Football League
Division Three (North). Bob spent four years
at Sealand Road, making 56 League
appearances. Nephew of Billy Middleton
(Aberdeen 1920-23) who also assisted Ayr
United and Dumbarton.

Appearances:
FL: 59 apps. 0 gls.
FAC: 7 apps. 0 gls.
Total: *66 apps. 0 gls.*
Honours:
1 Scot cap v Northern Ireland 1930.

Bob Middleton

Jimmy Millar

274

MILLAR, James

Role: Centre/inside-forward 1890-96 &
1900-04
5'9" 11st.12lbs.
b. Annbank, Ayrshire, 2nd March 1870
d. London, 5th February 1907

CAREER: Ayrshire schools football/
Annbank FC/SUNDERLAND Aug 1890/
Rangers May 1896/SUNDERLAND May
1900-1904/West Bromwich Albion trainer
July 1904-Apr 1905 (1 Lge app. Oct 1904)/
Chelsea trainer until his death.

Debut v Burnley (h) 13/9/1890

John Allan in the first volume of his great
1923 work, *The Story of the Rangers*,
graphically described Millar as follows. "A
rare companion with the heart of a boy and
as fond of fun, 'Jamie' held a firm place in
the affections of everyone at Ibrox. Not a
giant for strength, he relied for his success
solely on the expertness of his footwork.
He had a dainty touch and seemed to go
straight through the defence simply by tip-
tapping the ball from one foot to the other.
It was just art." Jimmy Millar was equally
revered at Sunderland, of course, as an
indispensable unit of four League
championship sides. (Incidentally, has his
career total of six Football League and
Scottish League championship medals - all
in the space of twelve years - ever been
surpassed? Certainly only Ned Doig can
match his Sunderland record of four
championship medals). His first
Sunderland spell took place in the
magnificent 'Team of All the Talents' era.
His debut came in Sunderland's first-ever
Football League match, and a week later he
scored twice in Sunderland's first League
win - a 4-0 victory at WBA. Here is Jimmy's
appearance record for the legendary
medal-winning seasons:

> 1891/92: 24 apps. out of a possible 26
> 1892/93: 23 apps. out of a possible 30
> 1894/95: 29 apps. out of a possible 30
> 1901/02: 32 apps. out of a possible 34
> Total: 108 apps. out of a possible 120

The 1892, '93 and '95 sides were largely
comprised of Scots, many lured south by
attractive wages and job offers. The 1892
regulars consisted of ten Scots and a lone
Englishman (Porteous) and he had been
recruited from a Scottish club. In the centre-
forward berth of the 'Nineties line-ups was
bustling Johnny Campbell, the adaptable
Millar taking one or other of the inside
positions. In February 1895 during a record
11-1 FA Cup win over Fairfield, Millar
became the first of only four Sunderland
players to score five in a game. In the
1901/02 side Millar, newly returned from
Rangers, led the Roker attack and finished
joint top scorer, Campbell by that time
being long retired. Naturally this was a
much changed team from those of the
'Nineties, only the perennial Doig and
Millar himself remaining. The 1892-95 sides
embraced comparatively few players: in
fact only 19 'regulars' while three others
made enough seasonal appearances to
qualify for a medal. Actually Millar's
durable first-class career extended over 15
years, perhaps a surprising fact considering
he was of only average physique and, in
view of his early demise, possibly
indifferent health. It is also a particularly
lengthy period at a time when ultra-robust
tackling often went unpunished and,
indeed, was anyway considered part of the
pioneer game. Jimmy's early and untimely
death was caused by one of the great early
century killers, tuberculosis. A colleague in
the 1892 and '93 championship sides was
William Gibson (q.v.), his brother-in-law.

NOTE: *In many sources the player's surname
appears as Miller. However the present writer
has seen a facsimile of his signature where
Jimmy himself used the Millar version.*

Appearances:
FL: 238 apps. 106 gls.
FAC: 22 apps. 17 gls.
Total: *260 apps. 123 gls.*
Honours:
*3 Scot caps/3 SL apps./(Sunderland) FL
champs 1892, 1893, 1895, 1902/
(Rangers) SL champs 1899. 1900/
SC winner 1897, 1898, finalist 1899.*

MILTON, Albert

Role: Left-back 1908-14
5'7" 12st.0lbs.
b. High Green, Sheffield, 1885
d. Killed in action, 12th October 1917

CAREER: South Kirkby Colliery Apr 1902/
Barnsley Dec 1907/SUNDERLAND May 1908
£350/Swindon Town May 1914.

Debut v Newcastle United (a) 5/12/1908

Thickset full-back Albert Milton was secured
from Barnsley after less than a season with the
Yorkshire club in which he made 15 Second
Division appearances. Considered at the time
as 'highly promising', that promise was duly
fulfilled, Milton going on to regular
membership of the great 1913 League
championship side. Albert, an ever-present
until mid-March, was unluckily injured and
missed both the climax of the championship
run-in and the Cup final that year, his place
going to another ex-Barnsley defender - Harry
Ness. Pithily described by Maurice
Golesworthy as "only a little 'un but as strong
as an ox and with legs like tree trunks."

> **Appearances:**
> *FL: 125 apps. 0 gls.*
> *FAC: 18 apps. 0 gls.*
> **Total:** *143 apps. 0 gls.*
> **Honours:**
> *(Sunderland) FL champs 1913.*

Albert Milton

MIMMS, Robert Andrew

Role: Goalkeeper 1986-87
6'2" 12st.13lbs.
b. York, 12th October 1963

CAREER: North Yorkshire Schoolboys (trials
in 1979 with Barnsley, Sheffield Wednesday
and Preston North End)/Halifax Town assoc
s'boy Oct 1979, app Apr 1980/Rotherham
United Nov 1981/Everton May 1985(Notts
County loan Mar 1986)(SUNDERLAND loan
Dec 1986-Jan 1987)(Blackburn Rovers loan Jan-
Mar 1987)(Manchester City loan Sept-Oct
1987)/Tottenham Hotspur Feb 1988(Aberdeen
loan Feb 1990)/Blackburn Rovers Dec 1990/
Crystal Palace Aug 1996/Preston North End
Sept 1996/Rotherham United Aug 1997(York
City loan Aug 1998)/York City Oct 1998,
appointed player-asst. manager May 1999.

Debut v Barnsley (a) 13/12/1986

Bobby Mimms

In August 1997
Bobby Mimms, an
ideally proportioned
and confident
goalkeeper, returned
to Rotherham
United, the club who
first launched him
into League football
as an 18-year-old. He
won England Under-
21 caps whilst at
Millmoor and cost
Everton £150,000 in
June 1985. As
understudy to Neville Southall at Goodison,
first team opportunities were at a premium,
and his brief association with Sunderland
occurred when he replaced Iain Hesford for
four consecutive games during December
1986. It was just one of four different loan

transfers he undertook during his Everton spell. Terry Venables paid £375,000 to take him to Spurs in February 1988, but it was at Blackburn where he enjoyed the best period of his career, helping Rovers into the Premiership following his £250,000 transfer in December 1990. Bobby played at the new Stadium of Light with York City in a 1998 Worthington Cup tie and, despite suffering relegation to Division Three in his first season, was retained and given additional duties as assistant to new manager, Neil Thompson.

Appearances:
FL: 4 apps. 0 gls.
Total: *4 apps. 0 gls.*
Honours:
3 Eng U-21 apps. 1985-86/(Everton) FAC finalist 1986.

MITCHELL, Robert

Role: Midfield 1973-76
5'10" 11st.0lbs.
b. South Shields, 4th January 1955

CAREER: Hebburn Youths/SUNDERLAND app, pro Jan 1972/Blackburn Rovers July 1976/Grimsby Town June 1978/Carlisle United Aug 1982/Rotherham United Mar 1983/Hamrun Spartans, Malta, late 1985/Lincoln City Jan 1986/Louth United Aug 1987/Spalding United Sept 1987/Boston United Jan 1988/Louth United Aug 1989/Grimsby Town Football in the Community officer.

Debut v Hull City (a) 3/11/1973

Afforded little chance to shine during his four years as a Roker professional, Bobby Mitchell had flourished in Sunderland's minor teams

before he eventually established himself with Grimsby Town. A sound, tenacious and often skilful midfielder, Mitchell proved a consistent performer for the Mariners, his 142 League appearances including an ever-present total of 46 in the Third Division championship side of 1979-80. Through

Bobby Mitchell

many stages of his career he was linked with manager George Kerr (brother of Bobby, captain of Sunderland's 1973 FA Cup-winning team), the two being associated at Grimsby Town, Rotherham United, Lincoln City and Boston United. His final career aggregate totalled 315 (including substitute appearances) and he scored 16 goals.

Appearances:
FL: 1(2) apps. 0 gls.
Total: *1(2) apps. 0 gls.*
Honours:
(Grimsby Town) FL Div 3 champs 1980.

MITCHINSON, Thomas W.

Role: Inside-forward 1962-66
5'7" 10st.11lbs.
b. Sunderland, 24th February 1943

CAREER: Sunderland Schools/SUNDERLAND app June 1960, pro Dec 1960/Mansfield Town Jan 1966 £10,000/Aston Villa Aug 1967 £18,000/Torquay United May 1969 £6,000/Bournemouth & Boscombe Athletic Dec 1971 £4,300/retired through injury Dec 1973.

Debut v Swansea Town (h) 1/9/1962

Tommy Mitchinson

Tom Mitchinson was engaged following a brilliant display for Sunderland Boys against their Newcastle rivals, developing into a handy reserve able to play outside-right also. He blossomed on leaving Sunderland, enjoying regular first team football with all of his subsequent clubs. "A clever constructive inside-forward" and "a steady probing player with a good eye" were typical critical comments. Tom's aggregate Football League record reads 280 appearances plus two substitutions, 36 goals. His transfer fee to Bournemouth was reported to be £2,300 plus a further £2,000 after 25 appearances, a condition that was met before injury forced retirement.

Appearances:
FL: 16(1) apps. 2 gls.
FAC: 2 apps. 0 gls.
FLC: 2 apps. 1 gl.
Total: *20(1) apps. 3 gls.*

MITTON, John

Role: Centre/wing-half 1920-24
5'11" 12st.0lbs.
*b. Cornholm, nr Todmorden,
Yorkshire, 7th November 1895
d. Burnham Market, Norfolk,
5th August 1983*

CAREER: Portsmouth Rovers/ Padiham FC/ Brierfield FC (Burnley am 1914 and a guest player for Bury 1916)/Exeter City June 1919/ SUNDERLAND Oct 1920 £250/Wolverhampton Wanderers May 1924 £500/ Southampton May 1927-cs 1928 £150, subsequently playing in Hampshire County League football before retiring in 1930.

Debut v Bradford City (a) 23/10/1920

A half-back blessed with height and a supple frame, Jack Mitton mostly played at wing-half while at Roker Park. He moved to Wolves when that club had just won promotion to Division Two, making 107 League and FA Cup appearances (six goals) and captaining the side on occasion. At Southampton, in the evening of his career, he had eight Football League outings. Jack also played cricket professionally (a bowler and tail-end batsman)

and played twice for Somerset in 1920. His brother, James, assisted Exeter City and Stockport County during the 1920s.

Appearances:
FL: 80 apps. 7 gls.
FAC: 2 apps. 0 gls.
Total: *82 apps. 7 gls.*

MONAGHAN

Role: Outside-left 1887-88
Debut v Morpeth Harriers 15/10/1887 (FAC) (scored)

Monaghan made many appearances for Sunderland in that pre-League season of 1887/88, which included all five FA Cup-ties. What is more, by slotting in half a dozen goals, he averaged more than one per tie. He scored a hat-trick in the above Cup debut, two a week later (also against Morpeth Harriers when a replay was ordered after a dispute) and one in an infamous replay against Middlesbrough at home on December 3, 1887 when Boro', who lost 4-2, lodged 'sour grapes' complaints, largely based on heresay, that Monaghan and two other Scotsmen - Hastings (q.v.) and Richardson (q.v.) had been paid to play. Keen to succeed in the English Cup many clubs of this era 'imported' good footballers and found them jobs locally - Monaghan worked on the new Town Hall - so they could both play and fulfil the competition rules. The investigating FA Council chose to duck the veiled issue of 'professionalism' and instead banned the trio for three months and expelled Sunderland from the Cup on the technicality the club had paid the players train fares from Dumfries. It is reasonable to say this saga was largely instrumental in Sunderland operating on a fully professional basis in the future.

Jack Mitton

Appearances:
FAC: 5 apps. 6 gls
Total: *5 apps. 6 gls.*

MONCUR, Robert

Role: Central defender 1974-77
5'10" 10st.9lbs.
b. Perth, Scotland, 19th January 1945

CAREER: West Lothian Schoolboys/
Newcastle United app Oct 1960, pro Apr
1962/SUNDERLAND June 1974/Carlisle
United player-manager Nov 1976, manager
Sept 1977/Heart of Midlothian manager Feb
1980/Plymouth Argyle manager June 1981-
Sept 1983/Whitley Bay coach Sept 1984/
Hartlepool United manager Oct 1988-Dec
1989.

Debut v Millwall (a) 17/8/1974

Manager Bob Stokoe persuaded Bobby
Moncur to join Sunderland in 1974 for £30,000
after an outstanding career with Newcastle
United and Scotland. In many ways it was a
mirror of a similarly successful move which
took Roker favourite Stan Anderson to
Tyneside a decade earlier. A gritty and
uncompromising central defender with the
ripe experience of over 350 senior appearances
for the Magpies, Moncur was 29 years old
when he began his new career as captain of
Sunderland. In splendid defensive partnership
with Dave Watson, and later with Jeff Clarke,

he successfully led Sunderland from Division
Two in 1976 after six seasons out of the top
flight. Indeed, Sunderland's defensive line-up
was so well organised and effective that only a
couple of draws prevented a one hundred per
cent home record. Moncur departed Roker in
November 1976 to become Carlisle United's
player-manager. In February 1980 he took over
as Heart of Midlothian manager, and in his
first full season at Tynecastle won the Scottish
Division One championship. A fine, all-round
sportsman, Moncur was twice winner of the
Footballers' Golf Championship and in his
48th year was a participant in the Whitbread
Round the World Yacht Race. He is presently
in the yacht charter business. He also currently
hosts a local radio phone-in show and is often
a visitor to the Stadium of Light.

Appearances:
FL: 86 apps. 2 gls.
FAC: 7 apps. 0 gls.
FLC: 3 apps. 0 gls.
Total: *96 apps. 2 gls.*
Honours:
*Scot Sch/1 Scot U-23 app. 1968/16 Scot caps
1968-72/(Newcastle United) FAYC winner
1962/FL Div 2 champs 1965/ICFC winner
1969/FAC finalist 1974/(Sunderland) Div 2
champs 1976.*

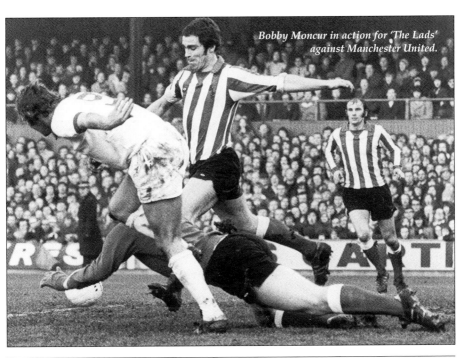

*Bobby Moncur in action for 'The Lads'
against Manchester United.*

on countless occasions but the moment seared into the nation's memory is a save many consider the greatest ever seen at Wembley. It stemmed from a Peter Lorimer rocket in the 1973 Cup final. Midway through the second half, with The Lads leading 1-0, Trevor Cherry's diving header was superbly saved by Jim but the ball rolled directly to the in-rushing Lorimer who shot fiercely at an apparently unguarded net; somehow Montgomery reacted, instinctively plunging across to touch the ball onto the crossbar before Malone cleared the danger. Lorimer later exclaimed: "I couldn't believe my eyes". The first break with Sunderland came in a month's loan at Southampton, which the player did not enjoy although getting five League outings. A similar loan to Birmingham City three months later, followed by a free transfer to that club when the loan period ended, was much more congenial. Monty played in 73 senior matches while at St Andrew's. It proved to be his final spell as a League player as he made no first team appearances for Nottingham Forest - (but collected a 1980 European Cup medal as an unused sub!) - nor when he returned to Roker as a player/coach in August that year. After his playing career ended Monty spent seven years working at the Meadowfield Sports Centre in Durham, coached at Newcastle and returned to Roker Park - where a hospitality suite had been named after him - as Director of Youth, before being surprisingly released in 1995. Most recently he has been employed as goalkeeping coach at Darlington. The biggest surprise, many would say travesty, though, is how such a great and brilliant 'keeper as Monty was never honoured with a full cap despite making it into the England squad. Jim was a model professional and a credit to the game. In May 1999 he received, alongside Bob Stokoe, a 'legend award' from Cup sponsors Axa as the goalkeeper who has made "the greatest contribution to the history of the FA Cup".

Appearances:
FL: 537 apps. 0 gls.
FAC: 41 apps. 0 gls.
FLC: 33 apps. 0 gls.
Other: 12 apps. 0 gls.
Total: *623 apps. 0 gls.*
Honours:
6 Eng U-23 apps./4 Eng Yth apps./
(Sunderland) FAC winner 1973/
Div 2 champs 1976.

MONTGOMERY, William

Role: Inside-forward 1907-09
5'7" 11st.0lbs.
b. Gourock, Renfrewshire, 1885
d. Oakland, California, USA,
21st November 1953

CAREER: Kilwinning Rangers/Rutherglen Glencairn/Bradford City Nov 1905/ SUNDERLAND July 1907/Oldham Athletic Oct 1909 £350/Rangers June 1912 £200/ Dundee Feb 1913.

Debut v Liverpool (a) 12/10/1907

A stocky Scot with at least a modicum of utility value, Montgomery's League appearances whilst on Wearside included an outing at outside-left and even one at right-back (against Bristol City in December 1908). Perhaps his best times were at Oldham where he was a regular in their Division Two runners-up team of 1909/10. Montgomery was in and out of the Athletic's side in the top flight during the following couple of season (42 appearances, 10 goals). A move back to Scotland proved unrewarding at first with only seven League outings in the Ibrox season, but he had 28 League games for Dundee in 1913/14.

Appearances:
FL: 10 apps. 2 gls.
Total: *10 apps. 2 gls.*

William Montgomery

MOONEY, Brian John

Role: Winger 1990-93
5'10 11st.2lbs.
b. Dublin, 2nd February 1966

CAREER: Home Farm/Liverpool Aug 1983
(Wrexham loan Dec 1985)/Preston North End
Nov 1987(Sheffield Wednesday loan July
1990)/SUNDERLAND Feb 1991-May 1993
(Burnley loan Sept 1992).

Debut v Nottingham Forest (h) 16/2/1991

A product of the celebrated nursery club
Home Farm, Brian Mooney won Republic of
Ireland international recognition at all levels
from Youth to Under-23, but in four years at
Anfield managed just one League Cup tie and
failed to graduate into Liverpool's League
side. His first senior appearance came during
a two-month loan spell with Fourth Division
Wrexham for whom he scored twice in nine

appearances. A move to Preston North End in
November 1987 afforded more opportunities,
and in the season that Sunderland won the
Third Division title, Mooney played in both
home and away fixtures against The Lads
scoring in the 2-2 draw at Deepdale in
February 1988. Three years on his transfer to
Roker Park cost £225,000, and whilst his debut
coincided with a rare League victory (one of
only eight during the season), Brian failed to
hold down a first team place during his two
years at Roker Park. He was released on a free
transfer in May 1993, and is believed to have
later returned to Irish football.

Appearances:
FL: 21(6) apps. 1 gl.
FAC: 2 apps. 0 gls.
Total: *23(6) apps. 1 gl.*
Honours:
Eire Yth/Eire 'B'/1 Eire U-21 app./
3 Eire U-23 apps.

MOORE, Gary

Role: Centre-forward 1964-67
6'0" 13st.0lbs.
b. Sunderland, 4th November 1945

CAREER: Sunderland Schools/
SUNDERLAND app May 1962, pro Nov 1962/
Grimsby Town Feb 1967 £8,000/Southend
United Nov 1968 £8,000 (Colchester United

Brian Mooney

Gary Moore

loan Mar 1974)/Chester Aug 1974 £6,000/
Swansea City July 1976-1978.

Debut v Wolverhampton Wanderers (a) 20/4/1965

Strapping strike forward Gary Moore began
his career at Roker Park, but spent the rest of it
in the lower divisions. He had been selected
for special FA coaching in 1963 but his
progress received a setback when injured in
the 1963/64 season and having to undergo a
cartilage operation. It is rare, thank goodness,
that a teenage player has to cope with this
particular surgery. Gary's longest club spell
with Southend produced a record of 156
League appearances plus six substitutions, 46
goals. After leaving senior football, Gary was
employed as a representative of a
pharmaceutical company for more than 17
years. In 1988 he became Blyth Spartans coach
for a time.

Appearances:
FL: 13 apps. 2 gls.
FAC: 1 app. 0 gls.
Total: *14 apps. 2 gls.*

MOORE, John

Role: Forward 1984-88
6'0" 11st.11lbs.
*b. Consett, Co Durham,
1st October 1966*

CAREER: Blackhall
Juniors/SUNDERLAND
app May 1983, pro Oct
1984(St Patrick Athletic loan Jan 1985)
(Newport County loan Dec 1985)(Darlington
loan Nov 1986)(Mansfield Town loan Mar
1987)(Rochdale loan Jan 1988)/Hull City June
1988(Sheffield United loan Mar 1989)/
FC Utrecht, Netherlands cs 1989/Shrewsbury
Town July 1990/Crewe Alexandra n.c. Jan
1991/FC Utrecht, Netherlands Mar 1991/
Scarborough Aug 1991-Apr 1992.

Debut v Chelsea (h) 30/3/1985 (sub)

John Moore

John Moore made his first appearance in the
week following Sunderland's defeat in the
League Cup final in 1985. In addition to his
debut he made three full appearances in
Division One, following Colin West's transfer
to Watford. Moore's only League goal was a
timely winner at Coventry City, but it was his,
and the team's, final success of the season.
Without a victory in the final seven matches

Sunderland fell through the relegation
trapdoor. Playing in the reserves in the
following season, he scored a 13-minute hat-
trick against Stoke City Reserves after coming
on as a second-half substitute. Sadly, despite
his toughness and aggression on the pitch, he
was unable to reproduce such fireworks at
senior level. He joined Hull City for £25,000
but failed to settle and, following a loan spell
at Sheffield United where he played in
midfield, made the first of his moves to FC
Utrecht for £30,000 in the close season of 1989.
Despite being associated with a dozen clubs at
home and abroad, including six on loan, his
aggregate League career was modest in the
extreme, totalling 70 appearances and eight
goals.

Appearances:
FL: 4(11) apps. 1 gl.
FLC: 1 app. 0 gls.
Other: 1(1) apps. 2 gls.
Total: *6(12) apps. 3 gls.*

MOORE, Malcolm

Role: Centre-forward 1967-69
5'10" 11st.0lbs.
b. Silksworth, Co Durham, 18th December 1948

CAREER: Dawdon Juniors/SUNDERLAND
Dec 1965 (Crewe Alexandra loan Mar 1970)/
Tranmere Rovers June 1970/Hartlepool Aug
1973/Workington Aug 1976-1977.

Debut v West Bromwich Albion (a) 2/4/1968

Rather strangely Sunderland fielded a couple
of locally recruited centre-forwards named

Moore in quick
succession during
the 1960s. Malcolm,
second and younger,
had led the attack in
the club's FA Youth
Cup-winning side of
1967, midway
through a near-five
year stay at Roker
Park. Like Gary
Moore he spent the
remainder of his
Football League
seasons in the lower
reaches. Malcolm
was usually first
choice with these

Malcolm Moore

clubs and, including his Sunderland figures, finished with a grand total of 250 League appearances plus 12 substitutions, in which he netted 60 goals.

Appearances:
FL: 10(2) apps. 3 gls.
Total: *10(2) apps. 3 gls.*

MOORE, William Grey Bruce

Role: Inside-left 1913-22
5'7" 10st.7lbs.
b. Newcastle upon Tyne, 6th October 1894
d. Plaistow, London, 26th September 1968

CAREER: Seaton Delaval/SUNDERLAND am Nov 1912, pro Aug 1914/West Ham United May 1922, retired cs 1929 and became the club's assistant trainer and then head trainer 1932 until his retirement in May 1960.

Debut v Sheffield United (a) 7/2/1914

Billy Moore

Billy Moore is remembered especially for his extraordinary length of continuous service to West Ham United: 38 seasons. But he had earlier been on Sunderland's books for a decade and is listed as their player in the roll-call of English amateur internationalists. Indeed, he scored twice on his amateur international debut in Brussels as England beat Belgium 8-1. Billy always shone as a neat provider of chances for fellow forwards while not neglecting to score himself when opportunity arose. His post-war link-up at West Ham with the England caps, Vic Watson and Jimmy Ruffell, was famous. In the Upton Park club's glamour 1922/23 season, when promotion to Division One and a first Wembley Cup final place were attained, he was an ever-present in both League and Cup, a run of 51 matches.

Appearances:
FL: 45 apps. 11 gls.
FAC: 1 app. 0 gls.
Total: *46 apps. 11 gls.*
Honours:
1 Eng cap v Sweden 1923/4 Eng am apps./(West Ham United) FAC finalist 1923

MORDUE, John

Role: Winger 1908-20
5'7" 11st.2lbs.
b. Edmondsley, Co Durham, 13th December 1886
d. Sunderland, 5th March 1938

CAREER: Sacriston FC/Spennymoor United/Barnsley Oct 1906/Woolwich Arsenal Apr 1907 £450/SUNDERLAND May 1908 £750/Middlesbrough May 1920/Hartlepools United May 1922/Durham City player-manager Feb 1923-Feb 1924/Ryhope Dec 1924.

Debut v Middlesbrough (a) 9/9/1908 (scored)

Mordue is a well-known footballing name in the North-East and Jackie is possibly its most distinguished bearer. A finely-tuned wingman of great pace with admirable accuracy of distribution and an eye for goal, Jackie's finest period was spent at Roker Park. He was the right-wing member of the famous Frank

Jackie Mordue

Cuggy/Mordue/Charlie Buchan triangle that set the critics drooling in pre-Great War seasons, the trio's intricate play a joy to behold. Jackie's goal tally was helped by his outstanding success from the penalty spot. He is arguably the only man in Sunderland's history to rival Gary Rowell and didn't miss from the spot until his 34th penalty - a quite remarkable effort in an era when goalkeepers were permitted to charge off their line. In his first season at Roker Jackie was one of the scorers in the stunning 9-1 win at Newcastle in December 1908 and he enjoyed another memorable day on Tyneside during the successful 1912/13 campaign when he scored twice in an FA Cup quarter-final replay. During 1912 he was capped twice by England, on one occasion partnering his talented team mate Charlie Buchan. Brother-in-law of James Ashcroft, the Woolwich Arsenal and England goalkeeper, it seems not unlikely the relationship was at least a factor in Jackie's move to the south in 1907. And the fact he became a world class Fives player makes an unusual bracketing of excellence in markedly contrasting sports.

Appearances:
FL: 266 apps. 73 gls.
FAC: 33 apps. 10 gls.
Total: *299 apps. 83 gls.*
Honours:
2 Eng caps/3 FL apps./(Sunderland) FL champs 1913/FAC finalist 1913.

MORGAN, Hugh

Role: Forward 1896-99
b. Lanarkshire, circa 1876

CAREER: Harthill
Thistle/Airdrieonians
Aug 1896/
SUNDERLAND Dec
1896/Bolton Wanderers
Feb 1899 £200/Newton Heath Dec 1900/
Manchester City Aug 1901/Accrington Stanley
July 1902/Blackpool May 1904-June 1905
when he left the first class game to join North
Wingfield St Lawrence (Derbyshire).

Hugh Morgan

Debut v Everton (a) 26/12/1896

Hugh Morgan appeared in four different attack positions but throughout his first-class career chiefly favoured outside-right or centre-forward. Hugh's was an up and down life, the 'ups' occurring when at Roker Park (" ... did much good work," said a 1903 observer) and at Bolton. Before this the *Athletic News* in 1901 reported "he is undoubtedly clever and can shoot well, but he lacks weight for First Division football." Morgan's high spots were in 1897/98 when Sunderland finished Division One runners-up, and 1899/1900 with Bolton winning promotion. As against these he sampled relegation blues with Bolton and Manchester City.

Appearances:
FL: 57 apps. 16 gls.
FAC: 3 apps. 1 gl.
Total: *60 apps. 17 gls.*

MORLEY, Jonathan Bell

Role: Outside-right 1907-08
5'9" 10st.9lbs.
b. Carlisle, 1883
d. Coalville, Leics,
26th October 1957

CAREER: Workington
Mar 1905/
SUNDERLAND May
1907/Burnley June
1908/Preston North
End Dec 1912-1915.

Debut v Aston Villa (a)
9/9/1907

Jonathan Morley

Jonathan Morley was a winger of willowy build who earned a big reputation in Lancashire after leaving Roker Park. For Burnley he totalled 96 League appearances (15 goals) and for Preston 75 (15 goals). The 1913/14 edition of *The Lancashire Daily Post Handbook* contains a eulogistic account of the player. " ... a master of mazy footwork ... one of the three cleverest outside-rights in England. Can do more in a yard of space than more men in half the field. Can shoot too, as a hat-trick proved at Glossop last year. Burnley people still wonder why such fine judges as the Turf Moor directors let him go." In North End's 1912/13 championship team Morley partnered the old Sunderland favourite, Alf Common.

Appearances:
FL: 5 apps. 1 gl.
Total: *5 apps. 1 gl.*
Honours:
(Preston North End) Div 2 champs 1913.

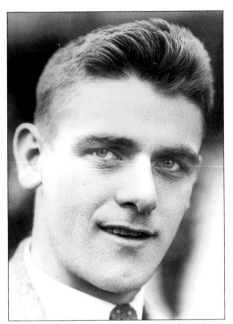

Sam Morris

MORRIS, Samuel Walker

Role: Right-half 1928-32
5'11' 11st.7lbs.
b. Prescot, Lancs., 16th April 1907
d. Nuneaton, Warwicks., 10th August 1991

CAREER: Prescot Cables/SUNDERLAND
Nov 1928/Charlton Athletic Sept 1932 £800/
Chester Oct 1933 £125/Bath City July 1935.

Debut v Arsenal (h) 1/1/1929

Sam Morris enjoyed a memorable debut when
Sunderland vanquished a Herbert Chapman
Arsenal side on New Year's Day 1929 by five
goals to one. Sam, collected and competent,
had a much greater run of top flight football at
Roker Park than he did with Charlton and
Chester in lower divisions. Indeed he was first
choice in 1931/32 (28 appearances) and played
in 19 in his final (1931/32) campaign. At
Charlton he had a dozen Second Division
outings and with Chester, of the Northern
Section, only five. He left the League scene
aged only 28.

> **Appearances:**
> *FL: 59 apps. 0 gls.*
> *FAC: 6 apps. 0 gls.*
> **Total:** *65 apps. 0 gls.*

MORRISON, Evelyn S.

Role: Centre-forward 1929-31
5'10" 11st.0lbs.
b. Wishaw, Lanarks.

CAREER: Hamilton Academy/Moorpark
Amateurs, Renfew(Motherwell trial)/
Stenhousemuir June 1927/Falkirk Jan 1928/
SUNDERLAND Nov 1929 £6,500/Partick
Thistle May 1931-cs 1932 £1,250, retired Oct
1932.

Debut v Grimsby Town (a) 23/11/1929

Evelyn Morrison started a remarkably prolific
scoring career at his school, Hamilton
Academy, alongside his brother, where they
won the Scottish Schools Under-16 Shield.
Junior Moorpark Amateurs were also
successful in Morrison's time, winning the
Scottish Amateur League and the West of
Scotland Amateur Cup with his personal
contribution a massive 150 goals in two
seasons. This kind of performance attracted
Scottish League scouts plus overtures from
Burnley and a trial with Motherwell. But to
Evelyn, soccer came a poor second to his
burgeoning business career, which concerned
the manufacture of briquettes (blocks of small
coal or compressed coal dust) in Shotts,
Lanarkshire. The player did, however,
eventually sign for Stenhousemuir. The
Scottish Second Division presented no
problems for such "a speedy, powerful
opportunist" who scored 30 goals in 23
appearances. The offer of a four-figure fee
from Falkirk elevated him to the Scottish top-
flight and he remained a scoring machine in
the higher grade, known and 'knighted' by
adoring Brockville fans as "Sir Evelyn". His
record speaks for itself: 75 goals in 58 League
matches. And in seasons 1928/29 Morrison
netted 29 in 16 consecutive league matches
between November 1928 and February 1929,
which may well constitute a first-class record.
Such marksmanship encouraged Sunderland
to expend a then extremely high fee. Morrison
was unwilling to cross the border, with only
the best endeavours of persuasive manager
Johnny Cochrane clinching the deal. There
were conditions, however. Morrison, business
interests uppermost, insisted on training in
Scotland, meeting his new team mates only on
match days. The arrangement did not work
and he played only 17 first team games for
The Lads. These produced a respectable seven

Evelyn Morrison

John Morrison

goals for Morrison but nothing approaching the fecundity of his Scottish League days. So Sunderland cut their losses, taking a much reduced fee from Partick Thistle. Morrison found no great success at Firhill either although, again, the figures were very respectable - 15 goals in 15 League outings. Leaving at the end of a single season and briefly courted by his old friends at Falkirk, Morrison hung up his boots, doubtless happy to return to his business activities on a full-time basis.

Appearances:
FL: 15 apps. 7 gls.
FAC: 1 app. 0 gls.
Total: *16 apps. 7 gls.*

MORRISON,
John Stanton Fleming

Role: Left-back 1919-20
b. Newcastle upon Tyne, 17th April 1892
d. Farnham, Surrey, 28th January 1961

CAREER: Charterhouse School/Cambridge University (Blue 1913, 1914 & 1920)/Corinthians in season 1912-13 and seasons

1919-20 to 1924-25 incl/Old Carthusians. Jarrow FC June 1913/SUNDERLAND am Dec 1919.

Debut v Sheffield Wednesday (a) 13/12/1919

John Morrison was an amateur of many parts evidenced by the fact he was a triple Blue - at soccer, cricket and golf. The latter honour must have had at least some bearing on him later becoming a noted designer of golf courses. Morrison captained the Corinthians during the 1920s when this famous amateur club, with its playing personnel consisting mainly of Oxford and Cambridge Blues, could call on several full internationalists. F.N.S. Creek in his authoritative *History of Corinthian Football Club* (Longmans 1933) says that John Morrison " ... was undeniably heavy and ponderous, yet he was a fine player on anything but hard or frozen grounds. He was remarkably fit for a big man who broke most of the accepted rules of training". He made four appearances for the Corinthians in 1912/13 and 70 from 1919/20 to 1924/25 inclusive, scoring one goal. Helping out Sunderland in a crisis in December 1919 he arrived for one game only to partner Bert Hobson at the back in a 2-0 victory. At cricket (a right-handed, mid-order batsman/wicket-keeper) he assisted Northumberland 1913-21 as well as Cambridge University and had one game for Somerset in 1920. His highest score was 233 not out for Cambridge University against the MCC at Cambridge in 1914. His last first-class match was for the Combined Universities in 1922.

Appearances:
FL: 1 app. 0 gls.
Total: *1 app. 0 gls.*
Honours:
1 Eng am app. v Wales 1920/Camb Blue (3 seasons).

MORRISON, Thomas Kelly

Role: Right-back 1935-36
5'9" 11st.0lbs.
b. Kilmarnock, 21st July 1904

CAREER: Troon Athletic/St Mirren Sept 1924/Liverpool Nov 1927 £4,000/SUNDERLAND Nov 1935-cs 1936, in 1936/37 assisting a village side (Gamlingay FC, Beds) until joining Ayr United June 1937/Drumcondra coach Aug 1939.

Debut v Preston North End (h) 9/11/1935

A strange but rewarding end to a first-class career in England. Tom, after nearly nine years

at Anfield, came to Sunderland and, hitherto a right-half, promptly won a League championship medal at right-back. He shared the right-back appearances equally with Bill Murray, both players registering 21. He had been in top grade football for some twelve years, a crisp tackling, constructive wing-half with a fine degree of consistency. Morrison made 132 Scottish League appearances for St Mirren and 240 in the Football League First Division in Liverpool's cause. He made no League appearances for Ayr United.

Appearances:
FL: 21 apps. 0 gls.
FAC: 2 apps. 0 gls.
Total: *23 apps. 0 gls.*
Honours:
1 Scot cap v England 1927/(St Mirren) SC winner 1926/(Sunderland) FL champs 1936.

MORRISON, William

Role: Right-half 1954-57
5'8" 10st.11lbs.
b. Edinburgh, 31st March 1934

CAREER: Merchiston Thistle/SUNDERLAND May 1951/Southend United Jan 1958/Bedford Town cs 1961.

Debut v Leicester City (h) 2/4/1955

Tom Morrison

Bill Morrison

Bill Morrison was a reserve right-half, recruited at age 17 and nursed for four years until making his League bow at 21. He proved a sound performer, making the bulk of his senior appearances (13) in season 1956/57. Morrison's time at Roker coincided with Stan Anderson's heyday so chances were limited. He did useful work for Southend, playing in 60 Third Division games and one FA Cup-tie.

Appearances:
FL: 19 apps. 0 gls.
Total: *19 apps. 0 gls.*

MULHALL, George

Role: Outside-left 1962-69
5'8" 10st.11lbs.
b. Standburn, Stirling, 8th May 1936

CAREER: Denny YMCA/Kilsyth Rangers/ Aberdeen cs 1953/SUNDERLAND Sept 1962 £23,000/Cape Town City, South Africa player-coach June 1969/Halifax Town trainer-coach Oct 1971, manager June 1972-Sept 1974/Bolton Wanderers chief coach Oct 1974/Bradford City manager Mar 1978/Bolton Wanderers asst. manager Mar 1981, manager June 1981-June 1982/Ipswich Town scout/Tranmere Rovers asst. manager July 1985-Feb 1987/ Huddersfield Town coach 1990, asst. manager 1992/Halifax Town manager 1997, Director of Football Aug 1998.

Debut v Rotherham United (a) 11/9/1962

George Mulhall was signed by manager Alan Brown for promotion-chasing Sunderland in the face of opposition from other top clubs. He was an experienced performer and had been a paid player from the age of 15, when he joined the well known junior club, Kilsyth Rangers. He moved into the big time two years later, signing for Aberdeen. The Pittodrie club had entered a vintage period (Scottish League champions in 1955 and four times Scottish Cup and League Cup finalists during the years 1953-59, lifting the League trophy in 1956). But George took little part in these triumphs, the Dons' regular left-winger of the time, Jackie Hather, a flying Englishman, then at his peak. George eventually took over in season 1959/60, and recorded 42 goals in 150 Scottish League and Cup matches. He won his first cap in that initial season as a senior player, the other two when at Roker. Oddly all six of his representative honours were against

George Mulhall

Irish opposition: the three internationals versus Northern Ireland while, for the Scottish League, he played twice against the League of Ireland and once against the Irish League. Two of these further honours were earned when a Sunderland player. George's two years' National Service occurred when at Aberdeen and were enlivened by Army football in company with other present and future Scotland internationalists such as the late John White, Alex Young and Alex Scott. During his Army service he also took up basketball and played in a team containing four basketball internationals which won the British Army championship. In 1962/63 George joined a Sunderland side, in which Brian Clough had scored 24 goals before the Christmas injury that ended his career and was pressing for a return to Division One. Direct in style, George possessed a fair turn of speed and an eye for goal scoring chances. He quickly formed a fine left-wing understanding with Northern Ireland cap, Johnny Crossan, as Sunderland narrowly missed out, but both made a substantial contribution to the promotion winning side of 1964. After seven great years at Roker, Mulhall's aquisition of honours did not end when he left British football: he starred in a Cape Town City side that won the South African league and cup. His career after leaving the playing arena has been long and varied. The high spots came at Bradford City (narrowly missing promotion in 1980) and saving Bolton Wanders from relegation in 1981 when Burnden Park was experiencing troublesome times. Bolton has been the venue for several of his administrative roles. The same point may be made as regards Halifax Town, where he has worked in several different capacities. In season 1997-98 George guided Halifax to the championship of the Vauxhall Conference, thus restoring their League status lost in 1993 and was recently awarded a testimonial match by the club against Sunderland at The Shay in July 1999 for his significant contribution towards their resurrection from non-League football. George's two brothers, Martin and Edward, both played football professionally. The former assisted Falkirk, Albion Rovers, Cowdenbeath and Brechin City. Edward 'stayed at home' playing for East Stirlingshire.

Appearances:
FL: 249(4) apps. 55 gls.
FAC: 19 apps. 5 gls.
FLC: 16(1) apps. 6 gls.
Total: *284(5) apps. 66 gls.*
Honours:
3 Scot caps/3 SL apps.

MULLIN, John

Role: Midfield/Forward 1995-99
6'0" 11st.5lbs.
b. Bury, 11th August 1975

CAREER: Burnley Schoolboys/Lancashire Schoolboys(trials with Manchester United and Blackburn Rovers)/Burnley assoc s'boy Mar 1990, pro Aug 1992/SUNDERLAND Aug 1995 (Preston North End loan Feb 1998)(Burnley loan Mar 1998)/Burnley June 1999.

Debut v Wolverhampton Wanderers (h) 26/8/1995 (sub)

John Mullin joined Sunderland as a promising, strong-running striker in a tribunal-set £40,000 deal in August 1995, with the fee rising in stages to £210,000 based on appearances. He made a bright start, scoring on his second full appearance in a 2-1 win at Luton Town.

Subsequently a catalogue of injuries restricted his opportunities. This factor, and the outstanding form of the senior strikeforce, combined to keep him on the fringe of the League side, although he scored in a memorable 2-1 Premiership win over Manchester United in March 1997 and also netted the last ever goal at Roker Park in May that year as Liverpool graced the 'Farewell to Roker' match. A switch to a central midfield role in the Reserves in 1997-98 proved successful, and his chance came early the following season when injuries to Lee Clark and Alex Rae gave John an extended first team run. His form was quite exceptional, particularly in a 2-0 win at Ipswich, where he opened the scoring and won the Sky TV Man of the Match award. Sadly, a groin injury sustained at Crewe in early November 1998

John Mullin

halted his progress. A rest period failed to cure the problem which eventually required surgery. After a four-month absence, John returned to Reserve team action in March and, although released by Sunderland at the season's close, was a scorer in the emphatic 4-1 victory against Derby County Reserves which secured the Pontins League Premier Division championship.

Appearances:
FL: 13(6) apps. 3 gls.
FAC: 0(1) apps. 0 gls.
FLC: 5(1) apps. 0 gls.
Total: *18(8) apps. 3 gls.*

MUNRO, Alexander Iain Fordyce

Role: Full-back 1981-84
5'8" 11st.8lbs.
b. Uddingston, Lanarkshire, 24th August 1951

CAREER: Drumchapel Amateurs/St Mirren 1968/Hibernian May 1973/Rangers 1976/St Mirren Nov 1977/Stoke City Oct 1980/SUNDERLAND Aug 1981/Dundee United Mar 1984/Hibernian Apr 1985/Dunfermline coach, manager 1989/Dundee coach/Hamilton Academical manager June 1992/Raith Rovers manager Sept 1996-Apr 1997/Ayr United coach 1997.

Debut v Ipswich Town (a) 29/8/1981

A committed Scottish international full-back, tough-tackling Iain Munro followed manager Alan Durban from Stoke City to Sunderland for £150,000 in August 1981. The 30-year-old defender was a polished enough performer with plenty of class and a fine positional sense, but is recalled by many Roker fans for his fearsome tackling. One observer considered him the "hardest player to appear for Sunderland for 30 years". A regular for two seasons, both of which saw Sunderland fighting to avoid relegation, Iain Munro lost his place early in 1983-84 and returned to Scotland where he subsequently moved into coaching and management.

Appearances:
FL: 80 apps. 0 gls.
FAC: 1 app. 0 gls.
FLC: 7 apps. 0 gls.
Total: *88 apps. 0 gls.*
Honours:
Scot Yth/7 Scot caps 1979-80/(Hibernian)
SLC finalist 1975, 1986.

MURDOCK, D.D.

Role: Inside-right 1885/86
Debut v Redcar (a) 24/10/1885 (FAC)

So far as is known Murdock played only twice for Sunderland in 1885/86: the above Cup-tie and the season's opening match. He was at inside-right on that occasion also, distinguishing himself by scoring two goals in a handsome 4-0 home win over North-Eastern FC on October 3, 1885.

Appearances:
FAC: 1 app. 0 gls.
Total: *1 app. 0 gls.*

Iain Munro

MURRAY, James Gerald

Role: Full-back 1983-84
5'9" 10st.12lbs.
b. Glasgow, 27th December 1958

Jamie Murray

CAREER: Rivet Sports/Cambridge United
Sept 1976(SUNDERLAND loan Mar 1984)/
Brentford July 1984/Cambridge United Sept
1987.

Debut v Tottenham Hotspur (h) 7/4/1984

Jamie Murray made his initial League
appearance, as a 17-year-old substitute, for
Cambridge United in their 1976-77 Division
Four championship campaign. It was his only
senior outing during that term, but he
appeared in 20 matches in the following
season, when Cambridge again won
promotion, as runners-up to Wrexham for the
Third Division championship. His loan to
Sunderland came after he had completed over
200 League appearances for Cambridge, but
he was injured during his single outing in
Division One for Sunderland, a 1-1 draw with
Spurs at Roker Park, and despite an otherwise
good impression, it did not lead to a
permanent engagement. In the close season he
left Cambridge for the first time and spent the
next three seasons at Brentford, totalling 134
League appearances, before returning for a
final spell at the Abbey Stadium. Aside from
his debut season, when he played just once,
Jamie Murray completed a further 363 League
appearances in eleven seasons, figures which
reflect his consistency of form and fitness.

> **Appearances:**
> *FL: 1 app. 0 gls.*
> **Total:** *1 app. 0 gls.*

MURRAY, John Winning

Role: Wing-half 1890-92
6'0" 13st.0lbs.
b. Strathblane, Stirlings., 24th April 1865
d. Accrington, 16th September 1922

CAREER: Wanderers FC/Vale of Leven/
SUNDERLAND Sept 1890/Blackburn Rovers
May 1892/retired Apr 1896.

Debut v Burnley (a) 27/9/1890

A doughty Scot with a daunting physique,
John Murray was also to be found at left-back.
His bulk was no deterrent to mobility,

however - a contemporary
Scottish critic reckoned him to
be " ... one of the best runners
and jumpers in the country".
And he was enthusiastic and
quite reliable. Murray's
retirement came about through

John Murray

the demands of his employment
in the calico printing trade, a calling he
followed all his working life. His son, Robert
W. Murray, also assisted Blackburn Rovers
(1909-11).

> **Appearances:**
> *FL: 38 apps. 1 gl.*
> *FAC: 10 apps. 0 gls.*
> **Total:** *48 apps. 1 gl.*
> **Honours:**
> *1 Scot cap v Wales 1890/(Vale of Leven) SC
> finalist 1890/(Sunderland) FL champs 1892.*

MURRAY, William B.

Role: Outside-left 1901-03
5'6" 11st.7lbs.
b. Forres, Morayshire, 1883

CAREER: Forres FC/Inverness/
SUNDERLAND Aug 1901/Northampton
Town cs 1903/Tottenham Hotspur May 1904/
Leeds City May 1906-1907.

Debut v Grimsby Town (h) 22/3/1902 (scored)

Willie Murray received a
goodly senior baptism in
1901/02, playing in seven
of the final eight League
fixtures of that season. It
would have been
especially beneficial too
as the Rokerites won the
championship and

Willie Murray

Willie's forward
colleagues included
luminaries such as Jimmy Millar and Billy
Hogg. That Willie responded is illustrated by
his selection for the Anglo-Scots against the
Home Scots in a Scotland trial. He had a
season of first team football at Northampton
in 1903/04 (27 Southern League outings) but
at Tottenham and Leeds acted mainly as a
reserve (21 Southern and eight Football
League appearances respectively).

> **Appearances:**
> *FL: 8 apps. 2 gls.*
> **Total:** *8 apps. 2 gls.*

MURRAY, William

Role: Right-back 1927-36
5'9" 11st.7lbs.
b. Aberdeen, 10th March 1901
d. Aberdeen, 14th December 1961

CAREER: Halls Russell's FC, Aberdeen
(Aberdeen FC amateur)/Cowdenbeath *
Sept 1921/SUNDERLAND Apr 1927 £8,000
incl David Wright/St Mirren Jan 1937/
retired Apr 1939 on appointment as
SUNDERLAND manager, an appointment
held until June 1957.
* *One source says he actually joined
Cowdenbeath on demobilisation from the Army
in Dec 1919.*

Debut v West Ham United (a) 1/9/1927

In the matter of lengthy service to
Sunderland Football Club few can match
Bill Murray, or indeed are ever likely to in
these later days of short and often
summarily terminated managerial
engagements. The combined sum of his
time on the playing staff and behind the
manager's desk amounted to 28 years.
Bill's senior playing career is neatly
bracketed between the two world wars. As
a teenager he served with the Gordon
Highlanders and, after demobilisation in
December 1919, cherished ambitions to
become a qualified mining engineer which
would have enabled him to take up an
appointment with a Shanghai shipping
firm. A promising footballer, several clubs
coveted his services, with Cowdenbeath his
eventual choice as the best prospect for
carrying on his professional studies.
However the lure of football proved so
strong all alternative career ideas were
abandoned. The Cowdenbeath club proved
ideal for an ambitions youngster and Bill
developed into a stylish full-back, unruffled
and highly consistent. He was also blessed
with remarkable freedom from injury. It has
been estimated he appeared in upwards of
600 senior games. This is quite feasible as
he made 490 appearances in the Football
and Scottish League First Divisions, plus
those for Cowdenbeath before he captained
them to promotion in 1924, and all the cup-
ties too. Murray arrived at Roker Park as a

seasoned defender aged 26. Sunderland
was a leading club usually in the top half of
the First Division and Bill soon fitted into a
defence whose other durable members
included Albert McInroy in goal and Ernie
England at left-back. In the course of time
Jimmy Thorpe took over in goal and Alex
Hall at left-back, and it was this defence -
Thorpe, Murray and Hall - that helped
attain runners-up and champions' slots in
successive seasons, 1934/35 and 1935/36.
Bill accordingly won a championship
medal in his last full season at Roker. But
some had reservations. A local football
annual for 1936/37 thought "the back
division conceded more goals than a
championship defence ought to". They
perhaps had a valid point: way down the
table in 13th position Bolton Wanderers
were the next club to ship in a greater
number of goals against. Anyway, James
Gorman of Blackburn Rovers was duly
signed in January 1937 as Bill Murray
transferred to St Mirren. Despite
approaching his 36th birthday, Bill was still
not quite a back number. He played 75
Scottish League games for the Paisley club
before hanging up his boots two years later.
He soon returned to Sunderland as
manager Johnny Cochrane's successor. It
was to be a long 18-year stint with the
seven-year war period as its prelude. When
peace returned Bill evolved accomplished
sides that lacked nothing in crowd-pulling
personalities - Len Shackleton was a prime
example. Of his eleven post-war seasons six
finishes were in Division One's top half, the
best in 1949/50 (third). And the Wearsiders
also reached the FA Cup semi-finals in 1955
and '56. The parting of the ways was a sad
affair. A League commission found the club
had made illegal payments to some
players. In April 1957 Directors were either
permanently suspended or suspended sine
die and the club heavily fined. Bill Murray
resigned the following June.

Appearances:
FL: 304 apps. 0 gls.
FAC: 24 apps. 0 gls.
Total: *328 apps. 0 gls.*
Honours:
(Sunderland) FL champs 1936.

McALLISTER, Alexander

Role: Centre-half 1896-1904
5'7" 12st.0lbs.
b. Kilmarnock, circa 1878
d. France, late February 1918

CAREER: Dean Park (Kilmarnock)/
Carrington Vale/Kilmarnock FC 1896/
SUNDERLAND Dec 1896/Derby
County June 1904/Oldham
Athletic cs 1905-1906/
Spennymoor United
July 1909.

Debut v Stoke (h)
20/2/1897

Sandy McAllister
was a one-time coal
miner who became a
pillar of Sunderland's
defence in the late 1890s.
Of only moderate height but heavily
built and strong he (as an early scribe
wrote in 1902) "won his spurs in the
(1896/97) Test Matches which he has
worn ever since with great success."
Sandy stayed at Derby only a season (24
League appearances) and ended his
senior career there. At Oldham, then
non-League, he was an ever-present in
1906/07, playing in 38 Lancashire
Combination matches (eight goals) plus
five FA Cup-ties (two goals). McAllister
had no first team outings with Killie so
it was Sunderland who introduced him
to senior football. He played in the first
game at Roker Park and tangible reward
for his loyal service was a championship
medal as Sunderland took the title in
1902. Obviously very popular at the
club: the Roker fans presented him with
a piano and gold watch when he scored
his first goal for them! Sandy died of
food poisoning whilst serving as a
private with the Northumberland
Fusiliers.

Appearances:
FL: 215 apps. 5 gls.
FAC: 10 apps. 0 gls.
Total: *225 apps. 5 gls.*
Honours:
(Sunderland) FL champs 1902.

McCALLUM, Donald

Role: Full-back 1904-05
b. Scotland, circa 1880

CAREER: Strathclyde/Queen's Park cs 1900/
Liverpool June 1901/Morton May 1903/
SUNDERLAND May 1904/Middlesbrough
Dec 1904/Port Glasgow Athletic Dec 1905/
Kilmarnock May 1906/Renton July 1908/
Lochgelly United May 1909/East Fife/Mid-
Rhondda Aug 1913/East Fife Aug 1914.

Debut v Aston Villa (a) 1/10/1904

Donald McCallum appeared on both flanks as
a full-back in his three League games with
Sunderland, on the left in the above debut and
on the right for the others. Right-back was his
usual berth throughout a wandering career.
He first sampled English football with a
couple of League appearances with Liverpool.
He had 25 for Middlesbrough plus a couple in
the FA Cup, and 25 with Killie up in Scotland.
Strong in his tackling and kicking, Donald was
under consideration for a cap appearing in a
Home Scots versus Anglo-Scottish
international trial.

Appearances:
FL: 3 apps. 0 gls.
Total: *3 apps. 0 gls.*

McCANN, Gavin Peter

Role: Midfield 1998-date
5'11" 11st.0lbs.
b. Blackpool, 10th January 1978

CAREER: Blackpool schoolboys/FA National
School of Excellence, Lilleshall/Everton
trainee July 1993, pro July 1995/
SUNDERLAND Nov 1998-date

Debut v Sheffield United (a) 28/11/1998 (sub)

Recruited by manager Peter Reid from his old
club, Everton, Gavin McCann was given his
first League outing with the Toffees by
manager Howard Kendall in September 1997.
His season, however, was marred by ankle
and leg injuries which restricted his Premier
League outings to five, plus six as substitute.
In the following season, new manager Walter
Smith brought in experienced midfielders John
Collins and Olivier Dacourt , and this factor
plus the strained financial climate at Goodison
Park led to Gavin's £500,000 move to the

Gavin McCann

Ally McCoist

Stadium of Light. Despite limited initial opportunities he has impressed in midfield with his all-round skills in tackling, covering, and an ability to use the ball constructively. He made his debut, as a substitute, in the outstanding 4-0 victory at Sheffield United, and opened his scoring account with the only goal of the game in the third round FA Cup tie at Lincoln City. With time and no little talent on his side, Gavin is expected to press his claim for a regular place in the Premiership during 1999/2000.

Appearances:
FL: 5(6) apps. 0 gls.
FAC: 1(1) apps. 1 gl.
FLC: 1 app. 1 gl.
Total: *7(7) apps. 2 gls.*

McCOIST, Alistair Murdoch

Role: Forward 1981-83
5'10" 12st.0lbs.
b. Bellshill, Lanarkshire, 24th September 1962

CAREER: Fir Park Boys Club, Motherwell/ St Johnstone on schoolboy forms, pro Aug 1978/SUNDERLAND Aug 1981/Rangers June 1983-May 1998/Kilmarnock Aug 1998.

Debut v Ipswich Town (a) 29/8/1981 (sub)

Ally McCoist made his debut for St Johnstone as a 16-year-old midfielder but when moved to a forward role his 23 goals in season 1980-81 soon had the scouts flocking to Muirton Park. He earned the Saints a record fee of

£400,000 when he signed for Sunderland in August 1981. Rangers, Wolves and Middlesbrough were among the disappointed clubs when new manager Alan Durban was successful in bringing the 19-year-old Scot to Roker Park. McCoist had quit his job with the Overseas Development Office to become a full-time professional, and he found the adjustment difficult. During his first season at Roker he scored only twice in League matches from 19 starting appearances and nine as substitute. One goal however was a brilliant curled shot past Southampton's Peter Shilton from the edge of the box. From a similar number of starts in 1982-83 he scored six goals but did not manage a League goal after October, during which month he had given a glimpse of things to come by netting in each of four consecutive League matches. The fans loved him and it was a mutual affair. The chants of 'Ally, Ally' were never far away, while McCoist has gone on record describing Sunderland's supporters as "the world's best". It was not until his cut-price (£180,000) transfer to Rangers in June 1983 that he developed into the goal machine who in 1998 passed the milestone of 250 goals for Rangers, winning countless club and international honours along the way. Outside of the game, the multi-talented McCoist, who is married to a Sunderland girl, has made videos, records, written a best-selling book and is a regular team captain on the popular BBC television quiz show *A Question of Sport*. The pressure of increasing media work and a persistent calf injury provoked some speculation regarding Ally's future in the game, but at the time of writing he looked set to remain with Kilmarnock for at least one more season.

Appearances:
FL: 38(18) apps. 8 gls.
FAC: 3(1) apps. 0 gls.
FLC: 5 apps. 1 gl.
Total: *46(19) apps. 9 gls.*
Honours:
(Scot Yth/1 Scot U-21 app.1984/58 Scot caps 1986-97/(Rangers) SL champs 1987, 1989, 1990, 1991, 1992, 1993, 1994, 1995, 1996, 1997/SC winners 1992/SC finalist 1989, 1990, 1994, 1998/SLC winners 1984, 1985, 1987, 1988, 1989, 1991, 1993, 1994, 1997.

McCOLL, Don

Role: Outside-right 1884-85
Debut v Redcar (a) 8/11/1884 (FAC) (scored)

Don McColl scored Sunderland's only goal in the club's first FA Cup-tie, which was lost 3-1. So he had the distinction of being Sunderland's first Cup goal scorer. He was not a regular player but later in the season appeared as goalkeeper - and conceded eleven! - (against Port Glasgow on January 3, 1885). They certainly were versatile in those far-off pioneering days!

Appearances:
FAC: 1 app. 1 gl.
Total: *1 app. 1 gl.*

McCOMBIE, Andrew

Role: Right-back 1898-1904
5'9" 12st.7lbs.
b. North Leith, Edinburgh, 30th June 1876
d. North Shields, 28th March 1952

CAREER: Inverness Thistle 1893/ SUNDERLAND Dec 1898/Newcastle United Feb 1904 £700, a record/retired Apr 1910 becoming Newcastle's asst trainer, promoted to trainer Jan 1928-cs 1930, general assistant to his retirement in 1950.

Debut v Sheffield Wednesday (a) 18/2/1899

Andy McCombie

A strapping full-back, Andy McCombie was a famous figure at the turn of the century. Although he did not disdain to use his physical advantages McCombie had brains too, and skills in ball manipulation, and he could take the left-back role. He was first choice during his five years with Sunderland, and his move to nearby Newcastle proved controversial, eventually leading to an enquiry by the FA and a suspension for certain Sunderland directors. The case concerned whether a sum of £100 handed to McCombie by the club to start up a business was a gift or a loan. Curiously, McCombie's final goal for Sunderland was on New Year's Day 1904 against Newcastle at Roker. When he returned to Roker as a Magpies man in Christmas 1904 he scored again - an own goal as The Lads won 3-1! In fact, Andy turned out as successful a Newcastle player as he had been at Roker Park, winning more club honours and making 131 League and FA Cup appearances in a Magpie jersey. And he went on to render 40 years service 'behind the scenes' - a quite remarkable spell of duty.

Appearances:
FL: 157 apps. 6 gls.
FAC: 7 apps. 0 gls.
Total: *164 apps. 6 gls.*
Honours:
4 Scot caps/(Sunderland) FL champs 1902/ (Newcastle United) FL champs 1905, 1907/ FAC finalist 1905, 1906.

McCONNELL, James English

Role: Wing-half 1905-08
5'8" 11st.8lbs.
b. Larne, Co Antrim, circa 1885
d. Belfast, 21st June 1928

CAREER: Cliftonville 1903/Glentoran 1904/ SUNDERLAND pro Aug 1905/Sheffield Wednesday Aug 1908/Chelsea Apr 1910 £1,000/South Shields Aug 1912.

Debut v Blackburn Rovers (h) 28/10/1905

A classy stylish Irishman, English McConnell appeared at centre-half in addition to the flank positions. At Sunderland he mostly played left-half. Following two years with Sheffield Wednesday he cost Chelsea a then very high transfer fee, one of several players secured in a

English McConnell

vain attempt to avoid relegation. A cartilage operation in April 1911 effectively ended this Stamford Bridge association. McConnell was selected for Ireland in January 1913 when with non-League South Shields but injury prevented the winning of what would have been his thirteenth cap. His brother, Victor, assisted Cliftonville and Belfast Celtic in pre-WW1 days. At the time of his early demise McConnell was a Belfast businessman.

Appearances:
FL: 39 apps. 0 gls.
FAC: 6 apps. 0 gls.
Total: *45 apps. 0 gls.*
Honours:
12 Irish caps.

McCREADIE, Andrew

Role: Centre-half 1894-96
5'5"
b. Girvan, Ayrshire, 19th November 1870

CAREER: Cowlairs/Rangers 1889-90/ SUNDERLAND May 1894, in exchange for William Gibson/Rangers Mar 1896/Bristol St George's June 1898/Wishaw Thistle Nov 1899.

Debut v Derby County (h) 1/9/1894

In later times it is doubtful whether a man 5 feet 5 inches tall would be even considered for the pivotal role. Back in the nineteenth century, though, Andy McCreadie's presence there would not have raised an eyebrow. Robert Neil of Hibs and Rangers, and also a Scotland cap, for example, at 5

Andy McCreadie

feet 4 inches was even shorter. In any event McCreadie's coolness, tenacity and work rate more than made up for lack of height at a time when Scots carried out, as well as believed, the sound maxim of keeping the ball on the ground. Andy loved to attack too and notched seven goals in the course of the 1895 championship campaign. Brother of Hugh McCreadie (Rangers and Scottish League).

Appearances:
FL: 42 apps. 8 gls.
FAC: 3 apps. 1 gl.
Total: *45 apps. 9 gls.*
Honours:
2 Scot caps/(Rangers) Joint SL champs 1891, SC winner 1894, 1897/(Sunderland) FL champs 1895.

McCULLOUGH, Robert

Role: Inside-right 1911-12

CAREER: Radley FC (Gateshead)/ SUNDERLAND am Sept 1911, signed for South Shields Aug 1913 (his name appears on the Sunderland players' list of 1913/14 but not that of 1914/15).

Debut v Newcastle United (a) 17/2/1912

Bob McCullough was an amateur whose one League appearance is memorable for the fact it was a local derby with the perennial rivals, Newcastle United. The Wearsiders lost 3-1, Harry Low scoring Sunderland's goal from centre-forward, a position he occupied on a number of occasions that term.

Appearances:
FL: 1 app. 0 gls.
Total: *1 app. 0 gls.*

McDERMID

Role: Right-half/inside-right 1888-89
Debut v Elswick Rangers (h) 27/10/1888 (FAC)

McDermid played right-half in the above Cup-tie (a 5-3 win) and at inside-right in the next round, against Newcastle East End at home (a 2-0 win). They scratched from the competition before meeting the next opponents, Sunderland Albion. McDermid played many times for Sunderland that season, particularly in the full-back berth.

Appearances:
FAC: 2 apps. 0 gls.
Total: *2 apps. 0 gls.*

McDONAGH, James M. 'Seamus'

Role: Goalkeeper 1985-86
6'0" 13st.9lbs.
b. Rotherham, 6th October 1952

CAREER: Rotherham United app, pro Oct 1970(Manchester United loan 1972-73)/Bolton Wanderers Aug 1976/Everton July 1980/ Bolton Wanderers Aug 1981/Notts County July 1983(Birmingham City loan Sept 1984) (Gillingham loan Mar 1985)(SUNDERLAND loan Aug 1985)/Wichita Wings, USA, Oct 1985/Scarborough Nov 1987(Huddersfield Town loan Jan 1988)/Charlton Athletic Mar 1988/Galway United, Rep of Ireland, player-manager/Derry City manager to May 1989/ Spalding United July 1989/Grantham Town early 1990/Telford United player-reserve team manager 1990-91/Arnold Town/Ilkeston Town Vet.

Debut v Blackburn Rovers (h) 17/8/1985

One of many transient players during the 1985-86 season - Lawrie McMenemy's first as Sunderland manager - Seamus McDonagh was, in fact, the first of three on-loan

goalkeepers to appear that term. His seven appearances were made consecutively at the beginning of the season, and they coincided with Sunderland's worst-ever start to a campaign which featured five straight defeats followed by two draws. He famously complained in one away game that the crossbar was too high, but not all the blame could be laid at the unfortunate McDonagh's door, as the team failed to score in the opening five fixtures. McDonagh had joined Sunderland on loan from Notts County where he was understudy to Mick Leonard. In a lengthy League career, the Republic of Ireland international most notably served Bolton Wanderers in two separate periods which took in 274 League appearances in his first spell, and in his final season (1982-83) even managed to get on the score sheet, netting in the 3-0 victory against Burnley at Burnden Park in January 1983. Seamus McDonagh played at senior level for nine clubs and totalled 471 League appearances. More recently he has had spells as a goalkeeping

Seamus McDonagh

coach with both Nottingham Forest and Leicester City. He was also employed in the insurance business but more latterly has run pubs in Nottinghamshire.

Appearances:
FL: 7 apps. 0 gls.
Total: *7 apps. 0 gls.*
Honours:
Eng Yth 1971/25 Eire caps 1981-86/ (Bolton Wanderers) Div 2 champs 1978.

McDONALD, J.

J. McDonald

Role: Inside-right/centre-forward 1884-86
Debut v Redcar (a) (FAC) 8/11/1884

McDonald appeared in Sunderland's earliest FA Cup-ties, which were at Redcar a season apart and resulted in defeats of 3-1 and 3-0 respectively. He was at inside-right in the first and centre-forward for the 1885/86 encounter. He played regularly in season 1884/85 occupying every forward position, and scored in the first game at the Abbs Field ground - a 2-0 win over Birtley in September 1884. The previous season he had scored in Sunderland's first ever triumph as Darlington were beaten 2-0 at Birtley in May 1884 in the replay of the Durham FA Challenge Cup final. The first game had been declared void following complaints from Darlington about crowd trouble. In 1885/86 he played centre-forward twice and, as far as is known, this was the extent of his Sunderland involvement.

Appearances:
FAC: 2 apps. 0 gls.
Total: *2 apps. 0 gls.*

McDONALD, Joseph

Role: Left-back 1953-58
5'8" 10st.6lbs.
b. Blantyre, Lanarks, 10th February 1929

CAREER: Lanarkshire schools and junior football/Bellshill Athletic/Falkirk Dec 1951/ SUNDERLAND MAR 1954 £5,500/ Nottingham Forest July 1958 £5,000/Wisbech Town July 1961/Ramsgate player-manager early 1963/Yeovil Town manager cs 1965-early 1967.

Debut v Sheffield United (h) 16/4/1954

Joe McDonald

Nicely summed up in 1955 as "a slight but very effective left-back, a good positional player and crisp tackler" and a "hard-to-beat full-back". Joe played in goal for his school, St Joseph's in Blantyre, and at right-back for Falkirk, the former especially useful later in the event of goalie injuries. He had an early taste of representative football when picked for the Lanarkshire Youth team against Glasgow Catholic Youth in 1946 and '47. Another minor honour came later, playing for Scotland 'B' against The Army. A first-teamer at Falkirk and Forest, he made 124 senior appearances for the latter.

Appearances:
FL: 137 apps. 1 gl.
FAC: 18 apps. 0 gls.
Total: *155 apps. 1 gl.*
Honours:
Gt Britain v Rest of Europe/2 Scot caps/ (Nottingham Forest) FAC winner 1959.

McDOUGALL, John

Role: Centre-half 1929-34
5'10" 11st.12lbs.
b. Port Glasgow, Renfrews, 21st September 1901
d. Port Glasgow, Renfrews, 26th September 1973

CAREER: Kilmalcolm Amateurs/Port Glasgow Juniors/Airdrieonians Nov 1921/ SUNDERLAND May 1929 £4,500/Leeds United Nov 1934-1937.

Debut v Manchester City (h) 7/9/1929

"One of the strongest and most reliable pivots in football" and "a glutton for work and generally does enough for two" were typical critical comments in the 1930s concerning this Sunderland skipper. Jock McDougall came to Wearside as a very experienced player with 262 Scottish League appearances (19 goals) for Airdrie to his credit. In this sequence the club had finished runners-up for four consecutive seasons (1922/23 - 1925/26 inclusive) and landed the Scottish Cup. Airdrieonians were

Jock McDougall leads the team out at Elland Road for the 1931 FA Cup semi-final with Birmingham. Bob Middleton is the goalkeeper is close pursuit.

then indeed a star-studded combination that included the immortal Hughie Gallacher and other luminaries such as Bob Bennie and Bob McPhail. Jock continued where he had left off after arriving at Roker Park, retaining all his consistency and other virtues. For Leeds United he made 59 Football League and FA Cup appearances. Before turning professional Jock had worked as a greenkeeper at the Port of Glasgow Golf Club. Elder brother of James McDougall (Liverpool and Scotland).

Appearances:
FL: 167 apps. 4 gls.
FAC: 17 apps. 1 gl.
Total: *184 apps. 5 gls.*
Honours:
1 Scot cap v N. Ireland 1926/2 SL apps./(Airdrieonians) SC winner 1924.

McDOWALL Leslie John

Role: Centre/left-half 1934-38
5'11" 11st.9lbs.
b. Gunga Pur, India, 25th October 1912
d. Tarporley, Cheshire, 18th August 1991

CAREER: Glenryan Thistle/Kilbarchan Thistle/SUNDERLAND Dec 1932/Manchester City Mar 1938 £8,000(WW2 guest St Mirren Oct 1939)/Wrexham player-manager May 1949/Manchester City manager June 1950-May 1963/Oldham Athletic manager June 1963-Mar 1965.

Debut v West Bromwich Albion (h) 24/11/1934

Les McDowall was with Sunderland at a time when the club had a plethora of above-average young half-backs. Consequently, his first team chances were few. Manchester City, teetering on the edge of relegation, were induced to pay what seemed to be an absurdly high sum for his transfer, but McDowall proved to be worth the outlay because of hard graft and organisational skills. He was still with City when they regained a top flight place after the War. After retiring and cutting his managerial teeth at Wrexham he returned to Maine Road for what seems an astonishing long spell in the modern age, of 13 years. Under his guidance City reached the FA Cup final in successive years, winning the trophy on the latter occasion. A quiet man but influential, he was architect of the famous Revie plan, which involved the employment of a deep-lying centre-forward (namely Don Revie). Les McDowall, born in India and the son of a Scottish missionary, originally worked as a shipyard draughtsman - in the War he reverted to this profession but this time the engagement was in an aircraft factory.

Appearances:
FL: 13 apps. 0 gls.
FAC: 1 app. 0 gls.
Total: *14 apps. 0 gls.*
Honours:
(Manchester City)FL Div 2 champs 1947.

Les McDowall

McGHIE, Joseph

Role: Centre-half 1906-08
5'8" 11st.7lbs.
b. Kilbirnie, Ayrshire, 22nd March 1884
d. Largs, Ayrshire, 8th September 1976

CAREER: Banquhat (Ayrshire) junior football/ Vale of Glengarnock Strollers 1905-06/ SUNDERLAND May 1906/Sheffield United Apr 1908/Brighton & Hove Albion Aug 1909/ Stalybridge Celtic June 1913.

Debut v Aston Villa (h) 8/9/1906

Joe McGhie was only part of a season with Vale of Glengarnock, a North Ayrshire League side, before a rare selection of senior clubs came knocking on his door. The selection is impressive enough to deserve a listing: Celtic, Kilmarnock, Third Lanark, St Mirren, Reading and Bradford City. And, of course, Sunderland who won his signature, and must have had a honey-tongued persuader to have done so. McGhie had just earned his junior international cap and helped to win the Ayrshire Junior Cup. A fine solid pivot, he soon became a Sunderland regular, making his League debut in the second fixture of 1906/07. Moving on to Sheffield United Joe stood in for the England international, Bernard Wilkinson, for a season (six League appearances) and then completed his first-class career at Brighton. In four years there he had 133 Southern League outings (three goals) plus seven FA Cup and one in the FA Charity Shield, and won a championship medal in the process.

Appearances:
FL: 41 apps.
0 gls.
FAC: 5 apps.
0 gls.
Total: *46 apps.*
0 gls.
Honours:
Scot Jnr int
1905-06/
(Brighton &
Hove Albion)
Sthn Lge
champs 1910.

PROMINENT FOOTBALLERS.

J. McGHIE,
SUNDERLAND.

McGINLEY, John

Role: Winger 1981-82
6'2" 13st.8lbs.
b. Rowlands Gill, Co Durham, 11th June 1959

CAREER: Ashington/Gateshead/
SUNDERLAND Jan 1982/Gateshead May
1982/Charleroi, Belgium 1983/Nairn County/
Lincoln City Sept 1984/Rotherham United
Sept 1986(Hartlepool United loan Jan 1987)/
Lincoln City Jan 1987/Doncaster Rovers June
1989/Boston United May 1990-92.

Debut v Stoke City (h) 10/2/1982

The transition from non-League Gateshead to
First Division Sunderland proved too much
for John McGinley when he was pitched
straight into the end of season fight against
relegation in 1981-82. The powerfully-built
wingman did, however, eventually make his
mark with Lincoln City, for whom he scored
33 goals in 150 League appearances in two
separate spells. Sadly his best season for the
Imps (15 goals in 38 appearances in 1988-89)
ended when he suffered an Achilles injury,
and was never quite so effective subsequently.

> **Appearances:**
> *FL: 3 apps. 0 gls.*
> **Total:** *3 apps. 0 gls.*

McGIVEN, Michael

Role: Central defender 1969-74
5'11" 11st.4lbs.
b. Newcastle upon Tyne, 7th February 1951

CAREER: Newcastle schools football/
SUNDERLAND pro July 1968(West Ham
United loan Nov 1973)/West Ham United Dec
1973-1978 £20,000/West Ham United training
staff/Ipswich Town training staff 1990/
Ipswich Town manager Aug 1992-May 1994,
after which he was appointed their Football
Development Officer.

Debut v Coventry City (h) 9/8/1969

Mick McGiven was a frizzy red-haired, hard-
tackling half-back who played a sound
amount of first team football at Roker Park. In
his initial season he was an ever-present
wearing jerseys number 2, 4 ,5 and 6, but
mostly the latter. Sunderland were relegated
that term so the remainder of his outings were
in a Second Division setting. With West Ham

Mick McGiven

he had the daunting prospect of succeeding
Bobby Moore, captain of England's World
Cup-winning team, eventually having a
prolonged stay at Upton Park thanks also to a
lengthy stay on the Hammers' training staff.
Mick served Ipswich similarly with a two year
managerial stint alongside mentor John Lyall.
Early on he had been right-half in
Sunderland's 1969 Youth Cup winning team.

> **Appearances:**
> *FL: 107(6) apps. 9 gls.*
> *FAC: 2(2) apps. 1 gl.*
> *FLC: 3 apps. 0 gls.*
> *Other: 7 apps. 2 gls.*
> **Total:** *119(8) apps. 12 gls.*

McGORIN, Isaac Moor

Role: Wing-half 1925-28
5'11" 11st.3lbs.
*b. Silksworth, Co Durham, 19th
October 1901*

Ike McGorin

CAREER: Thornley
Albion/New Silksworth
Colliery/ SUNDERLAND am Apr 1924, pro
Jan 1925/ Notts County Feb 1929 £500 incl
John Dowsey/Carlisle United Feb
1930/Shotton Colliery Welfare Aug
1931/Thurnscoe Victoria circa 1932/Thurnscoe
St Hilda's Nov 1933.

Debut v Newcastle United (a) 17/10/1925

Rather later than was customary in taking the
professional ticket, even in the Twenties,
McGorin however won a reputation as a
thoughtful, constructive wing-half. He could
take both flanks with equal dexterity and so
was an effective deputy for either Billy Clunas
or Arthur Andrews. Ike made only one
Southern Section appearance for Notts County
before returning north to assist Carlisle. He
did not fare much better there with three
senior outings. To return to his Wearside years,
13 of his 21 Football League appearances were
in his first full professional season,
1925/26.

> **Appearances:**
> *FL: 21 apps. 1 gl.*
> *FAC: 2 apps. 0 gls.*
> **Total:** *23 apps. 1 gl.*

McGREGOR, George W.

Role: Inside-right 1929-30
5'8" 10st.12lbs.
b. Saltcoats, Ayrshire

CAREER: Saltcoats Victoria/St Mirren
Aug 1927/SUNDERLAND May 1929/
Glasgow Benburb May 1931 (Norwich
City trial May 1931)/India of Inchinnan,
Scotland Oct 1935.

Debut v Portsmouth (a) 14/9/1929

George McGregor had his introduction to the
senior game in a St Mirren shirt, in that first
period playing five Scottish League First
Division matches and scoring one goal (season
1927/28). Sunderland retained George for
season 1930/31 but no further first team

appearances materialised and he reverted to
the Scottish junior scene.

NOTE: *A player named McGregor played twice
for St Mirren in 1928/29 but the initial 'A' is
appended to the surname in both Gamage and
Athletic News' annuals.)*

> **Appearances:**
> *FL: 1 app. 0 gls.*
> **Total:** *1 app. 0 gls.*

McGUIGAN, James

Role: Winger 1947-49
5'11" 11st.4lbs.
*b. Glasgow, 1st March 1924
d. Walton, Chesterfield, 30th March 1988*

CAREER: Junior football to Hamilton
Academical 1943-44/SUNDERLAND June
1947/Stockport County June 1949/Crewe
Alexandra Aug 1950/Rochdale July 1956-
1958/Crewe Alexandra trainer 1958, manager
June 1960/Grimsby Town manager Nov
1964/Chesterfield manager July 1967/
Rotherham United manager May 1973/
Stockport County manager Nov 1979-Apr
1982/Sheffield United coach Nov 1983-1987.

Debut v Stoke City (a) 20/3/1948

Jimmy McGuigan

Nominally an outside-right,
two of McGuigan's three
League outings for
Sunderland were on the
opposite wing. Towards the
end of his long Crewe
service as a player (1954/55)
he moved to right-half. A
1950 press comment said he
was a "clever Scottish type
of winger, he has a first-rate
shot but does not try it often
enough." And one the
following year: "an expert
penalty-taker, an uncommon
distinction for an outside-
right." All told he made 323 Football League
appearances (44 goals) of which 207 were for
Crewe. Jimmy's managerial career is more
than a touch unusual in that it was 'seamless',
i.e. he moved from club to club without a
barely discernible break, and it covered a
lengthy 22-year span.

> **Appearances:**
> *FL: 3 apps. 1 gl.*
> **Total:** *3 apps. 1 gl.*

McGUIRE, Douglas

Role: Forward 1987-88
5'8" 11st.4lbs.
b. Bathgate, 6th September 1967

CAREER: Celtic Boys' Club/Celtic 1984 (Dumbarton loan Feb 1988)(SUNDERLAND loan Mar 1988)/Coventry City Aug 1988, released Nov 1990/Cumnock Juniors Jan 1991/Queen of the South June 1991/Stranraer Mar 1995/Albion Rovers June 1996.

Debut v York City (a) 26/3/1988

Dougie McGuire

Dougie McGuire played once for Sunderland and was substituted, in the Third Division promotion season 1987-88. Although an outstanding junior, McGuire failed to graduate with Celtic, appearing only three times at senior level.

Signed by Coventry City for £40,000 in August 1988, he missed the whole of season 1988-89 due to glandular fever, finally making his Sky Blue debut twelve months after signing. Released in November 1990 after only four appearances (three as substitute) he returned to Scotland. Season 1996-97 began brightly in the modest surroundings of the Cliftonhill Stadium, Coatbridge, when McGuire netted a hat-trick for his new club Albion Rovers, against Arbroath in the first round of the Coca-Cola Cup. He was also on the scoresheet in the season's first two matches. Sadly his sparkling opening was not sustained and he did not feature in the League side after mid-season. He was last reported to be playing for a junior grade side in Ayrshire. (*NOTE: Junior grade in Scotland is roughly equivalent to non-League football in England*)

Appearances:
FL: 1 app. 0 gls.
Total: *1 app. 0 gls.*
Honours:
Scot Sch/Scot Yth.

McINALLY, Thomas

Role: Inside-left 1928-30
5'9" 12st.10lbs.
b. Barrhead, Renfrews., December 1899
d. Paisley, 29th December 1955

CAREER: St Mungo's Academy/Croy Celtic 1916/St Anthony's(Glasgow)/Barrhead/Celtic July 1919/Third Lanark Sept 1922/Celtic Aug 1925/SUNDERLAND May 1928/ Bournemouth & Boscombe Athletic Nov 1929/ Morton Oct 1930/Derry City Feb 1931/ Coleraine Mar 1931/Armadale Jan 1933/ Nithsdale Wanderers 1933-37/Celtic scout Jan 1948.

Debut v Burnley (a) 25/8/1928

Tom McInally was blessed with a talent that should have enabled him to rank higher in football's hall of fame than he did. As it was he became an international and won coveted medals. McInally at centre-forward - his other position - packed a vicious shot and was exceptionally fast (once beating a famed sprint champion, W B Applegarth, in 1920). His fine marksmanship still obtained when playing inside-forward, of course, bringing to the berth necessary combination skills if so minded. Tommy's trouble, it is said, concerned his temperament, shining for only half a game, training properly only at the behest of his great friend, Tommy Milligan, the British middleweight boxing champion of 1926-28, an avid Celtic supporter.

Sunderland made McInally their skipper in the hope of reforming him. To no avail. One straw in the wind: a recorded weight of 11st 2lbs. in 1919 had become 12st. 10lbs. in 1929. As one Celtic historian wrote, " a wastrel talent."

Tommy McInally

Appearances:
FL: 35 apps. 3 gls.
FAC: 1 app. 0 gls.
Total: *36 apps. 3 gls*
Honours:
2 Scot caps/(Celtic) SL champs 1922, 1926/SC winner 1927/SC finalist 1926, 1928.

McINROY, Albert

Role: Goalkeeper 1923-30
5'10" 11st.12lbs.
b. Walton-le-Dale, Lancs, 23rd April 1901
d. Houghton-le-Spring, Co Durham,
7th January 1985

CAREER: St Thomas School/Upper Walton (Preston District League) 1919/ Great Harwood/High Walton/Coppull Central (West Lancashire Leagues)/ Preston North End am 1921-22/Great Harwood/Leyland FC pro Nov 1922/ SUNDERLAND May 1923/ Newcastle United Oct 1929 £2,750/ SUNDERLAND June 1934/Leeds United May 1935/ Gateshead June 1937/retired cs 1939 but guested with Stockton and other North-East clubs during WW2.

Debut v Manchester City (h) 29/9/1923

A legendary figure from the Twenties, Albert McInroy was an outside-left at school. He was discovered as a goalkeeper with Upper Walton and never looked back. He broke into Sunderland's League side early in 1923/4 and was first choice until departing to rivals Newcastle six years later, where again he held the senior spot. The same applied later at Leeds and Gateshead so a grand total of Football League appearances came to a splendid 496. An agile 'keeper of supreme consistency, McInroy of course received many complimentary write-ups. Here is a smattering. "He is one of the smartest and most daring goalkeepers in England," (1926), "never foozles a ball, sets himself in such a manner that he is never bowled over by charging opponents" (1933) and "a bundle of agility as many a forward who has been robbed by his cat-like leap can testify." The only goalkeeper to be capped by England whilst with Sunderland, McInroy appeared alongside Roker team mate Warney Cresswell. Until Kevin Phillips and Michael Gray in 1999, it was the last occasion England had fielded two current Sunderland players. Albert worked as a packer at the Preston Co-operative Stores originally and later at the Leyland rubber works prior to turning professional. Latterly a famed 'mine host' at Newcastle, Gateshead and Houghton-le-Spring.

Appearances:
FL: 215 apps. 0 gls.
FAC: 12 apps. 0 gls.
Total: *227 apps. 0 gls.*
Honours:
1 Eng cap v N. Ireland
1927/(Newcastle United)
FAC winner 1932.

McINTOSH, Angus Munro

Role: Centre/inside-forward 1905-09
5'8" 11st.7lbs.
b. Birkenhead, 1884

CAREER: Assisted two minor Inverness sides before joining Inverness Thistle (Highland League)/SUNDERLAND pro Aug 1905/Bury Nov 1908/Aberdeen 1910-1914

Debut v Preston North End (h) 16/4/1906

Angus McIntosh lived in Inverness from the age of six. On leaving school he was apprenticed to an engineering firm, eventually in his spare time assisting Inverness Thistle as an amateur outside-right. Sunderland wished to obtain his services a year before the club actually did, the reason for the

Angus McIntosh

delay being McIntosh's wish to complete his apprenticeship. At Roker Park he played in all three inside-forward positions. On joining Bury in 1908 a Lancashire critic wrote that "as to his shooting powers generally, they are acknowledged to be of a high order, and as he also has a good turn of speed and an intelligent conception of the game as a whole he should serve his new club well." For Bury Angus played 36 Division One matches (13 goals) and for Aberdeen 65 Scottish League matches (22 goals). At both venues his position was almost invariably inside-right.

Appearances:
FL: 40 apps. 9 gls.
FAC: 6 apps. 3 gls.
Total: *46 apps. 12 gls.*

McINTOSH, John W.

Role: Centre-forward 1896-98
possibly b. Lanchester, Co Durham, 1876

CAREER: Pallion Star/Tow Law Sept 1895/SUNDERLAND Dec 1896/South Shields May 1898-cs 1900.

Debut v Burnley (h) 2/3/1897

A Tow Law amateur, John McIntosh joined Sunderland's paid ranks for a season and a half's service. His couple of League appearances were separated by eight months - the above debut, a 1-1 draw, and an away fixture with Wolves on November 13th 1897. Sunderland returned pointless from this encounter, losing 4-2.

Appearances:
FL: 2 apps. 0 gls.
Total: *2 apps. 0 gls.*

McIVER, Frederick

Role: Midfield 1971-72
5'7" 11st.0lbs.
b. Birtley, 14th February 1952

CAREER: SUNDERLAND app, pro Apr 1969/King's Park, South Africa May 1972/Racing Jet, Belgium/Sheffield Wednesday July 1974-May 1976.

Debut v Preston North End (h) 25/9/1971

As deputy for Keith Coleman, Fred McIver made his only League appearance in a high-scoring encounter with Preston North End at Roker Park. This game, incidentally, also marked the debut of 16-year-old Jimmy Hamilton (Sunderland's youngest outfield player) who ensured a winning bonus by scoring a last-minute goal in the 4-3 victory. Despite the promise shown by a star role in the Youth and Reserve teams, fair-haired Fred was one of nine Sunderland players to be given a free transfer at the close of his debut season. He left Wearside for soccer in the sunnier climes of South Africa. He then sampled European football before returning to the English League with Sheffield Wednesday. Relegated from Division One in 1970, the Owls enjoyed little success throughout the ensuing decade. McIver's two seasons at Hillsborough coincided with Wednesday's relegation from Division Two and their first ever season in Division Three in which a second successive relegation was only avoided by victory over Southend United in the season's final game.

Appearances:
FL: 1 app. 0 gls.
Total: *1 app. 0 gls.*

Fred McIver

McKAY, Robert

Bobby McKay

Role: Inside-right
1928-31
5'6" 10st.3lbs.
*b. Govan, Glasgow,
2nd September 1900*

CAREER: Ruarry Brae
Public School/
Parkhead White Rose/
Vale of Clyde/
Parkhead FC/Neilston
Victoria/Morton Sept 1921/Rangers June 1925
£1,750/Newcastle United Nov 1926 £2,750/
SUNDERLAND Oct 1928, in exchange for
Robert Thomson/ Charlton Athletic Dec 1930
£1,220/Bristol Rovers Nov 1932 £350/
Newport County June 1935-1936/Dundee
United manager July-Oct 1939/Ballymena
United manager 1947-1949. Also scouted for
Charlton Athletic for several years.

Debut v Manchester City (a) 6/10/1928 (scored)

Bobby McKay was a cute little Scottish inside-
right, much travelled and much to the fore
during the 1920s. "A bundle of tricks and a
clever pattern weaver," said one commentator
and another wrote in 1927 he was "one of the
most effective players Scotland has sent
south." Besides tactical awareness and the rest
he could take chances himself, registering a
hat-trick in his first appearance for Newcastle
and a couple on his Sunderland debut.
Bobby's first venture into management was
quickly ended by the outbreak of war and,
according to one source, his own call-up.

Appearances:
FL: 49 apps. 17 gls.
FAC: 2 apps. 0 gls.
Total: *51 apps. 17 gls.*
Honours:
*1 Scot cap v Wales 1928/1 SL app. v Irish
League 1926/(Morton) SC winner 1922/
(Newcastle United) FL champs 1927.*

McKENZIE, Archibald Denny F.

Role: Inside/outside-left 1895-96
b. Greenock, 1st May 1863

CAREER: Greenock & Port Glasgow
Schoolboys/Clyde/Millwall Athletic cs 1894/
SUNDERLAND May 1895/Millwall Athletic
May 1896/West Bromwich Albion July 1897/
Portsmouth Oct 1899.

Debut v Burnley (a) 9/9/1895

Archie McKenzie appeared at inside-left in his
debut and outside-left against Wolves at home
later that September, and that was the extent
of his Sunderland first team career. But it was
a different story elsewhere. In two separated
seasons with Millwall he was an ever-present
in the first and missed only one Southern
League match in 1896/97, his aggregate
figures for this competition being 35
appearances, 24 goals. Season 1894/95 should
be mentioned: McKenzie scored 17 goals in 16
outings. At West Bromwich he played in 51
First Division games, scoring nine goals. Both
at Millwall and West Brom, Archie usually
appeared at inside-left.

Appearances:
FL: 2 apps. 1 gl.
Total: *2 apps. 1 gl.*

McKENZIE, Thomas

Role: Centre-forward 1905-06
b. Petershill, Glasgow

CAREER: Petershill FC/Third Lanark cs 1903/
SUNDERLAND Oct 1905/Plymouth Argyle
May 1906/Portsmouth Feb 1907/Glossop
North End cs 1907-1908.

Debut v Woolwich Arsenal (a) 21/10/1905

Thomas McKenzie

A curious case this.
McKenzie won signal
club honours in each of
his first two seasons in
the first class game, but
afterwards, on migrating
to England, all was anti-
climax. At Roker Park,
following half a dozen
appearances as centre-
forward and one in either
inside berth, his goals haul was one. With
Southern League Plymouth things did look up
somewhat (ten goals in 20 outings). McKenzie
had identical figures with Portsmouth of the
Southern League and FL Division Two
Glossop: one goal in six appearances.

Appearances:
FL: 8 apps. 1 gl.
Total: *8 apps. 1 gl.*
Honours:
*(Third Lanark) SL champs 1904/SC winner
1905.*

McLAIN, Thomas

Role: Wing-half 1946-52
5'9" 10st.8lbs.
b. Linton, Roxburghshire, 19th January 1922

CAREER: Ashington/SUNDERLAND Aug
1946/Northampton Town June 1952 £3,000/
Wellingborough 1956.

Debut v Wolverhampton Wanderers (a) 26/12/1946

Tommy McLain

Tommy McLain's first
class career was
delayed thanks to the
War, during which he
served in Ceylon
with Tommy
Reynolds (q.v.).
Tommy was among
the fastest footballers
of his time - maybe
THE fastest - he had
won the Morpeth
Handicap shortly after demobilisation. For the
most part a reserve during his six years at
Roker Park, Tommy's best seasons were
1947/48 (22 First Division outings) and
1950/51 (17). A regular with Northampton
Town of the Third Division (South), his figures
were 96 Football League plus five FA Cup
appearances, 11 League goals.

Appearances:
FL: 67 apps. 1 gl.
FAC: 4 apps. 0 gls.
Total: *71 apps. 1 gl.*

McLATCHIE, Colin Campbell

Role: Outside-left 1898-1903
5'10" 13st.7lbs.
b. New Cumnock, Ayrshire, 2nd November 1876
d. 6th January 1952

CAREER: New Cumnock United/Lanemark/
Dean Park (Kilmarnock)/Kilmarnock FC Apr
1897/Preston North End June 1897/
SUNDERLAND Oct 1898/Grimsby Town Nov
1902/Lanemark cs 1903/Nithsdale Wanderers
Dec 1903/Lanemark July 1906-1913.

Debut v Wolverhampton Wanderers (a) 5/11/1898

Colin McLatchie possessed an imposing
physique that seems implausible in a wing-
forward position. Yet there it was. With his
direct style and blistering left foot shooting,

Colin certainly made
his presence felt
besides exhibiting the
winger's stock-in-
trade of accurate
centres. "A fine strong,
clever player," as one
commentator
remarked in 1902.
Before moving to
England, and after
returning, McLatchie

Colin McLatchie

plied his trade as a miner. He gave the
Ayrshire junior club, Lanemark, a goodly spell
of service spread over three instalments. Apart
from Sunderland, Colin's senior first team
action was modest: one League outing for
Killie, nine with Preston and nine at Grimsby.

Appearances:
FL: 122 apps. 28 gls.
FAC: 8 apps. 1 gl.
Total: *130 apps. 29 gls.*
Honours:
(Sunderland) FL champs 1902.

McLAUGHLAN, Alexander Donaldson

Role: Goalkeeper 1964-66
5'8" 11st.8lbs.
b. Kilwinning, Ayrshire, 17th July 1936

CAREER: Army football (Ayrshire
Yeomanry)/Ardeer Recreation Aug 1957/
Kilmarnock Sept 1958/SUNDERLAND Sept
1964 £12,000/Kilmarnock July 1967 £3,000/
Troon Juniors July 1971.

Debut v West Bromwich Albion (h) 2/9/1964

Short as goalkeepers go, Sandy McLaughlan
made up for any deficiency on that score by
agility, positioning and deft handling. One of
several distinguished custodians who guarded
the Killie net around this time. The roll-call
included Campbell Forsyth, Bobby Ferguson,
Alistair Hunter and Jim Stewart, all of whom
were capped by Scotland. (This is an
astonishing Killie record reminiscent of
Tranmere Rovers' capacity to unearth
outstanding centre-forwards between the
wars). When mentioning this illustrious
quartet it must not be forgotten our present
subject, Sandy McLaughlan, earned inter-
league honours. The 50th goalkeeper to play
League football for Sunderland, Sandy lost his

McLaughlan, regularly the pivot that term, made 24 appearances in the position. Nevertheless he seems to have had at least a modicum of versatility (like so many of these pioneers) as he turned out at outside-left against Grimsby Town in November 1888.

Appearances:
FL: 2 apps. 0 gls.
Total: *2 apps. 0 gls.*

McLEAN, Adam

Role: Outside-left 1928-31
5'7" 11st.0lbs.
b. Coatbridge, 27th April 1897
d. Glasgow, 29th June 1973

CAREER: Broomhill YMCA/Anderston Benburb Juveniles/Anderston Thornbank Juveniles/Celtic Jan 1917/SUNDERLAND Aug 1928/Aberdeen Oct 1930/Partick Thistle July 1933/retired cs 1934/Partick Thistle asst. trainer Nov 1938 and on that club's training staff for many years, eventually becoming head trainer. Later still had a spell as Thistle's assistant manager from July 1962.

Debut v Blackburn Rovers (h) 29/8/1928 (scored)

Adam McLean

Adam McLean was signed from Celtic a few months after his colleague, Tommy McInally. Adam had given the Glasgow club more than a decade of outstanding service - even now, seventy years on, he is regarded by Celtic historians as their best-ever left-winger. But he was by no means a one-position player, taking an inside berth on occasion, and he made several appearances for Sunderland at outside-right. To all of them he brought dribbling skills, accurate passing and shooting and an overall ebullience. It would seem McLean left Celtic only because of being offered much reduced terms, following a representation on the players' behalf, concerning wages offered for a summer tour. Adam spent his boyhood in Belfast, eventually moving to Greenock. He had played centre-

Sandy McLaughlan

place after conceding five at home to WBA on New Year's Day 1966 when he was - allegedly - still feeling the effects of the night before! In his final Roker Park season, 1966/67, Sandy did not make a single League appearance, the up and coming Jim Montgomery being an ever-present.

Appearances:
FL: 43 apps. 0 gls.
FAC: 2 apps. 0 gls.
FLC: 1 app. 0 gls.
Total: *46 apps. 0 gls.*
Honours:
1 SL app. v Italian Lge 1963/(Kilmarnock)
SLC finalist 1963.

McLAUGHLAN

Role: Centre-half 1888-89
Debut v Elswick Rangers (h) 27/10/1888 (FAC)

McLaughlan played centre-half in Sunderland's two FA Cup-ties of 1888/89. Both were won - the above game 5-3 and against Newcastle East End, also at home, 2-0 three weeks later. Sunderland were drawn against local rivals Albion in the next stage but withdrew before the match was played.

forward until going to Celtic and, soon afterwards, converted to outside-left. Doubtless his collection of caps would have been much greater but for the fact of being an exact contemporary of the unique Alan Morton. And the fact Adam was originally a Partick Thistle fan perhaps has more than a little to do with lengthy service at Firhill.

Appearances:
FL: 66 apps. 14 gls.
FAC: 4 apps. 2 gls.
Total: *70 apps. 16 gls.*
Honours:
4 Scot caps/3 SL apps./(Celtic) SL champs 1919, 1922, 1926/SC winner 1923, 1925, 1927/SC finalist 1928.

McMAHON, Hugh

Role: Outside-left 1937-39
5'8" 10st.8lbs.
b. Grangetown, Middlesbrough, 24th September 1909
d. Grangetown, Middlesbrough, October 1986

CAREER: St Mary's School/Upton FC / South Bank St Peter's(Derby County trial) (Hartlepools United trial)(Sheffield Wednesday trial Aug 1932)/Reading Sept 1932/Mexborough Town Dec 1932/Southend United May 1933/Reading June 1934/Queens Park Rangers May 1936/SUNDERLAND Nov 1937/Hartlepools United June 1945/ Rotherham United Sept 1947-1949.

Debut v Grimsby Town (h) 13/11/1937

Hugh McMahon

Hugh McMahon came to Sunderland after missing only one of QPR's Southern Section engagements in 1936/37. Before that he had made 21 League appearances in total with Reading and Southend. At Roker Park he understudied Eddie Burbanks and an injury stricken Jimmy Connor. Hugh's senior career, shortened like those of others of his generation by WW2, ended with regular places at Hartlepools and Rotherham. The latter were memorable for Rotherham finishing Northern Section runners-up in successive campaigns. Hugh had made a mark as Mexborough's centre-forward, switching to the extreme left-

wing berth at Southend. He had a brief association with Sheffield Wednesday early on, presumably a trial.

Appearances:
FL: 8 apps. 1 gl.
Total: *8 apps. 1 gl.*

McMILLAN, James

Role: Wing-half 1884-87
Debut v Redcar (a) 8/11/1884 (FAC)

James McMillan

Appeared in Sunderland's first five FA Cup-ties, which were spread over three seasons. He was inside-left in the above debut, left-half in 1885/86 and right-half in the trio of 1886/87 ties. McMillan appeared regularly in those early campaigns, right-half being his most favoured position. Earlier, in May 1884, he had captained Sunderland to their first trophy, the Durham Challenge Cup and also in 1884, was one of six Sunderland players in the very first Durham FA match against Northumberland FA. At the time of his death in 1930, James was Chairman of J. McMillan & Sons, sculptors to the masonic trade.

Appearances:
FAC: 5 apps. 0 gls.
Total: *5 apps. 0 gls.*

McNAB, Alexander

Role: Wing-half 1932-38
5'6" 10st.6lbs.
b. Glasgow, 27th December 1911
d. Halesowen, Worcs, September 1962

CAREER: Glasgow Schools/Tuesday Waverley/Bridgeton Waverley/Glasgow Pollock early 1932/SUNDERLAND May 1932/West Bromwich Albion Mar 1938 £6,750 (guested for Newport County, Nottingham Forest, Northampton Town & Walsall during WW2)/Newport County Apr 1946/Dudley Town Dec 1946/Northwich Victoria player-manager Sept 1948/retired cs 1949.

Debut v Aston Villa (a) 29/8/1932

Alex McNab

One of several young Scottish half-back discoveries in the 'Thirties, Sandy McNab was a slight, tireless, brave redhead. For all that, even though he was on the pitch the day the 1936 championship was clinched and helped rally Sunderland to their 1937 FA Cup victory, Sandy was only a regular for one season (1933/34), Alex Hastings, the club captain, monopolising the left-half spot. Indeed, the first of Sandy's two Scottish caps came a week after the Cup final when he played alongside Frank O'Donnell who had scored at Wembley to put Preston ahead. So, possessing such riches, the club felt able to let McNab go, receiving a handsome fee as a result. West Brom liked him too - a "marvellous pint-sized left-half whose tackling was done judiciously without losing any poise," as their historian recorded. He toured Canada and the States with the Scotland party in 1939 and was a Halesowen licensee at the time of his early demise. Originally Sandy had worked as a grocer's assistant.

Appearances:
FL: 97 apps. 6 gls.
FAC: 15 apps. 0 gls.
Total: *112 apps. 6 gls.*
Honours:
2 Scot caps/(Sunderland) Div 1 champs 1936,
FAC winner 1937.

McNAB, James

Role: Left-half 1958-67
5'9" 11st.7lbs.
b. Denny, Stirlings, 13th April 1940

CAREER: Stirlingshire schools football/Denny Rovers/Kilsyth Rangers/SUNDERLAND am Aug 1956, pro June 1957/Preston North End Mar 1967 £15,000/Stockport County May 1974-1976.

Debut v Ipswich Town (h) 20/9/1958

A pillar of the 1964 promotion team and obviously a real toughie, Jimmy McNab's catalogue of injuries included two broken legs and two broken noses yet he still managed to register over 320 first team appearances for the Wearsiders. Altogether, counting his Preston North End and Stockport spells, the League total rises to 536(3), a prodigious figure considering the injuries, and he popped in 20 goals. McNab showed his potential by winning Scottish schoolboy caps against England and Wales. The rich promise continued into junior circles where, interestingly, he appeared at outside-left for Kilsyth Rangers. A sizeable clutch of senior

Jimmy McNab's Testimonial match in 1999 was the first ever to be staged at The Stadium of Light.

club scouts were soon sniffing, half a dozen in fact, five Scottish and another from farther afield, Birmingham City. He had a run-out for Celtic when only 14 but they decreed he was at that time too young for an engagement. Sunderland, who were not among the clubs openly courting Jim's services, claimed him at 16 and he turned professional during the close season following his 17th birthday. Jimmy's progress through Sunderland's reserve side was such he made his League bow at 18 in September 1958. This match followed two shattering away defeats in which 11 goals were conceded (5-0 at Swansea and 6-0 against Sheffield Wednesday). The defeats were particularly traumatic, as indeed was the season with Sunderland tasting Second Division football for the first time. Jimmy's debut game was remarkable for the fact two other 1964 promotion heroes also made their senior bows: full-backs Cec Irwin and Len Ashurst. McNab switched to right-half for the next nine games until injury struck the teenager at Rotherham, with the first of his broken legs. Yet Jimmy returned for the third League match of 1959/60, and soon re-established himself. The arrival of the celebrated Jim Baxter saw McNab shift to inside-left putting the seal on a reputation for versatility: He had occupied all half-back berths, been a left-winger as a junior and was now an inside-forward. Later on he played left-back with Preston and Stockport County. He missed the first couple of games in 1959/60 but from then was first choice left-half, and despite the injuries, clocked up well over 300 appearances while at Roker Park. He was unlucky in the way of representative honours, being selected in March 1963 for a Scotland

Under-23 match called off through bad weather. For his other League clubs Jimmy played a substantial 222(2) for Preston and 30 with Stockport. At Deepdale Jim tasted the pleasure of promotion for the second time, Preston topping the Third Division in 1971 after suffering relegation the previous year. After leaving football Jimmy worked in the insurance industry. A measure of Sunderland's regard for the player was the staging of a Testimonial match which took place in May 1999. Jimmy appeared as a sub and scored from a perfectly executed penalty!

Appearances:
FL: 284(1) apps. 13 gls.
FAC: 20 apps. 1 gl.
FLC: 18 apps. 4 gls.
Total: *322(1) apps. 18 gls.*
Honours:
2 Scot Sch apps./(Preston North End) Div 3 champs 1971.

Jimmy McNab

McNEILL, Edward V.

Role: Goalkeeper 1953-54
b. Warren Point, Co Down, 26th March 1929

CAREER: Portadown/
SUNDERLAND Dec 1951
over £4,000/Portadown July
1954.

Ted McNeill

Debut v Portsmouth (a) 19/9/1953

On Wearside for two and a half seasons, all Ted McNeill's League outings were confined to the last, 1953/54. They consisted of his debut and then a consecutive half dozen commencing on October 31st and ending on 5th December. McNeill was standing in for Jimmy Cowan and did not have too happy a time, conceding 20 goals. Two of his seven matches were won, one was drawn and four lost.

Appearances:
FL: 7 apps. 0 gls.
Total: *7 apps. 0 gls.*

McNEILL, Robert

Role: Right/left-back
1894-1901
b. Glasgow

Robert McNeill

CAREER: Port Victoria/
Port Glasgow/Vale of Leven/Clyde 1892/
SUNDERLAND June 1894/Morton Nov 1901.

Debut v Burnley (h) 8/9/1894

A solid, stolid performer Robert McNeill was never of more value than in the '95 championship year when Donald Gow was mostly unavailable through injury. "He is more a determined than a showy or brilliant player," volunteered a 1902 critic. Rightly intimating the honest journeyman provides an essential (and sometimes a more important) accompaniment to a would-be flamboyant soloist. Robert became Sunderland's skipper at the turn of the century. A fine club man contributing seven years to the cause.

Appearances:
FL: 145 apps. 0 gls.
FAC: 12 apps. 0 gls.
Total: *157 apps. 0 gls.*
Honours:
(Sunderland) FL champs 1895.

McNESTRY, George

Role: Outside-right 1929-30
5'8" 10st.11lbs.
b. Chopwell, Co Durham, 7th January 1908

CAREER: Chopwell Institute (Arsenal trial July 1926)/Bradford Aug 1926/Doncaster Rovers May 1927/Leeds United Nov 1928/ SUNDERLAND Nov 1929 £200/Luton Town May 1930/Bristol Rovers May 1932/Coventry City June 1935/retired through injury 1937.

Debut v Leicester City (h) 16/11/1929

McNestry made League appearances with all his many League clubs but his career really took off on arrival at the Southern Section contingent. In other words, the final three. In a grand total of 256 Football League appearances (90 goals), 227 (88 goals) were made

George McNestry

in the colours of Luton, Bristol Rovers and Coventry. And of those Bristol Rovers claim 112 and 42 goals. George received an early senior blooding at Bradford Park Avenue aged 18 years, seven months. Although showing a good direct, assertive style, a penchant for penalty-taking and goal-scoring in general really became obvious at Luton, and his overall total is excellent for a wing forward. George's untimely departure from the game owing to a knee injury occasioned a £500 benefit from the Coventry club. He had figured in their Southern Section Cup-winning line-up as well as the championship side.

Appearances:
FL: 4 apps. 0 gls.
Total: *4 apps. 0 gls.*
Honours:
(Coventry City) FL Div 3 (Sth) champs 1936.

MacPHAIL, John

Role: Central defender 1987-91
6'0" 12st.3lbs.
b. Dundee, 7th December 1955

CAREER: Dundee/Sheffield United Jan 1979 (York City loan Feb 1983)/York City Mar 1983/Bristol City July 1986/SUNDERLAND July 1987(Hartlepool United loan Sept 1990)/

John MacPhail

Hartlepool United Dec 1990, appointed player-manager Nov 1993-Sept 1994/South Tyneside United manager.

Debut v Brentford (a) 15/8/1987

John MacPhail began with his hometown club, Dundee, recording 84 appearances following his debut versus Rangers at Ibrox in April 1976. In a four-year spell with Sheffield United he was a Division Four championship winner in 1982 and won a second such medal in his first full season with Denis Smith's York City side, who were runaway Division Four champions with 101 points in 1984. In a season with Bristol City he played in six of their eight Freight Rover Trophy matches including the Wembley final which was lost on penalties to Mansfield Town. Teaming up again with Denis Smith when he joined Sunderland for £23,000 in July 1987, MacPhail arrived at Roker during the lowest point in the club's history yet quickly won his third championship medal. In the successful Third Division campaign marked by prolific goalscoring - 92 were netted in 46 League matches - John's contribution was, for a central defender who had formed a solid partnership alongside Gary Bennett, a quite remarkable 16, including ten penalties. Indeed, he only missed once that season, an irrelevant failure in the final home game against Northampton. Two years later John played his part in the dramatic play-off semi-final victory over Newcastle and, although Sunderland lost to Swindon at Wembley, John achieved his ambition to play in the top flight as a result of the Robins' financial misdemeanours. Replaced by Kevin Ball after just one game at that level, he moved on to Hartlepool United, initially on loan and subsequently as player-manager. Still playing in season 1996-97 with South Tyneside United, John MacPhail is a partner in a South Shields-based kitchen installation business.

Appearances:
FL: 133 apps. 22 gls.
FAC: 5 apps. 0 gls.
FLC: 10 apps. 0 gls.
Other: 5 apps. 0 gls.
Total: *153 apps. 22 gls.*
Honours:
(Sheffield United) Div 4 champs 1982/(York City) Div 4 champs 1984/(Bristol City) FRT finalist 1987/(Sunderland) Div 3 champs 1988.

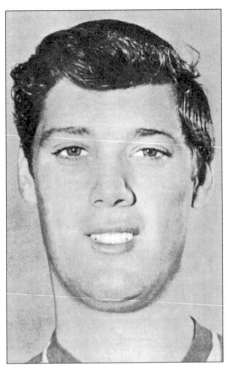

Willie McPheat

McPHEAT, William

Role: Inside-left 1960-63
6'0" 12st.7lbs.
b. Caldercruix, Lanarks., 4th September 1942

CAREER: Calder Youth/SUNDERLAND Sept 1959/Hartlepools United Sept 1965 over £1,000/Airdrieonians July 1966-1971.

Debut v Leeds United (h) 8/10/1960 (scored)

Before joining Sunderland, aged 16, Willie McPheat was out for almost a season with serious eye trouble, a detached retina. Nonetheless McPheat made his League debut at 18, scored in Sunderland's first League Cup tie at Brentford shortly after, and by early in season 1962/63 had made the full quota of senior appearances summarised below. This 'full-stop' was the result of a broken leg. Willie remained on Sunderland's books a further three years (which included the 1963/64 promotion campaign) then departed to nearby Hartlepool, where he played 14 Fourth Division games plus two substitutions, scoring two goals. Airdrie then got a bargain - Willie

arrived on a free transfer and gave the Lanarkshire club several useful years in Division One of the Scottish League. Tall and well built, Willie might have gone far but for that broken leg.

Appearances:
FL: 58 apps. 19 gls.
FAC: 9 apps. 3 gls.
FLC: 5 apps. 1 gl.
Total: *72 apps. 23 gls.*

McPHEE, John

Role: Outside-right 1929-30
5'7" 10st.6lbs.
b. Stirling

CAREER: Cowie Thistle Juveniles/ SUNDERLAND June 1929/Brentford May 1931/Albion Rovers June 1932-1936

Debut v Portsmouth (a) 14/9/1929

John McPhee figured in four early League matches of 1929/30 soon after leaving the amateur ranks, and failed to get a first team run-out with Brentford, then gearing up for their rocket-rise to Division One. McPhee did well for Albion Rovers, though, where he also played outside-left (he had been an inside-right as a junior). He was top scorer in the Coatbridge club's championship season and grossed 56 appearances (nine goals) in the following couple of top flight terms. Around this time described as "fast and dainty of movement ... discovered as a juvenile by Sunderland who released him before he had time to develop". Outside-right was definitely John's best position. An all-rounder: he had been an athletics champion at school and played an excellent game of cricket.

John McPhee

Appearances:
FL: 4 apps. 0 gls.
Total: *4 apps. 0 gls.*
Honours:
(Albion Rovers) SL Div 2 champs 1934.

McSEVENEY, John Haddon

Debut v Manchester United (a) 20/10/1951

Role: Outside-left 1951-55
5'7" 10st.2lbs.
b. Shotts, Lanarks, 8th February 1931

CAREER: Carluke Rovers/Hamilton Academical Dec 1948/SUNDERLAND Oct 1951 £5,000/Cardiff City May 1955/Newport County July 1957 - player exchange deal/Hull City July 1961 £1,000/retired June 1965/ Hull City training staff/ Barnsley manager Sept 1971-Oct 1972/Home Farm (Dublin) coach Feb 1973/Nottingham Forest chief scout/asst manager Dec 1973-Jan 1975/Waterford manager late 1975-Dec 1977/ Guyana national coach 1978/ Oman Sports Club coach 1979/ Rotherham United coach 1980/ Sheffield United asst manager-coach 1984/Plymouth Argyle scout 1986/Coventry City scout 1988.

A small competent Scot, John McSeveney had fine utility value and was able to occupy both wing and both inside-forward berths. "Full of energy and has a good shot," remarked one judge. Perhaps John's best playing periods were, a little oddly, the final ones, at Newport 171 League appearances, 53 goals, and Hull, 161 and 60 goals. It was at Hull he netted a first 20 plus seasonal goals total. In aggregate he made 442 Football League appearances and scored 134 goals. After leaving the playing arena John enjoyed a long and extremely varied career of coaching and managerial jobs. A truly all-round pro.

Appearances:
FL: 35 apps. 3 gls.
FAC: 3 apps. 1 gl.
Total: *38 apps. 4gls.*

John McSeveney

NAISBETT, A.

Role: Right-half 1899-1900

CAREER: Selbourne/SUNDERLAND Sept 1896/later assisted Sunderland Black Watch.

Debut v West Bromwich Albion (a) 28/10/1899

Naisbett is something of a mystery man in that his name does not appear at all in some sources, which could indicate some confusion between his surname and that of his contemporary, Tom Naisby, below. However, their positions don't tally, Tom being a goalkeeper and Naisbett a half-back. The latter's sole senior appearance, the debut match above, resulted in a 1-0 defeat. Naisbett was quite possibly an amateur.

Appearances:
FL: 1 app. 0 gls.
Total: *1 app. 0 gls.*

NAISBY, Thomas Henry

Role: Goalkeeper 1898-99 & 1905-07
5'8" 11st.10lbs.
b. Sunderland, 1878

CAREER: Sunderland East End/SUNDERLAND May 1898/Sunderland West End Sept 1901/Reading May 1903/SUNDERLAND May 1905/Leeds City Oct 1907/Luton Town cs 1910/South Shields Mar 1913/Darlington.

Debut v Blackburn Rovers (h) 3/4/1899

Tom Naisby

Tom Naisby was on the short side in stature for a goalkeeper but possessed a sturdy frame and reliability in performance. He stood in for Ned Doig a couple of times in 1898/99 before returning to local football. Two years later he started a splendid run with Reading of the Southern League becoming an ever-present in consecutive seasons, the second of which found the Biscuitmen in the runners-up spot. Such form rekindled Sunderland's interest and a return to Roker Park. Tom was first choice in 1905/06 but lost his place the following season to Bob Ward. Reserve football was often his lot at Leeds then he came into his own again with Luton, missing only three Southern League matches out of a possible 76 in 1910/11 and 1911/12. Tom obviously found Southern League air congenial!

Appearances:
FL: 37 apps. 0 gls.
FAC: 4 apps. 0 gls.
Total: *41 apps. 0 gls.*

NELSON, Colin Armstrong

Role: Right-back 1958-65
5'9" 11st.10lbs.
b. East Boldon, Co Durham, 13th March 1938

CAREER: Washington Grammar School/Usworth Juniors/Sunderland Technical College/SUNDERLAND Mar 1958/Mansfield Town Mar 1965-1966 £3,500.

Debut v Bristol City (a) 25/10/1958

After representing his school at all age levels Colin Nelson joined an Usworth Juniors' side that won everything in sight. A successful trial for Sunderland followed but he declined to sign having a stronger yen to qualify for the

Colin Nelson

pharmacy profession. However, after going to college he applied for a trial and joined the Wearsiders as a part-timer in 1958. This state of affairs continued, even though he had qualified as a pharmacist, until 1964 when he became a full-time player. Colin soon succeeded Jack Hedley as Sunderland's regular right-back, this situation continuing until February 1962 when Cecil Irwin moved increasingly into the picture. For Mansfield Town Colin made 38 League appearances. A resourceful back able to play on the left flank too.

Appearances:
FL: 146 apps. 2 gls.
FAC: 12 apps. 0 gls.
FLC: 10 apps. 0 gls.
Total: *168 apps. 2 gls.*

NESS, Harold Marshall

Role: Right/left-back 1911-20
5'9" 12st.9lbs.
b. Scarborough, 3rd qtr 1885
d. Scarborough, 26th June 1957

Harry Ness

CAREER: Sheffield Club/Parkgate/ Rawmarsh United/Barnsley May 1908/ SUNDERLAND June 1911/Aberdeen Apr 1920-1921.

Debut v Oldham Athletic (h) 28/10/1911

Harry Ness received a losers' medal in the 1910 Cup final and repeated the deed three years later wearing Sunderland's red and white stripes. The latter appearance was actually by courtesy of an Arthur Milton injury, a twist to the tale the fact Arthur was an ex-Barnsley left-back too. And the injury also enabled Harry to qualify for a championship medal. Rarely has an incapacitated player's hurt wrought such benefit upon another! Ness was a fine back though, effective in all the ways good defenders aspired to at the time, and was a Sunderland regular before the Great War halted his career in its prime. He made 81 League and Cup appearances for Barnsley. Son of a policeman a brother, J.R. Ness, turned out for Watford in season 1911/12. On leaving football Harry worked as a building contractor in his native Scarborough.

Appearances:
FL: 94 apps. 0 gls.
FAC: 7 apps. 0 gls.
Total: *101 apps. 0 gls*
Honours:
(Barnsley) FAC finalist 1910/(Sunderland) FL champs 1913/FAC finalist 1913.

NICHOLL, James Michael

Role: Defender 1981-83
5'9" 11st.1lb.
b. Hamilton, Ontario, Canada, 28th February 1956

CAREER: Belfast Central School/Manchester United am Nov 1971, app Oct 1972, pro Mar 1974(SUNDERLAND loan Dec 1981-Feb 1982)/Toronto Blizzard Apr 1982/ SUNDERLAND Sept 1982/Toronto Blizzard Apr 1983(Glasgow Rangers loan Oct 1983-Apr 1984)/Toronto Blizzard May 1984/West Bromwich Albion Nov 1984/Glasgow Rangers July 1986, appointed reserve team player-coach Mar 1987/Dunfermline Athletic July 1989/Raith Rovers player-manager Nov 1990/ Millwall manager Feb 1996/Raith Rovers asst. manager Feb 1997, manager June 1997.

Debut v Arsenal (h) 6/2/1982

Jimmy Nicholl was born in Canada, the son of Irish parents who moved to Belfast when he was around two years old. His distinguished and varied career encompassed three spells in Canada, and it was from Toronto Blizzard that he joined Sunderland in September 1982 for a fee of £250,000. He had earlier spent a brief, but reputedly expensive, loan spell with Sunderland who had paid his club Manchester United around £4,000 per game. In over a decade at Old Trafford he appeared in two FA Cup Finals and won 41 of his 73 Northern Ireland caps. Problems with documentation delayed Nicholl's first game for Sunderland following his transfer from Toronto Blizzard and he might have wished for the delay to have continued a little longer as Sunderland lost 8-0 at Watford in his first match! He spent less than a season at Roker and his best subsequent spells were with Rangers and Raith Rovers. In management Jimmy Nicholl guided Raith Rovers to the Scottish First Division championship in 1992-93 with the longest unbeaten spell in British senior football, four months and 19 matches from the start of the season. In 1994-95 a second

championship followed and Celtic were famously beaten in the Scottish League Cup Final. Indeed, such successes led to his being touted as a potential Sunderland manager during the Terry Butcher era at Roker. Jimmy did move to England, but an unhappy spell with Millwall ended when he and 18 other members of staff were dismissed by administrators in their rescue package for the crisis-hit Lions. Almost immediately welcomed back to the Raith Rovers fold as assistant to ex Sunderland captain Iain Munro, Jimmy took over as manager just four months later when Munro was dismissed.

Appearances:
FL: 32 apps. 0 gls.
FAC: 4 apps. 0 gls.
FLC: 4 apps. 0 gls.
Total: *40 apps. 0 gls.*
Honours:
NIre Yth/1 NIre U-21 app./73 NIre caps 1976-86/(Manchester United) FAC winner 1977/FAC finalist 1979/(Rangers)SPL champs 1987/SL winners 1987, 1988/(Raith Rovers) SL Div 1 champs 1992, 1995/(Toronto Blizzard) Soccer Bowl finalist 1983/NASL Championship finalist 1984.

NORMAN, Anthony John

Role: Goalkeeper 1988-95
6'2" 14st.5lbs.
b. Mancot, Flintshire, 24th February 1958

CAREER: Wales Schoolboys/Burnley from school, pro Aug 1976/Hull City Feb 1980/SUNDERLAND Dec 1988/Huddersfield Town July 1995, retired Aug 1997 to join Durham Police Force.

Debut v Portsmouth (h) 31/12/1988

Tony Norman began with Burnley, but in a four-year stay was kept out of the first team by England Under-23 goalkeeper, Alan Stephenson. A £30,000 move to Hull City kick-started his career which began with a clean sheet versus Millwall in Division Three on 16th February 1980. He was a promotion winner from Division Four in 1983 and from Division Three two years later. After winning two Wales Under-18 caps he made his full international debut, as a substitute, in a 1-0 victory against the Republic of Ireland in Dublin in March 1986. In the following month Tony was in the starting line-up against

Jimmy Nicholl

Uruguay at Cardiff, and had the satisfaction of maintaining a clean sheet. Signed by Sunderland in December 1988, his transfer - a Sunderland record at the time - was rated in the £500,000 bracket, and included a part-exchange element which took Iain Hesford and Billy Whitehurst to Hull. In a typically assured display of clean handling, Tony began his Sunderland career undefeated in a 4-0 victory versus Portsmouth on New Year's Eve 1988. A regular first team player in all but one of his seven seasons at Roker Park, his fantastic display of agility in an FA Cup fifth round replay at West Ham and the epic sixth round replay with Chelsea at Roker that followed did much to take The Lads on to Wembley in 1992. He left for Huddersfield in July 1995 and was warmly welcomed back in March of the following year but was unable to halt Sunderland's winning sequence - nine consecutive victories - in their run-in to the Division One championship. Norman retired from the game in August 1997 to join Durham Police Force. In September 1998 he helped run a Goalkeepers' Course organised by Sunderland at Monkwearmouth Comprehensive school, when the benefit of his top flight experience was passed on to youngsters up to 16 years of age. Tony now works for BBC Radio Leeds covering Huddersfield matches.

Tony Norman

Appearances:
FL: 201 apps. 0 gls.
FAC: 14 apps. 0 gls.
FLC: 8 apps. 0 gls.
Other: 4 apps. 0 gls.
Total: *227 apps. 0 gls.*
Honours:
5 Welsh caps 1986-88/
1 Wales 'B' app./
2 Wales U-18 apps./
(Sunderland) FAC finalist 1992.

OAKLEY, James Ernest

Role: Right-back 1922-30
5'7" 11st.6lbs.
b. Blyth, Northumberland, 10th November 1901
d. Northumberland, 3rd qtr 1972

CAREER: Seaton Delaval/Blyth Spartans Aug 1921/SUNDERLAND May 1922 £50/Reading July 1930/Northampton Town June 1931/Kettering Town Sept 1933/Birtley Aug 1935.

Debut v Newcastle United (h) 15/12/1922

It is a measure of Oakley's worth that, although the immaculate Warney Cresswell was available for five of his eight Roker years, he still made 90 senior appearances. He was, in fact, a first-rate reserve, a strong defender whose sole real defect was a lack of height. His seasonal League outings were usually in double figures, the highest count, 17, occurring in 1924/25. When Cresswell departed Jim did not get the regular right-back spot due to the arrival of Bill Murray. He made nine League appearances with Reading and 33 for Northampton Town - the former in Division Two and those for Northampton in Division Three (South). After football, James ran a hotel in Durham

Appearances:
FL: 84 apps. 0 gls.
FAC: 6 apps. 0 gls.
Total: *90 apps. 0 gls.*

O'DONNELL, Dennis

Role: Inside-right 1905-06
5'10" 10st.12lbs.
b. Willington Quay,
Northumberland, 1880

Dennis
O'Donnell

CAREER: Willington Athletic/Lincoln City Sept 1901 £47/SUNDERLAND May 1905 £350, a then Lincoln record/Queens Park Rangers May 1906/Notts County May 1907/Bradford June 1908-1909.

Debut v Blackburn Rovers (h) 28/10/1905 (scored)

Dennis O'Donnell signed following a solid four Second Division campaigns with Lincoln in which his goals' return totalled 31 from 118 appearances. O'Donnell had the capacity to take on all the attack positions. He appeared in over half Sunderland's League fixtures during 1905/06, a useful player in a moderate season when the club slipped from fifth place to 14th. He had an amount of first team football with his remaining senior clubs but stayed only one season with each. His brother, Magnus O'Donnell, an inside-left, was a colleague at Lincoln in 1904/05.

Appearances:
FL: 21 apps. 5 gls.
FAC: 1 app. 0 gls.
Total: *22 apps. 5 gls.*

OGILVIE, Gary F.

Role: Full-back 1988-89
5'11" 12st.2lbs.
b. Dundee, 16th November 1967

CAREER: Royals B.C./Dundee 1985/SUNDERLAND Mar 1988/Airdrieonians Feb 1989-1991.

Debut v West Ham United (a) 12/10/1988 (sub) (FLC)

Red-haired full-back Gary Ogilvie began with Dundee at 18 years of age, but had no senior experience when he joined Sunderland in late season 1987-88. Impressive enough in reserves action, he had his debut in the following term, but made just

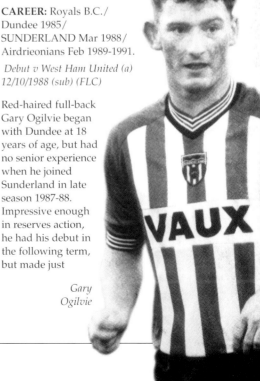

Gary
Ogilvie

three substitute appearances, leaving after eleven months at Roker to return to Scotland. Airdrieonians paid a reported fee of £10,000 for his transfer, but he made only eight senior appearances for the Diamonds in his two seasons at Broomfield Park.

Appearances:
FL: 0(1) apps. 0 gls.
FAC: 0(1) apps. 0 gls.
Other: 0(1) apps. 0 gls.
Total: *0(3) apps. 0 gls.*

O'HARE, John

Role: Centre/inside-forward 1964-67
5'8" 11st.2lbs.
b. Renton, Dunbartonshire, 24th September 1946

CAREER: Dumbarton schools football/ Drumchapel Amateurs/SUNDERLAND am cs 1962, pro Oct 1963/Derby County Aug 1967 £22,000/Leeds United Aug 1974 £50,000/ Nottingham Forest Feb 1975 £60,000 incl John McGovern (Dallas Tornado, USA loan 1977)/ Belper Town Aug 1981. Subsequently engaged in minor football: assisted Carriage & Wagon FC of Derby (East Midlands Regional League) in 1982/83 and managed two other sides in that district, Ockbrook and Stanton.

Debut v Chelsea (a) 29/8/1964

An admirable player, John O'Hare ranks among the best developed by Sunderland since World War Two. Totally unselfish and a magnificent team man, John had the ability and ball control to accept and retain possession in tight situations - virtues which outweighed some lack of pace and a modest strike rate in front goal. O'Hare joined Sunderland before his 16th birthday, turned pro at 17 and made his League debut a year later. The club was in the top flight for the whole of his Roker spell but, in the three seasons he gained first team experience, flirted uncomfortably with relegation. His main season at Roker was 1966-67, up-front alongside Neil Martin, when John was a regular and scored 11 goals in 35 League and cup outings. O'Hare was one of Brian Clough's early and significant signings as the newly-installed Derby County manager. Clough had shrewdly remembered coaching the player when responsible for Sunderland's youth team. It proved a most beneficial move for both men. John shared in the Rams'

John O'Hare

remarkable rise to glory, winning all his 13 Scottish caps, a League championship medal and a Division Two title during seven years at the Baseball Ground. Reliable and consistent, he missed only five League games in the first five years. As one commentator said "O'Hare may lack pace, grace and style but he is effective. Always ready to take a lonely role as chaser and an unselfish target man." He was a vital cog in the Rams' machine. When moved to midfield in 1972/73 to accommodate Roger Davies, he carried on without complaint and did well. Signed again by Clough during the colourful manager's later ill-fated short spell at Leeds, there was to be a third reunion with his managerial mentor, this time at Nottingham Forest. John arrived at the City Ground a month after Clough, accompanied by another ex-Derby man, John McGovern.

Ken Oliver

Aged 28, highly versed in the top-flight scene, O'Hare proved a rare bargain. He made 122(11) first team appearances, scored 20 goals and won a League Cup winners' medal. His last appearance for Forest was in the 1980 European Cup Final triumph against Hamburg in Madrid when he came on as a substitute. A perfect way to finish a senior career. John became involved with junior football following his departure from the senior scene. He was employed as a licensee for a time, later taking up a business appointment.

Appearances:
FL: 51 apps. 14 gls.
FAC: 5 apps. 3 gls.
FLC: 3 apps. 4 gls.
Total: *59 apps. 21 gls.*
Honours:
13 Scot caps/3 Scot U-23 apps/(Derby County) Div 2 champs 1969/ Div I champs 1972/(Nottingham Forest) FLC winner 1978 (sub first game, full game in replay)/ EC winner 1980 (sub).

OLIVER, James Henry Kenneth

Role: Centre-half/centre-forward 1947-49
5'11" 10st.12lbs.
b. Loughborough, Leics, 10th August 1924
d. Derby, 13th May 1994

CAREER: Brush Sports (Leics)/ SUNDERLAND Aug 1946/Derby County Sept 1949 £6,750/Exeter City Jan 1958/retired through injury May 1960.
Debut v Preston North End (a) 25/10/1947

Ken Oliver started as a centre-forward - three of his four League appearances in 1947/48 were in that position - but became exclusively a centre-half from 1948/49 onwards. Signed at a then sizeable fee by Derby, he succeeded the well-known Leon Leuty. At the Baseball Ground Ken acquired the nickname 'Rubberneck' because a long neck figured prominently in powerful headwork, his most obvious talent. He turned out for the Rams in all three divisions of the Football League, finishing with 193 League and FA Cup outings (one goal). At Exeter the figure was 96. Afterwards Ken became a director of a sports outfitting firm in Derby.

Appearances:
FL: 8 apps. 1 gl.
Total: *8 apps. 1 gl.*

OLIVER, John Sidney 'Dowk'

Role: Left-back 1886-92
b. Southwick, Sunderland, 1867

CAREER: Southwick FC/SUNDERLAND 1886/Middlesbrough Ironopolis June 1892/ Small Heath Apr 1894.
Debut v Morpeth Harriers (a) 16/10/1886 (FAC)
Debut v Burnley (h) 13/9/1890 (FL)

John Oliver holds a special place in the Sunderland scheme of things, being the only local to take a position in the Team of All the Talents. Oliver's ability is underlined by the fact of his selection for an international trial. Unfortunately in his final season, 1891/92, the first of Sunderland's League championships, he did not make sufficient appearances to qualify for

John Oliver

a medal. He had joined the club some years before its election to the Football League, proving a sturdy defender noted for powerful kicking. 'Dowk' refused the terms offered for 1892/93, hence the move to Ironopolis, a club attempting to establish the professional game on Teesside. For Small Heath (a club destined to become Birmingham FC in 1905) he made 62 first team appearances.

NOTE: *Although said to have originally joined Sunderland for season 1887/88 this is disproved by the date of his FA Cup-tie debut above.*

Appearances:
FL: 24 apps. 0 gls.
FAC: 16 apps. 0 gls.
Total: *40 apps. 0 gls.*

O'NEILL, Alan

Role: Inside-forward 1956-61
5'7" 10st.2lbs.
b. Leadgate, Co Durham, 13th November 1937

CAREER: Co Durham schools football/ SUNDERLAND am June 1954, pro Feb 1955/ Aston Villa Oct 1960 £10,000/Plymouth Argyle Nov 1962 £10,000/Bournemouth & Boscombe

Alan O'Neill

Athletic Feb 1964 £9,000/Cambridge United early 1966/South African football for 2 seasons before appointment as Drumcondra player-coach cs 1970.

Debut v Cardiff City (a) 17/11/1956

Originally named Alan Hope, he changed his surname to O'Neill in 1956 by deed poll, following the re-marriage of his mother. Alan was recruited by the Roker Park ground staff after playing for Sunderland Boys, getting his initial outing with the League team four days past his 19th birthday. Alan, though had no wish to make a career with his local club, making half a dozen requests for a move before Villa signed him. He made a dream debut for them, and in a local derby against Birmingham scored two goals, the first in a mere 25 seconds. (Possibly a debutant's record?) This was in a period when Aston Villa had just won the Second Division championship and were to win the 1960/61 League Cup but O'Neill was unable to displace either Bobby Thomson or Ron Wylie. For Plymouth Argyle he made 40 Football League appearances (14 goals) and with Bournemouth 37 (8 goals). A workmanlike forward who perhaps did not quite live up to early expectations.

Appearances:
FL: 74 apps. 27 gls.
FAC: 2 apps. 1 gl.
Total: *76 apps. 28 gls.*

O'NEILL, James

Role: Centre-forward 1961-62
5'10" 11st.1lb.
b. Lurgan, Co Armagh, 24th November 1941

CAREER: Mayharaming Juniors/ SUNDERLAND am June 1958, pro Nov 1958/ Walsall Dec 1962 £9,000/Hakoah (Australia) May 1965/Darlington Nov 1967, after a month's trial/Coleraine June 1968.

Debut v Bristol Rovers (h) 13/1/1962 (scored)

A stand-in for Brian Clough who, indeed, showed a Cloughie-like goals touch in his few appearances, two of Jimmy O'Neill's goals were scored on his debut. It was a similar story at Walsall, two in his initial game against Portsmouth. Jimmy did not have the best of luck, however, with the Saddlers. He played little during the 1963/64 campaign through illness and injury, and was unable to gain a

Jimmy O'Neill

Richard Ord

regular place in 1964/65. After a two-year stint in Australia, O'Neill made 20 Fourth Division appearances for Darlington, plus three substitutions, scoring four goals.

Appearances:
FL: 7 apps. 6 gls.
Total: *7 apps. 6 gls.*
Honours:
1 NIre cap v Wales 1962/2 NIre U-23 apps./ NIre Sch.

ORD, Richard John

Role: Defender 1987-98
6'2" 13st.5lbs.
b. Murton, Co Durham, 3rd March 1970

CAREER: East Durham and Durham County Schoolboys/Murton/Wheatley Hill/ SUNDERLAND assoc .s'boy Mar 1984, trainee June 1986, pro July 1987(York City loan Feb-Mar 1990)/Queens Park Rangers July 1998.

Debut v Southend United (h) 3/11/1987

Sunderland's best win for over thirty years also coincided with Dickie Ord's League debut against Southend United in November 1987.

It could hardly have been a more memorable introduction for the 17-year-old central defender as Sunderland won 7-0. Substituted after 68 minutes to make way for another debutant, Michael Heathcote, Ord had nevertheless announced his arrival at senior level in a most positive manner. Early comparisons to the great Charlie Hurley were premature and unhelpful, but his ability and versatility were never in doubt. Equally effective in central or left-sided defence or midfield, he was an ideal squad member, but his career really flourished after he claimed, then retained, the centre-back position. A Sunderland supporter, Dickie even featured in the title of a disc - "Who needs Cantona when we've got Dickie Ord" - released by Sunderland fans. In July 1996 he was unfortunate to miss playing in his own testimonial match against Steaua Bucharest due to injury, and although it was anticipated he would prove a most resilient defender during the 1996-97 Premiership season, Ord lost his way after twice being sent-off. He was then plagued by injury during season 1997-98, losing his first team place and then failing to regain it when restored to fitness. After eleven years as a Sunderland professional, Dickie Ord was transferred to Queens Park Rangers in the summer of 1998 for a reported fee of £675,000. Unfortunately Ord's Loftus Road career was blighted immediately as five minutes into QPR's first pre-season friendly he suffered a serious knee injury which required several unsuccessful operations. In July 1999 he was still sidelined with little prospect of any immediate return and his whole career in the balance.

Appearances:
PL: 33 apps. 2 gls.
FL: 190(21) apps. 5 gls.
FAC: 11(1) apps. 1 gl.
FLC: 17(4) apps. 0 gls.
Other: 5(1) apps. 0 gls.
Total: *256(27) apps. 8 gls.*
Honours:
3 Eng U-21 apps. 1990/(Sunderland) Div 1 champs 1996.

OUTTERSIDE, Mark Jeremy

Role: Full-back 1986-87
5'11" 11st.8lbs.
b. Hexham, 13th January 1967

CAREER: Ryton Comprehensive, Tyne & Wear/SUNDERLAND assoc. s'boy Sept 1981, pro Jan 1985(Blackburn Rovers loan Dec 1985)/Darlington July 1987-Sept 1988/ Newcastle Blue Star 1988/Hebburn FC/ Whitley Bay/Consett July 1995.

Debut v Oldham Athletic (h) 21/3/1987

A Sunderland professional at 18 years of age, Mark Outterside had joined the Roker staff straight from school but in an association just short of six years appeared only once at senior level. In a season with Darlington he appeared in 37(1) Division Four matches and additionally returned to Roker with his new team mates when Darlington were drawn to visit Sunderland in the first round of the

Mark Outterside

FA Cup. It was the first ever FA Cup tie between the teams and 16,892 spectators saw a brave fight by the Quakers who finally went down by 2-0. Mark Outterside was still only 21 years old when he left Darlington for non-League football.

Appearances:
FL: 1 app. 0 gls.
Total: *1 app. 0 gls.*

OVERFIELD, Jack

Role: Outside-left 1960-63
5'10" 10st.8lbs.
b. Leeds, 14th May 1932

CAREER: Leeds schoolboy football/Ashley Road Methodists (Leeds)/Yorkshire Amateurs (Sheffield United & Bolton Wanderers on amateur forms)/Leeds United May 1953/ SUNDERLAND Aug 1960 £11,500/ Peterborough United Feb 1963 £5,000/ Bradford City July 1964-1965.

Debut v Swansea Town (h) 20/8/1960

A tallish, slim wingman with ball control and plenty of speed to show most backs a clean

Jack Overfield

pair of heels, Jack Overfield came to Roker after service in good class amateur circles and for his home town Leeds United. At Elland Road he had played 163 League and Cup games, scoring 20 goals. Actually Jack was not a prolific scorer, a circumstance continued elsewhere including his time with Sunderland. A strange example of this occurred in 1956/57 when he scored in Leeds' opening League engagement and this was his only goal in a season when an ever-present.

Appearances:
FL: 65 apps. 5 gls.
FAC: 5 apps. 0 gls.
FLC: 4 apps. 0 gls.
Total: *74 apps. 5 gls.*

OWERS, Gary

Role: Midfield 1987-94
5'11" 11st.10lbs.
b. Newcastle upon Tyne, 3rd October 1968

CAREER: Lord Lawson Comprehensive School (Birtley)/Chester-le-Street Schoolboys/ SUNDERLAND app 1985, pro Oct 1986/ Bristol City Dec 1994/Notts County July 1998-date.

Debut v Brentford (a) 15/8/1987

Gary Owers joined Sunderland as a 16-year-old apprentice, and graduated through the ranks to make his first team debut in Third Division football under new manager Denis Smith in August 1987. Owers was an immediate success. A fierce competitor in midfield or at full-back, he made 37 League appearances in his first season and collected a championship medal as Sunderland won the title with 92 goals scored and a nine-point margin over second-placed Brighton & Hove Albion. For the following six-and-a-half seasons, many in midfield tandem with Paul Bracewell, Gary was a consistent and familiar fixture in the Sunderland team. An appearance in the 1990 play-off final and the 1992 FA Cup final, when he adapted to replace the injured John Kay at right-back and created two of Sunderland's best opportunities against Liverpool, were highlights of his distinguished spell at Roker which ended when Bristol City's manager Joe Jordan paid £250,000 for his transfer, which included Martin Scott in part-exchange, just prior to Christmas 1994. In season 1996-97 Bristol City reached the Division Two play-off semi-final but lost 4-2 on aggregate to Brentford. In 1997-98 however, they won automatic promotion as runners-up to Watford. At one time Gary was married to former British ice-skating champion, Joanne Conway.

Appearances:
FL: 262(9) apps. 25 gls.
FAC: 10(2) apps. 0 gls.
FLC: 27(1) apps. 1 gl.
Other: 8(1) apps. 1 gl.
Total: *307(13) apps. 27 gls.*
Honours:
(Sunderland) Div 3 champs 1988/ FAC finalist 1992.

Gary Owers

PAGE, John Abraham

Role: Outside-right 1919-20
5'6" 11st.lbs.
b. Sunderland, 1st qtr 1893

CAREER: Sunderland West End /
SUNDERLAND Jan 1920/Sunderland West
End May 1921.

Debut v Preston North End (h) 10/4/1920

Jack Page was a thickset, local outside-right
who spent one and a half seasons at Roker
Park. His League outings comprised three of
the final four League fixtures of 1919/20. All
were at home, Sunderland winning two and
losing the final game to Liverpool 1-0. On
Sunderland's books at the same time as Page
was his West End colleague Tommy Glidden.
The latter went on to win fame with West
Bromwich Albion as both player and
administrator in half a century at The
Hawthorns.

> **Appearances:**
> *FL: 3 apps. 0 gls.*
> **Total:** *3 apps. 0 gls.*

Jack Page

PALLISTER, William

Role: Right-half 1898-99
5'9" 12st.2lbs.
b. Gateshead

CAREER: Local junior
football to SUNDERLAND
Dec 1897/Lincoln City May
1902-cs 1905.

Bill Pallister

Debut v Bury (a) 31/3/1899

Bill Pallister made only one senior appearance
in his four and a half years at Sunderland, and
that at right-half (it was a 1-0 win at Gigg
Lane). At Lincoln all but three of his 61 Second
Division outings were at left-back, the others
being at right-back. At Sincil Bank too he
succeeded an old Sunderland favourite from
the great early 1890s days, Willie Gibson.

> **Appearances:**
> *FL: 1 app. 0 gls.*
> **Total:** *1 app. 0 gls.*

PALMER, Calvin Ian

Role: Back/Wing-half/Inside-forward 1967-70
5'10" 11st.5lbs.
b. Skegness, Lincs, 21st October 1940

CAREER: Skegness Town/Nottingham Forest
Mar 1958/Stoke City Sept 1963 £30,000/
SUNDERLAND Feb 1968 £70,000/South
African football 1970, first with Cape Town
City and later Hellenic FC where he was also
asst. manager/Crewe Alexandra Oct 1971-
1972.

Debut v Manchester City (a) 24/2/1968

Certainly among the most versatile players of
his day, Calvin Palmer was well able to make
a show in any outfield position, but was very
likely at his best in a wing-half slot. He
revealed high promise during his time on the
Forest ground staff, representing both the
Notts FA and the Thursday League. Calvin
gained prominence in 1960/61 with 27 League
outings replacing the injured right-half, Jeff
Whitefoot. He himself lost his place through
injury the following term and asked for a
transfer as a consequence. The same thing
happened again in 1962/63, after he had
become the Forest captain, and it was on the
cards West Bromwich Albion would sign him
in a £30,000 deal. However, Palmer did not

move for some months, eventually going to Stoke (196 League and Cup appearances, 27 goals). So Palmer arrived at Roker Park a seasoned performer but his stay was comparatively short.

Calvin Palmer

Appearances:
FL: 35(5) apps. 5 gls.
FLC: 2 apps. 0 gls.
Total *37(5) apps. 5 gls.*
Honours:
(Stoke City) FLC finalist 1964.

PARK, Robert

Role: Forward 1969-72
5'11" 9st.12lbs.
b. Coatbridge, 5th January 1952

CAREER: Coatbridge juniors/SUNDERLAND Jan 1969/retired through injury May 1975.

Debut v Arsenal (h)
18/10/1969

A versatile player, Bobby Park played inside-left in Sunderland's 1969 Youth Cup-winning side but most of his senior outings were at outside-right and he could cope in other positions. Tall and slim, Bobby compensated for a light weight with skill and courage. He also had an ability to deliver beautifully weighted passes, and one in 1970 that split the Derby defence for Gordon Harris to score particularly lives in the memory. He was regarded as being among the most promising young players of his generation when, on the opening day of the season in August 1971, he broke a leg playing left-back in torrential rain against Birmingham City. In 1972/73 he was all set for a return when he broke the same leg during a training session. Sadly Bobby had to eventually retire aged only 23, and was awarded a joint testimonial match with Ritchie Pitt against AZ67 Alkmaar of Holland.

Appearances:
FL: 50(15) apps. 4 gls.
FAC: 2 apps. 0 gls.
FLC: 1 app. 0 gls.
Other: 4 apps. 1 gl.
Total: *57(15) apps. 5 gls.*

Bobby Park in action for Sunderland at Ipswich.

PARKE, John

Role: Left-back/left-half 1964-68
5'9" 11st.4lbs.
b. Belfast, 6th August 1937

CAREER: Cliftonville/Linfield 1955/
Hibernian Oct 1963 £15,000/SUNDERLAND
Nov 1964 £33,000/Mechelen FC (Belgium) July
1968.

Debut v Sheffield United (a) 21/11/1964

John Parke was approaching a decade in
senior Ulster football before making the trip to
Edinburgh and joining Hibs. In that time John
had revealed a splendid versatility well
illustrated by his four Irish Cup finals. In them
he occupied a different position each time:
chronologically inside-right, right-half, left-
half and right-back. Also during those years
he had been awarded his first international
cap and represented the Irish League. It was
during his Roker Park stay that most of his
caps were garnered (11), joining late in 1964 a
club newly promoted to the top flight where
all his Sunderland days were spent. A capable
and valuable utility man.

> **Appearances:**
> *FL: 83(2) apps. 0 gls.*
> *FAC: 3 apps. 0 gls.*
> *FLC: 5 apps. 0 gls.*
> **Total:** *91(2) apps. 0 gls.*
> **Honours:**
> *14 NIre caps/1 Irish Lge app. v Lge of Ireland*
> *1959/(Linfield) IC winner 1962, 1963/*
> *IC finalist 1958, 1961.*

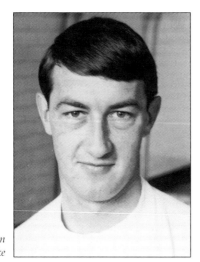

John
Parke

PARKER, Charles William

Role: Centre-half 1920-29
5'9" 10st.9lbs.
b. Seaham Harbour, Co Durham,
21st September 1891

CAREER: Seaham Young Albion/Seaham
Albion/Seaham Harbour FC(Blackpool
trial)/Stoke Jan 1914/SUNDERLAND Oct
1920 £3,300/Carlisle United player-coach
May 1929/Blyth Spartans Sept 1930/
Chopwell Institute 1931/Carlisle United
trainer July 1935.

Debut v Bradford City (a) 23/10/1920

With a height of 5'9" and a weight under 11
stones Charlie Parker hardly fitted the
stereotyped mental picture of a typical
centre-half of his day. Yet his skill,
perspicacity and consistency were such that
he was first choice pivot for seven of his
nine meritorious Roker Park seasons.
Charlie received a thorough grounding
during early days in his native Seaham,
ending up with Seaham Harbour FC,
members of the strong North-Eastern
League. He took a further step up the
football ladder joining Stoke in the
beginning of that fateful year, 1914. Stoke
had been a 'yo-yo' club right from its days
as a founder member of the Football
League and was immured in the Second
Division of the Southern League. Charlie
made his debut in Stoke's first team on

PARKER, Richard

Role: Centre-forward 1919-20
5'9" 11st.0lbs.
b. Stockton-on-Tees, 14th September 1894
d. Stockton-on-Tees, 1st January 1969

CAREER: Tilery School/Norton United 1913-
14/Thornaby Corinthians/South Bank/
Stockton/SUNDERLAND June 1919/
Coventry City Jan 1920 £1,500/South Shields
Oct 1920 £1,000/Wallsend Sept 1921/Queens
Park Rangers July 1922/Millwall Athletic July
1924/Watford Nov 1927 - cs 1928 £1,000/
Merthyr Town Mar 1929/Tunbridge Wells
Rangers 1930.

Debut v Aston Villa (h) 30/8/1919 (scored)

February 28, 1914 in a 2-1 home victory over Brentford. The following season he was a regular in their championship-winning side, making 22 out of a possible 24 appearances. He assisted the Potters in every wartime season and tasted his first Football League fare in the initial (1919/20) peacetime season, Stoke having been re-elected to the national scene. Charlie's form was excellent, a fact duly recognised by a selection for the 'Victory' international against Wales and an inter-league fixture for the Football League against the Scottish League. By then he was approaching 30, in an era which considered that age almost the end of the road for an outfield player. Sunderland, however, astutely recognised Charlie's worth by paying what then must have been the record fee for a half-back. At Roker Park over nine terms he averaged around 27 appearances per season but many years totalled between 30 and 40 games, mute tributes to fine consistency. Charlie was

pivot of a ubiquitous half-back line flanked usually by Billy Clunas and Arthur Andrews. It was a settled line that played in front of a solid defence: goalie Albert McInroy, and full backs Warney Cresswell (or Jim Oakley) and Ernie England. Charlie was Sunderland's vice-captain until Charles Buchan's transfer to Arsenal, then taking over the captaincy. He was perhaps a shade unlucky not to get a full cap but the great Joe McCall, and subsequently Sheffield Wednesday's George Wilson, barred the way. Charlie's younger brother, Fred, also a centre-half, assisted Nottingham Forest during the 1920s, winning a Division Two championship medal in 1922.

Appearances:
FL: 245 apps. 12 gls.
FAC: 11 apps. 0 gls.
Total: *256 apps. 12 gls.*
Honours:
1 Eng Victory app. v Wales 1920/1 FL app. v Scot Lge 1919/(Stoke) Sthn Lge Div 2 champs 1915.

Dick Parker was a man of many clubs who commenced his senior career at Roker Park with a debut goal in the club's opening League game after the Great War - a 2-1 win over Aston Villa. He subsequently served six Football League clubs, five of them from the Third Division (South). And it was at one of these, Millwall, that his best return came: 71 goals in 106 League and FA Cup appearances. At the Den too he established club records for a seasonal League total (37 in 1926/27) and for goals in a single League match (five versus

Dick Parker

Norwich City also in '26/27). Neither record has been broken at the time of writing, more than seventy years on. Dick Parker, speedy and skilled, believed in keeping the ball on the ground and shooting hard and often. "A strong forceful player and a consistent goal getter" as one commentator recorded in 1926. All told Parker scored 128 goals in 246 Football League outings. During the war Dick served with the Northumberland Fusiliers in France, and in an Army international versus Scotland scored a hat-trick

Appearances:
FL: 6 apps. 3 gls.
Total: *6 apps. 3 gls.*
Honours:
1 FL app. v The Army 1927.

PASCOE, Colin James

Role: Forward/Midfield 1987-92
5'10" 12st.0lbs.
b. Bridgend, Glamorgan, 9th April 1965

CAREER: Afan Nedd Schoolboys/Swansea City app, pro Apr 1983/SUNDERLAND Mar 1988(Swansea City loan July 1992)/Swansea City Aug 1993/Blackpool one month's trial Mar 1996/Merthyr Tydfil 1996-97.

Debut v York City (a) 26/3/1988 (sub) (scored)

A £70,000 transfer deadline day signing in March 1988, Colin Pascoe scored on his debut and his four goals in 8(1) appearances in the run-in helped Sunderland to win the Third Division championship. Earlier in the same season his 13 goals in 34 appearances had put Swansea City into the promotion frame, and

Colin Pascoe

following his departure they clinched a place in Division Three via the play-off finals. Although not quite 23 years old when signed, Colin was a full international and had experience in all four divisions of the Football League. He made his full League debut for Swansea City on his 18th birthday against Liverpool at Anfield and had scored 39 goals in 174 League appearances at the time of his move to Sunderland. Capped by Wales at three levels he won eight of his ten caps whilst on Sunderland's books, and was the club's first Welsh international since Ray Daniel in 1957. Colin returned to Swansea in August 1993 and in the following April helped them lift the Autoglass Trophy at Wembley. Ankle ligament injuries blighted his final season and he was released by Swansea in February 1996. Colin's aggregate League career, including substitute appearances totalled 397 and he scored 76 goals.

Appearances:
FL: 117(10) apps. 23 gls.
FAC: 4(2) apps. 0 gls.
FLC: 12 apps. 3 gls.
Other: 4 apps. 0 gls.
Total: *137(12) apps. 26 gls.*
Honours:
10 Welsh caps 1984-92/4 Welsh U-21 apps.
1983-84/6 Welsh Yth apps./(Swansea City)
WC winner 1983/AWT winner 1994.

PATERSON, John William

Role: Centre-forward 1921-25
5'10" 10st.8lbs.
b. Dundee, 14th December 1896

CAREER: Fort Hill/Dundee North End/Army football/Dundee FC 1918-19/Leicester City Dec 1919/SUNDERLAND Mar 1922 £3,790/Preston North End Oct 1924/Mid-Rhondda Sept 1925/Queens Park Rangers Jan 1926/Mansfield Town July 1928/Montrose Oct 1928.

Debut v Sheffield United (h) 4/3/1922

A big name in the immediate post-WW1 years and it took a large cheque to prise Jock Paterson from Leicester City in 1922. Despite being wounded five times while serving with the Black Watch he had recovered to charm spectators and critics alike with his resource, speed and shooting power. As one of the latter remarked in 1921 "Jock is one of the few forwards who can go through a modern defence on his own." This fine spell, which

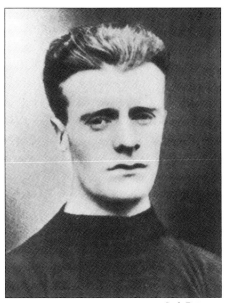

Jock Paterson

Tottenham Hotspur pro Nov 1906/Crystal Palace May 1909/ SUNDERLAND Apr 1911/ Leyton Jan 1912/ Woolwich Arsenal June 1912-cs 1913.

Debut v Oldham Athletic (h) 28/10/1911

A crack amateur, George Payne played five times for Hertfordshire in county matches just before turning professional. This change in status came about when Spurs gave him a trial against Oxford University and Payne performed so well that he was straightaway offered terms. But his career at White Hart Lane was blighted by injuries and he moved to Palace for his best spell as a pro (46 Southern League and FA Cup appearances, 31 goals: an outstanding return). Payne made 17 Southern League appearances for Leyton (four goals) and three in the Football League for Arsenal. He was severely wounded in September 1918 when serving with the Forces.

Appearances:
FL: 2 apps. 0 gls.
Total: *2 apps. 0 gls.*

won him a Scotland cap, had been preceded by scoring feats in Army football, during which time he represented the 61st Division. His best Sunderland season saw 21 League goals in 1922-23. With his last senior club, Preston, Jock joined in a season that saw them relegated from the top flight, and he failed to score in 17 League outings. Shortly before his move to Wales, Preston announced Jock was going to Raith Rovers as part of a deal for Alex James but Paterson refused the move.

Appearances:
FL: 74 apps. 37 gls.
FAC: 3 apps. 3 gls.
Total: *77 apps. 40 gls.*
Honours:
1 Scot cap v England 1920.

PAYNE, George Clark

Role: Inside-left 1911-12
5'8" 10st.6lbs.
b. Hitchin, Herts, 17th February 1887
d. Clacton-on-Sea, Essex, 21st August 1932

CAREER: Page Green Old Boys/ Hitchin Union Jack 1902/Hitchin Town 1904/Barnet Alston 1905/

PEACOCK, A.

Role: Inside-left 1888-89
Debut v Elswick Rangers (h) 27/10/1888 (FAC) (scored)

Scored twice in the above Cup-tie which resulted in a 5-3 victory for Sunderland. Peacock was partnered by a W. Peacock (q.v.) on this occasion, but it is not known whether the pair were brothers or otherwise related. A. Peacock also played in the other Cup-tie of that season (against Newcastle East End on November 17, 1888). The debut tie against Elswick started him on a long run of consecutive appearances at inside-left: 24 in total, the last of them on February 2, 1889. Four games at outside-left before this brought the total sequence to 28.

Appearances:
FAC: 2 apps. 2 gls.
Total: *2 apps. 2 gls.*

George Payne

PEACOCK, W.

Role: Outside-left 1888-89
Debut v Elswick Rangers (h) 27/10/1888 (FAC)

Partnered at inside-left in the above Cup-tie by A. Peacock, but whether they are related is not known. He had a number of other outings for Sunderland in that pre-League season. There were two runs of consecutive appearances: seven in December 1888 and seven in January-February 1889. But his appearances tally did not equal that of his namesake.

Appearances:
FAC: 1 app. 0 gls.
Total: *1 app. 0 gls.*

PEARCE, Reginald Stanley

Role: Left-half 1957-61
5'10" 11st.9lbs.
b. Liverpool, 12th January 1930

CAREER: Liverpool Marine (Liverpool FC am)/Winsford United/Luton Town Nov 1954 £1,000/SUNDERLAND Feb 1958 £16,500/Cambridge City July 1961/Peterborough United Aug 1963/Cambridge City July 1964/Boston FC cs 1966, released Sept 1966.

Debut v Preston North End (a) 1/3/1958

Reg Pearce joined Luton when nearing his 25th birthday after sampling a good class of minor professional football with Winsford United of the Cheshire League. The Hatters were then 'on a roll' finishing runners-up in Division Two in a thrilling season when only two points separated the top five clubs. Pearce made his debut before the season ended, going on to play a further 74 games (six goals) in the top flight before moving to Sunderland. That season, 1957/58, was perhaps Pearce's best for it was then his two inter-league medals were won and his considerable gifts as an all-round wing-half recognised. Sunderland were relegated that term and for the remainder of Reg's time they were a middling Second Division outfit. His final Football League spell was with Third Division Peterborough (28 appearances, two goals).

Appearances:
FL: 61 apps. 4 gls.
FAC: 1 app. 0 gls.
Total: *62 apps. 4 gls.*
Honours:
2 FL apps.

PEGG, Frank Edward

Role: Outside-left 1925-26
5'8" 11st.0lbs.
b. Beeston, Notts, 2nd August 1902
d. Bedford, 9th August 1991

CAREER: Sawley United (Blackpool trial Aug 1924)(Nelson trial Dec 1924)/Loughborough Corinthians early 1925/SUNDERLAND May 1925/Lincoln City May 1926/Bradford City May 1931/Norwich City June 1932/New Brighton Aug 1933/Yarmouth Town Aug 1934-Apr 1937.

Debut v Bolton Wanderers (a) 7/4/1926

Frank Pegg

Frank Pegg was apparently a prospect from his junior days with trials at two Football League clubs and a quick move from Loughborough of the Central Alliance to Roker Park. But Frank found himself third choice outside-left behind the two Bills, Ellis and Death. A move to Lincoln proved to be a good one, his hard - if often erratic - shooting much to the fore. His aggregate figures at Sincil Bank (115 appearances, 51 goals) would have been much higher but for a

Reg Pearce

bad injury sustained in the opening fixture of 1928/29. Pegg made only three appearances for Bradford City and six for Norwich, then missed a single game only in his New Brighton season, scoring eight goals. His spell at Yarmouth provided a highlight with the scoring of four goals in a match during November 1934

Appearances:
FL: 1 app. 0 gls.
Total: *1 app. 0 gls.*

PEREZ, Lionel

Role: Goalkeeper 1996-98
6'0" 13st.4lbs.
b. Bagnois Ceze, France, 24th April 1967

CAREER: Nimes Olympique, France/ Girondins de Bordeaux, France, 1993/ SUNDERLAND Aug 1996/Newcastle United June 1998(Olympique Lyonnais, France, loan Mar 1999).

Debut v Southampton (a) 19/10/1996 (sub)

Originally signed as cover for the unfortunate Tony Coton, Lionel Perez stepped into the breach when the senior goalkeeper suffered a compound leg fracture in the early stages of 1996-97. A flamboyant figure of stocky build, flowing locks and bared forearms, Lionel literally seized his opportunity with a string of heroic performances which earned him the supporters Player of the Year accolade - the first keeper to win the award since Chris Turner in 1985. Initially unorthodox, the bizarre Frenchman improved markedly in technique whilst remaining an excellent reflex shot-stopper. Born near to Marseille, Perez joined Nimes from school, and won promotion with them in 1991. (A team mate at Nimes was Eric Cantona). After three years with Bordeaux, he joined Sunderland for £200,000, and provided full value for his relatively modest fee. His extraordinary 'double save' in the home leg of the 1998 play-off semi-final with Sheffield United was simply magnificent, yet he was positionally at fault and blamed for Charlton's late equaliser from a corner in the thrilling play-off final that followed. Only

days after appearing in that Wembley heartbreak, Lionel was signed by Newcastle manager, Kenny Dalglish. Shortly after Ruud Gullit's arrival at St James Park, however, he promoted Steve Harper to number two behind Shay Given, leaving the Frenchman out of the picture. An opportunity to resurrect his career came in tragic circumstances. Luc Borelli, the Olympique Lyonnais goalkeeper, was killed in a road accident. His club asked Newcastle about the availability of Perez and, although the French transfer window had actually closed, permission was granted for his loan move to take place. Available from Newcastle on a free transfer, Lionel will be hoping to secure a permanent appointment in 1999/2000.

Appearances:
PL: 28(1) apps. 0 gls.
FL: 49 apps. 0 gls.
FAC: 4 apps. 0 gls.
FLC: 2 caps. 0 gls.
Total: *83(1) apps. 0 gls.*

Lionel Perez

PHILIP, George

Role: Centre-forward/inside-left 1914-15
5'9" 12st.0lbs.
b. Newport, Fife

CAREER: Junior football to Dundee 1911/
SUNDERLAND Apr 1914/Dundee June 1920-
21.

Debut v Sheffield United (h) 2/9/1914

George Philip

In the three seasons preceding his transfer to Sunderland George Philip had played in 68 Scottish League (Division One) games for Dundee, scoring 16 goals. This comparatively modest goals return is perhaps accounted for by his other position, centre-half. His term at Roker Park found him wholly a forward, the majority of his outings as leader of the attack. He missed only one game and produced an excellent goals return. George did not appear at all in the first post-war season, returning to his old club for season 1920/21, when he appeared 27 times in their Scottish League programme.

Appearances:
FL: 37 apps. 22 gls.
FAC: 1 app. 0 gls.
Total: *38 apps. 22 gls.*

PICKERING, Nicholas

Role: Midfield 1981-86
6'0" 11st.10lbs.
b. South Shields, 4th August 1963

CAREER: Harton Comprehensive School/
North Shields Schoolboys/SUNDERLAND
assoc s'boy Sept 1977, app, pro Aug 1981/
Coventry City Jan 1986/Derby County Aug
1988/Darlington Oct 1991/Burnley Mar 1993-
June 1994.

Debut v Ipswich Town (a) 29/8/1981

Pale-faced, slim and energetic, Nick Pickering became a fixture in Sunderland's first team after making his debut as an 18-year-old in the opening match of season 1981-82. England

PHILLIPS, Kevin

Role: Forward 1997-date
5'7" 11st.0lbs.
b. Hitchin, Herts, 25th July 1973

CAREER: Southampton assoc s'boy Oct
1987, trainee July 1989/Baldock Town cs
1991/Watford Dec 1994/SUNDERLAND
July 1997.

*Debut v Manchester City (h) 15/8/1997
(scored)*

A natural goalscorer with quick and nimble skills and every top striker's uncanny instinct for being in the right place at the right time, Kevin Phillips' speedy and incisive forward play has been a revelation since his bargain £325,000 transfer (reportedly since topped up to £600,000) from Watford in July 1997. He began with Southampton where he was considered too small for a striking role and converted into a full-back. Rejected after two years as a trainee he moved into the Beazer Homes League with Baldock Town, where he was re-instated up front by Ian Allison, the former Arsenal player and Baldock manager. Two goals in his first outing at centre-forward ensured his full-time defending days were over, and after a £10,000 move from Baldock to Watford his significant progress continued with 24 League goals in 59 appearances for the Hornets, despite an injury lay-off which lasted almost a year. 'SuperKev's' first season at the Stadium of Light was simply sensational. His total of 35 goals eclipsed the awesome record 34 scored by Brian Clough in season 1961-62. A purple mid-term burst in which he netted ten times in seven consecutive matches surpassed another record, set by Trevor Ford, who had scored in six consecutive games back in 1951. Despite his bitter disappointment at the club's failure to secure a place in the Premiership, recognition by England 'B' rewarded Kevin's outstanding first season in which he was voted Nationwide Player of the Year. As 1998-99 opened Kevin scored in all but one of the opening seven League fixtures and, despite injuries which restricted his League and Cup appearances during the season to 32, his total of 25 goals

Kevin Phillips with the Golden Boot awarded for being the First Division's joint top scorer in 1997/98.

(which included 23 in 26 League matches) saw him finish once again as the club's leading scorer. Called up by Kevin Keegan to play for England against Hungary in April 1999, Kevin partnered Alan Shearer, whose boots he had cleaned during those early days at Southampton. When Michael Gray was introduced as a substitute in the same match, it was the first time since 1926 that two Sunderland players had appeared together in an England shirt. Kevin scored his 50th goal for Sunderland against Bolton Wanderers on 20th March 1999. Since the war only Brian Clough has achieved 50 goals in fewer games for the club. Other highlights along the way included four at Rotherham United in an FA Cup third round tie in

January 1998. Another four goal blast (which included a 23-minute hat-trick) at Bury stylishly clinched promotion to the Premiership in April 1999. It will be fascinating to follow how the potent Phillips measures up against Premiership defences in 1999-2000. Few Sunderland supporters would bet against him rising to the challenge.

Appearances:
FL: 70 apps. 54 gls.
FAC: 3 apps. 4 gls.
FLC: 5 apps. 2 gls.
Total: *78 apps. 60 gls.*
Honours:
1 Eng 'B' app. 1998/1 Eng cap 1999/ (Sunderland) Div 1 champs 1999.

Youth honours were followed by 15 Under-21 caps and one full cap for England's 1983 tour to Australia. At either full-back or his favoured left side of midfield role, Pickering displayed remarkable maturity and vision during four-and-a-half seasons as a regular at Roker Park during the first half of the 'eighties decade. Never a great goalscorer, he did, however, end

Nick Pickering

his Sunderland spell with a remarkable flourish, netting a hat-trick in his penultimate game, a 4-2 home win over Leeds United. Coventry City paid £125,000 for him in January 1986 and in the following year he was a surprise FA Cup winner with the Sky Blues,

which made up for Nick's disappointment at collecting a losers' League Cup medal with Sunderland at Wembley in 1985. He had a much less rewarding time with Derby County who paid £250,000 for his transfer in August 1988. In three seasons at the Baseball Ground, Nick recorded only 35(10) League appearances, suffered from injuries and was given a free transfer to Darlington. Burnley paid £15,000 for him in March 1993 but he was released in June 1994 after just four League games. More recently he has acted as a summariser for Radio Newcastle and has also helped coach Wearside youngsters as part of Sunderland's Community Programme.

Appearances:
FL: 177(2) apps. 18 gls.
FAC: 10 apps. 0 gls.
FLC: 18 apps. 0 gls.,
Other: 2 apps. 0 gls.
Total: *207(2) apps. 18 gls.*
Honours:
1 Eng cap 1983/Eng Yth 1982/15 Eng U-21 apps. 1983-86/(Sunderland) FLC finalist 1985/(Coventry City) FAC winner 1987.

Ritchie Pitt (right) celebrates FA Cup success with Dennis Tueart and Vic Halom.

PITT, Richard Ernest 'Ritchie'

Role: Centre-half 1968-74
6'1" 12st.0lbs.
b. Ryhope, Co Durham, 22nd October 1951

CAREER: Seaham Schools/SUNDERLAND Nov 1968 (Arsenal loan Feb 1972)/retired through injury May 1975 but joined Blyth Spartans later that year.
Debut v Coventry City (a) 4/3/1969

Ritchie Pitt impressed as a schoolboy. Following a fine display in an English Schools trophy semi-final he was selected for England, subsequently appearing for the national Under-15 and Under-18 sides in the same season. Indeed, because of these early experiences he was the only member of the 1973 Cup winning side to have previously played at Wembley! Ritchie naturally graduated to Roker Park, becoming a member of the 1969 Youth Cup-winning team and making a League debut aged only 17. From then on his assured, skilful displays did not go

unnoticed and he was reckoned a possible future full international. But after a starring role in the 1973 FA Cup final he played only five games before receiving what appeared to be an innocuous knock to the right knee. Most unfortunately the injury forced retirement from full time football at the age of 24. A great loss to the game in general and Sunderland AFC in particular. Ritchie became a physical education teacher and worked in the Channel Islands before returning to the north east. He now teaches in Seaham and is currently actively involved in organising and running an ex-Sunderland Players' Association.

Appearances:
FL: 126 apps. 7 gls.
FAC: 10 apps. 0 gls.
FLC: 4 apps. 0 gls.
Other: 4(1) apps. 0 gls.
Total: *144(1) apps. 7 gls.*
Honours:
6 apps Eng Sch/(Sunderland) FAC winner 1973.

POOLE, John Smith

Role: Centre/left-half
1919-24
5'10" 12st.4lbs.
b. Codnor, Derbyshire, 1892
d. Mansfield, 21st March 1967

Jack Poole

CAREER: Sutton United/ Sutton Junction/Sherwood Foresters/ Nottingham Forest Mar 1917/SUNDERLAND May 1919/Bradford City May 1924, becoming their reserve side's player-coach Oct 1927, asst trainer 1930-Aug 1935/Mansfield Town trainer July 1935, manager May 1938/Notts County trainer-coach Aug 1944/Derby County trainer post-war until 1956/Sutton Town trainer Aug 1956.

Debut v Aston Villa (h) 30/8/1919

Jack Poole was a solid, reliable half-back with, like so many, a delayed peace-time debut. He had gained good experience guesting with Sheffield United and other clubs during the war period and no difficulty was encountered in translating to normal conditions. Indeed, manager Bob Kyle is reputed to have spotted his talent and taken the player on after watching him play football on the beach during the war when the Sherwood Foresters were based at Roker. Poole missed only one

game in 1919/20 and was a first team regular until the 1923/24 season. His fine consistency continued at Bradford City, an ever-present in his first couple of campaigns. On retirement from the playing arena Jack stayed in football with a succession of training appointments and a single stint in the manager's chair for Mansfield Town.

Appearances:
FL: 144 apps. 1 gl.
FAC: 8 apps. 1 gl.
Total: *152 apps. 2 gls.*

PORTEOUS, Thomas Stoddart

Role: Right-back 1889-94
5'9" 11st.10lbs.
b. Newcastle upon Tyne, 1865
d. Blackpool, 23rd February 1919

CAREER: Heart of Midlothian/Kilmarnock May 1885/SUNDERLAND June 1889/ Rotherham Town player-coach June 1894/ Manchester City Jan 1896/Rotherham Town Mar 1896/South Shore June 1896.

Debut v Blackburn Rovers (a) 18/1/1890 (FAC)

Tom Porteous holds a distinguished place in the Sunderland roll-call as the club's very first England cap in 1891 (i.e. honoured while on the playing staff). It came in a 4-1 win against Wales at Sunderland's Newcastle Road ground - the first full

Tom Porteous

international match staged in the city. He had learned his trade in Scotland, especially during the Kilmarnock years, and appeared in their 1886 Ayrshire Cup-winning line-up. A valued member of the Wearsiders' great Team of All the Talents 1890's side Tom was an ever-present in both his championship seasons. A Killie historian summed up Tom very well: "Measured his tackles to perfection, speedy with good ball control, he didn't just clear his lines but placed the ball to perfection."

Appearances:
FL: 79 apps. 0 gls.
FAC: 14 apps. 0 gls.
Total: *93 apps. 0 gls.*
Honours:
1 Eng cap v Wales 1891/
(Sunderland) FL champs 1892, 1893.

PORTERFIELD, John 'Ian'

Role: Midfield 1967-76
5'11" 11st.6lbs.
b. Dunfermline, 11th February 1946

CAREER: Lochgelly Albert/Lochore Welfare
1961/Leeds United app/Hearts trial/Rangers
trial/Raith Rovers 1964/SUNDERLAND Dec
1967 £45,000 a Raith Rovers record(Reading
loan Nov 1976)/Sheffield Wednesday July
1977/Rotherham United manager Dec 1979
(signed as player Jan 1980, no snr
apps.)/Sheffield United manager June 1981-
Mar 1986/Aberdeen manager Nov 1986-May
1988/Reading manager Nov 1989-Apr
1991/Chelsea manager June 1991-Feb 1993/
Zambia coach Apr 1993/Bolton Wanderers
asst. manager June 1996/Worthing manager to
Sept 1996/Oman manager Nov 1997.

Debut v Newcastle United (h) 30/12/1967

Ian Porterfield will forever be revered and
remembered on Wearside as scorer of the 31st
minute goal that upset all the odds and won
the 1973 FA Cup Final at Wembley against
mighty Leeds United. The goal came from a
Billy Hughes corner which fell beyond the far
post, where the leaping Dave Watson
distracted Leeds' defenders. The ball hit Vic
Halom's knee, and bounced to Porterfield

who, never a prolific scorer, calmly volleyed
over the goalkeeper with his right - and
weaker - foot. Ian had a splendid match, and
more than one reporter praised his elegance;
"coolly wielding his left foot and outshining
the similar weapons of Hunter and Gray".
No surprise then that as winner of the Golden
Boot for the goal, Ian requested a left footed
boot which for years was displayed in a
hospitality lounge at Roker Park. Ian took a
common Scottish route into the senior game
by joining Raith Rovers of the Second
Division. He made 115 appearances for the
Kirkcaldy club, scoring 17 goals, and his last
full season saw them runners-up and
promoted to the top flight. Ian's transfer to
Sunderland brought Raith their then record fee
- £38,000 plus a further £5,000 after 20
appearances. The Wearsiders obtained full
value as the player's probing intelligent
performances became a feature during the
next decade. Porterfield's progress was
interrupted in December 1974 - the day after a
dazzling display in a 4-1 win over Portsmouth
- by serious injuries sustained in a car accident
which included a fractured skull and broken
jaw. Nonetheless Ian reported back to Roker
within two months and played in the reserves
before the season ended wearing a protective
rugby skull cap. Towards the end of his
Sunderland spell Ian went on loan to Reading,

Ian Porterfield's Wembley winner against Leeds United in 1973.

Ian Porterfield,
FA Cup winner 1973.

343

lowly placed in Division Three, before severing ties altogether and signing for Sheffield Wednesday during the 1977 close season. Wednesday, a club with great traditions, were also languishing in Division Three, and took another two years to claw their way back up the League ladder. Ian, in his final playing fling, had 126(4) League and Cup outings, scored five goals and captained the side. A long and varied managerial career followed almost immediately. Ian quickly showed the necessary skills, guiding Rotherham United to the Third Division championship after only 18 months in office with '73 team mate Vic Halom as player-coach. Sheffield United who had fallen on hard times and just been demoted to Division Four soon secured his services. Ian presided over their championship the next season and, after a term of consolidation in 1982/83, again evolved a promotion side in 1983/84. The Blades were a middling Second Division side by early 1986, when Ian was dismissed for failure to maintain a promotion challenge. Six months later Ian succeeded Alex Ferguson as Aberdeen manager. This was an advancement of some magnitude as Porterfield inherited a squad of proven talent, and led them to the Scottish Cup semi-final and League Cup final in 1988. Little of note happened during his Reading period, so it came as a surprise when Chelsea engaged him. Ian's reign at Stamford Bridge lasted 20 months, ending in February 1991 following a run of 12 games without a win. His management strengths were said to be as a tactician, an ability to get on with players and the development of promising talent.

Appearances:
FL: 218(12) apps. 17 gls.
FAC: 19 apps. 2 gls.
FLC: 9 apps. 0 gls.
Other: 8 apps. 0 gls.
Total: *254(12) apps. 19 gls.*
Honours:
(Sunderland) FAC winner 1973/
Div 2 champs 1976.

POULTER, Henry

Role: Centre-forward 1931-32
5'10" 12st.2lbs.
b. Sunderland, 24th April 1910
d. Sunderland, February 1985

CAREER: Shiney Row Swifts/SUNDERLAND am July 1931/Exeter City July 1932/ Hartlepools United Aug 1936/retired through injury later in 1936.

Debut v Southampton (h) 9/1/1932 (FAC)

Harry Poulter came to football prominence with the Royal Navy at Portsmouth, Rosyth, and with the Atlantic Fleet generally, at home and in the Mediterranean. He joined Sunderland as an amateur and, rather unusually, made all his senior appearances in FA Cup ties. His two goals were scored in a

Harry Poulter

third round replay at Southampton, won 4-2 by Sunderland. In his first season with Exeter City he scored 16 goals for the Grecians' Reserves, who won the Western League championship. A confident leader with a strong physique, he was a fine opportunist and netted 33 goals in 50 Third Division South appearances. In 1935-36 he scored a hat-trick against Aldershot on the opening day of the season, but shortly afterwards was hospitalised with a stomach complaint. He made only one further appearance during the season, at the end of which Exeter were re-election applicants. During the close season it was reported he had been forced to give up football and had returned to Sunderland. He did, in fact, sign with Hartlepools United but did not appear at League level for them before finally retiring from the game.

Appearances:
FAC: 3 apps. 2 gls.
Total: *3 apps. 2 gls.*

POWER, Geoffrey Frank

Role: Inside-right 1920-21
5'6" 11st.12lbs.
b. Grangetown, Sunderland, 7th April 1899
d. Cleveland area, 1st qtr 1963

CAREER: Grangetown St Mary's/
SUNDERLAND Aug 1919/Blackpool Dec 1921
£350/Darwen Oct 1922/Fleetwood cs 1923,
then assisted a succession of other non-league
clubs that included Denaby United, Eston
United (Sept 1928), Scarborough and, for a
second spell, Grangetown St Mary's (Sept
1932).

Debut v Liverpool (a) 15/1/1921

Short in stature, though weighty, Geoff Power
was not easily brushed aside. A Charlie
Buchan understudy, Power came into the
League side when that worthy occupied the
centre-forward spot in the second half of the
season 1920/21. Of those nine appearances
most were either won or drawn. He had 19
Football League outings for Blackpool, then of
the Second Division, thereafter playing a
decade in minor circles. During the Great War
Geoff Power served with the Lancashire
Fusilliers.

Appearances:
FL: 9 apps. 0 gls.
Total: *9 apps. 0 gls.*

Geoff Power

*One of Lee Power's few
Sunderland appearances was
against Charlton Athletic at
Roker Park.*

POWER, Lee Michael

Role: Forward 1993-94
6'0" 11st.10lbs.
b. Lewisham, London, 30th June 1972

CAREER: Crofton Park School, Blackheath/
South London Schools/Norwich City assoc
s'boy Nov 1986, trainee July 1988, pro July
1990(Charlton Athletic loan Dec 1992)
(SUNDERLAND loan Aug 1993)(Portsmouth
loan Oct-Dec 1993)/Bradford City Mar 1994
(Millwall loan Jan-Feb 1995)/Peterborough
United July 1995(Heart of Midlothian loan Oct
1996)/Dundee Dec 1996/Hibernian Mar 1997
(Ayr United loan Apr 1998)/Plymouth Argyle
Aug 1998(Halifax Town loan Dec 1998)/
Halifax Town Jan 1999-date.

Debut v Derby County (a) 14/8/1993 (sub)

Since making his debut in League football
with Norwich City in April 1990, Lee Power
has been associated with a further twelve
clubs in England and Scotland. Qualified for
the Republic of Ireland by ancestry, he won a
record total of 13 Under-21 caps and was
voted the Republic's Young Player of the Year
in 1992-93. Blond-haired Lee scored prolifically

for Norwich at youth and reserve level but his immense potential has remained largely unrealised. Despite scoring a stunning goal in his first full appearance for Sunderland against Chester City at Roker Park, Lee's month trial did not result in a permanent offer, largely because despite publicly stating he wanted to buy him, manager Terry Butcher had no more available cash after spending more than £2 million during the pre-season. Power cost Bradford City £200,000 in March 1994 but appeared in only 27 League matches before moving on for a cut price fee of £80,000 to Peterborough United some sixteen months later.

Appearances:
FL: 1(2) apps. 0 gls.
FLC: 2 apps. 1 gl.
Total: *3(2) apps. 1 gl.*
Honours:
Eire Yth/13 Eire U-21 apps.

PRINCE, Thomas

Role: Inside/outside-left 1897-1901

CAREER: Selbourne/SUNDERLAND Jan 1898/retired May 1906.

Debut v Nottingham Forest (h) 23/4/1898

Tom Prince was on Sunderland's books for eight years and more but shows a meagre return in the matter of first team outings. His debut in the final fixture of 1897/98 (at inside-left) was followed by a second appearance nearly two years later in February 1900. Then a gap of thirteen months to the third (March 1901) and a final appearance the next week. Following the debut the other appearances Prince made were at outside-left.

Appearances:
FL: 4 apps. 0 gls.
Total: *4 apps. 0 gls.*

PRIOR, George

Role: Inside-right/centre-forward 1901-02
b. Edinburgh

George Prior

CAREER: Edinburgh St Bernard's Aug 1900/SUNDERLAND Oct 1901/Third Lanark July 1902.

Debut v Stoke (a) 9/11/1901

Less than a season at Roker Park, George Prior led the attack in League matches on three occasions and appeared at inside-right twice. The matches resulted chronologically in a defeat, a draw and three wins. And Sunderland scored a total of ten goals in those five games but none of them were credited to Prior, who returned to his native Scotland the following summer.

Appearances:
FL: 5 apps. 0 gls.
Total: *5 apps. 0 gls.*

PRIOR, Jack

Role: Outside-right 1922-27
5'9" 11st.4lbs.
b. Choppington, Northumberland, 2nd July 1904
d. Newton Abbot, Devon, 3rd qtr 1982

Jack Prior

CAREER: Blyth Spartans/SUNDERLAND Feb 1923 £250/Grimsby Town Feb 1927 £2,500/Ashington Aug 1932 £350/Mansfield Town Oct 1932 £350/Stalybridge Celtic July 1933/later to Pressed Steel FC (Oxford) as a permit player July 1935.

Debut v Manchester City (h) 30/3/1923

Jack Prior had a fair introduction to top grade football while at Sunderland, his best season being 1925/26 when he made 28 Football League appearances and scored eight goals. Jack was released late in the next term, at the time of Alwyne Wilks's signing, to commence his career's high point with Grimsby Town. The Mariners had recently won promotion to Division Two and were to advance further in 1928/29 on finishing runners-up to Middlesbrough. Jack played a big part in that promotion line-up. All told he appeared in 168 League and FA Cup games while at Blundell Park, scoring 36 goals. For Mansfield he made 32 Northern Section appearances (seven goals). In style fast and direct and expert in accurate middling of the ball. Brother of George Prior (Sheffield Wednesday & Watford, 1921-30) and uncle of Ken Prior (Newcastle United & Millwall 1952-57)

Appearances:
FL: 66 apps. 10 gls.
FAC: 4 apps. 1 gl.
Total: *70 apps. 11 gls.*

PROCTOR, Mark Gerald

Role: Midfield 1982-88
5'10" 11st.9lbs.
b. Middlesbrough, 30th January 1961

CAREER: Nunthorpe Athletic/Middlesbrough assoc s'boy Aug 1975, app, pro Sept 1978/ Nottingham Forest Aug 1981(SUNDERLAND loan Mar 1983)/SUNDERLAND May 1983/ Sheffield Wednesday Sept 1987/ Middlesbrough Mar 1989(Tranmere Rovers loan Mar 1993)/Tranmere Rovers July 1993/ St Johnstone Aug 1995/Whitley Bay Nov 1995.

Debut v Swansea City (h) 19/3/1983

Mark Proctor had a brief trial with Leeds United in 1975 before signing associate schoolboy forms with his hometown club Middlesbrough. A gifted midfielder with an assured touch on the ball, he featured regularly for 'Boro for three seasons following his League debut in August 1978. He won two of his England Under-21 caps when he was transferred to Nottingham Forest for £425,000. Initially on loan to Sunderland, manager Alan Durban paid £115,000 to secure his services. After a good first season at Roker, he was injured at Newcastle United on New Year's Day 1985 and sidelined for almost a year, missing out on a Wembley appearance in the League Cup Final against Norwich City. In 1986-87 he played an unhappy role in Sunderland's struggles, missing a vital penalty in a 2-3 home defeat by Barnsley that condemned The Lads to the relegation play-offs and then missed another in the second leg of the play-off with Gillingham that finally confirmed the drop. When Sunderland began their first spell in Third Division football in 1987-88, it was almost inevitable that Mark would be on his way and it was Sheffield Wednesday who returned him to Division One with a £275,000 transfer in September 1987. His homecoming to Middlesbrough for £300,000 in March 1989 came too late to save them from relegation but he soon returned to the top flight, following their promotion season 1991-92.

Appearances:
FL: 117(2) apps. 21 gls.
FAC: 6 apps. 0 gls.
FLC: 13 apps. 2 gls.
Total: *136(2) apps. 23 gls.*
Honours:
Eng Yth/4 Eng U-21 apps.
1981-82.

Mark Proctor

system to make a first-team debut when he came on as a substitute in the thrilling fourth round League Cup tie at Everton which ran into extra time and penalties. In fact, he was due to take the next spot-kick when Sorensen saved to win the tie. On January 27th 1999 Michael scored the winning goal for Sunderland Reserves against Liverpool Reserves, a fixture which attracted an attendance of 33,517, an all-time record for a Pontin's League fixture. In the Reserve team's championship campaign he scored twice in the title clinching fixture against Derby County Reserves, and was leading goalscorer with seven in 6(6) appearances.

> **Appearances:**
> *FLC: 0(1) apps. 0 gls.*
> **Total:** *0(1) apps. 0 gls.*

PRUDHOE, Mark

Role: Goalkeeper 1982-83
6'0" 13st.0lbs.
b. Washington, 11th November 1963

CAREER: Washington/SUNDERLAND app July 1980, pro Sept 1981(Hartlepool United loan Nov 1983)/Birmingham City Sept 1984/ Walsall Feb 1986(Doncaster Rovers loan Dec 1986)(Grimsby Town loan Mar 1987) (Hartlepool United loan Aug 1987)(Bristol City loan Nov 1987/Stoke City June 1993 (Peterborough United loan Sept 1994) (Liverpool loan Nov 1994)(York City loan Feb 1997)/Bradford City July 1997-date.

Debut v West Bromwich Albion (a) 11/12/1982

Michael Proctor

PROCTOR, Michael Anthony

Role: Forward 1998-date
5'11" 12st.7lbs.
b. Sunderland, 3rd October 1980

CAREER: Monkwearmouth School/ Sunderland Schoolboys/County Durham Schoolboys/SUNDERLAND assoc. s'boy Feb 1995, trainee Aug 1997, pro Nov 1997-date.

Debut v Everton (a) 11/11/1998 (FLC) (sub)

A Fulwell End season ticket holder during schooldays, Michael Proctor fulfilled his earliest ambition when he signed professional forms with his favourite club at 17 years of age. The blond-haired striker scored twice on his Reserve team debut v Leicester City in December 1997, and maintained an excellent goalscoring ratio in the Pontin's League in 1998-99. He became the eighth player from the club's youth

A much-travelled goalkeeper, Mark Prudhoe began with Sunderland initially as an understudy to Barry Siddall and Chris Turner. His only first team appearances were made in April and May of 1983 following Chris Turner's serious head injury at Norwich. Subsequent lack of first team football resulted in Prudhoe's £20,000 transfer to Birmingham City after three years as a professional at Roker Park. He subsequently found success with Darlington who regained League status by winning the championship of the

Mark Prudhoe

GM Vauxhall Conference in 1989-90. He was also ever-present in the following campaign when the Quakers won the championship of Division Four. A fee of £120,000 took him to Stoke City in June 1993, and he passed the milestone of 300 League appearances with The Potters. Since moving to Bradford City, however, he has found limited opportunities as understudy to the former Manchester United goalkeeper, Gary Walsh, but helps out on the coaching side too.

Appearances:
FL: 7 apps. 0 gls.
Total: *7 apps. 0 gls.*
Honours:
*(Darlington) GMVC champs 1990/
Div 4 champs 1991.*

PURDON, Edward John

Role: Centre-forward 1953-57
5'11" 12st.7lbs.
b. Johannesburg, South Africa, 1st March 1930

CAREER: Marist Brothers FC (Jo'burg)/ Birmingham City Aug 1950/SUNDERLAND Jan 1954 £15,000/Workington Mar 1957 about £6,000/Barrow Mar 1958/Bath City Aug 1959/Bristol Rovers July 1960/Toronto City, Canada 1961/Polish White Eagles, Toronto later in 1961/Toronto Roma 1963-64/New York Unknowns, USA 1965 for a season.

Debut v Cardiff City (h) 16/1/1954 (scored)

A personable, well-built blond striker, Ted Purdon was usefully versatile. He appeared in four of the attack berths for Birmingham - outside-right the exception - but centre-forward was unquestionably his best role. He came to England after scoring regularly for Marist Brothers, one of seven South Africans to sign for Birmingham in the space of two years and the one to remain longest (70

Ted Purdon

Football League and FA Cup games, 30 goals). Ted played a lot of first team football while at Roker Park, maintaining a fair scoring rate, including two on his debut in a 5-0 thrashing of Cardiff and a memorable hat-trick a week later as Sunderland hammered Arsenal 4-1 at Highbury. After sampling the lower division and non-League scene he emigrated to Canada, settling in Toronto and assisted several local sides. He eventually returned to his native South Africa, successfully pursuing a business career. Originally, before his football career, Ted had worked as a salesman in a Johannesburg store.

Appearances:
FL: 90 apps. 39 gls.
FAC: 6 apps. 3 gls.
Total: *96 apps. 42 gls.*

Niall Quinn

350

QUINN, Albert

Role: Inside-left 1947-48
b. Lanchester, Co Durham, 18th April 1920

CAREER: Esh Winning Juniors/
SUNDERLAND Nov 1946/Darlington May
1948-1951.

Debut v Grimsby Town (h) 30/8/1947

Albert Quinn was among seven players
occupying the inside-left spot during the
1947/48 campaign. Probably his best showing
was in a 5-1 drubbing of Liverpool on 15th
November. 1947 when he netted a couple of
goals. Quinn made 86 Northern Section
appearances during a three-year Darlington
stay, scoring 43 goals. He won many friends at
The Feethams, one commentator remarking on
his "good marksmanship and split-second
opportunism" and "an unselfishness which
helps to make plenty of opportunities for the
men alongside him". He possessed dribbling
skills and a telling body swerve in addition.

> **Appearances:**
> *FL: 6 apps. 2 gls.*
> **Total:** *6 apps. 2 gls.*

Albert Quinn

QUINN, Niall John

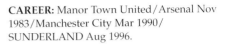

Role: Forward 1996-date
6'4" 13st.10lbs.
b. Dublin, 6th October 1966

CAREER: Manor Town United/Arsenal Nov
1983/Manchester City Mar 1990/
SUNDERLAND Aug 1996.

Debut v Leicester City (h) 17/8/1996 (sub)

Niall Quinn joined Arsenal from Irish junior
football in November 1983 and made his first
team debut some two years later, marking the
occasion by scoring against Liverpool at
Highbury. His best season with the Gunners
was 1986-87, when he made 48 League and
Cup appearances, scored 12 goals, and was a
League Cup winner against Liverpool at
Wembley. The arrival of Alan Smith from
Leicester City restricted Quinn's opportunities
thereafter, and he was largely out of the first
team picture when Manchester City paid
£800,000 for him, just prior to the transfer
deadline in March 1990. In his first full season
at Maine Road, Niall scored 21 League and
Cup goals - including two to relegate
Sunderland on the season's final day - and
whilst this proved the high point, his return of
77 League and Cup goals in 216(25)
appearances was a telling contribution to the
Light Blue's cause over six and a half seasons.
His international career blossomed at Maine
Road where he completed his half century of
Eire caps and twice represented the Republic
in World Cup competitions. Niall cost
Sunderland a then club record fee of
£1.3 million when signed in August 1996 on
the eve of the new season and The Lads' first
ever Premier League campaign. The 29-year-
old striker had rejected a financially tempting
offer from Malaysian club Selangor in order to
team up again with Peter Reid, his former
manager at Manchester City. Two goals at
Nottingham Forest in his first starting
appearance left him one short of a career
century of League and Cup goals. Sadly, a
serious knee ligament injury in the following
month sidelined him for six months and
restricted his first season's Premiership
appearances to a mere dozen, including four
as a substitute. On the first anniversary of his
move from Maine Road, where he made over
200 League and Cup appearances, Niall scored

Niall Quinn

Sunderland's first League goal at the Stadium of Light against his previous club, Manchester City. In the 3-1 win, debutant Kevin Phillips also scored and over the course of the season the 'Little & Large' pairing developed into one of the most prolific striking duos in the country. One of the best target men in the game, Quinn combines superb aerial ability with a sure touch on the ball and his exciting form during the season - which included the first hat-trick at the Stadium of Light with his treble against Stockport in March 1998 - was rewarded with a recall to international action. Season 1998-99 was truly memorable for Niall, the focal point of Sunderland's potent attack. During the campaign, in which he passed a career milestone of 350 League appearances, his contribution to Sunderland's impressive march into the top flight was outstanding. Twenty-one goals in League and Cup were his best return since season 1990-91 and this, plus his overall cheerful contribution to the team, saw the articulate, personable Irishman voted Player of the Year by the Supporters' Association. Fans even released a CD entitled "Niall Quinn's Disco Pants"!

Appearances:
PL: 8(4) apps. 2 gls.
FL: 71(5) apps. 35 gls.
FAC: 4 apps. 1 gl.
FLC: 5(2) app. 4 gls.
Total: *88(11) apps. 42 gls.*
Honours:
Eire Sch & Yth/5 Eire U-21 apps./1 Eire U-23 app./1 Eire B' app./67 Eire caps 1986-date/ (Arsenal) FLC winners 1987/ (Sunderland) Div 1 champs 1999.

RAE, Alexander Scott

Role: Midfield 1996-date
5'9" 11st.8lbs.
b. Glasgow, 30th September 1969

CAREER: Bishopbriggs BC/Glasgow Rangers
3 mth trial/Falkirk 1986/Millwall Aug 1990/
SUNDERLAND June 1996-date.

Debut v Newcastle United (h) 4/9/1996 (sub)

A combative, hard-tackling midfielder, Alex
Rae cost Sunderland £1 million from Millwall
in August 1996. Almost immediately, he cost a
further £1,000 when Sunderland fielded him in
a pre-season friendly at Whitley Bay. A
suspension carried over from his Millwall
days had been overlooked, and as a result he
did not make his Premiership debut until
September. Prior to his move to Wearside,
Alex had headed Millwall's goalscoring lists
for three consecutive seasons. On Alex's 20th
birthday he netted four goals, and also while
with The Lions was later voted into the PFA

Division One XI.
Nevertheless, he was
afforded few
opportunities in his first
season at Roker, despite
the fact the side were so deficient in
goalscoring, with only 35 registered in 38
Premiership matches. A prolonged run in the
side the following term caught the eye of
Scotland's selectors, leading to his appearance
in two 'B' internationals in late season.
Personal problems and knee ligament damage
restricted his appearances in 1998-99. Having
spent three weeks in a Hampshire clinic for
help with drink related problems Alex was
unfortunate to suffer knee ligament damage at
Blackburn in January 1999, cutting short his
successful come back. His brother once had a
trial with Sunderland.

> **Appearances:**
> *PL: 13(10) apps. 2 gls.*
> *FL: 36(4) apps. 5 gls.*
> *FAC: 3 apps. 0 gls.*
> *FLC: 5(1) apps. 2 gls.*
> **Total:** *57(15) apps. 9 gls.*
> **Honours:**
> *8 Scot U-21 apps. 1991-92/4 Scot 'B' apps.*
> *1996-98/(Sunderland) Div 1 champs 1999.*

RAINE, James Edmundson

Role: Outside-right 1906-08
5'11" 12st.8lbs.
b. Newcastle upon Tyne, March 1886
d. Davos, Switzerland, 4th September 1928

CAREER: Scotswood 1903/Sheffield United cs
1904/Newcastle United 1905/SUNDERLAND
Dec 1906/Glossop North End Apr 1908.

Debut v Manchester City (h) 22/12/1906

James Raine was a top amateur at a time when
amateurs were far from rare specimens in the
Football and Southern Leagues and well able
to vie with their professional colleagues.
Raine, educated at Trinity College, Harrogate,
and Sheffield University, played in good class
non-League football at an early age, had been
a devotee of the game from boyhood and
owed much to instruction from Sheffield
United's famous international winger, Walter
"Cocky" Bennett. An unflurried, confident
forward, Raine made four Football League
appearances for Newcastle United (one goal),
one with Sheffield United and 51 (three goals)

Alex Rae

James Raine

for Glossop North End. The last-named club was remarkable for the number of amateurs it called upon. James Raine served as a commissioned officer with the Durham Light Infantry during World War One, attaining the rank of major. Outside football he had a successful business career, becoming managing director of an iron and steel firm.

Appearances:
FL: 24 apps. 6 gls.
FAC: 3 apps. 1 gl.
Total: *27 apps. 7 gls.*
Honours:
10 Eng am apps./1 FL app v Irish Lge 1908.

RAISBECK, William

Role: Wing-half 1898-1902
5'10" 12st.2lbs.
b. Wallacetown, Stirlingshire, 1876

CAREER: Larkhall Thistle/Hibernian July 1896/Clyde Sept 1896/SUNDERLAND Dec 1896/Royal Albert Sept 1897/Clyde Oct 1897/ SUNDERLAND Aug 1898/Derby County May 1901/New Brompton May 1902/Reading June 1904-1905.

Debut v Preston North End (a) 3/9/1898

Bill Raisbeck appeared mostly at left-half with Sunderland but had appeared at centre-forward with Larkhall Thistle, Royal Albert and Clyde. In 1902 a critic wrote that Raisbeck " ... plays a strong & safe, if not brilliant game." Which makes rather

Bill Raisbeck

dismissive reading but it should be remembered honest journeymen often form the backbone of a good team. He had only three League outings with Derby followed by a goodly taste of Southern League fare for New Brompton (56 appearances) and Reading (14). Raisbeck came from a noted footballing family - it was said they could field a full side! Its most distinguished member was Alex Raisbeck, the great Liverpool and Scotland centre-half.

Appearances:
FL: 71 apps. 9 gls.
FAC: 5 apps. 0 gls.
Total: *76 apps. 9 gls.*

RAMSAY, Stanley Hunter

Role: Inside-left 1925-28
5'10" 11st.0lbs.
b. Ryton upon Tyne, Co Durham, 10th August 1904
d. Chipping Sodbury, Glos., 19th July 1989

CAREER: Ryton FC/Stargate Rovers/ SUNDERLAND May 1924/Blackpool Feb 1928/Norwich City July 1932/Shrewsbury Town player-manager June 1935/Dereham Town Aug 1936.

Debut v Sheffield United (a) 12/9/1925 (scored)

Stan Ramsay

Stan Ramsay was soon blooded into the top class game, first appearing in the fourth fixture of his inaugural season, celebrating the occasion by scoring in a 6-1 annihilation of Sheffield United. Stan held his own in a Sunderland side packed with top internationals and in March 1927 netted a memorable hat-trick against Leeds. Afterwards he appeared at left-back and left-half. Ramsay was a clever footballer - too clever for his team mates one Lancashire critic thought - and extremely fast. He showed an admirable versatility at Blackpool, moving to centre-half in the 1928/29 season. This adaptability continued during the Norwich years during which he captained their 1934 championship side when picking up a second divisional medal. After finishing with football Stan worked in Norwich, firstly as secretary of an old people's home and later as a tobacconist/newsagent.

Appearances:
FL: 23 apps. 14 gls.
FAC: 1 app. 0 gls.
Total: *24 apps. 14 gls.*
Honours:
(Blackpool) FL Div 2 champs 1930/
(Norwich City) FL Div 3 (Sth) champs 1934.

RAMSDEN, Bernard

Role: Right/left-back 1947-49
5'9" 11st.4lbs.
b. Sheffield, 8th November 1917
d. Terminal Island, Los Angeles, March 1976

CAREER: Hampton Sports (Sheffield)/ Sheffield Victoria/Liverpool am Mar 1933, pro Mar 1935/SUNDERLAND Mar 1948/ Hartlepools United Jan 1950/retired May 1950.

Debut v Stoke City (a) 20/3/1948

Sheffielder Barney Ramsden crossed the Pennines to spend thirteen years on Liverpool's books. Due to the war it was not until 1946/47 that he received any consistent first team selection with the Anfielders. Nonetheless a sound, reliable full-back on either flank, making 66 peacetime League and Cup appearances in the famous red jersey. Barney stood in for both Jack Stelling and Arthur Hudgell after joining Sunderland, twice for the former and on eleven occasions for Hudgell. Briefly with Hartlepools, Barney retired in 1950 emigrating later that year to the States and settling in California. During World War Two he guested for Brighton, Leeds United and York City.

Appearances:
FL: 12 apps. 0 gls.
FAC: 1 app. 0 gls.
Total: *13 apps. 0 gls.*

Barney Ramsden

RAYBOULD, Samuel F.

Role: Centre-forward/Inside-left 1907-08
5'10" 13st.0lbs.
b. Poolsbrook, nr Chesterfield, 1875

CAREER: Poolsbrook United/Staveley
Colliery/North Staveley(Chesterfield Town
trial Feb 1894)/Ilkeston United/Derby County
Apr 1894/Ilkeston Town Jan 1895 £10/
Poolsbrook United Oct 1897/Ilkeston Town
Feb 1898/Bolsover Colliery May 1899/New
Brighton Tower Oct 1899/Liverpool Jan 1900/
SUNDERLAND May 1907/Woolwich Arsenal
May 1908/Chesterfield Town Sept 1909/
Sutton Town Aug 1911/Barlborough United cs
1913.

Debut v Manchester City (h) 2/9/1907

An outside-right
converted into a centre-
forward whilst at New
Brighton, Sam Raybould
scored five goals in his
first couple of games in
that position. A quick
move to neighbouring
Liverpool ensued and it
was here where his
reputation was built
over the next seven
years. Sam played in 224
Football League and FA
Cup matches for the
Anfielders, scoring 127
goals. And at Anfield
he won three inter-
league medals - all
against the Scottish
League - and three
championship medals.
Given his physique and aggression it is not
surprising Raybould shone more when
leading the attack. His tally of 31 League
goals in 1902/03 remained a Liverpool record
for 29 years. He played inside-left also, a
circumstance repeated in his Roker Park
season.

PROMINENT FOOTBALLERS.

S. RAYBOULD,
SUNDERLAND.

Appearances:
FL: 27 apps. 13 gls.
FAC: 1 app. 0 gls.
Total: *28 apps. 13 gls.*
Honours:
*3 FL apps./(Liverpool) FL champs 1901,
1906/FL Div 2 champs 1905.*

READ, William Henry

Role: Outside-right 1909-11
5'6" 11st.7lbs.
b. Blackpool, 1885

CAREER: Junior football to Preston North
End/Blackpool cs 1907/Colne cs 1909/
SUNDERLAND Apr 1910/Chelsea May 1911/
Dundee Mar 1913, subsequently assisting
Swansea Town (there in season 1914/15).

Debut v Sheffield Wednesday (a) 30/4/1910

Bill Read's best spell of
first team football came
early: with Second Division
Blackpool (32 League
appearances, three goals,
plus a Cup-tie). Read was
associated
with some top
flight clubs but
a reserve player
at all of them. He had no senior
outings at Preston, and four each
with Chelsea and Dundee of the
Scottish First Division. These
match precisely his Sunderland
total. Read made his debut in the
final Football League fixture of
1909/10 and the remainder on
three consecutive Saturdays of
February 1911. At any rate he
finished with a flourish, scoring
twice in a 4-0 thumping of
Manchester City.

Bill Read

Appearances:
FL: 4 apps. 2 gls.
Total: *4 apps. 2 gls.*

REED, Graham

Role: Wing-half 1957-58
5'7" 10st.0lbs.
b. Kings Lynn, 6th February 1938

CAREER: King's Lynn FC/SUNDERLAND
am Aug 1954, pro Feb 1955/Wisbech Town
May 1959.

Debut v West Bromwich Albion (a) 23/11/1957

Five years on Sunderland's books, Graham
Reed's senior appearances were encapsulated
into one of them when he played three times

Graham Reed

those early pre-League seasons. Renney was apparently able to take any half-back role as the 11 appearances included single games at centre-half and left-half.

Appearances:
FAC: 1 app. 0 gls.
Total: *1 app. 0 gls.*

REVIE, Donald George

Role: Inside-forward 1956-59
5'11" 12st.9lbs.
b. Middlesbrough, 10th July 1927
d. Edinburgh, 26th May 1989

CAREER: Middlesbrough schools football/ Newport Boys' Club (Middlesbrough)/ Middlesbrough Swifts/Leicester City Aug 1944/Hull City Nov 1949 £20,000/Manchester City Oct 1951 £13,000 plus Ernie Phillips valued at £12,000/SUNDERLAND Nov 1956 £23,000/Leeds United Nov 1958 £14,000, appointed player-manager Mar 1961, retired from playing May 1963 and continued as manager until Apr 1974/England team manager Apr 1974-July 1977/coach to the United Arab Emirates July 1977-May 1980, afterwards coaching in Egypt.

Debut v Cardiff City (a) 17/11/1956

on the right flank and four on the left. The Rokerites were especially strong in the wing-half berths at the time with representative players such as Stan Anderson, George Aitken and Reg Pearce around and another international, Billy Elliott, then favouring the left-half spot. Graham, an East Anglian native, eventually returned to the area in the shape of the Southern League's Wisbech Town.

Appearances:
FL: 5 apps. 0 gls.
FAC: 2 apps. 0 gls.
Total: *7 apps. 0 gls.*

RENNEY

Role: Right-half 1888-89
Debut v Elswick Rangers (h) 27/10/1888 (FAC)

In season 1888/89 Renney played in all Sunderland's matches, eleven in number, up to and including that against Grimsby Town on November 10th. He then disappears from the scene, a far from unusual circumstance in

Don Revie was one of the big names in English football from the resumption after World War Two for the next 30 years and more. Much like Brian Clough he succeeded brilliantly in the managerial sphere after a playing career that had received international recognition. A skilful and intelligent footballer, Revie first came into prominence in Leicester's 1949 FA Cup run, unluckily missing the final through indisposition. Soon after that he moved to an ambitious Raich Carter-led Hull City where a loss of form conspired to bring a positional switch to right-half. An eventual transfer to Manchester City, a club that had bid for him in 1949, was the high point of his playing career. With the Blues he won his six caps, played in two FA Cup finals and was elected the 1955 Player of the Year. It was in his Maine Road spell too that the famous 'Revie Plan' evolved, with Revie, nominally centre-forward, operating behind his inside-forwards, a device perfected by the great Hungarian national side. It gave full scope to Revie's qualities of thoughtful distribution and control. But Revie was unhappy under

Don Revie

manager Les McDowall (q.v.) and Sunderland gave the 29-year-old a chance to resurrect his career. Unfortunately Revie's only full season at Roker in 1957/58 brought the misery of relegation despite his dozen goals and his two-year stay ended with a move to Elland Road. As a manager he famously turned a moribund Leeds Second Division outfit into a powerful, physical combination which won a string of honours under his guidance, with stars such as Billy Bremner, Jack Charlton and Johnny Giles the cornerstones. It is fair to say, however, Leeds were also too often runners-up including of course, the 1973 FA Cup final. Don Revie was awarded the CBE in 1970. Such solid success made a natural stepping-stone to the post of England coach but somehow, missing the day to day involvement with his players, he did not achieve in this major appointment and was castigated for abandoning the post in favour of a lucrative coaching contract in the Arab Emirates.

Appearances:
FL: 64 apps. 15 gls.
FAC: 2 apps. 0 gls.
Total: *66 apps. 15 gls.*
Honours:
6 Eng caps/1 Eng 'B' app./2 FL apps./ (Manchester City) FAC winner 1956, finalist 1955.

REYNOLDS, Thomas

Role: Outside-left 1946-53
5'4" 9st.2lbs.
b. Felling, Co Durham, 2nd October 1922
d. Gateshead, 13th March 1998

CAREER: RAF football/Felling Juniors/ SUNDERLAND July 1946/King's Lynn cs 1953/Darlington Dec 1954-1956

Debut v Charlton Athletic (a) 11/9/1946

Tommy Reynolds made his League bow at outside-right but eventually succeeded the long-serving Eddie Burbanks in his true position on the extreme left. Accurately summed up as "a little outside-left with plenty of speed and footballing skill", perhaps Tommy's dimensions were not quite so small as the figures above, recorded in 1950. A 1957 version gives them as 5ft 7ins, 10st. 10lbs. Tommy was recommended to Sunderland when serving with the RAF in Ceylon, the Wearsiders obtaining his signature although

Tommy Reynolds bred greyhounds and raced them on the Sunderland track.

facing competition from Middlesbrough. Tommy McLain (q.v.) served in Ceylon with Reynolds, whose League totals with Darlington read 42 Northern Section appearances, six goals. After retiring from football Tommy managed licensed premises in the Sunderland and Durham areas.

Appearances:
FL: 167 apps. 18 gls.
FAC: 4 apps. 0 gls.
Total: *171 apps. 18 gls.*

RHODES, Ephraim 'Dusty'

Role: Right/left-back 1902-08
5'11" 12st.7lbs.
b. Middlesbrough, 1882
d. Ealing, Middlesex, 30th September 1960

CAREER: Grangetown/SUNDERLAND May 1902/Brentford Apr 1908, player-manager Nov 1912-1919/Brentford trainer July 1922-1925.

Debut v Bury (a) 18/10/1902

A solid defender, 'Dusty' Rhodes provided consistent playing quality to his two professional clubs over a 17 year period. The major portion went to Brentford to whom he devoted behind-the-scenes labour in a managerial capacity and, later, trainer. The

'Dusty' Rhodes

three years in the latter post brought his Brentford years to fourteen. 'Dusty' captained the Bees from season 1909/10 onwards, becoming player/manager in 1912 and retained the post despite relegation to Division Two of the Southern League in 1913. All told he played 206 peacetime Southern League games (two goals) for Brentford, and was a regular member throughout the 1914/18 War (103 appearances, three goals). To his great credit 'Dusty' tried to join the fighting forces on at least four occasions but was rejected each time. So he spent the War in the Army Pay Corps and Army Records Office, continuing to run Brentford FC with the club secretary, Fred Halliday, in his spare time.

Appearances:
FL: 114 apps. 5 gls.
FAC: 5 apps. 0 gls.
Total: *119 apps. 5 gls.*

RICHARDSON

Role: Utility player 1887-88
Debut v Morpeth Harriers (h) 15/10/1887 (FAC)

Richardson played all five FA Cup ties Sunderland contested in 1887/88 and was part of the controversy involving two other Scots - Monaghan (q.v.) and Hastings (q.v.) - which led to Sunderland's expulsion from the Cup competition that season. The problems stemmed from a tie with Middlesbrough where, after a 2-2 draw, Sunderland won the replay 4-2 but Boro' protested that all three Scotsmen had been drafted in, breached the English Cup rules, and had indirectly been paid to play. The incident caused a considerable stir with two special commmissions investigating what happened. Sunderland argued the trio were amateurs but were found guilty of paying their train-fares from Dumfries. The club were ejected from the Cup competition and the players suspended for three months. It all did much to persuade Sunderland to operate on an open full professional basis thereafter.

Appearances:
FAC: 5 apps. 0 gls.
Total: *5 apps. 0 gls.*

RICHARDSON, James

Role: Centre-forward 1912-14
5'9" 11st.10lbs.
b. Bridgeton, Glasgow, 1885
d. Glasgow, 31st August 1951

CAREER: Glenitber FC/Blantyre Victoria/Kirkintilloch Rob Roy/Third Lanark 1907-08/Huddersfield Town Nov 1910/SUNDERLAND Aug 1912/Ayr United Mar 1914 £650/Millwall Athletic Mar 1921-1922 £250/Ayr United manager July 1923/Cowdenbeath manager June 1924-July 1925.

Debut v Newcastle United (a) 7/9/1912

It seemed strange that Sunderland should release Jimmy Richardson, a member of the 1912/13 contingent, so soon after that memorable campaign, albeit he attracted what must have been Ayr United's then record outlay. The answer came nearly 80 years later from Richardson's descendants in Volume One of the latter club's history.

Jimmy Richardson

The player's wife could not settle in Sunderland, a factor that has blighted so many transfers nationwide and doubtless will continue so to do. Jimmy himself was a valuable commodity if only because of an appetite for scoring goals. A habit that continued after leaving Roker Park and recognised by the Scottish authorities in the award of 1918/19 representative honours. Jimmy served in the Army during World War One, experienced trench warfare in France and was discharged during 1918 through stomach trouble.

Appearances:
FL: 35 apps. 20 gls.
FAC: 11 apps. 10 gls.
Total: *46 apps. 30 gls.*
Honours:
2 Scot Victory apps. 1919/2 SL apps. 1919/(Sunderland) FL champs 1913/FAC finalist 1913.

RITCHIE, Thomas Gibb

Role: Forward 1980-82
6'1" 12st.8lbs.
b. Edinburgh, 2nd January 1952

CAREER: Bridgend Thistle/Bristol City July 1969/SUNDERLAND Jan 1981(Carlisle United loan Mar 1982)/Bristol City June 1982/Yeovil Town Dec 1984.

Debut v Southampton 31/1/1981 (sub)

Elder brother of Steve Ritchie (Bristol City, Hereford, Torquay United and Scottish clubs in the 1970's), Tom Ritchie began with Bristol City as a 17-year-old and progressed quickly at Ashton Gate, making his League debut in Division Two against Millwall on 19 August 1972. Aside from his eighteen months with Sunderland, the lanky striker spent the best part of his career with Bristol City, scoring 132 senior goals in 494 (18) appearances. In the promotion season 1975-76 he was leading scorer with 18 in 42 League appearances. Rather significantly, when he left the Robins they were in Division Two and when he rejoined them a season and a half later they were in Division Four. Sunderland paid £180,000 for Ritchie after protracted negotiations, but he was slow to settle at Roker and failed to find the net in his first eleven appearances. He then scored a hat-trick in a vital relegation battle against Birmingham City. Despite a bright start to 1981-82, when he scored in both of the campaign's opening fixtures, he lost his place in mid-season and played out the remainder of the term on loan to Carlisle United, assisting the Cumbrians to promotion from Division Three, as runners-up to Burnley. Tom Ritchie was last reported to be settled in Clevedon, Avon and working as a postman.

Tom Ritchie

Appearances:
FL: 32(3) apps. 8 gls.
FAC: 3 apps. 0 gls.
FLC: 2 apps. 3 gls.
Total: *37(3) apps. 11 gls.*

ROBINSON, George Henry

Role: Outside-right 1927-31
5'8" 10st.9lbs.
b. Marlpool, Derbyshire, 11th January 1908
d. Blackheath, London, 15th January 1963

CAREER: Ilkeston Rangers/Ilkeston United/SUNDERLAND Apr 1927/Charlton Athletic June 1931 £650/Burton Town Apr 1933/Charlton Athletic May 1934 (guest player for Fulham, Sunderland, Lincoln City and Linfield during WW2)/retired Sept 1947 and appointed Charlton's asst. coach, becoming asst. manager Apr 1949.

Debut v Middlesbrough (a) 5/5/1928

Introduced in the final fixture of 1927/28, George could be termed a regular the next season with his 24 League outings (six goals), but he did not make any senior appearances in 1929/30 and only six in 1930/31, his last at Roker Park. George's transfer to Charlton Athletic was a great career move for him. He became a key man in the club's record rise to the top flight: an ever-present in 1934/35 and he missed only a single game the following year when runners-up in Division Two.

A neat, durable consistent performer, George spent a season at non-League Burton Town and was re-called (Charlton having cannily retained his registration) as his form was attracting other Football League clubs. He appeared a lot at inside-right for the London club, occupying that berth in the 1935 championship line-up.

George Robinson

Appearances:
FL: 31 apps. 8 gls.
FAC: 1 app. 0 gls.
Total: *32 apps. 8 gls.*
Honours:
(Charlton Athletic) Div 3 (Sth) champs 1935/
(Linfield) IC winner 1945 (as a guest).

ROBINSON, John 'Jackie'

Role: Inside-right 1946-49
5'9" 12st.0lbs.
b. Shiremoor, Northumberland, 10th August 1917
d. Shiremoor, Northumberland, 3rd qtr 1972

CAREER: Shiremoor FC/Sheffield Wednesday Oct 1934/SUNDERLAND Oct 1946 £5,000/ Lincoln City Oct 1949/retired through injury 1950.

Debut v Grimsby Town (h) 19/10/1946

By general consent Jackie Robinson was one of the Thirties major discoveries. He captivated critics and crowds alike with his natural grace, ball control, speed and scoring capability, and an assurance far beyond his years. He was a Wednesday regular at 19 and won his first England cap before his 20th birthday. The war, of course, took many of his peak years but during that time he turned in some brilliant games and scoring performances for the Wednesday. Robinson came to Sunderland when thought to be fading yet his figures show a penchant for

Jackie Robinson

Jackie Robinson

goal-scoring was still very much alive. He netted five goals in eight Northern Section appearances for Lincoln before fracturing a leg in a Christmas Eve 1949 encounter against Wrexham which caused retirement. It will be noticed signing dates with all three of Jackie's League clubs occurred in October.

Appearances:
FL: 82 apps. 32 gls.
FAC: 3 apps. 2 gls.
Total: *85 apps. 34 gls.*
Honours:
4 Eng caps/1 FL app. v Irish Lge 1939.

ROBINSON, Raymond Wilson

Role: Outside-right 1920-21
5'8" 13st.0lbs.
b. Blaydon, Co Durham, 3rd qtr 1895
d. Newcastle upon Tyne, 6th January 1964

CAREER: Scotswood (guest player for Grimsby Town 1915-16)/Newcastle United May 1919 £400/SUNDERLAND Aug 1920 £750/Grimsby Town May 1921/ SUNDERLAND June 1922/Eden Colliery Welfare Oct 1922, later in the 1920s assisting several other non-League sides including Lancaster Town, Liverpool Police, Shirebrook and Silverwood Colliery.

Debut v Sheffield United (a) 28/8/1920

Sunderland had an outside-right problem between the wars that persisted really until Len Duns emerged during the mid-Thirties. A very early attempt to fill the spot was the signing of Ray Robinson for a then significant fee from Newcastle United. A corporal in the Tank Corps in France during the Great War, he had been a first teamer at St James Park in 1919/20, clocking up 30 League and Cup appearances and scoring four goals. Robinson started as Sunderland's first choice but was soon replaced, by the season's end just making double figures in appearances, one of half a dozen players tried in the troublesome position. Grimsby knew of Robinson's capability from his spell as a wartime guest but here again his tenure was for a single season (nine

Ray Robinson

Northern Section outings). Robinson was unusually weighty for a winger.

Appearances:
FL: 10 apps. 2 gls.
TotaL: *10 apps. 2 gls.*

ROBINSON, Robert

Role: Goalkeeper 1929-31
5'9" 11st.3lbs.
b. Willington, 27th March 1910
d. Cross Hills, nr Keighley, Yorks, 22nd January 1989

CAREER: West Rainton School/Lambton & Hetton/South Hylton FC/South Hetton Colliery Welfare/Hebburn Colliery Welfare/ SUNDERLAND May 1926-Mar 1931/ Guildford City July 1931/Norwich City May 1932/Barrow July 1934/Scarborough June 1937, later assisting Gainsborough Trinity.

Debut v Liverpool (h) 14/12/1929

Robert Robinson represented Durham in county football prior to joining Sunderland, then waited three years understudying Albert McInroy before getting his senior baptism. This came soon after McInroy's departure to Newcastle and Robinson went on to make 26 League and Cup appearances in that (1929/30) season. In 1930/31 Bob Middleton and Jimmy

Robert Robinson

Thorpe came into contention with the result Robinson's contract was terminated in March 1931. Norwich City, a rising club, spotted him with Southern League Guildford and he was first choice for the Canaries in 1932/33 (34 Southern Section appearances) before losing his place to Clarence Wharton, an ever-present in their 1933/34 promotion team. Robert Robinson notably created a Norwich club record, making 15 consecutive appearances from his debut before tasting defeat. This record held until 1985/86. For Barrow he played in 32 Division Three (North) matches. A cool, confident goalkeeper.

Appearances:
FL: 34 apps. 0 gls.
FAC: 4 apps. 0 gls.
Total: *38 apps. 0 gls.*

ROBINSON, Robert

Role: Goalkeeper 1947-52
5'11" 13st.0lbs.
b. Newbiggin-by-the-Sea, Northumberland, 23rd June 1921

CAREER: Newbiggin FC/Burnley am/ SUNDERLAND Feb 1947/Newcastle United Aug 1952-June 1954 £3,000, subsequently returning to North-Eastern minor football.
Debut v Aston Villa (a) 1/9/1947

A reserve 'keeper at both Sunderland and Newcastle, Bobby Robinson understudied John Mapson at Roker Park, his best return being 18 League appearances in 1952/53. Opportunities were much rarer at St James Park,

Bobby Robinson pictured in action during a 1-1 draw at Villa Park in April 1949.

the man in charge the well-known Scottish cap, Ronnie Simpson and Robinson grossed only five Football League outings. Strange that Sunderland should have two goalies named Robert Robinson, albeit their periods of service are separated by two decades. But the Wearsiders also fielded two Charlie Thomsons, both half-backs and Scottish internationalists, their eras similarly separated.

Appearances:
FL: 31 apps. 0 gls.
FAC: 2 apps. 0 gls.
Total: *33 apps. 0 gls.*

ROBINSON, Robert Smith 'Whitey'

Role: Inside-right 1902-04
5'9" 12st.5lbs.
b. Sunderland, October 1879

CAREER: Sunderland schools football/ South Hylton/Sunderland Royal Rovers/ SUNDERLAND Nov 1902/Liverpool Apr 1904/Tranmere Rovers May 1913.

Debut v Stoke (a) 8/11/1902

A local find, 'Whitey' Robinson was acquired by Liverpool after the better part of two years at Roker Park to give long and distinguished service at Anfield. Always incisive and a snapper-up of a scoring opportunity,

'Whitey' Robinson

Whitey occasionally appeared at right-half. And, following the move of the noted Welsh cap, Maurice Parry, to Partick Thistle in 1909, became the regular right-half, still managing to score the odd goal. Robinson played 271 Football League and FA Cup matches for Liverpool in which he netted 65 goals. His best return came in a championship season: 23 goals in 32 Second Division outings, 1904/05.

Appearances:
FL: 24 apps. 7 gls.
Total: *24 apps. 7 gls.*
Honours:
(Liverpool) FL champs 1906/FL Div 2 champs 1905.

ROBINSON, William

Role: Centre-forward 1937-39
5'9" 12st.0lbs.
b. Whitburn, Co Durham, 4th April 1919
d. West Hartlepool, 7th October 1992

CAREER: Whitburn Schools/Hylton Juniors/SUNDERLAND am June 1934, pro Apr 1936 (guested for Charlton Athletic, Barnsley, Hamilton Academical, Luton Town and Stockport County during WW2)/Charlton Athletic May 1946 £1,000/West Ham United Jan 1949 £7,000/retired May 1953 joining West Ham's training staff until Nov 1957, when appointed asst. manager/Hartlepools United manager Nov 1959-June 1962.

Debut v Leicester City (a) 30/8/1937

A fine forward from boyhood - he was in the Sunderland Boys side that won the English Schools Shield in 1933 - Bill looked a veteran from a comparatively young age because of balding. In senior football he showed his mettle early, netting four goals in a handsome

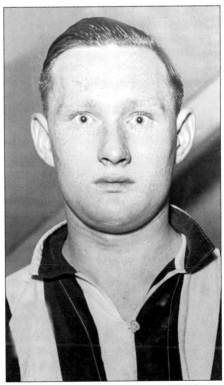

Bill Robinson

5-2 win over Manchester United in March 1939. He shone in wartime soccer, a high spot being a guest appearance at outside-right in the victorious Charlton Football League (South) Cup side of 1944. The London side wasted no time in adding Bill to their staff when peacetime conditions returned, and he played a significant role in the famous 1947 FA Cup win. Charlton also received a handsome profit on his cross-London move to West Ham where, following four excellent playing years, he played a major part in the club's acclaimed youth policy. Bill played in 60 League and FA Cup games (18 goals) for Charlton Athletic and in 105 (61 goals) for West Ham United.

Appearances:
FL: 24 apps. 14 gls.
Total: *24 apps. 14 gls.*
Honours:
(Charlton Athletic) FAC winner 1947.

ROBSON, Edward Riddell

Edward Robson

Role: Goalkeeper 1922-24
5'11" 12st.0lbs.
*b. Hexham,
Northumberland,
21st August 1890
d. Hexham,
Northumberland, 1st qtr
1977*

CAREER: Gateshead/ Watford June 1914 (guest for Sunderland during WW1)/ Portsmouth July 1919/ SUNDERLAND May 1922 £250/Swansea Town May 1924/ Wrexham June 1926/

ROBSON, Bryan Stanley

Role: Forward 1974-84
5'8" 11st.8lbs.
b. Sunderland, 11th November 1945

CAREER: Clara Vale Juniors/Newcastle United Nov 1962/West Ham United Feb 1971/ SUNDERLAND July 1974/West Ham United Oct 1976/SUNDERLAND June 1979/Carlisle United player-coach Mar 1981/Chelsea player-coach Aug 1982(Carlisle United loan Mar 1983)/ SUNDERLAND player-coach July 1983/Carlisle United July 1984, appointed asst. manager Aug-Oct 1985/Gateshead Oct 1985/ Newcastle Blue Star Sept 1986/ Manchester United scout 1987, coach 1988/ Hartlepool United asst. manager Oct 1988/ SUNDERLAND Community Officer Nov 1988/Manchester United asst. coach cs 1991/ SUNDERLAND asst. coach 1995, appointed Director of Youth 1997.

Debut v Millwall (a) 17/8/1974

Born within the shadow of Roker Park in 1945, 'Pop' Robson spent three separate playing spells with Sunderland. Initially recruited from West Ham United for a £145,000 fee in July 1974, the stockily-built balding striker was The Lads' leading scorer in 1974-75 with 21 League & Cup goals. He repeated the feat the following term with 15 as Sunderland won the Second Division championship. In his second spell at Roker, after

a £45,000 transfer from the Hammers, his scoring touch was undiminished as he again led the scoring charts with 22 League & Cup strikes in 1979-80. Returning for a third spell from Carlisle United at the advanced age (in footballing terms) of almost 38 years, he took only six minutes to score against West Bromwich Albion on his debut with a typical close-range finish. His last goal for the club, at Leicester in May 1984, earned him a record as Sunderland's oldest marksman at 38 years 182 days. Earlier in the season 'Pop' stood in as caretaker-boss for one match before the arrival of Len Ashurst. Robson's distinguished career began with Newcastle United - where typically he scored on his debut - and he enjoyed two successful spells with West Ham, highlighted by 28 League goals in 1972-73 and 24 in 1978-79. In terms of League goals alone, his career aggregate of 264 in 674 appearances ranks Sunderland's Director of Youth as one of the outstanding goalscoring forwards of his era.

Appearances:
FL: 146(8) apps. 60 gls.
FAC: 8 apps. 4 gls.
FLC: 10(2) apps. 3 gls.
Total: *164(10) apps. 67 gls.*
Honours:
3 Eng U-23 apps. 1967-69/1 FL app. 1970/ (Newcastle United) Div 2 champs 1965/ICFC winner 1969/(Sunderland) Div 2 champs 1976.

Grimsby Town July 1928/Rochdale Mar 1929-cs 1929.

Debut v Nottingham Forest (a) 26/8/1922

A capable goalkeeper, Ned Robson engaged in League soccer into his late 30s, his career taking in Welsh and widely separated, in a geographical sense, English clubs - and all four divisions plus a medal-winning Southern League season. A regular at Roker in 1922-23 with 32 League appearances, he lost his place

Bryan 'Pop' Robson

early the following term to Albert McInroy. Ned, however, had no senior outings with Grimsby Town. He made 112 Southern and Football League appearances for Pompey and his Football League tally for Swansea, Wrexham and Rochdale was 29, 70 and 12 respectively.

Appearances:
FL: 38 apps. 0 gls.
FAC: 2 apps. 0 gls.
Total: *40 apps. 0 gls.*
Honours:
(Portsmouth) Sthn Lge champs 1920/ (Swansea Town)Div 3 Sth champs 1925.

ROBSON, Thomas

Role: Centre-half 1958-60
5'11" 12st.7lbs.
b. Sunderland, 1st February 1936

CAREER: Junior football to SUNDERLAND on am forms June 1953, pro Sept 1957/ Darlington Aug 1960-1961.

Debut v Huddersfield Town (h) 28/2/1959

Nicely built and a locally born pivot, Tom Robson was a Charlie Hurley deputy so first team chances were not forthcoming very often. On moving to nearby Darlington, Tom found opportunities even rarer, a well established Ron Greener markedly first choice, and he managed only one Fourth Division appearance for the Quakers. Greener, by the way, went on to break Darlington's appearances record, his splendid total of 442 League outings remaining such forty years on.

Appearances:
FL: 5 apps. 0 gls.
Total: *5 apps. 0 gls.*

RODGERSON, Ian

Role: Midfield/Defender 1993-95
5'8" 11st.6lbs.
b. Hereford, 9th April 1966

CAREER: Pegasus Juniors(Hellenic League)/ Hereford United assoc s'boy, pro July 1985/ Cardiff City Aug 1988/Birmingham City Dec 1990/SUNDERLAND July 1993/Cardiff City July 1995/Hereford United cs 1997.

Debut v Portsmouth (h) 6/11/1993

Ian Rodgerson

to hold on to a first team spot and did not appear in the League side after playing at Notts County in early November. Released in the close season, he rejoined Cardiff City on a free transfer. Ian's father, Alan, was capped by England Schoolboys against Wales in 1954 and played for Middlesbrough. On his debut at Rotherham United in September 1958 Middlesbrough won 4-1, Rodgerson senior and Brian Clough each scoring twice.

Appearances:
FL: 5(5) *apps.* 0 *gls.*
Total: 5(5) *apps.* 0 *gls.*

RODGERSON, Ralph

Role: Left-back 1935-39
5'10" 11st.4lbs.
b. Sunderland, 25th December 1913
d. Sunderland, 18th April 1972

CAREER: Shotton Colliery/SUNDERLAND May 1935/retired May 1939.
Debut v Huddersfield Town (h) 18/4/1936

Ian Rodgerson began as a schoolboy with Hereford United, but in 1982 he was not offered trainee terms and spent the next three years as an apprentice plumber. Spotted for a second time by Hereford, he was offered a professional contract in July 1985. Always a versatile performer, but with a personal preference for right side midfield, Ian completed exactly one hundred appearances for Hereford United, 99 for Cardiff City and 95 for Birmingham. He joined Sunderland for a tribunal-set fee of £140,000 but was involved in a car crash within weeks of his arrival. The very bad shoulder injury that he sustained delayed his debut, and this was followed by a groin injury, all of which restricted him to just two full and two substitute appearances in his first season. Introduced as deputy for the injured Martin Smith at Tranmere in September of the following season, Ian failed

Ralph Rodgerson

An understudy for Alex Hall, Ralph Rodgerson made his League bow in the final three fixtures of 1935/36 going on to make single appearances in 1936/37 and 1938/39. A competent defender, Rodgerson's tally of appearances would possibly have been extended but for the arrivals of George Collin and Jimmy Gorman, both experienced backs. (Hall moved to right-back to accommodate the former.)

Appearances:
FL: 5 apps. 0 gls.
Total: *5 apps. 0 gls.*

ROGAN, Anthony Gerard Patrick 'Anton'

Role: Defender 1991-93
5'11" 12st.6lbs.
b. Belfast, 25th March 1966

CAREER: Distillery/Celtic May 1986/ SUNDERLAND Oct 1991/Oxford United Aug 1993/Millwall Aug 1995/Blackpool July 1997-June 1999.

Debut v Brighton & Hove Albion (h) 5/10/1991

Anton Rogan was a double winner with Celtic in their Centenary year (1988) and won a second Scottish Cup medal the following year. In the 1990 final however, he missed the decisive penalty in a 9-8 shoot-out defeat by Aberdeen. A powerful left-back with great pace and aerial ability, he was signed by Denis Smith for £350,000 in an early season welter of transfer activity which also saw the arrival of John Byrne and Peter Beagrie. A popular figure and reputedly hilarious dressing-room joker, Rogan had an impressive first season at Roker, culminating in a Wembley appearance against Liverpool in the FA Cup Final when he was handed a winner's medal by mistake. Sadly, a broken leg ended his second campaign in early November 1992 and in the close season he joined Oxford United for a reported fee of £250,000. Two years on he joined Millwall on a free transfer. Despite being the Lions' second highest goalscorer in 1996-97 with eight goals, and adding a further Northern Ireland cap to his total, he was released in the summer and

joined Blackpool. Unfortunately, after just two early season appearances he suffered a serious injury which kept him out of the first team picture for the remainder of the season.

Appearances:
FL: 45(1) apps. 1 gl.
FAC: 8 apps. 0 gls.
FLC: 1 app. 0 gls.
Other: 2 apps. 0 gls.
Total: *56(1) apps. 1 gl.*
Honours:
18 NIre caps 1988-97/(Celtic) SPL champs 1988/SC winner 1988, 1989, finalist 1990/ (Sunderland) FAC finalist 1992.

Anton Rogan

ROGERS, John

Role: Centre-forward 1923-25
5'7" 10st.7lbs.
b. Helston, Cornwall, 20th June 1895
d. Helston, Cornwall, 21st March 1977

CAREER: Aberdare Athletic June 1921/
SUNDERLAND May 1923/Norwich City Oct
1925 £250/Newquay, as a permit player, Sept
1926, later assisting Helston British Legion
July 1928.

Debut v Arsenal (a) 12/4/1924

John Rogers was actually an inside-right and
his Sunderland debut was made in that
position. But the remaining half-dozen League
outings and the two FA Cup-ties were as
leader of the attack. John had been an
Aberdare player prior to their election to the
Football League (June 1921 was the date he
signed a League form). In those first couple of
Southern Section seasons he played 59 games,
scoring nine goals, his form such that the
Wearsiders added him to their pay-roll. After
two years he was released, returning to
another Third Division South club, Norwich
City, where he made 12 Football League
appearances and one in the FA Cup (four
League goals) before returning to his native
Cornwall and the amateur scene.

Appearances:
FL: 7 apps. 2 gls.
FAC: 2 apps. 1 gl.
Total: *9 apps. 3 gls.*

ROOKS, Richard

Role: Centre-half 1960-65
5'10" 12st.0lbs.
b. Sunderland, 29th May 1940

CAREER: Sunderland Schools/Silksworth
Juniors/SUNDERLAND May 1957/
Middlesbrough Aug 1965 £20,000/Bristol City
June 1969-1972 £15,000/Willington player-
coach/Hadley United (Ipswich League)
manager Oct 1974/Scunthorpe United
manager Dec 1974-Jan 1976.

Debut v Norwich City (a) 3/4/1961

Dickie Rooks was perhaps the best known of
the several Charlie Hurley deputies. He
commanded an appreciable transfer fee on
moving to Middlesbrough, having recovered

Dickie Rooks

well from a cartilage operation in the mid-
1960s. Dickie was a regular first-teamer for the
'Boro' making 150 League and Cup
appearances (14 goals) and sometimes playing
at centre-forward during his first two seasons.
At Ayresome Park he tasted both the
disappointments of relegation (1965/66) and
the joys of promotion (1966/67). Dickie played
in well over a century of League and Cup
games for Bristol City following a surprising
departure from Middlesbrough that was
deplored by their fans. In the 1990's he helped
Sunderland with their Centre of Excellence
youth set-up.

Appearances:
FL: 34 apps. 2 gls.
FAC: 2 apps. 0 gls.
FLC: 4 apps. 1 gl.
Total: *40 apps. 3 gls.*

ROONEY

Role: Inside-right 1886-88
Debut v Morpeth Harriers (a) 16/10/1886 (FAC)

Of the pre-League contingent Rooney
appeared in more FA Cup-ties than the

ROOSE, Leigh Richmond

Role: Goalkeeper 1907-11
6'1" 13st.6lbs.
b. Holt, nr Wrexham, 27th November 1877
d. France, 7th October 1916, killed in action

CAREER: UCW Aberystwyth/
Aberystwyth Town 1898/Druids 1900/
London Welsh 1900-01/Stoke Oct 1901/
Everton Nov 1904/Stoke Aug 1905/
SUNDERLAND Jan 1908/ Huddersfield
Town Apr 1911/Aston Villa Aug 1911/
Woolwich Arsenal Dec 1911-May 1912/
Aberystwyth Town later in 1912/
Llandudno Town 1914.

Debut v Preston North End (a) 18/1/1908

Two of the most renowned pre-Great War
goalkeepers were Ned
Doig and L.R. Roose and
Sunderland employed
them both. The
incomparable Doig for a
remarkable 14 years, the
unorthodox, ever
surprising Roose for two
years, three months. The
latter, a financially secure
amateur, was the son of a
Presbyterian minister, a
bacteriologist and science
graduate of the University
College, Aberystwyth. He
was at one time taught by
H.G. Wells, but later decided
to take up medicine,
studying for the purpose at
King's College Hospital,
London, but never qualified
as a medico. As a footballer Roose was very
much an archetypal peripatetic amateur.
He won winners' and runners-up medals
(1900 and 1901) with different teams in
Welsh Cup finals before his tour of leading
and lesser Football League clubs. All told
he made 284 League appearance for his six
clubs, the bulk of them for Stoke (146) and
Sunderland (92). As indicated, the player's
overriding trait was his eccentricity and
renown for practical jokes. J.A.H. Catton, a

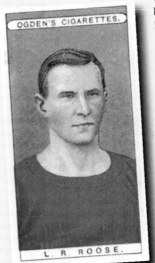

famed *Athletic News* commentator,
described him as "dexterous though
daring, valiant though volatile." Many
years afterwards, in 1960, it was said
"Roose could punch a ball farther than
most goalkeepers can kick it today, and his
erratic genius always kept a crowd at a
constant pitch of excitement." (The length
of his punches would have to be seen to be
believed!). And, despite his many virtues,
not knowing what he could do next may
have troubled some of his outfield
colleagues but his (now modern-day) habit
of rushing out to clear through-balls with
his feet was innovative. In December 1908
he played in The Lads' remarkable 9-1 win
at Newcastle conceding only a penalty.
A broken left wrist against the same
opponents in November
1910 when he was charged
by Jackie Rutherford was
his final game for
Sunderland. But Roose was
highly valued by the
Sunderland management
who planned to reward
him with a testimonial
match, but the FA scotched
this idea as being
unsuitable for an amateur.
Instead, he was presented
with an illuminated
address from Sunderland
supporters by the Mayor.
At the outbreak of World
War One Roose
immediately volunteered,
joining the 9th Battalion
of the Royal Welsh
Fusiliers as a private. At
the time of his death in action in the
Somme bloodbath Roose was a lance-
corporal and held the Military Medal.

Appearances:
FL: 92 apps. 0 gls.
FAC: 7 apps. 0 gls
Total: *99 apps. 0 gls.*
Honours:
*24 Welsh caps/1 Welsh am app. v Eng
1911.*

average. What is more, all his appearances were in the same position - inside-right - when other Sunderland outfield colleagues often took two or more. He played in all three ties of 1886/87 and the first two in 1887/88. Another facet: his five appearances covered but two opponents: Morpeth Harriers and Newcastle West End.

Appearances:
FAC: 5 apps. 0 gls.
Total: *5 apps. 0 gls.*

ROSTRON, John Wilfred

Role: Winger/Full-back 1977-80
5'6" 11st.2lbs.
b. Sunderland, 29th September 1956

CAREER: Sunderland Schoolboys/Arsenal assoc. s'boy Sept 1972, app July 1973, pro Oct 1973/SUNDERLAND July 1977/Watford Oct 1979/Sheffield Wednesday Jan 1989(Sheffield United loan Sept 1989)/Sheffield United Nov 1989/Brentford player-asst. manager Jan 1991/Gateshead asst. manager Oct 1993/Sunderland Ryhope Colliery Welfare manager Dec 1993-cs 1994.

Debut v Hull City (a) 20/8/1977 (sub)

Schoolboy international Wilf Rostron signed for Arsenal from school as a 16-year-old but returned home to Sunderland in a £40,000 transfer some five years later. A progressive wing-man with an eye for goal, his 11 goals in 34 appearances in 1978-79 included a hat-trick (with two late penalties) in the 6-2 demolition of Sheffield United at Roker Park in the season's penultimate home fixture which Sunderland needed to win by four goals to go top of the table. A change of manager the following term prompted the usual transfer activity and Rostron departed to Watford for £150,000 in October 1979. In a sterling stay of almost ten years at Vicarage Road, he was converted from winger to full-back and in all senior competitions clocked up 403 appearances and scored 30 goals during Watford's golden era. He was desperately unlucky to miss captaining Watford in the 1984 FA Cup Final, due to suspension.

Appearances:
FL: 75(1) apps. 17 gls.
FAC: 4 apps. 0 gls.
FLC: 5 apps. 1 gl.
Other: 1(1) app. 0 gls.
Total: *85(2) apps. 18 gls.*
Honours:
8 Eng Sch apps. 1972.

Wilf Rostron in action at Tottenham.

Ronnie Routledge

ROUTLEDGE, Rodney Wright

Role: Goalkeeper 1956-58
5'9" 11st.5lbs.
b. Ashington, Northumberland, 14th October 1937

CAREER: Northumberland schools football and Burnley FC juniors/SUNDERLAND Oct 1954/Bradford May 1958-1962.

Debut v Portsmouth (a) 1/5/1957

Known as Ronnie Routledge, this goalkeeper made his bow in the final fixture of 1956/57, the third choice 'keeper behind John Bollands and Willie Fraser. His other appearance was against Burnley, also away, the following October, when Sunderland sustained a heavy 6-0 defeat. At Bradford Park Avenue he played 39 Fourth Division matches (37 in 1958/59) and two Cup-ties.

Appearances:
FL: 2 apps. 0 gls.
Total: *2 apps. 0 gls.*

ROWELL, Gary

Role: Forward 1975-84
5'10" 11st.3lbs.
b. Seaham, 6th June 1957

CAREER: Seaham Northlea/Seaham Juniors/
SUNDERLAND app Aug 1972, pro July 1974/
Norwich City Aug 1984/Middlesbrough July
1985/Brighton & Hove Albion Aug 1986
(Dundee United trial Feb 1988)/Carlisle
United Mar 1988/Burnley Aug 1988-May 1989.
Debut v Oxford United (h) 13/12/1975 (sub)

Spotted whilst playing for Seaham Juniors,
Gary Rowell made his League debut in 1975-
76, the season in which Sunderland won the
Second Division championship. England
Under-21 honours quickly followed when he
was selected for the close season tour of

Scandinavia. He blossomed in 1977-78 with 18
League goals in 38(1) appearances and did
even better in the following term with 21 in 31
appearances. It was during 1978-79 that he
had the supreme satisfaction of scoring a hat-
trick against Newcastle United at St James
Park in a 4-1 victory. It was his first hat-trick,
and for a lifelong Sunderland supporter, it
could not have been bettered! Joy quickly
turned to despair, however, as in the following
months a medial ligament injury ended his
season. It also restricted his appearances to
just eight starts and some substitute outings in
the following 1979-80 term when promotion to
Division One was achieved. A regular during
the next four seasons in the top flight, Gary
notched another memorable treble against
Arsenal at Roker in December 1982. Arguably
the supporters most popular player of the past
25 years, Gary's energetic and often perceptive
contributions added greatly to the Sunderland
cause - not least through his healthy strike rate
in front of goal and clinical efficiency as a
penalty taker which saw him finish as the
club's top scorer on half a dozen occasions.
When eventually released by Sunderland, after
nine seasons, he joined Norwich City. Gary left
as not only The Lads' leading post-war scorer,
but also as one of only two post-war players
(the other is Len Shackleton) to have topped
100 goals. Injuries restricted him to just 2(4)
appearances and one goal for the Canaries,
who of course beat The Lads at Wembley in
1985 - Gary's only season at Carrow Road. As
an injured Canary player he brought the
League Cup over to salute Sunderland's fans
at the end of the game in what was clearly an
enormously emotional moment for him. Of his
subsequent moves, 10 goals in 27 appearances
for Middlesbrough was his best return. Since
retiring from playing, Gary has worked as a
financial consultant and in local radio, hosting
the Red'n'White phone-in on Sun FM. He is
still a regular Sunderland supporter.

Appearances:
FL: 229(25) apps. 88 gls.
FAC: 15 apps. 4 gls.
FLC: 19(2) apps. 8 gls.
Other: 3 apps. 2 gls.
Total: *266(27) apps. 102 gls.*
Honours:
1 Eng U-21 app. 1977.

Gary Rowell

ROWLANDSON, Thomas Sowerby

Role: Goalkeeper 1903-05
d. Darlington, 1880
d. France, 15th September 1916, killed in action

CAREER: Charterhouse School (Preston North End am 1900)/Cambridge University/SUNDERLAND Dec 1903/Newcastle United Oct 1905-1906. Like other leading amateurs of the time he assisted a variety of other clubs, notably the Corinthians (1903-10). Others included Bishop Auckland, Darlington and, of course, the Old Carthusians.
Debut v Wolverhampton Wanderers (h) 1/4/1904

A 1903 critique reads "This Old Carthusian scholar, who has toured with the Corinthians, is a resident of Trinity Hall, Cambridge. He is a most able custodian and did extremely well against the South African clubs. This well-known Blue can, as emergency, play a sound game at full-back". Rowlandson, a tall man, made only one League appearance for Newcastle United. But for the Corinthians, the crack amateur team then able to field many full internationalists, he played on 75 occasions. In the Great War he served with the Yorkshire Regiment, a commissioned officer reaching the rank of captain, and was the recipient of a Military Cross.

Appearances:
FL: 12 apps. 0 gls.
Total: *12 apps. 0 gls.*
Honours:
2 Eng am apps/Cambridge Blue 1903-04.

RUSH, David

Role: Forward 1989-94
5'11" 10st.10lbs.
b. Sunderland, 15th May 1971

CAREER: Sunderland Schoolboys/Durham County Schoolboys/Notts County Juniors/ SUNDERLAND trainee Jan 1989, pro July 1989 (Hartlepool United loan Aug 1991)

(Peterborough loan Oct 1993)(Cambridge United loan Sept 1994)/Oxford United Sept 1994/York City Jan-Nov 1997/Hartlepool United n.c. Sept 1998, pro Oct 1998-May 1999.
Debut v Fulham (h) 19/9/1989 (sub) (FLC)

Fair-haired David Rush captained Sunderland Schoolboys but arrived at Roker following a spell with Notts County juniors. A prolific goalscorer in youth and reserve team football, he nevertheless failed to establish a regular berth at senior level. His best season - 1991-92 - coincided with his FA Cup Final appearance against Liverpool, but his next regular spell of League action came with Oxford United, following his £100,000 transfer to the Manor Ground in September 1994. He enjoyed two good seasons (20 League goals in 77 appearances) which included promotion to

David Rush

Division One as runners-up to Swindon. His £80,000 transfer to York City in January 1997 was dogged by illness and injury and David appeared in just six matches before his contract was cancelled following breaches of club rules. A move back into League football followed almost a year later, when he secured a professional contract with Hartlepool United, following a month's trial.

Appearances:
FL: 40(19) apps. 12 gls.
FAC: 9 apps. 1 gl.
FLC: 1(1) app. 0 gls.
Other: 1(1) app. 0 gls.
Total: *51(21) apps. 13 gls.*
Honours:
(Sunderland) FAC finalist 1992.

RUSSELL, Craig Stewart

Role: Forward 1991-97
5'10" 12st.6lbs.
b. South Shields, 4th February 1974

CAREER: St Josephs Junior School, Hedworth/Jarrow & Hebburn Boys/South Tyneside Boys/SUNDERLAND assoc. s'boy May 1988, trainee July 1990, pro July 1992/ Manchester City Nov 1997(Tranmere Rovers loan Aug 1998)(Port Vale loan Jan 1999).

Debut v Watford (h) 2/11/1991 (sub)

One of Sunderland's promising juniors, Craig Russell signed schoolboy forms at 14 years of age, despite the interest of five other League clubs, including Manchester United. With Sunderland-mad parents and the fact he was once a mascot at Roker for a match against Liverpool it was perhaps an inevitable choice. Anyway, Craig has always claimed he was conceived the night of the 1973 Cup final! A strong-running centre-forward with an ideal physique, he progressed through the ranks to make a senior debut as a 17-year-old in November 1991. In the same week he had played in the FA Youth Cup and also made his debut in the Central League. A popular leading goalscorer in the Division One championship campaign of 1995-96 with 13 in 35(6) League appearances, including four in a match against Millwall, he found increased competition from the more experienced Paul Stewart in the Premiership season of 1996-97, especially so as Sunderland quite often

operated with only one man up front. Despite making only ten starts, he was joint top scorer with four goals in a season when only 35 League goals were registered. Linked with Manchester City in July 1997, a proposed £1.75 million move was shelved when personal terms were not agreed. In November of the same year, however, the deal was resurrected with Nick Summerbee moving to Sunderland in a £1 million exchange. Yet after only seven months at Maine Road, Russell was transfer-listed by new City manager Joe Royle. Asked to fill the unfamiliar role of left wing-

Craig
Russell

back by Frank Clark, he lost his way and was unable to help halt City's alarming slide into Division Two. No permanent move was however forthcoming and Craig, confined to the fringes, spent much of City's 1998-99 promotion season on loan, first at Tranmere with whom he lined up in a 5-0 defeat at the Stadium of Light, and later at Port Vale in a successful bid to beat the drop from Division One. His career figures display the all-time Sunderland record for substitute appearances.

Appearances:
PL: 10(19) apps. 4 gls.
FL: 93(28) apps. 27gls.
FAC: 6(3) apps. 2 gls.
FLC: 7(6) app. 1 gl.
Other: 2 apps. 0 gls.
Total: *118(56) apps. 34 gls.*
Honours:
(Sunderland) Div 1 champs 1996.

RUSSELL, James Walker

Role: Outside/inside-right 1935-38
5'9" 10st.4lbs.
b. Edinburgh, 14th September 1916

CAREER: Edinburgh Schools/Craigmer Juveniles (Edinburgh)/Carrickmuir Juniors/ Murrayfield Amateurs (trials with Queens Park and Heart of Midlothian)/ SUNDERLAND June 1934/Norwich City May 1938 £1,500 (guest player for Carlisle United and Middlesbrough during WW2)/Crystal Palace Dec 1946/New Brighton July 1947/ Fleetwood July 1949.

Debut v Derby County (a) 25/4/1936

An inside-right really, James Russell's last couple of League outings for Sunderland in September 1937 were on the right wing

deputising for Duns. Deemed an outstanding prospect as a schoolboy he translated his close control and accurate crossfield distribution to the senior scene. A reserve at Roker Park, the outstanding Raich Carter naturally first choice, Russell's subsequent move to Norwich was marred by niggling injuries and then war arrived to interrupt all footballing careers. As a teenager Russell worked as an electrical engineer. After leaving football he crossed the Atlantic living in Montreal and Detroit before retiring to Florida where he was still living in 1996 and related the following story to Norwich City historian Mike Davage: "My first manager Johnny Cochrane was laid-back and held very brief team talks. He would appear in the dressing-room just before the game with a cigar and a whisky glass and would ask: 'Who are we playing today?' The answer was 'Newcastle, boss', to which he replied, 'Oh, we'll stuff them', before closing the door and leaving us to it!"

Appearances:
FL: 5 apps. 0 gls.
Total: *5 apps. 0 gls.*
Honours:
3 Scot Sch apps.

James Russell (centre) seated between Raich Carter and Patsy Gallacher in a 1934 team photograph.

SADDINGTON, Nigel J.

Role: Central Defender 1986-87
6'1" 12st.2lbs.
b. Sunderland, 9th December 1965

CAREER: Monkwearmouth Schoolboys/
Silksworth Juniors/Coles Cranes FC/
Doncaster Rovers Sept 1984/Roker FC/
SUNDERLAND Jan 1986/Carlisle United Feb
1988-cs 1991.

Debut v Barnsley (a) 13/12/1986

A member of the Monkwearmouth Schoolboys
side that reached the final of the English
Schools Trophy in 1981, Nigel Saddington was
a teenage signing by Doncaster Rovers some
three years later. After just six League
appearances at Belle Vue he was released and
was playing in Wearside League football when
Sunderland recruited him in January 1986. He
had to wait almost a year for his first senior
appearance, the game at Barnsley also
marking the first appearance of goalkeeper
Bobby Mimms. Lack of first team
opportunities eventually resulted in his
transfer to Carlisle United. Ironically, his final
season of League football with the Cumbrians
eclipsed everything that had gone before. In 44

appearances in Division Four during 1989-90
he netted 10 goals, including five penalties. A
curious footnote is that Nigel has recently
purchased one of the houses built on the site
of the demolished Roker Park.

Appearances:
FL: 3 apps. 0 gls.
FAC: 1 app. 0 gls.
FLC: 1 app. 0 gls.
Total: *5 apps. 0 gls.*

SAMPSON, Ian

Role: Defender 1990-94
6'2" 12st.8lbs.
b. Wakefield, 14th November 1968

CAREER: Goole Town/SUNDERLAND Nov
1990(Northampton Town loan Dec 1993)/
Northampton Town Aug 1994(Tottenham
Hotspur loan May 1995).

Debut v Millwall (a) 24/8/1991 (sub)

Despite serving under four different managers
in as many seasons at Roker Park, Ian
Sampson strove in vain for an extended run of
first team action. Solid rather than spectacular,
he was a valuable cover defender with a

Nigel Saddington

Ian Sampson

robust style and a strong tackle. Following a mid-season loan to Northampton Town in 1993-94 he joined the Cobblers on a permanent basis following his release by Sunderland in the close season. Aside from a loan period to Tottenham Hotspur - specifically to appear in the much-maligned Inter-Toto Cup competition, Sampson has rarely been absent from the heart of Northampton's defence. In May 1997 he assisted in his team's promotion to Division Two via the Wembley play-off final. In a dramatic finale to the successful campaign, Swansea City were beaten 1-0 when Northampton's John Frain netted a 90th minute winner. Twelve months on, a second successive Wembley play-off final ended in heartbreak, Grimsby Town winning the last promotion place into Division One. Disappointments carried over into 1998-99, as Northampton failed to fulfil their potential and were relegated from Division Two. During the campaign Ian Sampson passed the milestone of 200 appearances for the Cobblers.

Appearances:
FL: 13(17) apps. 1 gl
FAC: 0(3) apps. 0 gls.
FLC: 1 app. 0 gls.
Total: *14(20) apps. 1 gl.*

SAUNDERS, Percy Kitchener

Role: Inside-left 1936-39
5'8" 10st.7lbs.
b. Newhaven, Sussex, 3rd qtr 1916
d. killed in action, 2nd/3rd March 1942

CAREER: Newhaven FC/SUNDERLAND October 1934/Brentford June 1939

Debut v Portsmouth (a) 13/3/1937

Percy Saunders' most fruitful term was 1937/38, starting with a run of seven consecutive appearances from the opening day and grossing 14 all told. He could also take the inside-right and left-half berths. For Brentford he played twice in the abandoned 1939/40 season (one goal) before the close-down. It seems a touch more poignant than usual to note that one born in the First World War - pointedly so in view of his second name, Kitchener - should lose his life in the Second.

Appearances:
FL: 25 apps. 5 gls.
Total: *25 apps. 5 gls.*

SAXTON, Arthur William

Role: Outside-left 1897-99
5'7" 11st.7lbs.
b. Long Eaton, Derbyshire in the 1870s

CAREER: Glossop North End May 1895/ Stalybridge Rovers June 1896/SUNDERLAND June 1898/Bedminster May 1899/Luton Town Aug 1900/Northampton Town May 1901/ Long Eaton St Helen's Aug 1902/Perks Athletic Nov 1902.

Debut v West Bromwich Albion (a) 19/2/1898

Made a name with Glossop, then a successful Midland League side, reaching Sunderland a year and half later via Stalybridge. Saxton did quite well when accomplishing the major transition to top grade soccer, sharing the outside-left spot with Jim Chalmers and, from the autumn of 1898, Colin McLatchie. Thereafter, with southern clubs, his career tapered off somewhat.

* A player named Arthur William Saxton made a single appearance at outside-right for Nottingham Forest on October 19, 1901, oddly enough against Sunderland. In a book entitled "Forest: The First

Percy Saunders

125 Years", published in 1991, Saxton's birth-place is given as Breaston, Derbyshire, and the date of birth as 28 August, 1874. Although it is not at the time of writing proven conclusively, it is considered more than likely to be the same man who wore a Sunderland jersey.

Appearances:
FL: 18 apps. 3 gls.
Total: *18 apps. 3 gls.*

SCOTSON, Reginald

Role: Right-half 1946-51
5'10" 10st.12lbs.
b. Stockton-on-Tees, 22nd September 1919
d. February 1999

CAREER: Ouston United, Co Durham/ SUNDERLAND Apr 1939/Grimsby Town Dec 1950 £5,000/Skegness Town June 1955.

Debut v Blackpool (a) 18/1/1947

A stalwart accurately delineated by a contemporary critic as "... one of the toughest half-backs in the game, a footballer who never stops trying." Reg had played centre-half as a junior, but was converted to right-half by the Wearsiders, filling in occasionally on the left

flank too. Grimsby's outlay of 1950 proved a good investment with Reg's wholehearted performance a feature at Blundell Park for four and a half seasons. While there he made 176 League and Cup appearances, scoring 6 goals.

Appearances:
FL: 61 apps. 1 gl.
Total: *61 apps. 1 gl.*

SCOTT, Henry

Role: Inside-right
1924-25
6'0" 11st.8lbs.
b. Newburn,
Northumberland,
4th August 1898

CAREER:
Bankhead
Albion/Newburn
Grange/
SUNDERLAND
June 1922/
Wolverhampton
Wanderers June 1925/Hull
City Nov 1926/Bradford June
1928/Swansea Town July 1932/Watford June
1933/Nuneaton Town July 1934/Vauxhall
Motors as a permit player Sept 1935.

Harry Scott

Debut v Nottingham Forest (a) 7/3/1925

A tall inside-right whose senior outings while on Wearside were limited to one, due to the availability of Buchan and the emerging Bobby Marshall. Harry fared much better at his next four clubs totalling 172 League appearances - all, incidentally, in Division Two. This was made up as follows: Wolves 35 (six goals), Hull City 29 (eight goals), Bradford 69 (20 goals) and Swansea Town 39 (seven goals). At his last Football League club, Watford of the Division Three South, he also made just a single appearance: the opening fixture of 1933/34. Harry was no demon goal scorer though an effective link man and provider for others.

Appearances:
FL: 1 app. 0 gls.
Total: *1 app. 0 gls.*

Reg
Scotson

John Scott

SCOTT, John

Role: Inside/outside-left 1890-96
b. most probably in Scotland

CAREER: Coatbridge Albion Rovers/
SUNDERLAND June 1890-1896/South
Shields Aug 1897.

Debut v Burnley (h) 13/9/1890

An important cog in the great
Sunderland machine of the 1890s that
won three League Championships in four
seasons. John Scott won medals in two of
them but missed out in 1892/93 as nine
appearances were insufficient for qualification
purposes. John's link-up with David Hannah
on the Wearsiders' left flank began in 1890/91,
both players ever-presents in that inaugural
League season. Afterwards he often appeared
at outside-left maintaining a fair scoring rate.

Appearances:
FL: 96 apps. 31 gls.
FAC: 14 apps. 3 gls.
Total: *110 apps. 34 gls.*
Honours:
(Sunderland) FL champs 1892, 1895.

SCOTT, Leslie

Role: Goalkeeper 1913-22
5'10" 11st.0lbs.
b. Sunderland, 2nd qtr 1895

CAREER: Co Durham schools football/
Fulwell/SUNDERLAND am June 1911, pro
Sept 1913/Stoke July 1922/Preston North End

Aug 1923-24. Subsequently a permit player,
e.g. joined Sunderland Corporation FC Sept
1929.

Debut v Sheffield Wednesday (h) 4/4/1914

Local lad Leslie Scott came in for Joe Butler in
the last five League fixtures of 1913/14 and,
consequent upon Butler's departure to Lincoln
City in the close season, was first choice in
1914/15, missing only one game. This was a
capital start for the accomplished young
'keeper: 42 League and Cup appearances out
of a possible 43, from one who had no
previous first class experience. After the Great
War, which claimed his best football years,
Scott had much first team exposure but now
had serious rivals in Tony Allen,
Dempster and, latterly, Willie
Harper. On leaving Roker
Park Scott enjoyed a
decent run in his term at
Stoke (20 League
outings) but only
managed a couple for
Preston in 1923/24.
By 1929 he was back
on Wearside and
reverted to amateur
status to work as a
storekeeper for
Sunderland Corporation.

Leslie
Scott

Appearances:
FL: 91 apps. 0 gls.
FAC: 4 apps. 0 gls.
Total: *95 apps. 0 gls.*

SCOTT, Martin

Role: Defender 1994-1999
5'9" 11st.7lbs.
b. Sheffield, 7th January 1968

CAREER: Lintsfield Juniors/Hind House/
Hillsborough Celtic/Sheffield Schoolboys/
Rotherham United app, pro Jan 1986
(Nottingham Forest loan Mar-Apr 1988)/
Bristol City Dec 1990/SUNDERLAND Dec
1994-June 1999.

Debut v Bolton Wanderers (h) 26/12/1994

Martin Scott was first associated with
Rotherham United as a 14-year-old, after
representing Sheffield Schoolboys at Under-10,
11 and 14 levels. Mainly at left back and
occasionally in midfield for the Millers, he

Martin Scott

made his League debut in May 1985, and four years later won a Division Four championship medal. Joining Bristol City for £200,000 in December 1990, he was ever-present in his first full season at Ashton Gate. His pace and strong tackling, coupled with an increasing strike rate, first interested Sunderland in the summer of 1994 when an initial bid of £500,000 was rejected. A follow up bid in December of the same year proved successful. A fee of £450,000 plus Gary Owers (valued at £300,000) finally being accepted. In Martin's first season Sunderland successfully fought off relegation and in his second the championship of the First Division was secured. His significant contribution included six goals in 43 League appearances. In the Premiership campaign that followed, a cruel catalogue of injuries restricted his appearances to just 15, and his problems continued in 1997-98, injury halting his progress shortly after he had completed his century of first team appearances. As deputy for Michael Gray, 'Scotty' played in 14 League matches in 1998-99, and additionally appeared in seven Cup ties. Nevertheless, much to his disappointment he was released in summer 1999 on a free transfer. Even more sadly, Martin's plans to

join newly-promoted Premiership outfit, Bradford City on a three year deal were dashed when his troublesome ankle flared up again and required yet more surgery.

Appearances:
PL: 15 apps. 1 gl.
FL: 89(2) apps. 8 gls .
FAC: 6 apps. 0 gls.
FLC: 12 apps 1 gl.
Total: *122(2) apps. 10 gls.*
Honours:
(Rotherham United) Div 4 champs 1989/
(Sunderland) Div 1 champs 1996 & 1999.

SCOTT, Matthew

Role: Right-back 1893-94
CAREER: Newcastle East End/
SUNDERLAND Oct 1892-93/later in the 1890s assisted South Shields.

Debut v Wolverhampton Wanderers (a) 6/1/1894

Recruited from local good class non-League soccer and only briefly with Sunderland. Chances for full-backs were hard to come by at the time with Scottish caps Donald Gow and Peter Meechan plus Tom Porteous and Willie Gibson around. Matthew Scott's sole League outing against Wolves resulted in a 2-1 defeat for the Wearsiders.

Appearances:
FL: 1 app. 0 gls.
Total: *1 app. 0 gls.*

SCOTT, Thomas

Role: Outside-right 1923-24
5'11" 12st.0lbs.
b. Newcastle upon Tyne, 6th April 1904
d. Bootle, 24th December 1979

CAREER: Swifts FC (Tyneside)/Pandon Temperance/SUNDERLAND Dec 1922/ Darlington June 1924/Liverpool Feb 1925/ Bristol City Oct 1928/Preston North End June 1930/Norwich City June 1932/Exeter City Oct 1934/Hartlepools United June 1936/Bangor City Aug 1937.

Debut v Chelsea (h) 17/10/1923

Although his initial couple of League games (for Sunderland) were on the right-wing it was at inside-right that Tom Scott became known. This was at Liverpool where he also turned

Tom Scott

out at centre-forward and in both left-wing berths, so he certainly did not lack versatility. At Preston Tom was commended for his whole-hearted play but criticised for slowness, a fault rectified at Norwich seemingly. However, his statistics for Bristol City (35 Football League appearances, six goals) and Preston (47 appearances, 23 goals) bear examination. All this led to his high peak with Norwich City (53 League outings 26 gls) that took in the winning of a championship medal. Here he was regarded as the brains of the attack, well maintaining an improved scoring rate. After leaving football Tom found employment as a Liverpool licensee.

Appearances:
FL: 2 apps. 0 gls.
Total: *2 apps. 0 gls.*
Honours:
(Norwich City) Div 3 Sth champs 1934.

SCOTT, Walter 'Buns'

Role: Goalkeeper 1911-13
5'11" 13st.0lbs.
b. Worksop, 3rd qtr 1886
d. Worksop, 16th September 1955

CAREER: Ashley House School/Worksop West End/Worksop Central/Worksop Town/Grimsby Town May 1907/Everton Feb 1910 £750/SUNDERLAND June 1911 £750/Shelbourne Oct 1913/Belfast United 1915 (guest player for Brentford and Millwall Athletic during WW1)/Worksop Town Aug 1919/Grimsby Town Feb 1920/Gainsborough Trinity June 1920/Ashington Apr 1921/later a permit player with Bebside Garden FC, Northumberland Sept 1924.

Debut v Middlesbrough (h) 2/9/1911

Scott was a goalkeeper of character, notably agile for a big man and possessed fine anticipation. Early in his first-class career 'Buns' entered the record books by saving

three penalties in a match against Burnley on February 13, 1909. All told he made in his two spells 104 Football League and FA Cup appearances for the Mariners. Everton paid what was then a hefty sum for a 'keeper (18 League outings) before he came to Roker Park for a similar fee. It was not however a happy stay, although he was first choice for most of the 1911-12 season. Sunderland made a poor start to their ultimately magnificent 1912-13 campaign with only a point from their opening four games which included two heavy defeats by reigning champions Blackburn Rovers. Scott was poor in the second of these a 2-4 reverse at Roker and the crowd got on his back. It still caused quite a stir two days later when the keeper was suspended - effectively sacked - by the club, officially for missing training. Convinced he was merely the scapegoat for the defeat Scott complained bitterly and publicly about his treatment. "Scott said he thought the directors had been forced into giving the notice through the hostility of a section of the crowd that visited Roker Park" reported the *Sunderland Echo*, adding: "He admitted not having shown

'Buns' Scott

his best form this season but contended that some of the spectators had not given him a chance, as at every match a certain clique gathered round the goal and throughout the game made use of offensive epithets towards him. This was enough to make any man downhearted and put him off his play." Scott though never played for the club again, but his talents were well appreciated in Ireland as seen by the tangible awards for Irish League representation. Walter's brother, Billy Scott, assisted Worksop Town too and also one of the Rotherham clubs.

Appearances:
FL: 34 apps. 0 gls.
FAC: 4 apps. 0 gls.
Total: *38 apps. 0 gls.*
Honours:
5 IL apps.

SCOTT

Role: Outside-left
1889-90
*Debut v Blackburn
Rovers (a) 18/1/1890
(FAC) (scored)*

In 1889/90, the last season before entering the Football League, Sunderland played 54 matches, which would be considered a large total even a century later. Scott occupied the outside-left berth in at least 29 of them - all the line-ups are not available - so can claim to be the

Scott

'regular' for the position. The tie mentioned above went to extra time, Blackburn running out 4-2 winners, and Scott was one of Sunderland's goal scorers.

Appearances:
FAC: 1 app. 1 gl.
Total: *1 app. 1 gl.*

SHACKLETON, Leonard Francis

Role: Inside-forward/outside-left 1947-58
5'8" 11st.5lbs.
b. Bradford, 3rd May 1922

CAREER: Bradford Schools/Kippax United/Arsenal ground staff Aug 1938 (loaned to London Paper Mills and Enfield for development)/returned home on outbreak of WW2/pro Bradford Dec 1940 (guest for Bradford City and Huddersfield Town during WW2)/Newcastle United Oct 1946 £13,000/SUNDERLAND Feb 1948 £20,050, a then record/retired through injury Sept 1957.

Debut v Derby County (a) 14/2/1948

When you talk to football followers of a certain age (not necessarily Sunderland supporters) and Sunderland AFC is mentioned, their eyes often light up or grow misty and they exclaim "Shack!" Even though the player left the football arena more than forty years ago, his memory lives on indelibly etched in the minds of those fortunate enough to have seen him. For Leonard Francis Shackleton was probably the greatest entertainer the game has ever seen, or indeed, is likely to. His wizardry with the ball, his trickery - which could mystify colleagues too - and repertoire of sheer unorthodox impudence were spell-binding. As one of his contemporaries said: "Once in possession, and few can match his dexterity at bringing the ball under control, the ball becomes his slave. All the skills of inside-forward play - dribbling, feinting, correct positioning and accurate passing are his to command." Len's career had been notable right from the

*Len
Shackleton*

Len Shackleton

Len Shackleton

There was however, no silverware to show for it. The highest place Sunderland reached in Shack's time was third in 1949/50 but the most successful can be counted as 1954/55, finishing fourth in the League and reaching the FA Cup semi-final (lost to Manchester City 1-0 on a mudbath pitch). The semi-final stage was scaled again the following term, but the Wearsiders were convincingly defeated 3-0 by Birmingham City. His five England caps were a criminally paltry return for such outstanding talent. In his final international 'Shack' scored with a cheeky chip over West Germany's 'keeper Herkenrath as England beat the World Champions 3-1, but it was common knowledge the publicly outspoken Yorkshireman was never popular with the crusty establishment selectors. In the season prior to Len's enforced retirement Sunderland finished 20th, a pointer to the relegation of a year later. Len was no mean cricketer either. He played, most notably as a bowler, for Lidgett Green in the strong Bradford League and, later, for Northumberland in the Minor Counties. On leaving football he became a journalist reporting on the local soccer scene first with the *Daily Express* and then the *Sunday People*. His forthright comments claimed much attention. So did the autobiography, "Clown Prince of Soccer", the title bestowed on him by an admiring press and public during his playing days. The book famously contained a chapter headed "The Average Director's Knowledge of Football". The rest of the page was left blank! He now lives in quiet retirement in Grange-over-Sands, spending winters in a holiday home in Tenerife. More recently 'Shack' opened the Visitor Centre at the Stadium of Light which enabled fans to watch it being built. Despite so many facts, it is the mental picture of the legendary 'Shack' that dominates the memory. Shoulders hunched, arms dangling, long shorts flapping, a half smile on his face daring opponents to take the ball away and knowing they very probably can't! Few footballers have given more lasting pleasure to spectators than this unique, genuinely charismatic player.

start. As a schoolboy he was the shortest, at four feet, ever to represent England. Thrilled to join mighty Arsenal as an amateur he was stunned after ten months when told by manager George Allison he would not make the grade! Unbowed, Len created a big reputation in wartime soccer so, by the time peace returned, he counted as 'red-hot property'. Newcastle United secured his signature for a record fee, reputed to be actually £13,000.0.3d. Surely no player ever had a more sensational debut for a new club. Not only did the team establish a new record with an incredible 13-0 annihilation of Newport County but Len netted six of them. Yet his stay at St James Park lasted a mere 16 months. It was said relations between maverick player and management were never easy. Be that as it may, 'Shack' (as he became widely known) joined big-spending Sunderland, again for a record sum - the first transfer fee, albeit by only £50, to top £20,000. The bids were requested in sealed envelopes and the story goes that Sunderland were tipped off about adding the extra fifty pounds. This time however, the stay was far happier and stretched nearly a decade, right through until a month into the fateful 1957/58 season that saw Sunderland's first relegation, and 'Shack' give in to a long-suffered ankle injury. During his ten Roker seasons Len played mostly at inside-left during the initial years, partnering 'Tich' Reynolds, and on Ken Chisholm's arrival moved to the right flank.

Appearances:
FL: 320 apps. 98 gls.
FAC: 28 apps. 3 gls.
Total: *348 apps. 101 gls.*
Honours:
5 Eng caps/2 Eng 'B' apps./3 Eng Sch. apps./ 2 FL apps.

SHARKEY, Dominic 'Nick'

Role: Centre-forward 1959-67
5'7" 11st.0lbs.
b. Helensburgh, Dunbartonshire, 4th May 1943

CAREER: Dunbartonshire Schools/
Sunderland am May 1958, pro May 1960/
Leicester City Oct 1966 £15,000/Mansfield
Town Mar 1968 £10,000, a Mansfield record/
Hartlepool July 1970/South Shields cs 1972.

Debut v Scunthorpe United (h) 9/4/1960

A slight build did not prevent Nick Sharkey
from consistently hitting the back of the net, as
illustrated by his better than a goal every other
game record. This was ably demonstrated in
his most memorable Roker Park term -
1963/64, when promotion was secured
(although he finished second top-scorer to
Johnny Crossan). Nick received his League
baptism very early, aged 16 years 311 days, a
few weeks before he joined the paid ranks.
However, he did not become a regular until
1962/63 having acted as understudy to Don
Kichenbrand, Ian Lawther and Brian Clough
in the meantime. Nick won a couple of
Scottish Schoolboy caps before Sunderland
snapped him up aged 15, rightly spotting his
abilities for team work, elusiveness and, above
all, goalscoring. He netted a prodigious 140
goals for the fifth team in his first season
before duly progressing towards that early
League debut. Nick's other high points at
Roker were the honour of Under-23 caps
(against England and France in 1964) and
equalling the club's 'most goals in a League
match' record (five in a 7-1 thrashing of
Norwich City on March 20, 1963), a feat
shared with Charlie Buchan and Bobby
Gurney. He also had a successful run at inside-
left after Harry Hood's arrival from Clyde late
in 1964. Sharkey's transfer to Leicester City
came after the centre-forward position became
crowded with John O'Hare, Harry Hood, and
the newly signed Neil Martin. Leicester, then a
mid-table Division One side, aimed to link
Nick with the well-known Irish international,
Derek Dougan. As it happened they played
together only once. Nick's chances at Filbert
Street afterwards were limited but he enjoyed
a free-scoring partnership in the reserves with
Jimmy Goodfellow which resumed at his next
club, Mansfield Town, an average Third
Division side, who outlayed their record fee
for his signature. In his second season they

Nick Sharkey

finished sixth and had a great FA Cup run,
reaching the 1969 quarter-final. Nick topped
the scoring list, mostly at inside-right. Sharkey
eventually came back to Co Durham, firstly to
Fourth Division Hartlepool (completing a
round of all League divisions) and then non-
League South Shields. For Hartlepool he
played 55(5) League games, scoring 12 goals.
On retiring from football he became a sales
representative for a leisure company, working
from Sunderland where he still lives today.

Appearances:
FL: 99 apps. 51 gls.
FAC: 12 apps. 8 gls.
FLC: 6 apps. 3 gls.
Total: *117 apps. 62 gls.*
Honours:
2 Scot U-23 apps./Scot Sch.

SHAW, Harold Victor

Harold Shaw

Role: Left-back 1929-36
5'10" 12st.5lbs.
b. Hednesford, Staffs, 22nd May 1905
d. Cambridge, June 1984

CAREER: Hednesford Primitives/Hednesford Town June 1920/Wolverhampton Wanderers May 1923/SUNDERLAND Feb 1930 £7,100/ retired through injury May 1938.

Debut v Newcastle United (a) 22/2/1930

A cultured left-back unlucky not to be awarded representative honours. Cool, good in positional play, neat and sure in tackling - he had all the qualities. Maybe the fact Harold Shaw did not play First Division football until reaching Roker Park weighed against him. And then England could call on a succession of outstanding left-backs: Sam Wadsworth, Blenkinsop and Hapgood. Yet the powers-that-be were cognisant of Harold's worth for he was selected and played in an international trial (for The Rest v England at White Hart Lane in March 1929). Harold had shown a precocious talent, making Hednesford Town's first team at 13 and Hednesford a member of the Birmingham League that provided opposition for such teams as the reserve sides of West Bromwich Albion and Wolves. For Wolves Shaw figured in 249 League and FA Cup matches but his name did not appear on a score sheet until donning a Sunderland jersey. Outside the game he worked as an engineer's fitter at Cannock Colliery.

> **Appearances:**
> *FL: 195 apps. 4 gls.*
> *FAC: 22 apps. 1 gl.*
> **Total:** *217 apps. 5 gls.*
> **Honours:**
> *(Wolverhampton Wanderers) Div 3 Nth champs 1924.*

SHAW, John T.

Role: Inside-left 1905-06

CAREER: Darlington/SUNDERLAND Apr 1906/Clapton Orient Oct 1906.

Debut v Middlesbrough (a) 13/4/1906

John Shaw was an amateur briefly on Sunderland's books and quickly given a tough League baptism in a local derby at

Middlesbrough, his sole appearance in the first team. Middlesbrough won the match 2-1.
NOTE: Clapton Orient had a J F Shaw who made 19 Second Division appearances in season 1908/09, mainly at centre-forward. He reputedly hailed from the North-East and signed from Wallsend Park Villa in 1908. It is possible this was Sunderland's John Shaw but not the J F Shaw dealt with below.

Appearances:
FL: 1 app. 0 gls.
Total: *1 app. 0 gls.*

SHAW, Joseph F.

Role: Centre-forward 1905-07
5'9" 11st.7lbs.

CAREER: Sunderland Schools/St Mark's (Sunderland) c.1898/Sunderland West End/ Armstrong College, Newcastle/Bishop Auckland/Darlington cs 1905/ SUNDERLAND Dec 1905/Hull City May 1907/Grimsby Town Oct 1909-10.

Debut v Middlesbrough (h) 1/1/1906 (scored)

A purposeful leader of the attack who netted nine goals in his first dozen League games for Sunderland and was tersely outlined by one critic as "not a showy player. Fearless in front of the posts, a custodian had to be alert or else he would find himself bundled in the net."
A teacher by profession, trained at Durham University, it is likely Joe Shaw's several transfers were dictated by moves to different schools. His statistics with the Humberside clubs read Hull City 48 Football League and FA Cup appearances, 22 goals; Grimsby Town six Football League appearances, 0 goals.

Appearances:
FL: 31 apps. 14 gls.
FAC: 4 apps. 1 gl.
Total: *35 apps. 15 gls.*

SHEPPEARD, Howard Thomas

Role: Inside-left 1953-54
6'1" 12st.5lbs.
b. Ynysybwl, Glamorgan, 31st January 1933

CAREER: Ynysybwl Boys Club Aug 1951/ SUNDERLAND Dec 1951/ Cardiff City May 1955 £9,000 incl Harry Kirtley and John McSeveney/Newport County June 1956 £1,000/Abergavenny Thursday 1958/Ton Pentre 1964/Brecon Corries 1965/retired 1967.

Debut v Preston North End (a) 24/10/1953

Tall Welsh inside-forward, Howard Sheppeard's years at Roker Park were spent understudying the likes of Len Shackleton and Ken Chisholm. Part of a triple deal on returning to Wales - obviously the makeweight with McSeveney and Kirtley largely accounting for the fee - Howard did not make the Cardiff first team. He had much more scope at Newport (31 Division Three (South) appearances, six goals) but had the misfortune to break a leg in his second season there during a reserve game. He skippered Abergavenny Thursday for a long while subsequently and settled in Pontypridd.

Appearances:
FL: 1 app. 0 gls.
Total: *1 app. 0 gls.*

Howard Sheppeard

SHERWIN, Harry

Role: Right/centre-half 1913-21
5'8" 11st.4lbs.
b. Walsall, 4th qtr 1893
d. Leeds, 8th January 1953

CAREER: Walsall Schools/Darlaston/
SUNDERLAND Dec 1913/Leeds United May
1921/Barnsley Mar 1925/Leeds United asst.
trainer June 1926/Bradford City trainer 1936.

Debut v Tottenham Hotspur (h) 14/3/1914

Harry Sherwin

A real tough customer, so it was said by fellow Sunderland players, Harry was a rugged centre-half described as "a rough 'un who used to butt centre-forwards away with his head". Later an important figure in Leeds United's first promotion line-up, Leeds knew all about Sherwin because he had guested - and created a great reputation - during WW1 for Leeds City (91 appearances all told and an ever-present in 1917/18). He had been a guest player with Sunderland Rovers in 1915/16. The formidable intermediate line of Leeds United's championship team consisted of Harry Sherwin, Ernie Hart (later of England) and the skipper, Jim Baker (brother of Alf Baker, Arsenal and England). Harry's other claim to fame was an appearance in the first-ever England Schoolboy international team.

Appearances:
FL: 28 apps. 0 gls.
FAC: 1 app. 0 gls.
Total: *29 apps. 0 gls.*
Honours:
1 Eng Sch app. v Wales 1907/
(Leeds United) Div 2 champs 1924

SHORE, Albert Victor

Role: Inside-forward 1919-21
5'9" 12st.0lbs.
b. Wednesbury, Staffs, 1st qtr 1897

CAREER: Harper, Son & Dean's (Birmingham works side)/SUNDERLAND Mar 1920/Stoke May 1921/Brierley Hill Alliance c.1922/later a permit player, eg. Cottage Spring FC (Wednesbury) Oct 1927/Whitburn.

Debut v Preston North End (h) 3/4/1920 (scored)

Victor Shore had a speedy introduction to the first-class game, making his debut a mere fortnight after joining Sunderland from the Midlands junior scene. What is more, he scored the only goal in a 1-0 win over Preston. He played both inside-right and inside-left in his few League outings while on Wearside. For Stoke he made three Second Division appearances during 1921/22. The Potters were runners-up that season with the inside-forward spots keenly contested.

Appearances:
FL: 5 apps. 1 gl.
Total: *5 apps. 1 gl.*

SHOULDER, James

Role: Left-back 1966-67
5'8" 10st.8lbs.
b. Esh Winning, 11th September 1946

CAREER: Esh Winning Juniors/
SUNDERLAND Feb 1964/Scarborough May 1969/Hartlepool Aug 1973-75. Later (1979) Darlington assistant manager.

Jim Shoulder

Debut v West Bromwich Albion (a) 25/2/1967

Not for the first time Hartlepool retrieved a former League player from a non-League source. In Jim's case an appreciable four years after leaving Roker Park. He responded with 62 Fourth Division appearances plus a substitution, scoring three goals. An understudy of Len Ashurst's while on Wearside, Len was Hartlepool manager at the time of Jim's signing for the club.

Appearances:
FL: 3 apps. 0 gls.
Total: *3 apps. 0 gls.*

SIDDALL, Barry Alfred

Role: Goalkeeper 1976-82
6'1" 14st.2lbs.
b. Ellesmere Port, 12th September 1954

CAREER: Bolton Wanderers app 1970, pro Jan 1972/SUNDERLAND Sept 1976(Darlington loan Oct 1980)(Vancouver Whitecaps, NASL loan May-Aug 1981)/Port Vale Aug 1982 (Blackpool loan Oct 1983)/Stoke City Jan 1985 (Tranmere Rovers loan Oct 1985)(Manchester City loan Mar 1986)/Blackpool Aug 1986/ Stockport County June 1989/Hartlepool United Mar 1990/West Bromwich Albion n.c. Aug 1990/Mossley FC/Carlisle United Nov 1990/Chester City July 1991/Preston North End Nov 1992/Bury nc Mar-Sept 1994/ Burnley nc Sept 1994/Lincoln City nc Nov-Dec 1994/Burnley nc Dec 1994-Mar 1995.

Debut v Aston Villa (h) 16/10/1976

Barry Siddall made his League debut as an 18-year-old in Bolton's Division Three championship side of 1972-73. In the following season he began as first choice goalkeeper and did so well that he immediately embarked on a run of 33 consecutive League games. Sunderland paid £80,000 for him in September 1976 to succeed one of the club's most celebrated players, record appearance holder Jim Montgomery. At 6ft 1in and over 14 stones, Barry Siddall was an imposing presence who dominated his area with a calm assurance and confidence. A popular figure at Roker, he was lauded for a last minute penalty save in a 6-2 win over Sheffield United that took Sunderland top in April 1979 and remained first choice until the autumn of the following promotion season 1979-80, when new £100,000 signing Chris Turner's

outstanding form won him the senior position. Siddall made his final League appearance for Preston North End against one of his former clubs, Port Vale in December 1992. He had appeared in 20 seasons of League football and clocked up 614 appearances, including at one stage playing in all four divisions during an eight month period. During his Sunderland days, Barry was a seven handicap golfer. In September 1979 he recorded a hole-in-one on the 140 yards, 13th hole on the South Shields course. Currently living in Kirkham near Preston, he works for the Royal Mail and keeps fit on his eight miles a day postal round.

Appearances:
FL: 167 apps. 0 gls.
FAC: 9 apps. 0 gls.
FLC: 11 apps. 0 gls.
Other: 2 apps. 0 gls.
Total: *189 apps. 0 gls.*
Honours:
Eng Yth/UEFA Yth Tourn winner 1972-73.

Barry Siddall

SIMPSON, William

Role: Right-half/inside-right 1898-99
5'9" 11st.10lbs.
b. Sunderland, 1877 or 1878
d. Lincoln, March 1962, aged 84

CAREER: Selbourne/SUNDERLAND May
1898-cs 1899 when he disappeared from first-
class football/Lincoln City June 1902/retired
through injury 1908.

Debut v Stoke (a) 25/3/1899

Obviously a two-footed
player ... on the right
flank for his Sunderland
appearances and, in his
six years with Lincoln,
moved to left-back from
centre-half. Simpson had
transferred to Lincoln
from his native North-
East with some
reluctance. However, he

William Simpson

prospered as an Imp, captaining the side, and
revealed commendable defensive qualities and
resolve when making 140 first team
appearances. A bad knee injury brought about
retirement. The reluctance in going to Lincoln
was, it would seem, temporary for he spent
the rest of his life in the cathedral city. After
leaving football he worked first in a local
engineering works and then as landlord of the
Roebuck Hotel, this last a very lengthy
engagement - 1921-47.

> **Appearances:**
> *FL: 3 apps. 1 gl.*
> **Total:** *3 apps. 1 gl.*

SLACK, Melvyn

Role: Wing-half 1964-65
5'8" 11st.8lbs.
b. Bishop Auckland, 7th March 1944

CAREER: Bishop Auckland Schools/
SUNDERLAND Mar 1961/Southend United
Aug 1965 £5,000/Cambridge United Jan
1969-71.

Debut v Stoke City (a) 24/4/1965 (scored)

Played centre-half for Bishop Auckland Boys
and successfully converted to right-back on
joining Sunderland. The staff then made a
further change, switching him to wing-half. It

Mel Slack

was there that Mel made his League bow in
the final couple of 1964/65 fixtures. He played
left-half on his debut, scoring in a 3-1 defeat,
and right-half against Sheffield Wednesday
four days later. A regular for Southend (107
Football League appearances plus four
substitutions, five goals), he moved to
Cambridge United a season and a half before
the club's elevation to the Football League.
Mel took part in Cambridge's first ever League
encounter. His Football League figures for the
club were 33 appearances and two
substitutions. An all-action, uncompromising
performer.

> **Appearances:**
> *FL: 2 apps. 1 gl.*
> **Total:** *2 apps. 1 gl.*

SMALL, John

Role: Right-half 1912-13
5'10" 11st.6lbs.
b. South Bank, Middlesbrough, 29th October 1889
d. Southampton, 9th December 1946

CAREER: St Peter's School/South Bank
schools football/South Bank North End/
Craghead United/SUNDERLAND Aug 1912/
Southampton Aug 1913/Thorneycrofts 1919/
Mid-Rhondda July 1920/Harland & Wolff Dec
1920/retired 1921.

Jack Small

Debut v Manchester United (a) 15/3/1913

Deputised once for Frank Cuggy in his single season at Roker Park. No mundane season this, however, with a 'Double' almost achieved and Jack Small's lone appearance at Old Trafford rewarded by an emphatic 3-1 victory. He became a popular figure at Southampton (51 Southern League and FA Cup appearances, two goals) with his wholehearted endeavour. John joined the RAMC in 1915, served in Salonika, and was invalided back to England after 16 months. He was a member of the Thorneycrofts side that sensationally drew with Burnley in the first round of the FA Cup in 1919-20, the latter a club that finished Division One runners-up the following May and as League champions in 1920-21.

Appearances:
FL: 1 app. 0 gls.
Total: *1 app. 0 gls.*

John Smeaton

SMART, Joseph

Role: Centre-half 1886-87
d. August 1930

Debut v Morpeth Harriers 16/10/1886 (FAC)

Sunderland's regular pivot in that second season of FA Cup participation, Smart played in all 11 opening fixtures that term, a run that included the side's three Cup-ties. The Wearsiders won the second tie against

Joseph Smart

Newcastle West End 2-1 but were ordered to replay after a protest, a game which West End won 1-0. Latterly, Joseph Smart was 'mine host' at The Aquatic Arms, Monkwearmouth.

Appearances:
FAC: 3 apps. 0 gls.
Total: *3 apps. 0 gls.*

SMEATON, John Raymond

Role: Inside-left 1938-39
5'8" 10st.11lbs.
b. Perth, 29th July 1914
d. Cleveland area, February 1984

CAREER: Stone Thistle/St Johnstone 1933-34/Blackburn Rovers June 1936/SUNDERLAND June 1938/Albion Rovers May 1946/St Johnstone cs 1947, player-coach cs 1948, retired May 1950.

Debut v Brentford (a) 24/9/1938

John Smeaton was a capable Scottish inside-left. He had made only eight Scottish League appearances (one goal) for St Johnstone prior to moving south. With Blackburn, then a middling Second Division club but one destined soon to win the championship, Smeaton received a measure of first team exposure (39 Football League outings, nine goals). A step-up to top flight football with Sunderland was well within Smeaton's compass, in spite of the presence of Carter, Gallacher and Harry Thompson, and he played regularly in that final pre-war season. After the war he returned to Scotland for a last few playing years, mostly spent with his first love, St Johnstone.

Appearances:
FL: 28 apps. 5 gls.
FAC: 5 apps. 1 gl.
Total: 33 apps. 6 gls.

SMELLIE, Robert

Robert Smellie

Role: Left-back 1892-93
b. Dalziel, Lanarks,
15th October 1865

CAREER: Clydesdale Colts/Hamilton Academical/Queen's Park July 1885/ SUNDERLAND July 1892/Queen's Park Feb 1893. An amateur and so, like others from the unpaid ranks, spread his assistance liberally. Thus, for example, we find him with Motherwell (Apr 1895) and Edinburgh St Bernard's (Jan 1896). President of Queen's Park 1910/11.

Debut v Accrington (a) 3/9/1892

Described in one newspaper writer's summing-up as a "resolute, hardy, never-say-die back", Smellie possessed no great subtlety, and was apt to rush his tackles but speed enabled quick recovery. A little prone too, it seems, to over-anxiety. This may have stemmed from a conscientious streak for he comes through as a first-rate clubman for Queen's Park. He assisted them towards the end of their glorious 19th century dominance.

Appearances:
FL: 23 apps. 1 gl.
FAC: 2 apps. 0 gls.
Total: 25 apps. 1 gl.
Honours:
6 Scot caps/(Queen's Park) SC winner 1890, 1893/SC finalist 1892 (played in first game only).

SMITH, Anthony

Role: Defender 1990-95
5'10" 11st.9lbs.
b. Sunderland, 21st September 1971

CAREER: Lambton & Hetton Boys/ Sunderland Schoolboys/SUNDERLAND trainee July 1988, pro July 1990(Hartlepool United loan Jan 1992)/Northampton Town nc Aug-Sept 1995.

Debut v Aston Villa (a) 6/10/1990

First associated with Sunderland's centre of excellence as an 11-year-old, Anthony Smith captained Sunderland's youth team and made his debut in Division One in 1990. In his second League appearance Sunderland recorded one of their best away victories, 6-1 at Bristol City. He made nine appearances in his debut season and often impressed, but thereafter was troubled by injury and rarely called upon. Substituted in his final appearance (the home game against Charlton

Anthony Smith

Athletic in August 1993), he was subsequently given a free transfer by manager Terry Butcher. A one month, non-contract arrangement with Northampton Town, managed by former Sunderland player and assistant manager Ian Atkins, failed to win Smith a permanent contract after he had made four first team appearances for the Cobblers.

Appearances:
FL: 19(1) apps. 0 gls.
FAC: 5 apps. 0 gls.
Total: *24(1) apps. 0 gls.*
Honours:
2 Eng Yth apps. 1990-91.

SMITH, John

Role: Inside-right
1889-92
b. Ayrshire
d. Newcastle-on-Tyne,
3rd February 1911

John Smith

CAREER: Kilmarnock cs 1885/Newcastle East End 1887/Kilmarnock later in 1887 - June 1888/SUNDERLAND Aug 1889/Liverpool May 1893/Sheffield Wednesday later in 1893/Newcastle United 1894/retired 1896.

Debut v Blackburn Rovers (a) 18/1/1890 (FAC)
Debut v Notts County (a) 15/12/1890 (FL)

A clever forward, one of the few old-timers whose Sunderland careers spanned the pre-League and League eras, John Smith had experienced both Scottish and North-Eastern football before reaching Sunderland, where he attained the honour of a championship medal. He never touched such heights again, having no first team outings with Liverpool, and for the Wednesday and Newcastle 18 Football League appearances (one goal) and 25 FL appearances (10 goals) respectively. After retiring, he became a licensee in the Byker district of Newcastle from 1898.

Appearances:
FL: 24 apps. 2 gls.
FAC: 7 apps. 1 gl.
Total: *31 apps. 3 gls.*
Honours:
(Sunderland) FL champs 1892.

SMITH, Kenneth

Role: Centre-forward 1950-53
5'11" 11st.12lbs.
b. South Shields, 21st May 1932

CAREER: Cleadon Juniors/SUNDERLAND am May 1948, pro Aug 1949/Headington United Aug 1954/Blackpool Dec 1954 £2,500/Shrewsbury Town Oct 1957 £5,000/Gateshead Nov 1958 £2,500/Darlington Dec 1959/Carlisle United July 1960/Toronto Italia, Canada cs 1961/Halifax Town Oct 1961-1962 (originally on a month's trial).

Debut v Fulham (h) 2/9/1950

Ken Smith caught Sunderland's eye with some prolific scoring for Cleadon Juniors and was given a first senior run-out at age 18. He had to wait a while for the second - two and half years in fact. This was against Portsmouth at Fratton Park in February 1953 and he celebrated the occasion by netting a couple of goals. Chances being few at Roker Park, with Trevor Ford and Dicky Davis on call, Ken moved on to First Division Blackpool following a few months at non-League Headington. Then a tour of lesser lights. Altogether he scored 68 goals in 156 League appearances.

Appearances:
FL: 5 apps. 2 gls.
Total: *5 apps. 2 gls.*

Ken Smith

SMITH, Martin Geoffrey

Role: Midfield/Forward 1993-1999
5'11" 12st.6lbs.
b. Sunderland, 13th November 1974

CAREER: Monkwearmouth School/Grange Park Juniors/SUNDERLAND assoc. s'boy Dec 1988, trainee July 1991, pro Sept 1992, released June 1999/Sheffield United July 1999.

Debut v Luton Town (h) 20/10/1993 (scored)

A star of the Sunderland Schoolboys side that reached the finals of the School FA Trophy in 1990, Martin Smith was additionally Wearside 200 metres champion as a 15-year-old. Very much a 'hot property' as a schoolboy, he resisted offers from six other League clubs including Arsenal and Manchester United, to sign for Sunderland as a 14-year-old in December 1988. One month short of his 19th birthday he made a dream League debut, converting a 19th minute free-kick into the Fulwell End goal, whose terraces he had frequented in boyhood. Under-21 honours followed in 1994 with an outstanding display at St James Park against Eire despite being loudly jeered when in possession. A Division One championship medal in 1996 was another obvious highlight. Sadly, a number of serious

injuries sapped his confidence and restricted first team appearances in his final two seasons. In his first League start of the 1998-99 championship campaign Martin scored two spectacular goals against Grimsby Town to help Sunderland to a 3-1 victory, but he failed to hold his place in the side and subsequently was marginalised in reserve. He was in fact joint leading scorer for the Pontin's League champions with six goals in 16 appearances. Out of contract with Sunderland at the end of the season, Martin was released in June and despite several other offers joined Sheffield United. Martin was reported as saying: "At least they play in red and white stripes".

Appearances:
PL: 6(5) apps. 0 gls.
FL: 83(24) apps. 25 gls.
FAC: 7(3) apps. 1 gl.
FLC: 9(6) apps. 2 gls.
Total: *105(38) apps. 28 gls.*
Honours:
1 Eng U-21 app. 1994/1 FL app. 1995/Eng Sch int/(Sunderland) Div 1 champs 1996.

SMITH

Role: Centre-forward 1886-88

Debut v Morpeth Harriers (h) 16/10/1886 (FAC) (scored)

A couple of seasons assisting Sunderland so Smith had one of the longer spells with the club in the pre-

Smith

League era. His first Cup-tie - a 7-2 rout of Morpeth Harriers - was a memorable occasion for him as he scored a hat-trick. Smith's inside-left partner, Lord, weighed in with another couple and the wingers, Erskine and Arnold Davison, notched one apiece.

Appearances:
FAC: 7 apps. 4 gls.
Total: *7 apps. 4 gls.*

Martin Smith

SNELL, Albert Edward

Role: Left-half 1952-55
b. Dunscroft, West Yorkshire, 7th February 1931

CAREER: Junior football in the Doncaster area/SUNDERLAND Aug 1949/Halifax Town Nov 1955-57.

Debut v Middlesbrough (a) 18/10/1952

Albert Snell was an 18-year-old debutant in a North-East derby at Ayresome Park which Sunderland won 2-1, making the day even more momentous for him. He could play right-half also and did once in a League outing (at Stoke in March 1953). Albert scored during his penultimate senior appearance at Roker Park against Chelsea in a see-saw draw. Back in his native West Riding he made 25 Division Three (North) appearances for Halifax Town.

Appearances:
FL: 9 apps. 1 gl.
Total: *9 apps. 1 gl.*

Albert Snell

SNODIN, Ian

Ian Snodin

Role: Midfield/Full-back 1994-95
5'7" 11st.0lbs.
b. Rotherham, 15th August 1963

CAREER: Doncaster Rovers app, pro Aug 1980/Leeds United May 1985/Everton Jan 1987(SUNDERLAND loan Oct 1994)/Oldham Athletic Jan 1995/Scarborough Aug 1997/Doncaster Rovers player-manager Aug 1998.

Debut v Burnley (h) 15/10/1994

An uncompromising midfielder, or full-back, Ian Snodin began with Doncaster Rovers but followed his outgoing manager, Billy Bremner, to Leeds United for £200,000 in May 1985. Although only 21 years old at the time, Snodin had made nearly 190 appearances for the Rovers, earning England Youth and Under-21 recognition, whilst still a Third Division player. Less than two years on he cost Everton £840,000 and helped them clinch the Football League championship in his first season. Severe hamstring injuries caused him to miss virtually all of season 1990-91 and 1991-92, but he had regained fitness when Sunderland's manager Mick Buxton signed him on loan in October 1994, in the midst of an injury and suspension crisis. After six appearances he returned to Everton and three months later joined Oldham Athletic on a free transfer. Released by the Latics after an injury-plagued season 1996-97, Ian joined Scarborough on a free transfer and made 33(2) League appearances in their promotion push which ended in disappointment in the play-off semi-finals. In August 1998 he returned to his roots to take over as player-manager of Doncaster Rovers for their inaugural campaign in the Football Conference. Elder brother Glynn made 532 League appearances, including 309 for Doncaster Rovers.

Appearances:
FL: 6 apps. 0 gls.
Total: *6 apps. 0 gls.*
Honours:
2 Eng 'B' apps. 1990/4 Eng U-21 apps. 1985/ EngYth int/(Everton) FL champs 1987.

SORENSEN, Thomas

Role: Goalkeeper 1998-date
6'4"
b. Odense, Denmark, 12th June 1976

CAREER: Erritso/Assens F.C./OB Odense, Denmark(Svendborg loan, full season 1997-98) (Manchester United trial)/SUNDERLAND August 1998 to date.

Debut v Queens Park Rangers (h) 8/8/1998

Signed for a near £1 million fee in the summer of 1998 to replace the popular Lionel Perez as Sunderland's goalkeeper, Thomas Sorenson enjoyed remarkable success in his first season at the Stadium of Light. At 6ft 4ins and with a build to match, Sorenson presents a formidable barrier to opposing forwards. In addition to his imposing presence, he is wonderfully agile and clean-handling goalkeeper who effectively commands his area. Groomed carefully through the Danish Under-21 squad he has now warmed the bench as a full international substitute and is widely tipped to succeed Peter Schmeichel as Denmark's goalkeeper. Thomas certainly furthered his claims in this direction during the 1999 championship season with a string of near faultless displays, accurately reflected by the 29 clean sheets recorded by him during the campaign. Certainly the eight-part documentry series produced by Danish TV channel, TV2, on the young goalkeeper's first season in England with Sunderland should make for very pleasant viewing with the added bonus of a happy ending!

Appearances:
FL: 45 apps. 0 gls.
FAC: 2 apps. 0 gls.
FLC: 9 apps. 0 gls.
Total: *56 apps. 0 gls.*
Honours:
25 Danish U-21 apps/
1 Denmark 'B' app./
(Sunderland) Div 1 champs 1999.

SPAIN

Role: Left-half 1887-89

Debut v Morpeth Harriers (h) 14/10/1887 (FAC)

Played in all five FA Cup-ties of 1887/88 and in the second of 1888/89 against Newcastle East End. Spain's name first appears - at right-half - in Sunderland line-ups towards the end of season 1886/87. In the next he played frequently on both flanks but the Cup-tie was his sole outing of 1888/89. For the record Spain was never in a losing Sunderland FA Cup side: the club's last ties in both seasons bringing a disqualification and a withdrawal respectively.

Appearances:
FAC: 6 apps. 0 gls.
Total: *6 apps. 0 gls.*

Thomas Sorensen

SPENCE, Alan Nicholson

Role: Centre-forward 1957-58
5'9" 11st.0lbs.
b. Seaham, Co Durham, 7th February 1940

CAREER: Co Durham schools and youth
football/Murton Colliery/SUNDERLAND am
Mar 1958, pro Sept 1958/Darlington June
1960/Southport July 1963/Oldham Athletic
Dec 1968/Chester Dec 1969/Southport reserve
team coach 1970, trainer 1971/Skelmersdale
United manager Aug 1972/Chorley manager
Oct 1974, general manager May 1979/Saudi
Arabia coaching appointment May 1982.

Debut v Blackpool (a) 5/10/1957

Seldom can a player
have had such a
down-to-earth
introduction to senior
football as that
experienced by Alan
Spence. It occurred
during the dire
1957/58 season which
saw Sunderland
relegated for the first
time. They conceded
97 goals, seven of
them (without reply) *Alan Spence*
at Bloomfield Road,

the scene of the Spence debut. He fared much
better elsewhere, of course, and when an
established performer it was remarked how
"his appetite for goals is undiminished". At
Darlington he set a club record by scoring in
seven consecutive games, while he proved
Southport's best-ever free transfer signing,
netting 98 goals, an aggregate club record
which included a seasonal best 27 in 1963/64.
In his youth Alan had twice represented
England Grammar Schools and, in 1958,
became an England Youth international. He
remained a part-time professional all his
career, qualifying as a teacher. He later left his
teaching appointment in Leyland to become
Chorley's commercial manager. His final
Football League figures were 285 appearances
plus eight substitutions, 123 goals.

Appearances:
FL: 5 apps. 1 gl.
Total: *5 apps. 1 gl.*
Honours:
Eng Yth.

SPENCE, John

Role: Half-back/forward 1890-91
Probably born in Scotland

CAREER: Kilmarnock/SUNDERLAND
October 1889/Newcastle East End July 1891.

Debut v Burnley (h) 13/9/1890

So far as can be ascertained John Spence
played no first team games for Kilmarnock: in
the late 1880s the club was still a pre-Scottish
League organisation. On joining Sunderland
during their final pre-League season he
appeared at right and centre-half and in both
full-back positions, so was obviously a man of
parts. Spence, in his League outings for the
Wearsiders, figured in turn at outside-right,
left-half (thrice) and centre-half, the versatility
act continuing. In passing one notes John
Spence's Football League career figures for
Sunderland are precisely similar to those of
namesake Alan (q.v.).

Appearances:
FL: 5 apps. 1 gl.
Total: *5 apps. 1 gl.*

SPUHLER, John Oswald

Role: Outside-right 1936-39
5'9" 11st.4lbs.
b. Sunderland, 18th September 1917

CAREER: Sunderland Schools/
SUNDERLAND am May 1932, pro Sept 1934/
Middlesbrough Oct 1945 (£1,500)/Darlington
June 1954 (£750)/Spennymoor United player-
manager Nov 1956/Shrewsbury Town
manager Feb-May 1958, after which he was
coach to Spennymoor United, West Auckland
and Stockton, the latter appointment from cs
1965.

Debut v Wolverhampton Wanderers (h) 26/3/1937

Started competing with another fine local
development, Len Duns, in 1937/38 and,
indeed, in that term made more League
appearances than Duns. In 1938-39 John's
outings were limited to 12, five of them at
centre-forward, a position he was to occupy
many times for Middlesbrough. The Teessiders had used him as a guest player during
the second world war, signing him on a
permanent basis shortly after peace returned.
It proved a wise investment: he made 241

John Spuhler

Football League and FA Cup appearances, scoring 81 goals during nine years at Ayresome Park. John's first seasons there were at outside-right, switching to centre-forward (and occasionally inside-forward) in 1948/49. As leader of the attack his main qualities of positional know-how and heading had greater scope. For Darlington he also played outside-right, centre- and inside-forward, making 67 League appearances (19 goals). John originally worked in the Roker Park office after leaving school. On quitting football he ran a sub-post office in Yarm near Stockton-on-Tees for eight years before going to live in Barnard Castle.

Appearances:
FL: 35 apps. 5 gls.
Total: *35 apps. 5 gls.*
Honours:
2 Eng Sch apps. 1932

STALEY, Clive Howard Victor

Role: Centre-forward 1921-22
5'8" 11st.7lbs.
b. Newhall, Derbys, 14th May 1899
d. Burton-on-Trent, 18th March 1985

CAREER: Newhall Swifts/ SUNDERLAND Mar 1921/ Stoke July 1922/Newhall Swifts 1922-23/Burton All Saints cs 1923 and still with this club in the late 1920s.
Debut v Manchester City (h) 14/1/1922

Victor Staley

Victor Staley's senior debut game - a 3-2 home defeat against Manchester City - was his sole senior appearance for he did not get a first team outing at Stoke. The free scoring Jimmy Broad was then leading the Potters attack while Charlie Buchan, Paterson and others were on the Sunderland roll call for the centre-forward spot.

Appearances:
FL: 1 app. 0 gls.
Total: *1 app. 0 gls.*

STANNARD, Paul

Role: Centre-forward
1921-24
5'10" 11st.7lbs.
b. All Saints, Warwick, 17th January 1895
d. Birmingham, 24th November 1982

Paul Stannard

CAREER: Tamworth Castle/SUNDERLAND May 1921/South Shields Dec 1923/Carlisle United c.1924/Workington Sept 1926/West Stanley August 1927/Jarrow c 1928.
Debut v Liverpool (h) 27/8/1921

Paul Stannard made most of his 14 senior appearances for Sunderland during his initial term at Roker Park, 1921/22, figuring in all of the first eight League fixtures. Perhaps his best display was against Huddersfield in September 1921 when he scored both goals in a 2-1 away victory. Afterwards it was back to the reserves, for the most part understudying Buchan and Jock Paterson. At South Shields, a club finishing in the top half of Division Two in 1923/24, he scored a goal in three League outings. Stannard netted 17 in his season with Workington, members of the North-Eastern League at the time.

Appearances:
FL: 13 apps. 2 gls.
FAC: 1 app. 1 gl.
Total: *14 apps. 3 gls.*

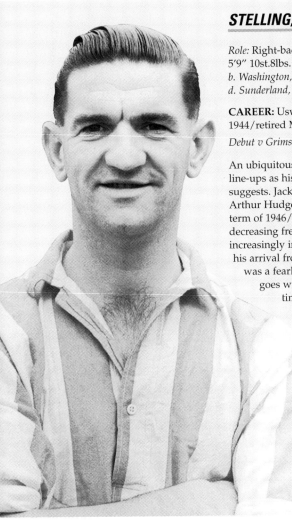

STELLING, John Graham S.

Role: Right-back 1945-56
5'9" 10st.8lbs.
b. Washington, Co Durham, 23rd May 1924
d. Sunderland, 29th March 1993

CAREER: Usworth Colliery/SUNDERLAND Nov 1944/retired May 1958.

Debut v Grimsby Town (a) 5/1/1946 (FAC)

An ubiquitous unit in the immediate post-WW2 line-ups as his impressive appearances total suggests. Jack's association with big money buy, Arthur Hudgell, commenced in that first post-war term of 1946/47 and continued with naturally decreasing frequency into 1955/56. (Hedley came increasingly into the picture on both flanks after his arrival from Everton in 1950). Jack Stelling was a fearless defender with a consistency that goes without saying. He had been a war-time discovery who played his very first match in a Sunderland jersey during the 1944/45 season against York City. A plumber employed at a nearby colliery originally, he worked for a construction company after leaving football.

Appearances:
FL: 259 apps. 8 gls.
FAC: 13 apps. 0 gls.
Total: *272 apps. 8 gls.*

STEPHENSON, James

Role: Outside-right/inside-forward 1921-22
5'6" 10st.9lbs.
b. New Delaval, Northumberland, 1st qtr 1895
d. Newcastle-on-Tyne, February 1958, aged 63

CAREER: New Delaval Villa/Aston Villa am May 1913, pro Apr 1914 (Leeds City guest during WW1)/SUNDERLAND May 1921 (£300, fee fixed by the FA, Aug 1922)/Watford Sept 1922 £500/Queens Park Rangers July 1927/Boston Aug 1928/Ashington Oct 1930/ New Delaval Villa Jan 1931.

Debut v Liverpool (h) 27/8/1921

James Stephenson

"A class act" wrote one Watford FC historian on the subject of Jimmy Stephenson. He warranted the praise: a progressive, able right-winger (he had a few outings for Sunderland at inside-forward but outside-right was his known position throughout a lengthy career). Watford saw the bulk of his peace-time activity; in five seasons at Vicarage Road he played 209 Southern Section and FA Cup matches in which he netted 20 goals. Stephenson came of footballing stock, a brother of the celebrated Clem (Villa and Huddersfield Town) and George (Derby County) both of whom were England caps. Additionally a nephew, Robert H. Stephenson, played cricket for Yorkshire and the Royal Navy. Jimmy joined the Royal Field Artillery in May 1917, saw much action with the 28th Brigade in Belgium and, after the Armistice, served in the Army of Occupation on the Rhine.

Appearances:
FL: 21 apps. 2 gls.
FAC: 1 app. 0 gls.
Total: *22 apps. 2 gls.*

STEVENSON, J.

J. Stevenson

Role: Right-half 1889-90

CAREER: Boldon Star/ SUNDERLAND c.1889.

Debut v Blackburn Rovers (a) 18/1/1890 (FAC)

Sunderland's regular right-half in 1889/90, the last season prior to the club's elevation into the Football League. The fixture list was extensive with 55 engagements and was not completed until May 21st. All appearances are not available but Stevenson was at right-half in at least 38 of them. His son, John Stevenson, joined Ayr United from Kilbirnie Hibs in July 1920 and first saw the light of day in Wigan.

Appearances:
FAC: 1 app. 0 gls.
Total: *1 app. 0 gls.*

STEWART, Duncan Smart

Role: Left-back 1922-23
5'8" 10st.6lbs.
b. Dundee, 8th September 1900

CAREER: Scottish junior football/ SUNDERLAND Sept 1922/Southend United May 1924-25.

Debut v Aston Villa (h) 28/4/1923

A couple of terms at Sunderland, making his only senior appearance in the penultimate League fixture at Roker Park, a goalless draw against Villa, Duncan Stewart found first team opportunities at Southend equally hard to

come by. He played right-back in the opening day of 1924/25 (a 3-0 home defeat against Charlton Athletic) and that was all, Tommy Sayles (40 Southern Section appearances) and Jim Donnelly (an ever-present 42) monopolising the Shrimpers' full-back appearances.

Appearances:
FL: 1 app. 0 gls.
Total: *1 app. 0 gls.*

STEWART, Paul Andrew

Role: Midfield/Forward 1995-97
5'11" 12st.4lbs.
b. Manchester, 7th October 1964

CAREER: Blackpool app, pro Oct 1981/ Manchester City Mar 1987/Tottenham Hotspur June 1988/Liverpool July 1992 (Crystal Palace loan Jan 1994)(Wolverhampton Wanderers loan Sept 1994)(Burnley loan Feb 1995)(SUNDERLAND loan Aug 1995)/ SUNDERLAND free Mar 1996/Stoke City June 1997-Aug 1998/Workington Sept 1998.

Debut v Port Vale (a) 30/8/1995 (sub)

Paul Stewart's first appearance in Sunderland's starting line-up - when on loan from Liverpool - ended after 36 minutes at Ipswich Town. The knee injury he sustained resulted in the curtailment of his loan and a return to Anfield. Stewart had cost Liverpool a hefty £2.3 million from Tottenham in July 1992, but failed to establish a regular first team place at Anfield. His loan to Sunderland following similar spells with Crystal Palace, Wolves and Burnley. Eventually released by Liverpool on a free transfer he joined Sunderland and made a significant contribution during the run-in to the Division One championship, his first ten appearances yielding seven wins and three draws. A knee injury blighted his season in the Premiership, which saw him finish as joint leading goalscorer with just four goals. Often left an isolated figure up front, his main strengths were his work rate and an ability to hold onto the ball in the opponents' half of the field. Released by Sunderland in the summer of 1997 Paul joined Stoke City on a free transfer and scored against his previous team-mates in the October fixture at the Britannia Stadium which the Lads won 2-1. Increasingly troubled by a thigh injury his season was virtually over by mid-term and he was released in the wake of Stoke's relegation from Division One. In September 1998 he signed a one-year contract with Workington of the North-West Counties League. At the outset of his career Paul Stewart scored 56 goals in 201 League appearances for Blackpool. Manchester City paid £200,000 for him but fifteen months later his value had soared to £1.7 million when Tottenham invested a record fee for his services. Midway through his four year spell at White Hart Lane his career blossomed following his successful switch from striker to midfield and he capped arguably his best individual performance for the club with a

goal in the 1991 FA Cup final. Full international recognition followed, but his subsequent big move to Liverpool did little to further his progress.

Appearances:
PL: 20(4) apps. 4 gls.
FL: 11(1) apps. 1 gl.
FLC: 3 apps. 0 gls.
Total: *34(5) apps. 5 gls.*
Honours:
Eng Yth/1 Eng U-21 app. 1988/
5 Eng 'B' apps. 1989/3 Eng caps 1992/
(Tottenham Hotspur) FAC winner 1991/
(Crystal Palace) Div 1 champs 1994/
(Sunderland) Div 1 champs 1996.

STEWART, Thomas *Worsley*

Role: Left-back 1904-05
5'11" 12st.7lbs.
b. Sunderland, 1881

CAREER: Sunderland Royal Rovers/ SUNDERLAND am May 1904, pro Jan 1905/ Portsmouth May 1905/Clapton Orient Aug 1906/Brighton & Hove Albion May 1908/ Brentford cs 1909-10.

Debut v Nottingham Forest (h) 2/1/1905

Tom Stewart

Recruited locally from a highly successful Sunderland Royal Rovers side that had topped the Wearside League for four successive seasons. Tom made his League bow as an amateur, joining the paid ranks the same month. The following season at Portsmouth proved barren (two Southern League outings), but a move to Second Division Orient a useful experience (54 Football League and FA Cup appearances). Back to the Southern League with Brighton, Tom skippered the team and was a stalwart in a successful fight against relegation from the top division (39 appearances plus one in the FA Cup). He made no first team appearances for Brentford in 1909/10, his final term in the first-class game.

Appearances:
FL: 3 apps. 0 gls.
FAC: 2 apps. 0 gls.
Total: *5 apps. 0 gls.*

Paul Stewart

STEWART

Role: Centre-half/outside-right 1887-88
Debut v Morpeth Harriers (h) 15/10/1887 (FAC)

Played in all the five FA Cup-ties of 1887/88: all but one in his main position of outside-right. The exception was the second clash with Morpeth Harriers in which he moved to centre-half (but scored a goal nonetheless in a 3-2 win). Stewart's name appeared quite frequently on the score-sheet that term - as will be seen the Cup-ties yielded an excellent return of four goals. Stewart continued at outside-right on and off into March 1888 when Arnold Davison took over for the final dozen fixtures, appearing during that sequence at inside-left on three occasions.

Appearances:
FAC: 5 apps. 4 gls.
Total: *5 apps. 4 gls.*

STONEHAM, John

Role: Goalkeeper 1923-26
6'2" 12st.0lbs.
b. Witham, Essex, 15th June (year not known)

CAREER: Carlisle United c.1920/SUNDERLAND May 1923/Nelson June 1927-Jan 1928.

John Stoneham

Debut v Cardiff City (h) 5/9/1923

A tall 'keeper versed in the arts of his trade by the time he reached Roker Park, John Stoneham was signed from Carlisle United, then a useful North-Eastern League outfit who had won the title in 1921/22; he made his senior debut early in his first season. Stoneham actually made his debut before that of Albert McInroy, whose brilliance was to keep him an understudy. His best return, 12 Football League appearances, came in 1925/26. At Nelson, a club destined to finish bottom of the Northern Section in 1927/28, John was again an understudy, this time to Sam Warhurst, later well known for long service to Southampton's cause.

Appearances:
FL: 14 apps. 0 gls.
FAC: 1 app. 0 gls.
Total: *15 apps. 0 gls.*

STRONACH, Peter

Role: Winger 1977-78
5'6" 12st.0lbs.
b. Seaham, 1st September 1956

Peter Stronach

CAREER: SUNDERLAND app July 1972, pro Sept 1973/York City June 1978-1980.

Debut v Bolton Wanderers (h) 17/9/1977

Peter Stronach was an outstanding schoolboy footballer who represented his country on eight occasions in 1972. Despite the brightest of starts, his glittering potential was never fully realised. In six years at Roker he played only three matches at senior level. He joined York City in June 1978, shortly after they had been re-elected to the Football League after finishing 22nd in Division Four in season 1977-78. Stronach was one of seven new signings and he appeared in a little over half of the season's matches, scoring twice. The following term proved to be his last whilst an 18-year-old team mate, John Byrne, (q.v.) made his very first appearance in League football.

Appearances:
FL: 2(1) apps. 0 gls.
Total: *2(1) apps. 0 gls.*
Honours:
8 Eng Sch apps. 1972.

STUCKEY, Bruce George

Role: Inside-right 1967-70
5'8" 11st.6lbs.
b. Torquay, 19th February 1947

CAREER: Junior football to Exeter City as an app, pro Feb 1965/ SUNDERLAND Nov 1967 £8,000/ Torquay United Feb 1971 £5,000/ Reading Nov 1973-77 (Torquay United loan Jan 1975) (AFC Bournemouth loan Mar-May 1977).

Bruce Stuckey

Debut v Southampton (a) 25/11/1967

A Devonian, Bruce Stuckey spent roughly a third of his first-class career in his native county and all but the Sunderland years in the South. Signed by the Wearsiders following a promising beginning at Exeter, Bruce was hardly a prolific goal scorer - he netted 21 in 232 League appearances plus 26 substitutions - his particular strength at Sunderland during the late 1960's lay in linking up with colleagues.

Appearances:
FL: 24(2) apps. 2 gls.
FAC: 1 app. 0 gls.
FLC: 2 apps. 0 gls.
Other: 0(1) app. 0 gls.
Total: *27(3) apps. 2 gls.*

SUGGETT, Colin

Role: Inside-forward 1966-69
5'8" 11st.0lbs.
b. Washington, Co Durham, 30th December 1948

CAREER: Washington Grammar School/ Chester-le-Street SFA/Co Durham Schools/ SUNDERLAND app Aug 1964, pro Jan 1966/ West Bromwich Albion July 1969 around £95,000/Norwich City Feb 1973 £75,000/ Newcastle United Aug 1978-June 1981 £65,000, retired through injury and was appointed asst-coach/coach Sept 1985/caretaker manager

Oct-Dec 1988/asst-coach to February 1994/ Bolton Wanderers, Berwick Rangers, Portsmouth scout/Ipswich Town Director of Coaching Mar 1995/ Ipswich Town youth coach, chief scout July 1998.

Debut v Stoke City (a) 18/3/1967

Colin Suggett was a player of consequence over a long period, starting as a much-honoured schoolboy cap. Indeed, he had played at Roker Park for Chester-le-Street Boys alongside Howard Kendall in 1964. It was the same team that produced another outstanding contemporary Roker jewel in Colin Todd. Suggett won an early reputation for scoring goals and quickly became something of a teenage star, thanks in no small measure to determination and exceptional pace. This in no way blunted a capacity to create chances for others, as later Jeff Astle and Tony Brown at West Bromwich and David Cross and Ted MacDougall of Norwich all profited from this ability. His first regular Sunderland season was 1967-68 with 14 League goals in 42 outings followed by a similarly consistent showing the following term. Sunderland however were having a thin time in Division One and needed the cash that came from what was sometimes claimed as the first £100,000 sale and was a then record transfer fee for WBA. It was first at the Hawthorns and later at Norwich, who also paid their record fee for his services, that Colin reverted to midfield where he became equally effective, playing a major role in the latter's promotion season of 1974-75 when he was voted their Player of the Year. Ankle ligament trouble compelled retirement at his final club, Newcastle, but an innate talent for youth coaching ensured long service at that club. Colin's talents were not confined to soccer, while at school he won county honours at basketball and athletics, specialising in the long jump, 220 yards and relay events.

Appearances:
FL: 83(3) apps. 24 gls.
FAC: 3 apps 1 gl.
FLC: 4 apps. 0 gls.
Total: *90(3) apps. 25 gls.*
Honours:
6 Eng Sch apps. 1964/Eng Yth 1965-67/ (Sunderland) FAYC winner/(West Bromwich Albion) FLC finalist 1970/(Norwich City) FLC finalist 1975.

Colin Suggett

SUMMERBEE, Nicholas

Role: Winger 1997-date
5'11' 11st.8lbs.
b. Altrincham, Cheshire, 26th August 1971

Career: Hillcrest G.S./Swindon Town trainee
Oct 1987, pro July 1989/Manchester City June
1994/SUNDERLAND Nov 1997 to date.

Debut v Portsmouth (a) 15/11/1997 (sub) (scored)

Nicky Summerbee joined Sunderland in a
£1 million rated exchange deal, with Craig
Russell moving in the opposite direction to
Maine Road. A versatile performer, his
strengths surround an ability to make ground
quickly on the flanks and centre accurately. In
his career to date, Nicky's running style - so
reminiscent of his England international father
Mike, has been seen to advantage in a variety
of roles from winger, wing-back to midfield.
He made a bright start when he scored on his
debut for Sunderland in an outstanding 4-1
away win against Portsmouth. His main
strength, however, has been his aerial supply
line to Niall Quinn, a former team mate from
Manchester City days. The scorer of
Sunderland's fourth goal, nine minutes into
extra time, in the heartbreaking Wembley
play-off final against Charlton Athletic in May
1998, Nicky was The Lads' first scorer in the
dramatic penalty shoot-out which ended 7-6 to
Charlton. It was his third visit to Wembley for
play-off finals. Although not a first team
player in his debut season, Swindon Town
beat Sunderland 1-0 in the 1990 final. Three
years later he was in the Swindon team that
beat Leicester City in a dramatic encounter.
After leading 3-0 the Robins had to rely on a
late penalty to win 4-3. In Sunderland's

Nicky Summerbee in action against Portsmouth in season 1998-99.

hugely successful 1998-99 campaign, Nicky was a key element in a strike force that scored 91 League and 17 Cup goals, supplying much of the ammunition for the goalscoring exploits of the central striking duo of Quinn and Phillips.

Appearances:
FL: 58(3) apps. 3 gls.
FAC: 2(1) apps. 0 gls.
FLC: 5(1) apps. 0 gls.
Total: *65(5) apps. 3 gls.*
Honours:
3 Eng U-21 apps. 1993/1 Eng 'B' app./
(Sunderland) Div 1 champs 1999.

SWINBURNE, Trevor

Role: Goalkeeper 1972-77
6'0" 14st.7lbs.
b. East Rainton, Co Durham, 20th June 1953

CAREER: Lambton & Hetton Boys/East Rainton Youths/SUNDERLAND app July 1968, pro June 1970(Sheffield United loan Dec 1976)/Carlisle United May 1977/Brentford Aug 1983/Leeds United June 1985(Doncaster Rovers loan Sept 1985)/Lincoln City Feb 1986, retired May 1987.

Debut v Orient (a) 30/4/1973

As deputy to Sunderland's always dependable 600-plus appearances goalkeeper, Jim Montgomery, Trevor Swinburne found few opportunities during his seven years as a professional at Roker Park. By complete contrast, he was rarely absent from the League side during six seasons with Carlisle United, where he totalled 248 appearances. Trevor hailed from a remarkable family of goalkeepers; father Tom was Newcastle United 'keeper in a career which spanned the second world war, and was England's goalkeeper against Scotland in wartime season 1939-40. Trevor's eldest brother Alan played for Oldham Athletic in season 1963-64 and was later on Newcastle United's books. After retiring from the game Trevor worked as a prison officer in Leicester.

Appearances:
FL: 10 apps. 0 gls
FAC: 1 app. 0 gls.
Total: *11 apps. 0 gls.*

SWINDLEHURST, David

Role: Forward 1985-87
6'2" 13st.13lbs.
b. Edgware, Middlesex, 6th January 1956

CAREER: Crystal Palace app, pro Jan 1973 (Derby County loan Feb 1980)/Derby County Apr 1980/West Ham United Mar 1983/ SUNDERLAND Aug 1985/Anorthosis (Cyprus) July 1987/Wimbledon nc Mar 1988/ Colchester United June 1988(Peterborough United loan Dec 1988)/Bromley FC manager June 1989, subsequently director/Whyteleafe manager 1996.

Debut v Blackburn Rovers (h) 17/8/1985

Dave Swindlehurst began with Crystal Palace and made his League debut as a 17-year-old in season 1973-74. He blossomed in the following term with 14 goals in 37(4) appearances and, at the time of his £410,000 transfer to Derby County, his Palace aggregate had risen to 80 goals in 258(16) appearances. On the day of his

Trevor Swinburne

Dave Swindlehurst

signing for Derby (following a two-month loan spell) the Rams lost their First Division status. After 33 goals in 125 appearances he was transferred to West Ham United for £160,000. In his first full season with the Hammers he scored 15 goals in 44(1) appearances but in 1984-85 was goalless and out of the first team when Sunderland signed him. He was the first goalscorer of the new season with two against Grimsby Town, but the opening five League fixtures had all been lost, without a goal being scored. For two terms he worked hard but often with little support and he departed Roker for the sunnier climes of Cyprus after two years as Sunderland prepared for their first ever campaign in the Third Division.

Appearances:
FL: 61 apps. 11 gls.
FAC: 3 apps. 0 gls.
FLC: 3 apps. 0 gls.
Other: 5 apps. 0 gls.
Total: *72 apps. 11 gls.*
Honours:
3 Eng Yth int apps. 1974/1 Eng U-21 app. 1976/(Crystal Palace) Div 2 champs 1979.

SYMM, Colin

Role: Half-back/forward 1969-72
5'9" 11st.8lbs.
b. Dunston-on-Tyne, Co Durham, 26th November 1946

CAREER: Redheugh Boys Club, Gateshead/ Sheffield Wednesday May 1965/ SUNDERLAND June 1969/Lincoln City June 1972/Boston United July 1975-cs 1978.
Debut v Coventry City (h) 9/8/1969

Product of a noted North-Eastern nursery, Colin was for the most part a reserve with Wednesday (16 Football League appearances and four substitutions, one goal) and Sunderland. He fared a lot better at Fourth Division Lincoln, making 60 League outings, nine substitutions and scoring seven goals. Described as a "neat and stylish midfielder" Colin was also eminently adaptable. In his nine starts in League encounters for Sunderland he occupied four different positions: left-half, outside-right, inside-right and inside-left. Not bad value for a free transfer signing. The Imps got him for nothing too.

Appearances;
FL: 9(5) apps. 0 gls.
FLC: 1 app. 0 gls.
Other: 2 apps. 0 gls.
Total: *12(5) apps. 0 gls.*

Colin Symm

TAIT, Thomas Somerville

Role: Right-half 1906-12
5'8" 11st.0lbs.
b. Carluke, Lanarks, 13th September 1879

CAREER: Cambuslang Rangers/Airdrieonians
May 1900/Bristol Rovers cs 1903/
SUNDERLAND May 1906/Dundee May
1912/Jarrow July 1914/Armadale Oct 1914.

Debut v Newcastle United (a) 1/9/1906

Tommy Tait was a canny Scottish wing-half
well versed in all aspects of his craft by the
time his country awarded a cap - when he was
31 years, 174 days of age to be precise. Tommy
had shone in a fine Bristol Rovers side which
had finished 3rd, 1st and 8th in Southern
League placings during his career at Eastville.
His aggregate figures there were 96
appearances, one goal. He served Sunderland
well too and it was maybe a little unfortunate
his Roker Park years occurred after and before
the honours-winning periods of the pre-WW1
era. Although not at the time of writing able to
record without doubt, we believe the player
was the father of Tommy Tait jnr. The latter,
an English schoolboy international, born

Tommy Tait

Hetton-le-Hole 1908,
achieved fame as a
scoring centre-forward
with Southport and
Manchester City in the
1920s.

Appearances:
FL: 180 apps. 2 gls.
FAC: 14 apps. 0 gls.
Total: *194 apps. 2 gls.*
Honours:
1 Scot cap v Wales 1911/
(Bristol Rovers) Sthn Lge champs 1905.

TAYLOR, Ernest

Role: Inside-forward 1958-61
5'4" 10st.4lbs.
b. Sunderland, 2nd September 1925
d. Birkenhead, 9th April 1985

CAREER: Sunderland Schools/Hylton
Colliery Juniors/Newcastle United Sept 1942
(also assisted Plymouth Argyle as a guest
during WW2)/Blackpool Oct 1951 (£25,000)/
Manchester United Feb 1958 (£6,000)/
SUNDERLAND Dec 1958 (£6,000)/Altrincham
Aug 1961/Derry City Nov 1961, retired Feb
1962/coach to New Brighton FC of
Christchurch, New Zealand Feb 1964-65 and
was also associated with the Surrey club,
Carshalton Athletic.

Debut v Cardiff City (h) 13/12/1958

Ernie Taylor was Sunderland-born but
Sunderland AFC was his last major club.
Unfortunately he also arrived at a sorry
juncture in their history - midway through the
grim first-ever spell in Division Two as the
Wearsiders finished 15th that season and were
a place lower in 1959-60. Things did improve,
however, in Ernie's final term, the club
climbing to a respectable sixth spot
commencing a challenge that climaxed with
promotion in 1964. Taylor arrived at Roker as a
vastly experienced practitioner of 33 and was
a first choice inside-forward - he took right
and left flanks equally well - until his final
term, 1960-61. Ernie began his senior career
with rivals Newcastle United during wartime.
He played in 26 games (seven goals) and
guested elsewhere before peace returned. He
got his first decent run in 1948-49, the season
after Newcastle's elevation to Division One. By
the time of his move to Blackpool, Taylor

was a recognised footballing personality. Standing only a fraction over 5ft 4ins in his size four boots, Ernie was a small, crowd-pleasing attacking entertainer. He won FA Cup medals with both Newcastle and Blackpool, distinguishing himself in two finals. His exquisite back-heeled pass enabled Jackie Milburn to score the only goal in 1951, while in 1953 he starred in the celebrated 'Matthews Final' when the Stanley Matthews-inspired Seasiders fought back from a 3-1 deficit to win 4-3. Taylor's partnership with Matthews was widely and justifiably acclaimed, with the pair's almost telepathic understanding and brilliant control a real delight. Blackpool had the best of Taylor; he played in 242 League and cup matches, scoring 55 goals. For Newcastle the League and cup figures were 117 appearances (21 goals). His sole cap occurred in his Blackpool period and a unique occasion it was - against the 'Magnificent Magyars' Hungarian line-up when England lost for the first time on native soil. His next

transfer also bore news value as Manchester United's first signing following the tragic losses in the Munich air disaster. The club needed an old head and Taylor did much to help re-knit a shattered side. At Old Trafford too he again tasted FA Cup excitement. Manchester United faced Bolton Wanderers at Wembley with Ernie at inside-right, but this time he had to settle for a runners-up medal. Still, how many players figure in three FA Cup finals in the space of seven years with three different clubs? His two-and-a-half year spell at Roker Park probably rather paled by comparison, as did stints in non-League and Northern Ireland football prior to his trip to New Zealand. Ernie returned to England, worked for Vauxhall Motors at Hooton in Cheshire and acted as adviser to the West Cheshire League club, Heswall. During the 1939-45 war he served in submarines in the Royal Navy. His brother, Eddie, played in the Willington team that won the FA Amateur Cup of 1950.

Appearances:
FL: 68 apps. 11 gls.
FAC: 3 apps. 0 gls.
Total: *71 apps. 11 gls.*
Honours:
1 Eng cap v Hungary 1954/1 Eng 'B' app. v Switzerland 1956/(Newcastle United) FAC winner 1951/(Blackpool) FAC winner 1953/ (Manchester United) FAC finalist 1958.

TAYLOR, Richard William

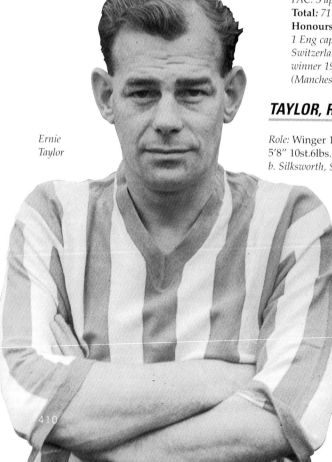

Ernie Taylor

Role: Winger 1971-72
5'8" 10st.6lbs.
b. Silksworth, Sunderland, 20th June 1951

CAREER: SUNDERLAND app, pro Oct 1968/York City July 1972-May 1973.

Debut v Blackpool (h) 13/11/1971 (sub)

Released by Sunderland on a free transfer after almost four years as a professional, Richard Taylor's solitary League outing was made as a substitute for Dennis Tueart in a goalless encounter against Blackpool at Roker Park. A move to Third Division

Richard Taylor

Tigers' interest was understandable as Jimmy's uncle, Arthur Temple, had been a Hull notability 1907-14). On going to Fulham any fears concerning a slight physique were dispelled, his speed and no nonsense approach combined with goal scoring ability an enticing mix. For the Craven Cottage club Jimmy netted a total of 61 in 168 League and FA Cup games, a handsome return for a wingman. This average was maintained at Roker Park. For Gateshead he scored four in 18 Northern Section outings.

Appearances:
FL: 31 apps. 13 gls.
FAC: 3 apps. 0 gls.
Total: *34 apps. 13 gls.*

THIRLWELL, Paul

Role: Midfield 1995-date
5'11" 11st.4lbs.
b. Springwell, Newcastle upon Tyne, 13th February 1979

CAREER: St Robert of Newminster School, Washington/Chester-le-Street Schoolboys/Durham County Schoolboys/Sheffield Wednesday School of Excellence, Gateshead Stadium/SUNDERLAND app Aug 1995, pro May 1998-date.

York City provided more opportunities for the speedy wingman, but he had joined a poor side who failed to record a win in their first eleven League engagements. Despite managing to narrowly avoid relegation, the end-of-season retained list was not a long one. Richard Taylor was one of the players released on a free transfer. During his single season at Bootham Crescent he had made 26(2) appearances and scored two goals.

Appearances:
FL: 0(1) apps. 0 gls.
Total: *0(1) apps. 0 gls.*

TEMPLE, James Leslie

Role: Outside-right 1931-33
5'6" 10st.4lbs.
b. Scarborough, 16th September 1904
d. during WW2

CAREER: Tyneside Juniors/Wallsend/Fulham Oct 1926/SUNDERLAND May 1931 (in exchange for Albert Wood)/Gateshead May 1933-34/Crook Town Aug 1935/Ashington Sept 1935/Murton Colliery Welfare Aug 1936.

Debut v Sheffield United (a) 26/9/1931 (scored)

When a tyro Jimmy Temple was vetted by both Newcastle United and Hull City but deemed "too small to make good". (The

Paul Thirlwell

Debut v York City (h) 18/8/1998 (sub) (FLC)

A return to Reserve team football followed Paul Thirlwell's mid-season injury lay-off, but the senior experience he gained in early season marked 1998-99 as a campaign of outstanding progress for the young central midfielder. An ability to pass the ball accurately, and at the right moment, drew early comparisons with Paul Bracewell, which was fulsome praise indeed. Following early season substitute appearances, Paul's full debut against Grimsby Town in the League Cup lasted for a full two hours, when extra time was needed to defeat the Mariners. One week later his full League debut followed, and he played a vital part in The Lads' excellent 3-0 victory against promotion rivals Bolton Wanderers at the Reebok Stadium.

Appearances:
FL: 1(1) apps. 0 gls.
FLC: 2(1) apps. 0 gls.
Total: *3(2) apps. 0 gls.*

THOMPSON, Andrew

Role: Outside-right 1904-05
b. Sunderland

CAREER: Sunderland West End/ SUNDERLAND Mar 1905/Queens Park Rangers cs 1905-07.

Debut v Everton (h) 18/3/1905

A local winger plunged into the big time very shortly after signing from Sunderland West End, Andy Thompson also appeared a week after this debut in an away fixture against Small Heath. Thompson's stay at Roker Park was brief, departing in the ensuing close season to London where he had a couple of terms with Queens Park Rangers. His record there reads 23 Southern League appearances plus one FA Cup-tie, one goal.

Appearances:
FL: 2 apps. 0 gls.
Total: *2 apps. 0 gls.*

THOMPSON, Frederick

Role: Goalkeeper 1895-96
5'9" 11st.4lbs.
b. South Hetton, Co Durham, 1873
d. Eastbourne, 13th January 1958

CAREER: Sunderland West End/ SUNDERLAND Aug 1895/Bury June 1896/ Bolton Wanderers May 1902/Luton Town cs 1903/Portsmouth May 1904/Fulham May 1905/Norwich City May 1906/Doncaster Rovers Nov 1908/Hartlepools United 1909-10.

Debut v Burnley (a) 9/9/1895

Fred Thompson

The most successful of the several Ned Doig deputies although the tangible success was confined to his Bury spell, the club he joined from Sunderland. As a critic then wrote Fred "proved one of the best men in the League" and that "he had no small share in the Bury triumph at the Crystal Palace" (in the Cup final). While at Gigg Lane he also participated in an England trial (for the North v the South in March 1900). He left Bury for neighbouring Bolton, then served a string of Southern League clubs, spending a bare year with each, never regaining his Bury peaks. At the time Fred was consistently sound, deservedly playing much first team football.

Appearances:
FL: 2 apps. 0 gls.
Total: *2 apps. 0 gls.*
Honours:
(Bury) FAC winner 1900.

THOMPSON, Harry

Role: Inside-forward 1938-39
5'10" 10st.8lbs.
b. Mansfield, 29th April 1915

CAREER: Carter Lane School/High Oakham School/Mansfield Invicta/Mansfield Town am June 1932/Wolverhampton Wanderers June 1933/SUNDERLAND Dec 1938 £7,500 (guested for Carlisle United and York City during WW2)/York City Dec 1945/

Northampton Town player-coach Nov 1946/
Ranheim FC, Norway coach 1946-47/
Headington United player-manager July 1949,
eventually retiring as a player but continuing
as manager to Dec 1958.

Debut v Liverpool (h) 17/12/1938

Harry Thompson played no senior football for
Mansfield but his form with their reserves
soon attracted Wolves' attention. He had his
League debut in 1935/36, making 69 First
Division appearances (16 goals) in all while at
Molineux. This was in an aspiring and
improving
Wolves side
destined to finish
runners-up in
1937/38 and
'38/39, and
Harry had the
experience of
partnering big
name players
such as Bryn
Jones and Dennis
Westcott.
Sunderland paid
a big fee for him
less than a year
before war broke
out. Harry joined

Harry Thompson

the Special Constabulary at the outbreak, later
serving in the RAF. He joined York City, for
whom he had 'guested' when stationed at
Marston Moor, before League football
resumed. Then soon to Northampton (38
Southern Section appearances) where he also
appeared at wing-half. After a short spell
coaching in Norway, Harry became player-
manager at Hednesford United. The club did
the Southern League and Cup 'double' in
season 1952-53 and in 1953-4 reached the
fourth round of the FA Cup. He resigned due
to ill-health in December 1958 and afterwards
worked for British Leyland until his retirement
in 1979. Harry presently lives in Oxford.
NOTE: *We are informed the player's surname is
actually Thomson. However, all pre-War and post-
War sources - which are many and include FL
seasonal lists for Sunderland - give it as
Thompson. This spelling has been retained with the
convenience of readers in mind.*

Appearances:
FL: 11 apps. 1 gl.
Total: *11 apps. 1 gl.*

THOMPSON, John William

Role: Outside-right 1907-10
5'8" 11st.7lbs.
b. Alnwick, Northumberland circa 1887

CAREER: Alnwick Town/North Shields
Athletic/SUNDERLAND May 1907/Preston
North End May 1910-cs 1912.

*Debut v Sheffield Wednesday (a) 26/12/1907
(scored)*

John Thompson had a
memorable Boxing Day
debut, netting a couple of
goals in an away victory
over Sheffield Wednesday.
On migrating to Preston the
*Lancashire Daily Post
Handbook* thought
Thompson would give the
North End attack "real

John Thompson

vitality and power". And went on to remark
he had "scored consistently as an outside
man" and was "fast, controls the ball well, and
knows the game thoroughly". The paragraph
concluded by saying "he scales 12 stone so
that he brings weight to the line as well as
skill". He made 58 League appearances for
Preston, scoring nine goals.

Appearances:
FL: 34 apps. 13 gls.
Total: *34 apps. 13 gls.*

THOMPSON

Role: Right-half 1884-85

Debut v Redcar (a) 8/11/1884 (FAC)

Appeared in Sunderland's first-ever FA Cup-
tie apparently out of position (the line-ups for
1884/85 for the most part in friendlies, are far
from complete). Thompson's other recorded
outings were six at right-back - including a
run of five, 31 January to 14 March 1885
inclusive - and one at left-back.

Appearances:
FAC: 1 app. 0 gls.
Total: *1 app. 0 gls.*

THOMSON, Charles Bellany

Role: Centre-half 1908-15
5'11" 12st.8lbs.
b. Prestonpans, East Lothian, 12th June 1878
d. 6th February 1936

CAREER: Prestonpans FC/Heart of
Midlothian April 1898/SUNDERLAND May
1908 *£350/retired May 1919.
*Signing occurred when there was a £350 limit
on transfer fees and Sunderland took a
'makeweight' player as well, also for £350. The
actuality was that Thomson cost Sunderland
£700.*

Debut v Manchester City (a) 1/9/1908

Not only one of the most illustrious names
in Sunderland's pre-Great War history, but
among the greatest of any era, Charlie
Thomson arrived from Hearts as an
established star with
a full decade of first-
class football behind
him. The transfer
enraged Hearts
supporters who
argued that,
although the player
had turned 30,
much remained in
those muscular
legs and sagacious
footballing brain.
The supporters
were quite right
as Charlie gave
Sunderland
seven years
sterling service
(and it could
have been more,
had war not intervened). Thomson
had joined Hearts a couple of months prior
to his 20th birthday. His wage was ten
shillings a week with, in addition, a job
arranged by the club, at an Edinburgh
baker's shop. The Tynecastle club was amid
a period of great success that stretched from
1891 to 1907. In that time they won the
Scottish League championship twice and
reached the Scottish Cup final six times,
(four as winners). When Charlie arrived
Hearts' staff was liberally sprinkled with
famous internationals. Charlie played in
three of the Cup finals, unusually occupying
a different position in each; centre-forward in
1901, right-back in 1903 and his ultimate,
renowned role of centre-half in 1906. It was
remarked at the time of the 1903 final:
"Thomson had not yet found himself",
meaning it was still undecided as to whether
right-back or leading the attack was the best
option. By his last (1906) Cup final both had
been discarded for his unchallenged role as a
master pivot. The dozen Scotland caps
earned before his move south merely
underlined the fact. Charlie's signing by
Sunderland was a major step in the creation
of a wonderful side that almost won the
'Double' of championship and FA Cup in

F. & J. SMITH'S CIGARETTES

SUNDERLAND.
C. THOMSON.

1913. Indeed, Thomson was the veritable core of the team. His physique was ideal for a centre-half and to this were added tenacity, ball skills and another natural advantage - a masterful character. This last quality made him an obvious choice as captain. Flanking Charlie on a regular basis from 1911/12 were wing-halves Frank Cuggy and Harry Low. This glittering Cuggy/Thomson/Low intermediate line achieved national fame for its all-round qualities, not least for feeding George Holley and company in a richly talented attack. In Thomson's seven peacetime seasons at Roker, Sunderland always finished in Division One's top half, were never lower than eighth, were third twice and champions once. And as noted, they reached the FA Cup final in the 1913 championship year. A 1-0 defeat by the League runners-up, Aston Villa, foiled the coveted Double. It was by all accounts a hard match with no quarter given and bitter personal duels between various opposing players. The ferocity of the exchanges between Charlie and Villa's equally combative centre-forward Harry Hampton were apparently the most fractious and earned both players a month's suspension at the opening of 1913/14. After leaving football Charlie worked as a licensee in his native Prestonpans.

Appearances:
FL: 236 apps. 6 gls.
FAC: 29 apps. 2 gls.
Total: *265 apps. 8 gls.*
Honours:
21 Scot caps/5 SL apps./(Heart of Midlothian) SC winner 1901, 1906/ SC finalist 1903/(Sunderland) FL champs 1913/FAC finalist 1913.

THOMSON, Charles Morgan

Role: Right-half 1931-39
5'8" 10st.6lbs.
b. Glasgow, 11th December 1910
d. Co Durham, 8th May 1984

CAREER: Glasgow schools football/Glasgow Pollok/SUNDERLAND June 1931/retired May 1940.
Debut v Blackburn Rovers (h) 3/10/1931

In the first half-century of League life, Sunderland AFC employed the services of two Charles Thomsons. Both were Scottish half-backs honoured by their country, both won League championship medals and played in a Cup final while at Roker. Not only that, their League and FA Cup appearance aggregates were almost identical. Physically, however, the pair were very different, the older man tall and weighty, the 1930's man small and light. A well-recorded feature in the evolution of the splendid 'Thirties side that carried off League and Cup trophies in consecutive years was the production of exceptional wing half-backs: Charlie Thomson, Alec Hastings and Alex ('Sandy') McNab. The trio, signed within a two-year period, were graduates from strong Scottish junior clubs and all became internationals. There was also a fourth - Les McDowall - talented but unable to get a look-in (14 senior appearances in six years), yet he brought a markedly higher fee when transferred in the same month as the experienced McNab (and proved a bargain for Manchester City). Charlie Thomson first played in Sunderland's League team in autumn 1931 but did not become a regular until the next season. Alec Hastings, a player more associated with the left-half position, often appeared on the right flank in 1931/32, with Joe Devine, an erstwhile inside-forward, at left-half. In 1932/33 Charlie had 32 outings, all at right-half, his chosen position. He could, nonetheless, take the left flank and, indeed, did so in four consecutive League matches in 1933/34, when Sandy McNab was given a long run of 24 games that stretched from August 1933 into the New Year of 1934. He was a Sunderland ever-present in successive seasons, 1934/35 and '35/36, and three times his seasonal appearances exceeded 30. In his last term the total dropped to 20 due to the grooming of the up and coming Arthur Housam. Thomson played in all nine ties of

Charlie Thomson (1930s)

416

the successful 1937 Cup run and a fortnight after the final won his only Scottish cap in a 3-1 win over Czechoslovakia. Charlie's playing style was nicely summed up by a commentator in the 1930s: "Here is a master craftsman who plays with his head as well as his feet. He sees an opening and generally puts the ball where it is most wanted, is dainty but surprises by the strength of his tackle." Charlie's last senior match was against Liverpool at Anfield on April 29, 1939 and possibly his last ever, as he did not appear in the three League games before war was declared and the competition's fixture list abandoned. He retired in the spring of 1940 aged only 29, doubtless with much good football still in him.

Appearances:
FL: 237 apps. 7 gls.
FAC: 27 apps. 1 gl.
Total: *264 apps. 8 gls.*
Honours:
1 Scot cap v Czechoslovakia 1937/ (Sunderland) FL champs 1936/FAC winner 1937.

THOMSON, Robert

Role: Left-back 1927-28
5'9" 11st.6lbs.
b. Falkirk, 24th October 1903

CAREER: Laurieston Villa/Falkirk Amateurs FC 1925/Falkirk 1925/ SUNDERLAND Apr 1927 (£5,000 including Adam Allan)/ Newcastle United Oct 1928 (in exchange for Bobby McKay)/Hull City July 1934 £340/ Marseille Aug 1934/ Racing Club de Paris later in 1935/Marseilles Aug 1935/ Ipswich Town July 1936/retired through injury sustained Aug 1937, becoming Ipswich Town's asst. trainer and then head trainer Sept 1938-May 1950.

Debut v West Ham United (a) 1/9/1927

Hailed as a discovery when with Falkirk. Such was Bob Thomson's progress he represented the Scottish League in March 1927 and, a month later, Scotland against the Auld Enemy. This a bare couple of years after

Bob Thomson

turning senior. Bob came to Sunderland less than a week after his international debut. His stay at Roker was comparatively brief, though understandable with Bobby McKay arriving in exchange and the seasoned Ernie England still on hand for the left-back job. Thomson had linked up with Falkirk as a half-back, moving to left-back with astonishing success in October 1926. Cool, stylish and fast, exploiting a clean kick, Bob was first choice at Newcastle for over two years (80 League and Cup games) but had only four Football League outings for Hull. Things looked up in Paris, the Racing Club a double trophy-winning combination in 1935/36. Ipswich was a non-League club in Bob's playing time and here his career-ending broken leg transpired, leading to an exceptionally long trainer's stint in Suffolk.

Appearances:
FL: 19 apps. 0 gls.
FAC: 3 apps. 0 gls.
Total: *22 apps. 0 gls.*
Honours:
1 Scot cap v England 1927/
1 SL app. v FL 1927.

THORLEY, Ernest 'Cliff'

Role: Outside-left 1932-35
5'10" 11st.0lbs.
b. West Melton, Yorks, 12th November 1913

CAREER: Wath National School/Dearne Valley/ Sandymount United/ Wath National Old Boys/Frickley Colliery briefly/ SUNDERLAND Sept 1932/Hull City Nov 1934/ Kidderminster Harriers July 1936/ Cheltenham Town c.1937/Bristol City Mar 1938-39.

Cliff Thorley

Debut v Middlesbrough (h) 22/3/1933

Cliff Thorley was a powerfully built outside-left - his weight had increased to 12 stone-plus by 1935 - and a Jimmy Connor understudy for a couple of years. Senior chances were accordingly few. He appeared thrice towards the end of 1932/33 with another outing in October 1934. The move to Hull City brought regular first team football (36 League and Cup appearances, five goals). Then two years at Kidderminster and Cheltenham in the Birmingham League and Birmingham Combination respectively before returning to the Football League scene at Bristol City (14 Southern Section outings, three goals). He left Bristol in March 1939 to join the Hull police force. Maybe the cognomen 'Cliff' was coined with the celebrity Cliff Bastin in mind, Bastin being a leading outside-left of the period.

> **Appearances:**
> *FL: 4 apps. 0 gls.*
> **Total:** *4 apps. 0 gls.*

THREADGOLD, Joseph Henry 'Harry'

Role: Goalkeeper 1952-53
5'11" 12st.3lbs.
b. Tattenhall, Cheshire, 6th November 1924

CAREER: Tarvin FC (Chester)/Chester FC Oct 1947/SUNDERLAND July 1952 £2,400/ Southend United July 1953 £750/retired cs 1963 but became a permit player during season 1963-64 with Southchurch Rovers of the Southend Borough Combination.

Debut v Charlton Athletic (h) 23/8/1952

Harry Threadgold's 16-year League career can be said to resemble a sandwich, goodly Third Division spells on either side of his season with top flight Sunderland. The latter found him first choice in a side that finished in the First Division's top half. He was, in fact, a continuous first teamer at all three clubs, with

THORPE, James Horatio

Role: Goalkeeper 1930-36
5'9" 11st.10lbs.
b. Jarrow, Co Durham, 16th September 1913
d. Sunderland, 5th February 1936

CAREER: Jarrow Imperial/Jarrow FC am cs 1930, pro Sept 1930/SUNDERLAND Sept 1930 £250, to his death.

Debut v Huddersfield Town (h) 25/10/1930

Even from a distance of 60 and more years the unhappy memory of this young man's untimely death during Sunderland's fine championship campaign of '35/6 is poignantly vivid. The circumstances were these: Jimmy Thorpe, had played in a rough 3-3 home draw against Chelsea on 1st February (just four days before his death) in which several players, including him, were injured. Although kicked a number of times in a second-half goalmouth melée, Jimmy had indicated to the referee he was fit enough to continue. He was, however, a diabetic who took insulin regularly, and even Raich Carter noted how Jimmy had lost considerable weight in the two years prior to his untimely death. An FA inquiry held later suggested Jimmy had died in a diabetic coma, sparked by a blow to the head during the game. Nevertheless, as one publication said,

"there is no doubt that this happening, coupled with injuries to other players, led to the alteration of the rule regarding the way a goalkeeper may be tackled". Players were no longer allowed to raise their feet to the ball once it was in the goalkeeper's hands. Jimmy worked as an engineer in the Jarrow shipyards, and had been a professional only a fortnight before he signed for Sunderland. He made his debut, aged only 17, and in 1933 was described as "a very promising youngster who under force of circumstances has had to take his place in Sunderland's first team before being quite ripe. A boy doing a man's work". Sunderland sensibly did not rush him into the side. but by the mid-1930's however, he was firmly established as the clear first choice and was making his 52nd consecutive appearance on that tragic February afternoon. Jimmy's death cast a dark shadow across Sunderland's triumph but he had easily made enough appearances (26) in 1935/36 to qualify for a League championship medal, which was duly presented to his widow.

> **Appearances:**
> *FL: 123 apps. 0 gls.*
> *FAC: 16 apps. 0 gls.*
> **Total:** *139 apps. 0 gls.*
> **Honours:**
> *(Sunderland) FL champs 1936.*

Jimmy Thorpe

Harry Threadgold

the last of which he made 319 appearances in Southend's goal during a decade at Roots Hall. Harry's Chester figure was 83 so his grand League aggregate comes to a considerable 437. An able, efficient custodian and also a useful boxer, Harry served in the Royal Marines during World War Two.

Appearances:
FL: 35 apps. 0 gls.
FAC: 3 apps. 0 gls.
Total: *38 apps. 0 gls.*

TINSLEY, Walter Edward

Role: Inside-left 1911-14
5'9" 11st.7lbs.
b. Ironville, Derbys, 10th August 1891
d. Ripley, Derbys, 7th March 1966

CAREER: Alfreton Town/Sutton Town/ SUNDERLAND Jan 1912/Middlesbrough Dec 1913/Nottingham Forest May 1921/Reading May 1924-27.

Debut v Woolwich Arsenal (h) 23/3/1912

Introduced by Sunderland to the senior game, Tinsley had a more notable career afterwards. Earmarked as the man to replace the injured George Holley in the 1913 FA Cup final it is said he got into such a state of nerves he was unable to play and Holley turned out instead

in front of 120,000 against Aston Villa when only half fit as Sunderland lost the chance of 'The Double'. Tinsley scored however, and hit the woodwork three times a few days later as Sunderland's 1-1 draw at Villa virtually ensured the championship title. He was a brainy forward and a strategist: as a Nottingham critic wrote in 1922 following Forest's Second Division championship "another of the exponents of the classical game, which he plays with unfailing cleverness and science". Forest were well aware of Walter's worth before acquiring him as he had been a wartime guest. Earlier still, at Middlesbrough where he had made his reputation, he proved no mean scorer (46 goals in 86 League outings). His Forest League figures were 61 appearances, 13 goals. At Reading, a veteran but still a valued figure in their 1925/26 promotion run, he also notched 13 goals, this time in 55 Football League matches.

Appearances:
FL: 10 apps. 3 gls.
Total: *10 apps. 3 gls.*
Honours:
(Nottingham Forest) Div 2 champs 1922/ (Reading) Div 3 Sth champs 1926.

Walter Tinsley

TODD, Colin

Debut v Leeds United (a) 7/9/1966 (sub)

Role: Central defender 1966-71
5' 9" 11st.5lbs.
*b. Chester-le-Street, Co Durham, 12th December
1948*

CAREER: Chester-le-Street Schools/
SUNDERLAND app July 1964, pro Dec 1966/
Derby County Feb 1971 £170,000/Everton Sept
1978 £300,000/Birmingham City Sept 1979
£250,000/Nottingham Forest Aug 1982
£65,000/Oxford United Feb 1984/Vancouver
Whitecaps, Canada May 1984/Luton Town
Oct 1984/Whitley Bay manager 1985/
Middlesbrough reserve team coach May 1986,
first team coach Sept 1986/Middlesbrough
manager Mar 1990-May 1991/Bradford City
coach Dec 1991/Bolton Wanderers asst.
manager June 1992, manager June 1995-Sept
1999.

Colin
Todd

A famous player from the 'Seventies whose
capacity to excite crowds was, and still is, an
uncommon thing for a defender. Colin had all
the required qualities in abundance; calmness,
a fluid turn of speed, a strong tackle and
superb constructive accuracy with his long-
distance passing out of defence. Allied to all
this outstanding ability was consistency and
fitness over a long career which resulted in
appearance totals of 637(4) plus over 100 more
in Cup-ties. Colin made his senior debut three
months before his 18th birthday and was soon
an established first teamer, widely recognised
as one of the most promising youngsters in the
country. These facts combine to raise the
question as to why, when he was only 22, the
Wearsiders parted with such a gem? The
answer must be a combination of
Sunderland's status as a mid-table Second
Division side and the size of the fee - then the
second highest ever and a record for a half-
back. Cute Derby manager Brian Clough knew
precisely what he was getting because of his
earlier association with Sunderland's young
talent. Todd proved a key aquisition for the
Rams, won the first of two championship
medals in his initial full season at the Baseball
Ground, and added the accolade of 1975's PFA
Player of the Year. Colin's move from Derby to
Everton when at the height of his immaculate
powers caused great resentment in the East
Midlands. In the event the player's stay at
Goodison lasted only a year. He lost his place
through illness, departing after a dispute with
Everton manager, Gordon Lee. His next club,
Second Division Birmingham City, proved far
more amenable, and third place in 1979/80
ensured the club's return to the top flight.
Todd also reached his landmark 500th League
appearance while at St.Andrew's. Colin
rejoined his old mentor, Brian Clough, at
Nottingham after three years. He was then
approaching his 34th birthday yet still made
36 Division One appearances for a side in the
country's leading half-dozen before his
swansong at Oxford and Luton. Honoured at
Youth level when an apprentice at Roker Park,
Todd played his first Under-23 international in
May 1968 aged 19, and in the course of 14 caps
at this level skippered the team. A satisfactory
prelude to the gaining of 27 full England caps.
Colin's post-playing career has had more ups
and downs than most. Middlesbrough rose
from Division Three to Division One in two

years from 1987 but went down to Division Two in 1990. At Bolton promotion from Division Two in 1993, Division One (1995) and Division One champions (1997) contrast with Premiership relegations in 1996 and again in 1998. His reign at Bolton's gleaming new Reebok Stadium which ended with his resignation in September 1999, did though, groom a number of young talented professionals, including his son, Andrew.

Appearances:
FL: 170(3) apps 3 gls.
FAC: 10 apps. 0 gls.
FLC: 4 apps. 0 gls.
Other: 4 apps. 0 gls.
Total: *188(3) apps 3 gls.*
Honours:
27 Eng caps/14 Eng U-23 apps./Eng Yth/ 3 FL apps./(Derby County) FL champs 1972, 1975.

TOMLIN, John

Role: Centre-half 1905-06
b. Seaham, Co Durham

CAREER: Seaham White Star/ SUNDERLAND June 1905/Middlesbrough Sept 1906-1908/later assisted Murton Red Star.

Debut v Aston Villa (h) 28/2/1906

John Tomlin

Tomlin had a solid introduction to senior football with Sunderland that encompassed the final 13 League fixtures of 1905/06. The run started extremely well with four wins which included a 7-2 thrashing of Wolves. The analysis of his appearances is six wins, two draws and five defeats, the heaviest reverse at Manchester City (5-1). Tomlin appeared only four times in a Middlesbrough line-up, consecutive appearances in September and October 1906, the great Andrew 'Daddler' Aitken then taking over after his arrival as player/manager from Newcastle United.

Appearances:
FL: 13 apps. 1 gl.
Total: *13 apps. 1 gl.*

TONES, John David

Role: Left-half 1969-73
6'2" 13st.0lbs.
b. Silksworth, Co Durham, 3rd December 1950

CAREER: Sunderland Schools/ SUNDERLAND May 1968/Arsenal May 1973-Dec 1974 (Swansea City loan Sept 1974) (Mansfield Town loan Oct 1974).

Debut v Lazio (a) 17/5/1970 (sub) (AIC) (scored)

Extremely powerfully built half-back whose few first team appearances were widely separated. There was a gap of two and a half years between John Tones' debut and his next outing, a home League match against Preston North End in December 1972. Indeed all his remaining appearances were in 1972/73. In his other Football League outing, at Nottingham against Forest, he played centre-half. Tones played no senior football for his next club, Arsenal, but on loan periods made Fourth Division appearances for Swansea (7) and for the eventual champions, Mansfield (3).

Appearances:
FL: 2(4) apps. 0 gls.
FAC: 2 apps 0 gls.
Other: 1(1) app. 1 gl.
Total: *5(5) apps. 1 gl.*

John Tones

TOSELAND, Geoffrey V.

Role: Outside-left 1948-55
6'0" 11st.6lbs.
b. Kettering, 31st January 1931

CAREER: Kettering Town/SUNDERLAND
Dec 1948/Kettering Town May 1955-1958.

Debut v Derby County (h) 6/9/1952 (scored)

Signed before his 18th birthday this tall left-winger had to wait nearly four years before making his League bow. When he did his remaining five appearances came quite quickly, the last being on November 29, 1952 against Spurs. Toseland's only goal was scored on his debut. Returning to Kettering Town, Geoffrey starred in their 1956/57 Southern League championship team, alongside player manager Tommy Lawton, and his 93 goals in 144 Southern League appearances was a club record for the Poppies.

> **Appearances:**
> *FL: 6 apps. 1 gl.*
> **Total:** *6 apps. 1 gl.*

TOWERS, Mark Anthony

Role: Midfield 1973-77
5'10" 11st.7lbs.
b. Manchester, 13th April 1952

CAREER: Manchester Schools F.A./
Manchester City app June 1967, pro Apr 1969/
SUNDERLAND Mar 1974/Birmingham City
July 1977/Montreal Manic Mar 1981/Tampa
Bay Rowdies/Vancouver Whitecaps Aug
1984/Rochdale n.c. Feb-May 1985.

Debut v Fulham (h) 16/3/1973

Tony Towers won six caps with England Schoolboys in 1976, the first of his eight Under-23 caps at 20 years of age, and made his full international debut at 24, winning three caps in the space of a month in 1976. A quicksilver midfield link man, scintillating on his day, Tony signed for Sunderland as part of an expensive package deal which involved Dennis Tueart (rated at £250,000) and Micky Horswill (£100,000) moving to Maine Road, with Tony, valued at £125,000, moving to Roker Park. He had crossed Sunderland's path during the 1973 Cup run, scoring for City before he was also sent off in the 2-2 fifth round tie at Maine Road. His sharp, incisive prompting from midfield added a much-needed variety to Sunderland's attack, and after narrowly missing out on promotion in 1974-75, he was a key member and team captain of the Division Two championship side one year later. In not untypical fashion, Sunderland lasted only one season in the top flight. In the close season, Towers moved on to Birmingham City for £140,000, and remained at St Andrews for a little under three seasons before spending much of the early 1980's playing in the NASL in America and Canada. His Football League career ended somewhat ingloriously with two half-game appearances for Rochdale (managed by ex Rokerite Vic Halom) in March 1985.

> **Appearances:**
> *FL: 108 apps. 20 gls.*
> *FAC: 6 apps. 0 gls.*
> *FLC: 6 apps. 2 gls.*
> **Total:** *120 apps. 22 gls.*
> **Honours:**
> *6 Eng Sch apps. 1967/Eng Yth/8 Eng U-23 apps. 1972-76/3 Eng caps 1976/(Manchester City) ECWC winner 1970/FLC finalist 1974/ (Sunderland) FL Div 2 champs 1976.*

Tony Towers

TRAIN, Raymond

Role: Midfield 1975-77
5'5" 10st.5lbs.
b. Nuneaton, 10th February 1951

CAREER: Bedworth United/Walsall app Sept 1967, pro Nov 1968/Carlisle United Dec 1971/ SUNDERLAND Mar 1976/Bolton Wanderers Mar 1977/Watford Nov 1978/ Oxford United Mar 1982(AFC Bournemouth loan Nov 1983)/ Northampton Town July 1984/Tranmere Rovers Aug 1985/Walsall Aug 1986, reg cancelled Dec 1986, subsequently appointed reserve and youth coach and, briefly, caretaker-manager from Dec 1988/Port Vale community officer Feb 1990/ Middlesbrough reserve team coach Apr 1990, chief scout cs 1994.

Debut v Orient (a) 13/3/1976

Ray Train, a curly-haired midfielder with seemingly inexhaustable stamina and enthusiasm, enjoyed a League career spanning two decades. He began and ended his playing days with Walsall, in between times appearing for eight other League clubs in a career that totalled in excess of 600 appearances and 30 goals. He joined Sunderland from Carlisle United - where he had been ever-present in their single season in Division One - for £80,000 in March 1976. His twelve League appearances in that term included seven wins and three draws, results which assisted Sunderland to win the championship of Division Two. Twelve months on he joined Bolton Wanderers for £35,000 and in 1978 he was able to toast a further promotion as Bolton won the Second Division championship. After joining Watford in November 1978, he proved good value for his £50,000 fee, assisting the Hornets to win promotion from Division Three in 1979. After captaining Oxford United for a spell, a series of fairly rapid moves ended at Walsall, for whom he made his final senior apperance at 36 years of age.

> **Appearances:**
> *FL: 31(1) apps. 1 gl.*
> *FAC: 1 app. 0 gls.*
> *FLC: 4 apps. 2 gls.*
> **Total:** *36(1) apps. 3 gls.*
> **Honours:**
> *(Sunderland) Div 2 champs 1976/*
> *(Bolton Wanderers) Div 2 champs 1979.*

Ray Train

TRAVERS, Bernard 'Barney'

Role: Centre-forward/inside-left 1919-21
5'10" 13st.0lbs.
b. Sunderland, 3rd qtr 1894
d. Sunderland, July 1949

CAREER: Sunderland Co-op Wednesday/Oak Villa/New Lambton Star 1913-14/Sunderland West End/SUNDERLAND Jan 1919/Fulham Feb 1921 £3,000/suspended for life Mar 1922/ Vienna Club, Austria as player-coach Apr 1922, subsequently briefly employed in Spanish football.

Debut v Aston Villa (h) 30/8/1919

Barney Travers was a strong, bustling type of forward usually leading the attack. An ever-present in that first post-war season, a sports journal in December 1919 described him thus. "There's no restraint about him. He means business, and he has the idea he may be able to do his side some good by jarring the nerves of the opposing goalkeeper. He is full of life and energy, and takes a great delight in football." Fulham paid a then substantial amount for Barney's services and it was

Barney Travers

greatly to be deplored his career ended in the manner it did. The ban arose from a bribery scandal concerning a vital promotion match towards the end of season 1921/22. Travers had joined the 4th Durham Light Infantry in 1914, was captured in August 1915 and became a prisoner-of-war until December 1918. After his departure from the game Barney ran a fruit and vegetable stall in the Sunderland area.

Appearances:
FL: 58 apps. 24 gls.
FAC: 5 apps. 3 gls.
Total: *63 apps. 27 gls.*

TROUGHEAR, William

Role: Right-back 1909-13
5'8" 11st.7lbs.
b. Workington, 1885
d. Heasingham, Whitehaven, 15th October 1955

CAREER: Workington Marsh Mission Juniors/Workington Town May 1907/SUNDERLAND May 1909 £10/Leicester Fosse May 1914/Flimby Rangers cs 1919/Workington 1922.

Debut v Blackburn Rovers (a) 6/11/1909

Billy Troughear

Billy's long-titled first club, the Workington Marsh Mission Juniors, achieved local prominence by winning both the Cumberland Shield and Cumberland League (West). A natural progression brought a step up to North-Eastern Leaguers, Workington and, that experience assimilated, a move to top flight Sunderland. Troughear established himself in Sunderland's League side during his first term, the debut above being forerunner of 26 consecutive appearances. His no nonsense approach made for effective

alliances with Agnew, Forster and Milton, and good form noticed by England selectors: he appeared in the 1910/11 White v Stripes trial. An aggregate century of Football League outings included only six for 1912/13 when the championship came to Roker Park for the fifth time, so a medal did not come Billy's way. A move to Leicester was not a great success (16 senior appearances), indeed the reverse as a poor Fosse side finished next to bottom and had to seek re-election. He guested for Preston North End and worked in munitions during the Great War, returning to Cumberland circles after it. The local soccer writer, Arthur Appleton, tells us that Billy Troughear was "inescapably destined in Sunderland to be called 'Tough-lugs'."

Appearances:
FL: 100 apps. 0 gls.
FAC: 8 apps. 0 gls.
Total: *108 apps. 0 gls.*

TUEART, Dennis

Role: Outside-left 1968-74
5'8" 11st.0lbs.
b. Newcastle-on-Tyne, 27th November 1949

CAREER: Newcastle Schools/SUNDERLAND Aug 1967/Manchester City Mar 1974 (plus Mick Horswill in exchange for Tony Towers and £225,000)/New York Cosmos, USA 1978 £250,000/Manchester City Feb 1980 £150,000/Stoke City Aug 1983/Burnley Dec 1983/retired cs 1984. Became a Manchester City director Dec 1997.

Debut v Sheffield Wednesday (h) 26/12/1968

Sunderland have been unusually well served on the extreme left flank down the years. Dennis Tueart, a major Sunderland discovery, is among the finest to have worn the red and white stripes. Dennis possessed a string of sterling qualities - speed, tight control and strong, accurate shooting all conducted in a manner quite correctly described as 'electric'. Unlike many outside-lefts he employed a useful right foot which provided additional attacking options. Dennis's years at Roker Park could hardly, with one glittering exception, be numbered among the club's more noteworthy. In his first full season at senior level the Wearsiders were relegated to Division Two, ended mid-table the next term, before - in Dennis's final three seasons -

finishing in the top half-dozen. The 'glittering exception' was, of course, the fairytale FA Cup victory of 1973. Tueart played a full role in that memorable triumph, partnering the adaptable Ian Porterfield, who scored the priceless Wembley winner. As well-documented, leading top flight sides Manchester City, Arsenal and Leeds United were all vanquished en route and Dennis took part in every round. There was always a buzz of anticipation among Sunderland fans whenever Dennis got the ball and the following season he scored two more of the fantastic goals that were his speciality. One came in Sunderland's first ever European tie when he skated through a host of bemused defenders on a run that began on the halfway line in the away leg against Hungarians Vasas Budapest. The second was a spectacular scissors-kick volley against Oxford only a few days earlier. Despite his seven years at Roker and a substantial appearance and goals total, it has to be said the two spells with Manchester City formed the greater part of Tueart's playing career. All his representative honours were aquired while at

Maine Road, even though he deserved a cap whilst at Sunderland, and his senior appearances and goals totals at City reached 259(10) and 107 respectively. His transfer to Manchester was rather complex. It involved Dennis (£250,000) and a 1973 Cup winning team mate, Micky Horswill (£100,000), moving in one direction with Tony Towers (£125,000) and an appreciable balancing sum moving in the other. Manchester City at the time were a First Division side to be reckoned with. In his first City spell they never finished lower than 8th, and in 1976-77 were pipped for the title by a single point. Dennis also participated in the club's two Cup finals of that era. His spectacular overhead scissors-kick won the 1976 League Cup and he was a substitute in the 1981 Centenary FA Cup showpiece. The spell in America which separated his stints with City was remarkable if only for the size of the fee involved. It must surely rank among the highest paid up to that time by an American club to a British one. Tueart's twilight career after his second Maine Road sojourn was brief, with a few outings for First

Division Stoke and Third Division Burnley. On leaving football Dennis pursued a successful business career. Working firstly in the launch and promotion of sports goods, he developed his own concern dealing with promotional packages, later taking up property interests and travel. He resumed active participation in football when appointed as a Manchester City director despite troubled times for the Blues. Three months later in March 1998 he was appointed Director of Football.

Appearances:
FL: 173(5) apps. 46 gls.
FAC: 17(1) apps. 3 gls.
FLC: 6 apps. 2 gls.
Other: 12 apps. 5 gls.
Total: *208(6) apps. 56 gls.*
Honours:
6 Eng caps/1 Eng U-23 app./2 FL apps./
(Sunderland) FAC winner 1973/
(Manchester City) FLC winner 1976/
FAC finalist (sub) 1981.

TURNBULL, Ronald William

Role: Centre-forward 1947-49
5'9" 11st.2lbs.
b. Newbiggin-by-the-Sea, Northumberland, 18th July 1922
d. Sunderland, 17th November 1966

Ronnie Turnbull

CAREER: RAF football to Dundee during WW2/SUNDERLAND Nov 1947 around £10,000/Manchester City Sept 1949 £11,000/ Swansea Town Jan 1951 £7,500/Dundee Mar 1953/Ashington Aug 1954.

Debut v Portsmouth (h) 29/11/1947 (scored)

Ronnie Turnbull made a simply sensational start to his Sunderland career by scoring all four goals in a 4-1 trouncing of Pompey. Not surprisingly, he was unable to maintain anything like such a rush. He had earned a reputation in Scotland as "a dashing go-ahead centre-forward", as one writer put it. He also turned out in both right-wing forward positions in League matches for the Wearsiders. Manchester City paid a fee similar to that expended by Sunderland two years earlier. At Maine Road he played in 31 Football League and FA Cup matches, netting five goals. With Swansea Ronnie regained much of his scoring touch (35 goals in 67 League outings), doing much to aid the Welsh club in their successful fight against relegation in 1951.

Appearances:
FL: 40 apps. 16 gls.
FAC: 3 apps. 2 gls.
Total: *43 apps. 18 gls.*
Honours:
(Dundee) SL Div 'B' champs 1947.

TURNER, Christopher Robert

Role: Goalkeeper 1979-85
5'10" 12st.2lbs.
b. Sheffield, 15th September 1958

CAREER: Sheffield Schoolboys/Sheffield Wednesday from school Mar 1975, pro Aug 1976(Lincoln City loan Oct 1978)/ SUNDERLAND July 1979/Manchester United Aug 1985/Sheffield Wednesday Sept 1988 (Leeds United loan Nov 1989)/Leyton Orient Oct 1991, asst. manager 1993, appointed joint manager Apr 1994-Apr 1995/Leicester City coach cs 1995/Wolverhampton Wanderers youth team coach/Hartlepool United manager Feb 1999.

Debut v Preston North End (h) 29/9/1979

Chris Turner joined Sheffield Wednesday from school and became a professional one month short of his eighteenth birthday. He appeared in all but one of League and Cup matches in his debut season, but subsequently shared the first team spot with Bob Bolder (q.v.) and had made 115 League and Cup appearances when Ken Knighton paid £100,000 to bring him to Sunderland. Agile, clean handling, and an excellent reflex shot-stopper, Chris lacked only the physical presence to dominate his penalty area, and initially found stiff competition at Roker from the more experienced Barry Siddall. Sunderland were promoted in Chris's first season and relegated in his last. Highlights in between included six successive clean sheets in 1982-83 (opponents including Liverpool, Manchester United and Arsenal). Only Montgomery in 1963-64 and Doig in 1901-02 and 1902-03 could match that. Also, his form in the League Cup run in 1984-85 was often inspired, most notably in the fourth round against Tottenham where, after keeping Spurs at bay virtually single-handed, he then made a vital penalty save in the replay. Sunderland lost form badly after defeat in the final; although Turner remained outstanding, the club were relegated. It was no surprise he was voted Sunderland's Player of the Year. In August 1985 Manchester United paid £275,000 for him, initially as reserve to Gary Bailey. Chris returned to Sheffield Wednesday in a £175,000 transfer in September 1988, and in 1990-91 was a member of the Owls' side that won promotion to Division One and lifted the League Cup, beating his previous club, Manchester United, 1-0 in the Wembley final. In more recent times he succeeded Mick Tait as manager of Hartlepool United, the League's 90th-placed club at the time of his appointment.

Appearances:
FL: 195 apps. 0 gls.
FAC: 7 apps. 0 gls.
FLC: 21 apps. 0 gls.
Total: *223 apps. 0 gls.*
Honours:
5 Eng Yth apps./
(Sunderland) FLC
finalist 1985/
(Sheffield
Wednesday)
FLC winner
1991.

TURNER, Neil

Role: Outside-right
1919-20
5'11" 10st.6lbs.
b. Hutchesontown, Scotland,
7th October 1892

CAREER: Petershill/
Leeds City Sept 1913/
Raith Rovers Aug 1914
(guest player for Glasgow Benburb during
WW1)/Vale of Leven Aug 1918/Kilmarnock
Sept 1918/SUNDERLAND Aug 1919/
Aberdare Athletic May 1920/Dundee June
1922/Bethlehem Steel, USA, Aug 1923.
Debut v Bradford (Park Avenue) (a) 17/4/1920

Neil Turner

A tall, slim forward, Neil Turner travelled a lot although he never achieved a regular first team place with any of his senior clubs. His best seasonal return by far was his 20 Southern Section appearances for Aberdare in 1921/22, their first Football League campaign, followed by nine in both his Kilmarnock and Dundee seasons. All the same Neil was well thought of - a Killie historian, for instance, remarked that he was "a speedy and tricky player with an eye for goal". And he appeared in every forward position bar outside-left for the Rugby Park club.

Appearances:
FL: 1 app. 0 gls.
Total: *1 app. 0 gls.*

Chris
Turner

URSEM, Loek A.J.M.

Role: Winger/Midfield 1981-82
5'9" 11st.4lbs.
b. Amsterdam, Netherlands, 7th January 1958

CAREER: AZ '67 Alkmaar (Holland)/Stoke
City July 1979(SUNDERLAND loan Mar
1982)/Haarlem (Holland) July 1983/
FC Wageningen/O.S.V. Velsen.

Debut v Middlesbrough (h) 3/4/1982 (sub)

Fair-haired Dutch midfielder Loek Ursem,
who was fluent in English, had impressed in
early days at Stoke, usually on the right of
midfield. His attacking flair was evident in his
return of seven goals in 24(4) League
appearances in 1980-81 but he had lost his first
team place by the time he arrived at Roker
Park on loan in March 1982. It was his second
link-up with Alan Durban, who had first
noted Ursem's talents in a youth international
tournament in Holland and subsequently
brought him to Stoke from AZ Alkmaar.
Although he expressed a desire to remain at
Roker Park, his four substitute appearances,
spanning about 45 minutes of football, were
not sufficiently impressive to win him a
permanent engagement.

> **Appearances:**
> *FL: 0(4) apps. 0 gls.*
> **Total:** *0(4) apps. 0 gls.*
> **Honours:**
> *28 Dutch U-21 caps.*

Loek Ursem

URWIN, Tom

Role: Outside/inside-
right 1929-35
5'6" 10st.0lbs.
b. Haswell, nr Sunderland, 5th February 1896
d. Monkseaton, Whitley Bay, 7th May 1968

CAREER: Sunderland Schools/
Monkwearmouth Colliery School/Fulwell FC
(Sunderland)/Lambton Star/Shildon am 1913,
pro Feb 1914/Middlesbrough Apr 1914 £100
(guest player for Fulham during WW1)/
Newcastle United Aug 1924 £3,200/
SUNDERLAND Feb 1930 £525, retired cs 1936
and for a time acted as coach to the club's
juniors and as a club scout.

Debut v Leeds United (a) 8/2/1930

A sprightly little
forward, equally
proficient at
outside-right and
left, Tom Urwin
appeared often at
inside-right for
Sunderland. He
was especially
noted for his
speed and
accuracy when
middling the
ball, and was
described at the
time as "a midget
winger who
could operate
efficiently down
either flank".
Tommy was a
member of the
distinguished

Tom Urwin

quartet that have assisted each of the North-
East's 'Big Three'. And in his case to some
purpose: besides his Sunderland quota he
made 200 League and FA Cup appearances for
both Middlesbrough and Newcastle (14 and 24
goals respectively). His first two England caps
were won at Middlesbrough on England's
1923 tour of Sweden while two more against
Belgium and Wales followed his move to
Newcastle in 1924. One of Tommy's favourite
true stories was that a telegram from the FA,
asking him to play for England, was never
delivered and his place was taken by Derby's
Alf Quantrill. He received benefits from all

three clubs which illustrates unusual durability. He played his final League match on April 22, 1935 (his first appearance since season 1931/32) when aged 39. Tommy, who represented County Durham and was in the Sunderland Boys side that won the English Schools Shield in 1910, worked as an engineer before turning professional. In the 1930s he had a tailor's shop in Sunderland. Later he held a clerical appointment in a Sunderland hospital, retiring in February 1962. During the 1914/18 War he had served with the Royal Field Artillery in India and Egypt.

Appearances:
FL: 50 apps. 5 gls.
FAC: 5 apps. 1 gl.
Total: *55 apps. 6 gls.*
Honours:
4 Eng caps/1 FL app. v the Scottish Lge 1927/ (Newcastle United) FL champs 1927.

USHER, Brian

Role: Outside-right 1963-65
5'11" 11st.5lbs.
b. Broomside, nr Durham, 11th March 1944

CAREER: Lambton and Hetton Schools/ SUNDERLAND ground staff 1959, pro Mar 1961/Sheffield Wednesday June 1965 £18,000/ Doncaster Rovers June 1968 in exchange for Alan Warboys/Yeovil Town cs 1973.

Debut v Huddersfield Town (a) 24/8/1963

Brian Usher was a tall wingman, an outside-right best remembered for his regular role in Sunderland's '64 promotion side when he missed only one game. On going to Roker he played mostly at outside-left and, later, inside-forward and right-wing. Brian was ranked fourth behind Hooper, Davison and Mel Smith in 1962/63 but particularly good form in the pre-season matches found him first choice for '63/64. He moved to Sheffield Wednesday following the acquisition of Mike Hellawell (55 League outings) then, after three years, to neighbouring Doncaster. Brian contributed a valuable five-year stint at Belle Vue including a promotion run (164 Football League appearances plus four substitutions).

Appearances:
FL: 61 apps. 5 gls.
FAC: 7 apps. 1 gl.
FLC: 3 apps. 1 gl.
Total: *71 apps. 7 gls.*
Honours:
1 Eng U-23 app. v France 1964/ (Doncaster Rovers) Div 4 champs 1969.

Brian Usher

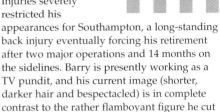

VENISON, Barry

Role: Full-back or Midfield 1981-86
5'10" 11st.12lbs.
b. Consett, Co Durham, 16th August 1964

CAREER: Stanley Schoolboys/
SUNDERLAND app July 1980, pro Jan 1982/
Liverpool July 1986/Newcastle United July
1992/Galatasary (Turkey) June 1995/
Southampton Oct 1995-Oct 1997.

Debut v Notts County (a) 10/10/1981

Barry Venison joined Sunderland from school
as an apprentice and rapidly progressed to
senior level winning England Youth
international recognition along the way. He
made his League debut at 17 and was
impressive enough to hold his place for four
months. An aggressive tackler with a highly-
developed competitive instinct, he was
comfortable in possession and a perceptive
passer out of defence. Club vice captain at the
time of the League Cup final in 1985, he had
the honour of captaining the team at Wembley,
when Shaun Elliott missed the final due to
suspension. After exactly 200 appearances in
The Lads' starting line-up, his first big-money
transfer was to Liverpool for £250,000. After
six successful seasons at Anfield, during which
time he won his two full England caps,
another £250,000 fee took him to Newcastle
United. He left after three seasons to link up
again with his former
manager, Graeme
Souness, in Turkey.
Injuries severely
restricted his
appearances for Southampton, a long-standing
back injury eventually forcing his retirement
after two major operations and 14 months on
the sidelines. Barry is presently working as a
TV pundit, and his current image (shorter,
darker hair and bespectacled) is in complete
contrast to the rather flamboyant figure he cut
in his playing days.

Appearances:
FL: 169(4) apps. 2 gls.
FAC: 7(1) apps. 0 gls.
FLC: 21 apps. 0 gls.
Other: 3 apps. 1 gl.
Total: *200(5) apps. 3 gls.*
Honours:
2 Eng caps 1995/10 Eng U-21 apps. 1983-86/
Eng Yth 1983/(Sunderland) FLC finalist
1985/(Liverpool) FL champs 1988, 1990/
FAC winner 1989/FLC finalist 1987/
(Newcastle Utd) Div 1 champs 1993.

VINALL, Edward John

Role: Centre/inside-forward 1931-33
5'10" 11st.0lbs.
b. Witton, Birmingham, 16th December 1910
d. Worcester, 26th May 1998

CAREER: Allan & Everitt's FC (Birmingham
works team)/Birmingham FC am Aug 1929/
Folkestone pro Sept 1930/SUNDERLAND Oct
1931/Norwich City June 1933/Luton Town
Oct 1937 (guest player for Walsall and
Coventry City during WW2)/Walsall July
1946/Worcester City Aug 1947, manager Jan
1948-Nov 1950/Aston Villa scout during the
1950s.

Debut v Middlesbrough (h) 31/10/1931

Jack Vinall was secured by Sunderland for a
reported 'useful cheque' from non-League
Folkestone the year after he had turned
professional. The Wearsiders tried him in four
of the five forward positions but qualities of

*Barry Venison (left) became the youngest ever
captain of a League Cup Final side when he led
Sunderland out against Norwich at Wembley in
1985 at the age of 20 years 7 months and 8 days.*

Jack Vinall

power shooting and thoughtful distribution were best employed in an inside role. He transferred to Norwich City where remarkably he was an ever-present in three consecutive seasons, 1933/34 - 1935/36, which included a championship year. His record as a Canary reads 177 League and FA Cup outings, 77 goals. Jack's last pre-war move, to newly-promoted Luton, produced League figures of 44 appearances, 18 goals. After the war he played a couple of Third Division games for Walsall and 11 (four goals) in the Southern League for Worcester City before becoming the latter club's manager. Jack worked as an

engineer before and after his footballing days. A younger brother, Albert Vinall, played for Aston Villa and Walsall during the immediate post-World War Two seasons.

Appearances:
FL: 16 apps. 3 gls.
FAC: 5 app. 1 gl.
Total: *21 apps. 4 gls.*
Honours:
(Norwich City) Div Sth champs 1934.

VINCENT, Robert G.

Role: Midfield/Defender 1980-81
5'10" 12st.1lb.
b. Newcastle upon Tyne, 23rd November 1962

CAREER: Newcastle Schools/SUNDERLAND app, pro Nov 1979/Leyton Orient May 1982/Brisbane Lions (Australia) early 1983/Whitley Bay Jan 1985.

Debut v West Bromwich Albion (a) 20/4/1981

An England Schoolboy cap versus Ireland in season 1978-79, Rob Vincent was a committed tackler who made two First Division appearances in 1980-81, during Mick Docherty's brief reign as caretaker-manager. Transferred to Third Division Orient in the close season of 1982, he appeared in 7(1) League matches and was released on New Year's Eve 1982. He then emigrated to Australia and spent two years with Brisbane Lions, returning in 1985 to sign for Whitley Bay.

Appearances:
FL: 1(1) apps. 0 gls.
Total: *1(1) apps. 0 gls.*
Honours:
1 Eng Sch int. app. 1979.

WADDLE, Christopher Roland

Role: Forward 1996-97
6'2" 13st.3lbs.
b. Heworth, Gateshead, 14th December 1960

CAREER: Pelaw Juniors/Whitehouse SC/
Mount Pleasant SC/Leam Lane SC/Clarke
Chapman/Tow Law Town cs 1978/Newcastle
United July 1980/Tottenham Hotspur July
1985/Olympique Marseille (France) July 1989/
Sheffield Wednesday July 1992/Falkirk Sept
1996/Bradford City Oct 1996/SUNDERLAND
Mar 1997/Burnley player-manager July 1997,
resigned May 1998/Torquay United n.c. Sept-
Nov 1998/Sheffield Wednesday coaching staff
Dec 1998.

Debut v Nottingham Forest (h) 22/3/1997

A Sunderland supporter as a boy, Chris
Waddle twice slipped though the club's
fingers following abortive trials in 1974 and
1980. His subsequent glittering career started
comparatively late, as he was 19 years old
when he accepted a twelve-month contract
with Newcastle United. In the event, he stayed
for five years, scoring 52 goals in 190(1)
League and Cup appearances and made his
full England debut in March 1985. Four
months later a fee of £590,000 took him to
Tottenham. In four years at White Hart Lane
he scored 54 goals in 212(4) League and Cup
appearances. A then record fee of £4.5 million,
making him the third most expensive
footballer of all time, took Chris to Olympique
de Marseille. He helped them to three
successive league championships and a place
in the European Cup Final in 1991. A return to
England in July 1992 with a £1 million transfer
to Sheffield Wednesday saw him honoured as
the Football Writers' Association Footballer of
the Year in 1993. Released by Wednesday in
the 1996 close season, spells with Falkirk and
Bradford City preceded his £75,000 move to
Sunderland in March 1997. Far from a spent
force at 36 years of age, the familiar
'hunchback' running style and the repertoire
of feints and tricks, allied to precisely-
weighted passes and crosses, were much in
evidence during his all-too-brief spell at Roker
Park. Although directly involved in five of the
seven goals scored during his sojourn, in
addition to scoring himself from a blistering
free-kick, he was unable to prevent
Sunderland's relegation from the Premiership.
In the close season he accepted the position of
player-manager of
Burnley. He had to wait
eleven matches for his
first victory and Burnley
struggled all season,
despite their illustrious player-manager's best
efforts to lift them from the foot of the Second
Division table. Relegation was finally avoided
on the last day of the season, but within a
week it was announced Waddle had resigned.
Currently coaching at Sheffield Wednesday,
Chris is also involved in media work. A more
recently reported possible playing comeback,
with non-League Boston United, appears to
have been without foundation.

Appearances:
PL: 7 apps. 1 gl.
Total: *7 apps. 1 gl.*
Honours:
*1 Eng U-21 app. 1985/62 Eng caps 1985-92/
1 FL app. 1988/(Tottenham Hotspur) FAC
finalist 1987/(Olympique de Marseille)
French Lge champs 1990, 1991, 1992/
EC finalist 1991, French Cup finalist 1991/
(Sheffield Wednesday) FAC finalist 1993/
FLC finalist 1993/FWA Player of Year 1993.*

Chris Waddle

WAGSTAFFE, Thomas Daniel

Role: Centre-forward 1922-23
5'7" 10st.6lbs.
b. circa late 1890s in Dinapore, India

CAREER: Fleetwood/SUNDERLAND Mar 1923 £550 (Oldham Athletic trial Aug-Sept 1924)/Fleetwood 1924-25 season/Crewe Alexandra Aug 1926/Mossley Aug 1927.

Debut v Manchester City (h) 30/3/1923

By scoring 28 goals in 11 matches for Fleetwood, Tom Wagstaffe built a reputation, inducing Sunderland to expend a significant sum for his signature. He was given a couple of run-outs with the League side - the second being against Burnley in April 1923 - otherwise he understudied Jock Paterson

Tom Wagstaffe

and Charlie Buchan. Wagstaffe was placed on the Wearsiders' transfer list after the 1923/24 season at £100. After a trial for Oldham and another spell with Fleetwood he returned to the League scene, making three Northern Section appearances for Crewe and scoring one goal.

> **Appearances:**
> *FL: 2 apps. 0 gls.*
> **Total:** *2 apps. 0 gls.*

WAINWRIGHT, Neil

Role: Midfield/Winger 1998-date
5'11" 10st.2lbs.
b. Warrington, 4th November 1977

CAREER: Crewe Alexandra assoc. sch Sept 1992/Wrexham trainee July 1994, pro July 1996/SUNDERLAND July 1998.

Debut v York City (a) 11/8/1998 (sub) (FLC)

Bought from Wrexham for £100,000 in the summer of 1998, Neil Wainwright had an early taste of first-team football with appearances in both legs of the First round League Cup ties against York City. Impressive performances in the Pontins League included a thirty minute hat-trick against Preston North End Reserves at Deepdale. Unfortunately, his progress was halted just prior to Christmas when he suffered a torn hamstring, an injury that

Neil Wainwright

proved slow to mend. A tall, slim wingman with a direct approach, Neil began on schoolboy forms with Crewe Alexandra but joined Wrexham as a trainee when he moved with his family to live in North Wales. A bright start at senior level with the Robins included scoring the winning goal on his debut at Blackpool, followed up by another winner at Millwall two weeks later. His form attracted many scouts to the Racecourse Ground, but Sunderland won the chase for his signature, despite reported interest from three Premiership clubs, including Newcastle United.

> **Appearances:**
> *FL: 0(2) apps. 0 gls.*
> *FLC: 2(1) apps. 0 gls.*
> **Total:** *2(3) apps. 0 gls.*

WAKEHAM, Peter Francis

Role: Goalkeeper 1958-62
6'0" 12st.0lbs.
b. Kingsbridge, Devon, 14th March 1936

CAREER: Devon schools football/Kingsbridge Grammar School/Torquay United youth team 1952, pro Oct 1953/SUNDERLAND Sept 1958 £5,000/Charlton Athletic June 1962 £4,000/ Lincoln City May 1965/Poole Town July 1966.

Debut v Grimsby Town (h) 1/11/1958

Spotted by Torquay United in local schools soccer, Peter Wakeham joined six months after his 17th birthday. He received his League baptism early - during 1953/54, his first term in the paid ranks. But Torquay nursed him carefully. He did not appear again until 1955/56 (three League outings) and was not first choice until the 1957/57 season. By this time Peter was spoken of as a 'keeper to watch and attracted scrutiny from higher echelons. Among the clubs most keen was Charlton Athletic, no doubt mindful how one of their greats, Don Welsh of England, had been recruited from Plainmoor between the wars. However, it seems Charlton were unwilling to meet Torquay's asking price but Sunderland were. Peter was physically ideal, at a whisker over six feet tall and lithely built. He gave Sunderland consistent and efficient service for five years as first choice goalkeeper until Jim Montgomery took over for his marathon 16-year run. He arrived at Roker Park in troubled times shortly into the inaugural Second Division season, yet left the summer after a top flight place was recaptured. Peter's best season with The Lads was undoubtedly 1960/61 when he missed only one League match, as Keith Hird got his sole first team game in the final fixture. The Wearsiders enjoyed an excellent FA Cup run to the quarter-final stage. Arsenal, Liverpool and Norwich City were beaten in rounds three to five, with only one goal conceded before a quarter-final against Spurs. The Londoners, in the latter part of their famous 'Double' season, drew 1-1 at Roker Park in front of a vast 61,326 crowd reportedly awesome in volume. The White Hart Lane replay, before an even bigger crowd, saw Spurs in rampant mood as 5-1 winners. Wakeham left Sunderland in the summer of 1962 for Charlton, the club which had angled for him when a tyro, with the fee not disimiliar to that which brought him to

Peter Wakeham

Wearside. He was a regular at The Valley in his first term, but afterwards understudied a 'keeper many considered inferior. Peter's last League move (and final season) was back north on a free transfer to Lincoln, where he made 44 Fourth Division appearances out of a possible 46. Peter's abilities were recognised at higher level when selected as stand-in for Fulham's Tony Macedo on a 1959 tour of Italy and West Germany. He did not play, however, but did in another representative match for an FA XI against the Royal Air Force.

Appearances:
FL: 134 apps. 0 gls.
FAC: 12 apps. 0 gls.
FLC: 5 apps. 0 gls.
Total: *151 apps. 0 gls.*

WALDRON, Colin

Role: Central defender 1976-78
6'0" 13st.13lbs.
b. Bristol, 22nd June 1948

CAREER: Bury app, pro May 1966/Chelsea June 1967/Burnley Oct 1967/Manchester United May 1976(SUNDERLAND loan Feb-May 1977/SUNDERLAND July 1977-Feb 1978/Tulsa Roughnecks (NASL) Apr 1978/

Colin Waldron

Philadelphia Fury June 1978/Atlanta Chiefs Apr 1979/Rochdale Oct 1979-cs 1980.

Debut v West Ham United (h) 5/3/1977

Burnley's captain at 21 years of age, Colin Waldron cost the Clarets £30,000 and the fair-haired centre-half spent his best footballing years at Turf Moor, clocking up in excess of 350 League and Cup appearances. A move to Manchester United, and a second link-up with Tommy Docherty - briefly his manager at Chelsea - proved unrewarding. After only four senior appearances he was loaned to Sunderland, managed at that time by former Burnley stalwart Jimmy Adamson. Colin arrived at Roker Park and was immediately thrust into the thick of the action. Sunderland beat West Ham United 6-0 on his debut, and a fortnight later his 70th minute winner accounted for Ipswich Town. A week on he was sent off at Aston Villa and served a two-match suspension. Despite a spirited battle, Sunderland were eventually relegated from the top flight. Needing a draw at Everton in the final fixture, they lost 2-0 and finished a point short of what would have been a miraculous escape. Appointed captain for the new season, in place of the departed Tony

Towers, Waldron lost his place eight matches into the campaign after a dismal start which saw the side with only one win to their credit. After spells in America he wound up his League career at Rochdale, managed by a former Burnley team mate, Doug Collins. Now settled in Lancashire, Waldron is working in the family book-making business in Nelson. A younger brother, Alan, was a midfield player who won a Third Division championship medal with Bolton Wanderers in 1973. Colin won his championship medal for Division Two in the same season.

Appearances:
FL: 20 apps. 1 gl.
FAC: 2 apps. 0 gls.
Total: *22 apps. 1 gl.*
Honours:
(Burnley) Div 2 champs 1973.

WALKER, Clive

Role: Winger 1984-86
5'8" 11st.4lbs.
b. Oxford, 26th May 1957

CAREER: Oxford Schoolboys/Chelsea app, pro Apr 1975/Fort Lauderdale Strikers 1979/ SUNDERLAND July 1984/Queens Park Rangers Dec 1985/Fulham Oct 1987/Brighton & Hove Albion Aug 1990/Woking FC Aug 1993/Brentford asst. manager Aug-Nov 1997/ Cheltenham Town Nov 1997.

Debut v Southampton (h) 25/8/1984

Former England Schoolboy international Clive Walker made his League debut for Chelsea in April 1977 and twenty years on assisted non-League Woking to complete a hat-trick of FA Trophy victories. A pacy wingman who liked to take the shortest route to goal, Walker scored 108 goals in 484 League appearances before retiring from senior football at the end of season 1992-93. His spell with Sunderland included a memorable hat-trick against Manchester United at Roker Park in November 1984. In the same season he finished as the club's leading goalscorer with 14 League and Cup goals. His efforts did much to take Sunderland to Wembley as he scored vital goals against Tottenham and Watford and two goals in the semi-final second leg against Chelsea at Stamford Bridge. In the final he sadly failed to score from the penalty spot and Norwich won the cup by a

Clive Walker

WALKER, John

Role: Right-back 1893-94

CAREER: Burnley c.1890/ Clyde cs 1892/ SUNDERLAND Aug 1893/ Stoke June 1894.

Debut v Sheffield Wednesday (a) 2/9/1893

Walker had a fair introduction to the new League's quality with Burnley, appearing in the third and fourth years of the competition. He played a total of 40 matches plus a couple of FA Cup-ties. Opportunities were much rarer in his Sunderland season with Peter Meechan, Donald Gow and Willie Gibson around, all players possessing, or who were destined to possess, representative honours. Walker made no senior appearances at Stoke.

Appearances:
FL: 5 apps. 0 gls.
Total: *5 apps. 0 gls.*

1-0 scoreline. Following Woking's FA Cup adventure in 1996-97, the 39-year-old was offered a new two-and-a-half year playing contract by the Vauxhall Conference side. Having added a fourth FA Trophy winners medal to his collection, and reached the runners-up position in the Conference in 1998, Clive has gone one better in 1999, and it will be interesting to see whether, at 42 years young, he continues to defy Father Time by featuring in League football with newly promoted Cheltenham Town in 1999-2000.

Appearances:
FL: 48(2) apps. 10 gls.
FAC: 1 app. 0 gls.
FLC: 11 apps. 6 gls.
Other: 1(1) apps. 1 gl.
Total: *61(3) apps. 17 gls.*
Honours:
2 Eng Sch int apps. 1972/(Sunderland) FLC finalist 1985/(Woking) FAT winner 1994, 1995, 1997/(Cheltenham Town) FAT winner 1998/Conf champs 1999.

WALKER, Nigel Stephen

Role: Midfield 1983-84
5'10" 11st.11lbs.
b. Gateshead, 7th April 1959

CAREER: Whickham/Newcastle United Apr 1977(Plymouth Argyle loan Jan 1982)/San Diego (USA) May 1982(SUNDERLAND trial Dec 1982)/Crewe Alexandra Jan 1983/ SUNDERLAND July 1983(Blackpool loan Mar 1984)/Chester June 1984/Hartlepool United June 1985/Blyth Spartans cs 1987, becoming manager Jan 1992/Dunston Fed 1992/RTM Newcastle Aug 1995.

Debut v Watford (h) 12/11/1983 (sub)

Nigel Walker

A County Youth representative at Rugby Union, Nigel Walker switched codes and was good enough to make his Newcastle United debut in the First Division as an 18-year-old. Sunderland gave him a trial following his return from playing in the USA but he was not signed permanently until eight months later. This followed a brief but impressive spell with Crewe Alexandra. Unable to graduate beyond the reserve side at Roker Park, he spent two months on loan at Blackpool and made a sensational debut, netting a hat-trick in a 5-1 win at Northampton Town. He subsequently spent a season with Chester City (41 League appearances, nine goals) and two seasons with Hartlepool United 77(5) appearances and eight goals. Released on a free transfer in May 1987 he moved into non-League circles. Awarded a first class honours degree in computer sciences by Northumbria University, he became a mathematics teacher at Lanchester Grammar School.

Appearances:
FL: 0(1) apps. 0 gls.
Total: *0(1) apps. 0 gls.*

WALLACE, Ian Andrew

Role: Forward 1984-86
5'7" 10st.12lbs.
b. Glasgow, 23rd May 1956

CAREER: York Athletic/Dumbarton cs 1974/ Coventry City Aug 1976/Nottingham Forest July 1980/Stade Brest (France) cs 1984/ SUNDERLAND Jan 1985/Maritimo (Portugal) June 1986/Melbourne Croatia (Australia) Mar 1987/Albion Turkagura, Australia/Melbourne Croatia manager/Albion Turkagura manager/ Dumbarton manager Nov 1986-Mar 1999.

Debut v Watford (a) 23/1/1985 (FLC)

A stocky, red-haired striker who began his professional career with Dumbarton, Ian Wallace's prowess as a marksman was quickly noted, leading to his £75,000 transfer to Coventry City in August 1976. He made his League debut, as a substitute, against Sunderland two months later. Happily, he made a full recovery from a sight-threatening car accident and as a bustling, oft times fiery, forward had recorded 57 Division One goals in 128(2) appearances for the Sky Blues when European Champions Nottingham Forest splashed out £1.25 million to take him to The

Ian Wallace

City Ground in July 1980. In four seasons his return of 36 League goals in 128(6) appearances was little more than modest, nevertheless he was Forest's leading scorer in three of his four seasons with them. Ian joined Sunderland after a spell in French football, made his debut in the League Cup quarter-finals and two months later, somewhat controversially, appeared at Wembley in the final of the competition when chosen ahead of Colin West who had scored three times in the two-legged semi-final. Relegation from the First Division followed and in the next season, under new boss Lawrie McMenemy, a further relegation was only avoided by the narrowest of margins. One of many players discarded in the close season, Ian played in Portugal and Australia before returning to his roots as manager of Dumbarton. Sadly, his 28 month stay at Boghead Park ended acrimoniously, his rift with the club's board resulting in his dismissal following a period of suspension. The dispute was reported to surround the club's action in transferring leading players, having also sold its ground, in desperate efforts to secure the future of The Sons, one of the founder members of the Scottish Football League, and joint champions with Rangers in the inaugural season, 1890-91.

Appearances:
FL: 28(6) apps. 6 gls.
FAC: 3 apps. 0 gls.
FLC: 1(2) apps. 0 gls.
Total: *32(8) apps. 6 gls.*
Honours:
3 Scot caps 1977-79/
1 Scot U-21 app. 1978/ (Sunderland) FLC finalist 1985.

WALLACE, Robert

Role: Inside-right 1928-29
5'6" 9st.7lbs.
b. Paisley, circa mid-1900s

CAREER: Cambuslang Rangers/ Cowdenbeath c.1926-27/SUNDERLAND Aug 1928 £100/Third Lanark July 1929/Bo'ness Aug 1931/permit player with Raleigh Athletic (Nottingham) Dec 1932.

Debut v Blackburn Rovers (h) 29/8/1928

A small, slight Caledonian, Bob Wallace arrived at Roker Park with half a dozen top flight Scottish League appearances and a goal to his name. He played in a run of five successive games for Sunderland in 1928/29 from the second fixture onwards before his return to Scotland a year later. Wallace's best return was at Bo'ness when he netted 28 goals in 35 Scottish League outings in 1931/32 - most creditable figures. It was, however, his swansong for Bo'ness were expelled during the following season, Wallace drifting into minor football.

Appearances:
FL: 5 apps. 0 gls.
Total: *5 apps. 0 gls.*

WALLACE, Thomas Hall

Role: Centre-half 1931-32
6'2" 12st.0lbs.
b. Jarrow, Co Durham, 1st July 1906
d. Sunderland, 12th April 1939

CAREER: South Shields schools and junior football/South Shields FC/SUNDERLAND Nov 1931/Burnley May 1933-1936.

Debut v Southampton (h) 9/1/1932 (FAC)

Unusually for an inter-war player with a single first team appearance, Tom's was in a Cup-tie. His chances were bound to have been restricted, a Scottish cap (Jock McDougall) and a future Scottish cap (Bob Johnston) being available. So Wallace moved to Burnley on a free transfer to obtain a fair slice of Second Division action over a three year period (61 appearances) plus six in FA Cup ties. He was a typical defensive pivot described at the time as "big, long and lanky, a useful build for the pivotal position. His motto: 'They shall not pass'." Tom had previously worked as a miner and unfortunately died young.

Appearances:
FAC: 1 app. 0 gls.
Total: *1 app. 0 gls.*

WALSH, William

Role: Centre-half 1946-53
5'11" 11st.11lbs.
b. Easington, Co Durham, 4th December 1923

CAREER: Horden Colliery/SUNDERLAND Sept 1946/Northampton Town July 1953 £6,000 incl Maurice Marston/Darlington June 1954/emigrated to Australia May 1955.

Debut v Charlton Athletic (a) 11/9/1946

Bill Walsh was signed a month into the new post-war era to give a longish seven-year service at Roker Park as a valued stand-in. He did not have to wait long for his senior debut - at left-back in the very same month as that signing. Like countless others, the war had delayed entry into the big time and Bill was nearing his 23rd birthday at his joining date. He had excellent physical dimensions for the preferred pivotal role. That first team place was, however, occupied by Fred Hall, signed only a month prior to Walsh, and he was the newly-appointed captain. Hall was a player with pre-war experience coveted by several clubs. Blackburn Rovers had no desire to lose him but reluctantly did so following a dispute over terms. So Walsh's role with The Lads was principally that of a reserve, yet he did have good League team runs. In two successive seasons he was first choice - 1949/50 (an excellent campaign when the Wearsiders finished third) and 1950/51. The appearances were 29 and 32 respectively and add up to approximately two-third of his grand total for Sunderland. He made no League appearances the following term, 1951/52, Hall being an ever-present. Walsh completed his League career with a couple of seasons in the Third Division; 19 appearances for Northampton Town of the Southern Section and, in a return to his native Co Durham, 28 for Darlington of the Northern.

Appearances:
FL: 98 apps. 1 gl.
FAC: 7 apps. 0 gls.
Total: *105 apps. 1 gl.*

Bill Walsh

WALSHAW, Kenneth

Role: Inside-left 1944-47
5'9" 11st.7lbs.
b. Tynemouth, 28th August 1918
d. Blyth, 16th May 1979

CAREER: North Shields and Army football/ SUNDERLAND Aug 1944/Lincoln City Aug 1947/Carlisle United Dec 1947/Bradford City Aug 1950-1951/assisted North Shields later in the 1950s.

Debut v Bury (FAC) (a) 29/1/1946 (scored)

Ken Walshaw played no League games in a Sunderland shirt, his first team matches a couple in the resumed FA Cup tourney of 1945/46. He transferred to Lincoln (in consideration of what was reported a 'four-figure fee') for the second post-World War Two season. Ken stayed at

Ken Walshaw

Sincil Bank only four months but long enough, and with appearances enough (17), to qualify for a championship medal. He returned north to Carlisle, remaining two and a half seasons with a return of 50 League outings, 15 goals. In his final Football League season, at Bradford City, Ken made nine League appearances, scoring three goals. He performed also at outside-left. It is worthy of note, too, that all his League appearances were in the Northern Section of the Third Division.

Appearances:
FAC: 2 apps. 1 gl.
Total: *2 apps. 1 gl.*
Honours:
(Lincoln City) Div 3 Nth champs 1948.

WARD, Robert

Role: Goalkeeper 1906-08
5'8" 11st.0lbs.
b. Glasgow area, circa 1881

CAREER: Abercorn/Port Glasgow Athletic June 1896/ SUNDERLAND May 1906/ Bradford Park Avenue June 1908/Marsden Rescue Aug 1909.

Debut v Liverpool (a) 15/9/1906

Of modest physical dimensions for a goalkeeper, Bob Ward was nevertheless very useful between the posts. He had spent a decade with Port Glasgow Athletic but had been recruited by that club when only in his mid-teens (Ward's age on joining Sunderland was said to be 25). Bob came into the side for the third League fixture of 1906/07 and missed only one game subsequently. In 1907/08 he shared goalkeeping duties with Tom Allan and the famous L.R. Roose. An odd sequence of goals conceded emerges from his final five appearances at Bradford Park Avenue: no goals conceded, one goal conceded, two goals conceded, three goals conceded, four goals conceded. We are indebted to Malcolm Hartley for spotting and pointing out this possibly unique sequence.

PROMINENT FOOTBALLERS.

R. WARD.
SUNDERLAND.

Appearances:
FL: 48 apps. 0 gls.
FAC: 6 apps. 0 gls.
Total: *54 apps. 0 gls.*

WARDLE, Henry

Role: Inside-left 1903-05
b. Sunderland

CAREER: Local junior football/ SUNDERLAND Sept 1902/South Shields May 1905/assisted North Shields later in the 1900s.

Debut v Wolverhampton Wanderers (h) 1/4/1904 (scored)

Harry Wardle, a local signing, made a bright start scoring one of the goals in a 2-1 home win over Wolves. He appeared also in the final two fixtures of that season. He played once in 1904/05: at Aston Villa, on October 1, 1904 when he netted his second League goal. A brother, J.W. Wardle, was known locally too - he assisted Southwick.

Appearances:
FL: 4 apps. 2 gls.
Total: *4 apps. 2 gls.*

WATKINS, Walter Martin 'Mark'

Role: Centre-forward 1904-05
5'8" 12st.8lbs.
b. Llanwnnog, Montgomeryshire, 1880
d. Stoke-on-Trent, 14th May 1942

CAREER: Caersws 1894/ Oswestry United 1896/Stoke Nov 1900/Aston Villa Jan 1904 £400/SUNDERLAND Oct 1904/Crystal Palace June 1905/ Northampton Town May 1906/ Stoke May 1907/Crewe Alexandra July 1908/ Stafford Rangers 1909/Tunstall player-coach 1911/Stoke 1911-1914.

Debut v Sheffield Wednesday (h) 22/10/1904 (scored)

A much travelled Welshman hailing from a farming family, Mark Watkins' many moves were punctuated by three to Stoke (although he played no first team football in the last). Possessing aggression and the ability to nurse his forwards and bring wingers into action, he had the utility value to take most attacking roles, and scored twice on his Sunderland debut. Manchester City tried to secure his transfer in 1903/04, which Watkins welcomed being desirous of linking up at club level with his great international colleague, Billy Meredith. However, City did not meet the £450 asking fee and Villa stepped in with a lower but successful bid. Mark had five brothers, the eldest of whom, A.E. Watkins, also assisted Aston Villa and was honoured by Wales on five occasions.

Mark Watkins

Appearances:
FL: 15 apps. 8 gls.
FAC: 1 app. 0 gls.
Total: *16 apps. 8 gls.*
Honours:
10 Welsh caps/
(Crystal Palace) Sthn Lge champs 1906.

Dave Watson

WATSON, David Vernon

Role: Centre-half/centre-forward 1970-75
6'0" 12st.0lbs.
b. Stapleford, Notts, 5th October 1946

CAREER: Nottingham Schools/Stapleford Old Boys/Notts County am June 1966, pro Jan 1967/Rotherham United Jan 1968 £8,000 plus Keith Pring/SUNDERLAND Dec 1970 £100,000/Manchester City June 1975 £175,000 plus Jeff Clarke/Werder Bremen, Germany June 1978 £200,000/ Southampton Oct 1979 £200,000/Stoke City Jan 1982 £50,000/ Vancouver Whitecaps, Canada Apr 1983/ Derby County Sept 1983/Fort Lauderdale, USA, May 1984/Notts County player-coach Sept 1984/Kettering Town Aug 1985.

Debut v Watford (a) 19/12/1970 (scored)

Dave Watson was among the outstanding centre-halves of the post World War Two era: cool, superb in the air, with an imperious stabilising influence. He was also durable, his League career approaching two decades beginning and ending at Meadow Lane, Nottingham. Over a quarter of this long period was spent with Sunderland, where he also displayed talents in his other position - centre-forward. Dave arrived at Roker with five seasons of Third and Fourth Division experience and one of Second. A hard school (both Notts County and Rotherham were usually enmeshed in the lower reaches of their respective tables), but this stood him in good stead for Sunderland's more exacting demands. Division Two provided the League fare for the whole of Dave's time on Wearside. In his first campaign, 1970/71, the club finished 13th but thereafter were always in the top half dozen and making a decent challenge for promotion. The high point of his Sunderland career was, of course, the glorious lifting of the FA Cup in 1973. It almost goes without saying that Watson's 'sheet anchor' displays at the heart of the defence were an indispensable contribution on the rocky road to Wembley. Dave's move to Manchester City two years after the Cup win counted at the time as a 'step up' for City were quite a force - they finished

runners-up to Liverpool in his second season, 1976/77, for example. An interesting fact, seldom if ever mentioned concerns Dave's first taste of Division One football. He made his top flight debut on 16th August, 1975 at Maine Road against Norwich City two months short of his 29th birthday when he already had 14 caps in his locker as Sunderland's most capped England international. A League Cup winners' medal constituted the chief reward of four years at Maine Road. There followed a miserable few months in Germany and a return to native soil via Southampton, also of Division One. While at The Dell, with the team usually in the top half of the table, he gathered a further 18 caps to add to the many already garnered elsewhere. Dave was to get a final couple more while serving his next club, Stoke City, also then a top division outfit. The caps totted up to a considerable 65 spread over a period of eight years with five different clubs, which established a record, subsequently equalled by goalkeeper Peter Shilton. The spell with Stoke saw the twilight of a long, illustrious career. Dave moved to Derby, who saw him as a likely bulwark in an unsuccessful struggle to avoid a drop into Division Three. Then came a return to his first love, Notts County, a club embroiled in a similar doomed cause. By the time he joined his final domicile, non-League Kettering Town, Dave had begun a successful business career. The secret of footballing longevity such as Dave Watson's must lie in a continuing high degree of fitness, plus fine judgement as to when to commit oneself and a wealth of natural talent. His tally of 657 League appearances speaks volumes. His wife Penny wrote a book about his career entitled 'My Dear Watson'.

Appearances:
FL: 177 apps. 27 gls.
FAC: 17 apps. 5 gls.
FLC: 7 apps. 0 gls.
Other: 8 apps. 1 gl.
Total: *209 apps. 33 gls.*
Honours:
65 Eng caps/
(Sunderland) FAC winner 1973/
(Manchester City) FLC winner 1976.

WATSON, Edward

Role: Right-back 1920-21
6'1" 11st.7lbs.
b. Sunderland, 1899

CAREER; Sunderland
Schools/Sunderland West
End/SUNDERLAND Jan
1920/Queens Park Rangers
May 1921/Rochdale June 1923-May 1924.

Edward Watson

Debut v Bradford City (h) 30/10/1920

Watson was a tall, slim full-back who
distinguished himself in schoolboy soccer. He
spent a season at Roker prior to moving to
London for a couple of years with Queens
Park Rangers. Watson made eight Southern
Section appearances while at Loftus Road, all
in 1922/23, one of them at right-half. Ben
Marsden monopolised the right-back
selections at that time. At Rochdale he had a
single Third Division (North) outing at right-
half against Barrow in December 1923.

Appearances
FL: 1 app. 0 gls.
Total: *1 app. 0 gls.*
Honours:
2 Eng Sch apps. v Scotland and Wales 1914.

WATSON, Ian

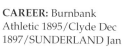

Role: Goalkeeper 1978-79
6'0" 12st.0lbs.
b. North Shields, 5th
February 1960

CAREER: North Shields
Juniors/SUNDERLAND
app, pro Feb 1978(Rochdale
loan Aug 1979)/Newport County Apr 1982.

Ian Watson

Debut v Burnley (a) 12/8/1978 (ASC)

As understudy to Barry Siddall, Ian Watson's
first team opportunities came very
infrequently. His only League appearance was
at Millwall in March 1979 when his assured
display enabled The Lads to score a 1-0 victory
and maintain a remarkable run of 14
undefeated away matches, in a season when
they finished just one point adrift from a
Second Division promotion spot. However, his
FA Cup outing in a fourth round replay with
Burnley at Roker became a nightmare of
nerves after he allowed an opening minute

effort to creep over the line as the visitors won
3-0. In the summer of 1979, Fourth Division
Rochdale paid Sunderland £12,000 for Alan
Weir and took Watson, by this time third
choice 'keeper at Roker, on loan. In a spell
which lasted some eight months, Watson
made 33 consecutive League appearances for
the Dale, returning to Roker in March 1980.
Fourteen months on he was released on a free
transfer. He failed to secure a League
engagement until April 1982 when Newport
County signed him as cover for Mark Kendall.

Appearances:
FL: 1 app. 0 gls.
FAC: 1 app. 0 gls.
Other: 1 app. 0 gls.
Total: *3 apps. 0 gls.*

WATSON, James

Role: Left-back 1899-1907
5'10" 12st.0lbs.
b. Larkhall, Lanarks., 4th
October 1877

CAREER: Burnbank
Athletic 1895/Clyde Dec
1897/SUNDERLAND Jan
1900/Middlesbrough Apr 1907-1910, latterly
acting as asst. trainer prior to joining Shildon.

Jimmy Watson

Debut v Glossop North End (h) 24/2/1900

Thought by many judges of the mid-1900s to
be the finest full-back in Britain, Jimmy
Watson was certainly in the running for such
an accolade with all-round qualities aided by a
powerful physique (his weight had reached 13
and a half stones by 1909). An all-action style
that involved extravagant arm and leg
movement earned him the nickname 'Daddy
Long Legs', a topical sobriquet from a famous
theatrical show of the period. The Scotland
selectors apparently subscribed to the 'best
British back' tag because four of his six caps
were for appearances against England, the
main clash of the then international calendar.
Jim in junior days had been courted by Hearts
but deemed Edinburgh too distant from his
native Lanarkshire, while a trial at Sheffield
United was unsuccessful. His form for Clyde,
however, brought about the move to
Sunderland, a club always on the look-out for
promising young Scots, and Jimmy missed
only one match in the 1902 championship
season. A year earlier he had missed only two

games as part of a solid defensive unit which conceded just 26 goals. On retiring he managed a Middlesbrough hotel before emigrating to Canada. It was reported that in September 1923 he had been appointed manager of a soccer club in British Columbia.

Appearances:
FL: 210 apps. 0 gls.
FAC: 15 apps. 0 gls.
Total: *225 apps. 0 gls.*
Honours:
6 Scot caps/Scot Jnr/
(Sunderland) FL champs 1902.

WATSON, James Jnr 'Dougal'

Role: Right-back/right-half 1903-05
5'10" 11st.9lbs.
b. Inverness, early 1880s

CAREER: Inverness Thistle/SUNDERLAND May 1903/Portsmouth Jan 1905/Chelsea Sept 1905/Brentford cs 1906.

Debut v Wolverhampton Wanderers (a) 24/10/1903

Dougal Watson was signed after what was reportedly 'splendid service' for Inverness Thistle in both wing-half positions. All his League outings at Roker Park were at right-half except the final one at right-back against Preston in December 1904. His other appearances were in season 1903/04: the debut above plus a consecutive run of three in March 1904. At Chelsea, engaged for their initial Football League season, he made 13 League appearances at centre- and left-half and one in the Cup at right-back, underlining his utility value. But Watson did not get a first team look-in for Brentford. The club already had a Watson - John of that ilk - a right-back in a run of Southern League outings that was to number 169 in the final count, and who should not be confused with James Jnr.

Appearances:
FL: 5 apps. 0 gls.
Total: *5 apps. 0 gls.*

WATSON, Willie

Role: Right-half/inside-outside-left
5'9" 11st.4lbs.
b. Bolton-on-Dearne, Yorkshire,
3rd March 1920

CAREER: Paddock Street School/ Huddersfield Schools and Junior football/ Huddersfield Town Oct 1937/ SUNDERLAND Apr 1946 around £7-8,000/ Halifax Town player-manager Nov 1954- Apr 1956 £4,000, when he also retired from playing/Halifax Town manager Aug 1964/ Bradford City manager Apr 1966-Jan 1968/ Wanderers (Johannesburg) manager Apr 1968-1972.

Debut v Everton (h) 12/10/1946

One of the select band that has represented his country at both cricket and football, Willie Watson started as an outside-left, making a First Division debut (at inside-left) in September 1938, aged 18, and playing outside-left in the final ten games of that last pre-war season. He came to Sunderland a few months before peacetime conditions returned, and was to win all four of his footballing caps whilst with The Lads. Willie's first cap marked a 9-2 win over Northern Ireland and his third was actually played at Roker Park against Wales. Willie was a superb performer whether as a wing-half or forward although many critics considered him best in the former berth with his ball-winning capacity and perceptive distribution. At cricket Willie assisted Yorkshire 1939-57 and Leicestershire 1958-64, playing for England in 23 Test matches. He was

Willie Watson

later a selector and was player-manager on an MCC tour to East Africa in 1963. He was neatly summed up as a "sound and stylish middle order left-hand batsman, fine outfield." Willie came of footballing stock: his father, William Watson, was left-half in the great Huddersfield Town 1919-26 team, winning three League championship medals (in consecutive seasons) and appearing in two FA Cup finals. His elder brother, Albert, also started with Huddersfield and he skippered Oldham Athletic post-war. He and Willie

opened a sports outfitting shop which many may recall in Sunderland's High Street East. Willie emigrated to South Africa in 1968 and developed business interests in Johannesburg. A great sportsman.

Appearances:
FL: 211 apps. 15 gls.
FAC: 12 apps. 1 gl.
Total: *223 apps. 16 gls.*
Honours:
4 Eng apps./3 Eng 'B' apps./2 Eng Victory apps.

Willie Watson (right) walks out to bat with Colin Cowdrey in the 2nd Test v Australia at Lords in 1956.

WAUGH, John

Role: Centre-forward 1913-14
5'11" 12st.4lbs.
b. Slamanann, Scotland

CAREER: Bo'ness/SUNDERLAND Dec 1913-1914(Guest player for Hearts, Motherwell, Dunfermline & Dundee Hibernian during WW1)/Newarthill Thistle July 1920/also had spells with Dundee, Dunfermline Athletic and Hibernian before joining Gillingham in Dec 1920-cs 1922/Guildford United cs 1922-1923.

Debut v Newcastle United (a) 27/12/1913

It does not fall to many one-match Rokerites to have as that match a Christmas derby against their greatest rivals. This was Waugh's lot, however, and in front of a 38,000 crowd. It must have been quite an occasion for him. After his short stay his movements are somewhat vague due to wartime conditions until he reached Gillingham. Here he was the regular centre-half, making 60 Third Division appearances and scoring four goals. Regarding Waugh's birthplace, it was given originally as Bo'ness, but in 1921 the *Athletic News* gives Slamannan. The two places are comparatively close.

Appearances:
FL: 1 app. 0 gls.
Total: *1 app. 0 gls.*

WEBB, Isaac

Role: Goalkeeper 1904-06
5'11" 12st.0lbs.
b. Worcester, October 1874
d. Winson Green, Birmingham, March 1950

CAREER: Worcester schools and junior football/Wellington Town/Small Heath 1898/West Bromwich Albion May 1901/SUNDERLAND Dec 1904 £250/Queens Park Rangers May 1906-cs 1908.

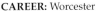
Isaac Webb

Debut v Sheffield United (a) 17/12/1904

West Bromwich Albion certainly provided the best segment of Ike Webb's career with 96 Football League appearances and five in the FA Cup. With his previous club, Small Heath, he had made his first half-dozen League outings. At Sunderland he was first choice on arriving until Tom Naisby's return in 1905. Webb was of spectacular bent, agile and quick to move off his line if a situation so demanded. A tendency to casualness at times could blemish otherwise excellent work. An apocryphal story is that he once played after sustaining a fractured skull. First team action for Queens Park Rangers was limited to the final ten Southern League fixtures of season 1906/07. Thereafter Charlie Shaw arrived to start a wonderful run of three ever-present campaigns and miss only three games until leaving in 1913 for much glory with Celtic. Isaac Webb remarkably came out of retirement in August 1918 to play in a wartime match for West Brom when aged 43.

NOTE: *It has been a common error for Alfred Webb, a contemporary goalkeeper who joined Lincoln City from Mansfield Mechanics in 1899, to be confused with Isaac. The fact they were two different players can be easily proved. Take season 1901/02 when both clubs were in Division Two. Isaac made 33 appearances in West Brom's championship line-up, and Alf was an ever-present in Lincoln's goal.*

Appearances:
FL: 22 apps. 0 gls.
FAC: 2 apps. 0 gls.
Total: *24 apps. 0 gls.*
Honours:
(West Bromwich Albion) FL Div 2 champs 1902.

WEDDLE, Derek Keith

Role: Centre-forward 1955-57
6'0" 12st.5lbs.
b. Newcastle upon Tyne, 27th December 1935

CAREER: Junior football to SUNDERLAND May 1953/Portsmouth Dec 1956 £6,000/Cambridge City 1959/Middlesbrough Aug 1961 £1,800/Darlington June 1962/York City July 1964-1966.

Debut v Huddersfield Town (a) 24/12/1955

A versatile forward with a commanding physique best employed, one would have thought, in leading an attack. However, at his last club, York, where Derek Weddle played most of his first team football (49 League and Cup games, 14 goals), he appeared exclusively at outside-right. There too he experienced promotion joys and relegation woes. Centre or inside-forward was Derek's role elsewhere. He

Derek Weddle

scoring three goals. His final season was spent with Hartlepool United, managed by former Sunderland player Michael Docherty. Weir failed to gain a regular berth in a side that narrowly achieved re-election to Division Four at the season's close.

Appearances:
FL: 1 app. 0 gls.
Total: *1 app. 0 gls.*
Honours:
4 Eng Yth apps. 1977-78.

WELSBY, Arthur

Arthur Welsby

Role: Outside-right/outside-left 1931-32
5'7" 10st.5lbs.
*b. Downall Green, Ashton-in-Makerfield, Lancs,
17th November 1902
d. Bryn, Lancashire,
24th April 1980*

CAREER: Ashton St Mary's/Wigan Borough am Jan 1924, pro Mar 1924/SUNDERLAND May 1931 £275/Exeter City May 1932/ Stockport County Aug 1934/Southport May 1935/Cardiff City May 1936/Wigan Athletic 1937/Mossley Feb 1938-1939.

Debut v West Bromwich Albion (a) 7/9/1931

Of the 170-plus players representing Wigan Borough in its ten-season Football League life, Welsby's return of 220 appearances (31 goals) is the highest by some distance. In fact only one other, John Moran, later of Spurs, exceeded the 200 mark with 201. Arthur, a versatile little performer, had appeared in both wing-half berths as well as wing-forward for the Lancashire club. For Sunderland, his only club above Third Division level, his debut was at outside-right, the other couple of League appearances on the opposite flank. Arthur had fair experience of 1930s Third Division soccer in both Sections at Exeter (39 games, eight goals) and Southport (21/1) but was a reserve with Stockport and Cardiff. He had originally worked as a coal miner and, after football, for a firm of hinge and lock makers, retiring when 65. Arthur played a fine tenor horn in the North Ashton Prize Band.

Appearances:
FL: 3 apps. 1 gl.
Total: *3 apps. 1 gl.*

was first choice at Darlington in spells (aggregate League figures - 36 matches, ten goals) and had a sampling of top division fare with Pompey (24 League appearances, 10 goals). At Middlesbrough the figures were three outings, one goal. He was latterly a part-time professional in order to follow his calling as a chiropodist.

Appearances:
FL: 2 apps. 0 gls.
Total: *2 apps. 0 gls.*

WEIR, Alan

Role: Defender 1977-78
5'9" 10st.0lbs.
b. South Shields, 1st September 1959

CAREER: SUNDERLAND app Apr 1976, pro May 1977/Rochdale June 1979/Hartlepool United Aug 1983-cs 1984.

Debut v Bolton Wanderers (a) 7/3/1978

Former captain of both Sunderland and England Youth teams, Alan Weir subsequently failed to establish himself at the highest level, despite a particularly good performance on his debut and indeed, only appearance for The Lads. He became Rochdale's record signing at £12,000 in June 1979 and in four seasons at Spotland recorded 96(1) League appearances,

WEST, Colin

Role: Forward 1980-85
6'1" 13st.11lbs.
b. Wallsend, 13th November 1962

CAREER: Wallsend Schools/County Durham Schools/SUNDERLAND app July 1979, pro July 1980/Watford Mar 1985/Glasgow Rangers May 1968/Sheffield Wednesday Sept 1987/West Bromwich Albion Feb 1988(Port Vale loan Nov 1991)/Swansea City Aug 1992/Leyton Orient July 1993(Rushden & Diamonds loan Jan 1998)/Rushden & Diamonds Feb 1998/Hartlepool United player-coach Oct 1999.

Debut v Tottenham Hotspur (h) 17/10/1981 (sub)

Powerful in the air and determined on the ground, Colin West, as a raw teenager, did much to preserve Sunderland's top flight status in his debut season. He insisted he would get goals if only given a chance and, true to his word, delivered with six goals in the final eleven fixtures to lift the side out of the bottom three, two points clear of Leeds United who were relegated along with Wolves and Middlesbrough. In the 1985 League Cup run, he was sensationally omitted from the Cup final team after scoring twice against Chelsea in the first leg of the semi-final, and once in the second leg. Less surprising was his transfer to Watford, later in the same month. A consistent performer and steady goalscorer throughout a lengthy career, Colin passed the milestone of 100 League goals in the colours of Leyton Orient in season 1993-94.

Appearances:
FL: 88(14) apps. 21 gls.
FAC: 3(1) apps. 2 gls.
FLC: 12(4) apps. 5 gls.
Total: *103(19) apps. 28 gls.*

Colin West

WHARTON, Sean Robert

Role: Forward 1988-89
5'10" 11st.4lbs.
b. Newport, 31st October 1968

CAREER: SUNDERLAND trainee Nov 1986, pro July 1987/Portsmouth trial May 1989.

Debut v Portsmouth (a) 8/4/1989

Sean Wharton's solitary first team appearance was made as deputy to Marco Gabbiadini at Portsmouth towards the close of season 1988-89. The first black player to graduate to first team level via the club's youth system, Sean was one of a number

Sean Wharton

of Welsh-born juniors on the staff. His signing followed scouting links established by manager Len Ashurst, who had previously managed Newport County. In the month following his debut Wharton was released by Sunderland and was immediately offered a trial by Portsmouth but this did not lead to a permanent engagement.

Appearances:
FL: 1 app. 0 gls.
Total: *1 app. 0 gls.*

WHELAN, William

Role: Left-half 1927-31
5'9" 11st.7lbs.
b. Airdrie, 20th February 1906
d. Sherborne, Dorset, 17th December 1982

CAREER: Coatbridge/Gartsherrie Athletic/
SUNDERLAND Apr 1927/Southend United
Apr 1932/Darlington June 1933-1935.

Debut v Birmingham City (h) 7/9/1927

Billy Whelan

Billy Whelan
understudied the
consistent Arthur
Andrews during the
latter's later Roker Park
years. He had a
promising start, having
but one reserve team
game before his League
debut. One critic wrote
"His display on that
occasion was impressive. He was easily the
best half on the field and, on that form, of First
League class". Two of his Sunderland
appearances (January 1930) were at right-half.
Proof that he possessed a good right foot - and
utility value - came at Southend. There Billy's
outings took in the final eight Third Division
fixtures of 1932/33 and he was at right-back in
all of them. For Darlington he appeared in the
League only ten times in a couple of seasons.

> **Appearances:**
> *FL: 19 apps. 0 gls.*
> **Total:** *19 apps. 0 gls.*

WHIPP, Percy Leonard

Role: Inside-right 1922-23
5'10" 11st.11lbs.
b. Gorbals, Glasgow, 28th June 1893

CAREER: West London Old Boys/Ton Pentre
cs 1920/Clapton Orient May 1921/
SUNDERLAND May 1922/Leeds United Nov
1922 £750/Clapton Orient June 1927/
Brentford May 1929/Swindon Town May
1930/Bath City July 1931, where he ended his
playing career.

Debut v Bolton Wanderers (a) 9/9/1922

For a decade Percy Whipp was a prominent
player in League circles, figuring in all three
grades. It is recalled he was a favourite subject

Percy Whipp

of the 1920s football cartoonists. Percy came to
Sunderland after his first spell with Clapton
Orient but left in a matter of months to join
the newly-constituted and ambitious Leeds
club. He was a member of their 1923/24
promotion side, making the transition to
regular top flight soccer without undue
difficulty. Percy left Elland Road (aggregate
154 League and FA Cup appearances, 47 goals)
following United's acquisition of the Scotland
cap, John White. His second Orient period
lasted two years bringing his total figures in
League and Cup for the London club to 94
outings, 26 goals. Whipp's final League terms
at Brentford and Swindon, when well into his
thirties, resulted in Southern Section totals of
seven (one goal) and nine (five goals)
respectively. He was a sharp alert forward,
good at headwork, and quick to capitalise on a
decent through-ball.

> **Appearances:**
> *FL: 1 app. 0 gls.*
> **Total:** *1 app. 0 gls.*
> **Honours:**
> *(Leeds United) Div 2 champs 1924.*

WHITBOURN, John Giles

Role: Goalkeeper 1904-05
5'11" 11st.8lbs.
b. Farnham, Surrey, 1885

CAREER: South Bank/SUNDERLAND Aug 1904/Tottenham Hotspur May 1905/Leyton Aug 1908-1912.

Debut v Nottingham Forest (a) 15/10/1904

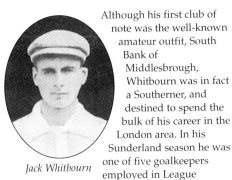

Jack Whitbourn

Although his first club of note was the well-known amateur outfit, South Bank of Middlesbrough, Whitbourn was in fact a Southerner, and destined to spend the bulk of his career in the London area. In his Sunderland season he was one of five goalkeepers employed in League matches, Ike Webb getting the lion's share. Moving to Spurs, Jack was again a reserve, playing in 19 Southern League encounters over three years at White Hart Lane. Whitbourn came into his own, though, on transferring to another metropolitan club, Leyton. Here he was the first choice 'keeper for four seasons, Leyton's last in the top division. He had Charlie Buchan as a colleague for most of 1910/11, that great player heading the scoring list with 15 goals from 23 appearances. On the subject of Leyton FC, the club is entitled 'Clapton Orient Reserves' in a Southern League history published in 1969, but the usual 'Leyton' appears in contemporary *Athletic News* and *Gamage* annuals.

Appearances:
FL: 3 apps. 0 gls.
Total: *3 apps. 0 gls.*

Dale White

WHITE, Dale

Role: Forward 1985-88
5'10" 11st.4lbs.
b. Sunderland, 17th March 1968

CAREER: Southmoor School/Sunderland Schoolboys/Durham County Schoolboys/ SUNDERLAND assoc. s'boy, app, pro Mar 1986(Peterborough United loan Dec 1987).

Debut v Sheffield United (a) 31/3/1986

Dale White was a member of the Sunderland Schoolboys team that shared the English Schools Gillette Trophy with Middlesbrough in season 1982-83. In the same term he scored for England Schoolboys against Northern Ireland and Wales. A regular goalscorer in youth and reserve football, he was unable to fulfil his potential at the highest level, his only goals in League football (four in 14 appearances) coming during his spell on loan to Fourth Division Peterborough United.

Appearances:
FL: 2(2) apps. 0 gls.
Other: 1 app. 0 gls.
Total: *3(2) apps. 0 gls.*
Honours:
5 Eng Sch apps. 1983.

WHITE, Thomas

Role: Inside-forward 1945-47
b. High Hold, 10th November 1924

CAREER: Chester Moor Juniors (Co Durham)/ SUNDERLAND Apr 1945/ Worcester City May 1947.

Debut v Grimsby Town (a) 5/1/1946 (FAC)

Locally born Tommy White was signed towards the end of the war. Four of his senior appearances were at inside-right, the exception being the last when he was at inside-left against Charlton Athletic on September 11, 1946. An oddity concerning these five

Tommy White

Billy Whitehurst began in League football with Hull City, who paid Mexborough Town of the Midland League £2,500 for his signature. A rugged player with few refinements, the ex bricklayer was nevertheless an excellent team man, lacking nothing in courage and commitment. He netted Hull City a handsome profit when Newcastle paid £232,000 for him in December 1985, and his wandering path took in nine different clubs for whom he scored 77 goals in 188 League appearances. His sojourn at Roker Park lasted just short of three months, following which he returned for a second spell with Hull City, as part of the Tony Norman transfer, having failed to link successfully with leading goalscorer Marco Gabbiadini in Sunderland's attack. Returning to Roker as a Hull City player some three months after his transfer, Billy was sent off the field following a clash with Sunderland's centre-half, John MacPhail. In 1997 Billy was reported to be 'mine host' at the Cricketers' Arms, near to Sheffield United's ground at Bramall Lane.

Appearances:
FL: 17 apps. 3 gls.
Other: 1 app. 0 gls.
Total: *18 apps. 3 gls.*

senior appearances is that all were in away fixtures. Tommy did well with non-League Worcester City, scoring 21 goals in 33 appearances.

Appearances:
FL: 2 apps. 1 gl.
FAC: 3 apps. 0 gls.
Total: *5 apps. 1 gl.*

WHITEHURST, William

Role: Forward 1988-89
6'1" 13st.0lbs.
b. Thurnscoe, Yorkshire, 10th June 1959

CAREER: Retford Town/Bridlington Trinity/ Mexborough Town/Hull City Oct 1980/ Newcastle United Dec 1985/Oxford United Oct 1986/Reading Feb 1988/SUNDERLAND Sept 1988/Hull City Dec 1988/Sheffield United Feb 1990(Stoke City loan Nov 1990)/ Doncaster Rovers Mar 1991(Crewe Alexandra loan Jan-Apr 1992)/Hatfield Main/Kettering Town/Goole Town/Stafford Rangers 1992/ Mossley/South China (Hong Kong)/ Glentoran Jan 1993/Frickley Athletic 1993, becoming manager Nov 1994.

Debut v Birmingham City (a) 17/9/1988

Billy Whitehurst

WHITELAW, George

Role: Centre/inside-forward 1957-59
5'10" 12st.8lbs.
b. Paisley, 1st January 1937

CAREER: Petershill/St Johnstone 1955/
SUNDERLAND Feb 1958 £4,500/Queens Park
Rangers Mar 1959 £5,000/Halifax Town Oct
1959/Carlisle United Feb 1961/Stockport
County Jan 1962, in exchange for Robert
Murdoch/Barrow Aug 1963.

Debut v Preston North End (a) 1/3/1958

"A rugged hard-as-nails leader who has
appeared in Division Two of the Scottish
League and all four division of the Football
League," wrote a popular commentator in
1964. George Whitelaw certainly moved
around after crossing the border, sampling six
clubs in six years. His most productive period
was spent at Halifax (22 goals in 52 League
outings). Something of an eccentric showman,
George had a good first touch and neat
passing abilities as well as a box of cheeky, fun
on field tricks with which he would entertain
the fans - tight-rope walking the white
touchline or pretending to fall over when
taking a throw in were just two. He certainly
impressed a young Frank Worthington (q.v.)
who confessed to being "completely and
utterly mesmerised" by George who in his
Halifax days he cited as "a big influence in my
approach to playing football with a smile on
your face." George's aggregate Football
League figures, including Sunderland, were
175 appearances, 60 goals. He could also take
an inside berth.

Appearances:
FL: 5 apps. 0 gls.
Total: *5 apps. 0 gls.*

WHITELUM, Clifford

Role: Centre-forward
1938-48
*b. Farnworth, Lancs,
2nd December 1919*

CAREER: Doncaster junior
football/Bentley Colliery
Welfare/SUNDERLAND
Dec 1938/ Sheffield United
Oct 1947 £9,000/Kings
Lynn July 1949.

*Debut v Blackpool (a)
25/1/1939*

Cliff Whitelum was born
in Lancashire but moved
to Doncaster with his
family when only five
months old. He played no
football after leaving
school until asked to turn
out for the local Co-
operative Sports Club side
in an emergency (he was
employed at the time by
the Society in their grocery
department). Cliff's
development from then on
was rapid, culminating in
a Sunderland trial and a

George Whitelaw

Cliff Whitelum

professional engagement before the trial month had elapsed. During World War Two, in which he served with the Royal Artillery for six-and-a-half years, he played much services football including representative appearances for the AA Command XI. His wartime soccer record which included 126 outings for Sunderland, was in aggregate 130 goals in 167 matches. Cliff once scored all six goals at Roker against Huddersfield in the 1943 Combined Counties West Riding FA Cup final first leg. Cliff resumed at Sunderland in peacetime as first choice centre-forward but moved to Sheffield United early in the following season for the Blades' then record fee. Rather surprisingly he stayed at Bramall Lane only a couple of years before joining non-League Kings Lynn. (Maybe the fact the Norfolk club had two months previously appointed a Blades colleague, Joe Cockcroft, player/manager had something to do with it.) Cliff had been summed up while at Bramall Lane as "lithe, elusive, quick-moving and packs a shot in each instep".

Appearances:
FL: 43 apps. 18 gls.
FAC: 7 apps. 2 gls.
Total: *50 apps. 20 gls.*

WHITFIELD, Michael

Role: Central defender 1982-83
5'8" 11st.0lbs.
b. Sunderland, 17th October 1962

CAREER: SUNDERLAND app July 1979, pro Oct 1980/Hartlepool United Aug 1983-cs 1984/Seaham Red Star.

Debut v Norwich City (a) 16/4/1983

Mike Whitfield was released by Sunderland shortly after making his senior debut in the closing stages of season 1982-83. He quickly joined forces with Mick Docherty, who had also departed Roker in the close season. It proved a traumatic experience for both player and manager. On December 26th Hartlepool won their second League match of the season, by which time Whitfield had made the last of his 15(1) appearances and manager Docherty had been sacked. The season ended in the 'Pool's 14th successful application for re-election. In Non-League circles Mike was later Player of the Year with Seaham Red Star.

Appearances:
FL: 3 apps. 0 gls.
Total: *3 apps. 0 gls.*

WHITWORTH, Stephen

Role: Full-back 1978-82
6'0" 12st.0lbs.
b. Ellistown, Leics, 20th March 1952

CAREER: Leicester City app July 1968, pro May 1969/SUNDERLAND Mar 1979/Bolton Wanderers Oct 1981/Mansfield Town July 1983/Barnet cs 1985.

Debut v Stoke City (a) 27/3/1979

A star in schools football, Steve represented England Schoolboys in 1967, and became a Leicester City apprentice in the following year. The locally produced full-back gave stalwart service to the Foxes, his 400 senior appearances including a run of 198 consecutive matches. He cost Sunderland £120,000 in March 1979, and successfully took over the number two jersey from Mike Henderson. The flame-haired defender helped Sunderland to win promotion in his first season, being the only ever-present team member during the campaign. Even so, Steve, a thoughtful and careful defender was oddly, never particularly popular with the crowd at

**Steve
Whitworth**

Roker. Departing in October 1981 to join
Bolton Wanderers, Steve appeared regularly
for two seasons, but left at the end of 1982-83
when Bolton were relegated to Division Three.
He joined Mansfield Town on a free transfer,
and his 80 appearances for the Stags took his
aggregate career total to 583 matches. Rather
surprisingly, for a back who had won
international recognition on the strength of his
smooth acceleration down the flanks and
perceptive promptings in attack, he scored
only two League goals. Both were successful
penalty conversions, recorded in the final
months of his lengthy senior career.

Appearances:
FL: 83 apps. 0 gls.
FAC: 3 apps. 0 gls.
FLC: 8 apps. 0 gls.
Total: *94 apps. 0 gls.*
Honours:
*5 Eng Sch apps. 1967/Eng Yth 1970/6 Eng
U-23 apps. 1972-75/7 Eng caps 1975-76/
(Leicester City) Div 2 champs 1971.*

WILKINS, Leslie

Role: Inside-right 1929-30
5'10" 12st.4lbs.
b. Swansea, 21st July 1907
d. Yeovil, Somerset, 4th qtr 1979

CAREER: Swansea Schools/Howard Villa/
Haford Juniors/Red Triangle (Swansea)/
Swansea Town May 1928/Merthyr Town June
1929/SUNDERLAND Nov 1929 £750/West
Ham United May 1930/Brentford Mar 1931/
Swindon Town cs 1932/Stockport County Aug
1933/Yeovil & Petters United 1934.
Debut v Grimsby Town (a) 23/11/1929

Les Wilkins was a schoolboy outside-right
who subsequently, in a roving career, went on
to reveal great versatility. For instance with
Brentford, a club where he recorded his
second best return in League matches, he
figured at inside-left and right-half. Elsewhere
he played in both wing-forward and wing-half
berths and in 1933 was listed as a right or left-
back. Wilkins, on the books of seven Football
League clubs in six seasons - averaging ten
months per club - grossed only 51 League
appearances (scoring 14 goals) in that time.
At only two, Brentford and Swindon, did the
totals reach double figures and, with two,
Swansea and West Ham, he did not play in the
first team. Sunderland secured him after he
had scored four goals in seven Southern
Section games for Merthyr Town, then of
Division Three (South), paying a significant
sum in the process. After leaving school,
Wilkins worked in the building trade before
becoming a professional footballer.

Appearances:
FL: 2 apps. 0 gls.
Total: *2 apps. 0 gls.*

WILKINSON, Reginald George

Role: Right-half 1923-24
5'8" 11st.7lbs.
b. Norwich, 26th March 1899
d. Norwich, 14th September 1946

CAREER: Thorpe Hamlet School/Norwich
CEYMS/Army football during WW1/
Norwich City 1919/SUNDERLAND June 1923
£1,000/Brighton & Hove Albion May 1924/
thereafter a permit player with Frost's Athletic
Aug 1934 and Norwich Electricity Works Sept
1936-1946.

Debut v West Ham United (h) 25/8/1923

Wilkinson's two senior outings for Sunderland were confined to the opening fixtures of 1923/24 but at his Third Division clubs a different story can be told. He had shown excellent form at Norwich (113 appearances, nine goals), while with Brighton he clocked up 396 (16 goals) in a decade of devoted service. The latter total included a remarkable consecutive sequence of 115. Reg's strengths included, besides obvious consistency, accuracy in passing the ball, deadly free kicks and penalty taking and being attack-minded. And he had a polished style. In the Great War, Reg served with the King's Royal Rifle Corps during which he

Reg Wilkinson

represented his battalion and corps at soccer. He literally went on playing to the end for he collapsed when assisting the Norwich Electricity team in September 1946, dying on the way to hospital. He was 47 years of age.

Appearances:
FL: 2 apps. 0 gls.
Total: *2 apps. 0 gls.*

WILKS, Alwyne

Role: Outside-right 1926-29
5'7" 11st.6lbs.
b. Staveley, Yorkshire, 4th September 1906
d, Doncaster, 3rd qtr 1980

CAREER: Brodsworth Main/Doncaster Rovers Apr 1925/SUNDERLAND Feb 1927 £1,500/Reading May 1929 £500/Barrow Oct 1929/Loughborough Corinthians Aug 1930/ Owston Park Rangers, Doncaster, Sept 1931 as a permit player.

Debut v Bradford City (h) 12/3/1927

One of the wingers recruited from Doncaster Rovers by Sunderland in 1927, Alwyne Wilks was the earlier arrival by a couple of months. This pair, the other being Len Hargreaves, had age similarities too: both were born in 1906 and died in 1980. Wilks, the management

Alwyne Wilks

hoped, would ease the Wearsiders' long-standing outside-right problem, and indeed he proved an adequate first choice from arriving to the end of 1927/28. George Robinson mostly got the selectors' vote the following term, at the end of which Alwyne moved to Reading. His stay with the Biscuitmen was short (no League appearances) nor was that at Barrow significantly longer (six Northern Section outings). Wilks, short and portly, in his prime had speed with sufficient weight to persistently harry defenders.

Appearances:
FL: 52 apps. 3 gls.
FAC: 3 apps. 0 gls.
Total: *55 apps. 3 gls.*

WILLIAMS, Darren

Role: Midfield/Defender 1996-date
5'8" 11st.0lbs.
b. Middlesbrough, 28th April 1977

CAREER: Viewley Hill Juniors/Cleveland Juniors/Middlesbrough FC School of excellence/York City assoc. s'boy Nov 1991, trainee July 1993, pro June 1995/ SUNDERLAND Oct 1996.

Debut v Arsenal (a) 11/1/1997 (sub) (FAC)

Darren Williams was out of contract with York City when, on the recommendation of Youth Coach Ricky Sbragia, he made a pre-season appearance for Sunderland Reserves in 1996. Initially unable to agree a fee for his services, Sunderland finally clinched a bargain deal of £50,000, with further payments based on appearances. The 19-year-old Middlesbrough born midfielder had some League experience, but was thought to have some time to wait for a first team place. In the event, Darren had established himself by the end of his first season. High spots were his first goal against Leicester City on his third appearance, and his late-season headed winner against his hometown club, Middlesbrough. Originally operating as an industrious midfielder, he subsequently slotted into the right full-back

Darren Williams

position and central defence with equal faculty. Such versatility made him an ideal squad member, and his value to the club was recognised with a new five-year contract in October 1998. Although a series of injuries restricted his first team opportunities in season 1998-99, he remained in the thoughts of the England Under-21 selectors, appearing against France at Derby's Pride Park in February 1999 despite having been unable to hold down a regular first team place with Sunderland.

Appearances:
PL: 10(1) apps. 2 gls.
FL: 54(10) apps. 2 gls.
FAC: 3(1) apps. 0 gls.
FLC: 7 apps. 1 gl.
Total: *74(12) apps. 5 gls.*
Honours:
1 Eng U-21 app. 1998-89/1 Eng 'B' app. 1998.

WILLIAMS, Harry

Role: Inside-left 1920-21
5'11" 11st.10lbs.
b. Hucknall Torkard, Notts, 1899

CAREER: Hucknall Olympic/SUNDERLAND am May 1920, pro Aug 1920/Chesterfield May 1921/Manchester United May 1922 £500/ Brentford Sept 1923 £300 (Sittingbourne trial Aug 1924)/Mansfield Town cs 1925.

Debut v Chelsea (a) 12/3/1921

Harry Williams

Harry Williams was introduced to the senior game by Sunderland after joining from the same junior club, and at the same time, as Bobby Marshall. Unlike Marshall, though, Harry stayed only a season departing to score Chesterfield's first goal in the newly-born Northern Section and accumulate nine in 28 outings. Good form brought the transfer to Manchester United, then an aspiring Second Division side. At Old Trafford Harry played in five of the opening 11 matches, scoring twice, before McBain and Lochhead took over the inside-left spot. With Brentford he had a fair showing. The Sittingbourne trial was just a blip - he did not join the Kent League club and played in a score of Southern section games in 1924/25. Harry's Bees record in the League totalled 43 appearances, seven goals.

Appearances:
FL: 1 app. 0 gls.
Total: *1 app. 0 gls.*

WILLIAMS, Paul Anthony

Role: Forward 1994-95
5'7" 10st.9lbs.
b. Stratford, London, 16th August 1965

CAREER: Aveley/Clapton/Fulham Dec 1984/ Woodford Town Oct Oct 1985/Charlton Athletic Feb 1987(Brentford loan Oct-Dec 1987)/Sheffield Wednesday Aug 1990/Crystal Palace Sept 1992(SUNDERLAND loan Jan 1995)(Birmingham City loan Mar 1995)/ Charlton Athletic Sept 1995(Torquay United loan Mar 1996)/Southend United Aug 1996- May 1998(Canvey Island loan Jan-Apr 1998).

Debut v Notts County (h) 21/1/1995

At the time of Paul Williams' loan to Sunderland from Crystal Palace he was reported to be available for transfer at a fee of £150,000. Nevertheless, after three outings - the last of which marked his 200th League appearance - he returned to Selhurst Park. The former accounts clerk won England Under-21 recognition whilst with Charlton Athletic, and cost Sheffield Wednesday a fee of £600,000 in

Paul Anthony Williams

August 1990. During his two years at Hillsborough he helped Wednesday to promotion and was a League Cup winner. He returned homewards to Crystal Palace in a part-exchange deal which took Mark Bright to Hillsborough, but his last two permanent transfers did not involve a fee. Released by Southend United in May 1998 following a lengthy loan spell with Canvey Island, Paul has since failed to find a League engagement.

Appearances:
FL: 3 apps. 0 gls.
Total: *3 apps. 0 gls.*
Honours:
4 Eng U-21 apps. 1989/3 Eng 'B' apps. 1990/ (Sheffield Wednesday) FLC winner 1991/ (Crystal Palace) Div 1 champs 1994.

WILLIAMS, Paul Leslie

Role: Defender 1988-93
6'0" 12st.2lbs.
b. Liverpool, 25th September 1970

CAREER: SUNDERLAND trainee July 1987, pro July 1989(Swansea City loan Mar 1991)/Doncaster Rovers 1993-Nov 1995.

Debut v Plymouth Argyle (h) 4/4/1988 (sub)

Paul Williams was a 17-year-old YTS boy when he made his League debut as a substitute. He replaced Brian Atkinson, one year older and also making his first senior appearance, in a late season Division Two fixture against Plymouth Argyle at Roker Park which was won 2-1. A promising player with a superb physique, Paul found opportunities

Paul Leslie Williams

scarce during his six years with Sunderland. His confidence was severely traumatised after an Old Trafford roasting at right-back from Manchester United's Lee Sharpe in January 1991, which saw him replaced at half-time. Loaned to Swansea City in March 1991, he made 12 consecutive League appearances, helping the Swans to avoid relegation from Division Three. In the following season back at Roker he played in the opening three League fixtures, but subsequently had only one further start and three substitute outings. Released at the close of the 1992-93 season he was signed by Doncaster Rovers but had appeared in only eight League matches when his contract was cancelled in November 1995.

Appearances:
FL: 6(4) apps. 0 gls.
FLC: 1 app. 0 gls.
Other: 2 apps. 0 gls.
Total: *9(4) apps. 0 gls.*

WILLIAMSON, John Robert

Role: Right/left-back 1914-15
5'10" 12st.7lbs.
b. Gateshead, 1887

CAREER: Annfield Plain Celtic/Stourbridge (also assisted Aston Villa reserves)/ Gainsborough Trinity 1913/SUNDERLAND May 1914-1915.

Debut v Notts County (h) 24/10/1914

Williamson made his debut at left-back with the remaining League appearances in his favoured right flank position. He arrived following a good season with Gainsborough Trinity, who finished runners-up in a strong Midland League - Trinity were back in this competition after failing to get re-election to the Football League in 1912. Williamson had a reputation as an expert penalty-taker and also possessed a useful physique. Another case of war intervening before a player's potential is fully assessed.

Appearances:
FL: 5 apps. 0 gls.
Total: 5 apps. 0 gls.

WILLINGHAM, Charles Kenneth

Role: Right-half 1945-47
5'7" 10st.11lbs.
b. Sheffield, 1st December 1912
d. Dewsbury, Yorkshire, May 1975

CAREER: Owler Lane School/Ecclesfield United/Worksop Town am 1928-29/ Huddersfield Town am 1930, pro Nov 1931/ SUNDERLAND Dec 1945 £5,000/Leeds United player-coach Mar 1947, retiring as a player May 1948 and continuing as a coach to 1950/Halifax Town coach for a spell from 1952.

Ken Willingham

Debut v Grimsby Town (a) 5/1/1946 (FAC)

A seasoned campaigner of 33 when signed by Sunderland soon after the war ended, Ken had been a star in the 'Thirties, winning many representative honours for his enthusiastic, tireless brand of wing-half play: he was Yorkshire's champion schoolboy half-miler and ran for England. He also played for England at shinty. At soccer Ken skippered Yorkshire Schools, joining Worksop Town, that constant well of young talent, when only 16. At Huddersfield, then a leading top flight side, he won a regular place in 1932/33, by the war's outbreak having amassed a total of 270 Division One and FA Cup-tie appearances. He made seven wartime appearances for England and, after retiring, was landlord of a hostelry in Hunslet, Leeds.

Appearances:
FL: 14 apps. 0 gls.
FAC: 6 apps. 0 gls.
Total: 20 apps. 0 gls.
Honours:
12 Eng caps/6 FL apps./
(Huddersfield Town) FAC finalist 1938.

WILLIS, David L.

Role: Left-half 1902-03 & 1904-07
5'8" 11st.7lbs.
b. Byker, Newcastle upon Tyne, July 1881
d. New Southgate, London, 26th May 1949

CAREER: Gateshead LNER/SUNDERLAND Oct 1901/Reading May 1903/SUNDERLAND July 1904/Newcastle United May 1907 £100/ Reading May 1913-1915/Palmer's FC, Jarrow, player-manager 1919/Raith Rovers trainer June 1921/Nottingham Forest trainer July 1925/Derby County trainer June 1933-June 1947.

Debut v Derby County (a) 1/11/1902

Rather unusually, Dave Willis had two separate spells with two different clubs, one of them Sunderland. Cool and hard-working, he was equally competent at right-half, his position in Newcastle's 1909 championship side and indeed the position on his Sunderland debut. His Cup final, however, was at left-half deputising for the injured Peter McWilliam. Dave literally spent almost the whole of his working life in the football world, his playing career followed by training engagements covering many years with three senior clubs. When stationed at Kirkaldy with Raith Rovers one of his young charges was the great future international, Alex James, later of Preston North End and Arsenal, who was to marry his daughter. Dave was active right up to the

Dave Willis

end, sometimes as a masseur in first-class cricket: he had been appointed to such a post for Derbyshire CCC shortly before he died. His son, Robert, assisted Blyth Spartans before joining Dundee in May 1921, moving back to England for engagements with Rochdale and Halifax Town.

Appearances:
FL: 47 apps. 2 gls.
FAC: 4 apps. 0 gls.
Total: *51 apps. 2 gls.*
Honours:
(Newcastle United) FL champs 1909/
FAC finalist 1911.

WILSON, ANDREW

Role: Forward 1896-97
5'9" 10st.6lbs.
b. Strathclyde area, mid-1870s

CAREER: Strathclyde FC/SUNDERLAND July 1896/Partick Thistle July 1897/Motherwell July 1899/Partick Thistle Apr 1900/Motherwell July 1902.

Debut v Bolton Wanderers (a) 26/9/1896

Apparently a man of parts, Andrew Wilson played inside-right on his debut and outside-left a week later against Wolves at home, having joined Sunderland as a left-back. Both matches were lost - 1-0 and 3-0 respectively. Like Dave Willis of Sunderland a little later, Andrew had separate periods with a couple of his senior clubs.

Appearances:
FL: 2 apps. 0 gls.
Total: *2 apps. 0 gls.*

WILSON, Hugh 'Lalty'

Role: Wing-half/inside-left 1890-99
5'11"
b. Mauchline, Ayrshire, 18th March 1869
d. 7th April 1940

CAREER: Mauchline FC/2nd ARV (Newmilns)/SUNDERLAND Sept 1890 £70 signing-on fee/Bedminster May 1899/Bristol City July 1900/Third Lanark May 1901/Kilmarnock Apr 1907/retired 1908.
Debut v Burnley (h) 13/9/1890

Hughie Wilson is a Sunderland immortal: he captained the celebrated 'Team of All the Talents', leading by example. For Wilson was a big man in all respects - long-striding, resourceful, sound in all aspects of his craft and, unlike many stars, always hard working. His one-handed throws were so tremendous they reputedly caused the law change to the two-handed variety. Wilson won three championship medals with Sunderland and was the only man to play in the club's first-ever League game and also the first match at Roker Park. Hughie was also capped by Scotland whilst at the club and, on a less illustrious note, was the first Sunderland player sent-off in a League game. Before signing for Sunderland, Hugh had represented Ayrshire on three occasions and Glasgow against Sheffield. Also Northumberland after joining Sunderland. The qualifications for assisting Northumberland (Sunderland being geographically in Co Durham) are not clear! Hugh skippered Bedminster, staying on the next season after the club merged into Bristol City (aggregate 88 League and FA Cup games, 29 goals). While with Kilmarnock he played in 22 Scottish League matches, scoring three goals. The Third Lanark figures are not available. The origin and meaning of the 'Lalty' nickname are likewise unknown.

Appearances:
FL: 232 apps. 40 gls.
FAC: 26 apps. 5 gls.
Total: *258 apps. 45 gls.*
Honours:
4 Scot caps/1 SL app. v Irish Lge 1902/
(Sunderland) FL champs 1892, 1893, 1895/(Third Lanark) SL champs 1904/
SC winner 1905/SC finalist 1906.

WOOD, Albert

Role: Inside-forward
1927-31
5'10" 11st.9lbs.
b. Seaham Harbour, Co Durham, 25th April 1903

CAREER: Seaham Harbour FC/
SUNDERLAND Aug 1927/Fulham May 1931,
in exch for J L Temple/Crewe Alexandra June
1935/Tranmere Rovers Aug 1936 £400/New
Brighton Feb 1938 £100/Hartlepools United
June 1939.

Debut v Tottenham Hotspur (a) 22/10/1927

At age 24 Albert Wood came to the senior
game comparatively late but soon received an
introduction to League fare. And he proved a
stayer, moving to Hartlepools shortly before
the war when 36. Albert, equally adept in both
inside-forward berths, was a forager, with a
ready shot and possessor of a deceptive body
swerve. His best Sunderland season came in
1929/30 (20 League appearances, eight goals)
and his best ever with Crewe (an ever-present
42, 14 goals). The Tranmere and New Brighton
records were 27 (11 goals) and 46 (11 goals)
respectively. So with the Fulham figures of 21
outings, nine goals, Albert Wood's aggregate
League record reads 176 appearances, 56
goals.

Appearances:
FL: 30 apps. 11 gls.
FAC: 2 apps. 0 gls.
Total: *32 apps. 11 gls.*

WOOD, Norman

Role: Left-half 1954-55
*b. Sunderland, 10th August
1932*

CAREER: Silksworth
Juniors/SUNDERLAND
May 1954/Silksworth
Colliery June 1957.

Norman Wood

Debut v Charlton Athletic (h) 12/2/1955

Locally-born Norman Wood was a young half-
back playing one first team game in a three-
year stay at Roker Park. Sunderland were
exceptionally well off at wing-half at the time
with Stan Anderson and George Aitken on
hand. The club finished fourth in Division

One, the season of Wood's appearance, but
were on a descending curve in 1955/56 and
'56/57. Norman later went into education,
working as a primary school teacher in
Sunderland.

Appearances:
FL: 1 app. 0 gls.
Total: *1 app. 0 gls.*

WOOD, William

Role: Left-back 1949-50
5'8" 11st.4lbs.
*b. Barnsley,
28th December 1927*

William Wood

CAREER: Spen Juniors/SUNDERLAND Oct
1948/Hull City July 1951 £5,000/Sheffield
United June 1952-1953.

Debut v Aston Villa (h) 1/4/1950

Despite transferring to Hull City for a sizeable
fee, Wood made no senior outings for the
Tigers. He moved to Sheffield United, again to
remain only a year. In that time he played in
five Second Division matches, the club
finishing as champions. Graham Shaw, later
England's left-back, made his debut for the
Blades that season, making 37 appearances,
with Fred Furniss at right-back an ever-
present.

Appearances:
FL: 1 app. 0 gls.
Total: *1 app. 0 gls.*

WORRALL, William Edward

Role: Goalkeeper 1910-11
6'1" 14st.7lbs.
*b. Thornaby-on-Tees,
Yorks, 1885*

CAREER: Shildon Athletic
1907-08/ SUNDERLAND
May 1908/Wingate Albion
Oct 1911.

William Worrall

Debut v Nottingham Forest (a) 18/2/1911

William Worrall was a goalkeeper of very
impressive physical proportions. During his
three years at Roker Park, Worrall's first team
activities were confined to the final dozen
League fixtures of 1910/11. He had less than a
season with Shildon Athletic of the North-

Eastern League, returning to that competition in the ranks of Wingate Albion. It appears a wage dispute with Sunderland was the cause, the *Athletic News* reporting in its club prospects features for 1911/12 that Worrall " ... after unsuccessfully claiming the maximum wage, has gone through the summer without his pay". Maybe the player had a case. In those 12 appearances four games had been won, five drawn and only three lost. Worrall had conceded 16 goals, five of them in the last match, a heavy 5-1 reverse at Old Trafford against Manchester United.

Appearances:
FL: 12 apps. 0 gls.
Total: *12 apps. 0 gls.*

WORTHINGTON, Frank Stuart

Role: Forward 1982-83
5'11" 11st.10lbs.
b. Halifax, 23rd November 1948

CAREER: Sowerby Bridge G.S./Halifax Schoolboys/Ripponden United/Huddersfield Town assoc. s'boy Apr 1964, pro Nov 1966/ Leicester City Aug 1972/Bolton Wanderers Sept 1977(Philadelphia Fury loan May 1979)/ Birmingham City Nov 1979(Tampa Bay Rowdies loan Apr 1981)/Leeds United Mar 1982/SUNDERLAND Dec 1982/Southampton June 1983/Brighton & Hove Albion May 1984/Tranmere Rovers player-manager July 1985/Preston North End Feb 1987/Stockport County Nov 1987/Cape Town Spurs Apr 1988/Chorley Oct 1988/Stalybridge Celtic Dec 1988/Galway United Feb 1989/Weymouth Sept 1989/Radcliffe Borough Oct 1989/ Guiseley player-coach Nov 1989/Preston North End player-coach 1990/Hinckley Town player-manager Sept 1990/Cemaes Bay 1991/ Halifax Town player-coach Aug 1991.

Debut v Ipswich Town (h) 4/12/1982 (scored)

Frank Worthington flitted only briefly across the Roker Park scene in the 1982-83 season. Nevertheless, he proved a bargain at £50,000 as he helped to lift a very moderate Sunderland side in their ultimately successful fight against relegation. He began with Huddersfield Town and was capped twice by England Under-23 in June 1972. Shortly afterwards he looked set to join Liverpool but failed the medical and was instead transferred to Leicester City for a fee in the region of £100,000. He scored on his debut, at Old Trafford, and went on to spend five very successful years at Filbert Street, scoring 78 goals in 237(2) appearances and winning eight England caps. Moving on to Bolton Wanderers in September 1977, he was the leading goalscorer in Division One in season 1978-79 with 24. He also won the 'Goal of the Season' for his sensational televised strike against Ipswich Town at Burnden Park in April 1979. Frank arrived at Sunderland from Leeds at 34 years of age. The gifted, elusive striker scored on his debut and generally enriched an otherwise mediocre season with his trademark repertoire of flamboyant ball skills and at times unpredictable machinations. An issue of the *Roker Review* in season 1982-83 featured an

Frank Worthington

interview with Frank who was quoted as saying "Football is a wonderful way to make a living - I still think it's a game to be enjoyed, a game where the individual can express himself and entertain the public." Those fortunate enough to have seen him on a good day will certainly endorse his philosophy. His amusing book *"One Hump or Two"* detailing his colourful on and off field life story proved a best-seller.

Appearances:
FL: 18(1) apps. 2 gls.
Total: *18(1) apps. 2 gls.*
Honours:
3 Eng U-23 apps. 1972/8 Eng caps 1974-75/ 1 FL app. 1973/(Huddersfield Town) Div 2 champs 1970/(Bolton Wanderers) Div 2 champs 1978.

WRIGHT, Arthur William Tempest

Role: **Left-half 1937-55**
5'10" 12st.6lbs.
b. Burradon, Northumberland, 23rd September 1919
d. Burradon, Northumberland, 27th May 1985

CAREER: Castletown Schools/Sunderland Schools/Hylton Colliery Juniors/SUNDERLAND ground staff mid-1930s, pro Sept 1936-1955 when he joined the club's training staff.
Debut v Leeds United (h) 16/4/1938

One of the all-time great servants of Sunderland AFC, Arthur Wright spent around two decades on the playing staff and had a peacetime appearance record approaching 300 despite the several seasons lost by World War Two. Arthur had been a schoolboy star, thrice honoured by England at this level. He made his League bow at 18 and had played 13 top flight matches by the time war broke out. Wright flourished when peace returned seven years later. A sports magazine in 1949 nicely analysed his play. "Gradually he developed into a fine attacking half-back - with a great shot (Sunderland people think it the strongest in England). He became adept at changing the point of attack besides being a sound, dependable and

Arthur Wright

clever defender". Arthur twice represented the Football League in 1948/49, when he was an ever-present for Sunderland, and was selected for the England touring side. But he was unable to go due to the illness of his young daughters. The chance of a cap did not occur again. A great pity.

Appearances:
FL: 270 apps. 13 gls.
FAC: 13 apps. 1 gl.
Total: *283 apps. 14 gls.*
Honours:
2 FL apps./3 Eng Sch apps.

WRIGHT, David

Role: Inside-left 1927-30
5'9" 12st.7lbs.
b. Kirkcaldy, 5th October 1905
d. Holdeness, nr Hull, August 1953

CAREER: Raith Rovers/East Fife/
Cowdenbeath 1926/SUNDERLAND Apr 1927
£8,000 incl. Bill Murray/Liverpool Mar 1930/
Hull City July 1934 £1,000/Bradford May
1935-1936.

Debut v Portsmouth (h) 27/8/1927

Scot David Wright was an inside man typical
of his period, able to play inside-right or lead
the attack in addition to his favourite inside-
left spot. Thoughtful in positional moves,
holding the ball before releasing to best
advantage, and a hard worker. No mean
dribbler either. David owned a bakery
business in his native Kirkcaldy, returning
there each close season to take charge. He was
leading scorer for Cowdenbeath in 1926/27
(17 in 35 Scottish League outings) and
generally a 'regular' at Liverpool (100 Football
League and FA Cup appearances, 35 goals).
With Hull and Bradford Park Avenue the
respective figures were 33 (11 goals) and 20
(one goal).

> **Appearances:**
> *FL: 52 apps. 7 gls.*
> *FAC: 1 app. 1 gl.*
> **Total:** *53 apps. 8 gls.*

David Wright

WRIGHT, Thomas

Role: Outside/inside-right 1948-55
5'9" 11st.0lbs.
b. Blandhill, Clackmannanshire, 20th January 1928

CAREER: Blairhall Colliery/Partick Thistle
Mar 1945/SUNDERLAND Mar 1949 £8,000/
East Fife Jan 1955, in part exch for Charlie
Fleming/Oldham Athletic Mar 1957 £700/
North Shields cs 1957.

Debut v Portsmouth (h) 12/3/1949

Tommy Wright made a name for himself as an
outside-right, eventually successful in the
inside berth and at centre-forward also.
Tommy, direct in style and never stinting in
effort, fitted well in Sunderland's attack. He
suffered a bad injury during his early time at
Roker Park but recovered to reach
commendable totals for both appearances and
goals scored, with a best return in 1953-54 of
18 League goals in 38 games. He was also
capped by Scotland against all the other Home
countries whilst with Sunderland. Tommy's
son, Thomas Elliot Wright, also assisted
Oldham Athletic and represented Scotland at
Under-21 and Youth
levels. He is uncle of
Jackie Sinclair
(Leicester City
and Scotland)
and Willie Sinclair
(Huddersfield
Town and Falkirk).

> **Appearances:**
> *FL: 170 apps.*
> *52 gls.*
> *FAC: 10 apps.*
> *3 gls.*
> **Total:** *180 apps. 55 gls.*
> **Honours:**
> *3 Scot caps.*

*Tommy
Wright*

WYLDE, Roger James

Role: Forward 1984-85
5'11" 11st.0lbs.
b. Sheffield, 8th March 1954

CAREER: Sheffield Wednesday app July 1970, pro July 1971/Oldham Athletic Feb 1980/ Sporting Lisbon July 1983/SUNDERLAND July 1984/Barnsley Dec 1984(Rotherham United loan Mar 1988).

Debut v Nottingham Forest (a) 1/9/1984

A polished centre-forward with deft footwork and an eye for goal, Roger Wylde scored 66 goals in 182 appearances for his hometown club, Sheffield Wednesday. Oldham Athletic paid £75,000 for him to replace ex Sunderland favourite Vic Halom, and he headed the Latics' goalscoring list in each of his three seasons at Boundary Park, scoring 51 goals in 109(4) appearances. Roger joined Sunderland after a season in Portugal and despite a bright start, which included a double strike against Crystal Palace in the FA Cup second round, and an inspirationally creative display in a Reserves 10-1 win over Blackpool, he was, rather surprisingly, transferred to Barnsley in mid season. His final League goal came during a brief loan spell with Rotherham United during March to April 1988 and brought his career total to 128 in 357 League appearances. He subsequently joined Stockport County as club physiotherapist.

Appearances:
FL: 8(3) apps. 3 gls.
FLC: 4 apps. 2 gls.
Total: *12(3) apps. 5 gls.*

WYLIE, Thomas

Role: Centre-forward/Inside-left 1936-37
5'7" 10st.7lbs.
*b. Linwood, Renfrewshire,
10th November 1907*

CAREER: Glasgow Benburb/ Motherwell June 1931/SUNDERLAND July 1936/Queen of the South July 1938.

Debut v Preston North End (a) 2/1/1937

Tom Wylie

Described in 1936 as a "close season capture from Motherwell where, despite his small stature, he proved himself a first class leader." Tom Wylie's height and weight were indeed modest but he was a ready made stand-in for Bob Gurney on three occasions in 1936/37 - his remaining four League outings that term were at inside-left. Tom's five-year stint at Motherwell gave him only 30 Scottish League appearances in which he scored an excellent 19 goals. In only one season did his appearances total attain double figures: the last, 1935/36, when he played in 18 matches, scoring 11 goals. However, Motherwell FC, from the late 'Twenties onwards, were a major force in Scottish football with first team places accordingly hard to come by. Wylie had the Scotland cap, Willie McFayden, to compete with. For Queen of the South he made seven League appearances, scoring one goal. He was a mechanic by trade.

Appearances:
FL: 7 apps. 3 gls.
Total: *7 apps. 3 gls.*

*Roger Wylde (top right) was one of a
trio of signings by Len Ashurst (left)
in the summer of '84. The other two are
Gary Bennett and Clive Walker.*

467

YORK, Andrew

Role: Left-back 1921-22
5'10" 11st.6lbs.
b. Tynemouth, 14th June 1894
d. Northumberland, 4th qtr 1977

CAREER: Bedlington United/Blyth
Spartans/Sleekburn Albion/SUNDERLAND
May 1921/Coventry City May
1923/Northampton Town Sept 1925/Lincoln
City Aug 1927/Newark Town Sept
1930/Scarborough Aug 1934.

Debut v Arsenal (h) 8/10/1921

A reserve at Roker Park, Andy York had only
moderate success with Second Division
Coventry City (17 League and FA Cup
appearances) and Third Division
Northampton (26). But he was extremely well
regarded at Lincoln (106 outings). A local
football handbook reported in 1929 that he
had " ... gradually developed a brilliant style
of football. Sound in judgement, good tackler,
strong kick, but always remembers that half
the success of a good clearance is in placing
well to a comrade." And note Andy was still
associated with good class non-League soccer
when turned 40.

> **Appearances:**
> *FL: 1 app. 0 gls.*
> **Total:** *1 app. 0 gls.*

Andy York

YORK, Charles H.

Role: Inside-right/Centre-forward 1903-04
5'9" 10st.6lbs.
b. Edinburgh, 1882

CAREER: Junior football to Reading Apr
1901/Derby County Mar
1902/SUNDERLAND Jan 1904/Heart of
Midlothian May 1904/Southampton Dec
1904/Sheppey United Mar 1906/South
Farnborough Oct 1906.

Debut v Sheffield Wednesday (a) 13/2/1904

Charles York

Charles York was
generally an inside-
right but made his
Sunderland bow as
leader of the attack. In
a first class career
taking in five clubs in
half a dozen years
York's most productive
period was with Derby
County. At the Baseball
Ground he played in 24
League matches plus three in the FA Cup,
scoring six League goals. And he appeared in
a Cup final, the Rams' third in five years, all of
which were lost. York had five Southern
League outings with Reading and no first
team activity for Southampton. A 1904
publication said he was " ... bustling but
somewhat lacking in pace".

> **Appearances:**
> *FL: 2 apps. 0 gls.*
> **Total:** *2 apps. 0 gls.*
> **Honours:**
> *(Derby County) FAC finalist 1903.*

YORSTON, Benjamin Collard

Role: Centre/Inside-forward 1931-34
5'5" 10st.11lbs.
b. Nigg, Kincardineshire, 14th October 1905
d. South Kensington, London, November 1977

CAREER: Kittybrewster FC (Aberdeen)/
Aberdeen Mugiemoss/Aberdeen Richmond/
Montrose Sept 1926/Aberdeen FC Mar 1927/
SUNDERLAND Jan 1932 £2,000/
Middlesbrough Mar 1934 £1,250(WW2 guest
St Mirren Nov 1939)/retired 1945/post-war
chief scout to both Bury and Barnsley.

Debut v Blackpool (a) 30/1/1932 (scored)

A short, chunky Scot, Benny Yorston was not particularly handicapped by his stature as he could outjump most defenders. The clever, quicksilver type, full of tricks, he was strong of leg and reckoned a second edition of Hughie Gallacher - praise indeed! All things considered those fees paid by Sunderland and Middlesbrough look extremely moderate. Benny was said to have been the inspiration that lifted Sunderland to mid-table in 1931/32 with a dozen goals in just 17 appearances. He had worked at Pittodrie in Aberdeen's office while assisting junior Mugiemoss and the Dons' third team. He also played for another local outfit, Richmond, moving on to Montrose before taking the full professional ticket with Aberdeen. Yorston's goal scoring in the Scottish League First Division was exceptional, being the top club scorer for four consecutive seasons and establishing a club record 36 in 38 outings, 1929/30. Overall figures in League and Cup for the Dons read 125 in 156 matches, superlative by any standard. For Middlesbrough he netted 54 in 159 Football League and FA Cup appearances. A broken leg in December 1937 did not halt Benny's career unduly for, after joining the Army Physical Training Corps in 1940, he guested for a number of clubs. These included Aldershot, Brentford, Reading, West Ham United and Lincoln City. He was the son of a trawler skipper and uncle of Harry Yorston (Aberdeen and Scotland). After leaving football Benny was employed in West London as a property agent.

Appearances:
FL: 49 apps. 25 gls.
FAC: 3 apps. 1 gl.
Total: 52 apps. 26 gls.
Honours:
1 Scot cap v Nth Ire 1931/1 Scot Jnr app.

Benny Yorston

YOUNG, David

Role: Central defender
1972-74
5'10" 10st.9lbs.
b. Newcastle upon Tyne, 12th November 1945

CAREER: Newcastle United Sept 1964/ SUNDERLAND Jan 1973/Charlton Athletic July 1974/Southend United Sept 1976/ Dartford Dec 1978-May 1980.

Debut v Brighton & Hove Albion (h) 6/1/1973

Within a couple of days, in January 1973, David Young and Ron Guthrie joined Sunderland for a joint fee reported to be in the region of £30,000. They were part of a double scoop by manager Bob Stokoe on local rivals, Newcastle United. Both had been fringe players at St James Park and, of the two, David did less well at Roker, if only for the fact that he spent the 1973 FA Cup final on the bench, having lost his place through injury to Ritchie Pitt, while Ron Guthrie played and collected a winners' medal. At either full-back or in central defence, Young could be relied upon for a workmanlike and efficient performance when brought into the first team. It was not until his move to Charlton Athletic, for a bargain £7,000, that he enjoyed

David Young

regular senior action. Immediately installed as captain, he led his side to promotion from Division Three in his first season at The Valley. He wound up his League career with two seasons at Southend United, helping them to promotion from Division Four and bringing his League career aggregate to 210 matches and three goals. David was later employed in sports centre management in the South of England

Appearances:
FL: 23(6) apps. 1 gl.
FAC: 4 apps. 0 gls.
FLC: 3 apps. 0 gls.
Other: 3(1) apps. 0 gls.
Total: *33(7) apps. 1 gl.*

YOUNG, John

Role: Centre-forward 1911-12
b. Burnbank, Lanarks.

CAREER: Burnbank Athletic/Bradford City Apr 1910/SUNDERLAND Nov 1911/Burslem Port Vale cs 1912/Hamilton Academical Oct 1913-1914.

Debut v West Bromwich Albion (h) 9/12/1911 (scored)

Jock, a recipient of junior honours when leading a strong Burnbank Athletic attack, was hailed as "the second Quinn" by the *Athletic News* on joining Bradford City. (Quinn was the great Celtic and Scotland centre-forward who, as one writer said: "gave no quarter and asked for none".) In the event Jock did well at Valley Parade, netting eight goals in ten First Division games, thus attracting Sunderland's interest. Young scored on his debut for the Wearsiders, afterwards sharing the first team spot with Harry Low and Tom Hall. He departed after the season ended for the then non-League Port Vale, scoring 11 goals in 20 Central League outings for the Potteries club in 1912/13. He re-entered the senior game with Hamilton Accies, notching a goal in four Scottish League (Division One) matches during 1913/14.

Appearances:
FL: 13 apps. 2 gls.
FAC: 2 apps. 0 gls.
Total: *15 apps. 2 gls.*
Honours:
Scot Jnr int.

YOUNG, Robert Thornton

Role: Left-back 1914-25
5'8" 12st.0lbs.
b. Brandon, Co Durham, 18th February 1894
d. Norwich, 8th September 1960

CAREER: Brancepath Villa/Esh Winning Rangers/SUNDERLAND am Feb 1913, pro Mar 1913/Norwich City trainer July 1927, manager Feb 1937-Jan 1939, and again in the war years 1940-46.

Debut v Bradford City (h) 10/4/1915

Bob Young was on the Sunderland players' roll for 13 years yet accumulated only a modest total of senior appearances even allowing for the lost World War One years. His sole first choice term was 1919/20 (24 League games). Nevertheless he was a sound defender and an excellent stand-by. Bob skippered the reserves in his final Roker Park years during which the North-Eastern League

Bob Young

championship was won (1924/25) and he himself represented that League against the Central League on three occasions. In the Great War he served with the Durham Light Infantry, was severely wounded and awarded the Military Medal for heroic action on 10th December 1916 at Cambrin. During World War Two Bob worked in the Treasurer's Department of the Norwich Corporation in addition to managing the wartime Canaries. From 1945 he managed a Norwich hostelry. Mention must be made to Bob's splendid length of service to Norwich City as both trainer and manager amounting to almost two decades.

Appearances:
FL: 50 apps. 0 gls.
FAC: 6 apps. 0 gls.
Total: *56 apps. 0 gls.*

ZOETEBIER, Eduard Andreas Dominicas Hendrikus Joseph

Z

Role: Goalkeeper 1997-98
6'2" 12st.12lbs.
b. Purmerend, Holland 7th May 1970

CAREER: Volendam 1987/SUNDERLAND June 1997/Feyenoord Jan 1998.
Debut v Bury (a) 23/9/1997 (FLC 2)

An early close season signing by Sunderland in 1997, Eduard Zoetebier - more commonly known as Edwin or 'Zoot' - was recruited for a reported £225,000 from Volendam in Holland. The fair-haired Dutch goalkeeper had spent his entire career with Volendam, making his first team debut at 19 and winning Holland Under-21 honours. Tall, athletic and brave, he faced a formidable barrier to his ambitions in first-choice 'keeper Lionel Perez, winner of the *Sunderland Echo* Player of the Year award in the previous season. In the event, despite accomplished performances in the reserves he made only two League Cup appearances, failed to impress in the second of these at Middlesbrough, and departed in frustration after only seven months on Wearside, returning to Holland in a £250,000 transfer to Feyenoord.

Eduard Zoetebier

Appearances:
FLC: 2 apps. 0 gls.
Total: *2 apps. 0 gls.*
Honours:
Holland U-21

APPENDIX 1999-2000

All updated Sunderland figures here are to the end of season 1999-2000. Other than the complete biographies of players new to Sunderland during 1999-2000, all other additional or amended information should be read in conjunction with the text on each individiual concerned in the main body of the book.

AISTON, Samuel James
Loaned to Stoke City Aug-Sept 1999, Shrewsbury Town Dec 1999.

ALLARDYCE, Samuel
Appointed Bolton Wanderers manager Oct 1999, two days after resigning his position with Notts County. In Apr 2000 Bolton were fined £45,000 for enticing Allardyce. The Trotters reached the FAC semi-finals and Division One play-offs but lost to Ipswich Town in the semi-final.

ANGELL, Brett Ashley Mark
Loaned to Notts County in Dec 1999. A £150,000 permanent move was proposed in Jan 2000 but subsequently called off, personal terms not agreed. Loaned to Preston North End in Feb 2000, Angell assisted them to promotion from Division Two.

ANNAN, Walter Archibald
Births details should read: *b. Carnworth, Lanarks, 1877*

ATKINS, Ian Leslie
Left Northampton Town in Oct 1999. The Cobblers subsequently won promotion under new manager Kevin Wilson. Atkins was appointed Chester City Director of Football in Jan 2000. Despite taking 23 points from 22 games after Atkins' arrival, Chester were relegated to the Conference League after 69 years as a Football League club.

BALL, Kevin
Left Sunderland to join Fulham in a £200,000 transfer in Dec 1999 after nine and a half years with The Lads and a total appearance record of 388 (equalling that of Bobby Gurney).
> **Appearances:**
> PL: 38(5) apps. 3 gls.
> FL: 294(5) apps. 19 gls.
> FAC: 16 apps. 0 gls.
> FLC: 23(3) apps. 3 gls.
> Other: 4 apps. 1 gl.
> **Total:** 375(13) apps. 26 gls.

BARRIE, Alexander W.
Further research reveals no second name. Birth details should read: *b. Hutchestown, Glasgow, 1882.*
Barrie was killed in action in France on 1st October 1918 when serving as a corporal in the 2nd Battalion Highland Light Infantry. He is buried at the Flesquieres Hill British Cemetery, Nord, France.

BELL, Richard
Birth details should read:
b. East Greenock, Scotland, 1915.

BOE, James
Career details should read: Wallsend Park Villa/ Rodsley FC/Scotswood May 1913/SUNDERLAND May 1914-1915, later assisted Southport Central.

BOULD, Stephen Andrew

Role: Defender 1999-date
6' 4" 14st 2lbs.
b. Stoke-on-Trent, Staffs, 16th November 1962

CAREER: Stoke City assoc s'boy 1979, app, 1979, pro 1980 (Torquay United loan)/Arsenal cs 1988/SUNDERLAND 1999.

Debut v Chelsea (a) 7/8/1999

Steve Bould

At 6ft 4 ins, and with a physique to match, Steve Bould has developed over the years into a cool, capable defender, outgrowing an early career tendency to give away free kicks in vulnerable positions. Steve was first attached to his local club, Stoke City, at 15 as an associate schoolboy: he became an apprentice in 1979 and a full professional the following year. After his senior debut in September 1981 he became a regular first team player in 1983-84, the previous total of League outings (23) consisting of 14 for Stoke and nine during a spell on loan to Fourth Division Torquay United. In his early seasons at Stoke he usually played right-back. Transferred to Arsenal for £390,000 during the 1988 close season, he linked up at Highbury with Tony Adams and, eventually, Martin Keown, to form one of the meanest defences on record. In 1990/91 Steve, an ever-present, saw only 18 goals conceded in a 38-match tourney. Such a dominant defensive network was the foundation of the Gunners' many trophy-winning exploits of the late Twentieth century. Brilliant in the air, Steve participated in the championships of 1989, '91 and '98 but missed other club honours through injury or suspension. Injury has rather dogged him throughout a long career. At Stoke a career-threatening back problem necessitated a major operation and, among others, he missed the first four months of 1991/92 with a damaged ankle, while his absence during the early months of 2000 coincided with Sunderland's drop in form. He has twice been honoured by England, making a late debut in 1993/94 aged 31 against Norway and Czechoslovakia after earlier winning a 'B' cap. He succeeded Kevin Ball as Sunderland club captain after the latter moved to Fulham.

Appearances:
PL: 19(1) apps. 0 gls.
FAC: 2 apps. 0 gls.
Total: *21(1) apps. 0 gls.*
Honours:
2 Eng caps/Eng 'B'.

BRACEWELL, Paul William
Dismissed by Fulham on 29th March 2000 after just ten months in charge. He follows Micky Adams (sacked Sept 1997) and Ray Wilkins (sacked May 1998) since Al Fayed took over the club.

BRIDGES, Michael
Scored 21 goals for Leeds United (19 in the Premier League). Leeds finished third in the Premiership and secured a Champions' League place.

BRODIE, Stephen Eric
Scored 16 goals for Scarborough in 1999-2000, helping them to finish in fourth place in the Nationwide Conference League.

BROWN, Harold Archer
Additional career information discovered:
High Grange FC/Shildon FC/SUNDERLAND Jan 1922 £650/Ledgate Park Sept 1922/Chilton Colliery Railway Athletic Oct 1922/Shildon FC c.1923/ Queens Park Rangers May 1924/Shildon Aug 1925/ Darlington Nov 1928/City of Durham FC/Witton Park Institute Aug 1934.

BROWN, Norman Liddle
Birth details should read:
b. Willington Quay, Co Durham, December 1884
d. Lewisham, 1st qtr 1938, aged 54.
Career details should read: Willington Athletic May 1904/SUNDERLAND Nov 1904/Brentford July 1907/Luton Town May 1908/Southend United cs 1909/Millwall Athletic Oct 1910/Newcastle City 1911/North Shields Athletic May 1912.

BURBANKS, William Edward
Leeds signing date should read 1953, not 1963.

BUTCHER, Terence Ian
In March 2000 was reported to have left his coaching role with Dundee United in order to take up a business appointment with a company launching a football website.

BUTLER, Paul
Made full international debut for the Republic of Ireland v Czech Republic in Feb 2000.

Appearances:
PL: 31(1) apps. 1 gl.
FL: 44 apps. 2 gls.
FAC: 4 apps. 0 gls.
FLC: 8(1) apps. 0 gls.
Total: *87(2) apps. 3 gls.*

BUTLER, Thomas

Thomas Butler

Role: Midfield 1999-date
5' 8" 10st.7lbs.
b. Ballymun, 25th April 1981

CAREER: Junior football to Sunderland, originally as a trainee.

Debut v Walsall (h)
14/9/1999 (FLC 2) (sub)

Young Thomas Butler is a former trainee who came on as a substitute during the first leg of a Worthington Cup-tie. He was also on the bench for the second leg at Walsall but did not get a run-out on that occasion. Hopefully another of Sunderland's Irishmen who will one day make the grade.

Appearances:
PL: 0(1) apps. 0 gls.
FLC: 0(1) apps. 0 gls.
Total: *0(2) apps. 0 gls.*

BYRNE, Chris Thomas
(Note amendment to forenames)
Loaned to Macclesfield Town Aug 1999.

COOKE, Terence John
Loaned to Wigan Athletic March 2000.

CORNFORTH, John Michael
Made a number of moves in 1999-2000: Swansea City nc July-Aug 1999/Cardiff City nc Aug-Nov 1999/ Scunthorpe United nc Feb 2000/Exeter City Feb 2000.

CRADDOCK, Jody Darryl
Despite the close season signings of Steve Bould and Thomas Helmer - which influenced Peter Reid's decision to allow Jody to spend a loan spell with Sheffield United - when his chance came, he seized it. In an extended run at the end of the season, Jody appeared in the starting line-up in 15 consecutive Premiership matches.

Appearances:
PL: 18(1) apps. 0 gls.
FL: 36(4) apps. 0 gls.
FAC: 2(1) apps. 0 gls.
FLC: 6(2) apps. 0 gls.
Total: *62(8) apps. 0 gls.*

DAVENPORT, Peter
In Jan 2000, following Sammy McIlroy's appointment as Northern Ireland manager, Peter Davenport was appointed manager of Macclesfield Town.

DIBBLE, Andrew Gerald
Loaned to Carlisle United (from Hartlepool United) Oct 1999.

DICHIO, Daniele Salvatore Ernest
Troubled for most of the season with a back injury, Danny was not seen at his best in 1999-2000, despite netting four goals in three League Cup ties. His

twelve Premiership appearances were all from the bench, and any repeat in 2000-2001 would see him overtake Craig Russell's club record of 56 substitute appearances.

Appearances:
PL: 0(12) apps. 0 gls.
FL: 18(32) apps. 10 gls.
FAC: 1(1) apps. 0 gls.
FLC: 7(1) apps. 6 gls.
Total: *26(46) apps. 16 gls.*

DI GUISEPPE, Marcos

Role: Forward 1999
b. Brazil, circa 1973

CAREER: Sport Boys (Brazil)/Batafogo (Brazil)/ Panathinaikos (Greece)/ SV Salzburg (Austria) 1995-97/Sport Boys Callao (Peru)/SUNDERLAND trial Sept 1999/ Walsall trial Oct-Dec 1999.

Debut v Walsall (a) 21/9/1999 (FLC 2) (sub)

Manager Peter Reid's continuing search for new players brought Brazilian forward Marcos Di Guiseppe to Wearside for an early season, two-week trial. International clearance was received in time to allow him to play at Walsall, where he replaced Neil Wainwright at half-time. Nine days later, he made a scoring debut for

Marcos Di Guiseppe

Sunderland Reserves against Mancester United Reserves at Gigg Lane, Bury, being replaced after 61 minutes by Michael Reddy. Despite making a generally favourable impression during his trial, Di Guiseppe was not offered a permanent engagement. The following month, he was offered a short-term engagement with Walsall, but again failed to impress, his one appearance in the Saddlers' colours actually lasting for just four minutes!

Appearances:
FLC: 0(1) apps. 0 gls.
Total: *0(1) apps. 0 gls.*

FERGUSON, Derek
Add to career: Partick Thistle Oct 1999/Adelaide Force, Australia, Nov 1999/Ross County Dec 1999.

Derek was sent off on his debut for Ross County, against his former team Partick Thistle. Ross County won promotion from Division Two of the Scottish League.

FLEMING, Charles
Sunderland signing date should read January 1955, not June 1955.

FORD, Anthony
Awarded the MBE in the New Year's Honours List. In March 2000 he became the only outfield player in the English game to complete 1,000 appearances. (Only three goalkeepers have played more; Peter Shilton 1,387; Ray Clemence 1,119; Pat Jennings 1,098).

FREDGAARD, Carsten

Role: Midfield 1999-date
b. Horshom, Denmark, 20th May 1976

CAREER: First played for Blovstrod IF/ Joined senior club, Lyngby, aged 10, played at all levels before a first team debut aged 18/ SUNDERLAND Mar 1999 £1.8m (West Bromwich Albion loan Feb-Mar 2000)

Debut v Chelsea (a) 7/8/1999 (sub)

Carsten Fredgaard enjoyed a long attachment to Danish senior club, Lyngby, before making a first team bow, in due course attracting attention from a miscellany of European clubs. These included in this country, besides Sunderland, Everton and West Ham United with others from Italy, Germany,

Carsten Fredgaard

Spain and France. Carsten's most obvious asset is speed, earning him the nickname 'Lightning' in Denmark. He is also something of a utility player. In addition to his favourite role - slotting in behind the two strikers - he can take both central and left flank midfield berths. Interestingly he started in juvenile football as a strike forward. A former colleague said Carsten has "speed like no on else, is skilful and has a great ability to go past players." Fredgaard scores a fair quota of goals. In 1998/99 he netted 16 in 33 appearances, and his aggregate figures for Lyngby read 33 goals in 120 matches. He made his full international debut in a 0-0 draw with Holland in Copenhagen in August 1999, coming on as a substitute. He did not join Sunderland immediately after his March 1999 signing, remaining the rest of the season at Lyngby to assist in their UEFA Cup endeavours. He was one of the runners-up to the former Manchester United goalkeeper,

Peter Schmeichel, in Denmark's 1999 Player of the Year awards. Between February and March 2000 Carsten was loaned to West Bromwich Albion but broke a rib whilst at the Hawthorns, returning to Sunderland after making five successive appearances.

Appearances:
PL: 0(1) app. 0 gls.
FLC: 3 apps. 2 gls.
Total: *3(1) apps. 2 gls.*
Honours:
3 Danish U-18 apps/9 Danish U-21 apps/
Denmark cap/Danish Lge tourist,
Sth America 1998-99.

FULLARTON, William Millwright
Birth details should read:
b. Tardeston, Glasgow, 1882

GABBIADINI, Marco
In another successful season with Darlington, Marco was leading goalscorer with 27 League goals in Division Three, prior to the play-offs. The club refused a transfer offer for him of £250,000 from Rushden & Diamonds during the season.

GIBSON, George Eardley
Sunderland signing date should read Apr 1932, not 1931.

GIVEN, Seamus J.J. 'Shay'
Shay's appearance for the Republic of Ireland against Greece in April 2000 took his total of full international caps to 24.

GODDARD, George Charles
Delete second name.

GRAY, Martin David
Transferred to Darlington June 1999.

GRAY, Michael
Mickey is now Sunderland's longest-serving player, since the departure of Kevin Ball.
Appearances:
PL: 63(4) apps 3 gls.
FL: 177(19) apps. 11 gls.
FAC: 11(1) apps. 1 gl.
FLC: 19(4) apps. 0 gls.
Total: *270(28) apps. 15 gls.*

GUNSON, Joseph Gordon
Death details should read 1991 not 1981.

HALL, Matthew
Birth details should read:
b. Renfrew, 1884.

HARDYMAN, Paul George
In Dec 1999 reported to be playing for Basingstoke in the Ryman Premiership. Appointed Assistant Youth Development Officer to Portsmouth April 2000.

HARRISON, Gerald Randall 'Gerry'
Loaned to Hull City Oct 1999, Burnley March 2000.

HAWES, Arthur Robert
Nelson signing date should read July 1930, not 1920.

HELMER, Thomas

Role: Defender 1999-date
6' 1" 11st. 13lbs.
b. Herford, West Germany, 21st April 1965

CAREER: Post SG/Bad Salzuflen/Arminia Bielefeld/Borussia Dortmund/Bayern Munich/SUNDERLAND July 1999(Hertha Berlin loan Aug-Dec 1999).

Debut v Arsenal (h) 14/8/1999 (sub)

A veteran German international signed by Sunderland in July 1999 on a free transfer under the Bosman ruling, Thomas Helmer arrived at the Stadium of Light bearing a reputation as one of Europe's most renowned defenders: dedicated, skilled, resolute and a keen competitor. A proposed

Thomas Helmer

earlier £1m move to Liverpool midway through season 1998/99 stalled because the player felt the time inopportune as regards his young family's educational arrangements. However, despite an impressive record over many years with two of Germany's leading clubs, Helmer's initial season at Sunderland was not the happiest. After only two early Premiership outings he, perhaps surprisingly, failed to integrate into the squad and subsequently returned to Germany on loan to Hertha Berlin with whom he then injured an Achilles tendon playing in the Champions' League. He finally returned to Sunderland in March but made no further first team appearances. Helmer learned the game's rudiments in the ranks of two local clubs, Post SG and Bad Salzuflen, his obvious promise at the latter attracting Arminia Bielefeld, a Bundesliga side. A couple of years in the higher grade brought a transfer to Borussia Dortmund, keen to exploit a still burgeoning talent. In a six-year stay a highlight was the winning of the German Cup in 1989 with Werder Bremen soundly beaten 4-1 in the final. Bayern Munich had to expend a large fee to secure his services in 1992 but it proved justified as the club won two German League championships and the 1996 UEFA Cup among other honours with Helmer's assistance. Helmer won his first international cap aged 25, the debut coinciding with the last time his country played labelled West Germany. In all this fine player earned 68 caps, a large total testifying to a consistency matching his other qualities.

Appearances:
PL: 1(1) apps. 0 gls.
Total: *1(1) apps. 0 gls.*

HOLLOWAY, Darren
A mid-term loan to Bolton Wanderers undoubtedly helped Darren to kickstart his season, following injury problems early on.

Appearances:
PL: 8(7) apps. 1 gl.
FL: 36(5) apps. 0 gls.
FAC: 2 apps. 0 gls.
FLC: 2 apps. 0 gls.
Total: *48(12) apps. 1 gl.*

IVES, Albert Edward
Birth details should read:
b. Newcastle upon Tyne, 18th December 1908.
d. Blyth, Northumberland, 3rd qtr 1980.

JOHNSTON, Allan
Did not feature with Sunderland in 1999-2000 due to his refusal to sign a contract extension, but added a further Scottish cap to his collection v Estonia in Sept 1999. Loaned to Birmingham City Oct 1999, Bolton Wanderers Jan 2000. In March was reported to have signed a pre-contract agreement with Glasgow Rangers.

JOHNSTONE, Robert
Birth details should read: *b. circa 1876.*

KAY, John
Assisted Workington in the Unibond First Division during 1999-2000.

KELLY, David Thomas
In an eventful season with Tranmere Rovers, David was a League Cup finalist, scoring at Wembley against Leicester City, one of his former clubs.

KILBANE, Kevin Daniel

Role: Midfield 1999-date
6' 0" 12st.7lbs.
b. Preston, Lancs, 1st February 1977

CAREER: Junior football to Preston North End, trainee July 1993, pro July 1995/West Bromwich Albion June 1997 £1.25m/ SUNDERLAND Dec 1999 £2.5m.

Debut v Southampton (h) 18/12/1999 (sub)

Kevin Kilbane is a left-sided midfielder exploiting pace truly described as blistering, while a powerful physique increases his opponents' difficulties. With manager Peter Reid keen on wing-play, Kevin could much

enjoy his time at the Stadium of Light. He joined his local League club, Preston North End, when it was in the doldrums. This once great club had been relegated to the lowest division immediately prior to his engagement as a trainee. They won the Division Three

Kevin Kilbane

championship three years later, Kevin playing 11 games in this his debut season. The next found him a regular first-teamer. Kilbane's move to West Bromwich Albion of Division One cost the Baggies their record outlay. He also soon attracted the attention of Premiership clubs on winning his first full international cap for Eire in September of that initial Hawthorns term. A substantial offer from Middlesbrough during 1998/99 came to nought. His overall performance for West Brom (where he was nicknamed 'Killi') contributed greatly to the emergence of Lee Hughes as an impressive striker. Kevin's explosive debut for Sunderland, shortly after his December 1999 signing, boded well for the future. He added a further two full caps to his collection v Czech Republic in Feb 1999 and v Greece in April 2000.

Appearances:
PL: 17(3) apps. 1 gl.
Total: *17(3) apps. 1 gl.*
Honours:
3 Eire caps/11 Eire U-21 apps/(P.N.E.) Div 3 champs 1995.

KUBICKI, Dariusz
In Sept 1999 it was reported that Dariusz was manager of Legia Warsaw, the club he first joined as a player in 1983.

LUMSDON, Christopher
Loaned to Blackpool Feb 2000.
Appearances:
PL: 1 app. 0 gls.
FL: 1 app. 0 gls.
FLC: 1(1) apps. 0 gls.
Total: *3(1) apps. 0 gls.*

MAKIN, Christopher Gregory
Chris scored his first Premiership goal for The Lads in the season's final fixture at Tottenham Hotspur.
Appearances:
PL: 34 apps. 1 gl.
FL: 61(4) apps. 1 gl.
FAC: 5 apps. 0 gls.
FLC: 11 apps. 0 gls.
Total: *111(4) apps. 2 gls.*

MALEY, Mark
  Appearances:
  FLC: 2 apps. 0 gls.
  Total: *2 apps. 0 gls*

MALONE, Richard Philip
Joined Ayr United cs 1964 from Shotts Bon Accord. Won a Scottish League Division Two medal with Ayr United in 1966.

MARRIOTT, Andrew
Continuing in the shadow of Thomas Sorensen, Andy made three League Cup appearances, and one Premier League appearance during 1999-2000.
  Appearances:
  PL: 1 app. 0 gls.
  FL: 1 app. 0 gls.
  FLC: 3 apps. 0 gls.
  Total: *5 apps. 0 gls.*

MILTON, Albert
Died Thursday, 11th October 1917, aged 31, whilst serving as a bombardier with 'B' Bty, 64th Bde, Royal Field Artillery in the Ypres Salient.

McCANN, Gavin Peter
In a season of outstanding progress, Gavin scored a number of vital goals from midfield. He was the runaway winner of Sunderland's Young Player of the Year award, polling over three-quarters of the votes cast. This despite the fact his season was ended prematurely by a serious injury sustained at Coventry City on 12th February 2000.
  Appearances:
  PL: 21(3) apps. 4 gls.
  FL: 5(6) apps. 0 gls.
  FAC: 3(1) apps. 2 gls.
  FLC: 1(1) apps. 1 gl.
  Total: *30(11) apps. 7 gls.*

McALLISTER, Alexander
Further information regarding his death has come to light. He died in Italy, not France, on 31st January 1918 when serving as a private in the 10th Btn, Northumberland Fusiliers. He is buried at the Giavera British Cemetery, Arcade, Italy. Details of McAllister's demise appeared in an Oldham Athletic programme dated 18th October 1966. A 73-year-old Mr Mather from Royton wrote in: "I played football with McAllister whilst serving in Italy during World War One. He had been a player with Oldham Athletic in their Lancashire Combination days. He died of food poisoning after eating an Italian cake, called polenta, made from Indian corn."

McNESTRY, George
d. Gateshead, 16th March 1998.

NUNEZ, Milton Omar Garcia

Role: Forward 1999-date
5' 5" 10st. 7lbs.
b. Honduras, 30th October 1972

CAREER: Comunicaciones (Guatemala)/ Nacional Montevideo (Uruguay)/PAOK Salonika, Greece cs 1999/SUNDERLAND

Mar 2000 £1.6m.

Debut v Wimbledon (h)
8/4/2000 (sub)

Milton Nunez

Milton Nunez's signing by Sunderland was the biggest deal completed on transfer deadline day, the fee of £1.6m set to rise by a further £1m, depending on appearances. The first Honduran to play in the Premiership, the powerfully-built inside forward has blistering pace, two good feet and an ability to outjump much taller opponents in aerial duels. Nicknamed 'Tyson' on account of his muscular build, the Spanish-speaking striker began with Comunicaciones, where he won two league titles. Transferred to former World Club champions Nacional, he added a further pair of league championships, signing off with a hat-trick against Vasco de Gama. A move to PAOK Salonika in summer 1999 proved unrewarding, manager Dusan Bajevic attempting to convert him into a full-back. There is no doubt Nunez faces a real challenge at the Stadium of Light, with Quinn and Phillips in pole position. It will be surprising, however, given 'Tyson's' proven track record in both domestic and international football, if he does not feature strongly in the coming season's Premiership campaign.

  Appearances:
  PL: 0(1) apps. 0 gls.
  Total: *0(1) apps. 0 gls.*
  Honours:
  29 Honduras caps.

ORD, Richard
Sadly, Dickie Ord's football career has ended, due to the injury he sustained in his very first training session with Queens Park Rangers. Five knee operations failed to bring him to the fitness required for full-time football, and he announced his retirement in January 2000.

OSTER, John Morgan

Role: Winger 1999-date
5' 9" 10st.2lbs.
b. Boston, Lincs, 8th December 1978

CAREER: Junior football to Grimsby Town originally as a youth trainee, pro July 1996/ Everton July 1997 £1.5m/SUNDERLAND Aug 1999 approx £1m.

Debut v Watford (h) 10/8/1999

John Oster is remarkable for the amount of representative football he has packed into a youthful career, and from an early age too, making the Wales Under-21 side at 17 years 8 months, three months <u>before</u> his Football League debut in November 1996. Oster is also notable for having served three senior clubs before reaching 21 and attracting a couple of seven-figure transfer fees in the process. At Grimsby John soon built a reputation, more than once described as "a flying winger", and one able to take either flank. The Mariners, relegated to Division Two in the season of John's debut, succumbed to Everton's

John Oster

overtures the following summer. He became a Premiership player bearing a £1.5m tag with a then aggregate 21 League appearances plus four substitutions, one in a League Cup tie. At Goodison he enjoyed a fair amount of first team football in his initial term. But in 1998/99 with a new manager (Walter Smith) at the helm, senior outings were less forthcoming and John grasped the chance of transferring to Sunderland as season 1999/2000 began. Lincolnshire-born, John qualifies for Wales by reason of his mother's family. He received his first full cap as a Sunderland player (and his third overall) in October 1999. At his then age, 20, his services to the Principality could be of long duration.

Appearances:
PL: 4(6) apps. 0 gls.
FLC: 3 apps. 0 gls.
Total: *7(6) apps. 0 gls.*
Honours:
Full & U-21 Welsh caps.

PEREZ, Lionel
Remained out of favour at Newcastle United, but had loan spells with Scunthorpe United (Oct-Nov 1999) and Cambridge United (Mar 2000).

PHILIP, George
More information on his early career has come to light: Dundee Wanderers/St Johnstone cs 1909/ Dundee cs 1910/SUNDERLAND Apr 1914/Dundee June 1920-21.

PHILLIPS, Kevin
Another season of outstanding progress for 'SuperKev' who rose spectacularly to the challenge of the Premiership by scoring 30 League goals - only the third player to do so - in 1999-2000. Runner-up for

both the F.W.A. Footballer of the Year and the P.F.A. award, Kevin was also included in the P.F.A.'s Premiership Select XI and was Sunderland Supporters' Player of the Year. Most importantly, he also committed his long-term future to the club by signing a lucrative five-year contract. Capped again by England v Belgium in October 1999 and confidently expected to feature strongly in England's Euro 2000 campaign.

Appearances:
PL: 36 apps. 30 gls.
FL: 70 apps. 54 gls.
FAC: 5 apps. 4 gls.
FLC: 5 apps. 2 gls.
Total: *116 apps. 90 gls.*

PORTERFIELD, John 'Ian'
Appointed national manager of Trinidad & Tobago in March 2000.

POWER, Geoffrey Frank
Further research has revealed no middle name on his birth certificate. *b. Grangetown St. Mary's* Amend career details to read:
Lancashire Fusiliers/SUNDERLAND Aug 1919/ Blackpool Dec 1921 £350/Chester-le-Street Oct 1922/ Fleetwood cs 1923/Wheatley Hill Colliery Dec 1924/ Scarborough/Scarborough Penguins/Eston United Sept 1928/Grangetown St.Mary's Sept 1932/ Allerton Instruction Centre Oct 1935.

POWER, Lee Michael
His contract with Halifax Town was cancelled in Nov 1999.

PRUDHOE, Mark
Loaned to Darlington Sept 1999, appointed player-coach to Southend United Nov 1999.

QUINN, Niall John
The pairing of Niall with Kevin Phillips as Sunderland's striking duo has continued to reap a rich harvest of goals. Between them they scored 44 of The Lads' 57 Premiership goals during 1999-2000 with Niall producing some of the finest football of his career. At international level, Niall has captained the Republic of Ireland and taken his total of international caps to 75.

Appearances:
PL: 43(6) apps. 16 gls.
FL: 71(5) apps. 35 gls.
FAC: 5 apps. 1 gl.
FLC: 5(2) apps. 4 gls.
Total: *124(13) apps. 56 gls.*

RAE, Alexander Scott
Alex's season ended on an unhappy note when he was sent off (after coming as as a 64th minute substitute) against Tottenham at White Hart Lane in the season's final fixture. During the season he passed the career milestone of 400 English and Scottish League appearances.

Appearances:
PL: 35(14) apps. 5 gls.
FL: 36(4) apps. 5 gls.
FAC: 4 apps. 0 gls.
FLC: 8(1) apps. 2 gls.
Total: *83(19) apps. 12 gls.*

REDDY, Michael

Role: Forward 1999-date
b.Kilkenny, Ireland, 24th March 1980

CAREER: Kilkenny/SUNDERLAND 1999
£30,000 initially.

Debut v Wimbledon (a) 12/10/1999 (FLC3) (sub)

Michael Reddy is an exciting young Irish prospect who could go far. He possesses power and great speed, enhanced by quickness from a standing start. His positional sense also impresses as does an eye for a goal opportunity. An unassuming youngster, Michael perhaps envisaged waiting two or three years

Michael Reddy

for a first team call-up, but instead had a taste of Premiership fare during 1999/2000, and an undoubted high spot was netting the equaliser in a North-east derby against Middlesbrough. Another fine moment was making his international debut for the Republic of Ireland Under-21 side v Greece in April 2000. Discovered for Sunderland by chief scout Andy King, Michael could easily have gone elsewhere in the North-east. He was booked for a Newcastle United trial in 1997/98 but, owing to a managerial crisis at the time, the trial never took place!

Appearances:
PL: 0(8) apps. 1 gl.
FAC: 0(1) apps. 0 gls.
FLC: 0(1) apps. 0 gls.
Total: *0(10) apps. 1 gl.*
Honours:
1 Eire U-21 app.

ROBSON, Bryan Stanley
Left his job as Sunderland Youth Coach in May 2000.

ROY, Eric

Role: Midfield 1999-date
b. Nice, France, 26th September 1967

CAREER: Cavigal Nice Sports as juvenile, later in Nice junior football/OGC Nice 1986/ Toulon 1992/Olympique de Marseille 1993/ SUNDERLAND Aug 1999 £200,000.

Debut v Leicester City (h) 11/9/1999 (sub)

Eric Roy is an elegant and richly experienced French midfielder with a style well suited to the English game, but nevertheless he took a little time to adjust to the Premiership. Roy rarely gives away the ball and, when in possession, distributes to advantage. He originally played as a striker but then discovered a

Eric Roy

midfield role more congenial. At Marseille Eric took part in a phenomenal 33-match unbeaten run. Another highlight was in the UEFA Cup run of 1998/99 but he unluckily missed the final through injury. By this time, of course, he had steadily built a solid reputation, being voted France's best midfield player in 1998. Son of a former French international, Eric also distinguished himself at tennis as a boy and, at 15 years old, was ranked in France's Top Ten for his age group.

Appearances:
PL: 19(5) apps. 0 gls.
FAC: 2 apps. 0 gls.
FLC: 3 apps. 1 gl.
Total: *24(5) apps. 1 gl.*

RUSSELL, Craig Stewart
During an early season loan spell with Darlington (Sept 1999), the Quakers were said to be keen to retain his services but were unable to afford the £100,000 asking fee. A second loan spell to Oxford United in Feb 2000 was followed in March by a loan to St Johnstone of the Scottish Premier League. However, after a scoring debut for the Saints, Russ sustained a hamstring injury, which ended yet another nightmare campaign. He is now said to be available on a free transfer from Manchester City.

RUSSELL, James Walker
d. Florida, USA, 17th August 1994.

SAUNDERS, Percy Kitchener
Amend death to read:
d. 2nd March 1942, killed in action in the Far East

SCHWARZ, Stefan Hans Jurgen

Role: Midfield 1999-date
b. Malmo, Sweden, 18th April 1969

CAREER: Kulladius FF 1985/Malmo FC 1988/Bayer 40 Leverkusen (Germany) during season 1989/90/Benfica 1991/Arsenal May 1994 £1.75m/Fiorentina (Italy) cs 1995/ Valencia 1998/SUNDERLAND July 1999 £3.75m.

Debut v Watford (h) 10/8/1999

Stefan Schwarz is not only Sunderland's most expensive signing to date but likely also their most cosmopolitan. Swedish, and the son of a German, married to a Portugese wife with a playing career that has taken in Sweden, Germany, Portugal, England, Italy and Spain, he believes the Italian game and Iberian spells greatly added to his all-round game.

Stefan Schwarz

A vastly experienced footballer, Stefan possesses a commensurate collection of caps and medals to show for it. After junior football he joined Malmo FC, the club he supported as a boy. He won his first cap in February 1990, before his 21st birthday and was eventually to captain his country. Stefan's first acquaintance with English soccer - the Arsenal season - ended, according to one account, because of his wife's desire for a warmer climate. He made 34 Premiership appearances in 1994/95 and picked up a European medal. Stefan is rightly numbered among Sweden's finest developments of the late twentieth century. Quick to size up a situation, exploiting a crisp tackle (which one writer likened to that of Tony Towers, the old Sunderland favourite) and invariably distributing wisely. A class man to have around.

Appearances:
PL: 26 apps. 1 gl.
FAC: 2 apps. 0 gls.
Total: *28 apps. 1 gl.*
Honours:
64 Swedish caps/(Malmo) Swedish Lge champs 1989/(Benfica) Portugese Lge champs 1991, 1994/Portugese Cup winners 1993/(Arsenal) ECWC finalist 1995.

SCOTT, Martin
In Dec 1999 Martin announced his retirement as a player, due to his persistent ankle injury problems. As the holder of an FA coaching badge, he was seeking a position within the game.

SMITH, Martin Geoffrey
Martin's stay at Sheffield United proved a relatively brief one as he was the subject of a £300,000 plus transfer to Huddersfield Town in Jan 2000. He had scored 15 goals for the Blades and the relatively low fee was accounted for by the fact that he would have been available on a 'Bosman' free at the end of the campaign. He finished the season with 19 goals, but Huddersfield ended disappointingly out of the play-offs in eighth position in Division One.

SORENSEN, Thomas
Whilst Thomas never looked likely to equal last season's record of 29 clean sheets in Division One, his continued progress earned him a first full international cap, for Denmark v Israel in Nov 1999.
Appearances:
PL: 37 apps. 0 gls.
FL: 45 apps. 0 gls.
FAC: 4 apps. 0 gls.
FLC: 9 apps. 0 gls.
Total: *95 apps. 0 gls.*
Honours: *Denmark cap.*

SUMMERBEE, Nicholas
Despite the loss of Scottish international left wingman Allan Johnston during 1999-2000, the outstanding form of Nicky Summerbee on the right flank ensured a continued supply of ammunition to The Lads' prolific striking duo of Quinn and Phillips.
Appearances:
PL: 29(3) apps. 1 gl.
FL: 58(3) apps. 3 gls.
FAC: 4(1) apps. 0 gls.
FLC: 6(1) apps. 0 gls.
Total: *97(8) apps. 4 gls.*

THIRLWELL, Paul
Paul's loan spell to Swindon Town from Sept to Nov 1999 provided his first extended run of League football, and his starting appearances in The Lads' final three Premiership matches rounded off a season of real progress.
Appearances:
PL: 7(1) apps. 0 gls.
FL: 1(1) apps. 0 gls.
FAC: 0(1) apps. 0 gls.
FLC: 2(1) apps. 0 gls.
Total: *10(4) apps. 0 gls.*

TODD, Colin
Appointed Swindon Town manager May 2000 and lost no time in recruiting assistants Andy King, Sunderland's chief scout plus former Mansfield Town manager, and ex Rokerite Malcolm Crosby.

TRAVERS, Bernard 'Barney'
Sunderland signing date should read July 1919 not January 1919.

WAINWRIGHT, Neil
Appearances in both legs of the League Cup ties against Walsall were Neil's only involvement in first team football with The Lads, but his outstanding loan spell with Darlington, from Feb 2000, helped take the Quakers to Wembley in the play-offs.
Appearances:
FL: 0(2) apps. 0 gls.
FLC: 4(1) apps. 0 gls.
Total: *4(3) apps. 0 gls.*

WILLIAMS, Darren
Appearances:
PL: 23(13) apps. 2 gls.
FL: 54(10) apps. 2 gls.
FAC: 3(1) apps. 0 gls.
FLC: 10 apps. 2 gls.
Total: *90(24) apps. 6 gls.*